P9-AQS-732

BLOOD OF BROTHERS

Also by Stephen Kinzer

Bitter Fruit: The Untold Story of the American Coup in Guatemala
(with Stephen Schlesinger)

BLOOD OF BROTHERS

LIFE AND WAR IN NICARAGUA

STEPHEN KINZER

SCCCC - LIBRARY
4601 Mid Rivers Mall Drive
St. Peters, MO 63376

WITHDRAWN

ANCHOR BOOKS
DOUBLEDAY
NEW YORK   LONDON   TORONTO   SYDNEY   AUCKLAND

For the people of Nicaragua.

For friends who helped me survive years of violence.

AN ANCHOR BOOK
PUBLISHED BY DOUBLEDAY
a division of Bantam Doubleday Dell Publishing Group, Inc.
666 Fifth Avenue, New York, New York 10103

ANCHOR BOOKS, DOUBLEDAY, and the portrayal of an anchor
are trademarks of Doubleday, a division of Bantam Doubleday
Dell Publishing Group, Inc.

Blood of Brothers was originally published in hardcover by G. P. Putnam's Sons
in 1991. The Anchor Books edition is published by arrangement with
G. P. Putnam's Sons.

Library of Congress Cataloging-in-Publication Data
Kinzer, Stephen.
Blood of brothers: life and war in Nicaragua / Stephen Kinzer.—
  1st Anchor Books ed.
    p.   cm.
  Reprint. Originally published in hardcover: Boston: Putnam,
  c1991.
  Includes bibliographical references and index.
  ISBN 0-385-42258-X
  1. Nicaragua—History—1979-   2. Nicaragua—History—1937–
1979.
I. Title.
F1528.K57   1992   91-42007
972.8505'3—dc20   CIP

ISBN 0-385-42258-X
Copyright © 1991 by Stephen Kinzer
ALL RIGHTS RESERVED
PRINTED IN THE UNITED STATES OF AMERICA
FIRST ANCHOR BOOKS EDITION: MAY 1992

1   3   5   7   9   10   8   6   4   2

ACKNOWLEDGMENTS

DURING MY thirteen years covering Nicaragua, more people opened their homes and hearts to me than I could possibly thank by name. It was from them that I slowly learned what it means to be Nicaraguan. They are the real heroes of this book, and to them I am eternally grateful.

Two especially wise Nicaraguans, Sergio Ramírez and Emilio Álvarez Montalván, were willing to spend long hours initiating an inquisitive correspondent into their country's secrets. To me they were not only public figures, but also friends, teachers, and debating partners. If I came to understand anything about the real Nicaragua, I have them to thank.

I also owe a debt to those who read the manuscript of this book, or sections of it, and shared their comments with me. They helped me shape an intimidating mass of material into a coherent narrative. For their time and insight, I am deeply grateful to Mary Ireland (Molly) Dougherty, Elissa Papirno, Steven Tullberg, Karen Brudney, Alejandro Bolaños Geyer, Cynthia Dench, and Caitlin Randall. In addition, my agent, Nancy Love, and my editor, Lisa Wager, contributed much valuable advice.

Also blessedly available when I needed them were James Linkin, Karen Segal, and James and Cathleen Douglas Stone.

My sainted mother, who for years tried bravely to ignore stories about journalists being injured and killed in Central America, also helped make this book possible. For her counsel, and for her love, I can only thank her again.

The staff of the *New York Times* bureau in Managua was always enthusiastic and resourceful. My co-workers there kept me going day after day, year after bloody year. More than a work crew, they were a family away from home. They made my reporting possible: Bertilda Cruz, Samuel Barreto, Luis López, Isaac Narvaez, Guillermo Marcia, Margarita Martínez, and Warner Zeledón.

CONTENTS

1. ARRIVAL   13
2. "GUN THE BANDITS DOWN"   23
3. A NATION REBELS   35
4. TRIUMPH   43
5. SANDINISTA DREAMS   56
6. GUERRILLAS IN POWER   69
7. ME AND E. G. SQUIER   86
8. LOOKING FOR CONTRAS   94
9. BUREAU CHIEF   114
10. CIA AND FRIENDS   136
11. LIFE DURING WARTIME   149
12. *COMANDANTES*   172
13. THE FAITHFUL   190
14. BASEBALL AND OTHER PASSIONS   209
15. ACTION DEMOCRACY   222
16. *TRABIL NANI:* THE MISKITO WAR   251
17. BLOODSTAINS   289
18. PLANE CRASH   309
19. AN AMERICAN MARTYR   324
20. OLIVER NORTH IN NICARAGUA   333
21. "PEACE IS A PROCESS"   341
22. ENDINGS   376

NOTES   395
BIBLIOGRAPHY   425
INDEX   442

USA

MEXICO

CUBA

HAITI
JAMAICA

BELIZE
HONDURAS

GUATEMALA
EL SALVADOR

NICARAGUA

COSTA RICA

PANAMA

COLOMBIA

0   400   800
MILES

MAP BY JANE SIMON

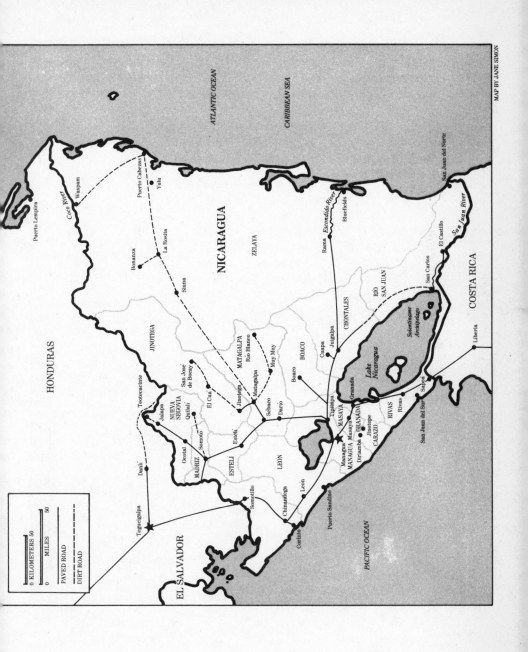

MAP BY JANE SIMON

1

ARRIVAL

SWEEPING MAJESTICALLY up from the plains of central Nicaragua, classic in its natural symmetry, lies the Masaya volcano, sulphuric steam ceaselessly rising from its cone as it has since the beginning of remembered time. Ancient peoples once gathered around the crater for human sacrifices to the gods they believed to live inside. Spanish conquerors fought bloody battles with Indian chieftains in the nearby foothills. The mad American adventurer William Walker rampaged through Masaya on his way to becoming president of Nicaragua. And early in the twentieth century, one of Nicaragua's nationalist heroes was killed there while leading a suicide attack against United States Marines.

I knew none of this as I arrived in Managua for the first time in November 1976. My flight landed at dusk, and on an impulse I turned to look toward the setting sun. There, rising from the distant horizon, loomed the volcano. I had heard that President Somoza occasionally dumped the bodies of executed rivals into the steaming crater. So as other arriving passengers walked toward the terminal, I stopped and gazed.

It was a stirring sight, perhaps all the more so for one who could not yet grasp its full meaning. In Nicaragua, geology is destiny. The Masaya volcano, like others scattered across the country, has erupted several times with terrifying violence, and is liable to erupt again at any moment. Even when the ground feels

13

still, tremors flutter through layers of rock below. Nicaragua is said to be the most seismically active spot on earth, and the turmoil underground has somehow infected the inhabitants.

Outside the terminal I stepped into an airport taxi, a giant-sized American car with long fins and a chrome hood ornament. As we pulled away, I tried to distinguish buildings in the shadows. The driver said nothing.

"I'm a free-lance journalist from the United States," I began in halting Spanish. "I can't afford a big hotel, but I'd like to be close to the center of things. Do you know an inexpensive place near downtown?"

There was a pause that grew embarrassingly long. I feared I had butchered the words so badly I hadn't been understood. But that was not the problem.

"First time in Managua?" the cab driver finally asked indulgently, as if he had heard it all many times before.

"Yes, my first visit," I replied. We continued another mile or two in silence. Outside, the warehouses that lined the airport highway were giving way to sprawling, vacant lots. It seemed we had passed out of the city entirely.

"Let me explain something to you," he said, waving his left arm out the window. "There is no center of things here. There is no downtown. Managua doesn't exist."

I was mystified, but held my tongue. A hot breeze blew through the cab's open windows. Occasionally, we passed what looked like hulks of destroyed buildings standing amid piles of rubble. There were no stores, no signs of bustle or nightlife. On a few streetcorners, small groups of people gathered where vendors sold hot food. I saw nothing overtly scary, but something in the air was disquieting.

"There's a place near here that's clean and not expensive," the driver said. "Tomorrow you can go out and look for yourself."

We arrived at a block of modest homes, and the driver pulled up to an unmarked door, got out, and rang the bell. He spoke to someone inside, and then beckoned me, told me that a room was available, and presented me to the landlady. I paid him and thanked him for his help. He had left me at what turned out to be a highly respectable guest house, where sheets were changed daily and lights went out punctually at 10:00 P.M. It was from there, without a premonition of what was ahead, that I set out to discover Nicaragua.

Shortly after dawn the next morning, I was awoken by the crowing of roosters. Downstairs, I found several other guests already eating breakfast around a large table, and I sat down to join them. Among my companions were two vacationing Mexican college students, a Venezuelan salesman, and a mining engineer from Canada who was studying ways to convert the power of Nicaragua's volcanoes into electric energy. Soon after I sat down, a young woman brought me a plate of fried eggs accompanied by rice and beans, together with a glass of strange-tasting fruit juice.

My fellow guests wanted to know what had brought me to Nicaragua. I told them I wanted to be a foreign correspondent, and had come to Central America to try my hand. They asked me what there was in Nicaragua to attract a foreign correspondent. I could only shrug my shoulders. They were asking too soon. I was twenty-five years old, and had come to Nicaragua with only an undergraduate degree in history, a desire to see the world, and a vague sense that the journalist's life might suit me. That day, I had nowhere and everywhere to go.

The sun was not yet high in the sky when I stepped outside, but Managua's tropical brightness was already searing. This was not the filtered northern sunshine to which I was accustomed, but an intense, almost painful brilliance. I felt a stab of pressure behind my eyes as my pupils struggled to adjust. In hasty retreat, I returned to my room to pick up my dark glasses. From that day forth, I never ventured into the Nicaraguan sun without them.

Since I had no points of reference or fixed destination, there was no sense in asking directions. I began to wander, and almost immediately, what the cab driver had told me the night before flashed into dreadful focus. Managua was devastated, as if it had suffered a firestorm. Block after block of buildings lay in ruin, with weeds sprouting up among the debris. Twisted and crushed signs marked the tombs of a hardware store, a hotel, a metalworking shop, and a restaurant. On some blocks, elegantly crafted marble front steps were all that remained of what had once been luxurious homes.

In the distance I saw an imposing church spire, and began walking toward it. When I arrived, I found that the spire and four outside walls were all that remained of what had once been Managua's Roman Catholic cathedral. There were no pews left, and bushes were growing through cracks in the floor. Sagging roof beams cast eerie, skeletal shadows onto the ground. Foliage enveloped the shattered altar. Statues of saints were headless and armless. Upstairs, in the rooms where bishops used to dress for Mass, I stumbled upon a family of squatters who had set up crude living quarters there. Naked children chased through the dust as women cooked over a smoky fire.

I was completely unprepared for this apocalyptic landscape, and could not at first connect it to anything I had read. The first person I asked told me that this was all earthquake damage, and his answer seemed fantastic and incredible. I remembered reading that an earthquake had shaken Managua four years earlier; Americans noticed it because the baseball star Roberto Clemente had died in a plane crash while bringing relief supplies. But the Dantesque scene before me was far beyond what could be grasped by distant newspaper readers. Ruin on this scale defied description and begged only for comparison, perhaps to Dresden after the Allied bombing. Thousands had perished in a matter of seconds, and the memories of countless lifetimes were wiped away. Now I understood why Managua had such a dazed and ghostly air. Walking through the rubble hour after hour, as I did those first days, was like exploring a maze of catacombs. I wondered how much of normal life could have survived such a cataclysm.

MUCH later, when I came to realize that Nicaragua abounds with implausible characters, I understood how appropriate it was that my first formal interview in Managua was with an emigré named Colonel László Pataky. A mutual acquaintance had given me his name, describing him as a knowledgeable local journalist. I telephoned him on one of my first days in Managua, and was invited to dinner that same evening. The colonel told me he lived quite near my guest house, and gave me directions so I could walk. When I knocked, the door was opened by my host himself, an imposing figure of a man with a stylishly trimmed beard, well into middle age, spreading at the waist but powerfully built. Most of his family was away, he told me as we entered, and we would be joined at dinner only by his young daughter, Anastasia.

László Pataky was a Hungarian-born Jew who had arrived in Nicaragua as a teenage refugee in the 1930s. As war spread through Europe, he had made his way from Managua to London, joined the Free French and fought with valor in North Africa. Later he ran guns to Zionist partisans in Palestine, and served as an Israeli officer in 1948. He then returned to his father, uncle, and brother in Nicaragua, determined to live out his years in peace and tropical comfort. He married a Nicaraguan woman, took citizenship, raised a family, and came to think of himself as fully Nicaraguan. He hosted a daily radio news program, which made him a minor political power and something of a local celebrity.

Our dinner was pleasant enough, with the colonel complaining about rising prices and other problems of the day. While he spoke, I scanned the collection of medals and military souvenirs that decorated the dining room, wondering what stories must lie behind them. As it turned out, the colonel did indeed have a story to tell that night. It was not a tale from across the sea, but rather an episode from the Nicaraguan revolution, a revolution that neither he nor I realized was underway.

We adjourned to the sitting room, and Anastasia politely took her leave. The colonel, who carried himself exactly as if he were in a European salon, poured two brandies and offered me one. We toasted each other, and he motioned me to a chair. He studied me, took a second sip of brandy, and then spoke.

"Are you aware of what happened to me?" he asked.

"I'm not sure I know what you mean," I replied.

He smiled, and then walked to a desk from which he withdrew a large cigar. After lighting it, he settled down across from me, cigar in hand and after-dinner drink at his side, his face only intermittently visible through clouds of smoke. I listened intently as he spoke.

Twenty-three months earlier, on the evening of December 27, 1974, Colonel Pataky had attended an exclusive after-Christmas reception at the home of a prominent Managua politician. Among the other guests were Nicaragua's foreign minister, the mayor of Managua, and the Nicaraguan ambassador to Washington, who was President Somoza's brother-in-law. Suddenly their chitchat was interrupted by gunfire and chaos. A squad of assailants shot their way past bodyguards outside, stormed into the house, and forced everyone to the ground. In a matter of seconds, the elegant party became a nightmare. Guests suddenly found their lives in the hands of commandos wearing red and black kerchiefs and shouting, "Long Live the Sandinista National Liberation Front!"

I had read only brief news reports about the assault Colonel Pataky was describing. He told the story in vivid detail, right down to the tidbit about the female guest who swallowed her $15,000 ring to keep it out of guerrilla hands. The party's host, José María Castillo, had been shot dead by one of the commandos as he ran toward a rifle hidden in his bedroom, and his body lay on his bed during the entire sixty-two-hour siege. President Somoza had rushed back from vacation to negotiate with the commandos, who threatened to begin executing hostages if their demands were not met. When the drama finally ended, Somoza had paid $1 million in ransom, agreed to publish a Sandinista broadside in local newspapers, and freed fourteen imprisoned rebels. A plane took the released prisoners, together with the thirteen-member commando squad, to refuge in Cuba. President Somoza responded by imposing martial law, which was still in effect.

Colonel Pataky warned me against reading too much into the episode. It proved that the Sandinista Front had some brave fighters, to be sure, and that they were able to deal humiliating blows to the regime. But their clandestine nature isolated them from the political process. It seemed entirely reasonable to speculate that the Sandinistas had gone their separate ways after arriving in Havana. Some were undoubtedly back in the Nicaraguan mountains, still dreaming wild dreams of insurrection. But their sporadic thirteen-year guerrilla campaign was no closer to success than when it had begun in 1963, and their movement had failed to make a substantial impact on national life.

Neither Colonel Pataky nor I knew that the Sandinista guerrillas aboard that dramatic flight out of Managua had regrouped in Cuba, pledged themselves anew to the cause of revolution, and systematically begun infiltrating back into Central America. They were beginning to burrow into Nicaraguan society, laying the groundwork for an uprising. But their work was invisible to naked eyes like mine and the colonel's. We could not have imagined that the Sandinistas would soon lead a national revolt, topple the forty-year Somoza dynasty, and seize the reins of state power. We did not guess that the man who had planned the spectacular Christmas party assault, Tomás Borge, would within a few years be Minister of the Interior, or that one of the gaunt prisoners hustled aboard the Cuba-bound plane, twenty-nine-year-old Daniel Ortega, would become Nicaragua's president.

After a second brandy, I rose to take my leave. Colonel Pataky offered to have his driver take me home. I thanked him, but said I'd rather walk.

"No," he said firmly. I was puzzled, and turned to face him.

"It's not a good idea," he told me, stabbing at the air with the butt of his cigar. "You shouldn't be walking on the streets. You're a young man. You're alone. It's nighttime. This is Managua. The wrong people might notice. Something could happen. To be safe, go with my driver."

I was taken aback by his insistence. Nothing I had seen or heard in Nicaragua suggested that such caution was necessary, and the colonel himself had seemed to dismiss talk that the country was in a violent or even pre-violent stage. His warning against walking four blocks through a quiet part of town disconcerted me even more than his account of being held hostage by masked guerrillas.

This was a time when Nicaragua was perceived by Americans, if it was perceived at all, as remote and peaceful. The very fact that so many educated people were not even certain which continent Nicaragua was on, or whether it was an island, appealed to me and gave me a sense that I was exploring uncharted territory. My evening with Colonel Pataky was my first inkling that Nicaragua was not the quiet backwater I had expected. As his driver took me on the two-minute trip to my guest house, I stared into the darkness and wondered what was lurking out there that could be so dangerous.

BEFORE setting out on that first trip to Nicaragua, I had managed to find the name of just one anti-Somoza leader, and had written him a letter requesting an interview. He was Pedro Joaquín Chamorro, editor and publisher of the opposition newspaper *La Prensa*. Soon after arriving in Managua, I telephoned him at his newspaper office. He had received my letter, and told me how pleased he was to hear that an American journalist was visiting Nicaragua. We fixed an appointment for later in the week.

On the day I was to meet Chamorro, I set out early from my guest house and began walking. Before long, I realized I was lost, and stopped into a filling station to ask if I was anywhere near *La Prensa*. A customer cleaning his windshield overheard my question. When I told him I was on my way to interview Chamorro, his tone became almost reverent, and he insisted that I ride with him.

As we drove, my benefactor remained absolutely silent, only smiling and nodding inscrutably to acknowledge my questions. He spoke for the first time when we pulled up to the newspaper's front gate.

"Mr. Chamorro is a brave man, and not everyone can be so brave," he said, and then sped away.

Chamorro was a man of action, not at all the figure one conjures from the phrase "newspaper publisher." Scion of a distinguished family that had produced four Nicaraguan presidents, he was only twenty years old when first forced into exile in 1944 by the ascendant Somoza clan. Soon after returning, he surged to the forefront of conflict with the Somozas, showing an instinctive talent for leadership.

The rivalry between Chamorros and Somozas, based originally on politics but thickly overlaid with personal hatred, soon took on aspects of a blood feud. When President Anastasio Somoza García was assassinated in 1956, his sons were certain Pedro Joaquín Chamorro was involved. They arrested him and other opposition leaders, and subjected them to long and bloody beatings over a period of months. The torture was conducted not in an isolated cell, but in a specially constructed room in the Somoza family home.

After his release, Chamorro had written a book about his experiences in Somoza's jails, and some Nicaraguans had smuggled copies home from Mexico. The most chilling section was an account of the time he spent imprisoned in a specially constructed zoo within the private Somoza compound. Cages there were built with two compartments, one for a big cat and the other for a political prisoner.

"Dozens of men spent days and even months locked up with lions, panthers, and jaguars in this garden of the modern Borgias," Chamorro wrote. "From the rear of the garden where I was caged, I could see the members of this extraordinary family pass by, and more than once I watched their innocent children enter with toys and dolls, practically facing the cages where men were pent up with beasts."

Chamorro endured the ordeal, and after five months was released on probation. At the first opportunity, he fled with his wife, Violeta, to Costa Rica, and again immersed himself in conspiracy. His life since then, marked by abortive uprisings and prison terms, had become an ever-escalating crusade against the Somoza dynasty. He threw himself into the family newspaper with the same vigor he had shown as a young agitator, churning out columns and editorials that burned with as much indignation as government censors would permit.

Among the many photos decorating Chamorro's office, I was struck by one taken during his guerrilla days. He was unshaven, and in his combat fatigues he looked lean and muscular. A rifle was slung over his shoulder. Years had passed, but obviously Chamorro still considered himself a fighter.

"Tell me about the Somoza regime," I suggested.

He nodded, much as a teacher nods to a new pupil at the begining of the semester's first class, leaned back in his swivel chair, and started to speak.

"It is a classic dictatorship, characterized by corruption, violence, disorder, and government-sponsored crime," Chamorro said. "I compare it to a Mafia gang, because it is dedicated first of all to self-enrichment. But this is a very special gang. The Somozas survive because they have support from your government, the United States government. They have powerful friends in Washington, sad to say. Ultimately they will fall, but only God knows how. Every Latin American dictatorship has fallen in a different way."

La Prensa was still publishing because the Somozas thought they would lose too much international prestige if they shut it down, but Chamorro told me he feared they might change their minds at any moment. He was provoking them with his militant editorials, as well as with anti-Somoza speeches he was delivering in various parts of the country. I asked him about the political coalition he was forging as a base from which to launch his next, still undefined political challenge.

"We have minimum and basic goals: ending the feudal dynasty and establishing a democratic republic in Nicaragua," he replied. "We're holding meetings all over the country. The police give us trouble, but we're out there working, preparing for the next stage."

Chamorro was not foolish enough to predict what the next stage would be, but he did say that he doubted the Somozas would ever allow themselves to be voted out of office. And there was one more thing.

"Don't forget that there is a Sandinista Front somewhere up in the mountains," he reminded me. "The government admits there are about a hundred of them, and other people say as many as five hundred. I personally detest their politics, but I can feel them out there. There's a war going on in this country between the Sandinistas and the National Guard. Don't believe anyone who tells you otherwise."

Copy deadlines were closing in on Chamorro, and I rose to leave. He urged me to publish something, anything, that might awaken Americans to what was happening in Nicaragua.

"The United States is the great, overwhelming factor in our national life, and you don't even know we exist!" he exclaimed, raising both hands over his head as if marveling at the absurdity.

We said goodbye, and I walked out into the shimmering midday heat. Could that extraordinary man, I asked myself, lead the charge that would oust the Somozas, and if so, at what cost? He seemed so modern, so worldly and so Western, yet he spent his days working to destroy a regime closely allied with the United States. I was finding Nicaragua more perplexing—and more alluring—as each day passed.

BEFORE leaving Managua at the end of November, I made repeated attempts to find someone connected to the Sandinistas, or at least someone who could tell me about them. That proved utterly impossible. Even the word "Sandinista" was taboo in public discourse. No one could risk showing public sympathy for the guerrillas, who, after all, were advocating nothing less than the violent destruction of the country's entire political and economic structure. Lawyers who had defended Sandinistas in political trials told me that guerrilla cells were totally inaccessible even to them. I resigned myself to not finding Sandinistas, and had to limit myself to civilians like Father Fernando Cardenal, a Jesuit priest from one of Nicaragua's oldest families.

A subcommittee of the United States Congress had lately held a hearing about human rights in Nicaragua, one of those esoteric topics that from time to time catch the odd legislator's attention. I was carrying a copy of the transcript with me, with Father Cardenal's name underlined. He had traveled to Washington to denounce the Somozas in the strongest terms, going so far as to issue a list of National Guardsmen who he said were torturers. Even more remarkably, he had returned to Nicaragua after testifying, virtually daring the authorities to arrest him. His cassock and his family background gave him a measure of protection, but nonetheless his friends worried about his safety. I located him without difficulty, and hired a taxi to take me to his home one afternoon. He lived comfortably, by himself, in a landscaped neighborhood beyond the zone of earthquake devastation.

Father Cardenal was tall and slender. His delicate features gave him a youthful appearance despite his white hair. Over several cups of strong coffee, he told me that Nicaragua was a land of misery, where a callous elite lived in luxury while masses of poor people suffered. He talked about his trip to Washington, his perception of the Somoza regime, and his fears for Nicaragua's future. He made a point of telling me that our conversation was on the record, and that I should feel free to quote him by name. Naturally I admired his courage, and told him so. But the truth about Father Cardenal did not dawn on me that day. Not until years later did I learn that he was a secret Sandinista, and that at the moment we spoke, he was engaged in a clandestine project of far-reaching importance.

Beginning in the late 1960s, a new, more socially conscious generation had come of age in Nicaragua. Sons and daughters of the ruling class, returning from schools abroad, were outraged by the deprivation they saw in urban slums and among peasants on their families' plantations. A strain of idealism appeared in circles where greed had long been the only motivating force. Many public-spirited young people volunteered to work for Catholic charities. For those who wanted to do more, who wanted to devote themselves fully to serving others, several priests began holding evening study groups at which they discussed ways of responding to life's ethical imperatives. Father Cardenal directed long consciousness-raising sessions with groups of altruistic young people who were searching for meaning in their lives. To outsiders, the sessions may have appeared spiritual and quite innocent, but, in fact, they had a very specific purpose: to persuade students that the way to live a Christian life at this moment in

Nicaragua was to become a Sandinista fighter. Father Cardenal's intellectual workshop produced many guerrillas, including some who went on to become senior Sandinista leaders.

DURING my last days in Managua, I walked through marketplaces, rode buses, and talked with everyone I met. After dark I sat in my room and typed. I wrote a short dispatch for the California-based Pacific News Service, and worked on a magazine article about the Somozas and their subservience to Washington. It was published in *The New Republic* under the title, "Nicaragua: A Wholly Owned Subsidiary."

One morning, shortly before I left Nicaragua, the Somoza family newspaper, *Novedades,* carried a front-page headline proclaiming the death of a "subversive leader" named Carlos Fonseca, along with a photo of the victim's body. The story reported that Fonseca had been shot dead in a skirmish in the north. I clipped the article, and read it over several times. The victim's name was only vaguely familiar. I had no idea that a tiny band of Sandinistas revered him, and would come to venerate his memory as if he were a deity.

The next day *Novedades* reported that another Sandinista leader, Eduardo Contreras, had died in combat along with several other guerrillas. Few knew it at the time, but Contreras was the very man code-named "Marco" who had led the commando squad that stormed the famous Christmas party two years before. I tried to imagine who these Sandinistas were, and guess what motivated them and moved them to such sacrifices. Reporting trips are supposed to be for finding answers, but I left Nicaragua unsatisfied and anxious to learn more.

2

"GUN THE BANDITS DOWN"

NICARAGUA'S HISTORY is an epic of tyranny and rebellion. The first Spanish governor was a fanatical despot named Pedrarias, who during the 1520s shipped thousands of Indians into slavery and slaughtered countless more. For amusement he staged gladiator-like games at which Indian chiefs were forced to fight packs of wild dogs. He taught Nicaragua the way of the boot and the rifle, and his legacy hangs over the country like an ancient curse.

The Spanish did not conquer Nicaragua without a fight, however. Indian warriors led by a legendary chieftain, Diriangén, fought valiantly against them, and even managed to drive them away for a time. Diriangén was Nicaragua's first resistance fighter, and his example, like that of Pedrarias, has resonated through the centuries. Tyrant and rebel: these are the archetypes of Nicaraguan history.

Central America gained its independence from Spain on September 15, 1821. For a time Guatemala, El Salvador, Honduras, Nicaragua, and Costa Rica were part of a single nation, the United Provinces of Central America. But their union fell apart, and in 1838 the Republic of Nicaragua came into being.

The central figure in nineteenth-century Nicaraguan history was not a Nicaraguan at all, but rather the messianic American adventurer William Walker. Though he has been all but forgotten in his native United States, Walker remains a vivid presence in Nicaragua. His campaign to build an empire in Central America captured the attention of millions, and briefly propelled him to the center of the world stage. It also fed a strain of anti-Americanism that was to become a permanent part of the Nicaraguan character.

Walker was born in 1824 to a devout family of Scottish Calvinists in Nashville, Tennessee. As a child he was shy and withdrawn, but an outstanding student. After abandoning promising careers in medicine, law and journalism, he moved to California. There he fell in with a group of adventurers who dreamed of conquering northern Mexico. Caught up in the racist fantasies that were implicit in the ideology of manifest destiny, he came to believe that Providence had chosen him to "liberate" Spanish-speaking nations and secure for them the blessings of rule by the white race.

"They are but drivellers," he wrote, "who speak of establishing fixed relations between the pure white American race, as it exists in the United States, and the mixed, Indo-Hispanic race, as it exists in Mexico and Central America, without the employment of force. The history of the world presents no such Utopian vision as that of an inferior race yielding meekly and peacefully to the controlling influence of a superior people. Whenever barbarism and civilization, or two distinct forms of civilization, meet face to face, the result must be war."

Walker's forays into Mexico proved disastrous, and nearly cost him his life. But he returned to California afire with the idea of conquest. In 1854 he learned that Liberal and Conservative bands in Nicaragua were fighting a civil war. Through an intermediary, he struck a deal with the besieged Liberal leader. Walker would lead a contingent of pro-Liberal soldiers to Nicaragua, and if the war was won, he and his men would be rewarded with money and land grants.

From waterfront taverns and boarding houses catering to luckless prospectors, Walker recruited a force of fifty-eight fighting men he dubbed "The Immortals." Full of enthusiasm, they set sail from San Francisco on May 4, 1855, and landed several weeks later at what is now the Nicaraguan port of Corinto. They were as strange a collection of misfits and idealists as ever set out to liberate any country.

Walker suffered some early setbacks, but after a four-month campaign he managed to capture the Conservative capital of Granada. By doing so, he established a strategic base in the heart of Central America. Stirring tales of his victories, and predictions that he would soon rule the entire isthmus, covered the front pages of newspapers. He became an international figure, and began to describe himself as an instrument of divine justice.

At first Walker ruled from behind the scenes, but within a year of his victory he decided to take the reins of power himself. He called a hurried presidential election, announced his candidacy, and counted votes in a manner that guaranteed his victory. On July 11, 1856, at the age of thirty-three, he was inaugurated president of Nicaragua.

Nicaraguans soon took up arms against the pretensions of a foreigner to rule their country. They were joined by soldiers from Costa Rica, Honduras, El Salvador, and Guatemala, all of whose rulers feared Walker's expansionist ambition. The multi-national force closed in on Granada, and though American fighters repelled its first assault, they could not hold out indefinitely. Walker was forced to surrender his prize. Before he retreated, however, he burned the city to the ground. One of his officers left behind a crude sign in the rubble, bearing the legend *Aquí Fue Granada*—Granada was here.

Walker knew little of Nicaragua's people or culture, but nonetheless he assumed the right to dictate its destiny. Mystically convinced of the righteousness of his cause, driven by an arrogance tinged with racism, he saw Nicaragua as a place where he could create a government in his own image. He was the first but not the last American whose irrational fantasies led them to unleash suffering and death upon innocent Nicaraguans.

FOR forty years after Walker's defeat, the Conservative party ruled Nicaragua, with the presidency rotating among heads of wealthy Granada families. The country's consuming dream during these years was that the great canal connecting the Atlantic and Pacific oceans would be built in Nicaragua. For a time, the dream seemed quite plausible. Detailed plans were drawn up, and excavation actually began at San Juan del Norte one October morning in 1889. It was a festive moment, marked by "the booming of cannon, cheers of crowds of all nationalities, the clinking of wine glasses, speeches and handshakes, dinners and receptions, services in the churches, and all the jollity natural to a general holiday."

Work on the canal continued for three years, but ultimately the project collapsed for lack of funds, and the United States went on to build its canal in Panama. Engineers had pronounced the Nicaragua route preferable, but financiers with interests in Panama launched a sophisticated lobbying campaign in Washington that robbed Nicaragua of its prize. Pro-Panama lobbyists portrayed Nicaragua as both geologically and politically unstable. The geological problems were represented by Nicaragua's many volcanos, and the political problems by the towering figure of President José Santos Zelaya.

The 1893 Liberal revolution that propelled Zelaya to power shook the foundations of Nicaraguan life. The Liberals were bent on reform, and Zelaya was a visionary nationalist and social crusader. He was also the first Nicaraguan president to defy the United States. For that heresy, he and his country paid dearly.

In photographs and drawings that survive, Zelaya appears a most formidable figure, tall and broad-shouldered, with penetrating eyes and a large face dominated by an elegantly twirled moustache. His sixteen-year rule was a period of unparalleled progress for Nicaragua. He poured resources into public education, encouraged foreign trade, and built roads, bridges, and government buildings. During his term, Congress extended political rights to all citizens including women, recognized civil marriage and divorce, and outlawed involuntary servitude. He paved the streets of Managua, lined them with street lamps, and then, as a crowning gesture, imported Nicaragua's first automobile. It came from France, together with a French chauffeur since there was no one in Nicaragua who could drive it. Riding the only car in the country along boulevards that he had built, paved, and illuminated, waving to awed crowds, the ruddy-cheeked president must have seemed a true prophet of progress.

Zelaya's belief in Nicaraguan nationalism inevitably led him into conflict with the United States. When he canceled or reduced the scope of concessions granted to several American mining and lumber companies, some influential figures in the United States became alarmed. They circulated rumors that Zelaya was making secret arrangements with extra-continental powers. At various times he was said to be negotiating with British businessmen for construction of a trans-isthmian canal, inviting Germans to invest in the Nicaraguan railroad system, and seeking a loan from Japan in order to avoid having to accept one from the United States. He became a favorite target for American politicians and editorial writers. President William Howard Taft denounced him as a "medieval despot."

In 1909, Zelaya moved to end a timber concession granted to the G. D. Emory Company, a Massachusetts-based lumber concern. President Taft decided he had seen enough of Zelaya, and resolved to force him from power. He recalled the American chargé d'affaires in Managua, and then sent gunboats to patrol near the Nicaraguan coast. Secretary of State Philander Knox, who as a private attorney in Pittsburgh had represented businessmen aggrieved by Zelaya, delivered the fatal blow. On December 1, 1909, he sent a letter to the Nicaraguan ambassador in Washington that became one of the most famous documents in United States-Latin America relations. The Knox Note, as it came to be known, was a direct notice that the United States wanted Zelaya's resignation. In it, Knox pledged that Washington would not rest until Nicaragua was ruled by "a Government capable of responding to demands . . . one entirely disassociated from the present intolerable conditions."

Although Zelaya was a dreamer, he never lost touch with reality. He understood immediately that he could not hope to survive in the face of such unequivocal opposition. In a brief telegram to President Taft dated December 4, he accepted the hopelessness of his situation and agreed to resign and accept exile. Soon afterward, a company of United States Marines debarked in Nicaragua and directed the installation of a new regime fully servile to Washington.

By eliminating Zelaya, the United States believed it had resolved the Nicaraguan "problem." The truth turned out to be quite different. American intervention sparked a patriotic surge. Impassioned Liberal leaders began to talk of taking up arms against the Marines and their client regime. One actually did so, and the mention of his name, Benjamin Zeledón, swells the hearts of Nicaraguan patriots to this day.

Zeledón was an earnest schoolteacher and judge who had greatly admired President Zelaya. He was outraged by the American intervention, and found Marine occupation deeply humiliating. Like-minded patriots began to gather around him, and in 1912 he forged them into a military regiment. The men took up positions on a hill near Masaya, and when Marines approached, they refused to surrender.

"With my resistance forces," Zeledón wrote to the Marine commander, "I will do what Nicaragua's dignity requires. Upon you and the leaders of your mighty nation will fall the tremendous responsibility that history will assign you, and the eternal reproach of having turned your weapons against the weak, who struggle to defend their country's sacred rights."

At dawn on October 3, 1912, Marines stormed Zeledón's position. Their charge was overwhelming, and in less than an hour they had won their objective. Zeledón and about thirty of his most determined followers continued firing as they retreated, drawing platoons of Marines into a day of sporadic fighting. During a break in the gunfire, he took time to write what became his final testament, a letter to his young wife, Ester.

"Surrounded as we are by gaping cannon and thousands of men prepared for assault, it would be foolish to expect anything other than death," he wrote. "I have no illusions. By taking up the rifle and refusing the humiliating offers of money and honors made to me, I signed my own death warrant. But if that sentence is carried out I will die serenely, because each drop of my blood spilled in defense of the nation and its freedom will give life to a hundred Nicaraguans who, like me, will take up arms against the betrayal of our beautiful but unfortunate Nicaragua."

Soon after writing those words, Zeledón was cut down by enemy fire. His brief but valiant rebellion had been crushed, but in death he sparked the rebellion to follow. Among the mourners at his funeral was a a young man named Augusto César Sandino. Staring into the coffin, Sandino felt indignation rising within him.

"Zeledón's death gave me the key to understanding our country's situation in the face of Yankee piracy," he wrote years afterward.

LATIN America has produced no more classic hero than Sandino. His six-year military campaign decisively shaped Nicaragua's political history, but he was much more than a political figure. By setting out to wage war on United States Marines, and by succeeding so well, he reshaped the consciousness of the Hispanic world. The story of his epic march toward glory is one of history's most stirring adventures.

Sandino was the illegitimate son of a small landowner and a domestic servant. He spent his youth at farm labor and left home soon after his twentieth birthday. In Honduras and Mexico, he worked for large American companies including United Fruit and South Pennsylvania Oil. In the Mexican boom towns of Tampico and Veracruz, he met trade union organizers, socialists, and anarchists. He heard not only radical anti-imperialist rhetoric, but harsh denunciations of Nicaragua for its submission to the United States.

"The other peoples of Central America and Mexico despise us Nicaraguans," Sandino wrote. "I felt deeply hurt when they called me a shameless traitor who had allowed his country to be bought and sold. At first I resisted those accusations, saying that since I was not a man of state, I did not deserve them. But later I reflected more deeply, and I came to understand that they were right, since I was a Nicaraguan and had a right to protest. Then I heard that a revolutionary movement had broken out in Nicaragua. I was working at the time for the Huasteca Petroleum Company at Tampico; it was May 15, 1926. . . . I told my friends that if Nicaragua had one hundred men who loved her as I do, our nation could recover its absolute sovereignty, stolen from us by the Yankee empire. My friends said that in Nicaragua there were that many and more."

Sandino returned to Nicaragua and found work at a gold mine in the northern village of San Albino. Impoverished laborers there were receptive to his ideas, and a group of them became his first comrades-in-arms. Declaring anti-imperialism as their cause, they began attacking military outposts along the Coco River in northeast Nicaragua. Their ultimate objective, Sandino declared, was nothing less than the expulsion of Marines from Nicaraguan territory.

"I believe I am doing my duty, and wish to write my future protests in blood," he proclaimed.

Sandino's rebel force, numbering several hundred men and boys, established a base at San Rafael del Norte, high in the cool Segovia hills near the Coco River, and began to learn the skills of war. Their first major target was the nearby town of Ocotal, where American Marines and their local allies had built a base. Many of the Marines were veterans of World War I, and their commander, General Logan Feland, had issued orders to "gun the bandits down mercilessly where they are encountered." Yet the chance to strike a blow against the United States had rarely been afforded to Nicaraguans, and Sandino's volunteers attacked with high spirits.

The guerrillas made skillful use of their eight machine guns, pressing systematically toward the center of Ocotal. After fifteen hours of fighting, they had forced defenders into a small area around the Marine garrison. Behind them, their peasant supporters rampaged wildly through the streets, destroying homes, looting shops and warehouses, and wreaking vengeance on those they considered collaborators and enemies.

Sandino wisely decided not to try to attack the concentration of troops gathered in and around the garrison. He had originally planned to burn Ocotal to the ground, but after hearing the pleas of residents he ordered his men to withdraw. His fighters obeyed, but many of the peasants accompanying them could not be induced to halt their plunder. Suddenly two American planes appeared overhead, followed by several more. They began dropping bombs on Sandino's followers, and then firing on them as they fled. The bombing lasted for about an hour. As many as three hundred Nicaraguans were killed, among them an unknown number of women and children. Ocotal thus earned the sad distinction of becoming the first town in the Western hemisphere to suffer military bombardment from the air.

"In all of U.S. history there has been no action of such indecency as we now see in Nicaragua," Governor Edward Dunne of Illinois wrote in a public protest.

OCOTAL is a living textbook for those who believe that history delights in patterns and symmetries. During one of my visits there, I met an elderly gentleman named José Ignacio Ponce, and asked him if he remembered anything about Sandino.

"I was right here in Ocotal the day of the attack," he told me, nodding and scratching his white whiskers. "I can tell you anything you want to know."

"Well, what happened?"

"It was a big battle, real big," Ponce recalled. "Many fighters. Most of them only had machetes. The fighting lasted all day. What was worst was the bombing. It was terrible. There were dead bodies everywhere. Vultures came to eat them."

"Did you see Sandino?"

"I saw him once, just for a few seconds. He was standing on that corner over there with some of his officers."

Ponce was pointing to a corner just a few yards away. I tried to envision the scene.

"What did Sandino look like?" I asked.

"*Muy bajito,*" the old man replied with a smile. Very short.

MARINE tactics in Nicaragua were harsh. Patrols often burned grain warehouses and killed cattle to deprive rebels of food. They also relied heavily on aerial bombing, by one estimate destroying seventy villages and hamlets in the two years following the Ocotal battle.

Sandino, not surprisingly, was fiercely anti-American, and attacked American property whenever he could. He described Marines as "murderous invaders" serving the "eagle with larcenous claws," and proclaimed himself "completely convinced that the North American people support and will always support the expansionist policies of their immoral governments."

The American journalist Carleton Beals, on assignment for *The Nation*, was one of the few Americans who interviewed and came to know Sandino. His dispatches helped stir indignation over the American role in Nicaragua, and made Sandino a figure of fascination in the United States:

> Several days ago I rode out of the camp of Augusto C. Sandino, the terrible "bandit" of Nicaragua who is holding the Marines at bay . . . I am the first bona fide correspondent of any nationality to talk to him face to face.
> "Do you still think of us as bandits?" was his last query as I bade him goodbye.
> "You are as much a bandit as Mr. Coolidge is a Bolshevik," was my reply.
> "Tell your people," he returned, "there may be bandits in Nicaragua, but they are not necessarily Nicaraguan."

The Marines were unable to suppress Sandino's rebellion, and as months and years passed they began to despair of ever defeating him. In the United States, the economy was collapsing into depression and public support for foreign military interventions was weakening. Facing military stalemate and rising protests at home, President Herbert Hoover made a momentous decision late in 1932: he would withdraw the Marines from Nicaragua. Sandino and his ragtag guerrillas had accomplished something unthinkable. They had not only won control of a vast territory in northern Nicaragua, but had managed to drive American soldiers from their homeland.

With the Marines gone, Sandino agreed to talk peace. He traveled to Managua for negotiations with President Juan Bautista Sacasa on February 2, 1933, and the two men spent the afternoon and evening together at the presidential residence. At 11:15 they emerged to announce that they had agreed on a peace treaty. Waiting crowds erupted in celebration at the news.

One man, General Anastasio Somoza García, was distressed at news of the treaty. Somoza García had been installed by the departing Marines as commander of the newly created National Guard, and he saw Sandino as a political rival. In the months that followed, he came to conclude that Nicaragua was not big enough for both of them. On the afternoon of February 21, 1934, he assembled a group of National Guard officers and told them that national security demanded Sandino's assassination.

That evening, Sandino was the guest of honor at a festive dinner hosted by President Sacasa. At ten o'clock, Sandino embraced the president and took his leave. With two of his generals, he was driven into the moonlit night in a government-owned Chevrolet. Soon after they left the presidential residence, they were stopped by a patrol of Guardsmen, rifles at the ready.

"Who gave the order?" asked a surprised Sandino. "The war is over."

No one answered. Guardsmen roughly pulled the three rebel leaders out of their car. Quickly they realized they were facing death.

"We're all brothers now, so why are you doing this?" Sandino appealed. "We've made peace, and we're going to work together to bring Nicaragua back to life. I haven't done anything except fight for this country's freedom . . . Call General Somoza. Let him tell me what he wants. Let him speak."

Sandino's plea was to no avail. He and his two comrades were ordered into the back of a National Guard truck, driven to a nearby military airfield, and shot. They were buried amid great secrecy, their bodies never to be found.

Sandino left an indelible imprint on the Nicaraguan psyche. By taking up the cause of nationalism and defending it so successfully against enormous odds, he gave Nicaragua a hero of great stature. His willingness to defy the United States was an almost unavoidable inspiration to future generations.

"I will not live much longer," Sandino correctly predicted early in 1934. "But there are young people who will continue my fight. They may do great things."

WITH his rival Sandino dead, General Somoza García was able to push his way to absolute power without difficulty. He forced President Sacasa aside, called an election for 1936, and imposed himself as the Liberal candidate. According to official results, 107,000 Nicaraguans voted for him and just 169 voted for his opponent.

Somoza García ruled oppressively and used his power to amass fabulous wealth. Nonetheless, he enjoyed unwavering American support, symbolized vividly by the lavish reception President Franklin Roosevelt gave him when he visited Washington in 1939. Roosevelt himself met the Nicaraguan leader as he stepped off a train at Union Station, and the two presidents, dressed formally and wearing silk top hats, drove together in an open car to the White House. Five thousand American military men in dress uniforms lined the route, ceremonial guns boomed, and a squadron of military planes flew overhead. Roosevelt explained the warm welcome by saying of his guest, "He's a son of a bitch, but he's ours."

Nicaragua's constitution forbade presidential re-election, but nonetheless Somoza García announced plans to seek a second term in 1944. His announcement set off such violent protests that he was forced to reconsider. Instead of running himself, he directed the fraudulent election of an elderly political ally named Leonardo Argüello.

In his inaugural address, however, President Argüello shocked everyone by declaring his political independence and asserting, "I have no commitments to anyone." In the days that followed, he lifted press censorship and declared his support for trade union organizing campaigns. Even more astonishing, he made plans to force General Somoza García and his military allies into retirement.

The general, faced with a crisis that threatened to end his career, struck back decisively. Abandoning all pretense of legality, he led a coup that ended Argüello's term after just twenty-six days. He made himself dictator, and normal political life in the country came to an end.

Several groups of Nicaraguans took up arms against the regime, including one led by young Pedro Joaquín Chamorro, but none came close to success. On September 20, 1956, the dictator traveled to Léon, traditional seat of the Liberal party, to be nominated for yet another presidential term. The next evening he attended a festive celebration at the city's largest public hall, the *Casa del Obrero*. At the height of the party, after he had danced a turn with a local beauty queen, a man stepped in front of him and began firing a small pistol. The gunman was immediately killed by presidential bodyguards, but he had shot well. Somoza was mortally wounded, and died several days later at an American hospital in the Panama Canal Zone.

"His constantly demonstrated friendship for the United States will never be forgotten," Secretary of State John Foster Dulles assured the widow in a consolation note.

The assassain was a twenty-six-year-old Liberal named Rigoberto López Pérez, who by his sacrifice became a martyr-hero of the anti-Somoza movement. He left a moving letter to his mother as a final testament. "I hope you will take all of this calmly," he wrote. "You should realize that what I have done is a duty which any Nicaraguan who truly loves his country should have carried out long ago."

The United States ambassador in Managua, Thomas Whelan, worked quickly to assure that the Somoza family would not lose power after the assassination. At his urging, Congress installed the late dictator's son, Luis Somoza Debayle, a beefy thirty-three-year-old graduate of Louisiana State University, as president. Luis ruled until 1963, and then gave way to his younger brother, Anastasio, known as Tachito.

Tachito Somoza had a reputation for swagger and cruelty, and he turned out to be the harshest of the three Somozas who ruled Nicaragua. Often he would personally drop in on torture sessions to see how the familiy's enemies were bearing up under abuse. By systematically extorting money from businessmen, he amassed a fortune far beyond those of his father and brother before him. His ascension to the presidency fulfilled Nicaragua's ultimate nightmare, and set the stage for escalating violence.

The Somozas were overjoyed when one of their old friends, Richard Nixon, won the White House in 1968. Nicaragua was the only country where Nixon had not been jeered when he toured Latin America as vice president a decade earlier, and like his predecessors he viewed Nicaragua as an important regional ally. His election assured the Somozas of a sympathetic ear in the Oval Office, but it also meant something far more tangible. Tachito had developed the wild idea that he could attract the furtive billionaire Howard Hughes to Nicaragua, and persuade him to invest there. As first step, he persuaded Nixon to appoint a Hughes protégé, Turner Shelton, as United States ambassador to Nicaragua. Using Shelton as an intermediary, Somoza opened contacts with Hughes and proposed a business partnership.

Hughes was interested, and late in 1972 he arrived in Managua. He and his aides took over an entire floor in the newly constructed Intercontinental Hotel, and they began negotiating with the Somozas, who owned nearly all of Nicaragua that was worth owning. Hughes was interested in building a trans-isthmian oil pipeline, and also wanted to buy a piece of the Intercontinental, a share in the Nicaraguan airline, Lanica, and according to rumor, much more. Tachito had apparently hooked a very big fish.

Hughes was in his hotel suite on the night of December 22, 1972, when the earthquake hit. All the hotel guests were naturally terrified, but Hughes's pathological fear of germs drove him especially wild. His aides frantically rushed him to the airport and packed him onto a waiting private jet. He never returned to Nicaragua, and abandoned his plans to invest there.

The earthquake was an enormous human tragedy, killing or injuring ten thousand people and leaving three hundred thousand others homeless. It also had a far-reaching effect on Nicaraguan politics. Tachito Somoza named himself chairman of a new National Emergency Committee, which assumed absolute control of the relief and reconstruction effort. He offered the vice-chairmanship to Archbishop Miguel Obando y Bravo, the Roman Catholic primate, but the archbishop suspected that Somoza had larceny on his mind, and refused to serve.

Planeloads of relief supplies began arriving at Managua's international airport within hours of the quake. All cargo was received by the National Emergency Committee, which became a kind of black hole from which precious little emerged. Sealed containers of food, medicine, and other goods from abroad, many of them marked "For Free Distribution Only," quickly turned up for sale at local markets. Somoza's men drove truckloads of donated building materials directly from the airport to warehouses owned by favored speculators and black marketeers. Guardsmen took advantage of the disorder to loot stores and showrooms.

At the peak of their power in the mid-1970s, the Somozas were said to be worth about one billion dollars. They owned more than ten thousand square miles of farm and grazing land in Nicaragua, as well as extensive properties in Guatemala, Honduras, and Costa Rica, and real estate in United States. Directly or through intermediaries, they also controlled railroad and steamship lines, factories, fishing fleets, gold mines, lumber companies and, certainly not least, Nicaragua's largest brewery. During the 1960s and 1970s, they made new and highly profitable investments in gambling, drug smuggling, and prostitution. Tachito Somoza's avarice, the extent of which became fully clear after the earthquake, reflected the decadence into which his regime had fallen. Public sentiment was newly outraged, and even once-neutral businessmen began to call for the dictator's ouster.

In July 1977 Somoza suffered a heart attack and was rushed to Miami for treatment. He spent two months recuperating there. When he returned home, he found many of his friends and allies worried about the future. They saw political trouble ahead, and urged him to use his health problems as an excuse to step down from the presidency, at least temporarily. He refused to consider their advice.

Watching from afar, I could sense that Nicaragua was headed for confrontation. I made a round of telephone calls to magazine and newspaper editors, and found several interested in buying stories about the gathering conflict. Then I bought a plane ticket and made my way back to Managua.

3

A NATION REBELS

I RETURNED to Managua late in 1977, and had been at my guest house for only a few days when the proprietress handed me a scrawled telephone message. The president of the Republic, General Anastasio Somoza Debayle, had scheduled a news conference that day, and I was invited to attend. Somoza had been portrayed to me as a cross between Caligula and Dale Carnegie, a tyrant with a modern veneer. I was eager for a look at him, and arrived early for the news conference. But at the door to the presidential suite, I was stopped by an elegant-looking woman.

"Young man," she said sternly, "certainly you cannot expect to enter dressed like that. You are here to see the leader of our nation. Come back with a proper suit and you will be admitted."

I looked around, and it was true that despite the suffocating heat outside, most of the arriving Nicaraguan journalists were formally dressed. No other foreigners were present. I was a lowly freelancer, still traveling with my Pacific News Service press card, and I saw that I would have to conform to local custom. Reluctantly, I made my way back to the guest house, where I had a light sport jacket hanging in my closet. When I returned to the news conference, sweating profusely, I was still without a necktie, but the woman at the door chose not to make a scene because the president was at that moment approaching the lectern.

Somoza's posture was stiff and erect. He wore a tailored charcoal-gray suit instead of the uniform I had expected, but years as a cadet and an officer had obviously marked him. On formal occasions like this he projected an air of brisk seriousness. His eyeglasses were modern, fashionably thin-rimmed. Only his slightly ridiculous pencil mustache suggested that he was something other than a wealthy investor or corporate executive.

When he reached the microphone, Somoza greeted us curtly and extracted some papers from a briefcase. He made a series of routine announcements about public works projects. Then, after speaking for only a few minutes, he called for questions. The first, from my friend Colonel Pataky, was about cotton prices. All the rest were equally innocuous. It was as if we were in a nation at absolute peace. No one asked about the Sandinista guerrillas, press censorship, prison conditions, or the three-year-old state of siege. The name Pedro Joaquín Chamorro was never mentioned.

CHAMORRO'S figure was looming larger than ever on the political horizon. His newspaper, *La Prensa,* freed from censorship when martial law was lifted in November 1977, relentlessly attacked the regime. In one series of articles, reporters from *La Prensa* traced Somoza's theft of earthquake relief supplies donated by foreign governments. Soon afterward, they unveiled the ghoulish workings of Plasmaferesis, a company run by Somoza cronies that bought blood from poor people and sold it abroad. The confrontation between Nicaragua's two giant figures became more intense and more personal.

"If I didn't make his headlines," Somoza wrote later, "my friends would say to me that Chamorro must be ill today."

Chamorro's newspaper columns reflected the breadth of his interests and his intellect. Even his most biting attacks on the regime were framed as civics lessons, discourses on the nature of freedom and the duty of individuals in the face of evil. Often he wrote of his expeditions to Nicaragua's interior, vividly describing the misery in which he found his fellow citizens living. Wherever he traveled, he stirred anti-Somoza passion. More than a newspaper editor, more than a politician, he was the outstanding figure of his generation. Many Nicaraguans expected that somehow, sometime, his moral authority would carry him to the presidency.

I tried to arrange another interview with Chamorro, but he was being honored in New York City. Columbia University had awarded him the Maria Moors Cabot journalism prize, signifying how far beyond Nicaragua's borders his fame had spread. Upon presenting the prize, Dean Elie Abel told the convocation, "If there is a journalist in the hemisphere who has been more consistent in his opposition to dictatorial government than Dr. Chamorro, we have not been able to find him."

In the course of his writing and speechmaking, Chamorro had coined several slogans that became part of Nicaragua's political language. *"Nicaragua volverá a ser república!"*—Nicaragua will be a republic again!—was his lifelong battle cry. In his columns, he liked to repeat another favorite maxim, *"Sin libertad de prensa, no hay libertad"*—Without freedom of the press, there is no freedom. And when asked about the personal risk he ran by hammering so insistently at the Somozas, he would reply, *"Cada quién es dueño de su propio miedo"*—Everyone is master of his own fear.

Chamorro had evidently mastered whatever fear was within him. When he drove to work on the morning of January 10, 1978, he was unprotected, as always. As he passed through the ruins of downtown Managua, a green Toyota pickup truck suddenly swerved in front of him. Two men jumped out, leveled shotguns, and began firing at him through his open driver's window. He slumped forward over the steering wheel as his car careened out of control. His assailants abandoned their truck, jumped into a waiting car, and sped away. Chamorro was rushed to a nearby hospital, but was dead on arrival.

President Somoza immediately expressed sorrow and regret, and even sent condolences to Chamorro's widow, Violeta. His public posture, of course, did not prevent Nicaraguans from blaming his regime for the crime. Some accused the dictator's son, Major Anastasio Somoza Portocarrero, who had often complained that his father was too tolerant of dissent. Others suspected Pedro Ramos, a Cuban exile who ran the blood-trafficking company, Plasmaferesis; Ramos had sued Chamorro for libel over his critical articles, and then left for Miami the day before the assassination. Whatever the truth, the Somoza dictatorship seemed fully unmasked. Pedro Joaquín Chamorro had embodied Nicaragua's hope for freedom. His murder surpassed all remaining limits, and profoundly shook the national conscience.

As thousands of angry mourners followed Chamorro's body through the streets of Managua to its final resting place, rioters ran wild in other parts of the city. One of their first targets was the Plasmaferesis building, which they sacked and burned. In other cities, young people hurled homemade bombs at military jeeps and fired on National Guard posts with small-caliber pistols and hunting rifles. Sandinista guerrillas arrived to join the fighting in Rivas and Granada, briefly holding parts of both cities. Businessmen, in their first concerted anti-Somoza protest, called a national strike to demand that Chamorro's assassins be found and punished.

It took Guardsmen two weeks to restore order. At the beginning of February, to demonstrate that the country was again at peace, Somoza held municipal elections. His candidates won in every city and town, without exception.

The next eruption came in the ever-defiant Monimbó neighborhood of Masaya. Several thousand residents turned out on the morning of February 21 to
rename a plaza in honor of Pedro Joaquín Chamorro, and they found Guardsmen waiting. Clashes were inevitable, and soon a full-scale riot broke out.
Guardsmen chased protesters through the streets, firing as they ran. Protesters
fought back with pistols, knives, firecrackers, rocks, and bottles. Street fighting
continued for three days. One group of residents somehow managed to build a
rudimentary bazooka out of metal scraps. Another group set fire to the homes
of Somoza supporters. In back rooms, mothers and grandmothers manufactured
crude pipe bombs filled with nails.

Finally President Somoza reached the end of his patience. Recognizing that
conventional infantry tactics were not working in Monimbó, he ordered a
frontal tank assault supported by helicopter bombing. Troops commanded by
General Reynaldo Pérez Vega, the National Guard's senior officer, smashed
through barricades and charged through the streets, firing wildly. Civilian casualties, though never precisely ascertained, were heavy. A form of peace was
finally restored to Monimbó, but no one who spoke to its residents could doubt
that this neighborhood would never be truly pacified as long as Somoza and his
National Guard were running Nicaragua.

Soon after the Monimbó uprising was crushed, I persuaded editors at the
Boston Globe to send me to Nicaragua for a short reporting trip. I found most
people still shocked by the Chamorro murder and the repression it had sparked.
Many seemed to have made up their minds to fight.

"Somoza is a savage, an animal!" one angry and resolute Monimbó housewife
told me. "He's going to pay for what he did to us. Maybe not today, but
tomorrow for sure."

While untrained civilians confronted Guardsmen on city streets, Sandinista
guerrillas in the remote northern mountains were escalating their military campaign. New volunteers, many of them burning with indignation over the Chamorro murder, swelled Sandinista ranks, and guerrilla squads in several areas
grew large enough to attempt major attacks. General Pérez Vega, who had
shown his ruthless efficiency in crushing the Monimbó uprising, was sent north
with orders to seek out and destroy guerrilla units.

General Pérez Vega's only regret was having to abandon his pursuit of Nora
Astorga, a tall, striking divorcée who had caught his eye several months earlier.
Unbeknownst to the General, Astorga was secretly a Sandinista agent. At first
she had been repulsed by his overtures, but soon she realized that she might be
able to take advantage of his interest by extracting information and passing it
along to her Sandinista friends. The Sandinista urged her to cultivate the relationship, and she did. When the general emerged in 1978 as the National
Guard's key counter-insurgency officer, they decided to spring a bloody trap.

Desperate to ease the military pressure General Pérez Vega was applying in the north, Sandinista leaders instructed Astorga to leave a provocative message with his secretary in Managua. She dialed his number on March 8, International Women's Day.

"Tell the general that something he's been very interested in for a long time can happen tonight," she told the secretary. "If it doesn't happen tonight, I can't guarantee that it ever will."

General Pérez Vega's response was immediate. In a matter of hours he was on his way back to Managua. When he arrived at Astorga's home, she offered him a drink, but he was eager, and suggested they adjourn directly to the bedroom. She agreed, and led him inside.

The general, believing his conquest was at hand, began to undress. He unbuckled the belt that held his pistol and laid it on a bedside bureau. But when he approached Astorga, she recoiled and shouted a revolutionary slogan. At that signal, two men wielding knives burst from a closet.

The general tried to resist, but since he was unarmed he had no chance. Soon he lay dead of stab wounds. His killers draped a red-and-black Sandinista flag over his mutilated corpse and then fled, taking Astorga with them. Their raid was a stunning success. It enhanced the Sandinista mystique, energized the opposition, and struck new fear into the hearts of Somoza and his servants.

As these events were reported in the world press, the dictator became increasingly irritated at foreign journalists, especially Americans. He complained that we ignored his good works, unfairly vilified his National Guard, harped excessively on his private wealth, and slandered him by suggesting that he was behind the murder of Pedro Joaquín Chamorro.

"They want to make me out to be a very devilish man," he protested once, "and I'm really just a simple farmer."

1978 was the year when I and other foreign correspondents realized that the crisis in Nicaragua would probably soon escalate into a very big news story. On my periodic visits, I began running into veteran Latin American hands like Alan Riding of the *New York Times* and Bernard Diederich of *Time* magazine. Even network television crews began appearing, a sure sign that Nicaragua was breaking into the American consciousness.

President Somoza viewed most foreign correspondents as enemies, and he usually turned down our requests for interviews. But when several of us were in Managua at the same time, he would sometimes relent and agree to meet with us as a group. On these occasions we would be invited to the presidential bunker, a fortified complex beside the Intercontinental Hotel. Past a patio and a set of glass doors, we left the tropical dust and heat behind and entered a suite of offices that could have been a corporate headquarters in midtown Manhattan. The air was cool and fresh, carpeting and upholstery were in tastefully matched patterns, and framed prints hung on the panelled walls. Arriving reporters were ushered into a windowless room and seated in cushioned leather chairs around a large, handcrafted wooden table. When all were present, Somoza would enter through a side door.

Knowing that many American correspondents spoke only broken Spanish, Somoza enjoyed starting these meetings by solemnly announcing, *"Vamos a hablar sólo en español"*—We're going to speak in Spanish only. As reporters looked at each other in dismay, he would break out in laughter.

"Don't worry, boys, just kidding," he would reassure us in vernacular English. "We'll talk whatever you want. What's on your minds?"

We prodded Somoza for insights into the burgeoning conflict, but if he had any, he kept them to himself. His patter was like a recorded statement, a string of the same cliches his family had used to win support in Washington for years. He reminded us that the Somozas had always been strong allies of the United States, and insisted that all of his critics were either Communist or Communist-inspired.

Usually I refrained from asking questions at these news conferences, but once I spoke up.

"It seems to many of us that you're facing a nationwide revolt," I suggested. "Are you sure you can survive in power?"

"I think we can take care of that particular insurgency," Somoza replied with an indulgent smile.

Despite the dizzying sequence of the Chamorro assassination, the wave of uprisings it sparked, and the murder of General Pérez Vega, the United States was still not paying much attention to Nicaragua. Foreign policy planners were preoccupied with more distant places, including the Philippines, Namibia, and even the Horn of Africa, where a crisis was thought to be brewing. Nicaragua never made it to the top of their priority list.

One Latin leader, President Carlos Andrés Pérez of Venezuela, urged the Carter administration to move decisively against Somoza, to force him from power while there was still hope of establishing a pro-Western regime in Managua. President Carter refused, arguing that any direct action against Somoza would constitute intervention in the affairs of a foreign nation, and thus violate his political principles. At one point Carter even sent Somoza a letter congratulating him for taking "important and heartening" steps toward democracy.

The letter boosted Somoza's confidence, but it did nothing to weaken the forces arrayed against him at home. Nicaragua had been in constant upheaval since Chamorro's murder. New anti-Somoza organizations were springing up, and with them a new generation of opposition leaders. It was no longer possible to hear a good word about Somoza anywhere.

THE Somozas recognized the value of democratic symbols, and they maintained a rubber-stamp Congress that met regularly at the white-columned National Palace. On the morning of August 22, 1978, most members were at their seats, listening to discussion of the next year's national budget. Speeches droned on, and no one heard the two olive-colored jeeps that screeched up to the Palace's side entrances.

Guardsmen posted at the entrances were jolted from their torpor as squads of soldiers jumped from the jeeps.

"Out of the way!" barked their leader, who wore an officer's uniform complete with several rows of ribbons. "The boss is coming!"

With an air of unquestionable authority, the officer pushed uncomprehending Guardsmen back, and briskly twisted their shotguns from them. Momentarily stunned, they looked expectantly for Somoza's limousine, but it did not appear. The arriving soldiers fanned out through the building, running down the corridors to pre-arranged stations. Quickly, though not quickly enough, the truth became clear. The soldiers were not soldiers at all, but Sandinista commandos.

By the time gunfire broke out, the commandos were already chaining the Palace doors shut behind them. There were only a handful of Guardsmen inside, and all quickly surrendered, escaped, or were shot. The chief commando, who turned out to be the flamboyant conspirator Edén Pastora, crashed into the stunned Chamber of Deputies, fired a burst of rifle fire at the ceiling, and shouted, "Guardsmen! Everyone on the floor!" Terrified legislators dove for cover under their desks.

It took Pastora's twenty-five commandos just four minutes to secure the building. All of the assailants realized that they would probably perish in the event of a National Guard counterattack. Preparing for that possibility, they selected three hostages they considered particularly odious, two prominent congressmen and a senior Somoza family functionary, to be shot immediately "in any eventuality."

Trapped inside the Palace were more than fifteen hundred government employees and private citizens. All were ordered to lie face down on the floors. Among them were sixty-seven members of Congress, including, inevitably, members of the Somoza family: Luis Pallais Debayle, the president's cousin, and José Somoza Abrego, son of the president's half-brother.

Sandinista commandos controlled their captives without trouble. The building was calm, except inside the Chamber of Deputies, where Pastora was delivering a bombastic speech to cowering legislators, denouncing them as "traitors to the people" for collaborating with the regime. Archbishop Obando, who served as the official mediator, arrived and appealed for calm. As he was leaving the chamber, Manuel Eugarrios, a reporter from La Prensa, suddenly appeared in front of him, proffering five rolls of film. Obando slipped them into a pocket of his cassock and carried them out. That afternoon, Eugarrios's spectacular photos were splashed on La Prensa's front page.

Somoza wavered for two days, but finally capitulated. To end the siege, he paid $500,000 ransom, permitted the publication and broadcast of a long Sandinista communiqué, and freed fifty-eight imprisoned revolutionaries, among them the veteran plotter Tomás Borge. A bus carried the victorious commandos and released prisoners toward the airport, and people poured from their homes to cheer as it passed.

Before stepping aboard the plane that Somoza had been forced to provide, Pastora defiantly ripped the kerchief from his face and turned to salute the ecstatic crowd. When he triumphantly waved his rifle above his head, people went wild, breaking through security lines and rushing forward to embrace their heroes. Operation Pigsty, as the National Palace assault was felicitously code-named, had been a complete and devastating success.

SANDINISTA leaders issued their long-awaited call to national insurrection less than three weeks later, on the morning of September 9. "The hour of the people's Sandinista insurrection has arrived!" they proclaimed over their clandestine Radio Sandino. "Everyone take to the streets!"

Sandinista organizers, who had infiltrated into a dozen cities, sprung into action. They seized the northern city of Estelí, and large sections of Masaya, León, and Chinandega. To rout them, Somoza ordered sustained bombing raids.

During the insurrection, I drove the streets of Managua as often as I dared. Guardsmen were short-tempered, ready to shoot at the slightest provocation. They were especially suspicious of young men. Often they summarily executed those they captured, then drenched their bodies with gasoline and set them afire. I came upon such a pyre after rounding a streetcorner one day. It was the first time I had smelled the stench of burning flesh and seen the bodies of human beings treated like garbage.

Many Nicaraguans had hoped the September uprising would topple Somoza, but it did not come close. The guerrillas were still no military match for the National Guard. Somoza, however, paid a high price for his victory. He had lost control of his country for the better part of a month, and won it back only by stooping to acts of barbarism, including aerial bombardment of cities. All who watched Nicaragua convulse could sense that the regime's days were numbered.

4

TRIUMPH

FROM THE moment of the September 1978 uprising, Nicaragua was no longer one country, but two. One was the real Nicaragua, seething with violent anger at the tyrant whose National Guard had just devastated six cities and killed nearly two thousand people. In this Nicaragua, everyone had now seen the National Guard's brutality at close range. The stench of death that hung over Managua, Masaya, León, Chinandega, Matagalpa, and Estelí symbolized the regime's decay, and the only questions remaining were how long the dictator could hold on, and how much destruction he would wreak before finally fleeing.

For news correspondents covering the conflict, however, it soon became clear that the Nicaragua we saw every day was not the only Nicaragua. Another one had been created in the Carter administration's imagination, and it bore frighteningly little resemblance to reality. This was a country facing little more than a nasty political quarrel, shaken by a spate of disturbances but not in true crisis. It was a Nicaragua awaiting a calmly reasoned, peaceful resolution of its problems.

Senior policymakers in Washington were trying to ignore Nicaragua, hoping that somehow the unpleasantness there would resolve itself. After the September uprising, they sent career diplomat William Bowdler to Managua to try to broker a settlement, but it was far too late. Nicaraguans were in no mood to compromise. They wanted Somoza out immediately and unconditionally, and Bowdler's mission of conciliation was doomed to failure.

One afternoon in December 1978, I visited the Coca-Cola bottling plant for an interview with its manager, Adolfo Calero. The plant was next door to *La Prensa,* and Calero had been a friend and sometime political ally of his erstwhile neighbor, Pedro Joaquín Chamorro. White-haired and courtly, opposed to Somoza but far from radical, he was a favorite of the American embassy. When I met him, he had recently spent twenty-four hours in jail on one of the dictator's whims.

"The problem is one man, and that man has to go," Calero told me. "If the Americans want to play a constructive role here, it would be to dump Somoza before the situation runs out of their control."

Leaders of several Latin American countries also urged the United States to abandon Somoza. Venezuelan President Carlos Andrés Pérez was especially insistent. "A Sandinista victory will open the door to Castro!" he warned one envoy from Washington. "This will end in Cuban hands. The shame is this could be avoided, but the United States has not been decisive enough."

General Omar Torrijos, the Panamanian strongman, was also frustrated by American policy. Torrijos had worked closely with Carter on a variety of issues, but on the question of Nicaragua they disagreed entirely. Carter favored a cool, legalistic approach, while Torrijos was impatient for action. He never saw the point of Carter's mediation effort, and told him so.

"It's a simple problem," Torrijos bluntly told Carter during one telephone conversation. "A mentally deranged man with an army of criminals is attacking a defenseless population." When Carter suggested that the Organization of American States be invited to join the mediation, Torrijos ridiculed the idea. "This isn't a problem for the OAS," he snorted. "What we need is a psychiatrist!"

UNLIKE American political leaders, newspaper editors in the United States and Europe took the September uprising very seriously. Few of them had much experience dealing with Central America, but it took no great insight to see that Nicaragua was in turmoil and likely to remain so. Soon journalists from the United States, Europe, and Latin America became a permanent presence in Managua and in the Nicaraguan countryside. We were on a sort of death watch, waiting for the shots that would signify the beginning of the next round of war. In February 1979 the hapless American ambassador, Mauricio Solaún, was withdrawn after only eighteen months on the job, and it became clear that the United States would not recover the control of events it had enjoyed for generations in Nicaragua.

Sandinista guerrillas had been gathering strength in the hills, and at the end of May they issued a new call to arms. "The hour of the decisive battle has arrived!" they proclaimed over Radio Sandino. "The dictatorship's days of oppression and death are numbered . . . The final bell has sounded. Let despots, killers, torturers, and Somozas tremble. The hour has come to answer to the people!"

In southern Nicaragua, hundreds of Sandinistas commanded by Edén Pastora attacked large National Guard concentrations. Guerilla units in other parts of the country also attacked in force. Stores and businesses closed, and street fighters took over neighborhoods in many cities. Wherever the Sandinistas managed to seize control, Somoza ordered planes and artillery to bomb them.

During the climactic weeks of the rebellion in June and July, I was in Managua filing stories for the *Boston Globe* and the *Washington Post*. Karen DeYoung, the regular *Post* correspondent, was sharing a house with several other journalists, and invited me to move in. Besides Karen, the reporters living there were Alan Riding of the *New York Times,* Bernard Diederich of *Time* magazine and the Washington *Star,* and Silio Boccanera of *Jornal do Brasil.* Alan and Karen had years of experience in Nicaragua, and Bernie not only knew Somoza but had written books about two kindred dictators, François "Papa Doc" Duvalier of Haiti and Rafael Trujillo of the Dominican Republic. I was a freelancer who had never held a full-time newspaper job, and at twenty-seven was by several years the youngest member of the household.

The safe house, as we called it, was in Villa Fontana, a modern, suburban-style section of Managua. A young Nicaraguan businessman, Martin Bárcenas, lived there, but like many of his countrymen who could afford to do so, he had sent his family abroad as a safety precaution. When I arrived, his house was already crowded. Martin slept on a king-size platform bed in the master bedroom. Karen occupied the children's bedroom while Alan, Bernie, and Silio slept in bedrolls on the living room floor. There wasn't much space left, and I was happy to accept Martin's offer to share his room.

Most mornings began with a search for news about Nicaragua on the Voice of America, the BBC, Radio Havana, or whatever other station we could pick up. Over breakfast, we would discuss what seemed to be happening, and try to decide how best to cover it. Alan had good ties to some well-informed Sandinistas, and he telephoned one of their strategists, Sergio Ramírez, every morning in Costa Rica to find out what was new. He and Karen circulated in opposition circles, and were able to piece together a fairly coherent picture of guerrilla strategy. While they were moving among hideouts, Bernie mingled with National Guard officers and government officials, trying to learn their plans. When an extra car was available and there was gas to fuel it, Silio would slip away to check conditions in nearby towns. That left me with the job of circulating around Managua to view damage, interview victims, and try to judge how much of the city was under control of one side or the other.

Our "assignments" naturally varied from day to day, but the story was unfolding on so many fronts that it would have been hopeless for any one person to try to cover it all. At mid-afternoon, as deadline time approached, we would find our separate ways back to Villa Fontana and exchange tidbits. Soon two or three or four typewriters would be clattering around the kitchen table, punctuated by questions when one of us was stuck. "Where was Somoza born?" one of us would call out, or "How old is Edén Pastora?"

It didn't take long for opposition leaders to learn that a single home in Villa Fontana was the center of operations for *Time,* the *Washington Post,* the Washington *Star,* the *New York Times,* and the *Boston Globe,* not to mention *Jornal do Brasil,* one of the most important newspapers in Latin America. Hardly a day passed without at least one prominent figure dropping in unannounced, either to hand us a written statement, grant an interview, or tip us off to something that was about to happen.

The most welcome visitor was Edmundo Jarquín, an energetic opposition leader who later held several important government jobs, including embassy jobs in Mexico and Spain. Jarquín was thoughtful, perceptive, and well-informed, but even more important, he somehow had access to gasoline. Covering a war without a vehicle is all but impossible, and vehicles need gas. Every day during June and July, hundreds of cars lined up outside Managua's filling stations, hoping against hope for a gallon or two. At our house, the only question was when Jarquín would arrive. When he did, we always had a fruitful chat, and as he was preparing to leave he would casually mention that he had a barrel full of gas in his truck outside. We always welcomed his insights, but we were at least equally grateful for his more tangible gifts.

Other than Jarquín, and the neighbor who monitored military radio frequencies for us, our most valued friend was Honey, the bilingual international telephone operator. Phone service had always been poor in Managua, and as violence spread, calling abroad became more and more difficult. Somehow Bernie Diederich found Honey, and struck up a business arrangement with her. For a healthy fee, she agreed to call our "safe house" every afternoon at deadline time and connect all our calls. At the end of our assignment in Managua, we threw her a party to show our gratitude.

Finding food was another constant challenge during those weeks. By mid-June, there was not a single store or restaurant open anywhere in Managua. Some food arrived from foreign charities, and some was brought from the countryside by farmers, but the main source was looting. Whenever National Guard bombs destroyed another store or warehouse, looters would arrive the moment the bombardment stopped. Each morning, they displayed their booty at a makeshift market that blossomed in front of an abandoned Esso station on the edge of town. The array of goods offered for sale there was entirely unpredictable. Depending on what kind of establishments had been looted the night before, buyers might find cases of wine, stacks of cherry jam, boxes of sanitary napkins, or brand-new axes and machetes. One day I found a vendor selling baseball gloves and catchers' equipment out of original boxes.

Although virtually the entire country was engulfed in war and Nicaraguans were dying by the hundreds, it was a single incident in a Managua slum that dealt Somoza his most devastating blow. On the morning of June 20, ABC television correspondent Bill Stewart and his crew, like other film crews from around the world, left the Intercontinental Hotel in search of new pictures to pique the interest of viewers back home. Stewart had been sent to Managua despite speaking no Spanish and having little experience in such dangerous surroundings.

The story Stewart was working on that day is one that is told in every war: the pathos of young soldiers. He had plenty of film of young Sandinistas, but needed footage of Guardsmen. The crew drove him to Riguero, a poor neighborhood where street fighting had been going on for several days. At a small outpost there, Stewart found a young-looking Guardsman plaintively playing a guitar, an ideal subject for his story. After filming the scene, he walked toward a handful of soldiers ahead, holding a white handkerchief in one hand and his press card in the other. Members of his crew, more familiar with the savage unpredictability of Guardsmen in battle, waited in the van.

As Stewart approached, one of the Guardsmen spun, pointed his rifle, and ordered him to the pavement. Stewart replied in the only Spanish he knew.

"*No Español,*" he said. "*Yo periodista.*"

The Guardsman pushed him down, kicked him in the ribs, and began to walk away. Then he stopped, as if he had forgotten something. He walked back to where Stewart was lying, casually raised his M-16, and fired a single shot into the back of his neck. Stewart's body jerked upwards, then lay still. He had died instantly.

Guardsmen who saw the killing motioned for the van's Nicaraguan driver, Pablo Tiffer, to approach, and he did. Tiffer heard one soldier tell another, "You fucked up, because that guy you killed was a gringo reporter."

The Guardsmen were silent for a moment. Then the one who had pulled the trigger came up with an idea to save the day. Pointing at the ABC crew and driver, he suggested, "Let's kill them all. We'll say it was the Sandinistas."

The other Guardsmen nodded in agreement, and Tiffer's heart sank. Quickly he offered a counterproposal. If the Guardsmen allowed them to live, he promised, they would tell the world that Stewart had been killed by a Sandinista sniper. The Guardsmen agreed, and allowed Tiffer and the other crew members to drive away.

News of the atrocity spread through the press corps within minutes, and a virtual riot broke out at the Intercontinental. Somoza's aides were anxious to control the damage, and the dictator quickly called a news conference. The atmosphere was hostile and combative. Somoza read a statement deploring the "sad and tragic event," and said he had information that the killer was a Sandinista sniper. Many reporters could not restrain their emotions, and shouted accusations at the tyrant. By evening, more than forty had decided that the risks of covering Nicaragua's revolution had become too great. They departed the next day in a bus caravan organized by the American embassy.

After nightfall, there was a stunning new development in the case. It turned out that Stewart's cameraman, sitting in his van a block away, had filmed the murder, capturing every detail. He had kept the film's existence secret until it was safely out of the country. That night, it was broadcast into millions of American living rooms, and millions more around the world. The film clip, which was televised in the United States accompanied by warnings that it should not be viewed by children, destroyed what little remained of Somoza's credibility.

On June 16, the Sandinistas announced that they had named a five-member junta to serve as Nicaragua's next government. The best-known of the five was Violeta Chamorro, widow of the martyred publisher. She had shown no interest in politics before her husband's death, but her presence seemed to symbolize the moral authority of the new junta. The other members were Alfonso Robelo, an energetic young entepreneur who had organized a series of anti-Somoza business strikes; Sergio Ramírez, a leftist writer and historian; mathematics professor Moisés Hassan, who held a doctorate in physics from North Carolina State University; and one guerrilla leader, Daniel Ortega.

The junta's initial statements were reassuringly moderate. Sergio Ramírez, who acted as spokesman, pledged that the new regime would "take the route of representative democracy" and strive for friendship with the United States. When Bill Stewart's murder shocked the world into recognizing Somoza's brutality, the Sandinista-backed junta seemed an ideal alternative.

Even at this late date, senior officials in the United States were unable to focus seriously on events in Nicaragua. President Carter traveled to Vienna for a summit with Soviet leader Leonid Brezhnev on June 15, and then to Asia for a week-long tour. Upon his return, he flew to his retreat at Camp David for a private review of his presidency, and remained there until July 14. The Nicaraguan crisis seemed overwhelmingly immediate to those of us in the middle of it, but in Washington it was perceived, if at all, only as one of many issues on a crowded agenda.

On June 21, the morning after Bill Stewart was murdered in Managua, Secretary of State Cyrus Vance addressed the Organization of American States at its august Washington headquarters. Vance acknowledged that Somoza's collapse now seemed imminent, but he still believed it was possible to prevent the Sandinistas from taking power. He urged the OAS to dispatch a "peacekeeping" military force to Nicaragua and launch a new round of negotiations.

Vance's proposal was laughably unrealistic. At the time he made it, Nicaragua was in flames. Thousands of people had died, and full-scale battles were raging on the streets of major cities. The Sandinistas had already named their junta. The idea of mediation, which implied compromise with the National Guard, was anathema to most Nicaraguans, and to the governments of most Latin American countries. The OAS rejected the idea without even taking a vote. Instead it approved a resolution unequivocally identifying the Somoza regime as "the fundamental cause" of Nicaragua's crisis and demanding its "immediate and definitive replacement."

That night in Nicaragua, Somoza held an extraordinary radio conference with senior National Guard officers. In the wake of the unprecedented OAS resolution calling for his ouster, he wanted to assure his men that he was determined to fight on. He ordered them all to be by their two-way radios at 10:30.

"This is Alfa Sierra Delta, stand by," Somoza began, using his military code name. "I ask each of you to acknowledge."

Nineteen field commanders responded when their code names were called. Somoza told them of the OAS vote, and denounced it as a "flagrant intervention into the internal affairs of Nicaragua."

"It doesn't matter to me what some countries that don't know the reality say," he told his officers. "We know the reality, and we must go forward."

In the days that followed, National Guard units were able to fend off some Sandinista attacks, notably in the south, where Guardsmen blunted Edén Pastora's drive on the provincial capital of Rivas. But the tide of battle inexorably favored the insurgents. They captured León, capital of the cotton-rich west, and then, a few days later, the farm town of Diriamba. In Managua, nervous Guardsmen rode through the streets at night in open jeeps, ready to shoot violators of the 7:00 curfew. Pillars of smoke rose over slum neighborhoods. On some days, mutilated corpses turned up along roadsides or at garbage dumps.

After the curfew hour, government planes appeared over Managua's eastern slums, which were in rebel hands. From our backyard in Villa Fontana, several miles away, we had a terrifying view. As we watched, the planes would circle above whatever section of the city was slated for that night's punishment. Once over the target area, they would begin dropping 500-pound bombs, which landed with powerful explosions. In the final days, Somoza's supply of bombs ran out, so the planes dropped drums of gasoline instead, rigged with incendiary triggers so they would burst into flames like homemade napalm.

When the bombing began each evening, a pall fell over our little group. No one said so, but we all understood that not far away, human beings were being incinerated for the crime of living in the wrong neighborhood. Along with thousands of Nicaraguans, we winced in horror at every explosion.

Despite the bombing, guerrillas holding positions in Managua's slums would not be dislodged. I was anxious to see what life was like inside their zone, but it was too dangerous a trip to make alone, and I could find no reporter willing to accompany me. Finally, one day late in June, our host at the Villa Fontana "safe house," Martin Bárcenas, agreed to come along. The farm equipment business he managed had its showroom inside what was now rebel-held territory, and he was anxious to know if it had been looted or destroyed.

We drove in Martin's car toward the east side of town, and pulled over to park as we approached no-man's-land. After walking a few hundred yards, we found a dozen helmeted Guardsmen sitting in the shade of a wrecked automobile. We explained who we were: a journalist curious about the tide of battle and a store manager worried about his business. Could we proceed?

No one was in command, and the Guardsmen looked at each other quizzically. Probably very few civilians had come by asking permission to enter the combat zone. They made no effort to stop us, nor did Guardsmen at two other posts we passed. At the last post, however, we were warned that we would have to walk half a mile to reach the first guerrilla position, and that snipers from both armies were hiding in bombed-out buildings along the way.

Martin and I advanced very slowly down the center of the highway, our eyes scanning the debris but seeing no one. Above our heads, we held large white banners made from torn bedsheets, hoping that whoever was watching from the shadows would recognize us as neutrals. I had driven down this stretch of road a hundred times without really studying it, but now I absorbed every detail, every structure, every utility pole, every street sign. The exaggerated slowness of our pace made me feel lightheaded and slightly dizzy.

I wondered if snipers were really watching us. It was logical that they would be, since neither side wanted enemies passing across the battle line. But these were rational snipers, I tried to tell myself, snipers who would recognize that Martin and I were harmless civilians.

As we advanced, one uncertain pace at a time, we tried to reassure each other with light banter.

"We're doing great, no problem," I told Martin.

"Absolutely right," he replied. "Like a stroll through the park."

After walking for what seemed like a very long time, we spotted the forward guerrilla post. It was a barricade made of paving bricks, pulled from the highway and stacked about four feet high in front of a corner pharmacy. As we approached, there was movement behind the barricade. I heard voices, and what I thought was the click of bolt-action rifles. Martin and I stopped in our tracks and looked at each other. After a moment, he began waving his white banner.

"Civilians!" he shouted. "We're civilians!"

There was no response. Everything looked empty and still. We nodded to each other and began to advance, walking even more slowly than before.

Finally we reached the barricade, and at that moment I impulsively fell to the pavement. I remained still for a moment as I recovered from the tension. When I looked up, I saw several boys staring and pointing weapons at me.

"Who are you?" asked a haggard-looking child of about ten.

"I'm a foreign journalist," I replied, rising to my feet and holding out my official press card.

The boy looked at it, and his eyes grew wide. Slowly I realized that my press card bore the large, triangular seal of Somoza's government.

"Guardsman!" he shouted, and swung the barrel of his single-shot rifle into my stomach.

Martin, who was being interrogated nearby, was startled to hear the word, and quickly turned to help. Calmly and authoritatively, he reasoned with the young guerrilla.

"This friend is a foreigner," Martin said. "He came here to find the truth about the Nicaraguan people's struggle. That seal is just a formality. We don't have anything to do with Somoza or the Guard."

The boy seemed intrigued, but kept his weapon pointed at me. "If I kill you right now," he mused, "I could tell my friends I killed an American."

The drift of his reasoning was not reassuring, especially so soon after Bill Stewart's murder. One of the diminutive fighters in our group decided to consult with higher authority, and dashed into a nearby house. Soon we were beckoned to follow.

Inside a dark room, we found a wiry guerrilla of about eighteen. He was wearing khaki fatigues, not street clothes like the youngsters outside, and an M-16 automatic rifle was propped against the wall beside him. When we told him our stories, he seemed sympathetic, though a bit incredulous.

"You came in here voluntarily, and you just want to walk around, see the sights, and then go back out?" he asked.

"Exactly," Martin replied.

"If that's all you want, I guess you can go ahead," he told us with a shrug. "I'm not responsible, just remember that."

From the streetcorner, Martin could see the building that housed his offices and showroom. We walked toward it, now less tense and without white banners because we were inside a controlled zone, and presumably in reduced danger. The showroom was intact, neither bombed nor looted. As Martin checked inside, I peered through doorways of abandoned homes nearby. Many residents had fled these slums when the fighting began, and most of those who remained were fighters. No civilians were visible anywhere, only exhausted young guerrillas lying behind barricades. Bombing had reduced entire blocks to rubble.

Martin and I stayed only half an hour in the guerrilla zone, afraid that bombing might begin at any time. We made our way safely back to his car, and as we drove away, my first thought was of the boy who had jammed his rifle into my abdomen, and the suffering he must have seen. Then I considered Somoza. He had decided that circumstances required him to bomb his own cities, and without compunction his National Guard was bombing them. It now seemed more unthinkable than ever that he or his supporters could be part of any future regime.

DURING June and July, the most entertaining show in Managua played every day in the lobby of the Intercontinental Hotel. Because the hotel was adjacent to Somoza's bunker, it was well defended, probably as safe a place as one could find in Nicaragua at that moment. Many members of Somoza's clique, including Cabinet ministers and members of Congress, had moved there after sending their families to Miami. They had little to do, and after breakfast each morning they congregated in small groups, smoking cigarettes and talking in hushed tones. The lobby took on an air of intrigue, and when I had a spare hour I would spend it there, watching as unobtrusively as I could.

Senior government functionaries passed in and out, often accompanied by bodyguards whose sidearms bulged beneath their dark jackets. Automatic weapons lay casually among the potted palms. Some people stood by the phone bank for hours at a time, waiting for calls that, so far as I could determine, never came. Others clutched locked briefcases, as if waiting for couriers to arrive. And for several hours each day, a casually dressed CIA agent held court in a cushioned wicker chair near the elevator. Nearly everyone who passed through the lobby stopped to exchange whispers with him, and occasionally he jotted a few words in a spiral notebook he carried in his back pocket.

One day as I was sitting in the Intercontinental lobby pretending to read a copy of *Novedades,* two strapping young men, both blond and speaking German, entered with small suitcases and approached the reception desk. They asked for a room, filled out registration forms, and disappeared into the elevator. Minutes later, a National Guard officer appeared in the lobby, accompanied by two orderlies carrying duffel bags. The three of them took the elevator to the same floor where the Germans had gotten off.

After half an hour, all five men reappeared. All were now dressed in National Guard uniforms. They strode through the lobby, climbed into a waiting jeep, and sped away. Apparently I had witnessed the arrival of two mercenaries. I never saw them again, and never learned what their mission had been.

On Sunday morning, June 24, I arrived at the Intercontinental to find one of my colleagues, a Dutch reporter, pacing the sidewalk outside. He had just heard a rumor that guerrillas had overrun the National Guard garrison in Masaya, twenty miles away, and were now in complete control of the city. I suggested we drive there to take a look, and he readily agreed.

Heavy combat, house-to-house in some neighborhoods, had raged in Masaya for twenty-five days. As we approached, we could see clouds of smoke hanging over downtown. Guardsmen at a forward post told us that Masaya had indeed fallen into Sandinista hands. They allowed us to drive around their emplacement, and we continued for about a mile until reaching the first guerrilla position.

There, behind a barricade of bricks and debris, we found fifteen or twenty ragged fighters, most of them barely into adolescence. They told us we could proceed, but only on foot. No private vehicles were now permitted to circulate in Masaya, nor were visitors allowed to walk unaccompanied. A fourteen-year-old girl wearing a green uniform and carrying an M-1 carbine was assigned to escort us.

Almost every one of the adobe houses we passed was pockmarked with bullet holes. Bazooka fire had blown away sections of many buildings. Heaps of tires and refuse smoldered in the streets, and stray animals foraged in piles of garbage. At strategic corners, exhausted young guerrillas dozed behind brick barricades. Some cradled rifles as if they were stuffed animals.

All was quiet, especially in the central plaza. The National Guard garrison, finally overrun and torched, was still smoldering. The brass plaque on the front wall was barely legible: "Built by the Government of General Somoza, 1941."

My visit to Masaya was the first time I had ever seen Sandinistas in control of an entire town. They ran a tightly disciplined operation, rationing food and water, controlling the use of telephones, and directing first-aid and cleanup crews with military efficiency. No essential goods could be bought or sold without their approval, and all residents were expected to obey their "dispositions" without question.

Sandinista fighters were driving about in pickup trucks, and one truck stopped near me as I walked through the silent streets. In the back was a middle-aged man wearing dark trousers and a soiled white undershirt. When he stepped down, I could see that his hands were bound. Two grim-looking guerrillas motioned him to walk, and he was marched around a corner and out of sight. I tried to follow, but the girl escorting me told me I could not.

I was never able to determine the identity of the prisoner I saw that day, but guerrillas who fought in Masaya later acknowledged that they had captured and executed several "enemies of the people" there. One of them was an infamous National Guardsman known as *Macho Negro,* who had been in charge of a police station where many Sandinistas were tortured and killed.

"People shouted indignantly for maximum punishment for this murderer, and tried to break through security lines in order to hit him," wrote one witness. "Upon hearing the charges, he said only, '*Comandante,* I have a wife and children; sentence me to thirty years, but don't shoot me.' It was too late. So much blood and so many lives mercilessly snuffed out demanded punishment. 'In the name of the Sandinista Front and the people, we condemn you to be shot. Take aim—fire!' A volley rang out, and the criminal fell. At the last moment, he stood straight and did not shake, bravely accepting his punishment."

Some of the Guardsmen forced to flee from Masaya were sent to man artillery batteries nearby, but most were dispatched to Managua. Guerrillas still controlled the eastern slums there, but they were worn down after nearly three weeks of fighting, and their supplies were low. Guardsmen had begun using tank battalions to blow barricades apart in one neighborhood after another, and bombs were falling day and night.

On the morning of June 28, we awoke to news that the guerrillas and their supporters had withdrawn from the Managua slums. At first we had trouble believing it, since Guardsmen had supposedly sealed off all escape routes. Soon it became clear, however, that guerrilla comandantes had led several thousand people through back streets and out of the city, toward the "liberated" city of Masaya. It was one of the most remarkable operations of the war, and was commemorated annually for years to come.

A few hours after Guardsmen moved in to retake possession of Managua's bombed-out slums, I toured the area on foot. The stench of corpses and rotting garbage was overpowering. Residents were trying to reclaim their homes from packs of dogs and swarms of insects. In some yards, arms and legs protruded from shallow graves.

Soldiers moved cautiously through the streets, holding their Galil submachine guns at the ready. Cars entering and leaving the area were carefully searched. Occasionally there were bursts of gunfire, suggesting that some guerrillas had remained behind.

Beside polluted Lake Managua, the decomposing bodies of eight blindfolded young men, their hands tied behind their backs and several of them still wearing red-and-black Sandinista kerchiefs, lay under the tropical sun. In another part of the city, ten boys who had been arrested by Guardsmen were found tortured to death by electric shocks. On one streetcorner, I approached a dazed-looking man who seemed on the brink of tears.

"I never thought this could happen," he mumbled as he gestured at the destruction that surrounded us. "I don't know. I don't know what to say. I don't know what to do. I don't even know where to start."

Despite the Sandinista retreat, Managua remained in a state of war. Snipers roamed the streets, and Guardsmen were safe only in daylight hours. Hundreds of people were encamped at the airport, hoping for a seat on any flight out. In front of the Intercontinental Hotel, street urchins sold sealed boxes of fine cigars and cases of rum at a fraction of their normal cost. The sound of rifle and artillery fire was almost constant.

As violence escalated, the tone of news stories and columns in La Prensa became ever more bitter and hostile. Somoza finally lost his patience, and sent Guardsmen to destroy La Prensa's building. They fired a few rockets into the building from point-blank range, then doused it with gasoline and set it ablaze.

Employees were able to escape, but in a matter of minutes the building was reduced to rubble, and *La Prensa* was no more.

Outside the capital, guerrillas were on the march, capturing more territory every day. León and Masaya were being governed by Sandinista "emergency juntas." Fighting was still fierce near Rivas, and large columns were advancing on the northern cities of Jinotega, Matagalpa, and Estelí, as well as on Juigalpa in the interior.

Everyone wondered how long the dictatorship could survive. Some foreign correspondents formed a betting pool, each paying five dollars to enter. The money would go to whoever came closest to guessing the date of Somoza's resignation, death, or flight into exile. I guessed August 4, not close enough to win.

A new American ambassador, Lawrence Pezzullo, arrived in mid-June, filling a post that had unconscionably been left vacant for four momentous months. In his first sessions with Somoza, Pezzullo was blunt.

"We don't see a solution without your departure," he told the dictator on June 27. "Without a statesmanlike act on your part, we are going to be caught in something which is going down."

For the first time, Somoza seemed receptive to the idea of quitting, and began asking what guarantees could be arranged for his family and associates. But the United States was still hoping to fashion some kind of compromise regime for Nicaragua, and Pezzullo retreated.

"I don't want you to leave tomorrow," he told Somoza. "Please don't move too precipitously. Let's keep the thing."

Events moved very quickly, however, and soon all understood that the end was at hand. On July 13, Ambassador Pezzullo arrived at Somoza's bunker for a decisive meeting. He had asked Somoza to summon Francisco Urcuyo, a senior member of Congress. When their meeting began, he turned to Urcuyo and asked if he was prepared to assume the presidency. Urcuyo said he was, and the arrangement was sealed without further discussion.

President-designate Urcuyo had achieved modest notoriety for his good fortune in avoiding Sandinistas. He had been invited to the 1974 Christmas party that was assaulted by commandos, but did not attend because of a conflicting engagement. And on the day guerrillas stormed the National Palace in 1978, he was out of the country. This time, however, luck would not save him. Thousands of well-armed fighters were converging on Managua from every direction. As the dictator and his men packed their bags and contemplated their defeat, Nicaragua was on the brink of the unknown.

SCCCC - LIBRARY
4601 Mid Rivers Mall Drive
St. Peters, MO 63376
WITHDRAWN

5

SANDINISTA DREAMS

IN THE years that followed the Somoza regime's collapse, family members and their retainers had much time to reflect on how they came to lose control of Nicaragua. Some of the reasons were self-evident. Over a period of decades, the Somozas had allowed social conditions to become intolerable. By perpetuating themselves in power, brutally repressing dissent, and indulging in the most brazen forms of corruption, they lost their claim to legitimacy. When the final uprising broke out in 1979, enraged citizens joined in such numbers that not even the military force of the National Guard could save the dynasty.

Straightforward and persuasive as that analysis may be, however, it fails to explain why Nicaragua, of all the countries in Latin America, erupted into national rebellion. Nicaragua, after all, was hardly the only country where masses of people lived in wretched poverty, where treasuries were looted by larcenous rulers, where political dissidents were tortured in prisons, and where elections were rigged to keep the ruling clique in power. Nor was Nicaragua the only place where guerrillas had taken up arms in hope of seizing power the way Fidel Castro had done in Cuba. But only in Nicaragua did revolution succeed. Only in Nicaragua was a regime and a way of life violently wiped away.

What made Nicaragua so different from other countries was the existence of the Sandinista Front, one of the most extraordinary revolutionary organizations of the twentieth century. At the moment of the dictatorship's collapse, no outsiders knew the true story of the Sandinista Front. Only over the years that followed were we able to piece it together. Whenever I met or interviewed people who had been part of the Sandinista underground, I asked them to tell me their stories. From them I learned how vast an endeavor their revolution had been, how much sacrifice it had required, and how deeply it had marked the men and women who lived through it.

Overthrowing governments was an established Nicaraguan tradition long before the Sandinista Front was conceived. Every regime that ruled Nicaragua in its first century and a half of independent life came to power by force of arms, the Somoza dictatorship being only the most recent example. History taught that such regimes could be overthrown only by force. No one had forgotten that it took a bullet to rid Nicaragua of the dynasty's patriarch, Anastasio Somoza García.

As the 1960s dawned, a new generation of revolutionaries was coming of age in Nicaragua, burning with anti-Somoza fervor. Radical newsletters and political broadsides began to circulate at high schools and on college campuses. Students clashed violently with police in several cities, and small guerrilla groups sprung up in the countryside.

Two especially thoughtful and highly motivated student leaders from Matagalpa, Tomás Borge and Carlos Fonseca, symbolized the new direction of Nicaraguan youth. Both had been in and out of prison for their political activities, and both were passionately anti-Somoza. They were groping for a strategy when, at the beginning of 1959, they heard the glorious and incredible news that Fidel Castro had won his guerrilla war against tyranny in Cuba.

"The victory of the armed struggle in Cuba, more than a joy, was the lifting of innumerable curtains, a flash of light that shone beyond the simple and boring dogmas of the time," Borge wrote later. "Fidel was for us the resurrection of Sandino, the answer to our reservations, the justification of the dreams of heresy of a few hours before."

Borge and Fonseca lived in Honduras during the early 1960s, and there they and another young Nicaraguan revolutionary, Silvio Mayorga, spent long hours together in political discussion. Finally they resolved to forge a new "political-military organization" called the National Liberation Front, named after the guerrilla army fighting French rule in Algeria. They conceived of a war like the Algerian war, a rebellion against both a political system and the foreign power that sustained it. Borge, Fonseca, and Mayorga became the first three members, pledging their lives to the cause.

Most of the new breed of Nicaraguan students, unlike their parents, were instinctively sympathetic to Marxism. They believed that Soviet Communism had vanquished poverty and social injustice, and the success of Castro's revolution in Cuba reaffirmed their Marxist faith. They also recognized Marxism as the principal enemy of the Somoza system and of those in Washington who had imposed it. To be Marxist in the 1960s was to be the thing most hated by Somoza and most hated by the United States.

But Carlos Fonseca and his friends recognized from the start of their improbable campaign that masses of Nicaraguans would never support an explicitly Marxist program. Nicaragua was a country of highly conservative peasants, shopkeepers, and small-scale entepreneurs. Any Marxist movement seeking to build a popular base would have to obscure its true nature and cover its radical message in native clothing.

Fonseca, having grown up in northern Nicaragua, was aware of Augusto César Sandino, and knew the story of his guerrilla resistance to United States Marines in the 1920s' and 1930s. He began reading about Sandino, and found his patriotic letters, especially those denouncing the evils of United States imperialism, almost religiously moving. In 1960 he compiled and published a booklet of extracts from Sandino's writings, pithy maxims such as, "My cause is the cause of my people, the cause of America, the cause of all oppressed nations."

Having found the hero for whom he was looking, Fonseca made a brilliant political decision. He added the word "Sandinista" to the name of his new revolutionary organization, making it the Sandinista National Liberation Front *(Frente Sandinista de Liberación Nacional, FSLN)*. No longer was it simply another band of Marxist rebels like those springing up in other countries. Now it had the aura of a truly Nicaraguan movement, one which any patriot would be proud to join and which only cowards would dare condemn.

With the success of Castro's revolution to inspire them, a band of about sixty students and ex-students led by Tomás Borge marched off to war in mid-1963. Their goal was to establish a *foco,* a remote camp from which guerrillas would set out to fight. Borge assembled the guerrillas in Honduras and then led them across the Coco River toward the Nicaraguan village of Raití. They foolishly revealed their presence by attacking National Guard patrols, and were quickly decimated. Other bands met similar defeats and in one decisive 1967 battle at a place called Pancasán in the remote northern hills, Silvio Mayorga was killed. These early Sandinista guerrilla campaigns were all military failures, but they established the Sandinista Front as a fighting force. After each defeat, the surviving leaders regrouped to decide when, where, and how to strike again.

Rural guerrillas were not the only Sandinista fighters. A handful of daring volunteers were assigned to live underground in Managua and foment "urban resistance." They carried out payroll holdups and bank robberies, the proceeds of which were used to support the insurrection. When guerrilla bands in the north were crushed in 1967 and the regime began proclaiming that it had broken the Sandinista insurgency, leaders of the "urban resistance" decided to show their defiance by striking a public blow against the regime.

As their victim, they chose Sergeant Gonzalo Lacayo, the National Guard's best-known torturer. Lacayo was known as an especially enthusiastic abuser of prisoners, and he relished his reputation. More than a few anti-Somoza plotters had entered his cells and never been seen again.

At 7:30 on the evening of October 23, 1967, a small Hillman sedan screeched up to Lacayo as he walked under a streetlight near his home.

"Gonzalo, hijo de puta!" shouted one of the four Sandinistas inside.

As the victim turned, rifle volleys rang out, and he fell to the pavement. One member of the squad jumped from the back seat to administer a coup de grace, but Lacayo had sixteen rifle bullets in his body and was already quite dead.

Years later, I learned that the head of "urban resistance" in Managua during this period was Daniel Ortega. He had planned at least a dozen holdups and robberies, and had participated in more than a few himself. Sandinista veterans told me that he was part of the squad that cut down Gonzalo Lacayo, and I asked him about it once. He freely accepted responsibility.

"Gonzalo was like a Nazi torturer," Ortega said. "The French resistance fighters used to kill people like him whenever they could. That is a patriotic act."

Guardsmen launched a highly successful anti-Sandinista crackdown in the late 1960s, capturing important guerrillas including Daniel Ortega, killing others, and forcing the remainder to flee into exile. The top Sandinista leader, Carlos Fonseca, became a general without an army, a dreamer taken seriously only by a handful of surviving disciples. But from his base in Havana, he resolved that the Sandinista Front would not fade away as so many other anti-Somoza movements had faded before.

At training camps in Cuba, Sandinista guerrillas learned the art of war alongside guerrillas from Paraguay, Argentina, Bolivia, El Salvador, and other Latin American countries. Ties among the various guerrilla groups, though loose, were fraternal. But beyond the Americas lay a world of even greater revolutionary potential, and Fonseca wanted to see what it could offer the Sandinistas. In 1969 he assigned two Sandinistas living in Havana, Gustavo Adolfo Vargas and his younger brother Oscar René, to find out.

The Vargas brothers were among the few full-fledged Sandinistas from economically secure backgrounds. They had fled Nicaragua after the killing of Gonzalo Lacayo, in which the elder brother had participated. Through the intercession of their father, a prominent physician, the brothers had been given asylum in Brazil. From there they found their way to Chile and ultimately to Cuba, where they joined the circle of Sandinistas gathered around Carlos Fonseca. For several months, they attended guerrilla training sessions alongside other Sandinistas. Then one day, Fonseca took them aside to give them a new assignment. He had decided to make them the first official Sandinista representatives outside the Western hemisphere. They were to operate under cover from

Geneva, where they would live as university students. Their first clandestine task would be to contact the Palestine Liberation Organization and try to forge a bond between the Palestinian movement and the Sandinistas.

While in Geneva, both Vargas brothers pursued advanced academic studies. They also devoted themselves assiduously to their undercover mission, and made quick contact with Palestinian guerrillas. Using Geneva as their base, financing themselves with family money, they made several trips to the Middle East to meet PLO leaders. They were warmly welcomed, and PLO officials invited them to bring a contingent of Sandinista fighters to the Mideast.

Sixteen Sandinista fighters arrived in Amman in mid-1970, and another group arrived soon afterward in Beirut. Most of them were hardened combat veterans, and several were assigned to offer specialized commando instruction to Palestinian recruits. In exchange for this help, Palestinians gave their new Nicaraguan friends free use of sprawling territories in Jordan and Lebanon over which they exercised virtually complete sovereignty. Here the Sandinistas honed a variety of military skills that were difficult to practice in more confined conditions.

On more than one occasion, Sandinistas fought alongside PLO guerrillas in skirmishes with Israeli troops. Several Nicaraguans also participated in airline hijackings led by PLO commandos. One of them, Patricio Argüello, was killed by Israeli security agents during a failed attempt to hijack an El Al passenger jet on September 6, 1970.

In future years, the Sandinistas were to maintain close ties with many foreign Marxists, particularly North Korea's Kim Il Sung, who proved to be their most faithful benefactor after Fidel Castro. But the tie between the Sandinista Front and the Palestine Liberation Organization was always especially warm. Both movements perceived themselves as fighting regimes that had been forcibly imposed upon them by foreigners, both found their ideological roots in Marxism, and both had concluded that armed struggle was the way to power. There was also another factor to strengthen the bond between them: the Somoza family's uncompromising support for Israel. Nicaragua was among the few third world countries that invariably supported Israeli positions at the United Nations and elsewhere. During the 1948 Middle East war, General Anastasio Somoza García had agreed to a secret arrangement under which weapons supposedly bought for Nicaragua's National Guard were sent to the nascent Israeli army. The Somozas and Israel developed a warm and cooperative relationship, and it was therefore not surprising that their respective enemies did the same.

As Sandinista fighters began returning to Cuba from extended periods of training in the Mideast and in North Korea, Carlos Fonseca decided it was time to test the climate inside Nicaragua once again. He dispatched several of his lieutenants to the mountains of Matagalpa and Estelí, assigning them the daunting and all but suicidal task of fomenting guerrilla war there. To another group he gave the assignment, no less dangerous, of infiltrating into Managua and trying to rebuild an urban underground. And he assigned one of his best lieutenants, Herty Lewites, to begin smuggling guns from California.

Lewites traveled to Los Angeles, rented an apartment, and began raising money from Nicaraguan exiles and sympathizers. With the money, he bought rifles and pistols at local sporting goods stores. Each time he accumulated fifteen or twenty, he packed them into the false bottom of his camper and drove them to Honduras, where he delivered them to couriers who sent them into Nicaragua on mules. Using this method, Lewites brought hundreds of firearms into Nicaragua during the early 1970s.

Sandinista fighters decided late in 1974 that they were strong enough to force the release of their imprisoned comrades. Their assault on the Managua Christmas party that year was a spectacular success. They managed not only to win freedom for a whole generation of guerrilla leaders, but also to catapult the FSLN back onto the political stage. Even more important, they showed idealistic young patriots that there was an organization they could join whose anti-Somoza credentials were impeccable. Scores and then hundreds were inspired to sign up.

Unlike traditional Nicaraguan opposition movements, the Sandinista Front was formally organized and demanded unquestioning obedience from its members. In most cases, the only way to join was to wait to be asked. Senior leaders, operating in utmost secrecy, periodically reviewed the credentials of prospective new members. Most of those who joined in the years before 1977 met violent deaths soon after signing up, and all who joined understood that death was their likely fate. Those who were assigned to guerrilla columns in the mountains rarely lived more than a year.

This was not a commitment attractive to dilettantes, and those who accepted it were people of extraordinary resolve and determination. One of them was Dora María Téllez, who was to lead the final Sandinista assault on León and become Nicaragua's most celebrated female guerrilla leader. *La Comandante Dora,* as everyone called her, was short and stocky, with close-cropped hair. Unlike other Sandinista women, she rarely used makeup and wore no jewelry other than a man's watch. Her female friends described her as warm and even sensitive, but in public, dressed always in uniform, she seemed very tough. Once I had a chance to interview her at length, and she told me about her decision to abandon normal life and become a clandestine revolutionary.

"When I was a girl in León, I dreamed of being the first woman doctor there," Téllez recalled. "But I was also very political. I was involved in anti-Somoza demonstrations starting when I was fourteen. I developed an intuitive understanding that I should support the Sandinista program, and when I got to college

I made contact with the organization. I started as a courier. After a while, being a student and a clandestine collaborator at the same time got to be too much. I decided to quit school and work full-time for the movement.

"One afternoon my Sandinista contact came over for a visit. He said, 'You're going to the mountains to fight.' I knew that meant certain death. Nobody survived more than six months in the mountains. I turned pale and broke into a sweat. I saw the absolute end of my life, the abandonment of fifteen years of wanting to be a doctor. My family is very important to me, and I'd never see them again, never go to a film or sit in a park again. I could have said I wasn't ready to go that far, that I would work at the medical school as a collaborator, and then help the movement as a doctor. But of course I said yes. I told the guy I would spend the next few weeks taking care of personal matters, but he said I had to leave in three days. Okay, I said, I'd just make a last visit to my parents. He said I couldn't even do that, so I told him I'd just say goodbye in a letter. 'No letters,' he told me. I spent the weekend in a daze."

No one came to pick her up on the appointed day, or on the day after. Finally, three days late, her contact appeared at her door in León and asked if she was ready to leave. She said she was, and grabbed the knapsack she had prepared.

"Forget it," the contact said. "You're not going to the mountains. That was just a test."

Having proven her loyalty, Téllez was granted her original request, and began life underground. Her job was producing Sandinista propaganda leaflets, a highly dangerous assignment since the mere posession of such material was clear evidence of subversive connections. She edited newsletters that were passed surreptitiously among Sandinista collaborators, mimeographed rebel communiqués, and produced hundreds of copies of internal Sandinista documents. In 1977, at the age of twenty-one, she was sent to Honduras for military training at a secret Sandinista camp, and there for the first time she put on the olive green fatigues in which she was to win renown.

Everyone accepted for membership in the Sandinista Front was given a pseudonym and assigned a control agent, who would be his or her sole contact with the organization. Cells were kept small, so that members who were captured would be able to disclose only minimal information. The seriousness with which they were expected to take their work was reflected in the oath administered to each: "Before the image of Augusto César Sandino and Ernesto Che Guevara, before the memory of the heroes and martyrs of Nicaragua, Latin America and all of Humanity, before history: I place my hand on the red-and-black banner that signifies 'Free Fatherland or Death,' and swear to defend the nation's dignity with arms in hand, and to fight for the redemption of the oppressed and exploited of Nicaragua and the world. If I fulfill this oath, the liberation of Nicaragua and of all peoples will be my reward; if I betray this oath, death in dishonor and disgrace will be my punishment."

This was how rigorous and disciplined a movement was secretly taking shape when I made my first visit to Nicaragua. For a foreigner, and even for most Nicaraguans, it was impossible to see the subversive power that was gathering beneath the calm of everyday life. Secrecy was always a cardinal Sandinista rule, and as a result, reporters who covered the insurrection could never fully understand the true nature and strength of the Sandinista Front.

Sandinista militants could not make themselves publicly known, but there were various ways for sympathizers to contact the organization. One was through Father Fernando Cardenal's circle of radical Catholics. He and other priests used their Christian Revolutionary Movement as a mechanism for recruiting Sandinistas. Their parishes and classrooms became centers of revolutionary activity, and many of the young people who gathered there went on to become guerrillas.

College campuses in Managua and León were also fertile ground for Sandinista organizing and recruiting. The Sandinistas formed a campus support group called the Student Revolutionary Front *(Frente Estudiantíl Revolucionario, FER),* and during most of the 1970s, FER members held principal student government posts. Encouraged by sympathetic professors, they staged protest marches, demanded improved conditions for Sandinista prisoners, and engaged in continuous political agitation. Groups of them began organizing in urban slums, quietly spreading the revolutionary gospel. On their campuses, which were protected from police search by laws that guaranteed university autonomy, they hid weapons and maintained clandestine printing presses.

Omar Cabezas, who rose from the León slums to become one of the most flamboyant and popular guerrilla *comandantes,* was among the Sandinistas originally recruited by a college friend. Cabezas was a popular FER leader in his early twenties when a schoolmate he admired, Juan José Quezada, approached him and asked if he was ready to make "a greater commitment to the people and to the organization." It was a moment he had anticipated and dreaded, as he wrote in a memoir years later:

> Blood of Christ! I thought. I know this shit, I know where this guy is coming from. I knew in my gut that sooner or later this had to happen; I'd heard talk of it I don't know how many times. Especially from the Social Christians, the professors, the fathers who sat down for a heart-to-heart with their daughters and sons who were coming to León and live in big fashionable houses and eat lunch at Mama Concha's. They would warn their kids to steer clear of politics, because politics gets you nowhere but into jail or the cemetery. Because politics is for grownups, not half-baked kids with no jobs and no income . . . I was scared shitless of getting myself killed . . . You numb yourself, because you don't want to think about that. Because it's better not to . . . I thought of so many things, and the more my imagination ran wild the more scared I got. But you'd better believe I was totally

composed in front of Juan José. I couldn't let him think I was a coward . . . I didn't have any firm political convictions. I knew nothing about theory. Worse, I had serious doubts about whether Marxism was a good thing or a bad thing. Finally, more out of confidence in Juan José than out of any personal conviction, 'Sure, hombre,' I said, 'certainly.'

It was more or less a question of manhood. What I mean is, I knew what I wanted: I wanted to fight the dictatorship . . . You know how I felt then? It was like being a little boy when they take you to school for the first time; it was as if that day marked the end of your childhood happiness. Because you have to become responsible . . . [I]f the organization you are joining is a revolutionary organization, and the revolution is a real revolution, then you're in to stay—until victory or death.

Although a wave of recruits joined the Sandinista Front after the exhilarating success of the 1974 Christmas party assault, the organization's capacity for growth was hindered by sectarian feuds that split its top leaders. Two of the younger leaders who emerged in the 1970s, Jaime Wheelock and Luis Carrión, expressed heretical doubts about the long-accepted theory that only a "prolonged people's war" launched from remote mountain *focos* could bring down the Somoza regime. Wheelock, who had spent time in Chile during the period of Marxist rule there, argued that Nicaraguan revolutionaries should come down from the hills, make closer contact with working people, and begin organizing laborers in cities and on plantations. For the first time, the Sandinista Front was confronted with a new, alternative analysis that fundamentally questioned its long-established dogma.

Luis Carrión, like Wheelock, brought a new intellectual perspective to the Sandinista Front. He had been named the outstanding sixth-grade student in the country in 1964, and later compiled the best record in his class at the rigorous Catholic high school he attended in Managua. His well-to-do parents sent him to Phillips Exeter Academy in New Hampshire for a year to prepare for college. He made the honor roll each term, and then enrolled at Rensselaer Polytechnic Institute in Troy, New York. His parents were distraught when he unexpectedly decided to drop out and return to Managua.

Handsome and fair-skinned, Carrión looked as though he would have been more at home at the Managua Country Club than among revolutionary guerrillas. He was the youngest and arguably the smartest of senior Sandinista comandantes.

"When I lived in the United States, I saw the great contradictions of life there," he told me once. "I saw that the relative luxury of a few countries had its necessary counterpoint in the misery and suffering of countries like Nicaragua. Individualism was taken to the extreme of people trying to climb over each other to get ahead. I wanted to try to build some kind of better society, and I decided that my own country was the logical place to start."

Carrión's family background was religious, and soon after coming home he joined a radical Catholic study group. Relatives sensed the direction in which he was moving, and at one point his father confronted him, vowing to cut him off and never speak to him again if he became a Sandinista. Even that threat did not sway him. One night, he stole his father's hunting rifles and fled to the hills.

Carrión's decision to become a rebel guerrilla, and the enlistment of other sons and daughters of the elite, gave the Sandinista Front a new infusion of intellectual power. But it also brought the organization to the point of schism as two hostile factions emerged within the Sandinista Front. One was known as the "prolonged people's war tendency" for its advocacy of traditional rural guerrilla tactics; the other was called the "proletarian tendency" because it advocated greater emphasis on mass organizing and urban warfare. Arguments between the two "tendencies" intensified and became tinged with personal animosity. In part, the schism was a clash between older leaders, most of them of modest backgrounds, and an insurgent faction of better-educated and often wealthier young people. Old-line leaders like Tomás Borge scorned Wheelock and Carrión as "petit bourgeois" wimps, unprepared for the rigors of Sandinista life.

"They cannot endure the rigor of guerrilla campaigns," Borge once wrote. "They are incapable of maintaining their dignity and solidness in harsh conditions, though they wet their pants with euphoria in the decisive battles."

The argument became so intense that it could have only one conclusion, and in October 1975 the inevitable happened: Wheelock and Carrión were expelled from the Sandinista Front. Carlos Fonseca, still the unquestioned Sandinista leader, was hard on both of them. He branded Wheelock a "vacillating militant" and "an invariable right-winger," and dismissed Carrión as "a person of bourgeois background and non-Marxist ideological formation."

Fonseca had been living in Cuba for more than a decade, making periodic trips to Eastern Europe, North Korea, and even China on behalf of his revolutionary cause. He had begun to lose touch with his homeland, and decided to make a trip back. After arranging intricate security measures, he traveled from Cuba to Honduras, and then crossed clandestinely into Nicaragua on November 6, 1975.

Guerrillas brought Fonseca to a hideout in Managua, and he spent several months there and in León. Later he and a group of comrades traveled northward, trekking through the rugged mountains to meet guerrillas and collaborators. It was only a matter of time before authorities learned of their presence. National Guard troops backed by American advisors launched a sweep through the zone where the provinces of Matagalpa, Jinotega, and Zelaya converge. Early on the evening of November 8, almost exactly a year after he re-entered Nicaragua, Fonseca and the eleven men accompanying him were found and attacked by Guardsmen outside the remote settlement of Zinica. Fonseca tried to cover his retreat by firing his .12-gauge shotgun, but he ran out of cartridges as Guardsmen advanced. In a moment the founder and guiding light of the Sandinista Front was cut down by rifle fire.

No single Sandinista leader ever emerged to fill the void left by Fonseca's death. Bickering among rival factions intensified, reaching its peak when a faction headed by Tomás Borge expelled another faction headed by Daniel Ortega and his brother Humberto. Their arguments were over the central question of what strategy the Sandinista Front should follow in its drive for power.

The Ortegas had been circulating a new "political-military platform" outlining innovative ideas about how a revolution could take shape. They argued that it was time for the Sandinistas to end their political isolation and to begin building alliances with political parties and other "bourgeois" opposition groups. That policy challenged the ideas of both existing Sandinista "tendencies." Its sponsors emerged as a third tendency, often called simply *terceristas*.

The key figure in forging and implementing *tercerista* strategy, other than Daniel and Humberto Ortega, was a unique member of the Sandinista Front, the only senior Sandinista who never put on a uniform or fired a shot in anger. He was the European-educated Sergio Ramírez, son of a small-town mayor in the town of Masatepe. Ramírez was living in West Berlin, working on a novel and considering an offer to join the film department at the Pompidou Center in Paris, when he read news accounts of the 1974 Christmas party assault. With the assault, the Sandinistas had ended their period of "accumulating forces in silence," and announced to the Somozas and the world that they were ready to renew their war. Their message reached Ramírez.

"I realized that if I didn't go back and join the struggle," he later said, "I would end up as just another intellectual lost in the jungles of Europe."

Ramírez returned to Central America, established himself in Costa Rica, and quickly contacted the Sandinistas. They accepted him as a member, but asked him to keep his membership secret and to cultivate a public identity as an independent patriot. This proved to be a masterful deception. Ramírez traveled widely during the late 1970s, gave highly articulate speeches and interviews denouncing the Somozas, and persuaded many leaders in Latin America and Europe that the Sandinista Front was dedicated to pluralism, liberty, and orderly social progress.

Ramírez was the key member of an influential anti-Somoza coalition called the Group of Twelve. The other eleven members—including two priests, a lawyer, an economist, and a leading Catholic businessman—were a cross-section of the Nicaraguan establishment, and their decision to campaign against Somoza had an important effect. The outside world, including journalists who covered the Nicaraguan conflict, believed the Group of Twelve to be simply an independent group of patriots. But in fact, Ramírez had carefully structured it so it would respond to Sandinista guidance whenever necessary. At least two members besides himself were secret Sandinistas, and two others had close family ties to the guerrilla movement. Yet in public, the group maintained a disingenuous modesty.

"This Group of Twelve is an unusual one," one of the members, Father Fernando Cardenal, told reporters at one point. "None of us is a politician. None of us has ever been involved in politics. None of us is interested in power."

Sandinista leaders also adroitly used the figure of Edén Pastora to give their movement a veneer of moderation. Pastora, widely known by his pseudonym "Comandante Cero," became a great hero following the spectacular National Palace assault, and he developed close ties with non-Marxist politicians in Latin America. His guerrilla column in southern Nicaragua included as many as two thousand men, and was supplied with the cooperation of Costa Rican President Rodrigo Carazo, Venezuelan President Carlos Andrés Pérez, and Panamanian leader Omar Torrijos. When he was named military commander of all Sandinista forces in October 1978, his influence seemed at a high point. In reality the title meant little, since his authority was limited to the southern front, but it allowed foreigners to believe that he was the top Sandinista.

By the end of 1978, everything was falling into place for the Sandinistas. The student movement was firmly under their control, as were the Group of Twelve and various other civilian fronts. Guerrilla columns were active in several parts of the country. The success of the Palace takeover in August had catapulted them to the forefront of the anti-Somoza rebellion. Momentum was on their side, and recruits were pouring in. Their one remaining debility was the persistent factional strife that had prevented them from forming a single, united command structure.

It was Fidel Castro, in his role as godfather to Latin American revolutionaries, who provided the pressure the Sandinistas needed to resolve their internal differences. Early in 1979, he made clear that he was prepared to provide large amounts of support to the Sandinistas, including weapons, in their final drive to power, but only if the three "tendencies" agreed to unite. With Carlos Fonseca dead, Castro was perhaps the only figure whose authority was respected by all Sandinistas, and he used it to demand their unity.

ONE afternoon in March 1979, Filadelfo Martínez, the Managua correspondent of the Spanish-language news agency Acan-Efe, was sitting behind his desk when a stranger burst through the door. The young man said he needed Martínez to accompany him immediately to an important news conference. He would say no more, and Martínez tried to brush him off. The man insisted, and to emphasize his seriousness pulled out a pistol and jammed it into Martínez's ribs.

The alarmed Martínez was led to a waiting car and driven to another part of Managua. Along the way, he was told that Sandinista guerrilla leaders had important announcements to make, and that they were assembling reporters by kidnapping them. They had drawn up a list of more than twenty Nicaraguan journalists, but as it turned out, only three were at their offices when abductors arrived. In a darkened room that had been converted into a Sandinista hideout, the three of them—Martínez and two radio announcers—were told to wait. After a time, they were introduced to a group of men who described themselves as the principal Sandinista underground leaders in Managua.

The Sandinistas had two pieces of business. First they read a communiqué denouncing efforts to replace Somoza with a non-Sandinista regime. Then they announced that rival Sandinista factions had ended their feud and agreed to unite under a joint leadership. A new National Directorate had been formed, equally balanced among the three "tendencies." The old-line "prolonged people's war" faction was represented by Tomás Borge, Henry Ruiz, and former campus activist Bayardo Arce; the rump "proletarians" were welcomed back to the fold, with Jaime Wheelock and Luis Carrión, together with urban organizer Carlos Núñez, taking seats on the Directorate; and the *terceristas,* who seemed to be the wave of the future within the movement, named as their three representatives Daniel Ortega, Humberto Ortega, and the Mexican-born Victor Tirado.

When the clandestine news conference ended, the journalists followed careful orders designed to protect the security of high-ranking Sandinistas inside. They slipped away without incident, but later Carlos Núñez, one of the Sandinistas who was present, wrote that the episode nearly ended in violence.

"The journalists never knew it, but as we crossed the street and reached the opposite sidewalk two [armored personnel carriers] emerged from the direction of Luis Somoza's mansion," Núñez recalled. "The situation became tense. The *compañeros* assigned to guard the area took up combat positions, their fingers on the triggers of their submachine guns. We were waiting only for the shout of 'Halt!' from the Guardsmen . . . They passed by us and continued up the street."

To many outsiders, it seemed later that victory had fallen into the Sandinistas' hands by luck, that they had stolen the anti-Somoza movement away from the politicians and civilian dissidents who were its rightful owners. But in the twisted political systems of countries like Nicaragua, harsh reality dictates that those who are most willing to shed blood are most likely to triumph. The Sandinistas did not win power because of what they did in a period of months in 1978 and 1979, but rather because they waged a relentless war for nearly two decades. Many Nicaraguans came to view them as the most dynamic, creative force in the country, and in the emotional final weeks of the 1979 uprising, they counted on the support of almost the entire population.

6

GUERRILLAS IN POWER

As THE anti-Somoza uprising reached its climax in mid-1979, almost all of Nicaragua was caught up in war. Trenches and barricades blocked streets in nearly every city, and the sound of combat was continuous in urban slums. Heavily armed guerrilla columns, each containing many hundreds of armed fighters, advanced on the capital from several directions. The only populated area truly controlled by the National Guard was the square mile around President Anastasio Somoza Debayle's fortified bunker.

Government had ceased to function, and the Cabinet ministers and congressmen ensconced at the Intercontinental Hotel had nothing to do but drink themselves into oblivion each day. Discreet entepreneurs at the hotel bar were offering new Mercedes-Benz automobiles at a fifty percent discount; the only conditions were payment in cash and immediate delivery in Managua. President Somoza held the Mecedes-Benz franchise, so it was clear that even members of his inner circle knew the end was approaching.

When Sandinista forces began capturing towns and cities, Somoza knew his only alternatives were to flee or make a last stand in his bunker. No one who knew him took seriously his repeated vow to fight until the end. Once he finally recognized that the end was at hand, he willingly followed the scenario for his departure laid out by Lawrence Pezzullo, the newly arrived American ambassador.

Late on the night of July 16, the dictator's aides fanned out through the corridors of the Intercontinental, banging on doors in search of congressmen. Those who could be found were hustled downstairs, and at one o'clock in the morning Congress was called into extraordinary session at a salon just off the main lobby. Somoza's brief resignation was read and accepted, and Francisco Urcuyo was sworn in to succeed him. Urcuyo stood erect as the presidential sash was draped across his chest, but the government whose leadership he was assuming was already a phantom.

After his pre-dawn inauguration, Urcuyo walked from the Intercontinental to Somoza's adjacent bunker. There he found the dictator bidding emotional farewell to his officers, many of whom were themselves preparing to flee. Somoza's parting advice to his successor was to break the agreement that the two men had just made with Ambassador Pezzullo, under which power would ultimately be turned over to the Sandinista-backed junta.

"You have to keep negotiating with Pezzullo until you get him to forget about the junta," he urged Urcuyo. "Don't forget that this junta is a Communist threat to Nicaragua, and you have to make Pezzullo see that. He's making a mistake!"

Urcuyo promised to do his best, and then made his way back to the hotel lobby, which was a scene of frenetic activity. Many Somoza functionaries who had lived there for weeks, hoping for some miracle to save the regime, now saw that there would be none. Suddenly they were in a race against time, and they began dashing toward the airport in order to make good their escapes before it was too late. About one hundred of them, the unsavory core of the regime that had tyrannized Nicaragua for more than forty years, boarded a Nicaraguan jet at dawn on July 17, and flew to Homestead Air Force Base in Florida. Somoza and his mistress—his wife had moved to Miami more than a year before—were among them.

Once safely in Florida, Somoza traveled to a villa he maintained at an exclusive enclave called Sunset Island. Reporters were waiting for him, and he obliged them with a brief, semi-coherent statement.

"The Nicaraguan people have not thrown me out," he insisted. "It is an insurrection orchestrated and backed by governments who are afraid of the Communists."

Back at the bunker, President Urcuyo was momentarily full of resolve. In meetings with Pezzullo and others during the day, he talked of his desire to stay in office for a period of months or longer. Too many long afternoons and evenings at the Intercontinental had evidently dulled his ability to perceive reality.

Sandinista forces were on the offensive, and their leaders had no reason to accept anything less than unconditional surrender. It was time for the United

States to apply pressure, and Deputy Secretary of State Warren Christopher showed he had not forgotten how. He telephoned Somoza at his villa and spoke bluntly. If Somoza did not force Urcuyo to play his pre-arranged role by giving way to the new junta, he warned, Somoza's permission to live in the United States might be revoked.

"You're not welcome here, because you haven't lived up to our arrangement," Christopher told the fallen dictator.

On the phone, Somoza was defiant. But after a few minutes of reflection he called Urcuyo with a plaintive message.

"Chico, I'm lost," he told the newly installed president. "Warren Christopher, the Deputy Secretary of State, just called to tell me that if you don't turn power over to the Reconstruction Junta, they'll turn me over to the Sandinista Front."

Somoza, apparently worried about what American authorities might do to him, left Florida the next day for the Bahamas. He departed in classic Somoza style, aboard a luxury yacht stocked with gourmet foods from specialty shops in Miami. His retainers paid all their bills in cash, from suitcases the Somoza party had carried out of Nicaragua.

In Managua, even Urcuyo now knew the game was up. Wandering through the abandoned bunker, he ran into a presidential aide, Humberto Sánchez.

"It's over, Humberto," he said, and began recounting his conversation with Somoza. As he was speaking, a telephone rang. Sánchez answered, and then passed the receiver to his boss.

"Mr. President, the American embassy is calling," he said.

Ambassador Pezzullo was on the line, and he wasted no time coming to the point. "Are you prepared to turn the government over today to the Reconstruction Junta?" he asked.

"No!" came Urcuyo's bold reply.

"In that case, you'll be the only one responsible for what happens to your country," Pezzullo retorted. "I'll have nothing further to do here, and I'll leave with my whole mission."

"You and President Carter, all you want is to for me to turn Nicaragua over to the Marxists, just like you did in Cuba!" Urcuyo shot back. "You say you're leaving, and I say you're leaving too late! You never should have come in the first place!"

Urcuyo tried to continue his harangue, but before he could say any more, the disgusted Pezzullo hung up. Humberto Sánchez, playing his role as courtier, then spoke.

"Mr. President, I agree with you that the vessel is sinking," he said. "I request permission to contact other Central American presidents in your name and ask them to send us planes to withdraw you, your family, and members of your government who so desire."

Urcuyo nodded his assent. The Guatemalan dictator, General Romeo Lucas García, agreed to send planes to pick up Urcuyo and his retinue. What remained of Nicaragua's government made its way to the airport on the afternoon of the 18th, and shortly after dusk three Guatemalan Air Force planes touched down. A colonel descended, found Urcuyo, and saluted him crisply.

"Mr. President, I have instructions from General Romeo Lucas García, president of Guatemala, to take you, your family, and other members of your party to Guatemala. Mr. President, I await your orders."

Only one set of orders was possible. Urcuyo boarded in the darkness and departed for exile. His presidency had lasted forty-three hours.

Sandinista leaders had never intended to negotiate with Urcuyo, because they knew he held no power. True power in Nicaragua rested with the National Guard, and if there were to be negotiations they would have to be with Guard officers. But on July 17 and 18, something happened which no one had expected: the National Guard disintegrated. Enlisted men abandoned their posts to return to their families, and even officers could be seen ripping off their uniforms and trying to melt into crowds. Some made hurried cross-border escapes to Honduras or Costa Rica, and others went into hiding. Many simply went home and waited to see what the new order would bring. Almost none remained to fight.

The Guard had been a personal instrument of the Somoza family for so long that once the Somozas were gone, nothing remained to hold it together. In the space of two days, an army that had terrorized its people for decades melted away and simply ceased to exist. Sandinista leaders had to accept the Guard's surrender from Lieutenant Colonel Fulgencio Largaespada, chief of the transit police.

All during July 19 and 20, battalions of jubilant Sandinistas poured into Managua. The youth and idealism that radiated from their faces was a perfect counterpoint to the aura of corruption and venality that had hung over Nicaragua for so long. By the tens of thousands, people poured from their homes to greet the conquering guerrilla heroes, to hug them and shower them with gratitude.

When the five junta members arrived, making their way to the newly baptized Plaza of the Revolution aboard a bright red fire engine, they found the plaza packed with ecstatic Nicaraguans anxious to join in celebrating the victory. It was a moment such as few nations ever experience. Masses of people from every social class viscerally identified with the new regime, and were determined to help it succeed. They saw the Sandinistas as liberators, and their faith in the new regime was boundless.

Sandinista leaders, like everyone else, were astonished by the National Guard's collapse. They had long expected to oust the dictator, but now it was beginning to dawn on them that they had done much more. To their amazement, they found themselves in absolute and unchallenged control of Nicaragua. There was no other force, military or political, with which they would have to share power.

"The Sandinista Front thought it was going to have a piece of power and no more," veteran militant Oscar René Vargas recalled years later. "We thought we were only going to be one factor in decision-making. We assumed we were going to have to negotiate with the Guard. But when the Guard fell apart, we found ourselves in complete command. It was a better situation than we had imagined in our wildest dreams."

Inside the National Palace, Sandinista guerrilla leaders, unshaven and with long waves of hair flowing over their shoulders, most of them still carrying their rifles, met privately and tried to comprehend the magnitude of what they had accomplished. The question on the table was simple: What should they do to take advantage of this glorious and entirely unexpected windfall of power? Jaime Wheelock was the first to answer.

"Declare socialism immediately!" Wheelock urged.

Others quickly jumped into the debate, which continued for several hours. It was agreed that Wheelock's suggestion was unwise, and that the Sandinistas' first task should be to consolidate their rule without alarming potential enemies. That meant they should stay in the background for a while, and allow the junta to function as if it were Nicaragua's true government.

The junta members seemed to represent a promising mix of ideologies and perspectives. Two of them, Alfonso Robelo and Violeta Chamorro, were true believers in Western-style democracy. Two others, the engaging essayist Sergio Ramírez and the American-educated Moisés Hassan, were appealing and slightly offbeat intellectuals. Only the fifth member, Daniel Ortega, had actually been a Sandinista fighter, and he represented a moderate, apparently social democratic wing of the FSLN.

This assessment of the junta, it turned out, was utterly mistaken. Unbeknownst to most outsiders, not only Ortega but also Ramírez and Hassan were committed Sandinista militants who had sworn a blood oath of allegiance to the organization. From the beginning, the junta was firmly under Sandinista control.

To run the machinery of government, the junta named a broadly representative Cabinet. Several of the new ministers had been members of the Group of Twelve, among them former university dean Carlos Tunnerman, who became Minister of Education, and economist Artur Cruz, who left his job at the Inter-American Development Bank in Washington to take over Nicaragua's central bank. A former National Guard officer who had led an unsuccessful coup against Somoza several years earlier and gone into exile, Bernardino Larios, became the new Minister of Defense. The only uniformed Sandinista given a seat in the cabinet was Tomás Borge, who was named Interior minister.

He had spent most of his life hiding from the law, and now, in one of those turnabouts that are the essence of revolution, he took control of the country's police apparatus.

The first days of revolutionary rule were chaotic. Arriving *comandantes* took over the Intercontinental Hotel, with Borge running the interior ministry from one floor while roommates Daniel Ortega and Sergio Ramírez planned political strategy on another. Cabinet ministers operated without any central direction. In many parts of the country, conditions quickly descended into anarchy. Looting went on for weeks, with only self-appointed "defense committees" to curb delinquency. Squads of armed ex-guerrillas arrived at many factories and farms, declared them "taken," expelled the owners and installed themselves in control.

THREE months after the Sandinista victory, I took a week-long drive through the dusty countryside. Nicaraguans were still mourning their dead, and still recovering from the shock of living through such destructive violence. In some villages, people insisted on showing me bombed-out neighborhoods or fresh gravesites, as if they themselves could hardly believe what Somoza had wrought. But everywhere the dominant emotions were positive. People wished the new regime well, and nearly all were confident that the Sandinistas would rule wisely and honorably.

On a back road a hundred miles north of Managua, a handful of children leapt to their feet as my rented car approached. I slowed down, and watched as they pulled a rope across the road to stop me. In a moment they were upon me, all laughing and shouting at once.

"We need a school!" begged a girl of about ten as she held out an empty coffee can. "Will you help?"

"Don't you have a school now?" I asked.

"Not here in town," she told me. "The school we go to is too far away. We can only go when there's no farm work. Now, with the revolution, we want our own school."

I asked if townspeople were working with the education ministry or some other government body, and no one seemed to know what to say. Finally one older boy spoke up.

"We went to a Sandinista meeting," he said. "The *compañeros* told us that we need good education, and that we should build schools. So we're going to build one here."

The kids applauded loudly as I dropped some money into the can. Like most other Nicaraguans at that moment, they were feeling a cathartic and liberating surge of energy. It seemed that now, finally, their country had a chance to escape from the cycle of poverty and frustration that had defined its history since the days of Spanish conquest.

Immense challenges faced the new regime. The Somozas had pillaged Nicaragua for years, and in their last weeks in power they stole whatever could be taken away or liquidated. Their greatest historical crime, however, was not larceny, but their refusal to develop the country they ruled. Nicaragua was blessed with resources, and with the power the Somozas held, they could have made it a model for Latin America and inscribed their family name among those of the continent's liberators. Instead they ruled cruelly and brutally, bequeathing to their successors a nation in physical, political, economic, and moral ruin.

In comparative surveys that measured living standards in Latin America, Nicaragua had always ranked at or near the bottom, often tied with Haiti for last place. Average life expectancy was fifty-three years. The principal causes of death were preventable diseases like diarrhea, tuberculosis, and tetanus. Clean water and sewage systems were unavailable in many rural areas. Two-thirds of children under the age of five suffered from malnutrition. Most young people could not read or write, and in the countryside only five percent completed the sixth grade.

Once in power, the Sandinistas set out to destroy the system that had created so much injustice. The program that best symbolized their zeal was the nationwide literacy campaign they launched in March 1980. Father Fernando Cardenal was named to oversee it, and for guidance he turned to Cuba, where a similar campaign had been launched following Fidel Castro's takeover twenty years earlier. Cuban administrators helped plan the Nicaraguan campaign and design the texts, and twelve hundred Cuban teachers traveled to Nicaragua to join the army of literacy teachers. Peace Corps volunteers from the United States were turned away because the Sandinistas mistrusted their motives, but there were contingents from several other countries, including Costa Rica, Spain, and the Dominican Republic. The bulk of the teachers, sixty thousand of them, were Nicaraguans, many of them teenagers. Answering the new government's call, they packed knapsacks and moved to rural villages where since time immemorial, education had been a privilege reserved for the elite.

Literacy teachers conducted their lessons from a textbook that was unabashedly political. Chapters had titles like, "Our Democracy Is the Power of the Organized People" and "The Revolutionary Workers' Organizations Promote Production and Guide the Revolutionary Process." Teachers were told that their role was not only to teach reading and writing, but also to raise the political consciousness of their students.

The tens of thousands of young Nicaraguans who became literacy teachers represented the best of their generation. Most came from homes that were at least comfortable, and had no real idea of the conditions in which many of their fellow citizens lived. During their months in rural isolation—rising before dawn to help with chores, teaching at night by the light of gas lanterns, and then sleeping in rustic hammocks or on mud floors—the young teachers saw Nicaragua's misery and desperation firsthand. Many returned highly politicized and determined to do more for the revolution.

During their first weeks in power, the Sandinistas carried out one of their most popular promises by expropriating all assets that had belonged to the Somoza family and those who had formed the dynasty's inner circle. With a single stroke, the new regime seized more than one hundred corporations and nearly two million acres of farmland. On the farmland, eight hundred state farms were established.

In their dreams, the Sandinstas had assumed that once peasants were liberated from oppression, they would work hard to make state farms succeed. Reality proved a rude shock. On nearly every one of the expropriated farms, productivity fell dramatically. Some laborers took "historic vacations" to which they considered themselves entitled after years of peonage. Others believed that since a worker's revolution had just seized power, workers were entitled to lighter schedules. Tractors and other farm machinery began to break down. Fertilizers and pesticides went undelivered, or sat too long in warehouses. Many of the new farm administrators, lacking even the most rudimentary experience, quickly ran their enterprises into hopeless debt.

Even when statistics from the harvests of 1980 and 1981 confirmed that farms still in private hands were realizing higher yields than those run by the government, Sandinista leaders emphatically rejected pleas that they allow peasants to buy plots of confiscated land for themselves. Encouraging private farming, they believed, would stimulate the kind of competition that smacked of capitalism.

"There have been many agrarian reforms that in one stroke have handed over the land," *Comandante* Jaime Wheelock said soon after the Sandinista takeover. "But this type of land reform destroys the process of proletarianization in the countryside, and constitutes an historical regression."

Other sweeping decrees followed the one under which the Somoza clan's property was seized. Sandinista leaders ordered the nationalization of all banks, credit agencies, and insurance companies, then all export businesses, and then the mining and forestry industries. They took these steps proudly, as matters of principle. Later they would concede that they had not fully considered all the practical implications.

The decree nationalizing the mining industry was unveiled at the remote town of Siuna, where for many decades an American-owned concern, La Luz Mines Limited, had been extracting gold and other minerals. Two junta members, Sergio Ramírez and Daniel Ortega, arrived in a small plane accompanied by a special guest, the Argentine novelist Julio Cortázar, one of Latin America's leading pro-Sandinista intellectuals. Ruddy-faced miners crowded curiously around, and cheered as the decree was read.

After the ceremony Ramírez began leafing through an old file cabinet, pulling papers out at random. One was a receipt for a payment made by La Luz management, accompanied by this typed notation: "General Anastasio Somoza, Excmo. Señor Presidente de la República de Nicaragua, Palacio Presidencial, Managua, Nicaragua. To pay Government Subsidy Tax of $10.00 for each kilo of gold shipped by La Luz Mines Limited from July 1, 1951 to December 31, 1951: $10,735.00."

In the same file cabinet, Ramírez found another revealing document. It was a sheet dated July 13, 1979, notifying a worker named José Villarreina that he was being fired from his job at the mine. An attached personnel record showed that Villarreina had been born in 1928 and had begun working for La Luz when he was twenty-four years old. By 1979, after more than a quarter century of continuous employment, he was earning the equivalent of thirty cents an hour.

"You are removed from your position at this business for legal reasons known to you," the printed dismissal sheet read. "You have violated your contract in this manner." Below was handwritten, "Death of Worker." A note explained that Villarreina had been killed instantly when a loose bucket smashed his skull, and that to avoid having to pay an indemnity to his family, the company had fired him several hours after his death.

Reading papers like those redoubled the Sandinistas' conviction that they were embarked on the course of justice. Many outsiders warned them that by nationalizing so much of the economy, they were setting the stage for disaster. But the Sandinistas ignored those arguments, acting instead to fulfill what they perceived as a profound historic obligation to free the poor from humiliation at the hands of the rich.

THE Sandinistas never hid their admiration for Fidel Castro, and immediately after taking power they established intimate official ties to Havana. Cuba sent large amounts of reconstruction aid to help Nicaraguans recover from the devastation of war, and Cuban airliners landed daily at the Managua airport. The planes carried not only emergency relief aid, but also hundreds of advisors who set to work creating a government structure for Nicaragua.

For anyone who had lived or worked in Cuba, the similarities were striking. Cuba had a national network of Committees to Defend the Revolution, and so Nicaragua established Sandinista Defense Committees. There had been a crash literacy campaign following the Cuban revolution, and so Nicaragua had to embark upon one. Cuba called its foreign ministry by the acronym Minrex, and so the Sandinistas called theirs Minex. The Communist party newspaper in Cuba, *Granma,* had a red-and-black masthead, so the Sandinista newspaper, *Barricada,* also appeared with red-and-black masthead.

Very soon, the Sandinistas began receiving shiploads of weaponry from Cuba, North Korea, Czechoslovakia, and the Soviet Union. Senior Cuban officers worked with Humberto Ortega and other leading Sandinistas to build Nicaragua's new army. Other Cubans, soon assisted by a small corps of specialists from

East Germany, assumed key roles in building and directing Tomás Borge's State Security police. Several Cuban advisors went on to take Nicaraguan citizenship, and assumed key posts in military and security agencies.

Fidel Castro was the great hero of Latin American revolutionaries, the font of wisdom and experience, revered by Sandinistas and hosts of others. He had been at the Sandinistas' side for years, and thus it was no surprise that his government developed such close ties to the new regime so quickly. Still, his influence in Managua deeply upset non-Marxists in the Sandinista government, and alienated influential leaders of other Latin American countries.

Few Sandinista *comandantes* had ever lived normal lives, much less faced the complexities of public administration, so it was not surprising that they looked for foreign help. Because they deeply mistrusted the United States for its histori-cal sins, there was no possibility of inviting American advisors into the highest councils of their government. Cuba was at the other extreme, the most trust-worthy and fraternal of nations. Cuban and Nicaraguan revolutionaries consid-ered themselves of the same flesh, and Cuba most closely approximated the country the Sandinistas sought to build. The Sandinistas understood the need to adjust their tactics to Nicaraguan realities, but their ultimate goal—as it had been for nearly two decades—was to make Nicaragua the second revolutionary Marxist state in the Americas.

"The idea was to form a party along Marxist-Leninist lines," junta member Moisés Hassan told me once. "If it was necessary to coexist with some business sectors, it would be coexistence on our terms. We would let them work, but not give them one iota of political power. Political power had to rest with the Sandinista Front, specifically with the National Directorate. There was never any intention of creating a pluralist project with a broad distribution of power."

One of the first Sandinista police operations was a roundup of every surviving National Guard soldier who could be found. There had been about ten thousand men in the Guard, of whom several thousand had fled the country in the days after their defeat. Those who remained had surrendered to the Red Cross or returned to their homes, believing that the new regime would not seek to punish them. But Sandinista leaders considered them criminals and potential counter-revolutionaries. They decreed the creation of a special tribunal to convict them, and as chief prosecutor they named Nora Astorga, the guerrilla heroine who had lured General Reynaldo Pérez Vega to his death a year earlier.

The Sandinistas had specific evidence against some Guardsmen, including prison wardens and officers who had ordered or participated in the bombing of cities. All of these were given thirty-year jail sentences, the maximum allowed by law. The rest, most of them ex-infantrymen in their teens or early twenties, were charged with two crimes: illicit association and "membership in a criminal organization." Though there was no evidence against them as individuals, they were judged guilty for having been Guardsmen, and sentenced to terms of at least ten years. Their trials were perfunctory and their convictions preordained. Some opposition leaders objected, but to no effect.

Sandinista *comandantes* maintained low public profiles in those first months. Occasionally Cabinet ministers would see or meet barely known figures like Luis Carrión or Bayardo Arce, who identified themselves as members of the Sandinista National Directorate and carried themselves with airs of authority. Very gradually, it became clear that the Directorate was a coherent, functioning body whose nine members viewed their role as guiding Nicaragua's government.

The Directorate had been formed in secret for the express purpose of directing a clandestine uprising. Its members, most of whom had lived underground for long periods of time, valued secrecy above all things. To survive their years on the run they had developed acute senses of paranoia, never trusting anyone outside their own tightly knit group. These became the impulses that guided their regime. No one knew where they met, or when, or how frequently, or what they discussed or decided. The country was being ruled by a mysterious body to which no outsiders had access.

Late in 1979 and early in 1980, the Sandinistas forced several non-Marxist Cabinet ministers to resign, replacing them with senior *comandantes*. Moscow-educated guerrilla hero Henry Ruiz became Minister of Planning, Jaime Wheelock took over the Ministry of Agrarian Reform, and, in the most important move of all, Humberto Ortega was named Minister of Defense. These changes deepened the alarm of non-Sandinistas in the government. Their only hope was to reassert their authority in the soon-to-be-created Council of State.

Before their victory, the Sandinistas had promised that they would share power with a thirty-three member legislature, the Council of State, until elections could be held. They issued a precise and carefully balanced list of which organizations would be represented on the Council. But once in power, they decided to alter the formula. The Council, they announced, would have not thirty-three members, but forty-seven. All the new ones would be Sandinistas.

By this maneuver, Sandinista leaders pushed Alfonso Robelo and Violeta Chamorro past the breaking point. Chamorro quit the junta on April 19, and Robelo followed three days later. "The FSLN has violated its trust and broken the political unity of Nicaragua," he declared.

Sandinistas replied by denouncing Robelo as a greedy capitalist without sympathy for the dispossessed. Attacks on him and his political party, the Nicaraguan Democratic Movement *(Movimiento Democrático Nicaragüense, MDN)*, became staples of Sandinista discourse. Henry Ruiz scorned the party as "eminently bourgeois," and Carlos Núñez described its members as "ideological fossils who belong in a museum."

For a time it even seemed that the Sandinistas were even preparing to shut down the country's resurrected newspaper, *La Prensa*. Editors and reporters there were locked in ideological conflict, and the paper was forced to shut down in April 1980. But in the face of strong foreign pressure, Sandinista leaders devised a compromise that pleased all parties. *La Prensa* was allowed to reopen under the control of resigned junta member Violeta Chamorro, and pro-Sandinista editors were given government help to establish a new paper, *Nuevo Diario.*

During these months, the Carter administration was trying uneasily to find a formula for coexistence with the Sandinistas. It was never a promising effort, mostly for reasons beyond the control of all participants. The United States had played an ignoble role in Nicaragua for more than a century, and it was precisely to fight a United States-imposed regime that the Sandinista Front had been formed. Sandinistas believed they were a form of incarnate revenge for the murder of Sandino and countless other outrages. Their moral authority was based on the fact that they were the only political faction that had never compromised with the Somozas or the United States. For them quickly to settle into friendship with Washington was never a real possibility. But President Carter wanted to make an overture anyway, and two months after the Sandinista victory he received junta coordinator Daniel Ortega and a high-level Nicaraguan delegation at the White House.

The meeting was cordial and free of rancor. Carter asked Ortega to tone down his rhetorical denunciations of the United States, and expressed hope that the Sandinistas would honor their commitments to democracy and human rights. Most emphatically, he urged the Sandinistas not to succumb to the temptation to begin aiding Marxist guerrillas in El Salvador or elsewhere.

Ortega assured Carter that his government was not aiding foreign guerrillas, and then brought up a concern of his own. According to reports he had received, anti-Sandinista groups were forming in Florida with the intention of launching armed attacks against Nicaragua. He said he suspected they were being advised by CIA agents.

Deputy Secretary of State Warren Christopher assured Ortega that the CIA was not involved in organizing exile groups and did not sanction their activities. History later proved that he was telling the truth, and so was Ortega. The United States was not then encouraging anti-Sandinista groups, and the Sandinistas had not begun shipping weapons to Salvadoran rebels.

Voices were already being raised in Washington, as well as in Central America, condemning the Sandinistas and demanding that the United States move to crush their regime. But President Carter was determined to offer them an olive branch. After his meeting with Ortega he asked Congress to approve a $75 million aid package for Nicaragua. The proposal was hotly debated, with the House of Representatives going into secret session for only the third time in its history to hear classified assessments of Soviet-bloc involvement in Nicaragua. Many legislators were dubious, but the majority overcame doubts and finally passed the aid bill after adding a series of amendments. The most significant of them required Carter to certify periodically that the Sandinistas were keeping their promise not to aid guerrillas in other countries. If at any point he could not do so, he would be required to stop disbursing the aid.

IN July 1980, revolutionaries from around the world converged on Managua to help the Sandinistas celebrate the first anniversary of their victory. They were guests of honor at a glittering party the *comandantes* threw on the evening of July 18, at what was once the Managua Country Club. Reporters were invited, and I arrived punctually. A band was playing at poolside, and waiters circulated through the crowd carrying trays of rum drinks and chilled seafood. Invitations had stipulated that guests wear formal clothes, but there was not a necktie to be seen. In Sandinista Nicaragua, "formal" dress was taken to mean either a military uniform or a clean, open-necked shirt and slacks.

The crowd was eclectic. Most striking were dozens of heavily decorated military officers from the Soviet Union, North Korea, Vietnam, and Eastern European countries. There were also, however, large contingents from Western Europe and Latin America. Former presidents José Figueres of Costa Rica and Carlos Andrés Pérez of Venezuela, both widely respected statesmen with impeccable democratic credentials, were prominent among the guests. So was the hemisphere's newest revolutionary celebrity, Maurice Bishop, who had recently seized power on the island of Grenada. In one corner, Hortensia Allende, widow of the Chilean Marxist leader, toasted Puerto Rican nationalist Lolita Lebrón, who had recently been released from an American prison after serving more than twenty years for firing gunshots into the House of Representatives. While one group clustered around the novelist Gabriel García Márquez, another surrounded Juan Chacón, a renowned twenty-seven-year-old guerrilla commander from El Salvador. Yasir Arafat of the Palestine Liberation Organization was delayed, and sent word he would arrive later.

The next morning, reporters rose early for the anniversary rally. As was customary on such occasions, we were required to report to the government press office four hours before it began. I stood in a line, showed my *Boston Globe* credentials, and was waved through.

Inside the press center, our effects were subjected to long and highly amateurish searches, and then we waited. Some correspondents dozed in their wooden chairs, some chatted idly, and others read books or magazines. Camera operators fiddled with their equipment. As the morning wore on and the room grew hotter, our boredom began turning to impatience.

By the time we were finally ushered to our places at the newly built July 19 Plaza, hundreds of thousands of Nicaraguans had assembled. Many had arrived before daybreak, traveling in convoys from outlying provinces.

As the sun rose, many of the celebrants covered their heads with scraps of newspaper to protect themselves from the shimmering heat. They were in a festive mood, and they applauded and cheered when Sandinista leaders, dressed in crisp new uniforms, arrived to take their places. Foreign guests arrived and were escorted to their seats, and at mid-morning the proceedings began. Large formations of soldiers and militia members, including several all-female units, marched past the reviewing stand. The crowd cheered loudly for representatives of the rebel movement in El Salvador and "the thousand times heroic people of Vietnam." But the greatest cheer erupted when Fidel Castro appeared and stepped to the microphone.

Castro had been told privately by United States officials that any anti-American bombast on this occasion would be considered "unfriendly and un-helpful," and his tone was moderate. He praised the Carter administration for its "intelligent and constructive policy" toward the Sandinistas, though he expressed "sincere regret" that the United States was not providing more than $75 million in aid.

"Really, sincerely, it is very little for the richest country in the world," he told the crowd.

Daniel Ortega also spoke that day, but he did not announce a timetable for elections, as some had hoped. Then, a few weeks later, his brother Humberto declared in a dramatic speech that the Sandinistas would never permit "false elections" in which "exploiters and oppressors" participated. Sandinista elections, he vowed, would be occasions to confirm Sandinista rule, not to "raffle off power."

Events moved quickly in the weeks following Humberto Ortega's speech. For the first time, groups of prominent Nicaraguans began to perceive the Sandinista regime as an enemy. Civilian leaders were losing their showdown with the Sandinistas, and in Miami, rightist exiles were talking of counter-revolution. Then on September 17 came a stunning event that everyone and no one had expected. Anastasio Somoza Debayle, the last of his line to rule Nicaragua, was assassinated while driving through the streets of Asunción, Paraguay.

Somoza and his mistress, Dinorah Sampson, had taken up residence in Asunción under the patronage of an old family friend, Paraguayan dictator Alfredo Stroessner. The fallen tyrant kept himself locked away from the public, spending his time tending to his private fortune, and was not visibly involved in politics. Evidently he planned his own personal security with the same laxity that had allowed Nicaragua's National Palace to be captured by guerrilla commandos. He regularly drove the same route to a downtown bank where he maintained an office, trusting that his armor-plated Mercedes would protect him from attackers. Perhaps he allowed himself to believe that the Sandinistas and their friends had forgotten about him. In any case, the armor in his Mercedes was not nearly strong enough to withstand the impact of the high-powered anti-tank rocket fired at it from only a few yards away. Somoza's body was so completely destroyed that Dinorah Sampson, who arrived at the scene moments afterwards, could identify it only by a wristwatch.

No clear evidence tying Sandinista leaders to the assassination was ever found, though many suspected their involvement. An Argentine guerrilla faction claimed responsibility. Few Nicaraguans were able to generate any sympathy for Somoza, but the shock of his murder underlined once again the high stakes implicit in Nicaraguan politics.

Former junta member Alfonso Robelo, home from a tour of European and Latin American capitals, had decided to mount one more political challenge to Sandinista rule. His Nicaraguan Democratic Movement called a political rally for November 9 in the town of Nandaime, and organizers began arranging transportation for thousands of supporters from faraway regions. As the date approached, it became clear that the rally would be a major event, the first true anti-Sandinista protest Nicaragua had ever seen. Few were surprised when Interior Minister Tomás Borge called Robelo to his office and told him the rally had been banned.

"I want to make clear that we have the arms, and are never going to put them down," he told Robelo. To underline the point, a gang of Sandinista youths was sent to loot and burn Robelo's headquarters in Nandaime.

Few Nicaraguans were more deeply outraged by what the Sandinistas had done than Jorge Salazar, a Matagalpa coffee grower who was emerging as one of the most articulate leaders of the incipient anti-Sandinista movement. Salazar was a natural leader, good-looking, personable, charismatic, and quick on his feet. During 1979 and 1980, he had organized a nationwide group of farmers that became part of the private sector coalition COSEP *(Consejo Permanente de la Empresa Privada),* and he soon rose to become an important COSEP strategist. By tirelessly traveling the back roads of his native Matagalpa, organizing peasants and taking their side in disputes with local authorities, Salazar became a hero to many poor people alienated by Sandinista farm policies.

Soon after Humberto Ortega's jarring speech in August, Salazar traveled to Miami to meet with exiles anxious to fight the Sandinistas. When he returned, he was approached by an acquaintance named Nestor Moncada. The news Moncada brought was too good to be true. He said he represented a group of dissident army officers who wanted to launch a coup, and asked if Salazar would help. Salazar met several times with the supposed conspirators, and finally agreed to join their plot.

On November 18, Moncada telephoned Salazar and said he had urgent information to share. The two men arranged to meet behind an abandoned filling station near the town of El Crucero, a few miles west of Managua. When Salazar arrived, Moncada produced a sack of automatic rifles, saying he needed Salazar to hide them. Salazar was alarmed, but before he could say more than a few words, police agents appeared. Shots rang out and Salazar fell dead, seven bullets in his body.

Jorge Salazar was the first and only prominent opposition leader killed by the Sandinistas. His death sparked protests, but since there was ample evidence that he had been involved in a serious conspiracy, the protests could not be too loud. The plot had been a Sandinista invention, but Salazar had fallen for the bait and paid for his misjudgment with his life. If Sandinista leaders were intending to show that they would tolerate dissent only within limits of the law, their message was clearly conveyed.

To kill Jorge Salazar was not the only major decision the National Directorate made in the autumn of 1980. The same month, they finally gave in to escalating appeals from Salvadoran guerrilla leaders. After resisting for more than a year, they quietly agreed to allow the use of airstrips in Nicaragua to supply rebel fighters in El Salvador.

Great solidarity already existed between the FSLN and Salvadoran guerrillas. The Salvadorans had donated several million dollars, earned as kidnap ransoms, to the Sandinista cause during 1978 and 1979. A number of Salvadorans had fought alongside the Sandinistas in climactic battles. Following the Sandinista victory, several Sandinista combatants returned the favor by joining the rebellion in El Salvador. But these few were acting independently, and Salvadoran pleas for material help from Managua were at first turned aside. Now, however, the Salvadorans were engaged in a "final offensive" of their own, aimed at toppling the regime before Ronald Reagan took office in January. The Sandinistas felt obliged to help.

During November and December, several hundred tons of weaponry, much of it from Cuba, was shipped to Salvadoran guerrillas from an airstrip at El Papalonál, a small outpost in the province of León. Daniel Ortega later claimed that the airstrip had been built without official authorization, and that those responsible were subsequently punished. But American officials doubted that such an operation could have been launched without official sanction. On January 9, Ambassador Pezzullo delivered a stiff protest to Tomás Borge. At first Borge protested the government's innocence, but he desisted after Pezzullo made clear how much he knew about the operation at El Papalonál, and about the use of Managua as a center for clandestine radio broadcasts into El Salvador.

The offensive launched by Salvadoran guerrillas in the last days of 1980 proved far short of final. Sandinista leaders had hoped that their aid would prove decisive in bringing about a second revolutionary victory in Central America, but their gamble did not pay off. Worse yet, it had a profound effect in Washington. Once President Carter was shown high-altitude photographs and other intelligence proving that the Sandinistas were sending weapons to El Salvador, he had no legal choice but to cut off aid to their regime.

When he did so, the Sandinistas were apparently taken by surprise. They quickly shut down *Radio Liberación,* the Salvadoran rebel station they had previously denied was located in Managua, and promised the Americans they would end all "funny business" at El Papalonál. But they were too late.

The Sandinistas' adventure into El Salvador proved ill-advised, since it provided the pretext for a cutoff of badly needed aid and ended an era of coexistence between Managua and Washington. The fact that the Sandinistas moved so quickly to halt their aid to Salvadoran guerrillas, and took such pains to assure the United States that it would not be renewed, suggested that they were ready to explore a new set of ground rules for relations with Washington. But on January 20, 1981, when Ronald Reagan took his oath of office as president, the United States abandoned all hope of being able to live peacefully with the Sandinista regime, and set out instead to destroy it.

7

ME AND E. G. SQUIER

MUCH OF Latin America was in violent upheaval during the late 1970s and early 1980s. Great events were unfolding from El Salvador, where civil war was raging, to Argentina, where drunken generals were planning to provoke war with Britain. But in Nicaragua, the big story seemed all but over. Inevitably, the broad coalition that had toppled Somoza was splitting apart, and discontent was spreading. Still, the country was being run by a group of young people who, though inexperienced and often misguided, were moved fundamentally by a desire to improve the lives of their fellow citizens—something that could not be said for governments in most nearby countries. There was every reason to believe that Nicaragua would slowly fade from the front pages and from the world's consciousness, and that the victorious Sandinistas would be left alone to discover that governing was an even greater challenge than organizing insurrection.

Had that happened, my love affair with Nicaragua would never have been consummated. Naturally my emotions had been seared by the human blood and suffering I had seen there during the revolution, but so had they been seared by the terrors and delights of other countries. Nicaragua was still foreign to me, a place where I had gone to cover a story just as I had covered stories from Key West to Patagonia. I presumed that it would become one of the many countries

I visited from time to time, understanding them well enough to write about them, but never sharing their most intimate secrets.

History and fate, however, conspired to bind me forever to Nicaragua. In January 1981, Ronald Reagan, one of the world's most outspokenly anti-Sandinista politicians, assumed the presidency of the United States. Reagan was a frightening match for the Sandinistas, because he saw the world in terms of stark good and evil, just as they did. During his campaign he made clear that if he was elected, the Sandinistas would face a very different and more hostile policy from Washington.

For years, Reagan had admired the Somoza dictatorship. In January 1978, only a week before Pedro Joaquín Chamorro's assassination, he told a national radio audience that Somoza was "getting a bad press," and asserted that his regime "has never been known as a major violator of human rights." The political platform on which he ran for president, approved at the 1980 Republican convention, included a special warning to the Sandinistas.

"We deplore the Marxist Sandinista takeover of Nicaragua," the platform said. "We oppose the Carter administration's aid program for the government of Nicaragua. However, we will support the efforts of the Nicaraguan people to establish a free and independent government."

Reagan took office at the same time that small, disparate groups of Nicaraguan exiles, most of them based in Miami, were beginning to talk of ways to oppose the Sandinistas. While Jimmy Carter was in the White House, neutrality laws restricting the activities of these groups had been strictly enforced, and the United States government gave them no public or private encouragement. As a result, the exiles confined themselves to holding small rallies and publishing broadsides denouncing the Sandinistas.

United States policy toward Nicaragua shifted dramatically following Reagan's inauguration. Central Intelligence Agency operatives began meeting with exile leaders in Miami, and before long presented them with an official, though secret, proposal. They said the CIA was ready to provide large amounts of aid to the anti-Sandinista cause, but on one condition. The exiles would have to unite with a group of former National Guardsmen who had fled Nicaragua and constituted themselves as the September 15 Legion.

At first the civilians in Miami were reluctant to make common cause with ex-Guardsmen, some of whom they held responsible for savage crimes during the 1978–79 insurrection. But the Americans insisted, and all understood that there could be no real anti-Sandinista movement without American support. Soon after Ronald Reagan's inauguration, the CIA invited a group of Miami-based exile leaders to meet in Guatemala with former Guard officers. At that meeting, CIA agents orchestrated the formation of a new organization, the Nicaraguan Democratic Force *(Fuerza Democrática Nicaragüense, FDN),* which was to become the core of the contra movement.

During those days, the most visible and appealing contra leader was a former Jesuit priest and university dean named Edgar Chamorro. Born in Granada to one of Nicaragua's oldest families, distantly related to the murdered newspaper publisher Pedro Joaquín Chamorro, he represented some of the best that Nicaragua had to offer. He had left the priesthood in 1969, won a graduate degree in education from Harvard, and returned home to start an advertising and public relations concern. He worked successfully in Managua until the Sandinista-led uprising put an end to normal life and business. Early in 1979, like many Nicaraguans with enough money to do so, he fled to Miami to wait out the war.

After the Sandinista takeover, Edgar Chamorro returned to Managua for a visit, but he found the new government too radical for his tastes. Instead of reopening his business there, he began building a new life in Florida, and there he fell in with other disaffected exiles. Chamorro was a social democrat whose ideology was roughly equivalent to that of Alfonso Robelo and other civilians who had lost faith in the Sandinistas. He believed that Nicaragua needed revolutionary change, but he could not accept the doctrinaire Sandinista style.

Recognizing Chamorro's talents, the CIA invited him to become official spokesman for the new FDN. It was a felicitous choice, because Chamorro presented the movement's most attractive face. He set up shop in Honduras, where contra footsoldiers were said to be encamped, though they had never actually been seen. His unofficial headquarters was the main hotel in Tegucigalpa, the Maya, which soon became a center of intrigue much as the Intercontinental in Managua had been a few years earlier.

Edgar Chamorro held court at the Maya during daylight hours, often floating lazily in the pool with his sunglasses on. From time to time he was called to the telephone, or to meetings in the poolside coffee shop, but usually he seemed to be just waiting for reporters. He argued the anti-Sandinista cause eloquently.

"Nicaragua needed a revolution, and it still needs a revolution," he told me as we sipped papaya juice beside the pool one morning. "All during my years at the university, I could see the evil of the Somoza tyranny, the way it ruled through blood and terror. I encouraged kids who wanted to work against Somoza, even if they wanted to become Sandinistas. The great tragedy of Nicaragua today is that the revolution is stalled. The Sandinistas took the first great step by getting rid of Somoza. But they're ruling the same way he did, holding all power to themselves. Somoza is gone, but we still don't have a democratic government. That's the next step, and that's what we're fighting for."

Slowly I came to understand the magnitude of what Chamorro and other leaders of the fledgling contra movement were undertaking. With covert financing from Washington, they were going to build a full-scale rebel army in Central America. It was an operation more ambitious than anything the CIA had ever attempted in the Western hemisphere. The only comparable effort had been the long and multi-faceted campaign against Fidel Castro's Cuba, but that had been a different sort of campaign, one based on assassination plots and commando raids. In Nicaragua, the CIA planned to launch all-out war.

Reagan's decision to wage war on the Sandinistas meant that during the years to come, I would be spending much time and energy in Nicaragua. It did not necessarily mean, however, that I would come to regard Nicaragua with any special warmth. I had begun contributing regularly to the *Boston Globe,* and *Globe* editors expected me to monitor events throughout Central America, the Caribbean, and South America. The vast territory I had to cover meant that I could not become too fully engaged in any one place.

My long stays in Nicaragua had been tantalizing. I sensed that this was a country with more to tell the world than it had been able to articulate, a country with a message both political and spiritual. For a time, I consciously resisted being drawn into its orbit. Finally, one overcast afternoon soon after Ronald Reagan's inauguration, I succumbed.

On that day, I was not in Nicaragua at all, but in Boston between assignments. One of my stops was the Brattle Book Shop, where, after tarrying over the fiction and poetry sections, I dutifully checked for books about Latin America. A clerk suggested that I climb to the third floor and see what might be available in the rare book vault.

There, in a quiet, musty chamber, I found original editions of hoary classics I had seen only in libraries, books about the Spanish conquest and South America's wars of independence. Standing among them was a thick black volume, its front cover almost severed by age, and its gold-leaf title so badly faded that only the word "Nicaragua" was legible. Gingerly I pulled it from the shelf and turned to the title page, which was covered by a sheet of translucent tissue. My eyes widened as I read the title: "Nicaragua: Its People, Scenery, Monuments, Resources, Condition, and Proposed Canal; With One Hundred Original Maps and Illustrations. By E. G. Squier, Formerly Charge D'Affaires of the United States to the Republics of Central America." The date of publication was 1860.

I had seen occasional references to Squier in other old books, and had heard his name once or twice from learned Nicaraguans. His book was nearly seven hundred pages long, and devoted entirely to Nicaragua. The table of contents alone ran five closely printed pages, and contained hundreds of entries.

Flipping through the chapters, I saw immediately how extraordinary a man Squier must have been. His book told what it was like to climb volcanoes, to confront alligators, and to search for ancient artifacts. He described sunsets and rainstorms, plants and animals, and encounters with Nicaraguans of every sort. Traveling on the backs of mules and aboard leaky canoes, he went to cockfights, joined in religious festivals, learned local folk dances, and even witnessed a revolution. Officially he was on a diplomatic mission, but he had been unable to confine himself to the merely political. The richness of Nicaragua had assaulted his senses and challenged his curiosity, and he made his stay there into a stirring adventure.

After holding the book for only a minute or so, I closed it and replaced it on the shelf. The price written inside the front cover was seventy-five dollars, but that wasn't all that held me back. I recognized instantly that Squier's book was a forgotten classic, undoubtedly the most exhaustive account of Nicaragua ever written. To buy it would imply a commitment such as I had never made to any single country.

I imagined that I would never again have a chance to buy Squier's book. I had never seen a copy for sale before, and never did again. It was a moment to make a commitment or to shrink from making one. I took the book down again and read the introduction, which was entitled "Preface to Revised Edition."

"Since the publication of the original edition of this work in 1852," Squier wrote, "the beautiful but hapless Republic of Nicaragua has been the theater of startling events which have concentrated upon it not only the attention of the American public, but of all civilized nations. It has been made the arena of aimless and not always reputable diplomatic contests . . . [U]nless the future shall strangely betray the indications of the present, it is destined to pass through a succession of still severer throes . . . Public interest and especially American interest in Nicaragua must therefore constantly increase; and the desire to know the characteristics of the country, its scenery and products, and the habits and customs of its people, can never diminish."

Squier was quite wrong, of course. Nicaragua had slipped from the American consciousness, and so had he and his masterpiece. But now, more than a century later, his discoveries were suddenly interesting again. I felt that he was beckoning me, that I had found a guide for my forthcoming venture into Nicaragua. Standing in the book vault that day, I resolved to do as Squier had done, to immerse myself in everything Nicaraguan. Suddenly decisive, I pulled the book from its shelf, briskly walked down to the cashier, and paid for it.

I read Squier's book slowly, dipping into it for a few pages at a time. Remarkably little seemed to have changed in Nicaragua over the years since he set pen to paper. He had found political leaders divided into hostile factions, with those out of power constantly plotting rebellion. León was already the country's intellectual capital, and Granada had long been established as its commercial center. The Masaya volcano was every bit as impressive then as now; Squier climbed its slope and pronounced the experience "singularly novel and beautiful." Most amazing of all was to read his account of the bandit who was terrorizing Nicaragua at the time he arrived, "a lawless, reckless fellow under proscription for murder, named Somoza." Squier was in Nicaragua as the outlaw chieftain Bernabé Somoza reached the peak of his power, and he had witnessed Somoza's collapse, just as I had watched the fall of another Somoza.

By the time I finished reading Squier's book, I was fired with enthusiasm for Nicaragua. President Reagan's inauguration and his avowed determination to destroy the Sandinistas had meant that I would be visiting Nicaragua regularly, and my discovery of Squier made the prospect vivid and exciting. Nonetheless, I was still worried that by concentrating too fully on Nicaragua, I would be shortchanging *Globe* readers who were anxious to follow events in other Latin American countries.

My duties as a *Globe* correspondent took me to more than a dozen Latin American countries. El Salvador, where rebel guerrillas were waging a full-scale war, was my most frequent stop. Among my other assignments were the 1980 exodus of Cubans from the port at Mariel and the 1982 war between Argentina and Great Britain. My job was close to ideal. The *Globe*'s foreign editor, David Greenway, who had been a celebrated correspondent in Southeast Asia and the Middle East, gave me free rein. Most of the time, he allowed me to choose the countries I visited and the topics I wrote about. If I wanted to ignore breaking news and concentrate on more unusual reporting, that was fine with him.

BECAUSE I spent most of my time traveling, I had no office or desk at the *Globe* building in Boston. When I stopped there to pick up my mail one autumn morning in 1982, a secretary at the foreign desk handed me a yellow telephone message slip. There was no message, only the name Craig Whitney and a New York phone number. I had never met Whitney, but I knew he was foreign editor of the *New York Times*. I dialed his number, and was soon introducing myself.

"Do you know who I am?" Whitney asked me.

"I do indeed," I replied.

After a few pleasantries, Whitney invited me to lunch in New York. Our meeting was friendly and professional. We chatted briefly about my background, and then he made a simple proposition. It was becoming plain, he told me, that Nicaragua was not going to calm down and return to normal just because the Somoza dictatorship had been overthrown. *Times* editors wanted to improve their coverage of Central America, and were looking for Spanish-speaking reporters who had worked in the region and understood the demands of daily journalism. I fit the bill, and Whitney asked if I would consider quitting the *Globe* to join the *Times*.

I made no direct answer, and Whitney did not insist. He suggested that I return home, give the matter some thought, and then call him back. My next few days were difficult. The *Globe* had been good to me, giving me more freedom than I would ever have if I accepted work at the *Times*. Yet the *Times* held a unique place in American journalism, and resisting an offer to work there was as difficult for me as it would be for almost any reporter.

All of this weighed on my mind as I returned to New York for a two-day series of interviews with *Times* editors. Whitney assured me that the interviews were largely a formality, and that my prospects were secure as long as I didn't make a fool of myself. As he promised, the editors who interviewed me on the first day had no sharp or rigorous questions. All that remained was for me to meet A. M. Rosenthal, the much-feared executive editor.

Tales of Rosenthal's withering rages and bursts of irrationality were legend far beyond New York, but my encounter with him was quite relaxed. He did most of the talking. Several times, we paused to watch a line of chorus girls who were practicing for a musical in a Forty-third Street loft across from his window.

"Do you want to come and work here?" Rosenthal finally asked.

"I'm interested, but I haven't made a final decision yet," I replied.

"Well, I don't offer jobs to people who aren't sure they want to work here," he replied. "When you're sure you want the job, let us know, and we'll go from there."

The prospect of working for the *New York Times* held great allure, but I was still hesitant. I remembered reporters in El Salvador who were under so much competitive pressure that they bolted from their breakfast tables at the sound of every distant explosion, forever fearing that one of their colleagues might report an incident that they had missed. Because the *Globe* did not insist that its reporters join the journalistic pack, I was able to eat uninterrupted breakfasts on most mornings, and to skip press conferences and other staged news events. I was free to roam the countryside without worrying whether I would miss some political development in the capital. Other correspondents, including those working for the *Times,* seemed constantly to be receiving telex messages ordering them to cover this or that story, or directing them to "match or deny" what someone else had filed. I had never received a single telex from the *Globe,* except one in mid-1982 telling me I was doing a good job covering the Falkland Islands war. Yet alongside all of this was the power and visibility of the *Times,* and its ability to help shape public discourse. The chance to become part of its corps of foreign correspondents would probably not come again.

I was still wrestling with this dilemma when the phone rang at my apartment in Boston. It was Craig Whitney. He had expected to hear from me within a couple of days after my return from New York, and now that a week had passed he wanted to know where we stood. Perhaps not entirely coherently, I began to explain my uncertainties. Whitney was not unsympathetic, but he wanted a decision. He made a final one-line pitch.

"If you're going to do this for a living," he told me, "you might as well do it here."

Whitney's logic was powerful. I paused for a brief moment, and then decided.

"OK, I'll do it," I told him.

"You want the job?" he asked.

"Yes, I want the job."

"Have you told the people at the *Globe?*"

"I haven't told anyone. I just made up my mind this minute."

"Well, call the *Globe,* and then call me back."

I did as he advised, and found *Globe* editors remarkably understanding. For years I had stared at *Times* by-lines, with their boldface capital letters and the authoritative-sounding agate legend, "Special to The New York Times." That would now be my signature.

New York Times policy dictates that new reporters not be promised specific assignments, much less assignments abroad. Normally they are sent to cover local news in New York while editors slowly make decisions about their future postings. I was told to expect at least six months of work covering New York City and learning the ways of the *Times,* but as it turned out, I was in Central America only weeks after being hired.

All the pieces were now in place for the adventure of my life. President Reagan's policies had guaranteed that Nicaragua would soon become one of the biggest news stories in the world. Squier had fueled my enthusiasm for the assignment, and sparked my ambition to learn all of Nicaragua's secrets. And the *Times'* decision to hire me meant that I would be able to concentrate my time and efforts in Nicaragua. The planets were aligned, and I approached my coming assignment as if shedding an old skin and trying to fit into a new and unfamiliar one.

8

LOOKING FOR CONTRAS

I ARRIVED early for my first day of work at the *New York Times.* My adrenaline level had been slowly rising as I packed my belongings in Boston and drove them down the Massachusetts Turnpike toward New York. When I walked through the revolving doors at the Times building on the morning of January 2, 1983, I felt a shiver of anticipation. The watchman didn't challenge me, which I took as a good omen.

By the 1980s, newsrooms of some large daily papers had come to resemble the offices of accounting firms or insurance companies, with rows of drones quietly clicking their days away behind word processors. At the *Times,* however, some vestiges of the pre-computer age still remained, and it was still possible to tell that journalists, not clerks, were at work there. Unkempt piles of papers covered many desks in the cavernous third-floor newsroom. Walls were adorned with union notices and odd photos, and the room exuded energy even when empty.

Beginning at mid-morning, reporters could be seen purposefully entering and leaving, pulling coats on or taking them off, some of them presumably working on stories that would become big news in a few days. Others leaned against walls holding coffee cups or munching on snacks, gossiping, discussing the day's news, and speculating about recent or impending editorial shakeups. By late afternoon, many would be hunched over their word processors, typing in bursts and glancing up at the clock every few minutes.

My first *Times* assignment, as it is for nearly every new reporter there, was to the metropolitan desk, which covers news of New York City and the surrounding area. Protocol dictated that reporters begin their service on the metro desk without any promise of a different assignment later, but in my case the veneer of protocol was thin. Everyone understood that I had been hired to cover Central America, and that my stay in New York would be brief. So long as I didn't make any mistakes or alienate any editors, I was privately assured, I would be on my way southward before long.

Winter mornings in New York were crisp and cold, but I loved walking the thirty blocks to work each day. From my sublet apartment near Central Park I would walk down Broadway toward Times Square, reveling in the throngs crowding the sidewalk around me. Knowing that I would soon be in another, very different place made New York all the more exhilarating. Though I had lived there before, the towering skyscrapers, the limousines, the fashions, and the frenetic pace of life dazzled me as if I were seeing them for the first time. Already, even before leaving the United States, I was beginning to perceive it with the eyes of a foreigner.

I found all of my local assignments fascinating, even the most mundane of them, because they were so different from the kind of work I would soon be doing in Central America. In New York there were facts, statistics, explanations, and people who answered telephones. Where I was headed, all was mysterious and unclear, and powerful people were dedicated to keeping it that way.

Late in February, I was sent to Ohio as part of a team of *Times* reporters who fanned out across the country to produce a series of articles about toxic waste dumps. I spent a pleasant week and a half in the Cincinnati area, poking around the site of an abandoned dump where carcinogenic chemicals were oozing into the earth from rusted barrels, and interviewing public officials in an attempt to find out how this little disaster had come to happen. A few days after I returned to New York, I was told that Craig Whitney, the foreign editor, wanted to see me.

Whitney and his crew sat at a cluster of desks only a few feet away from mine, but I had consciously avoided them for fear of seeming overeager. Now Whitney gave me the news I had expected, though not so soon: he needed me in Central America. It turned out that Pope John Paul II was about to tour the isthmus, and the *Times* was deploying correspondents to meet him at every stop. One additional reporter was needed, and I was the logical choice. Whitney told me to go home, pack a bag, and catch the next available flight.

As I walked uptown along the swirling avenues, I was already imagining what

I might do during my first trip to Central America as a *New York Times* correspondent. Officially I was going to cover the Pope, but I wasn't really interested in him. I was interested in contras.

PRESIDENT Reagan had by this time been in office for two years. He had long since concluded that the Sandinista government was a direct threat to American security, could not be "moderated," and would have to be dislodged by force. Reagan had sent Assistant Secretary of State Thomas Enders to Managua in August 1981 for a last-chance round of talks with the Sandinistas, but Enders came away empty-handed. He had offered what amounted to a straightforward deal: if the Sandinistas would alter their international behavior, contras training in the Florida Everglades would not be unleashed. Enders told the *comandantes* that if they wanted to head off an impending war, they would have to stop providing aid to Salvadoran rebels and other foreign guerrillas, and cut or substantially loosen their military ties to Cuba and the Soviet Union.

Considered coldly with the benefit of hindsight, especially in view of the devastation wreaked by the contra war, the deal does not sound entirely unappealing. But at the time, Sandinista leaders scorned it, replying to Enders with scathing denunciations of American intervention in Nicaragua that included long expositions about William Walker, Zelaya, and other figures with whom the envoy was probably only marginally familiar. The Sandinistas had fought for years to establish Nicaragua's independence from the United States, and for emotional as well as political reasons it was unrealistic to expect them to reach any accord with Enders. Making deals with the United States, especially deals coupled with implicit threats, was precisely what governments of Nicaragua had done for more than a century, and what the Sandinistas had sworn never to do. Throughout the country's history, heroic figures had been men like President Zelaya, like Benjamin Zeledón and Sandino, who had defied the United States for reasons of principle; traitors had been those like the Somozas, who accepted Washington's right to dictate the limits of Nicaraguan sovereignty.

Later I asked one Sandinista *comandante*, Bayardo Arce, if he had come to regret his government's decision to turn down Enders's offer.

"You can't put it in those terms," Arce replied. "We made our decision based on principles. It was not a matter of cold analysis, or else the choice might have been different. Remember what was the climate at that time. We were still in a wartime mentality. I myself was still running five kilometers every morning in order to stay fit for combat. Enders's proposal did not meet the requirements of that moment."

The Sandinistas had taken power for a reason, I understood Arce to be saying, and it was not to make compromises with men like Ronald Reagan.

* * *

IN the months that followed Enders's visit to Managua, United States policy toward the Sandinistas became clearly focused for the first time. Reagan aides spoke no more of peace overtures, and instead prepared for war. William Casey, the Director of Central Intelligence, began discreetly visiting Capitol Hill to inform members of Congress that covert operations against the Sandinistas were underway. Reports that anti-Sandinista commandos were training in Florida soon gave way to reports that the commandos were filtering into Honduras and making their way toward the Nicaraguan border.

On the night of March 15, 1982, saboteurs blew up two bridges in northern Nicaragua. That attack, which bore all the signs of CIA sponsorship, was the opening shot of the contra war. The Sandinistas responded by decreeing a nationwide state of emergency, imposing press censorship, curbing political freedoms, and stepping up surveillance and harassment of dissidents. Each side was fulfilling the other's worst fears, setting in motion the cycle of provocation and response that was to define relations between the United States and Nicaragua for years to come.

When defending the contra cause in secret testimony before congressional oversight committees, William Casey used an argument that no sentient observer could honestly have believed. He said the contras were not trying to overthrow the Sandinista government, but rather to disrupt the supply lines by which Sandinista weapons were being sent to guerrillas in El Salvador. Casey was thus asserting that the squads of Nicaraguan exiles he had assembled, armed, trained, and sent to camps in Central America were not actually fighting for power in their homeland, but were rather doing a kind of foreign policy favor for the United States. The argument was as absurd as it was false. In fact, the contras were being created to do precisely what Casey said they were not doing: fight the Sandinistas. By accepting Casey's outlandish rationale with a figurative wink, Congress gave its tacit approval to the contra project.

Legislators opposed to the contras tried late in 1982 to pass a bill cutting off their covert funding, and to prevent the bill from passing, the Reagan administration accepted official restrictions on its policy toward Nicaragua. In December, Congress voted overwhelmingly—the count in the House of Representatives was 411 to 0—for the first so-called Boland Amendment, which forbade the use of American funds on behalf of contras trying to overthrow the Sandinistas. Under its provisions, funds could only be used to support contras engaged in "interdiction" of arms caravans headed for El Salvador. The amendment, attached to a CIA budget measure, was unambiguous: "None of the funds provided in this act may be used by the Central Intelligence Agency or the Department of Defense to furnish military equipment, military training or advice, or any other support for military activities, to any group or individual, not part of a country's armed forces, for the purpose of overthrowing the government of Nicaragua or provoking a military exchange between Nicaragua and Honduras."

Rarely has such a powerful body cast a vote based on a subterfuge so widely acknowledged. Members of Congress certainly realized that no contra would ever sign up to fight under those conditions. To suggest that the contra army was being built solely to disrupt Sandinista gun-smuggling operations was an insult to the intelligence, as Reagan aides readily acknowledged in private.

I found Nestor Sanchez, a National Security Council planner involved in the contra project at its inception, quite frank when I interviewed him in Washington during one of my final *Boston Globe* assignments. Sanchez said the contra army was being formed to fight for the same demands that Enders had presented in Managua more than a year before. Speaking in terms not unlike those of his predecessors in administrations long past who also had trouble with Nicaragua, Sanchez offered advice to Nicaraguan leaders.

"Stop your support of insurgencies in other countries, and let them live in peace," he said. "Stop your military buildup, which scares all your neighbors. Just stop doing what you've been doing. When you knock it off, we certainly will."

For Sandinista leaders, who had memorized the infamous Knox Note and Zeledón's heart-rending patriotic testaments, who had sworn to follow Sandino's example and never kneel before the colossus, such talk was an unbearable affront. Like their heroes from generations past, they were ready to pay any price to establish what they viewed as Nicaragua's true independence.

Weapons from abroad soon began pouring into Central America. The Sandinistas started importing heavy artillery pieces and building up their stock of Soviet-made T-54 and T-55 tanks. In Honduras, mysterious cargo was being ferried in covered trucks toward the border area where contras were said to be building base camps. Nicaraguan towns near the border were fortified as hit-and-run contra raids increased. *Newsweek* ran a splashy cover story in November 1982 headlined "America's Secret War—Target: Nicaragua," in which it was alleged that several dozen CIA agents had set up shop in Honduras to oversee the contra operation.

When President Reagan stopped in Tegucigalpa to show support for Honduran leaders in November, all understood he was there to encourage the contras. Daniel Ortega saw immediately that the visit bode no good for his government.

"The embrace Reagan brings," Ortega warned in Managua, "comes full of blood, death, and tragedy for Central America."

It was apparent that a major CIA operation was unfolding along the Nicaragua-Honduras border, but its nature and dimensions were not yet clear. Sandinista leaders were making almost daily speeches denouncing Honduras for harboring contras, and logic suggested that their charges must be true. The contras tried to pretend they were an indigenous force operating strictly within

Nicaragua, but trips I had taken to Nicaraguan border towns like Jalapa and Teotecacinte led me to believe that was untrue. Townspeople had shown me how close the border was, and told me of former neighbors who had slipped across to join contra squads based on the other side. Refugees were flooding out of rural hamlets into Jalapa, telling stories of rampaging bands that pulled Sandinista activists from their beds and kidnapped or killed them, of buses ambushed and farms devastated by mortar attacks. All evidence indicated that the Honduran government, despite its public denials, had turned over a strip of its territory to the contras and their CIA overseers. Somewhere in the rugged hills north of Jalapa, just across the border, there had to be contra camps. No journalist had ever seen one, but all of us knew they must be there.

THE Pope's trip through Central America in March 1983 lasted only a few days. I covered his appearances in Panama and Belize, which were blessedly uneventful. My editors had agreed to let me snoop around the region for a while, and after the Pope departed I headed to Tegucigalpa, the Honduran capital. Landing at Toncontín airport there was always an adventure, because the runway is wedged between two mountain peaks and must be approached with great care. Local pilots were accustomed to the maneuver, but often an inexperienced passenger who looked out a window during the descent could be heard to gasp or recite hurried prayers.

Those of us who landed at Toncontín regularly, especially reporters, actually enjoyed looking out our windows at the tarmac below, because we could often see the silhouettes of giant C-47 transport planes, entirely without markings, parked at the far end of the airstrip. We had no evidence as to what kind of freight the planes were transporting, but in our hearts all of us believed they must be part of a clandestine CIA operation on behalf of the contras. As my Sahsa Airlines jet descended between the peaks that March evening, I saw several unmarked cargo planes parked on the side of the airport used by military aircraft.

At the Maya Hotel near the center of Tegucigalpa, most guests were Americans on mysterious missions. Just as United States agencies had not yet built their own airfield in Honduras and were forced to use the publicly visible strip at Toncontín, they had not found barracks and safe houses for their clandestine operatives, and so housed them at the Maya. The lobby took on an air of mystery quite like that which had pervaded the Intercontinental in Managua in the weeks before Somoza's fall. Young and fit-looking Americans, many sporting crewcuts and carrying olive green duffel bags, checked in and out by the hour. Mini-vans arrived from the airport carrying new guests at hours when I knew there were no commercial flights arriving.

One evening at the hotel bar, I noticed one of these men sitting alone, and ventured to ask what brought him to Honduras.

"Business," he replied after a moment's thought.

"Any special kind of business?" I inquired. He polished off what remained of his Jack Daniel's and called for the check.

"Just business," he told me with a half-smile as he stood to leave.

When not absorbing the intrigue that enveloped the Maya Hotel, I was about town dropping in on friends. The military-backed Honduran regime was built on mendacity, so its spokesmen were of no use to me. Without much difficulty, however, I was able to find honest citizens who rejected the corruption of their leaders, and I conversed at length with several of them, including a physician, a former Cabinet minister, a newspaper editor, and a retired military officer. All were wise men well versed in the ways of Honduras, and all told me the same things. The Reagan administration had obviously struck a private bargain with Honduran leaders, they said, under which contras were being allowed to build base camps on Honduran territory. Claims that the contras were operating wholly within Nicaragua were preposterous, and the suggestion that they were fighting to cut off the flow of weapons to Salvadoran guerrillas was even more so. The lattice of lies that had been constructed to hide the contra project from public view was obviously not fooling anyone in Honduras who wanted to see the truth.

The American embassy in Tegucigalpa was already becoming a key command center from which the clandestine contra war was directed. I called there to ask if Ambassador John Negroponte was receiving interviewers, and the next day was told that he was. There were several other American reporters in town, all on missions more or less like mine, and since we had all asked to see Ambassador Negroponte, he invited us by for a chat one morning. He had little to say, and my attention wandered until I found myself staring at a prominently displayed photo of the ambassador with former President Nixon, whose administration he had advised on Vietnam policy.

Officially, Negroponte was ambassador from the United States, but his true mission in Honduras was not diplomatic in any traditional sense of that word. He was there to direct a secret war, and to keep it secret as best he could. All of us at that day's interview had read recent news accounts identifying him as the chairman of a secret core group that was running the contra war, and none of us doubted that the accounts were true. As our conversation drew to a close, one reporter asked if Ambassador Negroponte could give us some reaction to the question we had all come to ask.

"I am not going to comment on stories there may have been with regard to allegations that we may have been involved in some way with the anti-Sandinistas," he replied curtly.

The next day I heard from the American embassy again. This time the caller informed me that one of the United States military attachés posted in Honduras had agreed to meet the press informally that afternoon. A military attaché working at the American embassy in Tegucigalpa had to know a great deal about the contras and their war, though he might pretend not to. His briefing would necessarily be a giant charade.

About half a dozen American reporters showed up for that day's briefing at the ugly concrete embassy compound. All of us had drifted to this part of the world with the same unstated ambition: to find a contra base inside Honduras, and thereby to expose the truth that the contras were not indigenous rebels, but cross-border raiders under foreign protection.

As we waited for the briefing to begin, we exchanged rumors about the contras and their secret camps. On a coffee table I found a copy of that day's local newspaper. It carried news of an indignant official statement just released by the Honduran government. Nicaragua had again accused Honduras of harboring contra guerrillas, and Honduras was again denying the charge.

"It is absolutely false that anti-Sandinista guerrillas have bases in Honduras or have used our territory to launch attacks against the regime of the neighboring country," the statement asserted.

The presence of contras in Honduras was an open secret, so most of the people who read that declaration probably realized it was untrue. It was offensive to logic as well as to honesty, and shamed the Hondurans who proclaimed it. Yet no one had evidence to prove it was false.

Our reporters' banter was interrupted when our host, a muscular army officer in his mid-thirties, appeared with a smile and introduced himself.

"I guess you're all interested in the contras, but we can't really tell you much about them," he began apologetically. "You've all heard these rumors that the contras have bases inside Honduras, but we don't have any definitive information on that."

One of my colleagues produced an Esso road map of Central America, and we began pointing to border towns in Nicaragua where contras had staged raids. No one had a map of Honduras, and the attaché volunteered to fetch one. He returned carrying an official map, framed and mounted behind glass, which he had taken from a wall in someone's office. "I guess this is the most detailed map we have," he told us.

I could barely contain my disbelief. Undoubtedly large and detailed maps of every section of Honduras, especially the border zone, were available at this embassy. The sight of this attaché propping up the framed geological map on a sofa, pretending to be unfamiliar with the names of towns near the border and claiming that the embassy had no better map, epitomized the clumsy deception on which the contra project was based. If the first big lie concocted by the Reagan administration to disguise its true intentions in Nicaragua was that the contras existed only to interdict arms shipments to El Salvador, the second was that there were no contra bases in Honduras.

Reporters at that day's briefing were impatient. Our strongest instincts told us that contra squads were based on Honduran soil. All available evidence confirmed our suspicion, and every Honduran we respected told us that we were right. Yet an American military officer, speaking in his official capacity, was telling us the opposite. We began pressing him. Everyone in town knew that the border area was crawling with contras, we insisted. Did he really expect us to believe that the United States government knew nothing about them?

"Let me ask you guys something," he said, flipping his looseleaf notebook shut. "If the contras really have bases inside Honduras, then how come nobody's ever seen one of those bases? You guys have been all over the area, and you haven't found a thing. Maybe you're barking up the wrong tree." He looked at us impassively for a moment, then stood up.

"So long, fellas," he told us with a smile and a theatrical wave. "Good luck!"

We didn't say much as we filed out through the embassy's triple security doors. Walking back toward the hotel, I felt frustrated. The border area where contras were operating was rugged and all but trackless. To find a clandestine military camp that was hidden there, especially one controlled by the CIA, would not be easy. I began to imagine how it might be done.

At least some of the bases, I reasoned, were sure to be in what was called the Las Vegas salient, a peninsula of Honduras that juts into Nicaragua near Jalapa. A dirt road ran through the salient, and the distance from that road to the border was only a few miles in some places. There had to be bases or contra installations of some kind in the narrow strip between the road and the border. A number of reporters had already traveled through the area and found nothing. But we all believed that contra bases were there, and we were convinced that if we kept looking, sooner or later one of us would hit paydirt.

I was expected back in New York soon, and was determined to try my luck in the border area before before returning. After the embassy briefing, I called Ken Silverman, a lanky, bespectacled free-lance photographer who was also passing through town. Would he be interested in some work along the border? He would. I arranged for a car rental, and at dawn the next morning, March 26, 1983, we met in the Maya Hotel parking lot and set out in search of contras.

Hours passed and the paved road gave way to dirt as Ken and I wound our way toward Danlí, the main town in the border zone. There and at nearby villages, we met Nicaraguan refugees who told us that contras were constantly crossing back and forth between Nicaragua and Honduras. These refugees, all poor peasants, complained bitterly about Sandinista rule, many saying their small plots of land had been confiscated or their farm animals seized by local Sandinista officials. They told us they supported the contras, but didn't know where we could find any.

We pressed ahead, taking unlikely-looking paths through abandoned fields until they faded into the woods, then returning to the road and trying again. Clusters of huts were few and widely scattered. Often we drove for miles without seeing a sign of human life. Rain fell intermittently, and mud splattered the car. We drank cans of fruit juice and talked about how sure we were that the contras were nearby, perhaps even watching us at that very moment through high-powered binoculars bought with American tax dollars. From wherever they were hidden, we felt their presence, and cursed them for concealing themselves.

Ken and I spent the better part of a day traipsing through the salient, and by late afternoon we had little to show but mud, which caked our shoes and formed mushy puddles on the floor of our rented car. What made our predicament especially frustrating was that many of the people we met told us that contras were indeed filtering through this area. No one knew where their bases were, but it stood to reason that they must be nearby. All we could see were wooded hills receding into the distance around us, but we knew there was more out there than hills. Dusk was approaching, and we decided to head back to Danlí and set out again the next day.

A few minutes after turning the car around, we saw two teenage boys hitchhiking by the roadside. We had been picking up every hitchhiker we saw, and I pulled to a stop. The boys climbed in, and were thrilled to hear that we were going all the way to Danlí. Evidently Danlí was the "big city" in their universe. They told us they were hoping for a good time there, and that they had risked punishment by sneaking away from their army base for the night.

There was a moment of silence as we bounced along. I turned to look at Ken, and he was looking at me. Ken spoke first, in a tone of studied nonchalance.

"Base?" he asked. "What base?"

"We're in the army," explained the older of the two youths. "Our base is back there, just off the road."

This conversation was becoming very interesting. These fellows were just the sort we had been seeking, and carefully Ken began to draw them out.

"You guys see a lot of contras around here?" he asked.

"*Bastante,*" replied the older boy. Lots of them.

Ken glanced at me, and I nodded to urge him onward.

"Any contra bases around here?" he asked casually.

"No, nothing like that," our passenger said. "The bases are somewhere else, not here."

I swore silently. Ken turned to face the boys in the backseat.

"You mean to say there aren't any contras based near here?" he demanded. "They don't even have supply posts here? Nothing?"

Both boys shook their heads sadly, as if genuinely sorry that they couldn't help us.

"No bases," said one of them. "Nothing at all. Just the little camp back at Matasano."

For the first and only time in my life, I thought I literally felt my heart skip a beat. Instinctively I shifted my right foot from the accelerator to the brake.

"What camp?" Ken asked quickly. "Where? Who's there?"

"The contras!" both boys replied in unison, as if Ken and I must be dunces.

I was already turning the car around as Ken grilled them, jumbling his Spanish as the questions flooded out. Quite willingly, obviously completely unaware of the implications of what they were saying, our passengers explained that about a hundred contras maintained a rustic camp in the hills behind a place they called Matasano, which appeared on no map I had ever seen. They said the contras had been there for several months, and that they operated in close cooperation with Honduran army units posted in the area. The older and more outgoing of the two youths told us that Honduran soldiers felt "a sense of brotherhood" with contras, and were helping them to obtain food and other necessities.

Ken lost no time in explaining to our young friends that he and I needed to see that camp. They agreed to direct us, and told us that the turnoff was not far ahead. I tried to concentrate on the twisting road, and Ken kept chattering with our passengers, but both of us were churning inside.

We drove past a strip of wooden shacks that turned out to be Matasano, and then at the direction of the boys in the back seat we turned onto an overgrown path that wound through a peaceful cow pasture. Night was falling. Half a mile from the road, we found our path blocked by a fence. Had we been alone, we might have thought twice about opening the gate. A real war was being fought here, and sentries would be armed. One of our passengers, however, bounded from the back seat and pulled the gate open, as if he had passed this way many times.

After driving a few hundred yards further, we were stopped by a grizzled, olive-skinned civilian carrying an AK-47 assault rifle, one of the world's most familiar guerrilla weapons. He was old for a fighter, perhaps forty, with white stubble on his leathery cheeks. As we approached, he walked to the middle of the path to block our way. I pulled to a stop, and the older of our passengers stepped out of the car.

After years of covering Nicaragua, I had developed an unconscious feel for who was Nicaraguan and who was not, and every instinct told me this sentry was Nicaraguan. This guy is a contra! I shouted silently to myself. He's in Honduras! And we're here looking at him!

I didn't hear what our friend told that sentry, but whatever it was, it worked perfectly. He climbed back aboard and said, "OK, let's go." The watchman smiled, holding his rifle at his side and using his free hand to wave us by. I smiled back, knowing that this poor fellow was making a terrible mistake by allowing me through, but grateful that his wits were not quicker. It was practically dark and I had been driving through mud and over mountains for more than twelve hours, but at that moment I was vividly alert.

"OK, we're coming to the camp now," one of the boys in the back seat said after we had driven about a mile past the sentry post. Ken and I looked silently at each other, both of us exploding with anticipation but struggling to preserve outward calm.

We turned a bend, and suddenly I could make out the shapes of people and tents. In a moment we were parked in front of a mid-sized earthen hut. Several men and women were sitting nearby, eating rice and beans from metal plates. Propped up casually against several trees were a variety of assault rifles, several American-made M-79 grenade launchers, and a grab bag of other weapons.

Instantly I realized that we had found what we were seeking. This was no Honduran army base, so it had to be a contra camp. Who besides contras, after all, would have armed squads based in the Honduran wilderness a few miles from the border with Nicaragua? I asked Ken if there was enough light for him to take pictures. No way, he replied. I hated to hear that, because for maximum impact I knew this story should be accompanied by a photo.

The four of us emerged from our car, and I offered a casual greeting to the puzzled-looking fighters, who were obviously not used to receiving unannounced visitors. It turned out that most of the contras based at this camp, and all their commanders, were away "on operations," and that the fifteen or so left behind were a kind of rear guard. This was fortuitous, since any responsible commander would have expelled us immediately from the area, or worse.

I didn't want to stay long enough to arouse suspicions, but I needed to take a quick look around. More than a dozen large tents served as barracks, and the hut in front of which we were standing was apparently some kind of supply center. All eyes were on me as I nodded toward its door with a friendly smile and suggested that I should take a look inside. No one said a word or moved to stop me. Perhaps they assumed I was with the CIA; what other gringo, after all, would be appearing at such a place?

What I saw inside that hut was no less thrilling to me than any treasure found in myth. Unopened wooden crates were stacked up to the rafters, each one labeled in large black letters as if for my convenience. "SHELLS FOR M2 OR M19 MORTARS," read some of the stenciled labels; "30 FRAGMENTATION GRE-NADES," read others.

By this time my initial adrenaline rush was wearing off, and I began to realize that it would be best for Ken and me to withdraw as soon as possible rather than continue to press our astonishing luck. I didn't want to give any of the contras time to think or make a radio call, and now that I had seen what I came to see, it was time to depart. In my mind I ran through the outlines of what I would write, and I realized there was one essential quote I did not yet have. To make my article airtight, I needed one of these contras to confirm explicitly that he and his comrades were Nicaraguan.

"Tell me," I asked as I was climbing back into my car, "are any of you guys Honduran?"

The man nearest to me snorted in disgust. "Hell no!" he replied. "We're all Nicaraguans."

That was precisely the line I had hoped to hear. We waved adieu, turned the car around, and headed back toward the road. When we reached it, Ken and I broke our silence and began talking to each other in English. Our situation, we agreed, was excellent. We had just uncovered a huge story that would have worldwide impact, and we had nearly everything we needed for a potent and irrefutable article. Only one problem remained: we still had no photo of the camp. A story of this magnitude, we agreed, should be supported by photographic evidence. Our only option was to return the next morning and hope against hope that we would be allowed to enter the camp again. For this we would need our young Honduran guides, and we resolved not to let them out of our sight.

Ken turned to them and explained the deal: we would drive them to Danlí, buy them dinner, and rent them a hotel room, if they would lead us back to the camp at first light. They asked which restaurant and which hotel we had in mind, and we told them they could have their pick. They were thunderstruck, and when we assured them that we were footing the bill, they began laughing in delight, as if they had stumbled onto a bonanza.

When we arrived at Danlí, our friends directed us to a modest inn which they apparently viewed as the height of luxury. The four of us dined together, and after consuming a bottle of rum between them, our Honduran friends danced a few unsteady turns around the floor to the accompaniment of mariachi music from a juke box. Soon they were in their room asleep. Ken and I rented the rooms on either side of them, and I left my door ajar so I would hear them if for any reason they sought to leave.

The reliable crowing of roosters awakened me at dawn, and soon the four of us had risen, eaten breakfast, and packed ourselves back into our much-abused rental car. Before we had gone far, the Honduran youths told us that they were due back at their army base, and wouldn't be able to return with us to the contra camp after all. Ken and I were disappointed, fearing that the photo we needed was beginning to slip away from us. We tried to persuade our young friends to change their minds, but they had a military duty and we were not so ungrateful as to demand that they shirk it. We left them at their base, and I foolishly decided to ask the commander a few questions. It took only a moment for him to start grilling me about my business in the area, and what I had been doing with two of his soldiers in my car. I quickly realized that I was only arousing suspicion, and mumbled excuses and thanks as I hastily withdrew. A close call, I told Ken as we drove away.

We had trouble finding Matasano that second day. For a while we wondered if we had become completely disoriented. We hadn't gotten a good look the night before, and in any case Matasano was nothing more than a few shacks along a back road. We feared we might have inadvertently driven past it, but after a couple of hours we came upon what we thought was the right place. The sun was fully visible on the eastern horizon, illuminating a ruggedly beautiful mountain scene. It was a Sunday morning. We found a small general store, and there we bought soft drinks and gasoline. The proprietress told us she had heard there was a contra camp nearby, but couldn't say exactly where. She said that the adjoining pasture had been abandoned for years, and belonged to a dairy company based in Tegucigalpa.

Before heading toward the camp, Ken carefully washed the mud from our windshield, and then laid his camera on the dashboard in front of him. If we managed to reach the camp again, we agreed, I would get out of the car and distract the contras' attention while Ken snapped his shutter as unobtrusively as possible. If we were stopped along the entry path, which was more likely, we would follow a similar drill, and Ken would snap whatever photo he could. Photographing contras in their camp would of course be ideal, but any picture of civilians carrying weapons of war in such circumstances would be powerful.

We set out on our way, finding the well-hidden pasture path after a few false starts. When we came to the gate, I stopped the car and gingerly stepped out. Wondering who might be watching, I walked up to the wooden gate, unlatched it, and pulled it open. Nothing happened. We drove slowly around the next bend, both of us nervous and scared. Suddenly we saw a patrol of soldiers coming toward us. They were not ignorant camp followers like those we had found the night before, but real contra guerrillas.

"This is it," I said to Ken. "I'm getting out. Take the picture fast, then we're out of here."

Three contra soldiers came toward me as I stepped away from the car. All were young, uniformed, and well armed. They pointed their assault rifles at me and fingered the triggers. I began to stammer, pretending to be lost. They looked very suspicious, and one of them called out to someone I couldn't see. A moment later, a jeep screeched up from the direction of the camp, and a man and a woman emerged. The man was in half-uniform, wearing a cap that said "Captain" on the visor. The woman looked even more fearsome. She was heavy-set, wore sunglasses even darker than mine, and looked angry.

"It's them!" she shouted to the man with her as she pointed in my direction. "These must be the guys who were here last night!"

Upon hearing those words, I knew it was time to retreat with dispatch. That was not so easily accomplished, however. The woman approached me and started asking insistent questions. Her companion, who was middle-aged and appeared to hold a command rank, listened intently. Both seemed to understand that an outsider had found them, and they weren't happy about it.

"Who are you?" the woman demanded, planting her hands on her ample hips and facing me. "What are you doing here? Who sent you? How did you get here last night?"

Protesting my innocence, I mumbled excuses and apologies: my friend and I had certainly not intended to upset anyone, we were just passing through, we wouldn't bother them again, we didn't understand the fuss. I said nothing to suggest I was a journalist, though my interrogators probably suspected it. After a few moments, I began edging backwards toward the car, hoping no one would do anything rash. The man in command pointed his finger at me and spoke for the first time. His voice was calm but authoritative.

"This is a totally restricted area," he warned me, jabbing his arm for emphasis. "You must never take this road."

It was not a friendly comment, but I found it an instant relief because it implied that Ken and I were going to be allowed to leave without trouble. The moment I slipped back behind the wheel, Ken had urgent advice for me.

"Don't bother to turn the car around," he said. "Just throw it in reverse and let's get out of here."

I did as he suggested, and we backed swiftly away. After we passed out of sight of the contras, I turned the car around. Only one question remained, and I asked it right away: "Did you get the picture?"

"I got it," Ken said with a grin. "We're in business."

It was not yet eight o'clock as we began racing toward Tegucigalpa. Mud spat from beneath our tires and dirty water spattered trees along the roadside as I drove as fast as I dared. Inside the car, Ken and I were jubilant, like high school ballplayers after winning a big game. As soon as we made it out of the cow pasture and beyond Matasano, we stopped looking behind us and started to shriek in exhilaration. There was no need for words. Both of us knew what we had accomplished, and Ken was obviously feeling the same thrill of satisfaction that I was. For several minutes, inarticulate howls were all we needed to communicate. The shock I should have felt when contras pointed their rifles at me suddenly hit home, now overlaid by the realization of what a big news story we had stumbled upon.

"That was them, man!" Ken shouted, as much to himself as to me. Both of his fists were clenched in ecstasy as he punched the air wildly. "We got 'em! We found 'em!"

He could not possibly have been more excited than I was. "Damn right!" I shouted back. "*Damn* right! Big story! Very big story!"

The trip through Danlí to the paved road took more than an hour, even at the unsafe speed at which I was driving. After we finished congratulating ourselves and each other, our first thought was of Ambassador Negroponte and the covert operation he was helping to direct. We had now seen with our own eyes what had been so widely suspected for months: that the United States had reached a secret bargain with Honduras to base contras near the border; that these contras were being supplied by the United States with factory-fresh arma- ments; and that the denials being issued every few days in Washington and Tegucigalpa were disingenuous lies.

When we finally reached the asphalt road, we began to calm down. As was my habit under such circumstances, I spent part of the return trip silently composing my first few paragraphs, so I would be ready to write as soon as I reached the hotel. Finally we arrived back at the Maya and parked our battered car. Ken took a taxi to the local Associated Press office to print and transmit his pictures, and I went up to my room to call New York. The editor on duty knew how I had planned to spend my weekend, so I was able to speak in oblique code.

"Remember those people I was looking for?" I asked her nonchalantly. "Well, I found them."

She understood immediately what I meant, but her tone was all business. "I assume this is frontable?" she asked, using *Times* slang for a story that deserves to be on the front page.

"Definitely frontable," I replied. "There are photos to go with it, and we're transmitting them now."

"Great," she told me. "Can you dictate a summary?"

Correspondents at the *Times* are expected to file summaries of their stories by midday so editors can have an idea of what to expect. I hadn't had time to prepare one, but that didn't matter in this case. The editor transferred my call upstairs to the recording room, where typists spend their days transcribing dispatches from far corners of the earth.

"Hi, it's Stephen Kinzer," I told the person who answered upstairs. "I'm in Tegucigalpa, Honduras. I have a summary for the foreign desk."

I heard a few clicks as the tape machine was switched on. "OK, go ahead," I was instructed.

"Dateline Matasano, Honduras," I began. "That's m-a-t-a-s-a-n-o. Nicara- guan contras have built a secret base camp in the hills near this remote mountain outpost. A reporter who visited there today found contra soldiers and crates of American-made ammunition. Frontable. One thousand words. With photos. That's all, thanks and end it."

I hung up and grabbed my typewriter, a tool of the trade already headed toward extinction but for which I still harbored a nostalgic affection. With my portable alarm clock in front of me so I could keep track of how much time remained until deadline, I began typing quickly on Maya Hotel statio- nery. When I had typed about five hundred words, the telephone in my room rang. A problem had cropped up in New York, where Ken's photos were being received. All the pictures showed me surrounded by contras, and thereby violated an old *Times* rule forbidding reporters to appear in news photos.

"There may be a rule, but this picture has got to go in the paper," I insisted. "This is history! The picture is absolutely necessary."

There was no argument, only some muttering about rules. After a series of consultations, editors in New York decided on a compromise. A picture was selected that showed only my back, and it was slated to run on an inside page instead of on page one, where the story would begin.

As this decision was being reached, I was frantically typing and at the same time trying to locate Ambassador Negroponte to ask him for comment. He was unavailable, but finally one of the messages I left was returned by his deputy, Shepard Lowman. I told him what I had seen, without giving him exact information, and asked how it jibed with official American policy.

"I'm sorry," he replied. "I'm just not in a position to help you out on that subject."

I incorporated Lowman's one-line comment into my story. As I wrote, I half-wondered, without any real reason, if someone would come crashing through the door to apprehend me before I was able to dictate it. But there were no further interruptions, and soon after I finished filing, Ken arrived with his prints.

"Everyone at AP was asking me what the pictures were, but I told them I couldn't say anything," he told me with a conspiratorial smile.

"What did Cuevas say?" I asked, referring to Freddy Cuevas, the veteran AP bureau chief in Tegucigalpa.

"I showed him the pictures and asked him if he knew who the people with guns were," Ken told me. "All he said was, 'They're not Hondurans, I can tell you that.' "

The setting sun was shining through my tinted hotel window, and Ken and I ordered drinks from room service as I awaited the call-back from New York that normally follows the filing of important stories. The editor who called had no major complaints, but wanted to adjust the lead paragraph to conform to *Times* standards of objectivity. My first sentence had read: "Nicaraguan insurgents fighting to overthrow the Sandinista government in Managua are operating from a camp in the hills above this hamlet near the border." As edited, the sentence was a bit longer, though arguably more precise: "Nicaraguans *described as* insurgents fighting to overthrow the Sandinista government in Managua *appear to be* operating from a camp . . ." Either way, the point was clear.

I invited Ken to dinner at the hotel steak house, where well-to-do Honduran couples often dine before heading upstairs to the casino for roulette and blackjack. As we dined, we imagined copies of the *Times* already rolling off the presses in New York, and the people in Washington whose breakfasts would, we hoped, be ruined the following morning. After dessert, we ordered a round of after-dinner drinks. Ken toasted me, and I toasted him. Never forgetting that dumb luck had been the key factor in our success, we also drank toasts to the two young soldiers who had led us to the contras. Both had readily given me their names, but I had chosen not to use them in my stories. Probably their commanding officer would realize that they were the culprits, but I didn't want to compound their possible embarrassment, and therefore left them anonymous.

Though I hadn't had much sleep for the last couple of days, I didn't feel at all tired. After bidding Ken good night, I took the elevator up to my room, changed into my bathing trunks, and padded down to the pool. The sky was dark, and Tegucigalpa's lights glistened below. I was alone in the stillness as I dove in and began swimming laps. In my mind I retraced what had happened, and suddenly it began to dawn on me that staying in Honduras was probably not a good idea for me at this moment. I climbed out of the pool, returned to my room, and set my alarm for 5 A.M.

The next morning I packed quickly, checked out of the Maya, and took a taxi to the airport. One counter was open, and I approached the attendant.

"When is your next flight out?" I inquired.

"To where, sir?"

"Anywhere, it doesn't matter."

"Well, there's a flight to Houston in about two hours."

"Are there seats available?"

There was a seat, and soon I was on my way. From Houston I made a connection to New York, and by nightfall Monday I was back at my West Side apartment. After showering and relaxing for a few minutes, I ventured downstairs to do something I had purposely avoided doing at the Houston and New York airports. I strolled down Seventy-second Street to Broadway, and at the corner newsstand there I bought a copy of that day's *New York Times.* I carried it into a snack bar, where I ordered a hot dog and a large cup of fruit juice. It fell open on the counter as I reached for mustard.

The front-page headline over my story was classically understated, but potent nonetheless. "At a Border Camp in Honduras, Anti-Sandinistas Are Wary of Visit," it said. Ken's photo appeared on page three, with an agate credit line identifying him as Singleton instead of Silverman. It showed several contras pointing their rifles at me. Standing in Manhattan eating my hot dog, I found the picture terrifying.

I reported for work at the metro desk on Tuesday morning, and picked up my local reporting almost as if I had never left. No one said anything about my story, which was quite normal in an environment where making news was held to be almost a contractual obligation. Elsewhere, however, reaction was more vocal.

In Washington, State Department spokesman Alan Romberg was asked about my story at his daily press briefing, and replied that he would "not address it one way or the other." He described the contras as "diverse, nationalist, and independent," but would say nothing more specific.

"It is a longstanding practice of this and other administrations not to address allegations of this sort," Romberg explained.

Congress was not in session that week, but at the United Nations, where the Security Council was considering charges of intervention in Nicaragua, my story provoked a ripple of interest. The ambassador from Poland, Wlodzimierz Natorf, arrived for the Monday session with a copy in his briefcase.

"Today the *New York Times* reveals new facts about the real involvement of Honduras in a master plan against Nicaragua," Natorf told the Council. "A real army of para-military forces has been recruited from abroad, from ex-Somoza Guardsmen, and is now being used in sabotage raids against agricultural, industrial, and other important targets in Nicaragua. Simple common sense is sufficient to confirm that those activities, and the groups conducting them, can exist only to the extent that they are financed, trained, and supported by external forces interested in overthrowing the legal government of Nicaragua."

Ambassador Enrique Ortez Colindres of Honduras had a difficult challenge during the debate. His role was to deny that his government was in any way collaborating with the contras, despite the highly persuasive contrary evidence that had appeared in that morning's newspaper. He chose to use the hoary Central American argument about the difficulty of patrolling long borders.

"My country has thousands of kilometers," Ortez declared. "Those who study international law, and any person who looks at Central America—even the reporter from the *New York Times,* to whom we shall refer and to whom we shall reply regarding the photograph that appeared in that newspaper today—must realize the problem of its borders."

To emphasize his government's good faith and innocence, Ortez announced that an official commission was being established in Tegucigalpa to determine the truth about what was happening around Matasano. Nothing further was ever heard of that commission.

The Security Council debate continued Tuesday, with the bearded young Sandinista ambassador, Victor Hugo Tinoco, a former guerrilla, leading the attack. That morning's papers had carried Alan Romberg's comments from the State Department, along with suggestions that the United States was involved in "psychological warfare" against the Sandinista regime. Tinoco took that statement as his point of departure.

"This is not psychological warfare," he asserted. "It is a real war promoted by the United States against Nicaragua. The automatic weapons, the C-4 explosives, and the grenade launchers made in the United States, on which Stephen Kinzer reported in yesterday's issue of the *New York Times,* are all real—and Mr. Kinzer was reporting on a visit he had made to a counter-revolutionary camp in Honduran territory. The Nicaraguans widowed, the children wounded, and the peasants decapitated as a result of aggression promoted by the United States are not the victims of psychological warfare."

On this second day of debate, Honduran Ambassador Ortez was more feisty than the day before. Evidently he had been in touch with Tegucigalpa and received instructions to be tough. He rejected all charges against Honduras, and in the course of his speech, he delivered a line that delighted me.

"I have special instructions from my government," he told the Security Council, "not to use reporters of the *New York Times* as witnesses."

In the following days, other news correspondents converged on the Matasano camp, which quickly folded up and disappeared, and on other camps nearby. Several of them found installations much larger that the small outpost I had discovered, and news of the contra network in Honduras spread across the world's front pages and television screens. No longer was it possible to argue that there were no contra installations in Honduras, or that the contras received no American help, or that their purpose was only to harass arms smugglers headed toward El Salvador. When Congress reconvened, on April 5, Nicaragua was a topic of heated debate in both chambers.

It was satisfying to have been able to contribute to the growing debate over American involvement in Nicaragua, and it resolved whatever doubts I may still have harbored about quitting the *Globe*. Yet in one respect it was less than fulfilling. What I had found was big news, but it did not tell much about Nicaragua. Like so much of the news from Central America, it was a foreign policy story that centered on Nicaragua's relations with its neighbors and with the United States. Those stories were of course important, but my interest in Nicaragua went beyond its current political problems. I wanted to learn and write about Nicaraguans as people, to immerse myself in their country as Squier had done, and to introduce them to a new generation of readers in the United States. The *Times* job in Central America was not yet officially mine, but I was growing more excited about it nevertheless.

When I first arrived in Central America more than six years earlier, I would not have believed that Nicaragua, a country many editors had barely even heard of, would one day become a laboratory for radical social change and an arena for confrontation between superpowers. Now that was happening, and I was going to Managua to watch it. Finding Nicaraguans in Honduras had been a thrill, but I wanted to find Nicaraguans in Nicaragua.

9

BUREAU CHIEF

BEFORE I had been back in New York a week, it dawned on my editors that there was now no *Times* correspondent anywhere in Central America. Given all that was happening there, someone had to be sent to fill the breach, and I was chosen. My suitcase was still lying half-unpacked on my bedroom floor, and I added a few clean shirts, zipped it back up, and by early April was back in Managua. The Intercontinental Hotel, where I was by now well known to doormen and other employees, had been partially renovated but still bore scars of the abuse to which reporters, generals, and other ruffians had subjected it during the chaotic months before Somoza's fall. I was given a room that overlooked the ruins of downtown Managua.

Two enormous news stories were unfolding in Nicaragua. Dramatic social, political, and cultural changes were reshaping the country as Sandinista leaders sought to wipe away the society that had existed for generations and replace it with a very different one. And as this was happening, a guerrilla force created and directed by the United States was escalating its military campaign and threatening to plunge the country into full-scale civil war. All normal life had been disrupted by these two overwhelming realities.

I arrived in Managua just in time for Easter, a holiday that Nicaraguans celebrate with special fervor. Archbishop Miguel Obando y Bravo, the outspoken Catholic primate, was to celebrate Mass in Niquinohomo, a quiet farm town twenty-five miles southeast of the capital. Obando had played a vital role in helping to bring down the Somoza dynasty, denouncing repression and human rights abuses so eloquently that he became a hero even to many Sandinistas. Like many of his countrymen, however, he was now deeply troubled by the direction of the Sandinista regime. He had begun accusing the Sandinistas of crimes like those for which he had once condemned the Somozas, and his charges stung. Sandinista *comandantes* responded by depicting him and other Catholic bishops as a reactionary, cloistered elite that did not truly represent the faithful. I was looking for snapshots of Nicaragua, pieces of the puzzle I was trying to fit together. Archbishop Obando's Mass at Niquinohomo would be a fine place to begin.

Sandinista authorities had told Obando that his Easter homily could only be broadcast on television and radio if he submitted a copy to censors in advance. He refused, leading some to suspect that he was preparing to use Easter as the occasion for a new attack on the Sandinistas. But in Niquinohomo he made no direct criticism of the regime, only a few allusions to food shortages and rationing. What was memorable that day was not what the archbishop said, but the delirious reception he received.

Niquinohomo has a special place in history as the birthplace of rebel hero Augusto César Sandino, but otherwise it closely resembles other mid-sized towns on Nicaragua's Pacific slope. Some families enjoy running water and electricity in their homes, but many do not. Only the main streets are paved. When I arrived early on Easter morning, the town was decked out in all its finery, and the central plaza was jammed. It seemed that every resident was out and about, each one dressed as well as fortune would allow, the men in white guayabera shirts and the women in frayed but clean cotton dresses. Many outsiders, anxious to see and hear Obando, had arrived from nearby towns. Bands played, firecrackers popped in bursts, and vendors did a brisk business in snacks and cold drinks.

An elaborate welcoming procession had been planned, but the plans degenerated into magnificent disorder when a cheer went up from the edge of town. In a moment, Obando's motorcade appeared and began slowly making its way through the adoring crowd. People pushed close, and Obando smiled and waved to them as his jeep approached the Church of Saint Anne. There, resplendent in brightly colored vestments, he stepped down and was immediately surrounded by the ecstatic crowd. People shrieked aloud and reached to touch his garments or the tips of his outstretched fingers, and aides had trouble clearing a path for him. More than two thousand people packed the church to hear him speak, cheering wildly as he stepped to the microphone. Finally he motioned for the crowd to be still, and began to speak.

"Maintain your faith in your church and in your bishops!" he boomed. That was enough to trigger another eruption of cheers, and so it went through the homily.

After the service, while young girls costumed as angels adjusted their halos for the delayed Easter parade, Obando adjourned to the parish hall for lunch with a group of friends and local Catholic leaders. Impressed at what I had seen, I decided to try to approach him for a quick interview. There were no other reporters around, so I slipped into the parish hall along with the official party. The archbishop agreed to give me a minute.

"You and the other bishops are being denounced every day in the press, and the government accuses you of terrible crimes," I began. "How is it that people are still so devoted to you?"

"More Nicaraguans are now attending church services than ever in our history," Obando replied. "Our mission is not political, but people are obviously drawing closer to their bishops in the face of this campaign against us. We are not going to allow the church to be divided. There is only one Catholic church. It is made up of believers who are in communion with their bishops and, through them, with the Pope. The others cannot be considered Catholic."

MY second snapshot of Nicaragua was from San Judas, a combative slum on the outskirts of Managua whose young people had been leaders of the anti-Somoza uprising. On the day I visited, a funeral procession was underway. The victims were two local youths who had been killed while on militia duty near the Honduran border. Hundreds of mourners were walking behind the open hearse. Relatives and neighbors wept, consoled each other, shook their fists, and chanted slogans condemning the contras.

"Imperialism will never turn us back!" some of them shouted.

"Revolution or death!" vowed others.

An elderly man in the crowd told me he was a carpenter and had known both of the victims. Why had they died? I asked him.

"The Yankees and the sellout bourgeoisie can't stand to see what's happening in Nicaragua," he replied simply. "We have to keep fighting against them."

Like most of the victims in this early phase of the contra war, the two San Judas youths had not been members of the regular army, but rather volunteers sent to the front for limited tours of duty after receiving only a few weeks of military training. The government was holding the army in reserve to resist a possible United States invasion, and militiamen were doing much of the fighting against contra bands. As a result, funerals like this one, for young men who were active members of local communities rather than professional soldiers, were being held in cities and towns across the country. They were vivid reminders that the contra war was not something remote, but rather a bloody reality for all Nicaraguans.

*   *   *

SNAPSHOT three: my meeting with two American congressmen who passed through Managua as part of a quick tour of the region. In the years to come, meeting intinerant members of Congress became part of my routine, much like listening to Archbishop Obando speak or attending Sandinista funerals. Most of the legislators who arrived were unimpressive, and came to Nicaragua only to confirm what they already believed. There was a certain cachet in being able to tell colleagues and constituents that one had actually visited Central America, though in truth the junketeers usually learned little or nothing during their brief stopovers. The two who visited in mid-April 1983, Robert Torricelli of New Jersey and Berkley Bedell of Iowa, were among the honorable exceptions. After four days of poking around on both sides of the Nicaragua-Honduras border, they had reached the obvious conclusion: that the Reagan administration was violating federal law by supporting contras who were fighting to overthrow the Sandinista regime.

"We visited refugee camps in Honduras where mothers of contras spoke with pride about the training their sons had received from Americans, and the weapons they had been given by Americans," Toricelli told me during a chat in the Intercontinental lobby.

His colleague, Bedell, who was one of the most thoughtful congressmen I ever encountered in Managua, seemed genuinely saddened by what he had seen.

"There is certainly no question we are supporting the contras," he told me over an afternoon drink. "We spoke to people who had been held prisoner by the contras and with other people familiar with their operations, and there was a clear pattern in their comments that leads inevitably to that conclusion."

The day after comments by Torricelli and Bedell appeared in print, Congressman Edward Boland, chairman of the House Intelligence Committee and author of the amendment that bore his name, told reporters in Washington that evidence against the administration was "very strong." But later that week, President Reagan himself flatly denied what had become obvious to all who cared to see.

"We are not doing anything to try and overthrow the Nicaraguan government," Reagan solemnly declared at a White House news conference. "We are complying with the law . . . Anything that we're doing in that area is simply trying to interdict the supply [of weapons going to El Salvador]."

SNAPSHOT four was my first ride aboard a Soviet-made military helicopter. A friend at the Sandinista defense ministry told me that a chopper would be heading to the northern village of San José de Bocay, where contras had been active, and that there would be a few empty seats. At dawn the next day, I was at the air force base adjacent to Sandino Airport in Managua. Most of the passengers were young soldiers, and the few civilians did well to wedge ourselves among their knapsacks and rifles. The ride took less than an hour, but I arrived exhausted. The copter vibrated terribly, and the noise of its rotor blades was deafening. A machine gun had been installed at the door, and a soldier manned it as we flew, constantly scanning the forests below in search of hostiles.

When we arrived at Bocay, the local Sandinista commander, Alvaro Baltodano, told us that his men had been chasing contras through the surrounding forests for weeks.

"Most of the enemy troops have returned to Honduras," he said, "but we expect them to regroup there and then try to infiltrate back into our territory."

The rugged terrain I had seen from above was ideal for guerrillas, and many of the contras were natives of the area and knew it well. This part of Nicaragua was girding for a long war. Soldiers were building barracks, technicians were installing a radio relay station, and heavy artillery pieces were being emplaced on nearby hills. I remarked to one soldier that living conditions in Bocay seemed quite primitive, and he laughed.

"Compared with the way we survive in the mountains, this place is like Manhattan," he told me.

SNAPSHOT five: Myriam Argüello, longtime Conservative party organizer, daughter and granddaughter of Conservative chieftains, and vigorous anti-Sandinista leader. Out of the dust and wilting heat of Managua, Argüello appeared for our interview at Conservative headquarters well-coiffed, carefully made up, and wearing a smartly tailored outfit set off by a string of pearls. Although trained as an attorney, she did not maintain a practice. She had never married, and now, in her mid-fifties, devoted most of her time to politics. For income she operated a flower and plant business. Sandinistas considered her a dinosaur, an anachronistic throwback to another epoch, a politician trying to live in a bygone time. She, in turn, had nothing but scorn for their revolutionary pretensions.

"The insurrection was a general repudiation of Somoza, not a movement in favor of any particular group," Argüello insisted as we sipped cups of strong black coffee in an upstairs office. "The Sandinistas were merely the armed group of the moment."

Life in Nicaragua, she told me, had not really changed much from the old days. Newspapers were being censored, political parties were forbidden to hold public rallies, and critics of the regime were subject to harassment and arrest. I could see that the Sandinistas had substantially restricted political activity, yet Argüello and politicians like her were still speaking out and doing what organizing they could. Unlike their counterparts in some nearby countries, they did not fear streetcorner abduction or midnight murder. Normal political activity had been restricted, but obviously some freedom remained.

*   *   *

MY next snapshot was of the Minister of Agrarian Reform, *Comandante* Jaime Wheelock, with whom I spent a highly enlightening afternoon. Former student activist, author of several tracts analyzing Nicaragua's subjugation over the years, reputedly quite radical, Wheelock greeted me courteously as I was ushered into his office at the ministry building, which had once been the headquarters of an insurance company. Thirty-four years old, trim, and teen-idol handsome in imported slacks and pastel polo shirt, he did not look much like the stereotypical Latin American revolutionary. On the wall of his office, I saw an unusual Nicaraguan license plate with five stars arranged in an arc. I asked about it, and Wheelock told me that it had belonged to President Somoza.

"After the triumph, we divided up souvenirs that had belonged to Somoza," Wheelock said. "I got the license plate, and I also got this."

He pulled down a long metal bar that looked like a fireplace poker. On the tip was a trademark outlined in iron. It was a branding iron with the mark of the Somoza family, which had been burned into the hide of uncounted cattle and into the fabric of the nation itself.

I told Wheelock that many Americans were trying to understand what the Sandinistas were doing in Nicaragua, and asked what insights he could offer. He bowed his head for a moment, and rubbed his temples while gathering his thoughts. Then he looked up and spoke.

"What guides *Sandinismo,*" he said, "is the conviction that our country, Nicaragua, has never been a country with real sovereignty or national independence. Nicaragua has been an appendage of the United States. We have been abused and humiliated. Nicaragua was kept dependent and backward, a country of illiterate farm laborers. Our function was to grow sugar, cocoa, and coffee for the United States. We served the dessert at the imperialist dinner table.

"*Sandinismo* represents the possibility that Nicaragua could exist for Nicaraguans," Wheelock continued. "Finally it is a group of Nicaraguans who are deciding where Nicaragua goes and what it does." He ticked off a list of American interventions in his country over the years, graciously sparing me the details, and then spread his arms wide to deliver the moral of the tale.

"We have to be against the United States in order to reaffirm ourselves as a nation," he said.

I was already familiar with the outlines of Nicaraguan history, and could hardly argue with Wheelock's eloquent answer. But if the new regime was so truly revolutionary, I asked, why was it repressing its critics and branding them as unpatriotic? Why did Sandinista leaders insist that anyone who opposed their regime was a traitor to the nation? Many frustrated Nicaraguans had asked me these questions, and now I was able to present them to someone who could give me an official answer. .

Wheelock did not try to correct my impression that Sandinistas considered their critics guilty of treason. On the contrary, he confirmed it, speaking slowly and enunciating each syllable.

"*Sandinismo* is Nicaragua," he told me. "*Sandinismo* is the Nicaraguan nation. You cannot oppose one and favor the other."

Having spent years covering Latin American dictatorships of all hues, I found Wheelock's formula frighteningly familiar. The Sandinistas had made a conscious decision to press ahead with their revolutionary program despite the upheaval it would cause. They were denouncing their critics with increasing bitterness and anger, even jailing some of them. Wheelock told me that those people represented a defeated class, an elite that for years had collaborated with the dictatorship and was now dedicated to fomenting discontent and "shining the boots" of American diplomats.

"In an act of infinite generosity, we invited the bourgeoisie to join our revolution," he said. "But they had always been against true revolution, and they immediately sought ways to dilute our program. Their aim was to retain a close relationship with the United States and support its imperial designs. These people have no business in Nicaragua. They are not Nicaraguans. They belong in Miami."

As we parted, Wheelock invited me to travel with him later that week to a village called Achuapa, where he was going to hand over plots of land to poor peasants. I accepted his offer to attend the ceremony, but told him I'd make my own travel arrangements. I wanted to rent a jeep and wander through the countryside by myself.

A few days later I drove northward from Managua, passing the airport and quickly reaching open country. The rainy season had not yet begun, and fields were parched and dusty. The only large patch of green I passed was in the rice fields of Sébaco Valley, an hour outside the capital; they were owned and irrigated by Samuel Amador, a wealthy landowner who had bent with the political winds and found a way to live with the Sandinistas. From there I drove on to where the road begins to climb through cool coffee plantations. My plan was to drive to the end of the paved road, and then get out and see where I found myself. The road ended in Jinotega, capital "city" of Jinotega province, where much of the contra war was being fought. It was just sixty-five miles from the Honduran border. Gunfire could sometimes be heard in the distance, and bands of contras had been sighted in the nearby hills.

One of the first people I met in Jinotega was a teenage girl named María Benito, who was carrying a plain clay jug in one hand as she walked down a side street. She told me she was from a large family that lived in a remote mountain hamlet, and that she had arisen before dawn that day and walked three hours to Jinotega in search of cooking oil. It was now midday, and she had visited every store and government-run cooperative in the area, but her jar was still empty. She was going to rest for a few minutes and then set out on her trek home.

A grocery store was on the next corner, and I stopped in to ask the proprietor if he had any cooking oil for sale.

"Cooking oil!" he exclaimed, his eyes widening as if I had mentioned the name of a long-lost relative. "Why not ask for soap and toilet paper also? Perhaps you would like a chicken or some rice? Well, my friend, you can ask the Sandinistas for those things, because you won't find them here."

That afternoon, I posted myself in a small general store for several hours, sitting on a dusty bench inside and trying to be as inconspicuous as an American in a sport shirt and sunglasses could be in Jinotega in 1983. Half the shelves were empty. Women from the outlying hills came looking for all manner of goods, and almost all left disappointed. Nearly every one of the fifty or so customers who passed through the store had something nasty to say about the Sandinistas. Most were from farm families themselves, and talked of how they had stopped growing food or raising animals because government-imposed controls were too onerous. As a result, in stores like this one there was no cooking oil, no chicken, no beef, no rice, no eggs. I had noticed eggs at a market in Matagalpa, half an hour away by car, and I asked the storekeeper why she did not send someone there to buy eggs for resale in Jinotega.

"Oh, no, you don't understand," she replied, pulling out a government price list issued to every store in the country. "In Matagalpa, I would have to pay the official price for eggs, and when I got them back here, I would have to sell them for that same price. I couldn't make back what I would have to spend for gasoline to drive to Matagalpa. If I charged a higher price, they would send a mob against me and paint 'House of Thieves' on my wall. That is why there are no eggs in Jinotega."

At a local Sandinista office, I found an official in charge of food distribution in Jinotega. I tried to goad him by telling him that the government was losing popularity because of its inability to feed people, but instead of arguing he glumly agreed. People were not following rules, he told me. They were not growing what they were supposed to grow, not selling their produce through government agencies, not respecting price controls.

"The mentality of the market woman is one of our most serious problems," he lamented. "They're oriented toward hoarding and speculating, and they can't accept the reality that we're living in a permanent state of emergency."

In Jinotega I could see the war's effect, but I wasn't close enough to see its face. To do that, I made my way toward the combat zone further north. I felt tense as I wound my way through the forested upland. Contras were operating in the hills here, and they did not seem to care much who they attacked. According to official Sandinista reports, contras had killed five hundred civilians in this area during the first six months of 1983, and had inflicted millions of dollars in damage by burning farms and warehouses, destroying vehicles, and blowing up mechanical equipment.

The towns of Jalapa and Teotecacinte sit in a valley dominated by hills that are inside Honduras. Once these had been sleepy outposts whose residents built their lives around the tobacco harvest, but now they were fortified garrisons where soldiers and militia outnumbered civilians. Rice and coffee fields between the two towns were pockmarked with trenches and foxholes. On the wall of an abandoned hut, someone had painted in large black letters: "We will not let any Yankee sons of bitches push us back."

Outside Jalapa, an abandoned tobacco farm called La Limonera was being used as a barracks for several hundred soldiers. Most were in their teens or early twenties, products of poor families, self-described revolutionaries eager to explain their fervor. I began talking to a seventeen-year-old militiaman with shoulder-length hair and two heavy cartridge belts draped over his shoulders. When I told him that many poor people seemed to be losing faith in the Sandinistas, he nodded in agreement and told me that he himself had plenty of complaints.

"But in every country, every government faces problems," he told me. "We have some matters to work out among ourselves, the Nicaraguan people. But all that is secondary now. Once again, our country is being attacked by the Yankee. As patriots, we have to unite and defend our independence."

The militiaman took me to a wooden shack that served as the base command post, and pointed to a sign above the door. The sign, painted in an unsteady hand, carried the famous quote from Sandino recalling his initial decision to take up arms against United States Marines. "I told my friends," Sandino wrote, "that if Nicaragua had one hundred men who loved her as I do, our nation could recover its absolute sovereignty, stolen from us by the Yankee empire. My friends said that in Nicaragua there were that many and more."

"We like those words," the young militiaman told me. "We think they refer to us, even though they were written before we were born. We are those hundred men and more that Nicaragua needs to keep the Yankee away from our door."

It was a long drive from Jalapa to Achuapa, the village to which Jaime Wheelock was bringing his land reform road show that week. As I rode through the countryside, I began to realize that contradictions were probably all I was ever going to find in Nicaragua. My search for the truth of what was happening there would never be fully successful, because in such a place there is always more than one truth.

What I was about to witness in Achuapa was a good example of Nicaragua's complexity. On the surface, this ceremony would reflect the Sandinistas' determination to keep one of their most sacred promises, that of turning land over to those who tilled it. But in fact, no peasants would be actually receiving full title to any land that day. They were being assigned to cooperatives, told what to grow, and required to sell all they raised—except for what they ate themselves—to government agencies at fixed prices. Some peasants found this kind of land reform liberating, but others considered the new conditions so unappealing that they quit farming altogether and drifted to Managua in search of better opportunities.

The sun beat down mercilessly on the Achuapa plaza as the town's entire population, swelled by the curious from outlying hamlets, waited for Wheelock and his party. Finally, in a cloud of dust, his caravan arrived. As he made his way through the crowd, I watched from a distance. The occasion was festive, and Wheelock, like any political leader about to give something away, was in high spirits. The crowd was animated, though not nearly as excited as the throng that had greeted Archbishop Obando in Niquinohomo.

As Wheelock passed near me, he shook the outstretched hand of a smiling farm laborer. When he had moved on, I asked the man, whose name was Eduardo Rojas, how his life had changed since the Sandinistas took power. He pointed to the adobe schoolhouse that had opened a few months before.

"My children are going to school," he said, shaking his head in amazement. "Can you imagine it? They'll get other ideas. Perhaps they won't be poor peasants. They'll be able to choose a different life for themselves—whatever they want. This is a total change. Without the revolution, it would never have happened."

Though only thirty-five years old, Eduardo Rojas looked withered and played out. His face was deeply lined, and many of his teeth were missing. All his life, starting when he was five years old, he had worked a small plot of land in the fertile hills outside Achuapa, sending half of what he produced to an absentee landlord as rent. That was how his father and his grandfather had lived, and he had expected nothing better for his children or grandchildren. Now things were suddenly different. The Sandinistas had seized the land around Achuapa from its former owner, compensating him with a plot of land in another part of the country that was formerly owned by the Somoza family. Rights to till the land were now being transferred to a cooperative made up of twenty-five peasant families, including the Rojas family. The government had not only built a school and a maternity clinic here, but was extending electricity to hovels like the one in which Mr. Rojas lived. He was full of hope for the future, and proud to call himself a Sandinista.

ON some days, the Nicaragua story became so baffling that reporters didn't even dare to guess the truth. Strange and unknowable things happened all the time. One began innocently in Managua on the morning of June 6, with a telephone call from the foreign ministry summoning reporters for what was described as a very important news conference at the foreign ministry.

Foreign Minister Miguel D'Escoto, looking unusually somber, greeted us from behind a long table at the ministry's auditorium. We expected to hear a statement from D'Escoto, but he remained silent. Suddenly, from out of nowhere, who should appear but *Comandante* Lenin Cerna, chief of the State Security police and probably the most feared man in Nicaragua. No one was ever comfortable in a room when Cerna was present, and reporters began to buzz. I had heard much about him, but never before seen his face.

As Cerna took a seat, I felt a chill. Sandinistas and anti-Sandinistas alike had described him to me as harsh and ruthless, and that was just the way he struck me. He nodded to acknowledge our presence, fiddled briefly with the microphone in front of him, and then proceeded to relate a tale that left everyone in the room speechless.

Cerna told us that his police had uncovered a CIA plot to murder Foreign Minister D'Escoto by sending him a bottle of Benedictine liqueur laced with toxic acids. The plot, he said, had been directed by three CIA agents working under diplomatic cover at the American embassy. All three had been expelled from Nicaragua that day.

D'Escoto was a lover of the good life, and presumably had consumed a fair amount of after-dinner refreshment in his time. But all of us knew that he was little more than a figurehead in a government where all important decisions were made by uniformed *comandantes*. It would make little sense to try killing him, though charging that someone had done so would undoubtedly make good copy in the foreign capitals where D'Escoto spent much of his time.

According to Cerna, the Nicaraguan woman recruited to present the poisoned Benedictine to D'Escoto was actually a double agent working for Sandinista security police. The CIA had recruited her while she was serving as a consular secretary at the Nicaraguan embassy in Honduras, and had given her implements of espionage which Cerna displayed like trophies, including two booklets for translating coded radio messages and a pad of note paper that dissolved upon contact with water. The woman was present at the news conference, and gave her name as Marlena Moncada. She said she had been given three lie detector tests by CIA control officers. After passing them all, she said, she accepted an offer of five thousand dollars for delivering the bottle of poisoned liqueur to D'Escoto.

Moncada said she had received a radio message telling her where to pick up the bottle, which had been left for her in an overgrown lot behind a Managua restaurant. At the designated spot, she found the bottle and a note, which Cerna read to us.

"Very important comply with following instructions," said the note, written in Spanish. "Protect bottle in a safe place, repeat safe place. Wait for opportune moment. Don't lose hope, but you mustn't lose much time in delivering it. Don't be afraid, have confidence, this will not leave any trace. Remember what was explained to you in your last visit. It will not have any immediate effect and is not fatal. I assure you no risk. You should notify as soon as you deliver."

None of us knew what to make of these charges. There was plenty of evidence in front of us, and part of the story sounded credible. Undoubtedly the CIA was trying to recruit Nicaraguan agents, and from what we had seen and heard it seemed likely they had recruited Moncada. Of the three Americans being expelled, one was known to some of us as the CIA station chief, and a second, a young woman working in the visa section, was also probably a spy. Yet it seemed too much to believe that the Americans were trying to poison Miguel D'Escoto.

Cerna told us that chemists had examined the contents of the Benedictine bottle, and had found that it contained a sophisticated mix of incapacitating agents. He said the chemists had reported that after ten days, anyone who drank from the bottle would experience difficulty in walking and breathing, would feel continuous nausea and abdominal pain, and would contract fever and other ailments. Later the victim would suffer convulsions, be unable to speak clearly and possibly die from respiratory failure. It would be "particularly difficult" to tell that these symptoms were not brought on by natural causes, Cerna said.

Reporters in the room wrote all this down, but most were incredulous. After Cerna finished his exposition, heads began to shake, and there were a few muffled wisecracks. Our chortling made it obvious that most of us doubted at least part of the story. The bottle of Benedictine in question, looking as though it were still full or nearly full, was sitting on the table between Cerna and D'Escoto, all eyes fixed upon it. The green liqueur cast an odd shadow on the table, and seemed to pose a challenge. Then from the back of the room, one of my colleagues, a typically irreverent Nicaraguan reporter, shouted, "Pass the bottle back here! We're thirsty."

That was all it took for the room to erupt. Reporters demanded that Cerna open the Benedictine, which we suspected was just as pure as any other bottle. Several of us even volunteered to take a swig, and the atmosphere in the hall began to deteriorate. Cerna, gaunt and intense-looking, was not amused. Perhaps he should have sent for glasses and called our bluff, but he did not. Instead, he spoke in a sharp tone that quieted us instantly.

"This is a matter of utmost gravity," he said. "Treat it as such."

Cerna rose to leave, followed by his agents and then by D'Escoto. Correspondents remained seated for a few moments, trying to make sense of what we had just seen and heard. I for one was never able to do so, and resigned myself to the fact that many of my questions about Nicaragua would never be answered. Reporters were allowed only fleeting glimpses of the secret spy-versus-spy war being fought between the Sandinistas and the CIA, but we suspected it was every bit as intense as the shooting war that was spreading across the north.

I had been in Nicaragua for nearly two months, and that afternoon when I returned to my room at the Intercontinental, I found a message from my editors in New York calling me home again. I filed my story about the Benedictine plot, and spent a last evening sipping papaya juice and reviewing what I had seen and done. As it turned out, those months were an excellent preview of what I would be doing for the next five years: listening to Archbishop Obando preach against the evils of collectivism, attending Sandinista funerals, meeting visiting American politicians, flying in helicopters to remote combat zones, interviewing revolutionaries and counter-revolutionaries, and traveling to small villages in search of news. It was a prospect not without its dangers, but now I was looking forward to it more eagerly than ever. For a correspondent in search of challenge, Nicaragua in the 1980s was an ideal assignment.

Back in New York, it was summertime and people were complaining about the heat, though to me the climate seemed refreshingly comfortable. I was diligent in my city reporting, and after work I spent my time enjoying art exhibitions, jazz concerts, and other sorts of amusement not available in Nicaragua. On the Fourth of July, as Americans were celebrating the two hundred and eighth anniversary of their independence and Nicaraguans were preparing to observe the fourth anniversary of the Sandinista revolution, I wanted to do something special. One of my Nicaraguan friends, Martin Barreto, was visiting New York, and I called to see what he was up to. We decided to spend Independence Day watching the New York Yankees play baseball.

Martin was one of my favorite upper-class Nicaraguans. Like many of his friends, he was completely bilingual and bicultural. He had recently graduated from Columbia Journalism School, and upon returning to Managua he had made himself invaluable to the shifting corps of American foreign correspondents there. Alert, intelligent, and energetic, he could arrange an interview with an inaccessible Cabinet minister, plan a trip to the countryside, and make plane reservations for supposedly sold-out flights. Martin did not come by his quick wits accidentally. He was a great-grandson of Leonardo Argüello, who had been president of Nicaragua for twenty-six days in 1947 before being removed by General Somoza García, and his father had been a prominent political figure who rose to become Minister of Internal and External Commerce in the 1970s. Evidently the father was close enough to the Somoza circle to perceive its decay.

"I would come home from school and my father would tell me I better study extra hard, because one day I would be competing against kids educated in Russia and Cuba," Martin once told me. "He used to tell us that we better appreciate everything we had, because one day the Communists were going to come and take it all away from us. He told us the time would come when the maid's children would be running Nicaragua."

As we rode the subway toward Yankee Stadium, Martin told me he was in the process of leaving Nicaragua permanently. His parents had already moved to Florida, and most of his schoolmates and friends were either there or scattered around the United States, Europe, and Latin America. He was not highly politicized, and though the Sandinistas had destroyed the way of life he had known as a youth, he bore them no grudge. Nicaragua needed change, and Martin knew it.

Our subway car was packed with baseball fans, and we followed the crowd through turnstiles and toward the sunswept stadium. As we arrived at our seats and gazed out across the pristine playing field, both of us broke into broad grins. I was marveling at how quintessentially American the scene was, and how fully it reflected the world I was preparing to leave. Martin, I imagined, felt New York beckoning and welcoming him.

An announcer told us that a special Independence Day show had been planned, and directed our attention to a couple of small planes circling so high above the stadium as to be almost invisible. A specially trained squad of Army parachute jumpers, we were told, was at that moment leaping from the planes. By maneuvering special panels attached to their chutes, these jumpers were going to float down and land directly on the ballfield. All heads craned toward the sky, and after a few moments, we could make out the shapes of parachutes being opened. They seemed to be drifting far away from the stadium in the brisk wind, but slowly they maneuvered themselves toward us. Martin and I gazed in admiration, along with the rest of the crowd, but as we watched, a terrible thought occurred to both of us.

"My God!" Martin shouted, startling some of our neighbors. "Do you know what those guys are getting ready for?"

"I know! I know!" I replied excitedly. "They're the guys who are going to invade Nicaragua!"

"These are the guys who are going to be landing in Matagalpa!" Martin shrieked, clasping his hands to his head. "These same guys! I can't believe it!"

Probably no one else in the stadium reacted to the parachutists as we did. To the rest of the crowd these jumpers were strictly showmen. But Martin and I had been reading about American military maneuvers in Honduras, and both of us knew that Honduran and American leaders would order an invasion of Nicaragua in a moment if they thought it could succeed. Who knew how close they were to giving that order? And if the order was given, wouldn't it be logical that the invading force include parachutists like these? I was trying to enjoy a day of respite, but already I was starting to see the world through Nicaraguan eyes.

The parachute jumpers did indeed land inside Yankee Stadium, all touching down within a few feet of second base. It was an impressive show, and the crowd cheered as they collected their chutes and jogged off the field. The trumpeter Chuck Mangione was introduced to play the national anthem, and then Yankee pitcher Dave Righetti took to the mound and began throwing. Martin and I settled back to watch Righetti perform, and he began mowing down batters. He did not allow a hit in the first eight innings, and in the ninth every fan was standing, cheering every pitch as he bid for a no-hitter. After the first out, a deafening cheer went up. Martin jabbed me in the ribs and pointed to the seats above us. Among the fans shouting and clapping was Richard Nixon.

"This is all too much!" Martin yelled over the din.

Righetti got his no-hitter, and in the subway station everyone was talking about his masterful performance. I was as impressed as anyone by Righetti's gem, but for me his pitching had been just one part of an extraordinary day. Surely this would be the last Fourth of July that I would be spending in the United States for a long time. That evening I watched fireworks from the roof of a friend's apartment building, and thought again of where I was headed. In New York, the booming of cannons and the bursts of brightness that illuminated the night sky were part of a harmless celebration. In Nicaragua they would be deadly.

I spent most of the summer of 1983 in New York, covering city news and meeting *Times* editors. Before too much time passed, however, I was sent south again, this time further afield than before. September marked the tenth anniversary of the military coup that had brought General Augusto Pinochet to power in Chile, and violent protests were expected. The *Times* was at that moment short-handed in South America, and since I had worked there as a free-lance reporter and a *Boston Globe* correspondent, I was dispatched to Santiago. Riots erupted as expected, and riot police fired tear gas and charged at demonstrators wherever they tried to assemble. After a couple of weeks there, I persuaded my editors to send me to Argentina to help cover the October election that ended a horrific period of military rule and brought the civilian Raúl Alfonsín to the presidency. Soon after the Argentine election, a foreign debt crisis erupted in Brazil and I was dispatched there to interview bankers and political leaders.

While in Brazil, I dined with the local *Times* bureau chief, Warren Hoge, who had just been named foreign editor to replace Craig Whitney. Hoge had a special interest in Latin America, and had actually reported from Nicaragua for a brief period following the Sandinista takeover. He assured me that upon assuming his new post, he would press to establish a news bureau in Nicaragua as soon as possible, and name me to run it. A *Times* bureau had recently been opened in El Salvador, but the correspondent there was overwhelmed with news about the Salvadoran conflict and could not be expected to cover Nicaragua as well. Opening new bureaus implied a major commitment, and it was not something the *Times* did lightly. Hoge, however, recognized that the story in Central America was growing to major proportions. No other newspaper had yet posted a full-time reporter in Central America, but he believed the *Times* needed two to do the job well.

Soon after Hoge assumed his new post in New York in the autumn of 1983, he called me aside and told me I could forget about covering local news. He instructed me to move my belongings to Managua, rent a suite at the Intercontinental Hotel, and start covering Nicaragua as if I were a bureau chief. I did as he said, and one day, just as he had predicted, I returned to my hotel room to find a cabled message from New York under the door. It said that my appointment as bureau chief had been finally approved by all concerned editors, thus making official what I had been half-promised upon joining the paper a year before. I read the cable slowly, several times, and then laid it on the bureau beside my bed. I can handle it, I told myself.

IN 1983 most Nicaraguans had still not fallen to the depths of deprivation and despair which they would reach in later years, but many were already unhappy and restive. Dissident politicians gave voice to this frustration, but those who felt it most fully were ordinary people whose lives had been thrown into chaos by the Sandinista whirlwind.

Nicaragua's economy was heavily based on what development specialists call "micro-businesses," the mechanics, knife sharpeners, bakers, seamstresses, and others who earn their livelihood from day to day, working out of their homes or tiny shops. These people depended on an invisible but intricate network of suppliers who imported small amounts of tools, raw materials, and other necessities from nearby countries. When the Sandinistas decreed that foreign trade was to be a state monopoly, they effectively declared war on these small-scale entrepreneurs.

In rural areas, where people were even more resistant to authority than in cities, Sandinista rule had disrupted long-established patterns of life and alienated many peasants. The new regime was building schools and clinics in places like Achuapa, and thereby winning the hearts of peasants like the man I had met in the crowd there. But their agricultural policies were based on the illusion that peasants are communally oriented and will work just as hard for the collective as they would for their own family. Jaime Wheelock and other Sandinista leaders viewed the existing system of food production in Nicaragua as anarchic, and so it was. But by trying to transform it so completely and so suddenly, they were underestimating the deeply ingrained conservatism of Nicaraguan peasants, who constitute not the country's revolutionary core, but actually its most counter-revolutionary social class. When Sandinistas began trying to regulate their lives and work, the result was predictable. All over the country, many peasants decided that farming was no longer a good business, and abandoned the land altogether. In Managua and other cities, most of them found work as middlemen or market vendors, joining the network of speculators and hoarders who were steadily pushing prices higher and making life more and more difficult for everyone.

Coffee was Nicaragua's most vital crop, and in December 1983 I traveled

north to watch the harvest begin. There was an acute shortage of field hands
to pick the crop that year. Thousands of discouraged peasants had fled the area,
either moving to cities or fleeing into Honduras. Many of those who remained
refused to work in the coffee fields because they feared contra attacks. Sandinista
comandantes were worried that they might lose part of the coffee crop, which
then accounted for forty percent of Nicaragua's foreign exchange earnings. To
assure that as much coffee as possible was picked, they had ordered a mass
mobilization of high school and college students. Every day during the first
weeks of December, singing, chanting students were arriving at remote government-owned plantations by the busload, ready to work.

At La Fundadora, a plantation once owned by the Somozas, several hundred
students were sleeping in ramshackle warehouses, rising before dawn in the
mountain chill, and gathering their wicker baskets for the trek to that day's
designated harvest area. They had been instructed on the rudiments of picking
and warned to harvest only red beans, leaving the green ones to ripen. Their
enthusiasm level varied from group to group. Some cheerily accepted what they
viewed as an opportunity to help their country, while others grumbled that they
were there under duress, since participating in such mobilizations was often a
prerequisite for graduation or advancement. I wandered up and down the rows
of coffee bushes, watching kids pull ripe beans from their stems and drop them
into baskets hanging from their waists. Militiamen armed with automatic rifles
patrolled every hilltop, a reminder that violence could break out at any moment.
Two thousand contras were said to be in the area, perhaps planning to disrupt
the harvest.

One of my Sandinista friends, Daniel Núñez, who had once been a private
farmer in this region, was helping to direct that year's coffee harvest. He was
always candid with me, and told me frankly that the official goal of picking
370,000 pounds of coffee beans was unrealistic. Officials in Managua had insisted that student pickers were highly motivated and would be just as productive as experienced peasants, but Núñez told me the opposite. The young people
goofed off a lot, he said, and some were actually damaging delicate coffee groves
by their carelessness. Yet Núñez considered their presence vital, not because
they were contributing to the economy but because they were sampling life in
the mountains and thereby developing "revolutionary consciousness." They
were confronting life as it was lived by peasants, and learning respect for farm
labor.

"These kids will be much better citizens after this experience," Núñez told
me. "Years from now, they'll come back to the mountains to show their children
where they came to cut coffee while the counter-revolution was going on."

The American-backed military campaign against the Sandinistas was still at
a relatively low level, but it had already succeeded in disrupting life throughout
Nicaragua. Farm work and travel on back roads had become dangerous. Cities

were not directly affected, but after American troops invaded the island of Grenada in October and toppled the Marxist government there, Sandinista leaders ordered major new defensive measures in Managua and provincial capitals. Military units drilled every night and on weekends in fields and public plazas. Factory workers were interrupted regularly for air-raid drills, work crews dug trenches along important highways, and Sandinista activists stockpiled food and weapons at scores of secret depots.

In Managua, I had taken to spending some of my spare time wandering around the San Judas slum, and one evening I found a public gathering underway at a large plaza there. From the shadows, I stood and watched. Three hundred local youths were marking their completion of a two-week militia training course, and outstanding achievers were being awarded prizes: Cuban magazines, paperback selections from the works of Lenin, and pamphlets containing speeches by Soviet leader Yuri Andropov. One of the winners, a teenager wearing a silver crucifix, wandered past where I was standing. I stopped him to ask why he had volunteered for military training.

"It's up to us to insure that in Nicaragua there will not be another Chile or another Grenada," he replied very seriously. "Our two weeks of training is not much compared with the years the Yankees spend at West Point, but there are enough of us to bury them."

The main speaker that night was a twenty-three-year-old college student named José Mena, who was in charge of military recruitment in San Judas.

"Your training will prove invaluable when the time comes to face Yankee soldiers," Mena told the crowd of young people and their parents, most of whom had witnessed or participated directly in the bloody fighting that convulsed San Judas during the anti-Somoza uprising. "We have all seen the progress our revolution has made despite the economic blockades, the burning of our crops, the bombing of our oil tanks, and so many other acts of aggression. We're determined to keep our economy functioning, and we're determined to defend the revolution!"

People clapped and broke into Sandinista chants. As they began to leave, Mena returned to the microphone and announced that ten of the three hundred new militia troops would soon be called to spend a week at a military base learning how to use artillery. "Given the emergency situation," he said, "I know there will be no shortage of volunteers."

He was right. Several wanted to sign up on the spot. One of them was a strapping young construction worker who told me he had built barricades and made gasoline bombs during the insurrection of 1978–79.

"Fighting and dying is part of revolution," he told me.

PRESSURES were increasing on all Nicaraguans, and many of those able to leave the country were doing so. The most urgent reasons were economic. Every week another farm or business was confiscated, another new set of rules restricting commerce was issued, and another vital item disappeared from the marketplace forever. All recognized that prospects for the future were bleak.

One day I accompanied junta coordinator Daniel Ortega on a walking tour of Managua, and watched as he tried to calm people's anger over food shortages. Ortega, dressed in rumpled fatigues, seemed unprepared for the barrage of complaints hurled at him. Several times he tried to argue that pressure from Washington was causing Nicaragua's troubles. No one was soothed. At one stop, people crowded around him shouting, *"Comandante,* we don't have meat any more! No meat, do you understand that?"

Several days later I was with Interior Minister Tomás Borge as he escorted a foreign dignitary through a marketplace on the edge of town. He was met just as rudely as Ortega had been. One woman loudly complained that she had been unable to find medicine for her sick children at any pharmacy or hospital.

"We don't have enough medicine to give you because we have to send so much to our soldiers," Borge shrugged. "The enemy cannot defeat us, but he is taking a toll on the country."

Bad economic times were not all that drove people out of Nicaragua. Many farmers, business administrators, and professionals were concluding that the Sandinistas would never allow them to shape their lives as they wanted. Those who believed that the Sandinistas were botching their chance to resurrect Nicaragua, or that they were dragging the country into an unnecessary war, or that their farm policies were cutting the heart out of the nation's economy, were day after day denounced as traitors. They constituted the class that government leaders contemptuously scorned as "the sellout bourgeoisie."

At a rally in Managua, I heard Leticia Herrera, who headed the nationwide network of Sandinista Defense Committees, define the Nicaraguan conflict in stark terms.

"There is no longer any middle ground in our revolution!" she told the wildly cheering crowd, her attacks gathering force as the applause intensified. "Now is the time to close ranks against the enemies of the people! And those enemies are not just the genocidal beasts stalking our mountains, but also the speculators, the people who spread rumors on buses and in markets, and the taxi drivers who force their passengers to listen to criticisms of the revolution."

That same week, an editorial in the pro-Sandinista newspaper *Nuevo Diario* drew the line just as clearly. "At this historical moment," the paper declared, "you are either on the side of the people and their revolution, or on the other side."

For those opposed to Sandinista rule who were still able to make ends meet, and who were not driven to leave Nicaragua by the stream of public attacks describing them as bloodsuckers and agents of imperialism, a new factor suddenly emerged late in 1983. The government announced that for the first time in Nicaraguan history, a nationwide military draft would be imposed. All young men between the ages of seventeen and twenty-one were ordered to register during October, and told that their military training would begin in January 1984. Minister of Defense Humberto Ortega said the draft would "strengthen the means of national defense," but to many Nicaraguans dissatisfied with the Sandinistas it was the last straw. The number of male students in many high schools dropped by as much as fifty percent as parents spirited their sons away, and foreign diplomats were swamped with applications from Nicaraguan friends seeking visas.

"I've put up with a lot of abuse and stayed here while a lot of things happened that I didn't like," one angry engineer told me. "But with this law, I'm leaving for good, because I don't want my sons to die fighting for a Communist regime."

The Sandinistas, not surprisingly, offered little sympathy to those who criticized the new military draft. "The attitude of the reactionary bourgeoisie is not surprising," *Nuevo Diario* said in an editorial. "They will always oppose any project or program aimed at consolidating the revolutionary process."

Christmas was approaching, and since there were shortages of everything in Nicaragua, it was not surprising that no toys were available for parents to buy their children. Because the government had forbidden private businesses to engage in foreign trade, most shops had little to offer. State-run commissaries were mobbed by government workers with special identification cards. They waited in line for hours to buy the allotted two toys, most of which were dolls and small trucks made in Eastern Europe. In what the government viewed as a concession to poor workers, the toys were sold at very low prices. But many of the workers, desperate for money to buy food and other necessities, quickly sold their toys to street vendors. The toys then turned up for sale illegally at markets in Managua and elsewhere, often at several times the official price. Soon everyone was angry, and another Sandinista attempt to help the poor by rationing and controlling prices was recognized as a failure.

Dionisio Marenco, a trained business administrator who was then serving as Minister of Internal Commerce, was forced to hold a news conference to answer charges that his agency had mismanaged the toy importation project, and that its employees had helped themselves to the best toys before they were placed on public sale. Appearing harassed, Marenco accepted responsibility for a "planning failure," but asked forgiveness on the grounds that "imperialist aggression" had forced the government to concentrate its efforts on defense rather than on the importation of non-essential goods. The crisis sparked by President Reagan's decision to invade Grenada was subsiding, but it had left its mark on Marenco and other Sandinista leaders.

"Here we are discussing dolls, miniature cars, and locomotives," Marenco sputtered, "when only four weeks ago the whole country was on the brink of war!"

* * *

ALL that I saw in Nicaragua during 1983 confirmed my view that very important news was going to be made there in the years to come. I was still observing from the outside, still taking snapshots and trying to analyze them. What I had seen thus far was confusing, but tantalizing. Now that I had been permanently posted in Managua, I was ready to begin studying harder, to try forming a more coherent picture of the process I was witnessing. Before I could begin, however, I needed to move out of the Intercontinental and into a home of my own. It was fine to be a bureau chief, but I was still without a bureau. The *Times* had no office in Managua, no files, no staff, nothing but a newly named correspondent.

Because plenty of people were leaving Managua, among them many families with comfortable and even luxurious homes, it stood to reason that there should be plenty of houses available for rent. That was not the case, however. Sandinista leaders snatched up all the best homes, either for themselves or for government offices. Homes that came onto the market were quickly rented by diplomats, relief workers, solidarity groups, and other foreigners who were converging on Managua. I spent days looking at houses, and finally turned to one of the real estate agents helping me and explained exactly what I wanted.

"I'm looking for a house that's bright and open to the sun, a place with a garden, not a dark, closed-in house like the ones you've been showing me," I told him.

The problem, the agent replied, was that most of the nicest homes in Managua were enormous, with six or eight bedrooms; finding a small one would not be easy. It was not impossible, however. The next day, the agent called and told me he had found a house I might like. We drove a few blocks from the Intercontinental and pulled up in front of a nondescript door. In Nicaragua, as in many parts of Latin America, houses are built around central courtyards, and it is often impossible to tell from the street what kind of a house one is passing. The real estate agent fumbled for the correct key and finally swung the door open. Instantly I knew this was what I wanted. There were two gardens, and the living and dining areas were open to the breeze.

"This is perfect," I said after having been inside only a few seconds. "I'll take it."

"You haven't even seen the place yet," the surprised agent replied. "Don't you want to look around, or at least find out how much rent they're asking?"

I obliged him by walking through the house. There were three bedrooms, making the house small by the standards of this neighborhood, and everything else I had hoped for. The house had been built and occupied by a physician who had recently taken a job with the Red Cross in Miami, and his two-room medical office was adjacent. I saw at once that I could convert the doctor's office into mine.

"I'm convinced," I told the agent. "Where do I sign?"

BLOOD OF BROTHERS 135

Nicaraguans are not accustomed to moving in such haste, and the agent was a bit uncertain. He told me that he had shown the house to a group of Swedes a few days earlier, and was waiting for them to decide if they wanted it.

"Forget the Swedes!" I urged him. "I'm telling you right now I'll take the place. What more do you need?"

"You Americans are really something," the real estate agent said with a smile. He said he would do his best, and the next day he called to tell me that the house was mine. The only formality was a meeting with the owners, who were picky about tenants. I flew to Florida, and we had drinks at a hotel bar in Miami. They asked me if I was some kind of pro-Sandinista agitator.

"No, nothing like that," I assured them. "This is the *New York Times*. We aren't involved on one side or the other."

"Oh, yeah?" asked the doctor. "What about *Comandante* Riding?"

In the Nicaraguan exile community, it was accepted as fact that American reporters had helped the Sandinistas take power and were now failing to alert the world to their abuses. Though Alan Riding, the *New York Times* correspondent who covered the 1978–79 insurrection, was deeply respected by his peers, some outsiders perceived him as a crypto-Marxist who had falsely and deliberately painted the Sandinistas as benign nationalists. He had not written a word about Nicaragua for years, but to Nicaraguan exiles and their American friends he was still a demon, a reminder of how pernicious the press could be. I took it as an object lesson, a hint of the controversy that was sure to follow anyone who ventured to cover so complex a country.

"Don't worry," I reassured the doctor and his wife. "I'm not working for the Sandinistas, I'm not a Communist, and I'll take great care of your house."

That sealed the bargain, and after a bit more chatting the doctor and his wife rose to take their leave. They said they would be happy to rent me their house, and we agreed that I would move in during January. Now I felt that my assignment was really beginning. I was anxious to return to Managua, open the boxes I had stored at friends' houses, and begin exploring for real.

10

CIA AND FRIENDS

By the time I arrived in Managua to begin my assignment at the end of 1983, I had already learned a fair amount about the Sandinistas, their motivations, their style of leadership, and their dreams for Nicaragua. They were messianic, intellectually arrogant, and in many ways out of touch with the poor people on whose behalf they claimed to govern. Nonetheless, they were addressing social ills that had afflicted Nicaragua for generations. They were making destructive mistakes and alienating many Nicaraguans, but still retained the strong support of many others.

No one will ever be able to say what the *comandantes* would have done with their historic opportunity in Nicaragua if they had not been confronted with civil war. They and their supporters have argued that they would have been able to unify the country and turn it into a peaceful, productive socialist democracy. Others doubt that the outcome would have been so positive. In any case, the Sandinistas would have been forced to adjust their policies with the passage of time, as every government does, or face the prospect of failure. If they insisted on holding power in the face of mass discontent, they might even have provoked an armed rebellion by frustrated patriots.

All of this must forever remain in the realm of speculation, because political life in Nicaragua was not allowed to develop normally following the Sandinista takeover. Senior officials of the Reagan administration, including President Reagan himself, reacted to the Sandinistas with a fervor that bordered on obsession. Fueled by that emotion, Nicaraguans were soon at war once again.

The contra army, like the Sandinista army before it, was forged in great secrecy. Journalists posted in Central America in the early 1980s could sense that a major covert operation was being launched, but most of what we heard was rumor. Only later did it become possible to reconstruct the story of the contras' beginnings. What follows is not a full account, since many secrets are still being kept, but rather a report of what I and other journalists managed to discover in dozens of conversations with contras, ex-contras, and their friends.

Nicaragua's counter-revolution began to take shape only weeks after Somoza's overthrow in July 1979. Many soldiers and officers of the defeated National Guard escaped to Honduras, and there they began to dream of another war. The central figure in their group was the charismatic Pablo Emilio Salazar, a legendary ex-Guardsman known as *Comandante Bravo*. He had been Somoza's most successful combat commander, the closest thing to a hero the Guard had produced. In Honduras he founded an organization called the Aid Committee for Nicaraguan Refugees, which he described as a humanitarian relief organization but which some saw as the nucleus of a new army. He seemed ready and willing to return to the anti-Sandinista fray.

No one understood Bravo's dangerous potential better than the Sandinistas. During their long years underground, they had become experts in counter-intelligence and the allied black arts. They had not hesitated to kill enemies when the need arose, and now it was arising again. They concluded that security required Bravo's elimination, and Interior Minister Tomás Borge, veteran of a lifetime of plots and intrigue, took on the contract as part of his job.

Borge approached one of Bravo's girlfriends, a bleached blonde named Barbara, and persuaded her to help set a trap. Barbara flew to Tegucigalpa, and on the afternoon of October 10, 1979, she telephoned Bravo at the out-of-the-way Tegucigalpa hotel where he lived. A few minutes later she arrived to pick him up.

Nothing more was seen of Bravo until four days later. Neighbors in an outlying section of the city called police about a stench in a nearby home, and when officers arrived they found congealed pools of blood and scattered human remains. Bravo's face had been mangled and much of the skin had been burned or peeled off, and it took forensic experts three days to identify his body positively.

The Sandinistas had eliminated one of their most dangerous potential enemies, and done in it in a way that sent a vivid message. Speaking on Nicaraguan radio the day Bravo's remains were finally identified, Tomás Borge sounded as if he had done just another day's work. "The head of that sector of the counter-revolution has been cut off," he said coolly. "The enemies of our people will fall one by one."

Ex-Guardsmen living in Honduras were shocked at Bravo's brutal murder, and many moved away. Several dozen gathered at an isolated Guatemala farm that was given the military-sounding name Detachment 101. They constituted themselves as the September 15 Legion and held occasional military drills, but they were far from a true military force. Some of them free-lanced as bodyguards or paid assassins.

With Bravo dead, a former National Guard colonel named Enrique Bermúdez began emerging as a majordomo of the men hanging around Detachment 101. Bermúdez was unusual among ex-Guardsmen because of his relative lack of taint. He had never been part of Somoza's inner circle, and had spent the late 1970s in Washington as Nicaragua's military attaché. During the Sandinista insurrection he had thus been far from the field of battle. In Washington he became friendly with a number of senior American military officers. He had commanded the small Nicaraguan contingent that joined United States Marines in the 1965 Dominican Republic intervention, and had all the right credentials for membership in the hemispheric fraternity of pro-American soldiers. Since the Sandinista takeover he had been living in exile, working for a time driving a magazine delivery truck in Miami.

Colonel Bermúdez met several times during late 1979 and 1980 with Luis Pallais Debayle, a cousin of Somoza's who had once been president of the Nicaraguan Congress. Pallais encouraged him to try to keep a force of ex-Guardsmen together, and provided several hundred thousand dollars to help him. At one point, Pallais even traveled to Paraguay to seek funds from Somoza himself. Somoza volunteered a million-dollar contribution, but was assassinated before he could produce it.

One of the ex-Guardsmen floating around Central America, Emilio Echaverry, had attended the Argentine Military Academy, and there he had met another foreign student, a Honduran named Gustavo Álvarez. In the years that followed, Álvarez rose to the rank of general and came to command FUSEP, the Honduran national police force. Now it was time for the two to renew acquaintances. Early in 1980, Echaverry traveled to Tegucigalpa for a chat with his old schoolmate. He asked if Álvarez was interested in supporting anti-Sandinista military actions, and Álvarez was immediately enthusiastic. They agreed on the first phase of what was to become a vast covert operation. Anti-Sandinistas in Miami were assembling crates of small arms, but had no-where to send them. Álvarez agreed to receive them in the name of the Honduran military, and then pass them on to ex-Guardsmen.

At around the same time, Luis Pallais Debayle was in Paraguay visiting his cousin, the lately deposed Somoza. While there, Pallais stopped in to see

Paraguayan dictator Alfredo Stroessner, and inquired whether he might be willing to help finance an anti-Sandinista insurgency. The aging Stroessner, who after years in power knew all the right questions to ask, wanted to know if the CIA was backing the project.

Pallais answered truthfully. The CIA, he said, was not involved. Stroessner then said he could not contribute, but he offered a piece of advice that was to prove invaluable.

"I think the Argentines can help," he told Pallais.

To journalists covering Latin America in the late 1970s, the very name of Argentina evoked shivers of horror. The generals who seized power there in 1976 were engaged in a systematic program of kidnapping and murder unlike any ever unleashed in the Western hemisphere. Police agents in civilian clothes abducted thousands of Argentines from their homes or from streetcorners, brought them to clandestine jails, tortured them to death, and then secretly disposed of their bodies.

The first time I suspected Argentine involvement with the contras came when I heard that there was a contra commander who used the pseudonym Krill. I doubted that any ordinary Nicaraguan would know that word, or that he would have heard it from an American. But I knew that krill, which are microscopic marine organisms, are plentiful off the coast of Argentina. I suspected that if there was a contra named Krill, he had probably been in contact with Argentines.

General Álvarez was particularly amenable to the suggestion that Argentines be invited to help forge the contra army, because he himself was a proud graduate of the Argentine Military Academy. During his studies in Buenos Aires, he had become a fervent believer in Argentine military doctrine. That doctrine, which had been adopted by military dictators in various Latin American countries, taught that the ideals of the Christian West were under worldwide attack by atheistic Marxists, and that the duty of men in uniform was to fight the spread of Marxist-influenced ideologies. Argentine military theorists believed that international Communism had infiltrated and taken over trade unions, student groups, cultural organizations, political parties, and even religious orders. Thus the job of an army was not only to guard against invasion by foreign troops, but also to repress undesirable political and social movements.

The Argentine doctrine was chilling in its simplicity, arrogating to military officers the right to decide which citizens could live and which must die. "A terrorist is not simply one who carries a gun or a bomb," explained the Argentine general Jorge Rafael Videla, who directed his country's torture/murder campaign when it was at its peak. "A terrorist is also someone who spreads ideas that are contrary to Western civilization."

Gustavo Álvarez enthusiastically embraced this principle. His credo— "Everything you do to destroy a Marxist regime is moral"—came straight from the Argentine military mind. It was with that credo that he set out to forge an anti-Sandinista army.

In April 1981, on his own initiative, Álvarez flew to Washington for meetings with CIA Director William Casey. In those meetings he sketched the outlines of what would become the contra war. His idea was to pull together the disparate bands of former National Guardsmen scattered around Central America and Florida; forge them into a coherent fighting force; provide them with weapons; build a network of bases for them in southern Honduras; and send them into Nicaragua to fight. The contras had little chance of actually defeating the formidable Sandinista army, Álvarez conceded, but they might be able to spark civil war within Nicaragua or provoke the Sandinistas into a military attack against Honduras. That would be all the justification the United States needed, he argued, to send troops to Managua and decapitate the Sandinista regime.

Casey was cautious at first. What Álvarez had to offer—a covert base for the contras adjacent to the Nicaraguan border, plus all the necessary military cover—was appealing indeed. Honduras was the ideal place from which to launch an anti-Sandinista insurgency. But for the moment, United States involvement had to be kept secret. American funds could quietly be found to pay for training contra field officers, Casey told Álvarez, but only if another country provided the trainers.

Hondurans were not considered able to provide sophisticated guerrilla training, so another country had to be enlisted in the project, a country where ex-Guardsmen could be sent to learn how to fight. It would be preferable if this country were a military dictatorship rather than a democracy, because that would give its army commanders freedom to carry out covert training without interference from legislators or journalists. Ideally it would be a country anxious to win Washington's good will, anxious to do a favor for which it might be rewarded. The obvious choice was Argentina.

The relentless efficiency of the Argentine killing machine shocked much of the world, and turned Argentina into an international pariah. President Carter had refused to sell weapons to the Argentine regime, dispatched his chief human rights advisor to Buenos Aires for an on-site investigation, and publicly criticized the murderous junta. But after Ronald Reagan replaced Carter in the White House, United States policy was abruptly reversed. No longer were Argentine generals reviled as killers who deserved to be treated as outcasts. Instead they were praised as patriotic officers who had brought order to a troubled country and who were now anxious to work closely with the United States. Argentina's geopolitical value was seen to outweigh the repressive bent of its rulers, and soon a full-scale rapprochement between Washington and Buenos Aires was underway.

As American and Argentine officials worked to draw their two countries together, they came to realize how similarly they viewed the world. All feared that Marxism was on the march in Latin America, and all were anxious to confront it. Many believed that Nicaragua, the newest leftist state in the hemisphere, was the logical place to begin.

An Argentine colonel named Osvaldo Ribeiro appeared in Miami at the beginning of 1981 with very good news for anti-Sandinista exiles. Ribeiro, known as *Balita* ("Little Bullet"), reported that his government was ready to provide military aid to ex-Guardsmen or anyone else preparing to fight the Sandinista regime. Soon afterward, Enrique Bermúdez traveled to Buenos Aires. There he met with the intelligence chief of the Argentine army, General Alberto Valin, and laid out his plan.

"We stated that the Sandinistas were a Marxist-Leninist regime and would build up a totalitarian government," Bermúdez recalled years later. Helping the contras, he told General Valin, was something "that the United States wanted to do, but could not find a way to do it." He said that some country had to "ease the way" for the United States, and that Argentina was the logical choice because its leaders "had been very successful against the urban guerrilla groups in Argentina, and had the prestige."

The sort of prestige that Argentine generals had won in the world was not the sort that most would seek, but Bermúdez felt a kinship with them. His visit to Buenos Aires was a great success. The Argentines agreed to begin secretly training field officers at bases in Argentina, and equally important, to recognize Bermúdez as commander of the incipient contra army.

"I was selected by them," Bermúdez would later recall. "I talked to the man in charge. He said to me, 'Bermúdez, we have studied your background. We trust you. And we are going to support you.' "

During 1981 the contra project finally became real. Three countries secretly agreed to divide key tasks among them, accepting an unwritten arrangement that became known as *la tripartita*. Honduras, where General Álvarez was becoming increasingly powerful, would allow the contras to build clandestine bases near the Nicaraguan border, and would receive arms and other supplies on their behalf. Argentina would train contra squad leaders at bases near Buenos Aires, and send advisors to Honduras to help them build a command structure. And the United States would provide clandestine funding, secretly funneling $15 million to Argentina during 1981 and 1982 to pay for training and equipping the first contras.

Now the groundwork had been laid, and it was time to begin building a military force capable of challenging the Sandinista army. First came the task of uniting the various contra factions, a task that was never fully accomplished. At a meeting in Guatemala in August 1981, several contra groups agreed to join Bermúdez in a new organization to be called the Nicaraguan Democratic Force

(Fuerza Democrática Nicaragüense, FDN). Around the same time, a flamboyant CIA officer named Duane Clarridge made his first visit to Tegucigalpa. He had been assigned by William Casey to oversee the formation of a contra army.

Clarridge was bulky of figure, fond of large cigars and bright-colored Hawaian shirts, and given to long discourses on the Red Brigades, against whom he had been pitted during his tenure as CIA station chief in Rome. From all that outsiders were able to determine, he knew nothing about guerrilla war, had never served in Latin America, and spoke only halting Spanish. Those qualities made him ideal for a job in which appreciation of subtleties would always be a liability.

Clarridge arrived in Tegucigalpa in mid-1981 accompanied by Colonel Mario Davico, deputy director of the Argentine military intelligence service. At a meeting with Álvarez and other senior Honduran officers, they formalized *la tripartita* and set the contra project on its way.

"I bring the greetings of my president," Colonel Davico began. "Argentina has faith in democracy and has decided to support Honduras and Nicaragua to be free. We are with you. We will do everything we can."

Clarridge spoke next. It was never determined to what extent his declaration was authorized, or if so, by whom.

"I speak in the name of President Ronald Reagan," he said. "We want to support this effort to change the government of Nicaragua."

One of the Honduran officers present, Colonel Rafael Torres-Arias, said frankly that he feared the United States would abandon Nicaraguan insurgents at some crucial moment, as it had done in Cuba and elsewhere. "We are concerned about a new Bay of Pigs," he told Clarridge.

The fears that Torres-Arias expressed would later prove well-founded, but at that moment Clarridge brushed them aside. Had Clarridge been motivated by honesty, he might have warned that political vicissitudes in the United States made this a risky venture, and that in a democracy it would be difficult to keep such a project secret forever. Instead he did just the opposite.

"Believe me, Colonel," he vowed, "there will never be a new Bay of Pigs."

It was in this almost casual manner that the United States agreed to join with General Álvarez and his Argentine friends in a military campaign against the Sandinista government. Although the United States was to spend hundreds of millions of dollars on the contra project, the project was not of American design, and in fact never had much design at all. General Álvarez clearly understood that the ex-Guardsmen he was helping to train and equip would never be able to topple the Sandinistas themselves; their purpose, he believed, should be only to foment upheaval inside Nicaragua and give American troops an excuse to invade and destroy the Managua regime. But no one in Washington ever accepted the inevitability of invasion, and therefore they were joining the contra program without sharing its most basic premise.

Although American involvement with the contras began without defined goals, and without any of the high-level discussion that would normally accompany such a momentous commitment, it had top-level approval almost from the start. During the second half of 1981, the safari-suited Duane Clarridge, who worked under the translucent alias "Dewey Maroni," and the lanky, balding proconsul John Negroponte spent much of their time establishing a logistical base for the contras in Honduras. CIA agents working under Clarridge consulted regularly with General Álvarez, who was setting aside large strips of land near the Nicaraguan border to be used as contra bases, and with Argentine military advisors who were arriving as trainers.

Seventy Nicaraguans were sent to Argentina for advanced military courses during 1981, and hundreds more were trained in Honduras by a dozen Argentine trainers who entered the country under cover provided by General Álvarez. The chief of the secret Argentine military mission was the energetic colonel called *Balita.* Operating from a large house in Tegucigalpa and freely spending the CIA money he was receiving, he became a vital link in the war preparations. In those months, Honduran, Argentine, and American agents forged a military force which could never have come together without outside help.

Toward the end of 1981, William Casey and other supporters of the contras in Washington recognized that the contra project had grown to the point where it required direct approval by President Reagan. A law passed in 1974 required presidents to sign secret "findings" when they ordered covert operations, and on December 1, 1981, President Reagan signed one, marking the first written United States commitment to the contras. Several days later, Casey briefed House and Senate intelligence committees on its contents, as required by law.

The "finding," which had been drafted by the CIA for Reagan's signature, was just three sentences long, but even at that length it was bursting with untruth. It did not report that the CIA had secretly committed itself to sponsoring an insurgency aimed at toppling the Sandinista regime, nor that it was working with senior officials of at least two foreign governments to that end. Instead it portrayed the contras as a force of five hundred men dedicated solely to interdicting arms headed for guerrillas in El Salvador.

Late in 1981, Honduras held a presidential election for the first time in a decade, and an affable country doctor named Roberto Suazo Córdova emerged as the victor. Like most Honduran politicians, Suazo recognized and deferred to American power. He also understood that in Honduras, being president did not mean what it meant in some other countries. The army held true power, and dictated to politicians whenever it chose.

Soon after taking office, Suazo was called upon to select a new commander-in-chief for the nation's armed forces. Following the advice of senior military officers as well as American diplomats and intelligence agents, he chose General

Álvarez. By doing so he secured Álvarez's position as the most powerful figure in Honduras, and thereby gave the contra project an implicit green light.

Honduras had long enjoyed a reputation as an oddly placid oasis among Central American nations. There had never been a serious guerrilla insurgency there, and political killings were very rare. Rural workers were fairly well organized, and while many were still wretchedly poor, they were never drawn to rebellion. Hondurans had peacefully resolved many conflicts that led to bloodshed in other countries, and government repression was relatively tame.

Once General Álvarez ascended to power, however, the relaxed style of Honduran political life changed dramatically. Beginning during his term as police chief and continuing while he served as the country's senior military commander, Álvarez supervised a small-scale version of the terror that swallowed up thousands of victims in Argentina. Under his direction, more than one hundred Hondurans were abducted and tortured to death in clandestine prisons. Some of the victims were leftists who hoped to launch an insurgency in Honduras, others were student leaders or anti-government activists, and still others had no known political backgrounds. Their disappearances served notice that the rules of Honduran politics were changing.

CIA officers planned the demolition of two Nicaraguan bridges in March 1982, training saboteurs especially for the operation and equipping them with detailed maps, night-vision goggles, and C-4 explosive. In Washington, William Casey privately admitted to congressional committees that his agents were involved. Some committee members were disturbed to learn that the CIA was building a full-scale insurgent army on the Nicaraguan border, and their confidence in Casey's judgment was not strengthened by his continuing inability to pronounce the word "Nicaragua." The best he could do was "Nicawawa."

In a sense there was no reason for Casey to do better. To him and to his longtime friend President Reagan, the identity of the country and its historical and cultural idiosyncrasies were not important. These countries, they believed, were best understood as battlegrounds on which a global ideological struggle was being waged. Inability or refusal to pronounce foreign names correctly was an apt symptom of the know-nothingism that lay at the heart of the Reagan administration's Central America policy. It exasperated some members of congressional committees. At one point, a staff aide exclaimed to Casey, "You can't overthrow the government of a country whose name you can't pronounce!"

As the war began in earnest, CIA planners decided that the contras needed civilian leadership. They set out to recruit a group of Nicaraguan exiles whose job would be to speak on behalf of the contra movement and to act as if they controlled it. These civilians would be figureheads, but their activities would help disguise the extent to which the contra movement was controlled by foreigners.

The CIA's plan was to form a contra directorate equivalent to the nine-man Sandinista National Directorate. Some members of the group would have military contacts, while others would be strictly political figures. Ideally they would span a range of anti-Sandinista opinion, and include people who had been known for their opposition to the Somoza dictatorship.

The contra leadership was unveiled at a press conference at the Hilton Conference Center in Fort Lauderdale, Florida. Seven Nicaraguans, all hand-picked by the CIA, solemnly proclaimed themselves the united leadership of the newly constituted Nicaraguan Democratic Force, the FDN. They had never worked together before that day, and some had never even met each other. As a group, they were only moderately impressive. One, Alfonso Callejas, had been a Liberal party leader and vice president of Nicaragua until breaking with the Somozas in 1972, and another, Adolfo Calero, was a veteran Conservative politician. The others were Lucia Salazar, widow of the slain anti-Sandinista plotter Jorge Salazar; Indalecio Rodriguez, a physician and former university dean; the ex-Jesuit Edgar Chamorro; Marco Zeledón, who had owned several businesses in Nicaragua; and Colonel Enrique Bermúdez of the defeated National Guard.

Before the press conference, CIA agents briefed the newly anointed contra leaders on provisions of the Neutrality Act. They warned the Nicaraguans not to say they wanted to overthrow the Sandinista regime, but rather that they were trying to "create conditions for democracy" in their homeland. If asked the source of their funds, they were not to answer. If asked whether they had been in contact with officials of the United States government, they were to lie and deny such contacts.

Edgar Chamorro was in some regards the most interesting member of the group. He had never been a political figure in Nicaragua, but had a background in advertising and was well prepared for the public relations challenge that faced the contras. He later became one of the few senior contras to quit the movement and write about its beginnings:

IN November 1982 I was approached by a CIA agent using the name "Steve Davis" and asked to become a member of the "political directorate" of the FDN . . . 1982 was a year of transition for the FDN. From a collection of small, disorganized, and ineffectual bands of ex-National Guardsmen, the FDN grew into a well-organized, well-armed, well-equipped, and well-trained fighting force of approximately four thousand men capable of inflicting great harm on Nicaragua. This was due entirely to the CIA, which organized, armed, equipped, trained and supplied us . . .

Our troops were trained in guerrilla warfare, sabotage, demolitions, and in the use of a variety of light weapons, including assault rifles, machine guns, mortars, grenade launchers, and explosives such as Claymore mines. We were also trained in field communications, and the CIA taught us how to use certain sophisticated codes that the Nicaraguan government would be unable to decipher . . . Even more critical to our military activities was the intelligence that the CIA provided to us

... With this information, our own forces knew the areas in which they could safely operate free of government troops. If our units were ordered to do battle with the government troops, they knew where to set up ambushes, because the CIA informed them of the precise routes the government troops would take.

AMONG the first targets the contras selected for their commando raids were several government-owned coffee plantations near the Honduras-Nicaragua border. They began swooping down on groups of coffee pickers, many of whom were Sandinista volunteers, with guns blazing. Among the contra commanders who led these raids was the one called Krill.

I later learned that Krill was a former Guardsman named Julio César Herrera who had managed to escape Nicaragua in the chaotic days following the Sandinista takeover. Together with some of his defeated comrades-in-arms, he had made his way to Honduras and become part of the first group of contras clustered around Enrique Bermúdez and his patron, General Álvarez. As I had suspected, he picked up the pseudonym "Krill" from an Argentine trainer, and with that name he became more infamous than Julio César Herrera had ever been. He had learned all the lessons that the Somozas taught National Guardsmen, and evidently the training he received from Argentines and Hondurans reinforced those lessons. One day in 1981, he snuck into Nicaragua to murder a local Sandinista official who had jailed his mother for seventeen days on charges of running contraband. He was known for uncontrolled fits of violence, directed not only at enemies but sometimes, in outbursts that led to death more than once, against his own contra brethren.

At a Sandinista coffee cooperative near the border outpost of Wuambuco, Krill and his squad lay in wait for coffee pickers one day in December 1981. When they spotted a group, they opened fire. Many of the pickers were armed, and some returned the contra fire to cover their friends' retreat. No one was killed.

When the shooting stopped, Krill and his men scouted the bushes for wounded Sandinistas. In a gully they found a middle-aged man and his wife, both bloody and terrified. The two were pulled out, and in short order their captors began beating them, demanding to know who they were and what they were doing. For long hours the two prisoners were tortured, and by the time they reached Krill's camp in Honduras several days later, both were nearly dead. At the base, their ordeal continued, and from all accounts they were not the only ones suffering such treatment. Eyewitnesses, including former contras, later described seeing prisoners at the camps tied half-naked to trees for days at a time, and hearing the screams of victims being abused nearby.

Both of the prisoners captured at Wuambuco were subjected to weeks of torment at a contra camp called Pino Uno. Then one day an acne-scarred contra torturer known as El Muerto ordered them to dig a hole and lie in it. When they did, he shot them dead and ordered their bodies covered with a thin layer of earth.

The two victims were Felipe and María Barreda, well-known Sandinista activists from Estelí. Felipe, fifty-one years old, was a comfortable small businessman who ran a jewelry shop and was active in church affairs. His wife, known to all as Mary, was also from a religious background. Both had been active in anti-Somoza activities, joining demonstrations and helping guerrillas however they could. After the Sandinista takeover, they became enthusiastic partisans of the government, devoting long hours to volunteer work as well as collaborating with State Security agents. They soon became two of the most prominent Sandinistas in Estelí. Organizing volunteers to pick coffee in a dangerous border zone, and then accompanying them to the fields, was typical of the kind of work they did.

Shortly before their capture, Mary Barreda had written a letter to workers at the state-run tobacco farm in Estelí, explaining that she would not be able to join them for Christmas dinner and asking them to accept her presence in the coffee fields as her Christmas gift to them.

"The little that I can pick will be translated, or rather converted into health, clothing, housing, roads, schooling, food, etc.," she wrote. "And it's for that that I'm going to pick coffee with all the love and enthusiasm of which I'm capable."

Contras like Krill and El Muerto were cold-blooded killers shaped in the violent, repressive tradition of the Nicaraguan National Guard. Their most bestial impulses had been encouraged by Honduran and Argentine trainers, and when they took to the field they unleashed all the bitterness and anger within them, turning it against whoever they happened to encounter. Some armies seek to control and channel the violence of their soldiers, but contra soldiers were taught quite differently. The form of warfare they adopted in their first years was straightforward terror, and episodes like the torture-murder of the Barredas were not anomalies but part of a pattern that gave them a fearsome reputation.

For a time it seemed that *la tripartita,* the secret Honduran-Argentine-American alliance that had turned the contras into a fully equipped and potent fighting force, would remain in place indefinitely. Suddenly and unexpectedly, however, the alliance collapsed, victim of political maneuverings that had little to do with the contra war. The chain of events began in Argentina.

Argentine generals had aided the contras in order to ingratiate themselves to the United States, and to build up a reputation as a new world power. By some standards, they were succeeding. But no one was prepared for the dramatic announcement beamed from Buenos Aires on April 2, 1982: Argentina had sent troops to occupy the Falkland Islands and declared that it would no longer accept British sovereignty there.

Argentina's decision to seize the desolate South Atlantic islands was based on a gamble. Members of the ruling junta in Buenos Aires had come to believe that at this moment of truth, the United States would support Argentina, or at least remain neutral. Intentionally or otherwise, the Reagan administration had led Argentine generals to believe such a scenario was plausible. Indeed, some of Argentina's friends in Washington, notably United Nations Ambassador Jeane Kirkpatrick, urged the administration to find some way to accommodate Argentina during the South Atlantic crisis. Ultimately they failed. The discredited junta in Buenos Aires was overthrown the day after surrendering, and a presidential election was called. Infuriated at the United States for its support of Great Britain, Argentine generals immediately began reducing their aid to the contras. When the civilian Raúl Alfonsín was inaugurated as president in December 1983, he ended the aid program entirely.

With the Argentines out of the contra picture, General Álvarez and the CIA were left to oversee the escalating war. Álvarez had become an intimidating figure in Honduras, a personalistic and highly ambitious dictator-in-the-making. The Honduran military had traditionally been run collegially, with senior officers making important decisions together, but Álvarez had begun to consider it a private fiefdom. He intruded into the delicate area of military promotions, helping his friends advance while frustrating the career plans of subordinates he mistrusted. At the same time he began actively promoting a new private business group, the Association for Honduran Progress, leading some industrialists and entrepreneurs to fear that he was planning to extend his power into non-military areas. He even established murky ties to the Unification Church of Rev. Sun Myung Moon, which began sponsoring conferences and other events in Honduras, and brought Colonel Bo Hi Pak, head of the Korean Central Intelligence Agency, to visit Tegucigalpa.

Concern about Álvarez's ambition fed a general disquiet in the Honduran officer corps. Still, he counted on the explicit and forceful support of the man who counted the most in Honduras, Ambassador Negroponte. The United States had gone so far as to award the general a "Legion of Merit" for his good works. No one had a clue that he faced serious trouble until the morning of March 31, 1984, when soldiers at the San Pedro Sula airport suddenly arrested, handcuffed, and pistol-whipped him, and then packed him off into exile. With unusual secrecy and precision, senior Honduran officers had voted to oust him, set a trap for him, and sprung it.

Now the Argentines and Hondurans who had nursed the contras through infancy were gone. The new Honduran ruling group was willing to continue supporting the contras, but from this point onward, their war became a fully American responsibility. A project dreamed up by retrograde Latin American military officers now fell under the control of the United States government.

11

LIFE DURING WARTIME

NO REPRESENTATIVE of an American daily newspaper had ever lived permanently in Nicaragua before, so it was natural that my presence provoked curiosity. Few Nicaraguans, I soon discovered, actually knew what the *New York Times* was—I was repeatedly introduced as the correspondent of *Time* magazine, and soon gave up trying to explain the difference—but they knew it was something important in the United States, and that was enough. Nicaraguans had learned through long experience that foreigners, especially Americans, held great power over their lives and over the fate of their nation, and often they treated me as though I might somehow be able to heal their ills or relieve their tribulations.

My standard of living, compared to that of most Nicaraguans, was more than opulent. I didn't live any better than the average middle-class American, and not nearly so luxuriously as wealthy people had lived during the Somoza years. Nonetheless, I had my own house, an air conditioner, a television, a jeep and a salary in dollars. By the mid-1980s, the only Nicaraguans living this way were the Sandinista *comandantes,* most of whom had settled into mansions confiscated from the old upper class, and a dwindling number of well-to-do Nicaraguan families still trying to live in the style to which they had become accustomed.

Just outside the whitewashed walls of my house lay the harsh reality of Managua. No one who lived there for any length of time during the 1980s could fail to be overwhelmed by the decay and sadness that enveloped the country. Instead of becoming more prosperous under Sandinista rule, as they had hoped, most Nicaraguans became quite palpably poorer. Jobs were hard to find, money was worth less each week, and violent crime increased steadily. Worst of all, the escalating contra war was tearing the country apart. Life inside the *Times* bureau was more than comfortable, but Nicaragua, the world outside the bureau, was where I worked, and life there was always hard.

The first major adjustment to life in Managua was to the city's physical desolation and relentless ugliness. Although more than a decade had passed since the earthquake, the city was still a wasteland. The Sandinistas laid out a park, cleared a fair amount of debris, and planted several groves of trees, but as the economy collapsed, plans for urban reconstruction were shelved. Only a few buildings had survived the quake, among them the old *Banco de America* headquarters, which had been taken over for use as government offices, and the pyramid-shaped Intercontinental Hotel. The rest of Managua was a random patchwork of unconnected neighborhoods scattered over a vast area of what had once been prairie and farmland. There was no shopping area, no central plaza, no downtown for strolling or window-shopping. No tended gardens, no unusual architectural flourishes, indeed almost no thing of beauty at all intruded on Managua's dreariness.

The earthquake had destroyed long-established traffic and street patterns, so when people built new homes they had to invent new addresses. Most streets in post-earthquake Managua had no names, and most houses had no numbers. Addresses were given by points of reference, and if one did not know thirty or forty basic ones, navigation was impossible. People gave directions to their homes or businesses from a particular restaurant, government office, statue, or other landmark. The official address of the *Times* bureau, for example, was: from the main gate of the military hospital, one block toward the lake and then one-and-a-half blocks down. Any experienced Managua driver could find that address with no trouble. "Down" and "up" had mysterious meanings which I never learned to decipher, but Managuans always seemed to understand them. If I was told to meet someone two blocks up from the Labor Ministry, I would simply drive to the Labor Ministry and ask some passer-by which direction was "up."

Other addresses were even more colorful. Once I asked a Nicaraguan friend for directions to his house, and he told me: "Turn onto the dirt road beside the UPOLI sign, drive to the end, and then look for the house under the tallest tree." Another time, I asked a young girl where in the Ciudad Sandino slum she lived. She hesitated for a moment.

"You remember where the puppy-dog died?" she asked finally. "I live ten *varas* up from there."

The use of *varas* to mark distances was another peculiar feature of Managua geography. The *vara* is an ancient unit of measure, supposedly based on the length of a famous nobleman's arm. It had fallen out of general usage in other Spanish-speaking countries at least a century earlier. A *vara*, I learned, was roughly equivalent to a yard or a meter, and soon I began to enjoy using the term. I felt as if I were speaking an elegant and archaic Spanish, the kind Don Quixote spoke.

Ascertaining an exact address was always a challenge. In all my years in Managua I never stopped losing my way. The process of giving directions was Socratic in form, as the host sought to find the proper place to begin. When explaining where I lived, for example, I would start by asking if my prospective guest knew the location of the military hospital. If the guest did not know the hospital, then I would begin asking questions: Did he or she know the Japanese embassy? How about the Libyan embassy? The Hoechst chemical company office? The Xolotlan pharmacy?

Often I would be on the receiving end of these process-of-elimination directions. Especially during my first year in Managua, I was regularly embarrassed by my ignorance of so many of the city's landmarks. People became frustrated or exasperated. If I didn't know where the Montoya monument was, they seemed to be asking me, nor where the Nicaraguan Development Institute had its office, nor where Enrique Sotelo Borgen worked, nor where Luis Sánchez lived, nor where the Monseñor Lezcano statue was, then how could I ever hope to cover anything in Managua?

The most challenging landmarks of all to locate were those that no longer existed. Dozens of important buildings and other points of reference had been destroyed in the earthquake, but Managuans talked about them as if they were still standing. The Pepsi-Cola plant, for example, had collapsed in the quake and its remains had long since been bulldozed away, but that did not prevent people in the neighborhood from saying they lived near the Pepsi plant. I sometimes bought airline tickets from a travel agency whose address was "Across the street from Retiro Hospital," but there was no longer a Retiro Hospital across the street or, for that matter, anywhere else.

The Peruvian writer Mario Vargas Llosa, who lived in Managua for a month gathering material for an essay, told me that he had once considered Tokyo to be the world's most impossible city, but that he was now prepared to award that title to Managua. Former Secretary of State Henry Kissinger, who passed through one day on a fact-finding mission, said Managua looked to him like the set for a movie about the aftermath of World War III. Most trenchant of all was one *New York Times* editor who passed through while I was there. He stayed for three days, and as I was driving him to the airport at the end of his trip, I asked his impression of Managua.

"When I first got here and rode to the hotel, my impression was that this was the ugliest place I had ever seen in my life," he told me. "After being here a few days and getting a chance to look around, I can be sure. It is the ugliest place I've ever seen in my life."

Being an outsider in Nicaragua meant that one was forever excluded from certain circles of knowledge. But being American meant that I was in a special category of outsiders, one loved and hated more passionately than most others. Every day the United States was denounced on radio by one *comandante* or other, but almost certainly the *comandante* would tape his denunciation while wearing imported American jeans, boots, and sunglasses. By day, young people attended political rallies, shook their fists, and sang the Sandinista anthem, pledging, "We fight against the Yankee, enemy of humanity"; by night, they danced to American pop songs or lined up to see American films, the more violent and chauvinistic the better. Consumers who disdained canned preserves from Bulgaria and other East-bloc countries happily paid a day's wages for an equivalent can from the United States.

Occasionally I encountered suspicious Nicaraguans who suggested I was some kind of United States government agent, but those encounters were rare. More typical was the market vendor who exploded at me one day as I was picking through produce at her stall.

"You Americans, I can't believe how stupid you are!" she shouted at me. I stopped to hear her harangue.

"You come here for a couple of days or a week, you live in some nice hotel, and maybe you go up north to pick coffee for a day," the woman began, shaking her finger in my face. "Then you go home to your little solidarity group or your church group and tell everyone how wonderful the revolution is. You people are so blind! You're forcing Communism on us Nicaraguans, don't you see? The Sandinistas are leading you around by the nose! You think everything looks so nice here, but we can't afford to eat in those places where you people eat. Poor people are suffering in this country! We don't have food for our children, but you don't see that because the Sandinistas don't show it to you! You're living in nice apartments in New York or Europe, and the idea of revolution seems so nice to you from over there. Open your eyes! Don't keep telling lies! Don't be useful idiots!"

The small crowd that gathered loved the woman's performance. Several bystanders even broke in to tell me how much they agreed with her. Finally I was able to defend myself, assuring the woman that I lived permanently in Nicaragua, did not work for a pro-Sandinista group in the United States, and had never picked any coffee or tried to force Communism on anyone. She was emotional, but never lost her sense of proportion. Like many people in Nicaragua, she was simply fed up with Americans who believed they knew what was best for her country.

"Just tell the truth," she admonished me as I bid her good day.

Shortages of food and a host of other products were chronic in Nicaragua during the 1980s. One item that became especially valuable was the lowly plastic bag. Cans and bottles disappeared soon after the revolution, since there was no money to produce or import them, and before long there were no paper cups, paper bags, cardboard boxes, or containers of any kind. Everything was bought and sold in plastic bags—vegetables and meat, eggs, herbs and spices, coffee, books, fertilizers, shoes, everything. Even the fruit drinks that Nicaraguans relied on to cool their days were served in plastic bags, and like all outsiders, I had to learn how to drink from them. There was a special technique to master. Vendors would ladle a portion of juice into a thin, transparent bag, and then deftly tie the top. The logical impulse for the uninitiated buyer was to untie the bag and try to drink out of the top, but following that impulse only guaranteed a sticky bath. The proper technique was to take a small bite out of a corner of the plastic bag, spit out the piece of plastic, and then drink through the hole.

One day I traveled to the town of Diriamba, forty miles west of Managua, to visit the state-owned Plastinic factory where the bags were made. Inside, the plant was loud, poorly ventilated, and half-dark. Most of the giant machines had been manufactured in the United States and were many decades old; several bore plates reading, "Gloucester Machinery, Gloucester, Mass." Huge crates of plastic pellets, the raw material from which the bags were made, were stacked against walls. The pellets, once bought in the United States, were now donated by friendly European countries, principally Bulgaria, and did not always arrive on time. When pellets were available, the factory was kept open twenty-four hours a day, but still it produced at less than fifty percent of capacity. I didn't understand how this could be, and the manager, Roberto Gómez, had to enlighten me.

"There is a lot of absenteeism," Gómez explained. "Salaries are so low that people don't bother to come to work. Trained technicians and engineers quit because they can make more money selling peanuts at the stadium than working here. Normally only about half our employees ever show up, so the factory never comes close to producing at full capacity."

The price of plastic bags, like the price of most other essential items, was set by the government. But because supply never met demand, and because the bags were so essential, eager consumers were willing to pay several times the legal price. A thriving black market developed, fed in part by shady middlemen with contacts inside the plant. Gómez told me that even some important officials had been involved. His predecessor as plant manager had been convicted of amassing large sums of money through illegal trafficking in plastic bags, and was serving a two-year prison term.

One of my friends in Managua was an executive at the Toña brewery, where one of the country's two brands of beer was produced. As the government tightened control over its dwindling supply of hard currency, he couldn't obtain enough dollars to buy the foreign products he needed to maintain the quality of his beer. Like many businessmen, he was caught in a strange financial trap: the government was the only place he was legally allowed to buy dollars, but the government didn't have any dollars available. The quality of his beer deteriorated, and to make matters worse, he was unable to hold on to his best and most experienced workers. He wanted to pay them reasonable wages, which would have meant at least doubling or tripling their legally fixed salaries, but the law forbade wage increases. For a time he let each worker take home cases of beer, which they could sell for cash at local markets, but such "payments in kind" were also restricted by law. It was a losing battle, and the workers' standard of living declined along with the quality of the beer. Ultimately my friend the brewer, who had worn a Sandinista uniform during the 1979 uprising, gave up and left Nicaragua.

Sandinista economic theory had a certain simplistic appeal. The *comandantes* envisioned a society in which central planning bodies, acting always on behalf of the poor, would regulate prices and wages and thereby reallocate society's resources. Prices for literally hundreds of products were set by an anonymous central body in Managua, and then enforced nationwide. The wage control mechanism was even more complex, based on an enormously detailed chart on which a value was assigned to every job in the country, and permissible wages listed in columns according to a worker's years of experience. Disgusted with these restrictions, many Nicaraguans abandoned productive labor and found work that allowed them to escape the controlled wage economy altogether. These people formed an important new economic class, the fastest-growing class in revolutionary Nicaragua. The work they did was given its own name, a wonderful transliteration from English: *bisnes.*

Sandinista newspapers were constantly demanding that authorities crack down on *bisnes,* and condemning those who had left their salaried jobs to become *bisneros.* They urged consumers to boycott goods being sold at illegal prices, but their appeals were hopeless while demand so far outstripped supply. Because salaries were tightly controlled, even the most marginally successful entrepreneur could make far more money than the highest-salaried professional or executive. Inflation raged so wildly that moving up a notch or two on the wage chart was no help; the only hope for economic advancement was to escape from the chart altogether.

Whenever a new shipment of goods arrived in Nicaragua, the government resolved that this time the goods would be sold to poor people at low prices, and would not leak onto the open market. The highly unpopular Ministry of Internal Commerce was usually in charge of distribution. It was committed to distributing goods through what it called "secure channels," meaning channels protected from market forces. This system was supposed to guarantee that government employees and members of Sandinista trade unions, farm organizations, and block committees would be able to buy goods at low, preferential prices.

The result was the same each time. A portion of the goods would always disappear, stolen by common thieves or diverted by unscrupulous government employees. What remained would be placed on sale at designated stores, and eligible shoppers would begin lining up before dawn on the appointed day. The fortunate among them would manage to fight their way to the front of the crowd. They would buy as much as allowed, carry their purchases directly to middlemen or *bisneros,* and sell them at a large profit. The next day, sometimes even the same day, the goods would be on public sale at prices as high as the market would bear.

These leaks in what was supposed to be a controlled economy drove Sandinista leaders to distraction. In speech after speech, they denounced speculators and *bisneros* in the most forceful terms, condemning them as bloodsuckers who were doing more damage to Nicaragua than the contras or the CIA. But the reality was unavoidable: few products were available, and thus people were willing to pay more for what there was.

None of the repeated efforts to combat *bisnes* came close to succeeding. Time after time, Sandinista police swept through the Eastern Market to clean out unlicensed vendors, but each time the vendors reappeared. Once squads of police arrived in the dead of night and physically destroyed more than a hundred illegal market stalls, breaking into warehouses and confiscating all the goods they found, but the effect was only temporary. Other strategies were more subtle, like the policy of granting space in the market only to vendors who had been certified as loyal by local Sandinista committees, but they proved no more successful. Even the idea of erecting a chainlink fence to enclose the legal vendors, and forbidding the transaction of business outside the fence, was a failure. Holes quickly appeared in the fence, and the market spilled back to its old size.

As it became clear that shortages and *bisnes* were going to become permanent facts of Nicaraguan life, people adjusted their lives accordingly. Enterprising people in cities found entirely new ways to earn money, such as hiring themselves out to wait in lines for other people who were slightly better off. In offices, the driver quickly became the most important person, the person upon whom everything depended. "Driver" was actually a misnomer, since these men rarely worked as chauffeurs. Their actual role was to run errands, a role that in most societies was simple and insignificant but in Nicaragua became absolutely vital.

So important was a good driver to the efficient functioning of an office or household in Managua that prospective employers fought over them. The driver who helped me inaugurate the *Times* bureau in Managua, Luis López, was a pioneer in his profession. He was a former bus driver with a nimble, agile mind, and under his guidance the *Times* office became one of the best-equipped in Managua. We had fluorescent lights that worked, we had beer and soft drinks available for guests, we had a functioning photocopy machine, and we even had toilet paper and soap in the vestibule. The credit for these luxuries, quite rightly, fell not on me but on Luis, who used the *Times* bureau as a canvas on which to display his special artistry. Alas, Luis succeeded too well. Among those who noticed his wizardry were local reporters and producers for NBC news, and one day they hired him away from me. Luis and I were saddened to part company, but he had to think of his family and couldn't turn down the lavish salary NBC was offering. While working for me, Luis was making more than a Cabinet minister; after moving to NBC, he made more than any three Cabinet ministers combined.

Before Luis left my employ, he introduced me to one of his boyhood friends, Guillermo Marcia, and recommended that I hire him as my new driver. Guillermo began work the next day. He was to become my closest Nicaraguan friend, but our relationship took root slowly. It took me several months to realize that Guillermo didn't understand much about my job or the concept of news reporting. I began to use our time together to explain how the *New York Times* worked, and he eagerly absorbed everything I said.

I knew Guillermo had fully emerged from his cocoon the day he shouted down a guard at the Salvadoran embassy in Managua. I had sent him to the embassy to see if he could obtain a visa for a visiting *Times* reporter who was traveling to El Salvador that afternoon. Unfortunately, there was a rule that visa applicants had to deposit their passports overnight. This was the kind of rule Guillermo was hired to evade.

Pulling up near the embassy gate, Guillermo stepped out of the jeep and confronted the guard, ignoring the line of visa applicants who had been patiently waiting for hours. There was much gesticulating, and voices were raised, but eventually Guillermo managed to talk his way through the gate and into the embassy. Once inside, he somehow persuaded the secretary to call a vice-consul, and finally he obtained the visa. Emerging after an hour, he was met by a naturally upset guard, who reprimanded him for behaving rudely and upsetting the day's routine. Guillermo, who had come to consider himself part of the *New York Times,* stopped dead in his tracks and shouted a withering retort for all to hear.

"Do you think there would be any freedom in any country in the world if it were not for the press?" he demanded.

The guard, who had not imagined that he was interfering with something so sacred, stood silent, as if accepting rebuke. Guillermo threw his arms over his head in a gesture of disgust and stalked away. It was a bravura performance.

Not only had he obtained the visa in record time, but when challenged he had justified himself with a passionate and eloquent defense of the journalistic profession.

Another of Guillermo's triumphs came the first time I asked him to try to find beef. *Comandante* Omar Cabezas and his wife were coming to dinner, and I wanted to make them spaghetti with meat sauce. A day in advance, I sent Guillermo out shopping. What he had to go through to find five pounds of beef was both a testament to his ingenuity and a reflection of how crazy life in Nicaragua had become.

Nicaragua had long been a cattle-rich country, and in pre-revolutionary days, most people ate beef at least once in a while. They usually could not afford butcher's prices, so an informal system of barter grew up. When one fellow in the neighborhood or village killed a cow, he would give part of the meat to friends and relatives, and sell the rest to neighbors or exchange it for other goods or services. Before long, someone else would be killing a cow, and return the favor. It was a moderately fair system, though naturally it did nothing to change the reality that wealthier people could eat much more meat than those who were poor. Its informality, however, offended the Sandinista sense of order. That anyone could kill a cow whenever he pleased, and then distribute the meat without any supervision, was perceived as a form of "anarchy." So the *comandantes* decreed a new system aimed at guaranteeing everyone equal access to beef.

Under Sandinista rules, no Nicaraguan was allowed to slaughter a cow without written permission from a government agent. Those with cows ready for slaughter were required to bring them to approved slaughterhouses and sell them there at prices fixed by the government. All beef obtained by such slaughter was to be placed on sale at local butcher shops, with the price kept low enough so everyone could afford to buy.

The idea probably sounded quite logical when the *comandantes* conceived it, but its practical effect was disastrous. Prices fixed by the government for the purchase of livestock were unreasonably low, and farmers simply found other ways to dispose of their cattle. Enormous herds were smuggled into Honduras and Costa Rica, where buyers were waiting to pay top dollar. And there emerged a new crime called *matanza clandestina,* clandestine slaughtering. In remote rural areas and in or near most cities, Nicaraguans could hire people to kill their livestock secretly, and distribute the extra meat to black-market buyers.

Because the total amount of meat produced in Nicaragua fell so dramatically, there was rarely any for sale in butcher shops. In many poor households, beef disappeared entirely from the diet. For those of us with access to money, however, finding it depended only on making the right connections. That was where "drivers" like Guillermo came in.

To begin his search for my beef, Guillermo wandered through marketplaces and back streets, asking quietly if anyone knew where some might be had. A few vendors may have wondered if he was a police agent, but through friends of friends he finally located someone who knew someone who was planning to kill a cow that night. Guillermo whispered along his order—five pounds of the good stuff—and money was surreptitiously passed.

When Guillermo did not show up for work the following morning, I suspected he must still be on the trail. Sure enough, he burst through the door at noontime with a triumphant grin on his face. In his hand he was holding five pounds of ground beef—in a plastic bag, no less!

"Wow, you got it!" I marveled.

"*Claro, jefe,*" he beamed. "*No hay problema!*"

It was never possible to know what item one might be seeing for the last time in Nicaragua. First cookies and snack foods disappeared from the marketplace, then breakfast cereals, then jams and peanut butter, and then canned milk. Wherever I went, older people spoke wistfully about their memories of some product or other that they had grown up with. The most commonly heard expression in Nicaragua during the 1980s was "*No hay,*" meaning "There isn't any." Many of the products Nicaraguans had been buying all their lives were no longer available. These chronic shortages disrupted the lives of almost everyone, and naturally hurt the Sandinistas' popularity.

The shortages meant real hardship for most Nicaraguans, but for foreign residents they were merely inconvenient. Managua quickly became the only Central American capital where basic goods were unavailable, and our efforts to compensate often bordered on the comical.

Only as Managua became slowly closed off from the outside world did most of us realize what items we really craved, and we would bring those items in with us whenever we returned home from Costa Rica, Honduras, Guatemala, or the United States. As flour and condiments became difficult to find, cake and muffin mixes were in growing demand. The New Orleans airport had a shop that sold nuts, and therefore many travelers who passed through New Orleans on their way to Managua arrived with a wide nut selection. In Miami, the chocolate-chip-cookie stand beneath the Omni Hotel was a regular stop for many travelers. As I arrived there to make a hurried purchase one afternoon on my way to the airport, I found myself in line behind the entire leadership of Nicaragua's Social Christian party.

At the Maya Hotel in Tegucigalpa one day, I was packing my suitcase with the door to my room open when the housekeeper passed by and looked inside. We chatted, and she asked where I was going.

"Back to Managua," I told her. "I live there."

"You live in Managua?" she exclaimed in horror. "Oh, you poor thing. Wait right here."

She disappeared, returning a few moments later carrying two rolls of toilet paper and a box of hotel-sized soap bars.

"Here, take these with you," she urged me as she left the gifts on my bureau. "And watch out for yourself in that place!"

Thousands of dollars in food and merchandise from abroad poured into Nicaragua every day, some of it brought legally by travelers and the rest smuggled in; every single trucker entering Nicaragua, I came to believe, was carrying at the very least a few pairs of jeans to sell on the side. For a time, Sandinista purists waged a serious campaign against this free-lance importing, but the campaign only drove smugglers further underground and pushed their prices even higher. Finally Herty Lewites, the former gunrunner who had become Minister of Tourism, was able to persuade the *comandantes* to put aside their political scruples and realize how much money there was to be made in the dollar trade.

Few of the Sandinista fighters who assumed high posts in the new regime were qualified for the responsibilities they assumed, and their administrative shortcomings cost the country dearly. Lewites, however, was a sterling exception. Fair-skinned and balding, son of a Jewish candy manufacturer who had emigrated from Poland in the 1920s, he was hardly a typical Sandinista. He was a quasi-intellectual who had joined the movement when it was made up mostly of tough street kids like Daniel Ortega, and over the years Ortega and other senior Sandinista leaders came to value his counsel highly. His influence increased as he built the tourism ministry into a potent money-making machine, an island of prosperity in Nicaragua's sea of economic woe.

Some Sandinista leaders saw the flood of foreign products being carried into Nicaragua as an ideological outrage, but Herty Lewites saw it as a business opportunity. Obviously there were many people in Nicaragua, natives as well as foreigners, who had dollars to spend and who wanted to spend them on items that were no longer available in stores. Each dollar these people spent for stereo equipment in Panama or chocolate bars in Miami, Lewites realized, was a dollar lost to Nicaragua. Given the country's desperate economic condition, such a loss was too substantial to overlook, and Lewites came up with a simple solution. In 1982, the Ministry of Tourism caused an overnight sensation by opening a hard currency shop in Managua, the first ever seen in the Western hemisphere outside of Cuba. The store became one of Nicaragua's most profitable institutions, a place where those with access to dollars could buy a host of items that were not available anywhere else in the country. By showing a passport or foreign resident card, or a Sandinista identity card, or sometimes simply by slipping the doorman a dollar bill, one could enter a world that seemed entirely separated from Nicaragua.

The dollar store had taken shape more quickly than most buildings in Nicaragua, though with the same secrecy that shrouded all Sandinista projects. Everyone took notice when work crews began clearing an overgrown field near Los Gauchos, a government-run steak house, and grading the land for construction. Nicaragua was already in an economic depression, although conditions were not nearly as serious as they would become in the late 1980s, and new construction projects were rare. After several months passed and sleek white walls began to spring up around the new complex, we sensed that something unusual was being built there. From the outside, the complex bore the unmistakable Lewites trademark: attractiveness. Every public works project undertaken by agencies other than the tourism ministry, it sometimes seemed, turned out to be ugly and inefficient, and to decay within months. But every project directed by Lewites, from small beachside hotels to the headquarters of his own ministry in Managua, was executed with taste and style.

Rumors began to circulate as to what was taking shape across from Los Gauchos. Then one day, without any ceremony or announcement, the doors opened. Soon everyone in Managua knew that the city now had its own hard currency shop, and that anyone with access to dollars could now escape the realities of Nicaraguan life and buy whatever items he or she desired.

Lewites had designed the dollar store's interior to resemble a supermarket in the United States. At the entrance, arriving customers picked up shopping carts, each of which carried a red plastic label saying it had been manufactured in Florida. When finished with their shopping, they pushed their carts to a cashier, who totaled their purchases on an electronic cash register and accepted payment—dollars only, of course.

This was nothing like the traditional way of shopping in Nicaragua, which entailed carrying one's basket or shoulder bag through a sweltering market where dogs and insects vied with customers for food, and picking through piles of produce to find something appealing. Foreigners felt comfortable at the dollar store, but for many poor Nicaraguans, wandering through the aisles constituted an intense sensory experience. Lewites once experimented with a policy of unrestricted admission, but the stampede was so great that he had to shut the doors.

The items that sold fastest at the dollar store were those basic staples, cigarettes and liquor, followed closely by disposable diapers, chocolates, and canned food. Business was brisk, and Lewites quickly built on his success. He opened a new section of the store to sell televisions, video cassette players, and other electronic equipment, then another section to sell clothing, then another for housewares like refrigerators and air conditioners, and then departments that sold sporting goods, auto parts, and even bicycles.

Nicaraguans who shopped at the Lewites complex obtained their dollars in several ways. Some worked for foreign companies that paid them in dollars. Others were farmers and fishermen who received "incentives" in dollars from the government after the local currency, the cordoba, lost its value. Still others received cash from relatives living in the United States or elsewhere. Once the dollar store opened, they began spending their dollars in Nicaragua instead of saving them to spend abroad.

Lewites succeeded because he recognized and accepted unpalatable realities which some other Sandinistas sought to avoid: that the cordoba had become utterly worthless, that it would ever be so, that a dollar economy was emerging in Nicaragua, and that fighting the trend was pointless. Naturally the opening of the store provoked protests, since it immediately created a two-class system in which those with access to dollars could live and eat far better than those who dealt only in the national currency. But the store was so successful that such objections were easily overruled.

To keep the dollar store stocked, Lewites worked with several dummy companies in Panama that imported goods from the United States and elsewhere for resale to Nicaragua. He simply prepared lists of what he needed and sent them to associates in Panama, who ordered the goods and then shipped them to Managua. One of the Sandinista agents in Panama was a friend of mine, and I was able to watch his net worth expand geometrically as the dollar store boomed. The last time I heard from him, he had bought a second yacht.

At the dollar store in Managua, Lewites charged high prices and realized a profit margin of about fifty percent. People nonetheless flocked to shop there, and to meet the demand, branch stores were opened in Granada, Matagalpa, and other provincial capitals. By the late 1980s they were generating more than twenty percent of the government's total hard-currency earnings.

Sandinista leaders had a ready justification for allowing the dollar complexes to thrive. In the face of so many pressures from the United States, they argued, they needed to capture foreign currency every way they could. Still, many Nicaraguans viewed the complexes as a sign of economic surrender. Their success meant that the Sandinistas had essentially given up on their own currency.

One day I met a tiny street urchin outside the door of the Managua dollar store. This youngster, like others who congregated in the area, earned small tips by helping customers with their packages. He approached me and mumbled something. Thinking he was offering to carry my grocery bag, I started to brush him off, but then I noticed that he was waving a 100-cordoba note at me. This seemed unusual, even though the note was worth only a few cents, so I stopped to hear him out.

"Do you have an apple you could sell me?" he asked.

Apples were one of the many items that had once been easily available in Nicaragua, but completely disappeared soon after the 1979 revolution. Herty Lewites had begun importing apples from Oregon, and as it happened I had bought a package that day. I reached into my bag and offered an apple to my young acquaintance. He seemed overwhelmed when I told him to keep his

hundred cordobas. I could see other ragged children watching us from behind
nearby cars. After a moment, I handed the whole package of apples to the boy.
He called to his friends, and they came running. As I pulled away from the
parking lot, I saw him beginning to distribute the fruit among his wide-eyed pals.
That day I drove home feeling unusually sad.

Once when I was in a supermarket in San José, Costa Rica, I wandered past
the fruit juice section and came upon a display of cranberry juice. I decided to
buy some and bring it home. I realized that carrying a single bottle wouldn't
make much sense, so I asked the store manager to sell me a case. He was puzzled
at first, but when I told him I lived in Nicaragua he understood immediately.
We found an empty cardboard box, carefully packed a dozen bottles into it, and
taped it tightly. At the airport, I checked the box as luggage and brought it home
without incident. Having cranberry juice around was a welcome taste of home,
and I bought more every time I passed through San José.

So far as I could gather, no Nicaraguan had ever tasted or even heard of
cranberry juice. I was reflecting on this esoteric topic during a flight home from
Costa Rica one day when I was struck by inspiration. The following day, I typed
a letter to Herty Lewites telling him that cranberry juice was very popular in
the United States and that it would definitely sell briskly at the dollar store. I
gave the letter to Guillermo to deliver, along with a bottle of the tart red juice
I had bought in Costa Rica.

Several months later I walked into the dollar store and, to my amazement,
found myself facing an entire shelf packed with bottles of Ocean Spray cranberry
juice. That day I bought half a dozen bottles, and over the following weeks I
made a point of buying several each time I visited. At first I feared no one else
would buy the stuff, but before long I began noticing that bottles were disappear-
ing from the shelf between my visits. Soon it began selling steadily, and before
long bottles of Cran-grape and Cran-apple juice appeared on the shelves. They
all sold well, and after a while I began to think of myself as a kind of Johnny
Appleseed. I congratulated myself for having introduced cranberry juice to
Nicaragua, but Lewites actually deserved the credit. Had there been ten or
twenty more clear-headed realists like him in the upper ranks of the Sandinista
Front, Nicaragua's history during the 1980s might have been profoundly different.

It did not take long for the tourism ministry to move into the restaurant
business, which like most other businesses was in a state of collapse. Many of
the small, working-class hangouts in Managua, the places where poor people
could buy a tortilla with something hot, had been run by ambitious, hardworking entrepreneurs who believed they deserved to profit from their labor.
Most of them closed during the early years of Sandinista rule, their owners
unable or unwilling to adapt to new conditions. As food shortages became more
widespread, the government began rationing meat and produce sold to restau-

rants, and forbade owners to buy from private distributors. Later all restaurants, bars, and cafés were ordered to set their menu prices according to government lists. Many of the most popular restaurants in Managua closed their doors, and others were absorbed wholly or partially by the tourism ministry. After a while Herty Lewites became not only the country's sole department-store operator, but also its principal restaurateur.

As restaurants and bars closed, other forms of entertainment also began to disappear. Cinemas, once favorite gathering places, were allowed to become filthy and unpleasant. Television, operated entirely by the government, offered an unappetizing mix of soap operas, crudely partisan news programs, Soviet and East-bloc propaganda films, and occasional old American features like "Gone With the Wind." Programming aimed at children was as mindless as that in the United States, composed mostly of inane American-made cartoons and sit-coms like "Mr. Ed." Nicaragua's symphony orchestra, which had been assembled and subsidized through the patronage of Hope Somoza, wife of the last dictator, dissolved when the dictatorship fell and was never reassembled.

The National Theater, which had also been built under Hope Somoza's patronage, was used for a few performances in the early 1980s, including a locally produced tribute to Sandino and a performance by a visiting symphony orchestra from Cuba. Inevitably, it fell into disrepair. In 1982 it was closed because the air conditioning had ceased working, and no parts were available to repair it. It took four years to find the parts, and the theater finally reopened with a performance of Bulgarian folk dances.

One of the many valuable commodities that became steadily scarcer in Managua was water. Each house was without water for at least two days each week. In the zone where I lived, Tuesday and Friday were dry days. This rationing was imposed, like so many Sandinista measures, with a simple and logical-sounding goal, that of saving water. In practice, however, the system fell victim to the anarchic impulses which are part of the Nicaraguan psyche. At nearly every home in my zone, all faucets were turned on full blast late Monday and late Thursday, and every available bucket, tub, and barrel was filled with water for use the following day. A certain amount would be consumed over the course of the day, but most would be dumped at nightfall, when water pressure was restored. So much water was wasted this way each week that I could not imagine the ration system was working. I tried to investigate, but found that statistics about water use were considered secret.

Cutoffs of water were usually announced in advance, but electricity cutoffs were not. As Nicaragua became poorer, it found itself unable to buy the petroleum it needed to keep electric current flowing. Venezuela and Mexico were selling oil to Central American countries at concessionary rates, but even those rates were too high for the Sandinistas to pay. Soon the Soviet Union was supplying nearly all of Nicaragua's petroleum, putting the country at the mercy of international shipping patterns. If a Soviet dispatcher had to hold a tanker in port for a couple of days, or if a paying customer appeared who suddenly wanted to buy oil earmarked for Nicaragua, or if inclement weather or unscheduled stops delayed a shipment, all of Nicaragua would grind to a halt.

Petroleum supplies were so tight that newspapers sometimes carried daily progress reports of tankers steaming toward Corinto with the precious cargo. When they were overdue and supplies ran low, officials would simply cut off electricity without warning, plunging entire regions into darkness. Often the same thing happened when there was supposedly plenty of oil on hand, and it was impossible to find out why.

These blackouts not only disrupted daily life, but also cost the country huge amounts of lost production. The problem was not simply that food spoiled in refrigerators, or that offices were left to function in sweltering darkness, or that hospitals were paralyzed and their refrigerated vaccines ruined, but that large factories and industrial plants were forced to shut down. It was quite common to arrive at the metal fabricating plant or one of the large textile mills or another place where hundreds of people were employed, and to find workers lounging around outside, waiting for power to be turned back on. Often the blackouts lasted for hours, and not infrequently for days on end.

Telephone service was no more reliable than water or electric service. Never was it possible to complete more than half the calls I needed to make within the city. Often I found myself writing notes to people who lived in other parts of Managua and dispatching Guillermo to carry them like a Pony Express rider. There were two phone lines at the *Times* bureau, but we considered ourselves fortunate when one was working. Neighbors would stop by to make calls when their phones were out of order, and returned the favor by allowing me into their homes when my phones went dead. Finding a working telephone, however, was only a start. Most frequently, the number dialed was either out of service or busy. If a call was completed and answered, there was every prospect that it would be a wrong number. Hardly a day passed at the *Times* bureau, for example, without someone calling and asking to make a reservation on Aeroflot, the Soviet airline.

Telephoning abroad, which more and more Nicaraguans did as their friends and relatives moved away, was even more challenging. For a while, direct international dialing was possible, but one day the Sandinistas announced that henceforth all long-distance calls would have to be placed through an operator. The reasons, of course, were never announced. Some speculated that the new system was a way of controlling the abuse of direct-dial lines by employees at government offices. Others guessed that it was a security measure, designed to give the government a record of who was calling who in foreign countries. Whatever the reason, the result was highly frustrating. After dialing 116 for the international operator, one would most likely hear a busy signal. Even hearing a ring was no guarantee that an operator would answer soon; I once watched an entire basketball game on television with the telephone receiver cradled on my shoulder, waiting for the overseas operator to answer. Sometimes it took ten or fifteen attempts to connect with an operator, other times fifty or a hundred attempts over a period of days.

Not all the problems that crippled the telephone and electric systems were the result of bureaucratic failures. As wire became scarce and then unavailable in Managua, people would sometimes creep into a neighborhood at night and cut themselves a 100- or 150-foot length of wire from the utility grid. Once when my phones stopped working, we discovered that the wire outside my house had been stolen. The government had no way to replace wire except in cases of most dire emergency, and I realized that unless I took matters into my own hands, my phones would probably never work again. Guillermo dropped his daily duties and went to scour Managua in search of telephone wire. It took many days, but after a series of adventures he appeared with a whole spool. It took a week for us to locate our telephone repair crew, the one we paid directly, but ultimately the operation was successful and my phones came back to life.

One morning when I awoke to find my telephone lines out of order, I looked down my street and was amazed to see a repair crew already working. Rarely did crews respond so quickly, so I inquired what special circumstance applied in this case. It turned out that the Libyan embassy, which was around the corner from our bureau, had also lost phone service, and the Sandinistas did not want to irritate Libya, one of the few countries that still gave them aid in hard currency. The repair took only a few hours, and after it was finished, the repairmen stopped into our office to chat with Guillermo. For their work outside the Libyan embassy, each of them had been given a handsome green book containing quotations from Libyan leader Muammar Khadaffy. They left the books in a pile in my office, and there they sat for months as we tried unsuccessfully to give them away.

Another chronic problem that afflicted Sandinista Nicaragua was public transportation. The government bought a fleet of buses from Brazil on credit, and then several dozen more from Argentina that bore the slogan, "Let's Take Care of These Buses," but the Ministry of Transport frankly admitted that the number never surpassed half of what was needed. Buses in Managua were not only packed tightly, but overflowed with passengers who rode on roofs and hung from windows. Pickup trucks, converted tractors, and even donkey carts were pressed into service, but still transportation was a nightmare, especially for poor people. A Nicaraguan might spend two hours each morning waiting in sweltering heat for a bus before finding one to squeeze into, only to arrive at work exhausted from the ordeal, certainly not in condition to do a decent day's labor.

One measure of Nicaragua's steady economic decline was that once something ceased to function, it usually never functioned again. If a streetlight went dark, it would most likely never be lit again, because there was probably no equipment to repair it. When a tractor broke down, it would most likely sit until it rusted away. I used to drive regularly past a large open field in Managua where dozens of buses were parked, each immobilized by some mechanical problem, none ever to see service again. There was no money to fix anything, or to maintain what was not yet broken.

Nowhere was this syndrome more visible than in the taxi fleet. Because bus service was so unreliable, people all over Nicaragua, and especially in Managua, did most of their local travel in collective taxis. These were not large, American-made sedans like the ones that waited on tourists at the airport or in front of the Intercontinental Hotel, but small Japanese cars. They were like normal taxis in that they had no fixed routes, but they accepted as many passengers as could be crammed inside. The taxis seemed to deteriorate before our eyes. By the late 1980s, many had no doors or windows, others were without fenders or hoods, and nearly all were crumbling with rust. They became so anemic that their drivers would often take circuitous routes to avoid hills, since the cabs could no longer climb steep grades.

As people waited in those interminable lines, and as they cursed water shortages, blackouts, and other deteriorating public services, their thoughts naturally turned to those responsible. After a period of years living under such conditions, many began to tire of explanations that had to do with American aggression and, quite naturally, began to blame the Sandinistas. The truth about who actually bore the blame was irrelevant at these moments. All that mattered was what people believed. Many were inclined to sympathize with the regime at first, but gradually they began to lose patience and grumble.

Economic troubles were not the only reason for spreading discontent. Sandinista leaders also paid dearly for their personal conduct, which profoundly and permanently alienated many Nicaraguans. By living flamboyantly and in luxury, or at least allowing people to believe that they did, they conveyed an impression of recklessness and immaturity that seriously undermined their authority.

Immediately upon taking power, the *comandantes* began acting in ways that reminded many people of their deposed predecessors. They confiscated many of the finest homes in Managua and moved into them, seemingly determined to live in a manner that would compensate them for all the deprivation they had suffered during their years as guerrilla fighters. Not only did they begin driving fancy cars, but they drove sleek, brand-new Mercedes-Benz sedans that were the most luxurious vehicles in Nicaragua. As it happened, Mercedes-Benz had been the preferred car of the Somoza elite, so the sight of Sandinista *comandantes* racing them around town conjured up especially repugnant memories. When on the road, they were always trailed by lengthy motorcades and surrounded by phalanxes of security agents, who wore orange gloves to wave outsiders away and raised their rifles to warn drivers who came too close. There are only a few main roads in Nicaragua, and before long everyone had seen the *comandantes* speeding between their mansions in automobiles that had once been reserved for the Somozas and their cronies.

Many journalists wrote about the strangeness of life in the Sandinista state. Among the more successful was Raquel Fernández of the official New Nicaragua Agency, whose thoughts were published in the pro-Sandinista newspaper *Nuevo Diario:*

> To live in Managua is a daily adventure, whether you are trying to get to work or home, to buy your beans and rice, to take a bus or to escape from one, to make a telephone call, or to resolve the slightest problem.
>
> Every day citizens are surprised by some unexpected change. These are not small changes that might pass unnoticed. In Managua, anything can appear anywhere. Things as supposedly immobile as neighborhoods, streets, avenues, plazas, parks, and monuments appear and disappear regularly. And all of this happens without a single notice in the newspapers or on radio, without explanations or excuses from anyone. As in Kafka's universe, these things happen without anyone appearing surprised or puzzled . . .
>
> It can easily happen, if you live in that thing which is commonly called Managua, that you leave your house for work in the morning and when you return, you find that in order to reach home sweet home, you must tiptoe across a fragile board laid across a deep trench that was not there ten hours before . . . Or perhaps you are afraid of walking through a lonely or abandoned area, until one day you go there and find a large and booming neighborhood where until yesterday there was only a barren field. In a matter of weeks or days or hours, the entire panorama changes as completely as if it were the work of a decorator.
>
> In the days of Somoza, everything was inaugurated. The laying of a section of pipe required the presence of a minister, or at least the director of a state agency . . . Anything larger required the presence of Somoza himself. Things reached the point where Somoza was inaugurating something every weekend . . . The Sandinistas, on the contrary, announce nothing . . .
>
> In the deepest bowels of ministries that deal with these matters, obscure and unknown persons draw up plans and design projects aimed at somehow improving this overflowing capital . . . When their studies are finally finished, a small crew of workers, armed with picks and shovels, begins doing something. Anyone who asks what they are doing receives the same response: "Who knows? Some damn thing!"

During my years in Managua, several of my more adventurous friends and relatives came to visit. The first to dare was my sister Jane, who arrived only a few months after I assumed my post. Her flight was with Taca Airlines, the Salvadoran carrier, and was due in Managua at 7 P.M. one starlit evening. I was at the airport in plenty of time, but the plane did not appear. No announcement was made, and there was no one to answer inquiries at the Taca counter. These delays were not uncommon, and I sat patiently with the waiting crowd for several hours. People began to drift away, and finally, at around ten o'clock, an airport employee announced that the Taca flight had been delayed in El Salvador and would not be arriving that night. I drove home wondering where Jane would be sleeping.

Hours later, I was roused from bed by a commotion in front of my house. I pulled on a bathrobe and stumbled through the darkness to investigate. Someone was pounding on my door. I opened it, and there stood Jane, her suitcase beside her. She glared at me, then started to smile and shake her head.

"No problem!" she said before I could apologize, raising her hands high in a gesture of surrender. "Just send me through El Salvador, get me to Nicaragua after midnight, and then don't be at the airport to meet me. I only speak ten words of Spanish, but it's fine! Just abandon me in the middle of the night in countries that are having civil wars! No problem!"

Some mishap at the El Salvador airport, it turned out, had delayed Jane's connection. She told me she had spent several hours sitting on the tarmac, sharing a bottle of rum with some Salvadoran maintenance workers, and had then wandered around the terminal for more hours. Finally she and the other passengers were permitted to board their plane and fly to Managua, but upon arriving most found themselves in the same predicament: no one was waiting to greet them, since an erroneous announcement had been made that the flight was canceled. Jane had passed through Sandinista customs, carried her suitcase out into the nighttime heat, and noticed what looked like a film crew piling into a van nearby. She walked over, and after being disappointed to learn that no member of the crew spoke English, she asked, "Kinzer? Stephen Kinzer?"

The crew, it turned out, was a free-lance outfit that worked with American television networks. The cameramen had no idea what Jane was talking about, but the Nicaraguan driver knew immediately. Ours was a small and tightly knit group, and that night I was grateful for it.

"Kinzer!" the driver exclaimed. *"Claro que sí!"*

Half an hour later, Jane was at my house banging on the door. The driver who had deposited her there was sitting in his van, waiting to be sure she managed to rouse me. I thanked him profusely, and then picked up Jane's suitcase and showed her in. We sat in wicker rocking chairs on my patio, and she seemed none the worse for her little ordeal.

"It was OK, don't worry about it," she assured me over a glass of tamarind juice. "Actually, it was kind of fun."

One of Jane's first surprises was the racket on my zinc roof. Sometimes we would hear a slow, scratching noise above our heads, and other times loud bangs. Iguanas were living in the neighborhood, and they liked to sun themselves on my roof. When a door slammed or there was some other loud noise, they would scamper noisily away.

Iguanas do not normally live in urban areas, but since the 1972 earthquake Managua had ceased to be a real urban area. Exotic animals like iguanas and bats and hummingbirds were common there, and farm animals roamed freely. Most Managuans were only a generation or two removed from the farm, if that, and when food became expensive and scarce, they thought nothing of keeping livestock in the vacant lots that surrounded their homes. The animals were not penned or tethered, and could often be seen moseying along main streets and standing in public plazas, as if they were waiting for the remaining humans to leave so they could have Managua to themselves.

Cows wandered at will, stopping to feed on the lush foliage whenever they pleased. A pair of them often spent the day at a lot next to the Japanese embassy on my block, and occasionally one of them wandered down to my house and peered through the open door into our bureau. Goats were also common, and small herds of them grazed peaceably in rocky fields near the interior ministry and behind the bakery at Plaza España. Chickens were even more plentiful, and at dawn roosters crowed loudly, as if we were living in some frontier farm town.

The frontier image was reinforced by the cattle drives that passed through town every few weeks. Dusty cowboys on horseback would drive fifty or a hundred of the hulking beasts down one of the city's principal avenues as if they were crossing an uninhabited prairie. City authorities, after much debate, once announced that they were permanently banning all livestock from the city, and stern notices were published in daily newspapers warning of severe fines and other penalties. People simply ignored the decree, and it never had the slightest effect.

All who lived in Managua had to adjust to its dreary ugliness. Many of us, foreigners as well as Nicaraguans, sought refuge in the beauty of nature. Nicaragua is sometimes called the land of lakes and volcanoes, but that is a stock tourist phrase that does not capture the fullness of the landscape's splendor.

Nicaragua has a geological history no less dramatic than its political history. Little of the western half of the country is flat. Gently rolling hills abruptly give way to forbidding mountain ranges that stretch for miles, impenetrable and spectacular. Multi-colored butterflies share the skies with tropical birds, and the land is alive with reptiles, amphibians, and all manner of four-legged creatures. Sunsets are lush and full of fiery color. Most memorable of all are the rainbows, which often appear following afternoon downpours. I found them brighter and crisper, and their colors more sharply separated, than any rainbows I had ever seen. Sometimes, to make the spectacle even more gorgeous, they formed circles rather than arcs.

There are two seasons in the Nicaraguan year. From September to April, all is dry and dusty, and trees slowly wither from lack of moisture. By April, the countryside is barren and brown, ugly, harsh, and inhospitable. Then suddenly the rains begin, and everything seems to bloom overnight.

Nicaraguan rainstorms were unlike anything I had ever witnessed. Watching them became my favorite form of entertainment. When the rain began, I would stop working and move to a part of my house where I could sit under a roof and watch the giant drops splatter on my patio a few feet away.

The end of April and the beginning of May is a period of anticipation in Nicaragua, as everyone waits for the first rainstorm. Newspapers publish lengthy interviews with meteorologists on their front pages, and inside they carry reports about gifted peasants who have devised mystical systems of weather prediction. Then one afternoon, with fury built up over six dry and dusty months, the skies open to release the season's first storm, always one of stunning force. Sheets of rain engulf Managua, and wildly flowing torrents tear destructively through poor and rich neighborhoods alike. Vehicles are trapped in mudslides, looters help themselves to goods from destroyed stores and warehouses, and thousands of private homes are inundated.

Nicaraguan rainstorms can be impressive to the point of inspiration. Water not only falls from the sky but also seems to spout from the trees and the streets. Parents keep their children indoors to prevent them from being carried away by raging currents. Rain makes so much noise on rooftops that conversation becomes difficult. Thunderclaps explode with deafening volume, and vivid bolts of lightning illuminate the sky. Usually the storms come late in the day, unleashing their power without warning and then stopping with equal suddenness, as if utterly spent.

The beauty of these storms does not mitigate their destructive power. The city has only a rudimentary drainage system, based on a network of ditches, some of them lined with concrete, that are supposed to carry rainwater into Lake Managua. Each year their inadequacy is proven anew, as water cascades down from nearby hills, quickly overflows the ditches and rushes through slum areas, sweeping away dwellings built precariously of cardboard and refuse. Patrons at restaurants, cinemas, and other public places often find themselves trapped, unable to return home because of washed-out streets or bridges. Electric power fails in most of the city, patients have to be moved from hospitals, and important factories and office centers are seriously damaged.

One year, at considerable expense, the government built a large convention hall so that it could play host to a conference of the World Inter-Parliamentary Union, an organization of legislators from around the world. The conference was scheduled for the beginning of May, and builders were thus directed to take special precautions against flooding. The conference, from which the Sandinistas sought to win a measure of international prestige, ended without trouble on a Saturday at midday, and the hall was closed after final speeches. But that evening, only hours after the conference ended, the first storm burst onto Managua. Waves of water flooded into the new convention hall, triggering a round of recriminations and finger-pointing among engineers and government officials. When Daniel Ortega arrived at ten o'clock to inspect the damage, he was walking in water up to his knees.

The rainstorms seem to have an emotional effect on many Nicaraguans. In the countryside, peasants take them as signals of rebirth, the way that people in colder countries view the advent of spring. Some men bare their chests and prance outdoors during the first storm, echoing an ancient Indian ritual. The advent of the rainy season has even become an archetype in Nicaraguan literature. "The atmosphere, polluted by dust and ash, becomes clear and brilliant after the rain falls," wrote the commentator Octavio Robleto in one of his essays about Managua. "Windows can be opened because the air is amiable." Azarias Pallais, a prominent poet who died in 1954, recalled that it was on the night of the first storm that the elderly maid who raised him would tell the strangest tales of the year. "Another of the miracles of the rain is that it puts a new mantle on my city, as if washing it," Pallais wrote. "I feel that I am in one of those austere and impeccable Dutch cities, a clean city without dust, brand-new and blessedly neat."

At first light on the morning after one of these downpours, I set out to wander the streets, and I found Managua devastated but also cleansed. A few people were still trying to make their way home. Others were digging automobiles out of mud banks or trying to resurrect damaged homes. Beside one of the drainage ditches where cement panels had been ripped from their moorings like tissue, people were picking through debris, hoping to find objects of value swept away from other places. Behind one of my favorite restaurants, Rincón Criollo, the owner was surveying his losses. All he could say was all that any Nicaraguan could say when reflecting on the unkindness of fate.

"The Lord giveth and the Lord taketh away," he said. "That is life."

12

COMANDANTES

FLOATING ABOVE Nicaraguan life, directing the nation from behind a curtain no outsider could penetrate, were the nine Sandinista *comandantes* who called themselves the National Directorate. They held what amounted to absolute political power, and their word was law on every matter. Yet until the moment they took over in July 1979, they were clandestine revolutionaries and hence completely unknown to most Nicaraguans. Only one of them, Tomás Borge, whose prison hunger strike had been a rallying point for radicals in the mid-1970s, was at all prominent, and no one knew much about him except that he was a dedicated Sandinista.

When Somoza was ousted in July 1979 and the five-member junta was sworn in to replace him, most people assumed that the junta would be Nicaragua's new government. Even two of the original junta members, Alfonso Robelo and Violeta Chamorro, made that error in judgment. The truth was that the National Directorate, a group most Nicaraguans did not even know existed, held ultimate political control, and that the junta was only a facade through which it ruled. This became clear within a few months after the Sandinista victory, and when it did, curiosity about the Directorate became intense. People began realizing that these nine obscure Nicaraguans, most of them in their mid-thirties or younger, now held the fate of the nation in their hands.

172

By definition, Sandinista leaders had led lives far different from those of most Nicaraguans. Some had briefly held paying jobs, but nearly all had been full-time conspirators for many years. They had spent extended periods in exile, mostly in Fidel Castro's Cuba. Their need to work deep underground sealed them off from the mainstream of Nicaraguan life. They developed a kind of fervent mysticism about their cause that they called *mística,* a quasi-religious dedication that set them quite apart from conventional politicians. They believed they were a "vanguard" which, through valor in the anti-Somoza struggle, had won moral authority to rule.

The National Directorate, Nicaraguans soon learned, was not the group of political and military leaders who had guided the Sandinista Front through its two-decade struggle for power. There was no such group, and never had been. The Sandinista Front had been composed of independent and even antagonistic factions since Carlos Fonseca's death in 1976. It was only in March 1979, after Fidel Castro insisted that feuding Sandinista leaders unite, that the nine men who were to assume national leadership came together. Thus, these were not nine people who had worked shoulder to shoulder planning the revolution as journalists had first believed. They were a group of men who shared basic principles, but who had been denouncing and purging each other for years. It was not until after the Sandinistas had won their war, in fact, that the National Directorate even met at full strength for the first time.

To many outsiders, the oddest aspect of the Directorate was that the heroic Edén Pastora was not one of its members. We understood Pastora to be one of the most senior Sandinistas, and while the rebellion was underway the Sandinista Front encouraged that belief. But the truth, as we slowly learned, was that he had never been part of the Sandinista inner circle. Other leading Sandinistas never fully trusted him. In the first place, his political motivation was always suspect. He had a background of family loyalty to the Conservative party, which many Sandinistas scorned as a party of traitors. He had worked with various anti-Somoza groups, not just the Sandinista Front, and when revolutionary activity ebbed he would return to his shark fishing business rather than accept life underground or in Havana. Above all, he was too flamboyant and undisciplined to be a good Sandinista. The same freewheeling ego that helped make him such a popular figure marked him as dangerously individualistic in the eyes of other *comandantes.*

From the first weeks of Sandinista rule, Pastora was shunted aside, given positions of secondary importance—deputy minister of the interior, then deputy minister of defense. He could have remained in Nicaragua, enjoyed the perquisites of power, and made a career as a parlor Marxist, regaling sympathetic audiences in Europe and Latin America with fiery rhetoric. Instead, he tired of the routine. One day in July 1981, he slipped out of Nicaragua on a small plane, telling aides he was meeting a girlfriend in Panama and would be back shortly.

Once safely in Panama, he announced that he was through with the Sandinista Front and that he had cut all ties to the regime in Managua. In a cryptic letter, he hinted that he was preparing to join guerrillas in Guatemala or some other Latin American country.

The mercurial Panamanian leader, General Omar Torrijos, was the closest political friend Pastora ever had. Both were prodigious drinkers and womanizers, and over many long nights at Farallón, Torrijos's seaside villa, they formed an intimate bond that was personal as well as political. Torrijos had a vision of non-Marxist revolution in Central America, of regimes like his own that sought to maintain political and economic freedoms while channeling public resources to the poor. Pastora was the man who could transform this vision into reality as a guerrilla leader, and the two made a promising team. Torrijos would supply the political shrewdness, the money, and the international protection for new revolutions, and Pastora would organize and help direct them. Both men had begun to sour on the Sandinistas, and both wanted to undercut Sandinista-style revolutions in other countries by offering a different kind.

Torrijos lived chaotically, and he governed Panama the same way. He was a country boy at heart, and loved nothing better than dropping into small villages in his helicopter for first-hand views of Panamanian life. At the end of July 1982, he traveled to the village of Coclecito to inspect a new lumber mill. As his copter was returning to Panama City through a driving rainstorm, it suddenly plunged toward earth and crashed. All aboard were killed.

Torrijos's death left Edén Pastora without a political mooring. From Panama he drifted to Cuba, where he made contact with a Guatemalan guerrilla group, the Revolutionary Organization of the People in Arms *(Organización Revolucionaria del Pueblo Armado, ORPA)* and decided to join its struggle to overthrow the Guatemalan military regime. Seeking funds for ORPA, he traveled to Algeria and then to Libya, where Muammar Khadaffy promised him $5 million. The money was never forthcoming, and in any case ORPA leaders were not keen on the idea of Pastora coming to fight in Guatemala.

Soon Pastora began to focus his attention back on the Sandinistas. He had become highly critical of their close ties to Cuba and the Soviet Union, which he said violated their pledge of nonalignment. For a while no one paid attention to his denunciations. Most Nicaraguans were stunned when he announced in mid-1982 that he was taking up arms not against the Guatemalan or Salvadoran regime, but against his former comrades, the Sandinistas. His emergence as an anti-Sandinista guerrilla leader marked the closing of a remarkable circle. In just three years, the man we once believed was running the Sandinista Front had become its sworn enemy.

In the months after issuing his declaration of war on the Sandinistas, Pastora was elusive, rarely spending more than one or two nights in the same bed. It took me some effort to track him down, but finally, working through friends of friends, I arranged to meet him one night late in 1982 at his home outside San José, Costa Rica. One of his aides picked me up at my hotel in a nondescript sedan, and we drove toward the cool hills outside town. At the end of a long drive guarded by armed men stood Pastora's rambling manse, part residence and part command post. Although the hour was late, there was much noise and activity. Jeeps and armored cars came and went, radios squawked, telephones rang, and men read coded messages into short-wave microphones. Detailed maps of Nicaragua covered the walls inside. On one porch, a Galil assault rifle was propped against a tricycle that belonged to one of Pastora's many children.

At that time Pastora was forty-five years old, but he looked fit to fight. Tall, fair-skinned, and handsome, he nonetheless had a roughness about him. When he entered the room where I was waiting, I instantly sensed the aura that had made him the most popular of Sandinistas.

Pastora beckoned me into his small office, where an automatic rifle hung on the wall and a pistol lay within easy reach. The only decoration was a portrait of Omar Torrijos, and I asked about it. Pastora held up his hand to show me a diamond-encrusted ring.

"Torrijos gave me this," he said softly. "Torrijos was the man. He had a project for Central America."

He reminisced about Torrijos for a while, then turned to other topics. Soon, inevitably, our conversation turned to the 1978 National Palace takeover that had catapulted him to worldwide fame. If Somoza's Guardsmen had decided to storm the Palace, I asked, would he and the other commandos actually have killed the high-ranking hostages they had captured?

"Absolutely," he replied. "When you choose people for a mission like that, they only need to have two qualities. They have to be ready to die, and they have to be ready to kill."

For several hours, Pastora treated me to a stream-of-consciousness monologue on the nature of revolution, the duty of revolutionaries, and sundry other topics.

"That gang in power in Managua today is a bunch of frauds!" he shouted at one point, pounding a fist on his desk. "None of those Sandinista leaders ever participated in a major battle. They sat back while others fought! Only by realizing this fact can you understand why they were corrupted so easily."

Sandinista leaders had accused Pastora of having no ideology, and I asked him if it was true.

"I remain what I have always been, an anti-imperialist revolutionary," he replied. "I can die peacefully because I have followed my conscience. If I could be born again, I would do everything just the same."

ONCE Pastora dealt himself out of the Managua regime, journalists and other outsiders tried to figure out which *comandante* would ultimately emerge as the principal Sandinista leader. By process of elimination, we narrowed the number down considerably. Whoever was to become Nicaragua's strongman would have to emerge from the National Directorate. The Directorate had nine members, and some of them were unlikely choices.

The hell-raising student leader Bayardo Arce was young, inexperienced, and unknown. So were prep school graduate Luis Carrión and urban organizer Carlos Núñez. Another member of the Directorate, Victor Tirado, had accumulated sterling revolutionary credentials over many years, but had been born in Mexico and was thus probably disqualified from national leadership. That reduced the number of prospects to five, and we cut the number further by eliminating Humberto Ortega, who had shown his willingness to defer to his older brother Daniel. As the Sandinistas began their subtle, drawn-out private battle for personal power, there were only four possible victors.

Two of the four who might have come to lead Nicaragua fell by the wayside during the early years of Sandinista rule, one because of his professional failures and one seemingly by choice. Jaime Wheelock, the self-styled intellectual who had urged his comrades to "declare socialism" the day they took power, struck many who met him as a fine combination of thinker and doer. As Minister of Agrarian Reform, Wheelock was in one of the most visible and most crucial government posts. He had no direct experience in agriculture, but he had read a lot of books, and that made him more qualified for the job than any of his Sandinista brethren. Agriculture is Nicaragua's lifeblood, and if Wheelock had done his job well he might have become the brightest Sandinista star. Instead he failed spectacularly.

Nicaraguans realized that a large measure of blame for their country's economic collapse was due to the host of pressures applied by the United States. Even Sandinista leaders themselves, however, acknowledged that they themselves bore a share of the blame, and as time passed they assigned more and more of the blame to Wheelock. He had imposed a complex system of regulations that upset rural life and led thousands of peasants to give up farming altogether. By the time the Sandinistas finally began abandoning those policies in the mid-1980s, irreparable damage had been done not only to the Nicaraguan economy, but also to Jaime Wheelock's political prospects.

The next remaining *comandante* was the most mysterious, Henry Ruiz. Little was known about his background, other than that he had been an outstanding student, joined the Moscow-line Nicaraguan Socialist party as a youth, and attended Patrice Lumumba University in Moscow. Most important, he had been the legendary guerrilla leader called Modesto, one of the few Sandinistas whose image reached mythic proportions.

Outsiders often assumed that Sandinista *comandantes* had won their positions by surviving years of miserable guerrilla war, but as Pastora loved to point out, that was not really true. Most had lived relatively comfortable lives in exile during much of the anti-Somoza struggle. Modesto was the exception, the Sandinista who had actually lived and fought the way Sandinistas were supposed to have lived and fought.

Three weeks after the Sandinista takeover, Ruiz set off on a mission to four countries that were projected as major benefactors: the Soviet Union, Bulgaria, Algeria, and Libya. He returned with only a series of "technical agreements," the contents of which were never revealed, and without the promises of largesse for which some *comandantes* had hoped. Soon afterward, he was named Minister of Planning, a job for which he was completely unprepared. With guerrilla warfare his only real experience in life, he was entrusted with the complex task of drawing up economic plans for reconstructing a war-devastated nation.

As the economy began to fall apart, Ruiz shared some of the blame that was heaped on Wheelock. Later his ministry was abolished and he was made Minister of Foreign Cooperation, assigned to carry Nicaragua's tin cup from one donor country to another. He never made a serious bid for power within the Sandinista Front, and unlike other *comandantes,* he avoided the press and seemed to disdain the staged adulation of Sandinista rallies. He rarely appeared in public, lived without ostentation, and seemed to accept being pushed aside. I never came to know him, but from afar I sensed that after years of fighting in the mountains, he was not fulfilled by life as a bureaucrat. He seemed more connected to the real world than some of his comrades, more aware of the breadth of the tragedy that was enveloping his country. When a Nicaraguan reporter asked him once to assess the results of Sandinista rule, he replied not with the usual slogans but with a laconic observation of his own.

"Governing has not been our best success," he said.

By the time the Sandinistas had been in power for a few years, only two *comandantes* were still serious candidates for national leadership, Tomás Borge and Daniel Ortega. Both had devoted their lives to the cause of revolution. They shared a passionate belief in the basic principles laid down originally by Carlos Fonseca: deep antipathy toward capitalism and toward the United States, and a conviction that Marxism held the key to social progress in Nicaragua and the rest of Latin America. If asked separately to give their views on Fidel Castro, or on the role of American corporations in the world, or on any other important international or domestic question, Ortega and Borge would give very similar replies. Yet they were longtime rivals, separated not only by years but by profound differences of character.

Daniel Ortega was often described as the leading moderate within the Sandinista Front, in contrast to the supposedly more radical Tomás Borge. Ortega and those around him, after all, had conceived the strategy of alliances which brought the Sandinistas to power, rejecting Borge's thesis that victory could only be won by waging "prolonged people's war." The notion that Ortega was a moderate was reinforced by his good behavior on the five-member junta, where he showed himself to be reassuringly rational and open-minded.

Borge, by contrast, assumed the newly created post of interior minister. Because the distasteful tasks of domestic repression and counter-intelligence fell to him, he was blamed most directly for Sandinista human rights abuses. I always believed, however, that Ortega would have been just as implacable a jailer as Borge if that had been his job. The image of the two men as cultural opposites, a crusty old hard-liner and an innovative moderate, persisted mostly because they themselves encouraged it. Borge liked being perceived as a super-spymaster who saw all and knew all. Ortega, for his part, enjoyed basking in the praise of political and religious leaders from Europe and Latin America, some of whom even persuaded themselves that he was simply a social democrat in third world guise.

There was a swagger about Tomás Borge that could be either reassuring or terrifying. Physically he was not imposing, especially when compared to the charismatic Pastora. He was short and stubby, with fleshy cheeks and large ears. His hairline receded and his waist thickened as the years passed, but he never lost his air of command. He was always playing one role or another. In many ways he was the most cultured and sophisticated member of the National Directorate, the only one who had read Flaubert and Dante, and he was also one of the few among them who mixed easily with ordinary people.

Borge was born in the northern city of Matagalpa on August 13, 1930, son of a bookish father and a mother who ran a small general store. Like many Sandinista *comandantes,* he was distressed from an early age by the social injustices around him, and angered by the repressive arrogance of the Somozas and their American supporters. He joined his first protest at the age of thirteen, and at sixteen was first imprisoned.

When talking about his childhood, Borge often recalled the popular novels of the German author Karl May as important to his developing consciousness. May wrote simple good-versus-evil stories set in the American West, and Borge was attracted by the romantic purity of Western life. In one interview, he went so far as to declare, "I was led to the revolutionary life by reading an author named Karl May.

"I was about twelve years old when I read his books, and they affected me profoundly," he said. "In the May Westerns, the heroes were archetypes of nobility—they were courageous, audacious, personally honest. I wanted to be like them. But since in Nicaragua we didn't have the Great Plains of the North American West, and since the injustices we were facing were different from those in the Western novels, I decided to confront *Nicaraguan* injustices."

Borge attended law school in León, but he found politics far more interesting than jurisprudence. In 1956 he was among thousands of Nicaraguans arrested in the police crackdown that followed the assassination of President Anastasio Somoza García. He was allowed out of jail to serve his sentence under house arrest, and soon escaped, setting out on a revolutionary odyssey that would take him to Costa Rica, Mexico, Honduras, Peru, Colombia, North Korea, and Cuba over the next twenty years.

Although Borge participated in several early guerrilla campaigns, he was by his own account only an average fighter, unable to carry heavy loads or adapt fully to the rigors of mountain life. Instead he became a master conspirator, an expert in the black arts and a specialist in arcane techniques of espionage and counter-espionage. What he learned served him magnificently when he became Minister of the Interior.

Borge ran his ministry like a personal fiefdom. The National Directorate had assigned him the task of guarding the regime's security, and he assumed it with gusto. He often said that he had found clandestine life fascinating. To all appearances, he found his work in government equally so.

Borge's most fearsome instrument was the State Security police, run by his shadowy amanuensis Lenin Cerna. State Security was the core not only of the interior ministry, but of the entire Sandinista regime. The regime was, after all, under attack by the United States, and was presumably the target of many covert CIA operations. An effective secret police was essential to its survival, and under Borge and Cerna the police were nothing if not effective. They foiled every major CIA effort to bring the contra war into urban areas, and kept the internal political opposition in permanent uncertainty and fear.

The State Security police force was a corps of Sandinista shock troops, the first and last line of defense against subversion. In the Somoza era, the number of secret police agents in Nicaragua had never exceeded a few hundred, but under the Sandinistas, they numbered more than three thousand. Some were assigned to infiltrate political parties, human rights groups, trade unions, and other possible centers of anti-Sandinista activity. Others were trained in tapping telephones, secret taping and filming, and other black arts. Still others became interrogators and investigators, roaming the countryside looking for contra collaborators. Most mysterious of all were those who had been sent to enlist in the contra army, and were risking their lives to transmit secret information about contra plans and operations. Several of them were caught and executed, but many were never unmasked.

"They are in the entrails of the enemy," Borge once said of his spies inside the contra army. "They are revolutionaries who pass themselves off as counter-revolutionaries. It is the greatest sacrifice possible for someone with ideals, someone convinced that revolution is the best possible option."

Once, half in jest, I asked Borge if it was true that he had penetrated every level of the contra army. He looked at me quite seriously, and then pointed his index finger skyward as he liked to do when making a point.

"Hasta la CIA tengo infiltrada," he said—I even have infiltrated the CIA. I asked what he meant, but he would say no more.

Borge was the only senior Sandinista who had survived serious and sustained torture while in Somoza's jails. Some said the dictator had particularly hated Borge and was determined to break his spirit. Whatever the reason, Borge suffered inhuman brutality. For nine months he was kept in a heavily air-conditioned isolation cell with a hood over his head, chained to the floor so he could not stand upright, and was subjected to constant beatings.

"Nine months hooded and handcuffed," he recalled years later. "Nine months in total darkness. Nine months of black that made García Lorca's green seem hideous to imagine. Nine months naked. Nine months of freezing, and with the noise of the air conditioner filling my ears. Nine months of eating rotten beans once a day."

Borge was thus not only a secret police chief with years of experience as an underground fugitive, but also a jailer who had been confined in the worst kind of prisons. Perhaps most fitting of all, he was a former conspirator now assigned to detect and suppress conspiracies.

The centerpiece of Borge's security system was El Chipote, a subterranean prison buried under a hill behind the Intercontinental Hotel in central Managua. There, in the same complex where Pedro Joaquín Chamorro and other anti-Somoza activists had been tortured in years past, suspected counter-revolutionaries were thrown into tiny, dark cells, subjected to highly repetitive interrogations for hours on end, and often told that their close relatives had been killed or that they themselves were about to be executed. Many of the country's leading political figures were "graduates" of El Chipote, and they told frightening stories.

One friend of mine who had served a term at El Chipote was a Nicaraguan labor organizer named Larry Schoures. He was never charged with a crime, but interrogators told him that his trade union organizing was "against the people's interests." They said he could make amends by becoming an informer for State Security, and warned him that if he refused, police would kill his nine-year-old son. After ten days of threats and interrogations, guards told Schoures that he had been judged a traitor and sentenced to death. He was dumped into a dark isolation cell for some days. Then suddenly he was released without explanation.

The Schoures case was typical of the way Borge treated bothersome agitators. At El Chipote, which was used principally as a detention and interrogation center rather than a long-term prison, all detainees were political, and few were held longer than a month or two. Some were sent to trial and given jail terms, but most were released after authorities decided they had been sufficiently intimidated.

Stories about what took place inside El Chipote and other State Security detention centers were repeated throughout Nicaragua, and they led many people to decide that mixing in politics was not worth the danger. One Sandinista official who worked with Borge, a lawyer named Plutarco Anduray Palma, once suggested to me that spreading this fear was precisely the point of maintaining such centers.

"People are afraid just to be going into El Chipote because it has a somewhat fearsome reputation," he explained. "That has a psychological impact by itself."

Borge had decreed an end to the old-style forms of torture that had been used in Latin America for generations, and which he himself had suffered. In their place he had implanted a much less bloody though arguably more effective system of coercive pressures. Rather than have his prisoners kicked and beaten, tortured with electric prods, or burned with cigarette butts, he had them sealed into poorly ventilated dark closets, where heat was intense and inmates lost their sense of time. Confinement was interrupted at odd intervals for long, draining interrogations and for threats against either the inmate or the inmate's family. It was a new and more sophisticated form of abuse, one that Borge pioneered.

"They told me that I was encouraging people to act against the revolution, that I would never see my family again, and that I would be in jail for twenty years," labor leader José Altamirano told me after serving fifty-five days at El Chipote. "There was no physical torture, only complete darkness and silence so you lose your senses."

Borge cast his net wide when he looked for enemies. Occasionally he singled out some real or perceived rival for special abuse. One of the victims was Sofonias Cisneros, who headed a national organization of parents of children attending religious schools. The organization often criticized Sandinista educational policies, complaining in one public statement that official grammar school study plans were full of "more and more Marxist-Leninist teachings." The public paid little attention to these declarations, but they apparently irritated Borge. He sent police to monitor Cisneros's speeches, and then one evening ordered his arrest.

Cisneros was taken to El Chipote, where he was locked into a small cell for several hours. Then, he wrote afterward, a "big, strong soldier" appeared before him, surrounded by several aides. The soldier ordered him to undress, and then began punching and kicking him. Later Cisneros wrote an account of his ordeal:

> . . . Then he asked me, "Do you know who I am?" I answered no, because in truth, without eyeglasses and in the half-light, it was impossible for me to recognize him. He then put a gun to my temple and told me: "Well, I am *Comandante* Lenin Cerna, and you are a son of a bitch who is going to die right here!" . . . At that point, *Comandante* Cerna began to punch and kick me all over while he said, "Why do you attack the revolution? Why don't you respect the *comandantes*? Why do you ridicule the heroes and martyrs?" . . . I noticed that *Comandante* Cerna and

his henchmen were not trying to get answers to the questions they asked, and that the questions were simply to accompany the blows and verbal abuse. The henchmen hit me only rarely, and the entire session was under *Comandante* Cerna's control. He is the one who hit me hard on the face, the ears, the back of the head, the chest, the abdomen, and the wounds on my back . . .

At one point, *Comandante* Cerna asked me how old I was and I said I was sixty. "You're already an old man, you son of a bitch," he replied. Finally, after having left the room for a moment, he came back and told me: "Look, I'm going to let you go, but don't go around making statements or saying dumb things, because if you do I'll have you killed in the streets like a dog, you and your entire family!" He asked me how many children I had and where they were. He said: "The best thing for you is to leave Nicaragua, and keep your mouth shut even when you're gone, because wherever you are we can get you. You saw how we liquidated Somoza!" He then ordered his henchmen to throw me into the street naked.

One day, during an interview, I asked Borge about the Cisneros case. I expected him to feign ignorance, or to dismiss Cisneros as a liar. That would have been the reflexive reaction of most Latin American police ministers. But on this occasion, Borge was in no mood to dissemble. On the contrary, he was disarmingly direct.

"Do you know what that man Cisneros did?" he asked me.

"I have no way of knowing," I replied. "I don't even think Cisneros knows."

"He knows perfectly well," Borge said firmly. "That man gave a speech saying that [Sandinista hero] Luis Alfonso Velasquez was a street urchin and that Carlos Fonseca was a pot-smoker!"

"Is that enough to earn a sixty-year-old man a beating, personally administered by the chief of State Security?"

"I'll just tell you one thing. That man is lucky he was interrogated by Lenin Cerna and not by me."

Borge was a master of psychology, both mass and individual, and had a deep understanding of the importance of symbols. He never denied, for example, that he was a committed atheist, and he enjoyed recalling how, as a child, he had rejected his mother's suggestion that he study for the priesthood. Some religious leaders, especially Catholic bishops, thought of him as a veritable anti-Christ, since he was the one who expelled priests when they displeased him, restricted the broadcast of religious services, and directed slander campaigns against clerics who opposed the regime. What more perfect hobby for Borge to profess, then, than collecting crucifixes?

All who came to Borge's interior ministry office were ushered into a waiting room where dozens of crucifixes were displayed in specially built cases that lined the walls. Some were primitive and some exquisitely carved, some Nicaraguan and others gathered on trips abroad. The image of Christ's suffering pervaded the room, and visitors were normally given a few minutes to absorb the sensation before being ushered in for their audience.

Because Borge enjoyed playing so many different roles, one could never be sure what his costume would be on any given day. Often he dressed in simple fatigues, sometimes affecting a matching cap, with a pistol at his hip. On ceremonial occasions he sported star-studded epaulets. When he addressed police officers or accompanied them on operations, he wore a police officer's outfit. At a fire in Managua once, he appeared in a full firefighter's suit, complete with helmet and rubber overcoat.

Every Tuesday afternoon, Borge spent several hours meeting with humble people seeking favors. Sessions like these have been traditional in Latin America since the days of Spanish rule, when the *patrón* was the source of all wealth. They had been institutionalized by dictators of every political stripe, including the various Somozas. To many revolutionaries they symbolized the corruption of dictatorships, systems in which individual favors were used to ease the pressure of social injustice. If another *comandante* had tried to conduct such sessions he might have been roundly criticized, but they fit perfectly into Borge's style.

One Tuesday I arranged to sit and watch Borge dispense his favors. I drove to the imposing interior ministry building, which in pre-revolutionary days had housed the state-run electric company. Over the main entrance was painted the Orwellian slogan, "Guardian of the People's Happiness."

An armed guard of about sixteen stood behind the tinted doors and ascertained my business before admitting me. After passing through a metal detector, I was summoned to an elevator and escorted into an upstairs waiting room. Borge appeared in plain slacks and a striped shirt rolled up to the elbows. There was a spring to his step, and as he called for the first supplicant he lit a cigar.

A young man in fatigues, missing a leg, entered the room. Borge asked him his name and home town, and listened to the story of his war wound. The youth spoke slowly and emotionally, and was near tears when he told Borge he had been unable to find a job since being discharged from the army. Borge listened sympathetically, and reminded the young man to comport himself as a hero, since his wound was a badge of valor. They chatted briefly about the cruel necessity of war, and as they parted, Borge promised to find something for him.

The next visitor was a blind man who said he could not live on the salary he earned at a state-owned match company, because blind employees were paid less than those who were sighted. After hearing details of the two-tiered wage structure, Borge became indignant. On the spot he promised to outlaw such discrimination, and he was as good as his word. During a break later that afternoon he telephoned the Minister of Industry, and they agreed that henceforth state enterprises would pay equal salaries to blind and sighted people. That was how public policy in Nicaragua was often set.

One after another unfortunate Nicaraguans filed in to see Borge and tell him their troubles. The audience had been screened by his aides, so there were none of the pleading mothers of prisoners who often surrounded him when he appeared in public. Most of the petitioners were asking for something pathetically simple but nonetheless vital, like a lottery vendor's license or a sheet of zinc for roofing, and none left without a promise of help.

Borge's last visitors that day were a group of ragged children from the town of Masatepe. They were energetic and restless after the long wait outside, wide-eyed at meeting Borge but not at all intimidated by him. They explained that they were a baseball team, but that they had no equipment.

"Boys, Nicaragua is a poor country, and you can't expect to have uniforms for baseball," Borge told them. "You can play perfectly good baseball without uniforms."

"Forget uniforms!" several of the boys replied at once. "We need a bat and a ball and some gloves!"

"Well, that's different," Borge told them, withdrawing his cigar. "You have to have a bat and ball."

He paused for a moment, and then asked, "Which one of you is the catcher?" When one boy raised his hand, Borge called him over, placed a hand on his small shoulder, and began speaking to him seriously.

"Always remember that the catcher is the most important member of the team," he said. "Some people in the stadium don't understand that, but the players know. The catcher sees everything that's happening, and he has to be the smartest player. He tells the pitcher what to throw, and tells the infielders and outfielders where to stand. Catchers have to understand the game well. That's why they make the best managers."

I wondered if Borge was talking about himself. The young boys, however, took his words as sporting advice.

"We're going to see if we can find you some equipment," Borge told them. "It won't be much, but enough to start with. Remember that the future of Nicaragua belongs to you, and that your job is to be good revolutionaries. Do you know what that means?"

The boys were silent, perhaps not wanting to risk a wrong answer that might endanger their gift.

"Being a good revolutionary," Borge told them, "means being a good friend, a good student, a good son, and a good ballplayer."

For visitors to Nicaragua, Borge was certainly the most interesting *comandante* to meet, the one whose discourse was the most eclectic and unpredictable. Women especially were drawn to him, and he made no effort to hide the fact that he was drawn to them also. Just as he somehow managed to persuade many foreigners that he was a gentle, benign poet who dreamed of nothing but human freedom, he seduced some of Nicaragua's most attractive women as well as an even larger number of foreigners. Several other *comandantes* were also known for the number of their sexual conquests, but none seemed as compulsive, or as highly successful, as Borge.

"As far as my sexual habits and options, I am definitely a man who likes women," Borge once told a Sandinista television interviewer. "I like women because they are better than men. For a long time I have realized that there are certain differences between male and female natures. Women are made of better wood than men. We men are made of pine, the wood that is used to make coffins. Women are made of ebony, and ebony is used for works of art. Anyone who appreciates woman as fully as I believe I do, who appreciates her virtues, her generosity, her loyalty, her extraordinary force, is naturally going to enjoy woman as a sex, as a concept, and is naturally going to give himself to a woman."

The contrasts between Borge and his chief rival, Daniel Ortega, were unmistakable. Borge was short, paunchy, and balding, a dandy who never missed his weekly facial massage. Ortega stood tall and broadshouldered. In his early years in power he looked as though he rarely visited a barber, much less a masseuse. He was unkempt, ill at ease, and painfully inarticulate. With his walrus moustache and dark glasses, he seemed sullen and unapproachable.

In countries ruled by military men, it is axiomatic that those who command the most military power will emerge victorious. By this formula, Borge's greatest asset was not his wit or his powers of oratory or persuasion, but his control over the interior ministry. He directed a potent political police force that had been organized and trained by specialists from Cuba, East Germany, and Bulgaria. He also controlled the regular uniformed police, the prison system, and the customs and immigration services. Most intimidating of all, he commanded a force of several thousand elite combat troops who reported to him alone.

In the chaotic first months of Sandinista rule, Borge seemed to be the man who was holding the country together, the one most clearly in control. But within a few months, Daniel Ortega began working to make himself Borge's equal and, ultimately, to elbow him aside. His first and most important success was installing his younger brother Humberto as Minister of Defense. From that moment, Borge had to confront not just Daniel Ortega but an entity that came to be known as "the Ortega faction."

The Ortegas' family background was a microcosm of modern Nicaraguan history. Their father had been an active supporter of Sandino, and was briefly imprisoned in the early 1930s. According to family legend, General Somoza García had sent him a packet of money after his release, hoping to win his support, but he refused it. Somoza then sent him a telegram with the simple message: "Eat Shit."

American intervention in Nicaragua had already made the elder Ortega deeply anti-Yankee, and his treatment at Somoza's hands further stiffened his convictions. He was a man of somewhat bohemian bent. Though he held several jobs during his life, he seemed unsuited to conventional work, preferring to read, write, and reflect. He spent his early years in Granada, but chafed at the aristocratic style of life there. Not long after his release from jail, he packed his few belongings and left for a new life on the frontier. After some wandering, he settled in the rugged mining town of La Libertad, near the geographic center of Nicaragua. His prospects were uncertain until he met Lidia Saavedra, a pretty young woman from a successful local family. She also had strong anti-Somoza convictions, and the two were a natural match. They married after a brief courtship, and their first child, Daniel, was born on November 11, 1945.

The Ortega household, while more stable than many in Nicaragua, was in many respects quite typical. Money was hard to come by, living conditions were poor, and medical care was an unheard-of luxury. The father finally found a job at an American-owned gold mine called La Esmeralda, but the mother had to work continuously, selling snacks and fruit juices from a streetcorner stand. She gave birth to six children, and was devastated when first one and then a second died of infectious diseases. Political trouble also dogged the family. When the father lost his job at La Esmeralda, he and his family left town, lived for a time in the provincial capital of Juigalpa, and then found their way to Managua. There, the family settled in a working-class neighborhood whose very name evoked the country's nightmare: Colonia Somoza.

Anti-Americanism permeated the Ortega household. Sandino's war against United States Marines and the treacherous manner in which he was murdered had made a deep imprint on both parents. Both blamed the country's under-development, and hence the misery of its people, on the Somoza dictatorship and its sponsors in Washington. The father even chafed at selling American soft drinks at the family refreshment stand.

"At that time, there was a generalized anti-U.S. sentiment here, and it affected me very strongly," Daniel Ortega once recalled. "I saw myself as a young Nicaraguan nationalist: anti-imperialist, anti-Yankee. My neighborhood friends were the same. We were anti-Coca-Cola, anti-comic book, against everything, good and bad, represented by the United States, except baseball. I remember once when I was about sixteen, we were at a demonstration near the Managua Cathedral. Things got very violent. Guardsmen were shooting at us and throwing tear gas. So as we fled, we ran up the steps of the cathedral. Inside, by chance, we encountered an American, dressed in military uniform, about to marry a Nicaraguan woman. In a rage, we surrounded the wedding party. Then we tried to attack the groom. We broke up the wedding . . . All we saw was, as we would say, a bad Yankee. We just didn't want any kind of Yankee here."

The director of Nicaragua's official radio station, *Voz de Nicaragua,* was an ex-guerrilla named Carlos Guadamúz, who had been one of Ortega's childhood mates. Sometimes when I talked with Guadamúz, I asked him to tell me stories about those early years. He told me that with a few other teenagers, he and Ortega had formed what amounted to an anti-military street gang, engaging in such direct forms of protest as blowing up National Guard jeeps and placing small bombs near the homes of pro-Somoza politicians. All members of the gang were arrested periodically, and Ortega was once jailed for fire-bombing cars that belonged to the American embassy.

"We never had a real youth or a normal youth," Guadamúz told me one day as we sat in his dark office at the radio station. "We decided to start something and not to stop until it was done. We were very radical in those days, very serious. We were going to make revolution no matter what the cost."

I asked Guadamúz which other members of the gang I might interview, and he shook his head.

"Daniel and I are the only ones who survived," he said. "All the rest were killed along the way."

After a period as small-time terrorists, Ortega and his friends came to realize that they could never hope to have a political impact unless they were part of a coherent organization. When the Sandinista Front was formed in the early 1960s, they joined immediately. Sandinista leaders encouraged Ortega to become a student leader, and he began delivering anti-Somoza speeches at high school rallies. During a trip to Guatemala in 1964, when military repression was at a peak there, he and several of his friends were jailed and beaten after police became suspicious of them. Among his fellow inmates were about forty Guatemalan peasants from a region where guerrillas had been active.

"One day, they took all the peasants away," he recalled years later. "Not long after, a news item appeared in the paper saying that the vehicle in which these peasants were traveling had 'turned over' on the highway and they were all killed. Who knows what really happened to them?"

Guatemalan authorities finally decided to turn Ortega and his friends over to the National Guard in Nicaragua. The Guardsman waiting for them at the northern border was the notorious torturer Gonzalo Lacayo, whose brutality symbolized all that the Ortegas hated most about the National Guard and the Somoza dictatorship. During the entire trip from the border to Managua, Lacayo mercilessly clubbed and beat the prisoners. They arrived semi-conscious, were held for a few weeks, and then released.

Not long after surviving that arrest, Ortega enrolled in law school. He planned to use his cover as a student to recruit new Sandinistas, but he dropped out after being named to direct the "urban resistance" in Managua. In August 1967, after losing several of his operatives to Gonzalo Lacayo's tortures, he planned Lacayo's spectacular assassination, himself firing one of the automatic rifles that brought the victim down in a hail of bullets. Guardsmen were already looking for him on bank robbery charges, and at the end of 1967 they captured him at a Managua hideout. He spent the next seven years in jail.

As life in prison goes, Daniel Ortega's incarceration was not especially harsh. He was badly beaten in the days following his arrest, as Guardsmen sought to force secrets from him, but after he had been tried and sentenced his life became fairly routine. His mother became active in groups that demanded rights for political prisoners, and partly as a result of hunger strikes and protest marches staged by such groups, Ortega and other Sandinista prisoners were treated with a modicum of humanity. Yet despite all this, seven years in prison, particularly if they came between the ages of twenty-two and twenty-nine as they did for Daniel Ortega, must necessarily sear a person's psyche. Forever afterward, Ortega bore a scar near his right eye from a cut inflicted during his 1967 interrogation, and I always assumed that his years in jail had also left other, less visible scars.

Ortega was one of the Sandinista prisoners freed in December 1974 as ransom for the high-society hostages who were taken captive by commandos during their famous Christmas party raid. Immediately upon his release, he flew to Cuba with the other prisoners and stayed there, slowly recovering from his ordeal, for more than a year. He was not so disoriented that he required psychiatric care in Havana, as did Lenin Cerna and some of the other released prisoners, but it took months for him to become accustomed to walking outdoors or sleeping without interruption.

During the Sandinistas' first years in power, in his role as "coordinator" of the junta, Ortega received a stream of foreign visitors. Many were fawning admirers, but among them were also writers, thinkers, and political leaders who had lived lives very different from his. Almost alone among Sandinista leaders, he seemed to grow before our eyes. His public comments became steadily more sophisticated, and it was obvious that he was fully applying himself to his job and determined to master it.

One of Ortega's most successful maneuvers was to force Borge to give up control over his combat units. There was never any overt indication that these units might have been used to support Borge in an internal confrontation. Nonetheless, many Sandinistas were uncomfortable with the idea of maintaining two fighting forces, and they supported Ortega in his drive to centralize all military forces under the Ministry of Defense.

While he was working to curb Borge's power, Ortega also worked assiduously to increase his own. He placed friends and allies in important posts, both in the government and in the hierarchy of the Sandinista Front. At the same time, he built strong relationships with influential foreign leaders, especially with Fidel Castro, who was deeply revered by all Sandinistas.

The most important reason for Ortega's ultimate victory over Borge, however, was that other *comandantes* never managed to overcome their mistrust for Borge. He was Nicaragua's master conspirator, and no one knew it better than his Sandinista comrades. They were glad to have him as Interior Minister, but they wanted to elevate him no further. Ortega was a far more reassuring figure.

Borge might have launched some bold challenge to Ortega and forced a public showdown, but he chose not to do so. He never stopped believing that he was better qualified for national leadership than Ortega, and sometimes he was overheard making derogatory wisecracks about his younger comrade. Ultimately, however, he accepted Ortega's emergence, though he in no way relinquished his right to help run Nicaragua. On the contrary, he insisted on remaining the country's policeman and ideological arbiter. He never fully trusted his comrades, and they in turn never fully trusted him.

13

THE FAITHFUL

LOST IN the hills of Nicaragua's rugged interior, the farm village of Cuapa is so small that it does not even appear on the government-issued road map. Only a few hundred hardy souls live there, and the dirt road that is their sole link to civilization is rough and strewn with rocks. Cuapa is one of countless tiny hamlets where, until 1979, peasants farmed tiny plots exactly as their parents and grandparents had. With the Sandinista victory, their lives, like those of most Nicaraguans, were turned upside down.

If Cuapa was a typically anonymous Nicaraguan village, then Bernardo Martínez was perhaps the classic anonymous Nicaraguan. He was born in Cuapa, and in his forty-nine years he had never ventured more than a few miles away. For sustenance he depended on a small plot of land that he tilled each day, and on a couple of chickens and a cow. Devoutly religious like most of his neighbors, he never missed going to church on Sunday. When political upheaval upset his life in the early 1980s and there seemed no way to resist the Sandinista whirlwind, he drew even closer to the church, finding in his Roman Catholic faith a refuge from the forces shaking Nicaragua. He would certainly have lived and died unnoticed if the Virgin Mary had not appeared before him in the hills outside Cuapa.

At first, Bernardo Martínez was afraid of the Virgin, and told no one about his encounters with her. But again and again, during his daily walks to and from his farm in late 1980 and early 1981, she appeared in his path, always bathed in radiant light. Finally he confided in the priest who visited Cuapa on Sundays. The priest, in turn, informed his ecclesiastical superiors. They took the report quite seriously, and sent investigators to Cuapa. Soon news of the apparition leaked out. Villagers erected a rustic shrine on a hillside where the Virgin had appeared. Visitors began to arrive, anxious to see the place and to soak up whatever holiness might remain there. Soon Nicaraguans by the hundreds began making pilgrimages to Cuapa, and Bernardo Martínez found himself a center of attention.

I chose a Sunday to make the rugged four-hour drive to Cuapa. When I arrived at mid-morning, the town was full of pilgrims. It had not occurred to anyone to sell T-shirts or trinkets commemorating the miracle, but villagers were doing a brisk business in cold drinks and other refreshments. The hillside shrine, which was the center of everyone's attention, was simply a semi-circle of white rocks around a small clearing. Men, women, and children stood reverently before it, holding hands and bowing their heads. People sang hymns, clutched Bibles, and hugged each other. Some fingered rosary beads and whispered fervent prayers, while others gathered rocks or clumps of earth to take home as souvenirs.

Soon after noon, there was a commotion from the direction of the village. A group of people made their way toward us, among them a priest. The crowd began to buzz. People were saying, "It's him. It's Bernardo."

Once each day, Bernardo Martínez emerged from the parish house where he had been living since the commotion began. He was small and stooped, and most of his teeth were missing. As he approached, dressed in a freshly laundered white shirt, the already highly emotional crowd was moved to the brink of rapture. There was absolute silence as people waited for Martínez's first words.

"The Virgin was dressed in white," he began, and that simple sentence was enough to elicit shrieks from several women.

After the crowd calmed down, Martínez continued. "She seemed to be about fifteen or sixteen years old," he said, setting off another round of gasps. It was as if people were shocked by any physical description of someone whom they had only known as a mysterious force or an object of adoration.

"I asked her, 'Why are you here?' and she told me she had a message for the world and for Nicaragua. 'Do not preach the kingdom of God unless you are building it here on earth,' she said. 'The world is threatened by great danger. Nicaragua has suffered much, and that is why I am here.' Later she asked for prayers for the unbelievers, and for peace in the world. She said, 'I am the mother of all sinners, and a mother never forgets her children. I have not forgotten the people of this earth.'"

Martínez spoke for only about five minutes, but by the time he finished much of the crowd was in tears. Several people had fainted. Townspeople told me that the same scene was being re-enacted every day as pilgrims flocked to hear about the Virgin of Cuapa and see the spot where she had chosen to appear.

After returning to Managua, I visited Father Bosco Vivas, a spokesman for Catholic bishops, and asked his view of what was happening in Cuapa. He reminded me that the Virgin had appeared under strikingly similar circumstances in Lourdes, France, and in Fatima, Portugal.

"Bernardo is a simple man," Father Vivas told me. "It is difficult to believe that he alone could invent such impressive, beautiful, and profound descriptions."

That week, the opposition newspaper *La Prensa* published an editorial portraying Martínez as a specially blessed Nicaraguan. "Anyone who hears Bernardo's tale has to believe it, if only a little bit," *La Prensa* said. "It is a tale of peace." Archbishop Obando, the country's senior Catholic leader, was also inclined to credulity. "The Virgin has never appeared to great intellectuals and thinkers," he reminded reporters after Mass one Sunday. "She has always shown herself to humble people."

In another country, even one whose people were equally devoted to Catholicism and veneration of the Virgin, such an episode might have remained a religious curiosity. But in the polarized environment of Sandinista Nicaragua, politics intruded into everyone's life, and soon the Virgin's appearance in Cuapa became a matter of heated political debate. The message that Bernardo Martínez had supposedly received from the Virgin, doubters were quick to point out, was not simply one of Christian love, but actually a political message directed against the Sandinista regime. The Virgin had used code words that were popular among anti-Sandinista activists. The "great danger" to which she had supposedly referred was taken as a reference to Marxism, and her warning about unbelievers and those who were not building God's kingdom was evidently aimed at the Sandinistas.

"All of this is nothing more or less than an attempt to delude and divert public opinion from the real problems that confront our country at this moment," the pro-Sandinista newspaper *Nuevo Diario* asserted. "The story about a supposed apparition is intended to deceive true Christians, and to divert their attention away from reactionary attacks against us."

Sandinista *comandantes* struck the same note in a series of public speeches, and pro-Sandinista priests warned parishioners not to believe stories about apparitions. Still the pilgrimages continued. Finally the interior ministry issued a decree forbidding the reporting of miracles in the press unless they had been previously accepted by the Vatican, thereby effectively banning press coverage of events at Cuapa.

The Sandinistas had good reason to try to stifle the news from Cuapa. As they consolidated their political power, they had crushed many opponents and managed to co-opt many others. Traditionally powerful business groups had been intimidated by the jailing of their most prominent leaders. Labor unions were forbidden to strike or hold protest rallies. Critics in the press knew that if they criticized too forcefully, they would be silenced. Political parties were in disarray, with some of their leaders already in exile and the rest unable to organize freely. The only non-Sandinista institution that managed to remain intact through the 1980s, and indeed to become stronger and more powerful, was the mainstream Catholic church. Archbishop Obando and his fellow bishops, it soon became clear, were Nicaragua's real anti-Sandinista leaders. They had the resources, the moral authority, and the institutional base that the rest of the opposition lacked. Politicians, journalists, business leaders, and other civilians who opposed the regime could be bought off or repressed as necessary, but the church could not so easily be brought to heel. Sandinista *comandantes* correctly viewed the bishops, and especially Archbishop Obando, as their most potent political rivals. Their confrontation with the bishops was spiritual as well as political, touching on basic questions of good and evil.

For decades and centuries, Catholic priests and bishops in Nicaragua had willingly cozied up to those in power and blessed their repressive and unjust regimes. But from the earliest days of Spanish conquest, there had also been brave clerics who dared to speak out in defense of the poor. The first voice to be raised against the slaughter of Nicaraguan Indians was that of the heroic friar Bartolomé de las Casas, whose anguished protests to the court in Madrid were eloquent challenges to the prevailing belief that natives were subhuman savages. Spanish adventurers in Central America managed to have the bothersome priest recalled to Madrid, but were soon faced with an equally outspoken clerical enemy, Antonio de Valdivieso, who arrived from Spain in 1544 to become archbishop of Nicaragua. The brutal conqueror Pedrarias was no longer in power, but his successor and son-in-law, Rodrigo de Contreras, proved every bit as cruel.

Archbishop Valdivieso did not hesitate to confront Contreras. He publicly accused the Spanish commander of stealing land from natives and then killing them or selling them into slavery. Authorities in Madrid held a series of hearings into the archbishop's accusations, finally recalling Contreras and issuing a decree stripping him of his rank and authority. His sons Pedro and Hernando, who had remained behind in Nicaragua, were infuriated by the family's fall from power, and determined to take revenge. On the morning of February 26, 1549, Hernando Contreras burst into the parish house in León, where he found Archbishop Valdivieso playing chess in the courtyard. As he charged forward, the archbishop tried to escape, but could not. He fell before Contreras's sword, dying for his humanistic beliefs and becoming Nicaragua's first Catholic martyr.

Ever since then, there have been Catholic priests in Nicaragua who courageously denounced injustice. In countries where political and social institutions were stronger, these priests might have enjoyed the luxury of avoiding public life. But Nicaragua never developed vigorous political parties or other centers of independent thought, and so the Catholic church emerged as the only true center of opposition. Whatever the regime in power, there were always clerics ready to shelter its enemies.

During the Somoza period, many of Nicaragua's most influential priests were from the Jesuit order. Many of them supported the dictatorship, and some were known as intimate advisors to the Somoza family. Through their influence, the order was given a large plot of land in Managua in the early 1960s and allowed to build the Central American University, which became one of Nicaragua's most important centers of higher education. What President Anastasio Somoza Debayle had not foreseen was that the university, known as the UCA, would also become a hotbed of political agitation. Its rector, Father Leon Pallais, a Jesuit loyal to the regime, was unable to control burgeoning Sandinista activism on the campus during the 1970s, much to Somoza's outrage. At the same time, the Jesuit order was being shaken by change, both in Nicaragua and elsewhere, and the UCA faculty became steadily more radical.

Jesuit priests prominent in Nicaragua during these years were a highly educated and sophisticated group. But although they were the only clerics seen regularly on the Managua social and diplomatic circuit, they were hardly the only ones working in Nicaragua. Slowly and without fanfare, another, very different Catholic order was making a profound mark on Nicaraguan life.

The Salesian order, founded by the nineteenth-century Italian friar Don Bosco, is devoted to educating young people. It operates schools throughout Central America, including three large ones in Nicaragua. Unlike Jesuits, Salesian priests are not normally thought of as intellectuals. While Jesuits mixed with Nicaragua's elite, Salesians worked in slums and working-class neighborhoods, devoting their time to helping boys and girls who lacked the advantages that might have allowed them to attend Jesuit institutions.

Salesians were a quiet group, known for getting along well with everyone. Thus when one of their number, Bishop Miguel Obando y Bravo of Matagalpa, was named archbishop in 1970, no one expected any important changes in the church's role in Nicaragua. He was the first native-born archbishop in Nicaraguan history, and President Somoza privately called him *"mi indito"*—my little Indian.

No estimate could have been more mistaken. The first sign of trouble came when Somoza sent the archbishop a new Mercedes-Benz; instead of using it, Obando had it auctioned off, and donated the proceeds to Catholic charities. The dictator then sent a long black limousine, but the archbishop returned it. Following the 1972 earthquake, when Obando refused to become vice-chairman of Somoza's larcenous National Emergency Committee, their split became more pronounced. In 1974, Obando and his fellow bishops issued a pastoral letter

Susan Meiselas/Magnum

Anastasio Somoza Debayle was the most brutal and corrupt of the three Somozas who tyrannized Nicaragua for nearly half a century.

The Somozas' most prominent enemy was valiant newspaper publisher Pedro Joaquín Chamorro. His assassination in January 1978 triggered a national uprising.

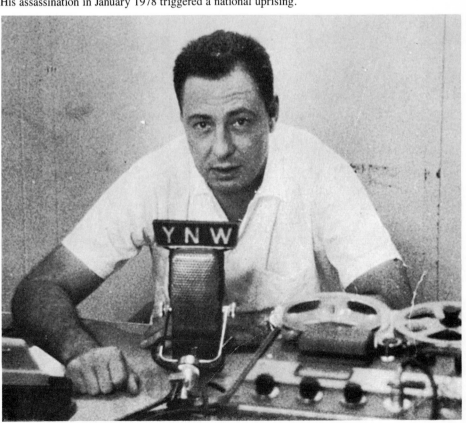

La Prensa

Carlos Fonseca, a radical law student from Matagalpa, founded the Sandinista National Liberation Front.

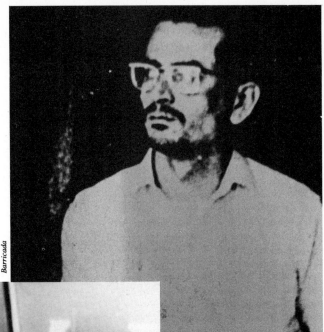

Barricada

Sandinista commandos led by Edén Pastora ("Commander Zero") dealt the Somoza regime a crushing defeat by capturing the National Palace in August 1978.

Barricada

La Prensa

Somoza was finally overthrown in July 1979. The five members of the revolutionary junta that replaced him were, from left, essayist Sergio Ramírez (in white shirt); mathematics professor Moisés Hassan (partially obscured); Violeta Chamorro, widow of the martyred publisher; guerrilla leader Daniel Ortega; and businessman Alfonso Robelo (with beard).

Within a few months, Nicaraguans realized that real power was in the hands of nine Sandinista *comandantes* who called themselves the National Directorate. From left: Tomás Borge, Victor Tirado, Daniel Ortega, Humberto Ortega, Henry Ruiz, Jaime Wheelock, Bayardo Arce, Carlos Núñez and Luis Carrión.

Peter Morgan

Four historic figures helped shape Nicaragua's destiny. Clockwise from top left: William Walker, the American adventurer who seized control of the country in 1855; President José Santos Zelaya, a visionary nationalist who was forced from power by the United States; Rubén Darío, one of the finest poets ever to write in Spanish; and Augusto César Sandino, who led a six-year guerrilla war against United States Marines in the 1920s and 1930s.

Barricada

Daniel Vázquez Díaz

Barricada

Soon after the Sandinistas took power in 1979, a counter-revolutionary or "contra" army began taking shape in Honduras. Its patron was General Gustavo Álvarez, above, commander of the Honduran military. The principal contra leader, Enrique Bermúdez, right, had been a colonel in Somoza's defeated National Guard.

Juan Carlos Piovano

The contra army was financed and directed by the United States government. Its most powerful sponsors were President Reagan and Director of Central Intelligence William Casey.

World Wide Photos

Ken Silverman

In March 1983 I stumbled upon a contra camp near a Honduran hamlet called Matasano. This photo was published in the *New York Times*.

Peter Morgan

Most of the footsoldiers in both Nicaraguan armies were teenagers from poor families. Above, Sandinistas on patrol near the Honduran border. Below, contras training at a clandestine camp inside Nicaragua.

Juan Carlos Piovano

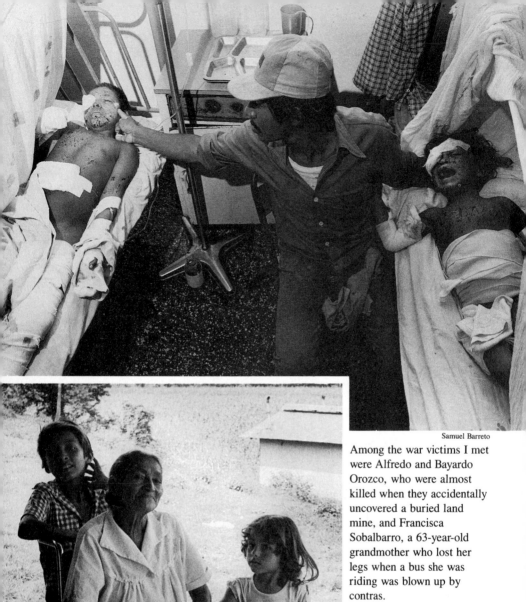

Samuel Barreto

Among the war victims I met were Alfredo and Bayardo Orozco, who were almost killed when they accidentally uncovered a buried land mine, and Francisca Sobalbarro, a 63-year-old grandmother who lost her legs when a bus she was riding was blown up by contras.

Stephen Kinzer

Miguel Cardinal Obando y Bravo was enormously popular, but Sandinista leaders attacked him relentlessly for his refusal to condemn the contras.

Peter Morgan

Minister of Culture Ernesto Cardenal, one of the most outspoken Sandinista priests, was publicly reprimanded by Pope John Paul II during his 1983 visit to Managua.

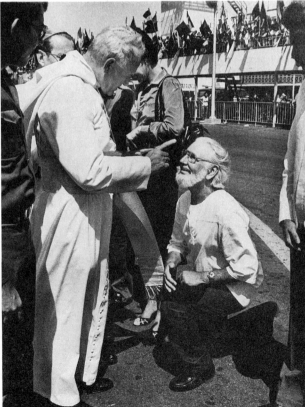

Mario Tapia

Funerals for war victims, like this one in San José de Bocay, reflected the relentlessness with which Nicaragua was tearing itself apart.

Arturo Cruz was the opposition candidate for president in 1984.

La Prensa

Juan Carlos Piovano

The two most powerful Sandinista leaders were President Daniel Ortega and Interior Minister Tomás Borge.

Barricada

The Sandinista army was commanded by Daniel Ortega's brother Humberto, an avid baseball fan who was proud of his pitching skill.

Guillermo Marcia was my companion on dozens of trips to remote parts of Nicaragua.

Juan Carlos Piovano

The principal Miskito Indian leader, Brooklyn Rivera, roused crowds whenever he was allowed to speak in public.

Stephen Kinzer

Susan Meiselas/Magnum

During one of my visits to the Miskito homeland, I dove into the Coco River to sample its legendary powers. In this photo, Nicaragua is on the right, Honduras across the river at left.

Not all my assignments were as refreshing as my dip in the Coco. Here Sandinista police escort me away from a group of striking construction workers I wanted to interview.

Carlos Durán/*Barricada*

In 1986, Sandinista soldiers shot down a C-123 transport plane bringing supplies to the contras. They captured an American crewman, Eugene Hasenfus.

The only American to be killed by contra gunfire was Benjamin Linder, a 27-year-old engineer from Portland, Oregon, whose hobby was circus performing.

Barricada

Costa Rican President Oscar Arias, shown with his wife, Margarita, devised the plan that showed Nicaraguans a way out of war.

Peter Morgan

In March 1988, contra and Sandinista leaders finally signed a peace treaty. Among those present at the midnight signing were Defense Minister Humberto Ortega, in uniform at left; President Daniel Ortega, third from left; the two official witnesses, Organization of American States Secretary-General João Baena Soares and Miguel Cardinal Obando y Bravo; and contra leaders Adolfo Calero, signing the treaty, and Alfredo César, standing at right foreground.

Samuel Barreto

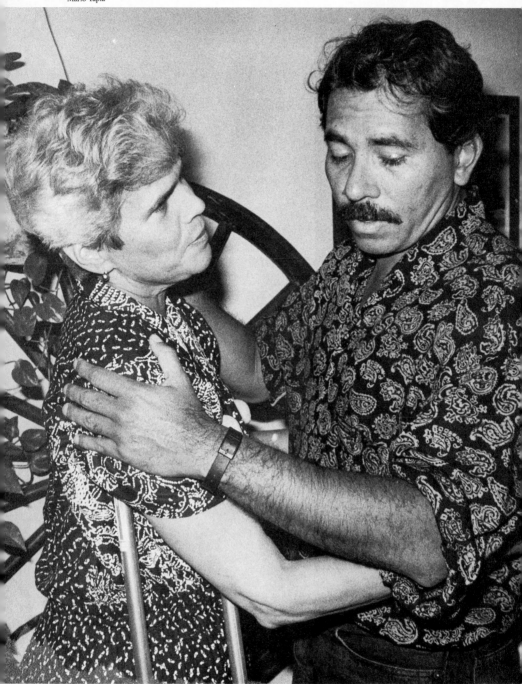

President Daniel Ortega called a national election for February 25, 1990. In a stunning upset, he lost to Violeta Chamorro, and ten years of Sandinista rule came to an end.

questioning the legitimacy of that year's presidential election, and Obando refused to attend Somoza's subsequent inauguration.

At the beginning of 1977, when National Guard troops were in the midst of a major offensive against Sandinista rebels, the bishops issued a statement far more direct and accusatory than any they had ever issued before. It charged that Guardsmen had imposed a "state of terror" in many rural areas, and that in particular they were capturing, torturing, and killing Catholic missionaries. The statement was widely publicized in Nicaragua and elsewhere, and with it Obando and the other bishops cut their remaining ties to the regime. They formalized the break a year later by suggesting that Somoza resign his presidency as a way to pacify the country. Then on June 2, 1979, as the Sandinista-led insurrection was reaching its peak, they went so far as to pronounce armed revolutions legitimate "in the case of evident and prolonged tyranny that gravely threatens the fundamental rights of the person and the common good of the nation."

Immediately following the revolutionary victory, the bishops offered a Mass of thanksgiving that was attended by virtually every important Sandinista leader. Less than two weeks later, they issued a pastoral letter welcoming the new regime and pledging to work with it "in a spirit of brotherhood." Soon afterward, they produced a more detailed and stirring statement that welcomed the advent of the Sandinista era as an "exceptional opportunity for announcing and bearing witness to God's kingdom."

Sandinista *comandantes* returned the bishops' embrace. In a communiqué issued in 1980, they officially acknowledged the role Catholic leaders had played in the insurrection, praising Archbishop Obando for having "courageously denounced the crimes of the dictatorship." There had been much hopeful talk throughout Latin America during the 1960s and 1970s about the possibility of modernizing backward countries by applying a combination of Marxist and Catholic doctrines, and in Nicaragua that radical notion seemed about to be tested. On the surface at least, Archbishop Obando was as open to the idea as any archbishop in the hemisphere.

Miguel Obando was born in 1926 in the mining town of La Libertad, the same frontier outpost where Daniel Ortega would be born nineteen years later. His father worked as a foreman at the El Chaparro gold mine, and his mother, from whom the future archbishop inherited his dark skin and Indian features, was from a poor rural family. Only two of her children, Miguel and a younger brother, Jesus, survived infancy.

The boys' father, Antonio Obando, had attended a seminary and was devoutly Catholic. Few Nicaraguans kept Bibles in their homes in those days—Scripture was considered the province of deacons and priests—but in the Obando household Bible readings and prayer sessions were daily rituals. At the age of twelve, with his parents' blessing, Miguel left home, crossed Lake Nicaragua in a steamship, and arrived in Granada to enroll at the Salesian school there. Soon he decided to enter the priesthood, and after graduating he traveled to El Salvador to begin religious studies. While he was there, his father died of a respiratory ailment apparently related to his work at the gold mine. His mother died later, in 1970, and his brother left Nicaragua at a young age.

"He wasn't formed by his family," his longtime secretary Josefa Valenzuela once told me. "He was formed by the Salesians."

After his ordination, Father Obando followed a career path typical for a Salesian priest. He spent several years as a classroom teacher, specializing in physics, math, and Latin. Later he became a baseball coach, and then served as director of a seminary in El Salvador. He returned to Nicaragua in the 1960s, and in 1968 was named auxiliary bishop of Matagalpa.

Obando quickly became something of a local legend in his mountainous diocese. In contrast to the elderly bishop, who rarely left the provincial capital, and to the majority of Nicaraguan prelates, Obando rode ox-carts and pack animals through the alternately muddy and dusty back country, preaching in remote parishes where no one of his rank had ever ventured before.

In 1968, soon after Obando was named to his post in Matagalpa, Nicaragua's Archbishop Vicente González y Robleto died. That same year, at a historic summit in Medellín, Colombia, Catholic bishops from throughout Latin America approved a series of resolutions urging that the "liberating gospel" of Vatican Council II be spread throughout the Western hemisphere. In a singular burst of enthusiasm, priests and other religious workers from Mexico to Brazil adopted a "liberation theology" that led them to immerse themselves in social activism and, in many cases, to challenge established political orders they considered unjust. The Somozas, who had enjoyed cordial support from Archbishop González, sought assurances from the Vatican that his successor would not be radical or hostile. They knew of Obando as a provincial cleric devoted to pastoral work, and did not object when Pope Paul VI named him archbishop in 1970. By the time they realized the profundity of their miscalculation, it was too late. Archbishop Obando was on his way to becoming the most beloved figure in Nicaragua.

It might have been possible for Sandinista *comandantes* to build a long-term alliance with Archbishop Obando and his fellow bishops, but it would have taken much compromise by all parties. Many leading Sandinistas were lapsed Catholics who had found a political doctrine that satisfied their spiritual needs more fully than traditional religion. They viewed bishops in their multi-colored regalia as relics of a past and pre-rational era. Obando, for his part, was repelled by the Sandinista belief that conflict among social classes was inevitable. In sermon after sermon, he called for reconciliation of "the Nicaraguan family," and condemned the doctrine of class struggle as abhorrent and anti-Christian.

There were some clerics in Nicaragua, including many Jesuits, who made leaps of political faith in order to support the Sandinista regime. They often spoke of how completely other political models had failed to meet Latin America's needs, and how tragic it would be if the Sandinista experiment were to fail. Archbishop Obando, however, would not leap. Like many Nicaraguans, he was jarred and alienated by the rush of change that shook Nicaragua following the Sandinista takeover. By late 1980 he had stopped attending government functions, and his homilies and other public statements began taking on a sharper, more critical tone. He showed himself to be essentially a traditionalist who believed that society could not be transformed by political reform alone; that messianic political movements were a delusion; and that true social regeneration must necessarily have a religious base.

Early optimism about the prospect of a church-state alliance to rebuild Nicaragua was based partly on the presence of four Catholic priests in high-level government posts. They were Fernando Cardenal, the Jesuit I had met during my first trip to Nicaragua, who directed the 1980 literacy campaign and later became Minister of Education; his brother, the poet Ernesto Cardenal, who was named Minister of Culture; Edgard Parrales, who served briefly as Minister of Social Welfare and was then named ambassador to the Organization of American States; and Foreign Minister Miguel D'Escoto, a member of the Maryknoll order. All four had supported the Sandinistas for years, and all were fervent believers in the imperatives of what came to be called liberation theology. The church's true mission on earth, they believed, was to battle social injustice and strive to build a Christian utopia on earth.

The four priests working in high government posts insisted that not only was there no contradiction between their religious vocations and their Sandinista jobs, but that their religious faith was precisely what had made them Sandinistas. Yet their beliefs and religious practices were sometimes highly unorthodox.

"Now we know," Ernesto Cardenal declared once while celebrating a baptism, "that original sin is the division of society into classes ... I command you, spirit of egoism, of capitalism, of Somozism, to come out of this child." As he poured water on the baby's forehead he concluded, "Now I give you your revolutionary membership."

Ernesto Cardenal, whose shoulder-length white hair, black beret, and eternally beatific expression gave him the appearance of a kind of revolutionary guru, became one of Nicaragua's most forceful advocates of liberation theology. He was disarmingly candid, and seemed to enjoy shocking visitors with his radical views. "Our only solution is Marxism," he liked to say. "That's our only hope for freedom."

Once during an interview with Archbishop Obando, I asked him why he had originally embraced liberation theology. He frowned.

"I was enthusiastic at the beginning," he said ruefully. "I thought liberation theology could help people, and could play a role in reducing the enormous gap between rich and poor. But now, watching it in practice, I think this is very unlikely, because I see that it foments class hatred."

The first overt sign that the church-state honeymoon was ending came in May 1980, as the revolutionary coalition was splitting apart. Sandinistas were consolidating their political power, and the two practicing Catholics on the five-member junta, Alfonso Robelo and Violeta Chamorro, had quit in protest. Obando decided that it was time for the four priests serving in government posts to resign and return to their pastoral duties, and he sent them notices ordering them to do so. They refused, citing their "unbreakable commitment to the people's Sandinista revolution."

Later the four priests agreed not to exercise their religious functions while they remained in public office, but they never fully accepted Obando's authority. In the eyes of the church hierarchy, their defiance was unpardonable. Obando declared that the four had placed themselves "in an attitude of open rebellion and formal disobedience to legitimate ecclesiastical authority."

Before long, Sandinista leaders came to recognize that the archbishop had become, and in all probability would remain, their most important domestic enemy. Various *comandantes* took turns replying to his charges. As time passed, Tomás Borge became his principal antagonist. Perhaps the other *comandantes* had decided that Borge was the only one among them with the intellectual agility to confront the archbishop. Certainly he was one of the few who had thought deeply about theological matters. In any case, the job of monitoring religious leaders, and repressing them when necessary, fell to him, and he accepted it eagerly.

"They have never been true Christians, never!" Borge thundered in one speech denouncing Nicaragua's bishops. "I sincerely believe that we Sandinistas respect Christ much more than these false Christians, Pharisees, and traitors to the cause and true creed of Christ."

As both Borge's speeches and Archbishop Obando's Sunday homilies became tougher, the confrontation between church and state escalated. Borge forbade television broadcast of Obando's sermons, and Obando responded by forbidding all other priests to celebrate Mass on television as long as he was not allowed to do so. Several times, gangs of rowdy Sandinistas gathered around cars carrying Obando or priests who supported him, shouting insults and sometimes throwing rocks and other objects. In mid-1982, the Sandinista government refused to permit the United States Agency for International Development to send financial aid to charities controlled by Obando, arguing that the money would be used for political purposes. When bishops received a letter from Pope John Paul II expressing his solidarity, the interior ministry forbade its publication or any reference to it in the press. The Catholic radio station referred to it anyway, and was ordered shut for a month as punishment. Soon afterward, in coordinated actions one Sunday morning, Sandinista protesters took over more than a dozen churches where they said counter-revolutionary doctrine was being spread, launching sit-ins that lasted several weeks.

The anger generated by the intensifying religious conflict was reflected almost comically in a bizarre episode on August 11, 1982. On that day, a well-known young priest named Bismarck Carballo, whose vocal allegiance to Archbishop Obando had made him a hero to anti-Sandinistas, paid a call on a female acquaintance in a quiet section of Managua. He had been inside for several minutes when the front door was suddenly pushed open, and several State Security agents in civilian clothes crashed in. They either found Father Carballo unclothed and engaged in "unpriestly relations," or forcibly stripped him, and then threw him out onto the street. Several dozen conveniently assembled Sandinista activists chased the naked priest through the neighborhood, jeering and shouting insults. A Sandinista film crew had been posted nearby, and explicit footage of the street chase was broadcast on Sandinista television news programs. Watching it sent the bishops to new heights of outrage.

Nicaraguans had barely assimilated the "case of the naked priest," as reporters dubbed it, when a much more serious clash broke out, this time in the eternally rebellious city of Masaya. Sandinista authorities had repeatedly threatened teachers at the Salesian school there, whom they charged with spreading anti-government propaganda. In mid-August crowds of Sandinistas began gathering in front of the school building, shouting revolutionary slogans and damning the Salesians for not supporting the regime. Students and parents arrived to confront them, and tempers flared. At one point a shot rang out, apparently from inside the school, and one of the demonstrators, a peasant who had been bused to Masaya from a nearby village, was killed. Pandemonium broke out, demonstrators and counter-demonstrators began fighting, and police reinforcements had to be called from Managua to restore order. Immediately afterward, Tomás Borge ordered the school confiscated from the Salesians—an order he later rescinded—and expelled two Salesian priests who had been teachers there. For a time it seemed as if church-state relations were at the lowest possible ebb.

THE emergence of the contras as a military force inside Nicaragua posed a dilemma to Archbishop Obando and his fellow bishops. The archbishop had specifically pledged, in his 1980 New Year's message, that he would impartially denounce whatever human rights abuses he saw. Yet he had become so viscerally anti-Sandinista, so convinced that Sandinista rule was fundamentally evil, that he found himself unable to condemn the contras. He may have disapproved of their methods—though he never said so—but he could not avoid a certain sympathy for their cause. So as reports of contra atrocities began to surface, Archbishop Obando held his tongue. He did not protest when contras invoked his name to justify their war, and in his homilies he never accused them of cruelties or brutality. When contra squads abducted and murdered civilians and even religious workers, he and the other bishops were silent.

This posture infuriated Sandinista leaders, and they launched counter-attacks on various fronts. Some of their attacks were directly aggressive, like the entrapment of Father Carballo and the disruption of services at churches whose pastors were politically suspect. Others were more affirmative, aimed at encouraging pro-Sandinista Catholics. The government supported several institutes and study centers that became the backbone of Nicaragua's "popular church." Revolutionary priests who directed these institutions insisted that they were motivated by Christian principles, but Obando scorned them as pawns of the regime.

Despite Sandinista efforts, the "popular church" never attracted support from more than a small minority of Nicaraguan Catholics. Perhaps eighty percent of Nicaraguans were Catholic, and of that number the overwhelming majority was poor, highly traditional, and intensely loyal to Archbishop Obando. The proportion of priests sympathetic to liberation theology was somewhat larger, perhaps reaching as high as one-third, though few were as outspoken as the four clerics in government. What was called the "popular church" was not actually a coherent entity, but a political force that appeared and faded as politically necessary. Its leaders willingly joined Sandinista political campaigns whenever called upon, and at other times occupied themselves with other concerns.

Many of the most vocal "popular church" activists in Nicaragua were foreigners without much understanding of local traditions, but some were prominent Nicaraguans who had devoted their lives to the struggle for justice. One of them was Reynaldo Tefel, who as a young student in New York had met and worked with the radical Catholic activist Dorothy Day. Tefel never wavered in his conviction that Catholicism was fully compatible with revolutionary politics. He had worked closely with the martyred Pedro Joaquín Chamorro, and became a Sandinista supporter after Chamorro's death. In the 1980s he served as Minister of Social Welfare, and also wrote sharply worded articles and pamphlets criticizing Obando and the other bishops. In one broadside, he denounced their theology as "by nature counter-revolutionary, conservative, and devoid of conscience." Nicaraguan Catholics, he wrote, needed "to forge a new man out of Saint Peter, Marx, and Sandino."

Archbishop Obando considered ideas like these nothing less than diabolical. Not only did they place secular figures, and atheists at that, on a level with saints of the Roman Catholic church, but they directly questioned clerical authority. Tefel and other radical Catholics were arguing that Catholics could reject their bishops and still be good Catholics, a doctrine no bishop could accept.

Faced with steady pressures from the regime, the bishops drew closer together. Even those rumored to be uncomfortable with Obando's militantly anti-Sandinista stance were alarmed by the challenges to their authority from Tefel and other government officials. Then early in 1983, they learned that they would have the opportunity to rally around the ultimate symbol of Catholic unity, Pope John Paul II. He was planning a tour of Central America, and had announced plans to stop in Nicaragua.

News of the Pope's upcoming visit electrified Nicaraguan Catholics. He would become the first pontiff to set foot in Nicaragua, and he was arriving at a time of profound church-state hostility. All knew of his Polish background and antipathy to Marxism, and of his letters encouraging Obando and the other bishops. Yet Vatican officials had announced that the Pope's trip was to be strictly pastoral, and bishops in each country were informed that he would not refer to political matters. In other countries that assurance was received happily, but the Sandinista *comandantes* found it insulting. To their way of thinking, no moral person, much less a religious leader of the Pope's stature, could come to Nicaragua without denouncing the contras. To do so would in itself be a political statement. Once it became clear that the Pope would not condemn the contras during his trip, or even refer to the fact that a war was underway, the National Directorate decided to show its disgust by planning a welcome he would not soon forget.

The drama began only moments after John Paul stepped down from his chartered Alitalia jet at Sandino Airport on the morning of March 4. His first act, as was his custom when landing in a country for the first time, was to kneel and kiss the tarmac. Then, as a breeze blew his robes about him, he was led to a receiving line where Sandinista leaders were waiting to greet him. He made his way down the line without incident until coming to Father Ernesto Cardenal. Father Cardenal, not satisfied with a discreet greeting, dropped to his knees, grasped the Pope's hand, and sought to kiss his ring.

John Paul recoiled and pulled his hand away. Then he pointed his index finger at the kneeling Father Cardenal, and shook it like a schoolteacher scolding an errant pupil. He knew that Father Cardenal had defied his archbishop, which by Catholic doctrine put him in defiance of the Vatican.

"Usted debe arreglar su situación con la iglesia," the Pope warned Father Cardenal. You need to correct your situation with the Church.

From the airport John Paul traveled to León, where he delivered a sermon without incident. All attention was focused on Managua, where a huge crowd had assembled at the city's largest public plaza. When the Pope arrived, resplendent in a pristine white cassock, he found himself sharing the dais with the entire National Directorate, as well as a host of other Sandinista dignitaries. Only a few minutes after beginning his sermon, he was interrupted by scattered catcalls. Then, as he asserted the duty of all Catholics to obey their bishops, the catcalls escalated into organized chanting of revolutionary slogans. Authorities had arranged for a group of several hundred Sandinista militants to fill the space directly in front of the podium, and when the shouting began, technicians turned down the Pope's microphone and began amplifying the crowd noise.

"Queremos la paz, queremos la paz!" they shouted, and the Pope stopped in astonishment. He glared down at the demonstrators. It was immediately evident that the noise was coming from a small, organized group, and that the disruption had been planned in advance. Some of the chants, in fact, were being led by Sandinista police officers.

The Pope sought to continue, but could barely be heard above the amplified protesters. Then the crowd took up another favorite Sandinista chant, the one demanding people's power. *"Po-der po-pu-lar, po-der po-pu-lar,"* they shouted, and as they did so, all nine of the ruling *comandantes* raised their fists above their heads and joined in. The Pope looked first stupefied, then angry. His jaw stiffened, and he called for order.

"Silencio!" he demanded, shaking his right arm above his head. *"Silencio!"* The *comandantes* finally quieted down, and the protesters followed suit. Jeering continued, however, and the Pope was clearly enraged. He completed his homily, which as promised made no reference to the contra war, and left Nicaragua immediately.

Because of his years of resisting pressures from the Marxist government in Poland, John Paul had been instinctively sympathetic to Archbishop Obando, but it was his experience in Managua that permanently solidified their relationship. The Pope was now prepared to believe the worst about the Sandinistas. A government that would orchestrate the disruption of a Papal Mass, he concluded, must be capable of any outrage.

With the passage of years, Sandinista leaders came to regret and privately apologize for many of their adventures, but to my knowledge none ever had second thoughts about the decision to confront the Pope so directly. To have allowed the Pope to deliver his message freely, they believed, would have been a sign of weakness, since in their eyes he was part of the coalition arrayed against them. "This is the Pope of the West, the Pope of imperialism," *Comandante* Jaime Wheelock told me in an interview soon after the incident. Ernesto Cardenal, whose airport reprimand had made international headlines, was even more scornful. "It has been said," Father Cardenal asserted in a speech several months afterward, "that the Pope is very thankful to the CIA for the work it has done in Poland, and that the Pope has come to repay the CIA in Central America."

The Sandinistas' harassment of Pope John Paul had an enormous international cost. Television footage of the Pope being shouted down was transmitted around the world, and the effect was instantaneous. The *comandantes'* audacity seemed to confirm all that Ronald Reagan and their other enemies had said of them: that they were arrogant punks with no respect for even the most sacred of institutions, and that their beliefs clashed directly with those of the overwhelming majority of Nicaraguans. Doors in the United States, Europe, and Latin America that had been open to the Sandinistas began to close, and onetime friends began emerging as critics. Many political and religious leaders who had withheld judgment about the Sandinistas for years now believed they had decisive evidence to dismiss them as wild and irrational.

Within Nicaragua, large groups of people had lost confidence in Sandinista rule after the packing of the Council of State in April 1980 and the subsequent repression of what was to have been the first opposition political rally. Internationally, the disruption of the Pope's Mass in Managua had a comparable effect. No single decision the *comandantes* ever made was as permanently devastating to their worldwide prestige.

SEVERAL months after the Pope's tumultuous visit, Sandinista leaders jolted the nation again by imposing universal military conscription for the first time in Nicaraguan history. Many young men did not want to serve in the Sandinista army, and many sought advice from local priests. At least some priests sheltered draft-dodgers or helped them cross illegally into Honduras or Costa Rica. Then, in another defiant pastoral letter, Obando and the other bishops took a ringing anti-draft position. The Sandinistas, they asserted, had undermined the army's legitimacy by converting it into "an instrument of forced political indoctrination."

On October 30, 1983, the Sunday after the bishops issued their anti-draft statement, bands of Sandinista militants stormed into more than a dozen churches in and around Managua. They disrupted services, shouted insults at priests and worshipers, threw rocks, and ignited bonfires. The next day two Salesian priests, both of them administrators at the Salesian school in Masaya, were expelled from Nicaragua after being charged with aiding draft evaders.

The following Sunday, I attended a mid-morning Mass in the outlying neighborhood of Las Brisas. Father Bismarck Carballo, who had recovered from his humiliation at the hands of Sandinista demonstrators a year earlier, was the parish priest. Carballo had achieved a special status because he had been singled out for punishment by the Sandinistas, and Nicaraguans who opposed the regime flocked to hear his sermons. He was young, handsome, energetic, and a stirring anti-Sandinista orator. His church and others like it were virtually the only places for protest still available in Nicaragua. On that morning, parishioners clapped loudly and called his name as he approached the altar, breaking into extended chants of "Long Live Father Carballo!" and "Long Live Christ the King!"

When the crowd was finally quiet, Carballo began his homily. "We all know that the church is suffering in Nicaragua today!" he cried, and parishioners shouted their agreement. "The church is being persecuted!"

Father Carballo gave the faithful all they had come to hear, and after the Mass parishioners swarmed around him. It was nearing eleven o'clock, time for me to make my way across town to hear what Archbishop Obando had to say that day. At his church, the crowd was a bit more refined than the one at Las Brisas, but no less enthusiastic. The archbishop began his sermon by lamenting the takeovers of churches the week before, which he described as "a sad spectacle" that had subjected church-goers to "an afternoon of hell." Recalling that the Sandinistas had proclaimed themselves friends of peace, he spread his arms heavenward and insisted that he too sought peace.

"I pray for a peace in which hatred is not the motivating force in society!" he boomed, and the church shook with applause.

Bishops in outlying provinces were also becoming more outspoken. In Chontales, where the contras had a base of popular support among ranchers and cowboys, Bishop Pablo Antonio Vega charged that State Security agents were abusing innocent civilians. Further north, in Jinotega, Bishop Pedro Vilchez issued an open letter charging that Sandinista troops were committing "tortures, rapes, and killings" with impunity.

As I traveled through war zones, I found evidence to support the bishops' charges. Police agents were arresting people by the dozen and holding them indefinitely on the flimsiest of suspicions, especially in areas where contras were active. Catholic religious workers were always suspect, since they traveled widely and were, at least in their great majority, supporters of the archbishop. Yet I also found evidence of appalling abuses by contras, including some cases that confirmed the worst of what was being reported in Sandinista newspapers.

One of my tours took me to the area around Ocotal, 135 miles north of Managua and just a few minutes drive from the Honduran border. Several of the largest contra bases inside Honduras were close by, and bands of raiders were sweeping through the area. The day before I arrived, they had burned the Nicaraguan customs post at El Espino, one of the two official crossing points between Nicaragua and Honduras. Authorities had evacuated more than a thousand residents of El Espino and nearby villages, but contra snipers were preventing them from reaching the destroyed border post.

I arrived in Ocotal only a few days after a force of about two hundred contras had attacked and tried to seize it. The operation was extremely ambitious, and if successful would have been a spectacular victory. Official reports published in Managua had claimed that contras never came close to the town itself, but residents showed me signs to the contrary. There had been heavy fighting in several neighborhoods, and families had been forced to take cover under beds while firefights raged outside. Many people I met were still in shock, stunned to realize how close the war had suddenly come.

Several funerals were held in Ocotal that day. The first was at a dark and miserable shack on the outskirts of town. Friends and relatives were grieving over the open casket of twenty-year-old Francisco Cruz, who had been killed in the recent fighting. The most composed person in the dirt hovel was a dignified woman who told me she was Francisco's mother. I asked her who she blamed for her son's death. To my surprise, she told me the Sandinistas, not the contras, were guilty.

"The troops came to our house yesterday to ask if Francisco would do guard duty in the neighborhood, and he went with them," she said. "But instead, they took him straight into the heaviest combat, and this morning they called me to the hospital to pick up his body. To die in battle is one thing, but when they give you a rifle you don't even know how to use, and then put you on the front lines, that is unjust."

As I left the Cruz home and walked toward the center of Ocotal, I came across a parade of about a hundred angry mourners, many wearing red-and-black Sandinista headbands and shouting slogans like *"Viva Sandino!"* and *"Muerte al Imperialismo!"* They were following the flag-draped coffin of Jose Salgado, who, like Francisco Cruz, had been among defenders killed during the attack. At the central plaza, his coffin was laid on the back of a pickup truck, and people crowded close to hear fiery speeches pledging eternal resistance to the Yankee. The nation was at peril, the speakers declared, and no patriotic Nicaraguan could ignore the call to duty.

"Tonight, this very night, the process of arming the revolutionary people of Ocotal will begin!" a Sandinista military officer vowed. *"Patria Libre o Morir!"*

Everyone applauded, and there was another round of chants before the coffin was driven slowly away toward the cemetery. I sat in the plaza for a few minutes. It was an unusually pleasant place, and I imagined that at one time it must have been quite a restful oasis. Some benches still remained, and there were signs that the graceful trees had once been carefully tended. There was even a water fountain, out of order and crumbling, with a dirty but still legible brass plaque above it. The plaque read: "Gift of the people of the United States. To commemorate the friendship between the people of Nicaragua and the people of the United States."

After dark in northern Nicaragua, the weather actually turns chilly, and I wore a light sweater as I wandered through Ocotal's streets that evening. As the night wore on, a small crowd began gathering near the military post that faced the central plaza. In the moonlight I made out the profile of the local parish priest, a full-bearded Spaniard. We chatted for a few minutes. He had heard that a shipment of weapons was about to arrive, and that rifles would be distributed to local Sandinistas so they could fight if Ocotal were attacked again.

"There are plenty of contra supporters around here," the priest told me. "Some kids from this town have actually gone to join the contras. Many people here, maybe even most people, are angry with the Sandinistas. But the contras have these people absolutely terrified. They're running wild through the countryside, kidnapping and killing people, torturing, destroying homes, burning crops. Nobody knows who the next victims will be. It's frightening to see."

Soon a military truck pulled into the plaza, and at the sight of it people began to cheer. The truck was loaded with unopened wooden crates of Soviet-made AK-47 assault rifles. An officer from the Ocotal barracks signed for the shipment, and then pried one of the crates open as people crowded around. He pulled out one of the sleek, still-oily rifles, admired it for a moment, and then waved it over his head.

"With these weapons, we will defend our revolution!" he cried. *"Patria Libre!"*

"O morir!" came back the shouted reply, and people began to clap. Some apparently expected officers to begin distributing the rifles then and there, but the Sandinistas were never that foolish. They liked to tell the world that they had distributed weapons to "the people" for self-defense, but that actually meant that caches of weapons were under the control of local Sandinista organizations. Had rifles been given out to the crowd that night, a goodly number of them would undoubtedly have wound up in contra hands. Fully realizing this, the officer in charge ordered that the weapons be carried into the barracks, and there they were placed under lock and key.

In Ocotal and other large towns near the Honduran border, war was becoming part of everyday life. Sounds of mortar fire echoed through the air for hours on end, and strange airplanes appeared in the skies and then disappeared without explanation. Young people were being drafted into the Sandinista army, and others were fleeing to join the contras. Peasants were abandoning their land, afraid to continue farming in conflictive areas. Week after week, the bodies of young people cut down by gunfire were being lowered into the rich Nicaraguan soil.

ON Easter Sunday 1984, almost exactly a year after the Papal visit, Archbishop Obando's church was packed. I found a place to stand near a side door. From there I watched as Obando stepped to the microphone to deliver his homily. He looked stern, but that day as always he was greeted with an outpouring of enthusiastic affection.

After waiting patiently for the applause to subside, Obando began to speak. Nicaragua's nine Catholic bishops, he told parishioners, had just completed a period of reflection. They had produced a lengthy pastoral letter urging the government to open talks with contra leaders, thereby breaking a rigid Sandinista taboo.

"All Nicaraguans inside and outside the country, regardless of ideology, class, or partisan belief, must participate in this dialogue," Obando said, reading from the letter. "We believe that Nicaraguans who have taken up arms against the government must also participate in this dialogue. If not, there will be no possibility of a settlement, and our people, especially the poorest among them, will continue to die."

The Easter letter sparked an immediate storm of Sandinista protest. Tomás Borge called it "criminal," and *Barricada* denounced the bishops as "sanctified hypocrites." A few days later, junta member Sergio Ramírez roused cheers and coined a new slogan when he vowed, "Our only dialogue will be through the barrel of a gun!"

To outsiders who were still hoping that full-scale confrontation in Nicaragua could be avoided, the bitterness of the internal debate was frightening. In Europe, particularly in heavily Catholic Spain and Italy, public and official sympathy for the Sandinistas had declined precipitously in the wake of the Pope's misadventure in Managua, and it fell further as the church-state conflict dragged on. The same pattern was repeated in many parts of Latin America. And in Washington, even politicians inclined to tolerate the Sandinistas were upset by the verbal attacks on Catholic bishops following their Easter letter. "This is not the language of tolerance or religious freedom," said one of them, Senator Edward Kennedy. "These are not the words of people who are genuinely committed to pluralism. This is not the rhetoric of a leadership determined to bring peace and reconciliation to all of the people of Nicaragua."

Archbishop Obando's principal complaints against the Sandinistas—that they were intolerant, instinctively repressive, and contemptuous of traditional religion—were essentially correct. No one who cared for human rights could fail to cheer when Obando denounced mass jailings, mistreatment of prisoners, forced relocations, and other Sandinista outrages. His had been an inspirational voice for justice during the Somoza years, and had accumulated unparalleled moral authority among Nicaraguans. But when he refused to use that authority impartially, it slowly began to weaken. Archbishop Obando was probably the only Nicaraguan who could have followed all aspects of the contra war and reported credibly on abuses committed by all parties. He could have made his church a temple of truth in a country awash in lies. Instead he chose to denounce only the Sandinistas, and to ignore contra abuses. By doing so, he lowered himself into the political arena and robbed Nicaraguans and the world of a potentially glorious moral leader.

Clerics active in the "popular church" were guilty of comparable myopia. For years they had denounced Catholics who attached themselves to power elites and forgot their commitment to the persecuted. But once the Sandinistas came to power, they themselves succumbed to that very temptation. They accepted favors from the regime and willingly endorsed its every action. While Obando and other bishops spoke out on behalf of prisoners and other victims of the regime, the "popular church" remained silent. It became an appendage of the Sandinista Front, and never gained legitimacy in the eyes of most Nicaraguans.

Fierce as the church-state debate became, it never seriously threatened the *comandantes'* hold on power. Yet they could sense that things were not going well for them in the court of world opinion. The religious conflict cost them dearly, and as the contra war escalated they began casting about for a new strategy and a new image.

Both Tomás Borge and Daniel Ortega took important international trips at the end of 1983. Borge traveled through Western Europe, meeting with political leaders and speaking to packed houses in Spain, Italy, and the Netherlands. Soon afterward, Ortega visited Mexico, Panama, Venezuela, and Colombia, the four countries that had formed the so-called Contadora Group several months earlier in an effort to find a negotiated solution to crises in Central America. Many of the leaders with whom Borge and Ortega met sympathized with the Sandinista cause, but nearly all expressed distress at how undemocratic the Managua regime seemed to have become.

Sandinista leaders concluded that it was time for them to do something dramatic, something that would strengthen their democratic credentials and allow them more effectively to refute President Reagan's repeated charges that their rule was oppressive and dictatorial. The solution they found was one that many Latin American military leaders had found before: they called an election. Many people all over the world, they had discovered, believed that elections were synonymous with democracy, and would think much better of the *comandantes* if they had the stamp of electoral approval. The Sandinistas now saw the value of playing the game of images that the Western world was asking them to play.

14

BASEBALL AND OTHER PASSIONS

MANAGUA WAS calm after sundown, and I often spent my evenings in a wicker rocking chair, reading and trying to relax. One night soon after my arrival, I was sitting quietly when I heard what sounded like an eruption of cheers in the distance. I listened for what might follow, but there was nothing. Imagining that some political rally was underway, I pulled on my shoes and headed out to investigate. Before I had gone far, I realized that the cheering was not for politics, but for something Nicaraguans held more dear: baseball, their king of sports.

I arrived at Rigoberto López Pérez Stadium, bought a ticket, and made my way inside. The stadium was shabby and in need of repair, but that did nothing to dampen the crowd's enthusiasm. Men and women of all ages were caught up in the game, shouting encouragement to their favorite players.

As one thickly muscled batter stepped to the plate, a boy sitting next to me told me that this was Ernesto López, Nicaragua's best power hitter. I watched López take two strikes, and then swing perfectly at a slow curve. He made contact, and as the left fielder raced back, the crowd rose to its feet. When the ball cleared the fence, people jumped and shouted for joy. Sad as this country had become, I realized, there were still a few things left to cheer about, a few ways to lighten the heavy burden of being Nicaraguan.

Enveloped in war and tragedy, forced every day to confront the ugliest aspects of life, many Nicaraguans had trouble maintaining their equilibrium. Each day was worse than the one before, and no one dared to predict when the free-fall might end. The entire nation was sinking into a deep state of depression and lassitude. All who lived there shared in the few diversions still available, baseball chief among them.

"There's so much you want to forget," a college student named Ivan Martínez told me one evening as we watched a game together at the Managua Stadium. "This is as close as you can come to forgetting it all."

With the sole exception of Roman Catholicism, no institution is as deeply rooted in Nicaragua as baseball. More than simply a pastime, it has for generations been a way for Nicaraguans to define themselves and hold themselves together as a nation. People play baseball in the most remote hamlets and the most miserable urban slums. Baseball metaphors permeate political speech, and the history of Nicaraguan baseball is widely believed to reflect the nation's history. Famous stories of glory and defeat on the playing field have become part of Nicaragua's heritage. During long years of repressive rule, baseball has absorbed many of the energies and emotions that might, in better times, have been turned to civic or social causes.

The first baseball teams in Nicaragua were organized by an American businessman in Bluefields in the mid-1880s, and within a few years there were teams in most large towns. Adán Cárdenas, a leader of the Conservative party and former president of the Republic, organized the first team in Managua. President José Santos Zelaya, a Liberal, founded the first league, which included a team called "Youth" and another called "The Insurgency." By the early twentieth century, baseball was well established as Nicaragua's favorite sport.

"The ball park on Sunday is the main meeting place in Managua," one visiting American wrote in his diary in 1916. "Sometimes our American Marines play in the game, or more frequently umpire it. You see the native players grow excited and sometimes stab or kill one of the nine."

I soon realized that understanding Nicaraguan baseball would help me understand Nicaragua, and I set out to learn about it. Whenever I spent time with Nicaraguans, I asked them about baseball. At the stadium in Managua, I often arrived early so I could chat with the most enthusiastic fans. I also met several of the radio announcers who broadcasted the games, and occasionally one of them interviewed me between innings.

"With us now is the distinguished correspondent of the *New York Times,* Stephen Kinzer, who is enjoying tonight's game," the broadcaster would say. "So tell us, Kinzer, how does the game look to you?"

I never had much of value to say during these interviews, but I enjoyed being part of the spectacle. When the games were over, I sat and listened as old-timers rehashed classic stories about Nicaragua's great victories and defeats on the ballfield. Of all the stories, I found none so moving as the one about "that error."

Nicaragua began sending teams to international baseball competitions in the 1930s, and by the 1940s was recognized as one of the world's baseball powers. When the Nicaraguan national team arrived in Colombia to play for the world amateur championship in 1947, many believed it could win. But in one of the final games, a substitute third baseman named Jaguita—his real name was Juan Manuel Vallecillo—allowed a grounder to roll through his legs. Nicaragua lost the game, and went on to finish third in the tournament, behind Colombia and Puerto Rico.

Jaguita's error was in the second inning of a nine-inning game, so his teammates had plenty of time to make up for it. But they could not, and soon a myth grew up that Jaguita had cost Nicaragua its best chance at a world championship. He returned home in shame, and though he played baseball for many more years while earning an honest living as a stevedore in Corinto, he was forever branded as the man who had committed "that error." His friends and neighbors tried to help him forget, but he never stopped hearing insults from boorish or drunken fans, insults that sometimes reduced him to tears. A Nicaraguan reporter visited him at home in April 1988, a few months before his death, and asked him what he had to say to his fellow Nicaraguans.

"Stop blaming me," he pleaded.

Baseball had become the way Nicaragua expressed itself to the world. Nicaraguans understood that their country was small, poor, backward, and living under the thumb of a foreign power. They desperately wanted to redeem themselves, to show the world that they were outstanding in something. Thus the baseball team's failure to win a championship in 1947 was a heavy blow to the nation's self-confidence. Many took it as further confirmation that Nicaragua and Nicaraguans were consigned forever to failure, humiliation, and defeat.

Since that moment, Nicaraguan governments have sought in vain for a way to win a baseball championship. The closest they came was in 1972, when Nicaraguan fans had their most sublime moment. I was never able to talk baseball with a Nicaraguan for more than a few minutes without hearing about Nicaragua's historic triumph over supposedly invincible Cuba during that year's world championships. Nearly everyone I met claimed to have been in the Managua stadium that December day.

"I don't believe I have the capacity to convey the greatness of this victory," sportswriter Edgard Tijerino wrote. "It was a dramatic and incredible triumph of a team that knew less over a team that knew more . . . The Cubans had every advantage. They were a complete team with devastating power, and they were better trained, stronger, and more experienced. But in that game, Nicaragua had more fire and more dynamism . . . A dream came true. Nicaragua defeated Cuba. Quixote prevailed over Einstein."

Baseball thrived during the rule of the Somoza family. The Somozas, all of whom had been educated in the United States, were great fans, and sponsored their own team in the Nicaraguan league, *Cinco Estrellas*. When the Sandinista Front swept to power in 1979, baseball remained a top government priority. Minister of Defense Humberto Ortega emerged as the new baseball czar. Like the Somozas before him, he attended many games, assumed responsibility for selecting managers, and sponsored a team of his own, *Los Dantos*, on which he bestowed special favors. As the civil conflict dragged on and people became more and more disgusted by things military, *Los Dantos* became the most unpopular team in Nicaragua. Finally the army emblem was removed from players' uniforms.

Baseball inevitably suffered from the political upheaval that tore Nicaragua apart during the 1980s. Many young men who might normally have spent their time learning to hit and throw had joined one of the warring Nicaraguan armies, or had fled to avoid serving. The most celebrated of those who fled was a teenage infielder from Managua named Brant Alyea. I was watching him bat during a game one day when I heard a group of men behind me speculating about his future.

"Alyea's good, and he gets better every game," one of them said.

"He's too good," replied another man. "I give him two years more in Nicaragua. Then he'll find a way to get to the States."

"Two years, hell!" said someone else. "I give him one year, at most."

Less than a month later, friends told me that Alyea had managed to slip out of Nicaragua. Later we learned that he had signed a professional contract with the Toronto Blue Jays, who paid him a six-thousand-dollar bonus and assigned him to a minor league team in Medicine Hat, Alberta. He was a long way from the warm Managua sun, but he had found an escape from the crushing realities of Nicaraguan life, and his teammates and fans wished him well.

Nicaraguans not only closely followed their local baseball heroes, but also kept track of major league teams in the United States. Newspapers carried daily reports of major league games and published regular features about American players. Sandinista leaders considered this a form of cultural imperialism, and soon after taking power they asked editors of *La Prensa* to stop covering American baseball. The editors refused, saying their readers would be furious at such a step. Finally the Sandinistas relented, and before long they began printing news of American baseball in their own newspapers.

Almost every day during the season, it seemed, one newspaper or another ran an article about Denis Martinez, Nicaragua's greatest baseball hero. Martinez had once starred for the Granada team, and pitched in a Nicaraguan uniform during the 1972 world championships. He was one of a handful of Nicaraguan players who made it to the major leagues, and the only one who was truly successful there. The Nicaraguan press avidly followed his career with the Baltimore Orioles, his recovery from alcoholism, and his rebirth as a star for the Montreal Expos. Among the most common headlines on Nicaraguan sports pages were "Denis Pitches Tomorrow," "Denis Pitches Today," "Denis Wins," "Denis Loses," and the ever-reliable "Denis Doing Fine."

During the 1980s, baseball took on a new importance for Nicaraguans. It served to distract them from the harsh realities of their daily lives, and anchored them in a simpler and calmer past. Baseball was a refuge from reality, though in the end a very incomplete one, as Omar Cisneros, one of the country's most talented managers, once reminded me.

"It's fun, and I love managing a baseball team, but I read the papers too," Cisneros said after one game. "There's too much dying, too much suffering. You can't get it out of your mind."

Baseball was an obvious key to the Nicaraguan soul, but it was only a beginning. I took my assignment as a chance to immerse myself in all things Nicaraguan. Wherever I traveled, I asked questions about local history and traditions, and prodded people to show me whatever old documents or other keepsakes they might have around.

After a while it became known that an American journalist in Managua was interested in such things. People with items to sell began knocking on my door. Without at first realizing it, I became something of a collector. I bought scores of old stamps, some of them depicting stately scenes of Managua before the 1931 earthquake, others showing baseball scenes, and many bearing portraits of political figures. Through the stamps, and through a collection of old Nicaraguan currency I also built up, I could tell the whole story of the nation's history. Older stamps and banknotes showed such figures as the Indian chieftain Diriangén, while newer ones showed rebels like Benjamin Zeledón, Sandino, and Carlos Fonseca.

Besides stamps and coins and banknotes, I collected old photographs, dogeared political tracts, and even some pre-Colombian artifacts unearthed by peasants. My favorite artifact was a small two-headed alligator chiseled from jadeite. It seemed to reflect Nicaragua's eternal uncertainties, and I kept it on my desk as a kind of good luck charm.

My favorite spot to visit in Nicaragua was the stately Masaya volcano. I could drive there in half an hour, following a paved road to the summit. Steam and smoke were always rising from inside, sometimes in dense clouds, other times in a thin white plume. It was one of Central America's most impressive sights.

When Spanish explorers climbed to the summit of the Masaya volcano in 1529, they found the crater full of boiling lava. "I beheld at the bottom of the second crater a fire, which was as liquid as water, and the color of brass," wrote one of them. "This fire appeared to be more violent than any I had ever seen before . . . I cannot believe that a Christian could behold this spectacle unmindful of hell and unrepentant of his sins."

The lava slowly cooled, and when the American travel writer John Lloyd

Stephens visited Masaya in 1840, the volcano was dormant. Stephens imagined its commercial potential. "At home this volcano would be worth a fortune," he wrote, "with a good hotel on top, a railing to keep the children from falling in, a zigzagging staircase down the sides, and a glass of lemonade at the bottom."

Thick clouds of steam began rising from the crater at the beginning of the twentieth century. For a time people feared it might erupt violently, as had other Nicaraguan volcanoes in 1835 and 1850, but it never did. The sight of its constant smoking, however, always inspired awe in visitors, myself included.

There was one other place in Nicaragua I particularly enjoyed visiting. It was a permanent exhibition of giant stone idols, arranged in an eerie double file behind an ancient convent in Granada. The idols, made between A.D. 800 and 1200, depict disturbing man-beasts, some of them seeming to be humans in the grasp of wild animals. Many theories have been advanced to explain their origin and meaning, all of them speculative.

Spanish explorers came upon the idols during expeditions to the volcanic islands that dot Lake Nicaragua. The first person to study and catalogue them was the intrepid American diplomat E. G. Squier. He shipped some of them to the Smithsonian Institution in Washington, and later wrote about them.

"They are plain, simple, and severe, and although not elaborately finished, are cut with considerable freedom and skill," Squier wrote. "[One] seemed like some gray monster just emerging from the depths of the earth, at the bidding of a wizard-priest of an unholy religion . . . [Another] was a study for a Samson under the gates of Gaza, or an Atlas supporting the world."

Time and mistreatment took their toll on the statues, and the drawings in Squier's book show much more detail than was visible a century later. But the idols had lost none of their power to impress. For me, the Masaya volcano and the stone idols on display in Granada were two of the most memorable sights in Nicaragua.

During the years of contra war I visited nearly every Nicaraguan town and village, as well as many hamlets not noted on any map. My white jeep, with ever-enthusiastic Guillermo Marcia at the wheel, became a familiar sight on back roads. For days at a time, Guillermo and I would roam the hills of Jinotega or the prairies of Chontales searching for news.

One day, at the end of a rugged road in Chontales, we arrived at a small settlement called La Embajada. We noticed a handful of people gathered outside one shack, and went to investigate. Lying on a bed inside was a small boy with a bloodstained bandage around his head. Neighbors told us that he had been hit by shrapnel the day before, and that his skull had been torn open. La Embajada was beyond the reach of medical care, so the boy's parents could do nothing but wait for him to die.

After a few minutes of hurried arranging, Guillermo and I agreed to drive the boy immediately toward civilization. He was only half-conscious, and we wondered if he would survive the trip. We carefully carried him into our jeep and then raced to the nearest Red Cross center, where it was determined that he needed to be sent to the hospital at Juigalpa. I kept track of his progress, and learned that he slowly recovered and was ultimately able to rejoin his family. Guillermo and I had saved his life, and given him a chance to return to his world of poverty, isolation, and violence.

On trips to the countryside I usually slept on floors, in wooden bunks, or in hammocks. After a couple of days, my body would be covered with rashes and insect bites. Often I was sick from one unknown ailment or another. Illness was a constant companion to foreigners in Nicaragua, just as it was to Nicaraguans themselves. It could not have been otherwise in a country where governments had ignored public health problems for generations, where there were no real sanitary standards, and where few qualified doctors or nurses remained.

Only twice during my five years in Managua did I contract diseases serious enough to require my evacuation to the United States. Once I was incapacitated for a few days after being stung by a scorpion. At other times, I simply adjusted to feeling poorly. I had extended headaches and body pains, and sometimes felt so lethargic that I had to drag myself out of bed in the morning. Often I was sick to my stomach for days on end. Most of these ailments, I realized, were caused by what I ate and drank when visiting peasants in remote areas. Their food was unclean and their drinks crawled with bacteria and other toxins. But when they offered to share with me, they were making heartfelt gestures, often at great sacrifice. I always accepted.

MOST of my travels in Nicaragua took me to places where news was being made, but whenever possible I visited less likely corners of the country. One spot that had always fascinated me was El Castillo, the historic fort that guarded the San Juan River. After reading so much about its role in Nicaraguan history, I hated the thought of leaving Nicaragua without seeing it.

"El Castillo!" exclaimed Guillermo when I proposed the trip. "Rafaela Herrera!"

"Who?"

"Rafaela Herrera!" he repeated. "She's the heroine of El Castillo."

I pressed for details, but Guillermo had forgotten much of the Nicaraguan history he learned in school. That afternoon, rummaging through books in my office, I learned that Rafaela Herrera had helped save Central America from conquest by Great Britain in 1762, and that she was the most celebrated woman in Nicaraguan history. Her father had been the commandant of El Castillo when British vessels attacked, and he was killed early in the battle. Subordinate officers were about to surrender the fort when Rafaela, just nineteen years old, rallied them to arms. A four-day artillery battle followed, and the British were finally forced to withdraw. They left behind, according to one Nicaraguan history text, "many dead, several wrecked ships and, above all, a glorious place in Nicaraguan history for the bravery of a woman, Rafaela Herrera."

It took Guillermo and I a full day to drive from Managua to the remote provincial capital of San Carlos. There I found one of the local Sandinista administrators sitting on a patio overlooking Lake Nicaragua, listening to music on his Walkman. We chatted for a few minutes, and I asked him if it would be possible for me to travel downriver to El Castillo.

"We could probably find a boat for you, and a boatman to get you down the river, but finding fuel is more difficult," he replied. He promised to investigate, and a little while later I dropped off a couple of reggae tapes to encourage him.

After two days of waiting, we heard good news. Local authorities had decided to grant us a permit for travel to El Castillo, and to sell us a tank of fuel. With a local boatman to guide us, we were underway by mid-morning. As we pulled away from shore, I thought of how cruel fate had been to San Carlos. If the great canal had been built through Nicaragua instead of Panama, San Carlos would probably have become a thriving center of international commerce. Instead it was poor, desolate, and forgotten.

Soon after San Carlos faded behind us, however, I began to realize that in one sense the decision not to build a canal in Nicaragua had been a great blessing. The San Juan River was never ravaged by development, and remained resplendent in its natural glory. Early travelers like Squier and Mark Twain had described the river basin as an earthly paradise, and on the day I made my trip it looked just as they pictured it.

The tropical rain forest through which the San Juan River snaked was a lush wonderland teeming with life. As we motored slowly downriver, graceful white herons swept from beneath overhanging cypress and banyan trees. Vividly colored butterflies flitted among the coconut palms. Alligators lay side by side on the muddy bank, absorbing the damp heat. Half a dozen turtles the size of dinner plates drifted by on a giant tree stump.

Two hours after setting out, we turned a bend in the river and the stately fortress came into view. It was perched high on a hill, ancient and crumbling but still an impressive sight. We pulled to the shore, showed our travel permit to the lone soldier on duty, and began to climb toward the fortress.

Long years of neglect and vandalism had taken their toll on El Castillo, but the remaining walls were still thick and solid, and there were still gun turrets to show where cannon had once been emplaced. We found several cells apparently used to confine prisoners, as well as remnants of underground tunnels.

Gazing down at the river, I could feel history washing over me. At this spot Rafaela Herrera had turned back the British advance into Central America, and here William Walker's adventurers had done battle a century later. Tens of thousands of Americans had passed this spot on their way to the California gold fields. Surely no edifice in Central America had seen more drama than El Castillo.

Our boatman was anxious to begin the return trip, lest we be caught on the river after nightfall. He navigated carefully among the shoals, floating tree trunks, and other obstacles. The sun was setting as we arrived back at San Carlos. That evening, I found my Sandinista friend and told him I wanted to make one more boat trip before returning to Managua. My destination was another place I had heard about but never visited: the Solentiname archipelago in Lake Nicaragua.

There are more than thirty islands in the archipelago, only the largest of them inhabited. In the early 1960s, the radical poet/priest Ernesto Cardenal had built a small chapel there, and introduced highly unorthodox forms of Catholic worship. In long dialogues with parishioners, he equated the Somoza dictatorship with Herod's tyranny, and compared Sandinista guerrillas to Christ and his apostles. Secretly he became a Sandinista himself, and allowed a squad of guerrillas to train at his island sanctuary. The guerrillas launched a bold attack on San Carlos in October 1977, and in retaliation President Somoza ordered the Solentiname chapel destroyed.

When Ernesto Cardenal was named Minister of Culture in the Sandinista government, he focused international attention on a remarkable art colony that he had helped to establish at Solentiname. He had brought paint and canvas there for the first time, and encouraged residents to paint what they saw around them. Soon more than a dozen of them, mostly women, emerged as talented painters. Reflecting Father Cardenal's influence, some of their early paintings had political themes, showing such scenes as Christ being arrested by National Guardsmen. But most depicted the rich beauty of the islands, with bright green and blue tones predominating. Their style was primitive, the best of them reminiscent of Henri Rousseau.

No permits were required for travel to Solentiname. Our boat trip took barely an hour, and we docked in front of the local guest house. Monkeys, parrots, and macaws chattered above us. There could be no more inspiring spot for an artist seeking to capture the richness of tropical life.

The Solentiname painters worked in or near their own homes, and I was able to visit several of them. All were grateful to Father Cardenal, who had not only founded the art colony but also arranged exhibitions in many parts of Latin America and Europe.

"Ernesto discovered that we could paint," said Maria Silva, the first artist I met. "At the beginning we had no idea there was a market for paintings like these, but now we can't turn out enough to meet the demand."

In a simple wooden shack I found a painter named Eylin Guadamúz Pineda at work. She had set up her easel in front of her window, which looked out across verdant overgrowth and the vast lake.

"I'll keep painting forever, even if I don't earn a cent," she told me. "I don't know if what we paint is good art or bad art. All I can say is that it's very satisfying. It lets us express what is inside us."

I admired several of Mrs. Guadamúz's finished paintings, and as I was preparing to leave she asked if I'd like to buy one.

"Are you allowed to sell them?" I asked her, knowing that commerce in Solentiname paintings was regulated by the government.

"These two I can sell," she replied.

The two small canvases she showed me were dense landscapes, thick with foliage. One showed monkeys picking mangoes off a tree.

"How much?" I asked.

"You have dollars, right?"

"Yes, I have dollars."

"How about one hundred dollars for the pair?"

The paintings were not the best ones I had seen that day, but I had a chance to buy them directly from the artist, at the studio where she had painted them. I agreed, paid the asking price, and brought the paintings home with me. There they became part of my growing collection of things Nicaraguan.

I was always on the lookout for insights into Nicaragua, and sometimes I found them in the classified advertisements at the back of *La Prensa.* Nearly all of the ads were placed by people who had decided to abandon Nicaragua, and were selling their belongings to raise cash. Many began with the euphemism *Por Motivo de Viaje Vendo*—Selling Because I'm Going on a Trip. By the mid-1980s, these ads filled column after column, testifying to the hopelessness many Nicaraguans had come to feel for their country's future. They offered items ranging from silverware and medical instruments to tires and machetes.

One day my eye was caught by an advertisement that offered several sets of books for sale. Among them was one listed as "Rubén Darío, complete works, 5 vols." I circled it.

Since first arriving in Nicaragua, I had noticed the unusual prominence of poetry. In every town I found people who considered themselves serious poets, and who were able to discuss poetry with clarity and sophistication. Many could recite long verses by great Nicaraguan poets of generations past.

"I can't say exactly why this happened," Michelle Najlis, a young Nicaraguan poet, once told me. "But I know it has something to do with Rubén."

In learning about Nicaragua, I had heard frequent mention of Rubén Darío. I knew that he was considered Nicaragua's greatest literary figure, and that many considered him the finest and most influential poet ever to have emerged from Latin America. Politicians of every stripe laid claim to his legacy. At the centenary of his birth in 1967, the Somoza regime had organized an international symposium in his honor. Sandinista leaders also embraced his memory, and no one was surprised when President Daniel Ortega invoked "the divine Rubén" in his 1984 inaugural address.

Despite all this, I had read only a few fragments of Darío's poetry. The advertisement offering a set of his complete works sounded appealing, and I arranged to visit the seller. The books were elegant. They had been printed in Spain, bound with fine leather, and gilt in gold. I paid forty dollars for the five volumes.

Of all the adventures I had in Nicaragua, the most magical and most unexpected was discovering Rubén Darío. I began by reading a handful of poems recommended by my Nicaraguan friends, and was astonished. Darío used the Spanish language with breathtaking deftness, and led me to a new understanding of its expressive power. I immediately set out to learn more about him.

On my trips northward to cover war news, I had often passed a road sign pointing toward the town of Darío. I knew that the town had once been called Metapa, and that the name had been changed to honor its most famous son. One day, soon after buying the books, I followed the sign, and in a few minutes found myself in a medium-sized town where streets were paved and utility wires reached most houses. I easily found the low adobe building where Rubén Darío was born on January 18, 1867. Inside, an elderly curator invited me to view a small wooden cradle and some old photographs. The two rooms were sparsely furnished, with only a few artifacts on display.

"León stole our glory," the curator told me with a smile. "Rubén was born here, but his home was León. Go there if you want to learn about him."

León is Nicaragua's traditional intellectual center, the home of its oldest university and many of its most cultivated families. Rubén Darío grew up there among erudite men and women, and as a small boy he sat quietly through many long discussions of literature and philosophy. He published his first verses in local newspapers while in his early teens, and became known as the "child-poet." Soon he was given a post at the National Library in Managua, where he devoured classical French and Spanish literature. In 1888 he burst onto an unsuspecting Europe with *Azul,* a short but dazzling collection of stories and poems written in fresh, melodic rhythms. His later works were of surpassing beauty, confirming all of his early promise. Praise followed him during his years in South America and Europe, and at the time of his death in 1916, shortly after his final return to León, he was the leading literary figure in the Spanish-speaking world. From wretched and faraway Nicaragua had sprung this brilliant vagabond spirit, a poet deeply versed in the classics, enamored of French and Italian culture and master of a musical sense that allowed him to fashion some of the loveliest verses written in any language.

"That such a thing could happen makes you believe either in God or Darwin," the Nicaragua poet Carlos Martínez Rivas once mused.

Darío lived most of his life outside Nicaragua, but he always remained deeply attached to his native land. He greatly admired the progressive-minded President José Santos Zelaya, and served the Zelaya government as a diplomat and propagandist. Like many Nicaraguans, he was angered by the United States intervention that toppled Zelaya in 1909.

In many of his poems and essays, Darío showed deep political passion. He lamented the "treacheries of ambition" that had kept Latin America backward and in upheaval, and ceaselessly defended the cause of pan-American unity. During the Sandinista era, government leaders sought to portray him as having been strongly anti-Yankee. They published leaflets and posters carrying his poem "Ode to Roosevelt," which includes these lines:

> You are primitive and modern, simple and complex;
> you are one part George Washington and one part Nimrod.
> You are the United States,
> future invader of our innocent America
> with its Indian blood, an America
> that still prays to Christ and still speaks Spanish . . .
> Roosevelt, you must become, by God's own will,
> the deadly Rifleman and the dreadful Hunter
> before you can clutch us in your iron claws.

"Ode to Roosevelt" was written in 1905, just four years before the United States forced President Zelaya from power. It was the Sandinistas' favorite Darío poem, the one they most often quoted. But in my set of Darío's complete works, I found another poem that conveyed a very different view of the United States. It was called "Salutation to the Eagle," and after reading it I understood why it was never printed in any Sandinista-sponsored anthology. In it, Darío sings to the "magic eagle who loved Walt Whitman so much," and urges Latin America to "learn constancy, vigor and character from the Yankee." He speaks to the United States:

> Welcome, magic eagle with wings great and strong,
> Extend your great continental shadow southward . . .
> May Latin America receive your magic influence
> And may a new Olympus be born, full of Gods and heroes!

The greatest of Darío's poems are not political at all, but deal with universal themes. In his early work, he was preoccupied with beauty, love, and sensual pleasures. Later he showed a more introspective side, brooding over the ephemeral quality of life and pondering his destiny "to be, and to know nothing, and to have no certain path."

Although the political upheaval of the 1980s took its toll on the cult of Darío in Nicaragua, and although the "Rubén Darío Honor Guard" no longer met for readings as it had in decades past, there remained a loose-knit group of Nicaraguans who seriously studied Darío and continued to publish new studies of his work and his dramatic, alcohol-shortened life. My favorite among these "Dariologists" was José Jirón Terán, a shopkeeper in León who had devoted thirty years to collecting editions of Darío's work and books about him. Jirón had more than three thousand volumes crammed into musty bookcases that lined every room in his house and spilled over into his sister's house next door. Upon request, he could discourse at length on the role of Greek mythology in Darío's poetry, Darío's view of God, Darío's debt to the French symbolists, and a hundred other such topics.

Though the writer Rubén Darío belongs to all who read his work, Darío as a legend belongs above all to Nicaragua. He was the first figure to make Nicaraguans proud of their nationality, to encourage them to believe that a Nicaraguan could accomplish as much as anyone else or more. When he died, Nicaraguans staged the most elaborate funeral in their history. For six days his body was displayed to weeping crowds, guarded by alternating groups of soldiers and students. Thousands of mourners followed his funeral cortege.

When first I discovered Darío's poetry, I could not understand how such a titanic and majestic artist had remained so obscure in the United States. His audacious rhyme schemes, singsong rhythms, and daringly modern use of language placed him on a level with the poets he most admired, among them Whitman, Verlaine, Edgar Allan Poe, and Victor Hugo. Yet he remained all but unknown in the English-speaking world. The reason, I came to realize, was that the transcendent beauty of his verses was entirely lost in translation.

Darío resists and defies translation, yet among Spanish speakers, his reputation is secure. He is universally recognized as the figure who liberated the Spanish language from centuries of stiffness, and inspired generations of writers to follow. Among the many who have directly acknowledged his influence are Federico García Lorca, Pablo Neruda, and Gabriel García Márquez.

I often imagined that the classic Nicaraguan would be a baseball player with a dog-eared book of Darío poetry protruding from his back pocket. Though I looked for that person, I never found him. But at the baseball stadiums, in the remote countryside, and in the poetry of Darío, I found clues to the spirit of a nation often victimized and repressed, several times on the brink of greatness, and ever searching for its destiny.

15

ACTION DEMOCRACY

IN THE eyes of most Americans, Arturo Cruz would be the ideal Nicaraguan. In his youth he had abandoned a promising military career to join conspirators trying to overthrow the Somoza dictatorship. He forged a close personal and political bond with the valiant newspaper publisher Pedro Joaquín Chamorro, and the two served prison sentences together for their anti-Somoza plotting. The injustices of Nicaraguan life turned Cruz into a revolutionary, but he never sympathized with Marxist ideology. He had lived in Washington for many years, greatly admired the United States, and was free of the anti-Americanism that radiated from most Nicaraguan radicals.

Sandinista leaders respected Cruz's revolutionary credentials, and after taking power they entrusted him with a series of high-level positions, in which he served with distinction before breaking with the regime for reasons of conscience. He soon became the most respected non-Sandinista political figure in Nicaragua. When it became clear that a presidential election would be held in 1984, he immediately emerged as the logical opposition candidate.

Many Nicaraguans dared to hope that somehow the election campaign could contribute to the cause of peace. Fighting between Sandinista and contra forces was steadily escalating, civilian deaths were mounting, and there was every indication that both sides were preparing for a protracted conflict. The election was a magnificent chance to upset the momentum carrying Nicaragua toward full-scale war.

No Nicaraguan government had ever allowed its enemies to come to power through elections, and there was no reason to expect the Sandinista government to do so. The *comandantes* themselves said as much, asserting openly that they were not prepared to surrender the power they had won at such a cost. But the country was facing the gravest crisis in its history, and patriotism demanded that all Nicaraguans do their utmost to avert conflagration. For a time it seemed that Arturo Cruz and Daniel Ortega were poised to make a historic compromise for peace. At the crucial moment, however, they failed, and their failure condemned Nicaragua to civil war.

IF Ortega was the exemplar of Latin America guerrilla leaders, proud of his anti-Americanism and his military power, Cruz was the classic civilian dissident. Born in 1923 to a landowning family in the provincial capital of Jinotepe, he grew up in a turbulent political environment. The Cruz clan had been traditionally Liberal, but broke with the Liberal party in the 1930s to protest the Somozas' excesses. Young Arturo excelled as a student, and was selected to enter the newly established Military Academy in Managua, which was then under the command of an American officer. He graduated in 1944 with a National Guard commission, but refused to serve after concluding that the Guard had become a private instrument of the Somoza clan. Instead he enrolled at Georgetown University in Washington, D.C., where he earned an undergraduate degree in two and a half years, attending school during summers in order to finish more quickly.

In 1947, when Nicaragua's newly elected President Leonardo Argüello announced his intention to defy the Somoza family and establish democracy in Nicaragua, Cruz rushed back to Managua to support him. Argüello's bold challenge lasted just twenty-six days, and Cruz was one of those arrested in the wake of his overthrow. He was jailed for four months, and after his release he returned to Georgetown. There he earned a graduate degree in economics, became a fan of the Redskins football team, and acquired the habits and opinions that would later make him so congenial to Americans.

One afternoon while living in Washington, Cruz happened to walk past the front of the White House. The occupant at that time was Dwight Eisenhower, a friend of the Somoza regime, and Cruz could not contain his anger.

"Down with Eisenhower!" he shouted at one of the White House guards. "Eisenhower supports dictatorship in Latin America! Down with him!"

The guard, no doubt accustomed to such harangues, watched without moving. Cruz stood still, half expecting to be dragged away by a squad of police. Nothing happened, however, and he shouted a few more insults. Still there was no response, and finally he moved on. In his homeland and in many other Latin

American countries, he realized, such conduct would be enough to justify imprisonment or worse. Yet in the United States it was freely permitted. The incident made a deep impression on him, and was one of many that led him to profound faith in the principles of Jeffersonian democracy.

Returning to Nicaragua after winning his graduate degree, Cruz fell in with a circle of impatient young Conservatives, among them Pedro Joaquín Chamorro and Reynaldo Tefel, who were devoted to anti-Somoza agitation. Chamorro described their ideology as "nationalist and social revolutionary." They quickly attracted police attention, and several were arrested following an unsuccessful attempt on the life of President Anastasio Somoza García in 1954. Cruz served eleven months without charge, and after his release he lowered his political profile. He worked for several private companies, and then in 1969 left Nicaragua to begin a career at the Inter-American Development Bank in Washington. There he might have remained permanently if his country had not called.

Although never a Sandinista himself, Cruz had always felt visceral sympathy for all movements aimed against the Somoza dictatorship. In 1978, when Sandinista leaders sought prominent civilians to form the dissident coalition known as the Group of Twelve, Cruz was among the first they invited, and he joined immediately. After winning their insurrectional victory the next year, the Sandinistas appealed to him to quit his job in Washington and assume the presidency of the looted Central Bank. He agreed, and within days after the Sandinista takeover he was immersed in frantic negotiations with creditors from all over the world, many of whom were threatening to close off Nicaragua's credit lines as punishment for Somoza's failure to make payments during the uprising.

My first interview with Cruz was during those chaotic early months. We met at his cluttered Central Bank office, where he was still trying to determine the magnitude of the financial disaster left in the wake of the Somoza regime's collapse. There was a briskness about his manner that was unusual in Nicaragua. Fifty-six years old, solidly built, with wavy black hair receding from his forehead and wearing oversized tortoise-rim eyeglasses, he looked as if he could have been a central banker from a wealthy, developed country.

Our interview was somewhat disjointed because Cruz was being interrupted every few minutes to take phone calls or answer urgent telex messages from foreign bankers, but I sensed immediately that he was well prepared for his responsibilities. He not only understood international finance, but was obviously excited about the once-in-a-lifetime experiment that was unfolding around him. Seeing a person of such ability and passion working in government was enough to fill anyone with hope for Nicaragua's future.

*   *   *

WHEN two of the five junta members, Violeta Chamorro and Alfonso Robelo, quit their posts in May 1980, some opposition leaders feared that the two would be replaced with militant radicals. Instead, Sandinista *comandantes* named two men with honorable backgrounds in the Conservative party. One was Rafael Córdova Rivas, a lawyer who had defended Sandinista prisoners during the Somoza era, and the other was Arturo Cruz.

Córdova Rivas proved pliable, willing to say and do whatever the Sandinistas asked, but Cruz was quite different. He never directly criticized Sandinista leaders in public, but in private meetings he clashed with them repeatedly. After ten months of losing arguments, he resigned from the junta and announced that he was through with government. But he had been in private life for only a few days when the *comandantes* approached him and asked him to take another sensitive post: ambassador to the United States.

The appointment, and Cruz's acceptance, surprised some people, but all welcomed it. Sandinista leaders appreciated the diligence Cruz had shown at the Central Bank and on the junta, and recognized that his stature and experience in Washington could benefit them. Other Nicaraguans admired his commitment to free enterprise and liberal democracy. But although he was widely considered one of Nicaragua's most capable public citizens, his friends doubted that he would be comfortable serving the Sandinistas for long.

I was one of many who had admired Cruz from afar. At this moment, on the eve of his departure for Washington, I was curious to know his feelings. Through mutual friends I sent word that I wanted to interview him, and one evening he called and offered to stop by for a chat.

In April 1981, it still seemed possible that the conflicts shaking Nicaragua might be resolved without violence. President Reagan had moved into the White House, but he had not yet begun publicly supporting the idea of anti-Sandinista insurrection. Within Nicaragua, many critics of the regime still hoped for accommodation, and Cruz's appointment as ambassador encouraged them. No one was better equipped to negotiate an agreement between Washington and the *comandantes,* if agreement was still possible.

At that time, I was staying at the Intercontinental Hotel, where guests were either given a room that faced forward, overlooking the ruins of what had once been downtown Managua, or one facing back, toward the ominous State Security complex that included El Chipote prison. I was in a room facing forward, and as I waited for Cruz to arrive I gazed out my open window at the destroyed city. Cruz knocked at precisely the appointed time, not half an hour or an hour late as was the Nicaraguan custom. We shook hands and he sat down in a frayed armchair, lit a cigarette, and placed himself at my disposal. I asked him to tell me what he really thought of the Sandinistas.

"The government is in the hands of intelligent, honest patriots," he told me.

"I have never questioned that, or their deep sense of honor. But they need to revise some of their political views. It's difficult for young revolutionaries to understand the deep, deep discontent that exists here."

It was hardly the kind of statement one expected from a newly named ambassador, and I wrote down every word. Without waiting for more questions, chain-smoking and occasionally rising to stare out over the ruins, Cruz launched into a disarmingly candid monologue that crystallized the position of Nicaraguans who had once supported the Sandinista revolution, but were now worried about its course.

"Some very unfortunate things are happening here in Nicaragua, and I'm not going to Washington to cover them up," he began. "The Sandinistas need to make the transition from being soldiers to being political leaders. They need to understand that political opposition is not only tolerable, but indispensable for a stable society. If they don't, they run the risk of being thrown out of power."

Cruz was known as a devout Catholic and an admirer of Archbishop Obando, and had even visited the rustic shrine to the Virgin Mary at Cuapa. As we spoke that evening, he seemed especially anguished over the rising tensions between Nicaragua's political and religious leaders. The *comandantes* would never be able to unify the country, he predicted, as long as they were in conflict with Catholic bishops.

"I know of many, many small businessmen and others—not Somoza cronies or self-centered millionaires—who are profoundly upset over what they see as efforts by the government to take over from the church the task of moral guidance," he said. "Many of these people, who we need for our future development, have left the country for this reason. When their six-year-old comes home from school with slogans about Sandino and ideas that the bourgeoisie is nothing but a gang of traitors who hate their country, then that's the last straw."

Cruz spoke for more than an hour. I was amazed at his openness, and when he finished his cathartic monologue, I waited a moment to allow him to catch his breath. He pulled out a handkerchief, wiped his brow, and lit another cigarette.

"You sound more like a critic of the regime than a supporter," I ventured.

"All of my concern is because I love my country, and because I desperately want this experiment to succeed," he replied. "I would never put myself in a position of opposing the revolution."

A few days later, Cruz assumed his new post at the Nicaraguan embassy in Washington. From his first days there, many of his closest friends and relatives believed he was embarked on a hopeless mission. Soon he came to agree with them. As he was trying to assert that the Sandinistas were trustworthy moderates, the regime in Managua was turning tougher by the day. Cruz found he had no real influence over the *comandantes,* and finally concluded that he could serve them no longer. On a Saturday in mid-November, just six months after taking over as ambassador, he flew to Managua, personally delivered his resignation, and then returned to Washington.

I was in the United States between *Globe* assignments when Cruz announced his resignation, and managed to reach him by telephone after he returned from his weekend trip to Managua. He agreed to receive me the next day at the embassy building on New Hampshire Avenue, where he would be packing his belongings. When I arrived there, the mood was somber. A secretary escorted me upstairs, and I found Cruz leafing through a file of papers. When he turned to face me, he stood silent for a moment, shaking his head sadly. I thought of our conversation in Managua, and imagined that he also was remembering it. Too many of the fears he had expressed for Nicaragua's future were being fulfilled.

"This ritual of speeches, mass rallies, and Cuban-style revolution has been a total failure," he sighed. "Combined with the strident rhetoric coming from the United States, this could produce in Nicaragua a result which I dread even to think about. The deterioration of support in Washington for my country is almost total."

It was a grim prognosis, and Cruz seemed pained to pronounce it. I asked him what he would like to see in Nicaragua.

"The Sandinistas have a challenge: to build a political system acceptable to their own ideology, but also to that of the majority of Nicaraguans, who do not want Communism," he replied. "I repeat, they do not want Communism."

Anti-Sandinista exiles based in Miami had already made overtures to Cruz, urging him to denounce the Sandinista government and join their cause. I asked him about his future plans, and he heaved another of his world-weary sighs.

"All I really want is to disappear slowly from public life," he said.

From the time he resigned his diplomatic post that week until the *comandantes* decided to call a presidential election more than two years later, hardly a word was heard from Arturo Cruz. He worked quietly at the Inter-American Development Bank, holding himself above the Nicaraguan political fray. Yet he never lost his following at home. Opposition leaders recognized that his unique credentials would make him a most appealing political candidate.

In January 1984 the Sandinistas announced that they would convene an election later that year. Nicaraguans would be asked to choose a president, a vice president, and ninety members for a new National Assembly, all for terms of six years. With that announcement, the campaign season opened. From Managua, I telephoned Cruz in Washington, and he told me he might agree to run for president if his candidacy "could contribute to a national consensus that could stop the spilling of blood in our country."

WHILE the few hundred people who constituted the Nicaraguan political class planned strategy for the coming campaign, many of their fellow citizens were caught up in a far more brutal conflict. Congress had approved $24 million in aid to the contras late in 1983, and by the beginning of 1984 armed clashes were being reported almost daily. Contra raiders were striking at farm cooperatives and small military outposts, and CIA squads supporting them were attacking coastal targets from fast-moving speedboats. In a series of alarming successes, anti-Sandinista units destroyed an offshore oil pipeline at Puerto Sandino, blew up petroleum storage tanks in Corinto, and even bombed the international airport in Managua. Then suddenly there was a new escalation, one that no one had expected, and Nicaragua burst onto the world's front pages again.

Corinto, Nicaragua's principal seaport, lies on the Pacific coast ninety miles northwest of Managua. Activity at the port, like economic activity all over Nicaragua, was a shadow of what it had been in pre-revolutionary days. Two or three freighters a week docked there, usually carrying donated cargo from Europe or the Soviet Union.

Early in March, journalists in Managua began hearing rumors that contras had planted mines in Corinto harbor. Sandinista newspapers carried vague references to "incidents" caused by "artifacts" there, but the government issued no official statement. After a Dutch dredger was damaged in Corinto harbor, Sandinista spokesmen suggested that a mechanical malfunction might have been responsible.

A few days later another freighter, this one of Panamanian registry, was also reported to have had trouble in Corinto. The defense ministry issued a statement saying the freighter had been damaged by "an external explosive charge." Never in any statement did the Sandinistas use the word "mine." I found their ambiguity puzzling, and decided to drive to Corinto and investigate.

The cotton harvest was at its peak, and trucks piled high with tightly bound bales were backed up at the docks, waiting to unload their precious cargo onto foreign vessels. I had arrived with a straightforward question, and expected a fairly easy day's work. But at local military headquarters, I found officers unusually evasive. Some pleaded ignorance, and others refused even to receive me. Finally I managed to corner the deputy commander of Sandinista forces in the area, a young lieutenant named Francisco Cajina.

"I just want you to answer to a simple question," I told him. "Are there mines in the harbor out there or not?"

Lieutenant Cajina winced. "Difficult, difficult," he muttered. "I don't really know how to answer."

"There's nothing difficult about it at all," I countered. "Just say yes or no."

"I really can't help you," the lieutenant insisted.

"Why not?"

"Because I haven't received instructions on what answer to give."

"Can't you answer without instructions?"

"No, not in this case."

"Why not?"

"It's all very delicate, that's why not."

Obviously Lieutenant Cajina was not going to be much help, so I bid him good day and began wandering around Corinto, stopping to talk to street vendors, off-duty stevedores, and whoever else I encountered. All told me that the harbor was indeed mined, and that mines had damaged several vessels during recent weeks. The mines, they said, were apparently of low explosive content, not powerful enough to sink an ocean-going vessel.

At an unmarked waterfront office I found a Dutch shipping agent who agreed to be interviewed as long as I concealed his identity. Not only did he confirm that both of the ships damaged in Corinto had hit mines, but he showed me a report that had already been prepared by specialists from the Netherlands who had come to investigate. The report concluded that the mines planted in Corinto harbor were of a type activated by the sound or vibration of passing vessels, and that each one was about six feet long and contained about 220 pounds of explosive. Sandinista authorities had refused to publicize these facts for fear that doing so would scare other ships away.

In Honduras, contra leaders took credit for the mining operation, but in truth they had nothing at all to do with it. The entire operation had been planned and carried out by the Central Intelligence Agency, using foreign-born Hispanic commandos known in the trade as UCLAs–Unilaterally Controlled Latino Assets. Nine ships were ultimately damaged in waters off Corinto, Puerto Sandino, and Bluefields. Among them was a Soviet freighter, several of whose crewmen were seriously injured.

As the truth of United States involvement in the mining became known, protests began pouring into the White House, and before long the Reagan administration was facing a firestorm of criticism. Foreign political leaders reacted with dismay and, in some cases, outrage. The United Nations Security Council debated the issue for four days, and at the end of the debate the United States was forced to use its veto to prevent adoption of a strong censure. The International Court of Justice voted 15–0 to condemn the mining, with an American judge concurring.

The reaction in Washington was just as fierce. The vice-chairman of the Senate Select Committee on Intelligence, Senator Daniel Patrick Moynihan, resigned his post in protest, and the chairman, Senator Barry Goldwater, fired off an unusually blunt "Dear Bill" letter to CIA Director William Casey.

"I am pissed off," Goldwater wrote. "I don't like this. I don't like it one bit from the president or from you . . . This is an act violating international law. It is an act of war. For the life of me, I don't see how we are going to explain it."

The episode did more than rhetorical damage to the Reagan administration's Nicaragua policy. Both the Senate and the House of Representatives overwhelmingly approved resolutions condemning the mining, and many legislators took the occasion to make their first anti-contra speeches. Several vowed never again to support aid to the contras, and in a remarkable reversal, the same Congress that had approved $24 million in contra aid only a few months earlier now voted to reject President Reagan's request for $21 million more. Prospects for peace seemed to brighten. The presidential election in Nicaragua, it appeared, was coming at a very propitious time.

Contra leaders were upset by the cutoff of American aid, which came just as they sensed for the first time that they were making military headway. But not all of their problems were in Washington. Though their army was growing in size, swelled by young men fleeing Sandinista rule, its leadership group never expanded beyond a small clique of ex-Guardsmen led by Enrique Bermúdez. Several of Bermúdez's senior officers were infamous for their brutality, and inside Nicaragua they had no constituency whatever. They had one chance to brighten their image and broaden their political appeal, but they refused to take it because it implied compromise with their most formidable rival, the renegade Sandinista hero Edén Pastora.

Pastora was famous not only for his bravery, but also for his insistent individualism. He had never been able to accept Sandinista discipline, and his break with the regime in Managua strengthened his image as an idealistic maverick. When he announced plans to lead an anti-Sandinista uprising, many Nicaraguans, including his former Sandinista comrades, took him quite seriously. During 1983 he built a military force in southern Nicaragua, directed from sanctuaries inside Costa Rica. Soon his force became a counterpart to the Nicaraguan Democratic Force (FDN), which the CIA and Bermúdez were directing from Honduras.

Bermúdez and Pastora were embarked on the same anti-Sandinista mission, and logic dictated that they combine their efforts. They were never able to do so. Instead, their old antagonisms flared to the surface, and they fought bitterly. Bermúdez and his men considered Pastora a crypto-Communist and probable Sandinista agent. In return, Pastora swore publicly that he would never unite with the "fascist" and "genocidal" ex-Guardsmen.

Costa Rican authorities, anxious to preserve their country's fragile neutrality, told Pastora early in 1984 that he was no longer welcome on Costa Rican soil. They pressured him to move, and he made new overtures to the FDN, offering to transfer his entire operation to Honduras and place it under FDN command. In exchange, he demanded that all former Guardsmen be removed from command positions in the contra army, which would have meant purging forty-six of the forty-eight senior FDN commanders, including Bermúdez. The contras would then need a new commander-in-chief, and for that post, the immodest Pastora offered himself.

I flew to Tegucigalpa late in April to see how these overtures were being received. The political balance there had been unexpectedly upset by the coup against General Álvarez. Álvarez had been a strong FDN backer, and despised Pastora. Once he was deposed and packed off into exile, prospects for a broadened contra movement seemed to improve. New Honduran military leaders thought the idea of merging the FDN with Pastora's force made sense.

"They want Pastora to come here," contra spokesman Edgar Chamorro told me. "They feel that he's being pushed out of Costa Rica and needs a place."

But at a meeting between Honduran army officers and FDN leaders, attended also by an American intelligence agent, the FDN flatly ruled out accepting Pastora as a comrade. They offered a long list of objections, but the issue came down to a very simple question: who was going to run the contras? Colonel Bermúdez and his fellow FDN commanders would be out of work if Pastora's conditions were accepted, forced to return to anonymous lives in Miami. They were not prepared to turn their guerrilla army over to someone else, and especially not to Pastora.

The stalemate continued for several days, and one afternoon Edgar Chamorro called my room at the Maya Hotel and asked if I was still following the story. I told him I was. He said he had a friend who wanted to give me a few interesting opinions. Such mysterious propositions were quite normal in Central America, and I told Chamorro I would be happy to hear anything interesting. He said his "friend" would be knocking on my door in about fifteen minutes.

Soon afterward I heard footsteps in the corridor outside my room, and then a single, loud knock. I opened the door and saw the wide girth of Frank Arana, a contra publicist who reporters had unkindly dubbed *Comandante Sandwich.* Arana was a mid-level figure whose opinions were not especially valuable, but I thought he might have some useful tidbits, and stepped out of the doorway to allow him room to pass. Instead of entering he turned to look backward, and I saw that he was not alone. Two young men, obviously bodyguards or security agents, were checking the corridor. I was puzzled for a moment, but suddenly all became clear as Enrique Bermúdez himself emerged from the shadows, dressed in casual civilian clothes. The FDN commander, then fifty-one years old, was powerfully built with jet-black hair, his face angular and scarred by acne.

"Colonel Bermúdez has a couple of things he wants to get off his chest," Arana told me after shutting the door behind us. I nodded, and Bermúdez began an intense monologue.

"You know, Kinzer," he said, "I was outside Nicaragua during the Sandinista revolution, and when the Sandinistas took over, I could have just settled calmly in the United States with no problem. But when I saw what was happening in Nicaragua, I made a decision to fight. I abandoned my family to come here, and I'm ready to make any sacrifice to wipe out the Marxist-Leninist tyranny in my country. I built this FDN up from nothing, and now there are people talking about taking it away. These are people who never contributed anything to the anti-Sandinista movement, and in fact even served the Communist regime! They're nothing like me. I'm not an egomaniac. I didn't come here looking for fame or publicity. Why should they be able to push me out?"

"So you won't accept Pastora under any circumstances?" I asked.

"The FDN always welcomes recruits," Bermúdez replied. "But we're not about to surrender to an outsider we don't respect."

At that point, Bermúdez rose to his feet and thanked me for the chance to unburden himself. Our encounter had lasted all of five minutes. He was in the midst of a busy week, and had no time to tarry.

The final word in this internecine dispute was naturally that of the CIA, which paid the contras' bills and made all of their important decisions. Pastora was a self-declared socialist and anti-imperialist known for his unpredictability; Bermúdez and the other FDN leaders were fervently pro-American and willing to take orders from Washington without question. It was an easy choice. Pastora, the only figure who might have given the contras legitimacy and transformed their movement into a popular crusade, was forced aside.

By choosing to support Colonel Bermúdez and his FDN over other contra factions, the United States threw in its lot with the single most detested group of Nicaraguans. American planners never seemed to grasp the simple fact that Nicaraguans hated the National Guard, and would never support an insurgency directed by ex-Guardsmen. Edén Pastora, in contrast, was arguably the most popular political figure in Nicaragua, and in many ways he made an ideal contra leader. But the CIA mistrusted him for his leftist politics, his background as a Sandinista, and his well-known aversion to taking orders. Bermúdez and his ex-Guardsmen were much more reliable clients.

Back in Costa Rica, Pastora insisted that he would find a way to carry on his fight. His prospects were bleak. Not only were his men being harassed by Costa Rican police, but the CIA had cut off the $150,000 monthly stipend it had been providing him since he declared war on the Sandinistas a year earlier.

"There are strong pressures by the CIA," he told a radio interviewer in San José. "They have blocked all help to us. For the past two months, we have not received a bullet or a pair of boots. We have not received anything."

A few days later, speaking on Costa Rican television, Pastora reiterated his vow never to ally with ex-Guardsmen, no matter how desperate his situation became. "The CIA will have to kill me first," he swore.

Pastora was not allowed to hold news conferences in Costa Rica, so he devised a typically dramatic alternative. His idea was to invite journalists to travel north to the Costa Rica-Nicaragua border, cross the San Juan River in canoes, and then assemble inside Nicaraguan territory. There he would appear and deliver his harangue against the CIA, the Sandinistas, and his other enemies.

It was late on the night of May 29, 1984, when Pastora's aides began telephoning journalists in San José, the Costa Rican capital, to invite them to the unusual news conference. Twenty-four reporters and photographers accepted the invitation. By pure coincidence, I was not among them. I visited San José regularly, but that week I happened to be at home in Managua.

The journalists assembled on the morning of May 30 at the Hotel Irazú, where Pastora's men were waiting. Their caravan of jeeps made its way northward into the verdant rain forest, and after several hours reached the San Juan River. The journalists and their guides boarded waiting canoes and crossed into Nicaragua without incident.

By the time they reached their destination, an isolated outpost called La Penca, darkness had fallen. They set up their equipment inside a shack built above the river on stilts. When Pastora walked in, television lights flashed on. He seated himself behind a wooden table, waited for a cup of coffee to be placed before him, and began to speak. After only a few seconds, several of the journalists heard a strange electronic whine. Before they could react, there was a brilliant flash followed instantly by a tremendous explosion.

In the hours of horror that followed, the Central American press corps lived through our worst tragedy of the 1980s. Pastora and one of his senior aides, both seriously hurt, were rushed aboard a speedboat and taken to a guerrilla hospital, but it was hours before anyone came to the aid of injured reporters. Two died slowly, waiting for help that never arrived, and a third succumbed in a hospital bed six days later. Nearly all the journalists present were hurt, several of them very badly. One of those killed was an American, Linda Frazier, who worked for the English-language *Tico Times* and was married to the Associated Press bureau chief in San José.

The bomb, it turned out, was a powerful homemade device containing both dynamite and C-4 plastic explosive. It had been carried to the news conference by a gaunt, bearded terrorist posing as a photographer and using a stolen Danish passport. He had slipped away from the crowd of reporters seconds before detonating the explosion by remote control, and the moment it went off, he hurled the detonator into nearby bushes and collapsed in feigned shock. The next day, while being treated at a hospital in the Costa Rican town of Ciudad Quesada, he was photographed in a wheelchair calmly smoking a cigarette, and even gave a radio interview describing the bombing. After his discharge a few hours later, he and one of the actual victims shared a taxi back to San José. There he checked out of his hotel and disappeared.

One of the reporters injured at La Penca was the British freelancer Susan Morgan, who lived in Managua and with whom I had often worked. At first it was reported that Susan was doing fine at the Ciudad Quesada hospital. Luckily for her, one of our colleagues, Rod Nordland of the *Philadelphia Inquirer*, was dubious.

Nordland had spent a full day reporting and writing about the bombing in

San José, and after filing his story, he began to worry about Susan. He decided to drive to Ciudad Quesada, a trip of several hours. It was midnight when he arrived, and hospital guards would not admit him. As he was arguing, someone from inside called to him, and he was allowed to enter.

A nurse at the hospital had just received an extraordinary telephone call. The caller, who was still on the line, was a doctor who said he had flown from Miami to San José aboard a specially equipped air ambulance with orders to bring Susan Morgan to the United States. He said the operation was being paid for by *Newsweek* magazine, for whom Susan had been covering the La Penca press conference.

Nordland took the phone, spoke for a few minutes, and then hung up. The doctor had given him some medical terms to throw around, and he managed to persuade hospital administrators that he too was a doctor. He demanded to be taken to Susan's room, and they agreed. Susan was in shocking condition. The force of the bomb blast had broken both of her knees, both of her shoulders, both of her elbows, and all of her fingers. She was severely burned, and her face had been deeply cut by shrapnel.

After a moment with Susan, Nordland decided she had to be taken immediately to a more modern hospital. Her doctors argued that she was already in good hands, but finally they gave in. Nordland rushed her to San José in a rented ambulance, helped carry her aboard the evacuation plane, and accompanied her to a hospital in Florida. She remained there for three months and underwent several operations, but never fully recovered.

No one ever discovered who had chartered the plane that flew Susan out of San José. Editors at *Newsweek* had no reason to do so, since they believed their correspondent to be unhurt. Rod Nordland swore he hadn't done it. Apparently one of Susan's friends or colleagues had called the charter company in *Newsweek*'s name and ordered the plane dispatched. *Newsweek* editors were at first angry, since such flights are not cheap, but they calmed down upon learning how badly Susan was hurt, and paid the bill without complaint.

Several of the journalists who survived La Penca, including Susan Morgan, came to believe that Pastora's enemies within the contra movement, possibly in league with the CIA and/or other clandestine services, were behind the bombing. Others suggested the Sandinistas had ordered it, or that it had been carried out on their behalf. Several private investigations were launched, but none produced conclusive evidence. Those who were seriously interested in finding the truth, including the victims, did not have the resources for an exhaustive probe. Those who had the resources apparently lacked motivation.

Pastora survived the attempt on his life, but he was seriously injured. His leaderless army went into virtual hibernation. To speak of the contras was now to speak of the FDN and Bermúdez, its newly strengthened commander.

But although the CIA had reaffirmed its faith in Bermúdez, nothing had changed inside Nicaragua, where ex-Guardsmen were still considered pariahs and where people were looking forward to the upcoming presidential election with increasing hope. If the election campaign could set Nicaragua on the way to democracy, they reasoned, political passions would cool and support for the contras would fade. What Nicaraguans now wished for was some sign that the United States was prepared to accept a political solution. To everyone's surprise, that sign came on June 1, when no less a personage than Secretary of State George Shultz arrived in Managua for a talk with Daniel Ortega.

Shultz was in the midst of one of the interminable turf wars that marked foreign policy planning in the Reagan administration. He was one of the few officials in Washington who believed it might be worthwhile to try negotiating with the Sandinistas, but he was so outnumbered within the administration that he felt obliged to keep his Managua trip secret until the last moment, lest his rivals scuttle it. His airport meeting with Ortega lasted two and a half hours, and he later described the tone as "businesslike and civil." There were no breakthroughs, but an agreement was reached to begin a round of bilateral negotiations.

"We are proceeding on the premise that a negotiated settlement is possible, and that practical reasons exist on all sides to reach agreement," Shultz wrote in his report of the conversation. He was hardly airborne, however, before other Reagan advisors began undercutting his initiative. A "senior official" quickly told reporters that at the White House, news of Shultz's overture to Managua had been greeted with "a feeling of no great enthusiasm."

In Nicaragua, the beginnings of a political campaign were already visible. Billboards for opposition parties had begun appearing along roadsides, carrying slogans like "God, Order, Justice" and "The Future Is Ours." Politicians were debating the rules that would govern voting. Anti-Sandinista organizing was tolerated in some areas, though elsewhere it was repressed, apparently at the whim of local authorities.

If Nicaraguans needed a reason to hope the election would succeed, they had only to read news reports from the northern and central provinces, where contra attacks were continuing without respite. When I toured the northern border area in mid-June, one Sandinista commander told me he guessed there were three thousand contras inside Nicaragua, and at least that many more grouped in Honduras awaiting orders to move. Major attacks had been launched against the towns of Ocotal, Waslala, and San Rafael del Norte, resulting in millions of dollars in property damage. In several cases, attackers had gone directly to the homes of Sandinista officials, told them they had been judged guilty of repressive abuses, and executed them on the spot.

Anxiety about the war and the military draft contributed to public discontent, but the most common complaints were economic. Wages were being held below the poverty level, and unemployment was widespread. Total export earnings had fallen to half the pre-Sandinista level. At stores and marketplaces, nearly every basic product was unavailable or in short supply. Foreign aid was dropping each year as donors lost confidence in the Sandinistas. The $1.6 billion national debt that had taken the Somoza tyranny forty years to accumulate jumped to $3.5 billion in the first five years of Sandinista rule. Public frustration was rising steadily, and when strikes were temporarily legalized as part of the government's effort to improve the political climate, workers at several factories immediately walked off the job, demanding wage increases of at least one hundred percent.

For a time the *comandantes* had tried to deny the enormity of the economic collapse, but by 1984 they were acknowledging it in public. Minister of Internal Trade Dionisio Marenco candidly urged Nicaraguans to adjust to shortages, since they were going to be a permanent part of national life.

"From a tractor to a soft drink," Marenco said at a news conference, "we have to get used to using and drinking what is available."

The sad state into which Nicaragua had fallen by 1984 was exemplified by what happened at that year's regional celebration of Central American independence. It was a custom for outstanding young athletes from all five Central American countries to carry a "torch of freedom" through the entire isthmus. The torch began its route in Guatemala in early September, and was carried by groups of runners through El Salvador, Honduras, and Nicaragua, with ceremonies at each border. Nicaraguan runners had been carefully selected from the ranks of Sandinista youth groups, and when they arrived at the Costa Rican border, they assembled to listen to patriotic speeches. But when the border gate was opened to allow transfer of the torch, as horrified Sandinista Cabinet ministers watched, nearly the entire twenty-five-member Nicaraguan team grabbed its momentary chance and bolted into Costa Rica. Once on Costa Rican soil, the runners said life in their homeland had become unbearable, and appealed for political asylum.

As the election approached, Sandinista leaders found themselves torn by contrary impulses. In order to show the world that they tolerated dissent, they had to ease restrictions on civil and political rights, and to allow forms of protest that had been forbidden for years. Yet in their hearts, they still viewed the opposition as unpatriotic and treasonous.

Nowhere was this conflict more evident than in their dealings with the opposition newspaper *La Prensa,* which had become a powerful symbol of press freedom not only in Nicaragua but throughout the world. It would have been impossible for the Sandinistas to shut *La Prensa* during the election campaign, because doing so would have destroyed their credibility as democrats. Nonetheless, they waged a permanent campaign to limit its impact, a campaign that cast the country's ideological conflict in sharp relief.

Control over the Nicaraguan press was one of Interior Minister Tomás

Borge's responsibilities. Borge established a press censorship office in a confiscated house about a mile from his ministry. His rule of thumb was simple. "The revolution tolerates ideological pluralism," he asserted, "as long as it does not endanger the revolution's political power."

Borge's campaign against *La Prensa* was waged patiently and on many fronts. His principal weapons were cutbacks in paper supply, reduced allocations of foreign currency needed to buy ink and other supplies, and harassment of editors and correspondents. His agents also intimidated newsdealers in the countryside, leading many to agree to stop selling *La Prensa*. One day in 1984, an unknown attacker even fired a rocket at the printing plant in Managua.

Once the contra war began in earnest, Borge imposed prior censorship on *La Prensa*. Editors were required to submit every article in every day's paper to the interior ministry, and only those that were approved could be published. Early each afternoon, editors would prepare a large packet containing all the material they proposed to publish that evening, and deliver it to the censorship office on the other side of Managua. Some hours later, the packet would be returned, accompanied by a list of which articles had been deemed unprintable.

Borge and other Sandinista leaders believed that editors of *La Prensa* sympathized with the contra cause, and they were not far wrong. *La Prensa* was not simply a newspaper, but a focus of political opposition. Its ideological challenge to the regime was direct and unapologetic, and its pages were always as full of anti-Sandinista propaganda as possible. Editors sought every opportunity to portray the regime in a negative light, and rarely published a single word of praise for any government program or any Sandinista official.

Borge ordered his censors to use a heavy hand, and they did. Many of the topics that had interested Nicaraguans for years, like prison conditions or deteriorating public services, were now ruled off limits for all comment in *La Prensa*. Most stories about Nicaragua received from wire services were also deemed unacceptable. And coverage of foreign news was expected to respect a certain etiquette, not offending Cuba, the Soviet Union, or Nicaragua's other benefactors.

When it was announced that a national election would be held in 1984, opposition leaders began demanding that restrictions on *La Prensa* be eased. For a time the Sandinistas ignored their pleas, and applied censorship as usual. In the first half of the year, they forbade publication of statements by Catholic bishops, banned all coverage of the bomb attack on Edén Pastora, and even refused to allow publication of photographs showing flood damage caused by rainstorms in Managua.

As the election drew closer, however, the *comandantes* began to realize that they would never be able to claim their election had been free if they did not liberate the press. Yet the contra war was still raging, and the CIA was presumably as active as ever in its covert efforts to destabilize Nicaraguan society. Borge was in no mood to lift censorship entirely, but as a compromise he ordered his censors be more permissive. In mid-1984 articles began appearing in *La Prensa* that had not appeared anywhere in Nicaragua for years. Anti-Sandinista leaders were given space in every day's paper, and they used it to castigate the regime.

Nicaragua's political parties were weak, disorganized, and ill prepared for the historic challenge facing them. Ideological enmity and personal rivalries kept them in constant internecine conflict. Thus when the time came for opposition leaders to make their momentous choice of a presidential candidate to oppose Daniel Ortega, none had the slightest idea how to proceed.

Sandinista authorities had decreed that all candidates who wanted to run in the November election would have to be inside Nicaragua by July 25, and register their candidacies by the following day. When a group of West German politicians visited Managua in early July, they asked opposition leaders who their presidential candidate would be. They were amazed to learn that there was not only no candidate, but no process by which to select one.

The Germans, stepping in where no one else seemed interested, prodded two prominent opposition leaders, Azucena Ferrey of the Social Christian party and Enrique Bolaños, president of the business coalition COSEP, to meet and discuss the matter. The two met without public notice and without any formal mandate from anyone, in what Bolaños later called "the darkness of a tunnel." They made a list of five possible candidates: the economist Arturo Cruz; contra leader Adolfo Calero; Ismael Reyes, longtime head of the Nicaraguan Red Cross; Alfonso Robelo, the former junta member now allied with Edén Pastora; and Eduardo Rivas Gasteazoro, an old political warhorse. The two political leaders looked over their list, and Bolaños offered his opinion of the prospective candidates.

"Number One is okay with COSEP," Bolaños said. "Number Two has his finger on the trigger, no good. Number Four is the same as Number Two. Number Five is very ill. So Numbers One and Three are okay with us, in that ·order."

Ferrey agreed, and on July 11 she flew to Washington to offer the nomination to Cruz. It was not the first time the thought of running for president had occurred to him. Reporters had been telephoning him periodically to hear his views about the approaching election, and we had found him ready to run. What we did not know was that several months earlier, Cruz had met for dinner at Germaine's, a stylish Vietnamese restaurant in Georgetown, with a senior State Department official, L. Craig Johnstone, to discuss the election campaign. That night, Johnstone had asked Cruz directly if he would accept a presidential candidacy, and Cruz said yes.

Within the Reagan administration, there was deep division over how to deal with the election in Nicaragua. Johnstone and other State Department officials, apparently including Secretary of State Shultz, hoped the opposition would participate. They reasoned that if the campaign was fair, opposition candidates might do quite well, and that if it turned out to be fraudulent, the world would learn that the Sandinistas were not to be trusted. But at every turn, this group was stymied by other Reagan advisors who favored a more militant, confrontational policy. Led most prominently by United Nations Ambassador Jeane Kirkpatrick, these advisors argued that the Sandinistas were Communists, that Communists never permitted free elections or any form of true democracy, and that therefore they should be met only on the field of battle, not at the negotiating table or at the polls.

This same internal debate undermined the peace talks that Shultz and Ortega had agreed to launch. The talks were held at Manzanillo, Mexico, beginning early in 1984, and represented a magnificent opportunity for both parties. Largely because of American intransigence, however, the opportunity was lost. United States negotiators offered ludicrously unbalanced peace proposals, knowing full well that they would be rejected. Their militance led to the talks' failure, and contributed to the parallel failure of peace efforts by the four-nation Contadora Group.

One of the saddest results of the atrophy of political institutions in Nicaragua was the reflex of many opposition leaders to look to Washington for support in times of trouble. Throughout Nicaraguan history, the United States had intervened at decisive moments, and politicians came to consider the United States a permanent factor in national politics. When the Sandinista Front came to power, those who opposed Sandinista rule immediately turned to Washington for support. Once President Reagan was in office, support began to flow freely. Wittingly or otherwise, many opposition groups became partners of the CIA. While excoriating the *comandantes* for their deference to Moscow and Havana, they eagerly awaited orders from Washington, preferably accompanied by dollars.

The Sandinistas did not look upon the election as a genuine chance for Nicaraguans to determine their future, any more than the Reagan administration did. They viewed themselves as the "vanguard" of the Nicaraguan people, the culmination of a century of Nicaraguan history, and did not admit the possibility of ever relinquishing power. True democracy, they argued, required that nations be run by truly democratic parties, and in their judgment the Sandinista Front was the only such party in Nicaragua. By this circular argument, it would be patently anti-democratic for the Sandinistas ever to surrender power.

"Democracy is not something that takes place at election time, and democracy is not choosing among candidates as if they were products in a supermarket," Tomás Borge once asserted. "Democracy has to come from an organization that raises people's consciousness and encourages their active participation."

* * *

BOTH of the most powerful forces entering the election campaign, the Sandinistas and the CIA, were determined to use it for their own purposes, which had
nothing to do with determining the true sentiments of Nicaraguan voters. Yet
despite these formidable obstacles, there was still a prospect that the campaign
could contribute to national reconciliation. Journalists and diplomats in Managua imagined a scenario in which the opposition would finish with thirty or forty
percent of the vote, producing some new and attractive leaders along the way,
and emerge as a cohesive and constructive political force. Whether that would
be possible depended largely on Arturo Cruz.

The night of July 25, when Cruz finally arrived in Nicaragua, was a tense
moment. Sandinista security agents filled the airport and surrounding areas,
prepared to deal with what the government feared would be a huge welcoming
crowd. Inside the terminal, reporters wondered what to expect. Someone made
a ghoulish reference to the Filipino opposition leader Benigno Aquino, who had
recently been murdered at the Manila airport as he returned home to launch
a dissident presidential campaign.

Cookie Hood, the Nicaraguan-American manager of the local CBS bureau,
spun around angrily. "Don't you *dare* say that!" she cried, shaking her finger
at the offending reporter. "Don't you dare even mention that *name!*"

As it turned out, only a few hundred Cruz supporters showed up that night.
When their hero emerged, they squealed in delight and rushed toward him. For
several minutes they surrounded him, chanting *"Democracia sí, comunismo
no!"* Finally his friends managed to rescue him, whisking him into a waiting
car that sped away into the darkness.

At a two-hour news conference the next day, Cruz embraced the sweeping
opposition political platform issued several months earlier. It demanded that the
Sandinistas effectively dismantle their regime by relinquishing control over the
police, the army, the court system, and the press, and also that they open talks
with contra leaders. Cruz, however, seemed to view the platform as a statement
of long-term goals, not pre-conditions for his participation in the election. He
told reporters that his most fervent desire was "to put an end to the fratricidal
war." All of his comments suggested that he had arrived with a conciliatory
attitude, determined to use the election campaign as a vehicle to raise civic
consciousness and forge a genuine opposition movement. He praised advances
made by the Sandinistas in education and health care, and said he approved of
their nationalization of the banking system. If elected, he said, he would invite
some Sandinistas to join in his government. He even described himself as a
Sandinista at heart, and declared, "The revolution is irreversible." In the back
of the room, I noticed Enrique Bolaños and several other business leaders
shifting uncomfortably in their seats, casting quizzical glances at each other.

The next day, which was also the final day for registration of presidential candidates, several hundred opposition activists gathered at a Managua movie theater to ratify the choice of Cruz as their standard-bearer. They had been summoned by the Democratic Coordinator, a coalition of anti-Sandinista political parties, business groups, and trade unions that had emerged as the principal opposition force within Nicaragua. Many of them were people I had met and interviewed during my travels to outlying provinces.

As I scanned the waiting crowd, I caught sight of someone waving toward me. It was Alvin Guthrie, a former airport baggage handler who had risen to head one of the country's largest non-Sandinista labor federations. Guthrie, descended from Caribbean islanders, was one of Nicaragua's few black political figures. He was an outspoken Cruz supporter, eager for a political fight, and ready to turn his union members into campaign workers.

"I need to talk to you," Guthrie told me urgently. He put an arm around my shoulder, and led me away from the other delegates.

"Listen, I've been noticing that you and Cruz seem to know each other," Guthrie said when we were out of earshot. "Is he a good friend of yours?"

"He's not really a personal friend," I replied. "We've known each other over the years, but only on a professional basis."

"But can you get to him?" Guthrie insisted. "Can you talk to him? Do you have any influence with him?"

"I don't know what you mean," I told him. "What's the problem?"

Guthrie shook his head, looked back over his shoulder at the milling crowd, and then spoke again.

"Cruz is under a lot of pressure from people who don't want him to participate in the election," he said. "We're going to have a meeting this afternoon to decide. Unless Cruz takes a strong stand himself, we're out of the campaign. We need to get to Cruz now. He's got to stay in Nicaragua and see this thing through to the end."

"Alvin, I sympathize with you, but you're talking to the wrong guy," I told him. "Aren't there Nicaraguans you can ask, or other people who have real influence?"

"I wouldn't know of any," Guthrie said sadly. "I guess you can't help. It's really too bad."

As he walked away, I marveled at how clumsily this historic process was being managed. The convention soon came to order, and political speeches began. Orators denounced the Sandinistas, praised Cruz, and predicted overwhelming victory at the polls. When the candidate himself finally rose, he was greeted with thunderous applause, and declared nominated by acclamation. In his acceptance speech, he gave the first indication that he was not going to register his candidacy that afternoon. He scorned the deadline as a form of "political blackmail," and said he would not join the campaign unless the Sandinistas agreed to open talks with contra leaders.

The closed-door meeting of opposition leaders that followed the public convention was a great opportunity for Cruz. If he had been serious about running, and if he had been able to summon the necessary fortitude, he could have seized the gavel, proclaimed that as nominee he was now empowered to make decisions, and insisted that the campaign proceed. But in the first of a series of actions that made many of his admirers wonder if they had misplaced their confidence in him, he quietly accepted the split decision of Democratic Coordinator leaders, and refused to register his candidacy.

Nonetheless, Cruz insisted that he was still running for president. In the days that followed, he made unannounced visits to several towns, and was warmly welcomed. Crowds of rowdy Sandinistas arrived looking for trouble, but retreated after being confronted with larger and equally rowdy pro-Cruz crowds. The campaign, though still unofficial because Cruz was not a registered candidate, seemed to be gaining momentum. Sandinista leaders were suggesting privately that they might allow Cruz to register his candidacy even though the official deadline had passed. Even Archbishop Obando was encouraged.

"Why don't you politicians give it a try?" the archbishop urged Cruz during a private meeting. "Why don't you find a way to do it?"

Rather than continue campaigning after his initial successes, however, Cruz decided to return to Washington. He had spent less than two weeks in Nicaragua, and his departure threw the incipient campaign into disarray. There were several other presidential candidates in the race against Daniel Ortega, but Cruz was the only one who counted, and now he was gone.

From Washington, Cruz issued a series of statements condemning the Sandinistas as undemocratic and pointing out quite correctly that the electoral system they had established made an opposition victory impossible. The Sandinistas had overwhelming advantages, beginning with their control of the press, the police, and the three-member Supreme Electoral Council charged with overseeing the campaign. They had set the voting age at sixteen to take advantage of their support among young people, and had insisted that soldiers, who were required to attend Sandinista "political education" classes and were cut off from contact with the opposition, be allowed to vote at special polling places adjacent to military bases. Mayors and provincial governors used their control over ration cards and business permits to discourage people from supporting the opposition.

In some areas, Cruz supporters were harassed by police and even arrested for political organizing. When they became too aggressive, Sandinista officials sent political gangs called *turbas* to break up their campaign meetings, throw rocks through their windows, paint slogans on their walls, or attack them on the street. Many Latin American and European political leaders recognized that no fair election could be held under these conditions, and several of them decided to press the Sandinistas for new concessions.

During the weeks that followed, Cruz shuttled among Latin American capitals, enlisting foreign help for his cause. In mid-September he arrived back in Managua, sounding like a candidate. As president, he declared, he would end the confiscation of farms and businesses, issue an amnesty for political prisoners, abolish all restrictions on the press and, most appealing of all, decree "the gradual and total demilitarization of Nicaragua."

Of all the foreign leaders who tried to forge a compromise between Cruz and the Sandinistas, President Belisario Betancur of Colombia proved the most determined. Betancur had recently signed a preliminary agreement with guerrillas in his own country, and hoped he could use his diplomatic skills to mediate the electoral dispute in Nicaragua. After many telephone calls to Managua, he began making progress. Through him, the Sandinistas signaled their willingness to meet several opposition demands. If Cruz agreed to participate in the campaign, they told Betancur, they would ease press censorship, move polling places away from military installations, and allow opposition parties to inspect voting lists. They even suggested they might be willing to postpone the election so the opposition would have time to organize. Betancur, sensing that a breakthrough might be at hand, arranged a dramatic summit to resolve the matter.

The three-day summit, which represented an extraordinary opportunity for peace in Nicaragua, opened September 30 in a hotel suite overlooking Copacabana beach in Rio de Janeiro. Cruz himself represented the opposition, and *Comandante* Bayardo Arce represented the Sandinista Front. Several prominent outsiders attended as witnesses and guarantors. One of them, Carlos Andrés Pérez, had given the Sandinistas decisive help during their 1978–79 uprising, when he was president of Venezuela. Two others, former Norwegian defense minister Thorwald Stoltenberg and German parliamentarian Hans-Jurgen Wischnewski, both of whom had closely followed events in Central America, were symbols of the European aid that Nicaragua might expect if it could resolve its internal conflicts.

Both Cruz and Arce were nervous and uncertain during the talks, neither one trusting the other. Prodded by Pérez, however, they made surprising progress. Arce agreed to modify some of the more glaring inequities of Sandinista electoral law, and said he was prepared to accept postponement of the election until January. Cruz said that under those conditions, he would officially enter the race. A draft agreement was produced, and it seemed success was at hand.

"This is the most exhilarating day in my whole life," Cruz gushed as the agreement took shape. "We actually have a chance to have an election and stop the war."

Back in Managua, opposition leaders were following the talks anxiously, with Cruz reporting to them regularly by telephone. They knew that their telephone conversations were being monitored by the interior ministry, and they ordered Cruz to sign nothing until they could meet with him privately. Cruz had no doubt that he could persuade his allies to accept the agreement, and for a brief, intoxicating moment, all seemed in order. No one ever fully understood what happened next, but several years later, I met Thorwald Stoltenberg at a dinner in Managua and asked him for his account.

"We thought we had succeeded, and that the agreement was complete," Stoltenberg said. "People were sipping cognac and congratulating each other. Everybody was happy. Suddenly Bayardo Arce stood up, shook a few hands, and said he had to leave. Then he went out and announced that the negotiations had collapsed. All of us were completely astonished. I'm still not sure exactly what was behind it all."

For some reason, the Sandinista *comandantes* had decided that further concessions, especially postponing the election, were no longer acceptable. Daniel Ortega had just made a speech at the United Nations predicting that American troops would invade Nicaragua within the next two weeks, and apparently he viewed the Rio de Janeiro talks as part of a Machiavellian plot designed to set the stage for invasion. Stoltenberg traveled to Managua to plead with Ortega to relent, and a few days later, the German Social Democratic leader Willy Brandt, a longtime friend of the Sandinistas, arrived with the same plea. Both were turned down, and another opportunity to resolve the Nicaraguan conflict, or at least to shift it from the military to the political realm, slipped tragically away.

Sandinista leaders bore ultimate responsibility for breaking off the talks in Rio de Janeiro, and, by extension, for the failure of the election. Cruz, however, could have saved the day if he had been willing to take the bold stand many of his friends expected of him. He had known all along that he had no chance of defeating Ortega for the presidency, and that the election would be less than pristine. What had made him so appealing was that he seemed to understand there was a purpose in running even if he could not win. He seemed to realize that building democracy in Nicaragua was going to be a long-term project, and that he could make a great contribution by leading a vigorous and honest opposition. If he had agreed to participate in the election despite all the obstacles placed in his way, he would have run a strong campaign and attracted much sympathy for the abuses to which the Sandinistas would probably have subjected him. He would have finished with a third of the vote or more, and become Nicaragua's undisputed opposition leader. As a losing presidential candidate, he would have been guaranteed a seat in the new National Assembly, and from that position he might well have become the statesman his country needed so desperately. But he flinched at a crucial moment, refusing to re-enter the campaign and thus retreating from the historic challenge before him. Never again would Nicaraguans turn to him for political leadership.

With Cruz definitively out of the race, journalists began to notice the other candidates running against Ortega. Only one of them, Virgilio Godoy of the

Independent Liberal party, had a substantial following. The United States, which had been pleased at Cruz's withdrawal from the campaign, now wanted Godoy to withdraw as well. Three weeks before the election, Ambassador Harry Bergold received a cable from Washington ordering him to visit Godoy and deliver that message. Bergold, an anti-interventionist at heart, met Godoy at his party headquarters. There they spoke behind closed doors.

"I'm here because I've received a cable from Washington," Bergold said. "I'm supposed to tell you that you should pull out of the presidential campaign. But I'm not going to do that, because I've got too much respect for you. I personally think you should do whatever you and your party believe is right."

It was an odd way to deliver a message, but probably the best Bergold could do, considering his need to balance conviction with duty. The Independent Liberals held a convention the following weekend, and one delegate after another rose to complain that Sandinista harassment had made it impossible for them to organize campaign activities. A group of young party workers circulated a letter urging Godoy's withdrawal on the grounds that under Sandinista election rules, "we have as much chance as a cat who is tied into a sack and thrown into the river." At the end of the day, delegates voted 94–20 to quit the race.

The Conservative party had nominated the physician and writer Clemente Guido as their presidential candidate, and many of his supporters wanted him to follow Godoy's lead and withdraw from the campaign. Party leaders met in convention to vote on the issue. They seemed ready to vote in favor of withdrawal when several dozen young thugs invaded the convention hall. The youths, who claimed to be members of a Conservative youth group but were actually Sandinistas, overturned furniture and chased party leaders from the hall, chanting *"Elecciones! Elecciones!"*

A few minutes later I caught up with one of the pro-Sandinista Conservatives, Rafael Córdova Rivas.

"Is this democracy?" I called out to him.

"This is action democracy!" he shouted back. "Get used to it!"

Two weeks before the election, the Sandinistas reached a secret agreement with the remaining opposition candidates. Under the agreement, all candidates agreed to stay in the race, work for a high voter turnout, and restrain their criticism of the military draft law. In exchange, the Sandinistas gave each one a campaign contribution of five million cordobas, the equivalent of about $18,000 at the official rate. By this mechanism the Sandinistas became hidden financial sponsors of candidates who claimed to be trying to oust them from power.

One day as the election approached, Guillermo and I traveled north to the coffee capital, Matagalpa, to attend an Ortega campaign rally. The streets were decked with red-and-black banners. At the local Sandinista headquarters, workers wore red-and-black hats and T-shirts. Dozens of government-owned trucks, mobilized to bring rural farm laborers to the rally, were parked near the open field where Ortega was to speak.

Before the rally began, journalists were invited to meet with the local Sandinista military commander, Javier Carrión. His briefing was a sobering reminder that while the electoral charade was being played out in Managua and provincial capitals, a real war was raging in the countryside. In the provinces of Matagalpa and Jinotega alone, Carrión told us, there had been forty firefights during September and October, costing the lives of 110 contras and fifty-two Sandinista soldiers.

Outside, a crowd had gathered to await Ortega. When his motorcade arrived and he stepped up to the wooden platform, the applause was no more than polite. His first order of business was to hand out a round of land reform titles to peasants who had been brought to Matagalpa for the purpose. Then a young militiaman presented him with a portrait, and a visiting Canadian clergyman ceremoniously awarded him a "medal of peace." Finally the candidate was ready to speak, and he shook his fist as he approached the podium. On each of his cheeks were painted slashes of red and black.

For several minutes, Ortega led the crowd in a sustained chant for people's power: *"Po-der Po-pu-lar! Po-der Po-pu-lar!"*

Ortega's speech sounded like that of any incumbent politician. He ticked off his party's achievements and pledged more progress in the years to come. In an emotional crescendo, he launched a scathing attack on the Reagan administration.

"The United States government is sponsoring a campaign of death aimed against Nicaragua!" he cried. "They are sending gangs of criminal mercenaries to attack us! They say we're anti-democratic, but we know what real democracy means. Democracy is literacy, democracy is land reform, democracy is education and public health! That is what we have always stood for, and what we stand for today!"

Ortega had found his rhythm, and the crowd was finally with him. "We have not betrayed the original program of the Sandinista Front!" he declared. "That is why we know that when Nicaraguans go to the polls on November 4, they are going to say, 'Sandino yesterday, Sandino today, Sandino forever!' "

On November 3, the evening before the election, I was sitting at home with a couple of friends when my doorbell rang. I opened the door, and there stood Bianca Jagger, ex-wife of Rolling Stones star Mick Jagger and one of the few Nicaraguans to have won a measure of international celebrity. With her was José Francisco Peña Gómez, a populist politician from the Dominican Republic who was then serving as mayor of Santo Domingo. They made a striking couple. Jagger was carefully dressed, pale, delicate, and reed-thin. Peña Gómez, his black skin glistening in the darkness, was fat, rumpled, and jovial. Both had come to witness the election, and they had decided to drop by for a chat. I invited them into my garden, motioned for them to sit down in my pair of wicker rocking chairs, and served them fruit drinks.

Bianca said little, but Peña Gómez was full of trenchant observations. He said he thought Arturo Cruz had made a great mistake in quitting the campaign, and recalled the struggles of his own political party in the Dominican Republic.

"For twelve years we didn't participate in elections because they were a fraud run by a dictatorship," he told me. "Those were years we lost in the fight to democratize our country. Finally we agreed to run, in the worst of conditions. Our presidential candidate was arrested, our offices were burned, and we had campaign workers murdered. But after many sacrifices, here we are in power. Parties don't want to give up power; that's a general rule. You have to take the best conditions you can get and then make a fight of it."

Election day was a Sunday. Guillermo showed up at dawn and we set out through the countryside. I spent the day interviewing voters in several provincial capitals and more than a dozen towns and villages. Everyone I met understood perfectly well what the election meant and what it did not mean. Many remembered other elections in which the outcome was preordained. Few Nicaraguans, indeed, had ever known any other kind.

Sandinista supporters were anxious to be interviewed. They told me that by voting for Ortega they were "strengthening revolutionary power" and sending a message of defiance to Washington. Finding people who would admit to favoring an opposition candidate was more difficult, though I encountered many who weren't interested in voting at all.

"There isn't anyone to vote for," a fruit vendor in Granada told me with a shrug. We spoke for a minute or two, but when two young men approached she fell silent. Both were local Sandinista activists, and both told us they had just voted for Ortega.

"By holding an election," one of them said, "we're taking an argument away from those who want to invade us."

"Arturo Cruz is a traitor," added his friend. "He wants us to negotiate with the murderers who are killing our people."

The results of the election were not exactly as expected, with the Sandinistas winning only sixty-three percent of the votes cast. Tomás Borge had promised to "cry in a public plaza" if the Sandinistas did not win at least seventy percent, but he never kept that promise. A total of 1.17 million voters, seventy-five percent of those registered, went to the polls.

There was no way for outsiders to determine if vote counts were genuine, but the Sandinistas showed themselves unusually sensitive to allegations of fraud. The newspaper of the Communist party, *Avance,* was ordered shut indefinitely after it published a statistical analysis purporting to prove that returns from several provinces had been falsified. To prevent the appearance of other such articles, and to serve notice that the period of relative press freedom was ending, interior ministry officials delivered a tough new set of guidelines to *La Prensa*. Its first provision was a ban on all references to the election "in terms that directly or indirectly express or suggest citizens' abstentions, fraud, manipulation of figures, or lack of confidence in electoral authorities."

JUST two days after Nicaraguans went to the polls to elect Daniel Ortega, citizens of the United States voted in a presidential election of their own. Ronald Reagan easily won a second term, crushing his Democratic challenger, Senator Walter Mondale, who had pledged to end support for the contras if elected. Among those who celebrated were William Casey and his associates at the CIA. As a hint of what was to come, they decided to give the Sandinistas a scare on the very night of Reagan's re-election.

It was late when the telephone rang at my house that night, too late for most Nicaraguans to call. I lifted the receiver and heard the sequence of clicks that announced an international call. After a few seconds, I could make out the voice of one of my editors in New York.

"What do you know about the Sandinistas getting a shipment of Russian fighter jets?" he asked.

"I don't know anything," I replied.

"Well, it's all over TV tonight that the jets are coming into Nicaragua right now."

"Probably not true," I warned him. "Don't believe it."

"The story's coming from the White House, apparently."

"That makes it even less credible," I said. "I wouldn't advise you to play it up too big."

"OK, I guess someone will call you in the morning," the editor said, and we bade each other good night.

I awoke early the next day, and turned on the radio news as I was dressing. On every station, announcers were buzzing about the dramatic charges from Washington. The night before, it turned out, an urgent news bulletin had been flashed across the United States: Soviet jets were about to arrive in Nicaragua. The television audience was unusually large that night, since millions of Americans were following the election returns. Many of them naturally found the bulletin alarming. It suggested that Nicaragua was joining Cuba as part of a new Soviet-backed military alliance in the Caribbean basin, and that the Sandinistas, with Soviet help, were building an air force capable of threatening the United States.

Most Americans had no real basis on which to assess the news, but the way it was presented, interrupting the vote count on the night of a presidential election, lent it great urgency. In Managua, journalists knew enough to dismiss it almost out of hand. The *comandantes* had made no secret of the fact that they were actively seeking fighter jets, which they wanted to use against contra supply and reconnaissance planes. *Comandantes* Daniel Ortega, Henry Ruiz, and Bayardo Arce had all traveled to foreign capitals pleading for jets, but all had returned empty-handed. Soviet generals had wisely decided that MiG fighters were too combustible a weapon to be placed in Sandinista hands, and once the Soviets had demurred, the Bulgarians, North Koreans, and Libyans felt obliged to follow. At one point the Sandinistas tried to obtain Super-Mystère jets from France, but that deal fell through when the manufacturers realized that the Sandinistas had no money and were hoping to buy on credit.

Diplomats in Managua, including military analysts at the American embassy, watched these developments closely, and none had detected the slightest hint that jets might be on their way. That morning, I spoke with several of them, and also with a couple of mid-ranking Sandinistas whose word I had come to trust. All confirmed my own reaction, and that of other journalists in Managua, that the dramatic report from Washington could not be true.

The more I reflected on the story that was unfolding that day, the more frustrated I became. There was every indication that the story had been fabricated by CIA operatives or officials of the Reagan administration. By covering it in any way, we were giving it credence. Yet the commotion it caused made it impossible to ignore.

Within a few days, it became clear that the Sandinistas had no fighter jets, and were expecting none. That news, however, did not filter into the American consciousness. If CIA propagandists had concocted and planted this story in order to spread the idea that the Sandinistas posed a dangerous threat to United States security, they had succeeded. President Reagan said the episode showed that Sandinista leaders "are contemplating a threat to their neighbors in the Americas." Casual television viewers could be forgiven for coming away with the same conclusion.

In Managua, where the Sandinistas were already warning that an American invasion was imminent, the election-night bombshell from Washington sparked a new wave of fear. *Comandante* Carlos Núñez told a specially convened gathering of foreign correspondents that the baseless allegation was part of a Reagan administration plan "to prepare conditions for an invasion." An editorial in *Nuevo Diario* said the United States was threatening "military action against Nicaragua similar to that carried out against the island of Grenada." When an American warship moved into position off Corinto, Foreign Minister Miguel D'Escoto warned that "something bigger" might be in the offing.

"If by Thanksgiving Mr. Reagan has not invaded Nicaragua, we'll have something to be thankful for," D'Escoto said.

Sensing that the Sandinistas had been jolted, the White House devised a new way to flaunt American power. Beginning in early November, SR-71 spy planes that regularly flew over Nicaragua were directed to perform maneuvers that would produce sonic booms over the capital. Soon the booms became the talk of the town.

One morning president-elect Ortega met with reporters to warn that we were facing "one of the most critical moments, or the most critical moment, that the Nicaraguan revolution has experienced." The instant those words were out of his mouth, a thundering sonic boom shattered the air. The SR-71 made two booms in rapid succession, ka-BOOM ka-BOOM, and Ortega turned indignant.

"This outrages our people!" he told us angrily.

There was never any real plan in Washington to invade Nicaragua, either then or at any other time. President Reagan showed himself always willing to castigate the Sandinistas in public, but never prepared to assume the political cost of carrying out his implicit threats. Nonetheless, post-election pressures and Sandinista reaction to them sent Nicaragua into sudden upheaval at the end of 1984. Air raid drills were held daily in many factories and government offices. Thousands of students about to depart for work in the coffee fields were told they would instead be donning military uniforms and preparing to defend Managua.

Many ordinary people had become tired of these warnings and mobilizations, and no longer took them seriously. But the Sandinistas, determined to take every precaution, turned Nicaragua upside down in the weeks following the election, at a cost of millions of dollars in lost export earnings. Thus the pressures from Washington served a purpose.

"You Americans sure know how to throw a small country into turmoil," one European diplomat in Managua told me with grudging admiration.

The Nicaraguan election had done nothing to resolve the country's conflicts. President Reagan and his advisors were still convinced that the Sandinistas could be overthrown by force, and as long as they believed that, peace overtures were impossible. To warn the Sandinistas of what lay ahead, Ambassador Bergold visited the foreign ministry to deliver a blunt message.

"From now on, you have to understand that everything will center on the contras," Bergold said. "That is our main instrument."

16

TRABIL NANI: THE MISKITO WAR

A WOMAN'S piercing scream from near the river bank jarred my colleague John Lantigua and me from our reverie near the Miskito Indian village of Saupuka one morning. We turned in time to see a young mother race out of the jungle toward her thatched hut. She was shrieking wildly, and in her arms she was carrying a limp and apparently lifeless infant.

"Baby fell in the river!" cried a young Indian standing near us.

We ran toward the hut, and as we ran I wondered if I could try to save the child with artificial respiration. Bounding up the wooden steps, we burst into a dark room where the distraught mother was kneeling over her motionless child. One side of the child's face was red and badly swollen. He had not fallen into the river, but rather been bitten by some tropical creature, probably an insect. Artificial respiration would be no help, nor would anything else I could do.

From the shadows stepped a young Indian woman, about the same age as the anguished mother. The crowd parted, and she knelt over the infant, waved her hands back and forth over his body, and began softly chanting. Everyone fell silent and watched, some clasping their hands to their faces in expressions of awe. After a few minutes, the woman produced some flower petals and scattered them over the infant's tiny body, chanting all the while. I knew enough of the

251

Miskito language to know that she was not chanting in Miskito, and the villagers, all of them Indians, seemed nearly as amazed as I was at the spectacle.

For about ten minutes, the woman's singsong voice filled the tropical air. Several times she showered the infant with colored petals, or gently slapped his chest. Her body swayed back and forth, and with her hands and arms she seemed to be trying to coax something evil out of the innocent baby's body.

Then, at first imperceptibly, the baby's head began to move. He opened his eyes, kicked both his feet, and started to cry. The mother shouted for joy and hugged her baby, and the rest of us watched in astonishment. All believed we had witnessed a resurrection.

Lantigua and I stood silently for several minutes as the villagers slowly returned to their work. He had been in Central America for several years and was now writing for the *Washington Post,* and I had been around even longer, but neither of us had ever seen anything like this.

"What just happened?" he finally asked me. I had no answer.

Later, when the shock had worn off, we approached the woman who had worked the miracle. When I asked if she was a healer, or had some special powers, she laughed aloud.

"I'm not a healer, and I don't have the slightest idea what I did," she said. "I was in a refugee camp, and I saw a lot of healers. They chanted and used flower petals, so when I saw that nobody else was helping that baby, I decided to try."

"But what were you singing?" Lantigua asked.

"Who knows?" shrugged the woman. "It was just nonsense syllables. I never learned any of the real ones. But I guess it worked."

As we prepared to leave Saupuka, a young Indian, apparently sensing our emotional response to that day's drama, approached and offered to clear up our doubts.

"What happened to that baby was my fault," he said.

"How could it have been your fault?" I asked.

The Indian looked downward, seeming deeply contrite, and spoke quietly.

"Last night, there was a sign that something bad was about to happen," he said. "I was outside, and I saw a black man walk into one of the huts. When he came out, he was a blue tiger with black marks. That was a demon who turned himself into an animal. I should have recognized it as a warning to be careful. But I never told anyone, and so that poor baby almost died."

EVERY trip I made to the Mosquito Coast was filled with that kind of strangeness. It was an ancient, indigenous world full of ritual and mystery, part of Nicaragua only geographically. For centuries its residents knew little and cared less about events in Managua. The isolation of their homeland protected them, and allowed them to develop a self-contained and unique culture. Like native peoples throughout the world, they have been abused by various conquerors. When their history is written, the era of Sandinista rule will be the blackest chapter.

Sandinista leaders ultimately came to acknowledge that their policy toward the Mosquito Coast had been disastrously misconceived. In speeches and other public statements, they apologized for it more frequently and more emphatically than they ever apologized for any of their other errors. The apologies were amply justified, because Sandinista policies devastated Miskito culture and cost the lives of many hundreds of Indians.

Not everyone who contributed to the devastation was candid enough to apologize, however. The Central Intelligence Agency, seizing on Indian discontent, trained and armed groups of Miskito fighters and encouraged them to join the contra war. American intervention helped turn the lush Mosquito Coast into a bloody battleground, but that did not prevent President Reagan, not otherwise known as a defender of indigenous peoples, from professing support for the Miskito cause. On one occasion, during a speech in which he asserted his empathy with the oppressed, he went so far as to declare passionately, "I am a Miskito Indian."

The Mosquito Coast encompasses all of Nicaragua's long Atlantic shoreline, plus the vast expanse of adjoining swamp, savannah, and rain forest. It is perhaps best understood if one imagines it as a Caribbean island that, by some geological catastrophe, drifted toward Central America and found itself part of a foreign nation. Patterns of life along the coast are entirely different from those in the rest of Nicaragua, and people who live there approach the world from a spiritual perspective alien to other Nicaraguans. Most are of either African or indigenous racial stock, speak English, profess the Protestant faith, and deeply admire the United States. They constitute less than ten percent of Nicaragua's population, and have always mistrusted "the Spanish" who are the other ninety. When Sandinista guerrillas overthrew the Somoza dictatorship in 1979, coast people, as they call themselves, did not consider the change particularly important. As far as they were concerned, one group of "Spanish" had simply replaced another.

The barriers separating Nicaragua's two halves were not only linguistic, cultural, racial, and religious, but also physical. Rugged and trackless wilderness, including a dense jungle nearly as big as the Republic of El Salvador, keeps the two sides apart. For years, the Mosquito Coast was supplied by freighters from New Orleans and other Caribbean ports, and foreign-owned companies provided most of the paid employment. Residents looked eastward, toward Jamaica and New Orleans, rather than westward toward the interior of their own country. No paved road ever connected them to Managua, and they never asked that one be built. Spanish-speaking Nicaraguans, it seemed to them, were perpetually fighting, oppressing, imprisoning, and killing each other. Coast people wanted as little to do with them as possible.

Early ancestors of the Miskito Indians are believed to have migrated northward from South America, settling first on what is now Nicaragua's Pacific plain. Around the tenth century they were expelled by stronger tribes, and ultimately found their way to the eastern shore. There they lived off the bounty of sea and rivers, cultivating what few crops they needed, until the arrival of the first explorers. Miskitos were probably the Indians who welcomed Christopher Columbus when he landed at Cape Gracias a Dios in 1502, and the hospitality they showed to him anticipated their good relations with European settlers. They were especially warm toward the British, whose expeditions from Jamaica began arriving regularly in the late seventeenth century. They admired the order and grandeur that Britain represented, not to mention the prosperity that seemed to follow her imperial expansion.

Late in the seventeenth century, a delegation of Miskitos traveled to Jamaica to appeal to the British governor for official protection against pirates, Spaniards, and other enemies. The Miskitos asked to be considered British subjects, and swore their loyalty to the Crown. In the competition for power in the Caribbean basin, these Indians were a potentially valuable ally, and they were welcomed into the empire.

British authority over the Mosquito coast was established gradually. The first treaty between Britain and the Miskitos was signed in 1710, British commercial agents began arriving in the 1730s, and by 1750 there was a resident British superintendent, named by the Governor of Jamaica. British lumber companies, attracted by the giant mahogany trees that abounded near Nicaragua's eastern coast, established lucrative export operations there, and small British-style towns began springing up. Descendants of pirates, many of whom had been born in England or Scotland, also settled along the coast, as did blacks from Jamaica and other British-influenced islands. They and the Miskito Indians mixed reasonably well, and together gave eastern Nicaragua a decidedly non-Spanish flavor.

Through the eighteenth century and well into the nineteenth, Britain held sway over the Mosquito coast, ruling through a hereditary line of Indian "kings" who never wavered in their loyalty to the Crown. Some of the kings were figures of ridicule, often found drunk by foreign visitors, but others were men of intelligence who enjoyed great prestige among their people. One of the most popular was George Augustus Frederick, who ruled from 1845 to 1864.

"His education, received at Jamaica, was quite equal to that of an ordinary English gentleman," wrote a British traveler who met him. "With it he had acquired a refined taste, hardly to have been expected; he was never without one or two volumes of our best English poets in his pocket, and availed himself of every unoccupied moment to peruse them. I do not want it to be supposed that civilization had made him effeminate in the slightest degree; on the contrary, he was the best shot, and canoe's man, in the whole country; and though regarded by his people with the affection of children for their father, his slightest word or look was law, and woe to him who disobeyed either."

George Augustus Frederick was to be the last Miskito king. Once Nicaragua emerged as an independent nation, its leaders sought to assert their authority over the coast region, which they considered part of their national territory. In 1860 they finally persuaded Britain to sign a treaty ending its two-century hold on the Mosquito Coast.

For many years Nicaraguan authorities paid almost no attention to the Mosquito Coast. The vacuum left by British withdrawal was filled not by Spanish-speaking Nicaraguans, but by American entrepreneurs, who established logging camps and banana plantations along the coast and turned the region's principal town, Bluefields, into a bustling commercial center. Bluefields was connected by regular steamship service to New Orleans, and also became a frequent port of call for vessels from Baltimore, Philadelphia, and New York. Soon it boasted a fourteen-piece brass band which specialized in playing American tunes, a bottling company that produced ginger ale and seltzer, and even a daily English-language newspaper, *The Bluefields Messenger*. Advertisements in the *Messenger* suggested the town's prosperity, like this one published in the 1880s: "Finest and complete assortment of Wines, Liquors, and Cigars. Cold and Warm Lunches. Imported Fancy Eatables. Regular meals from 9 to 10 A.M. and from 3 to 4 P.M. Lunch at any hours. Also a variety of all the most popular Fancy and Mixed Iced Drinks: Cocktails, Punches, Souris, Fizz, etc."

Beginning in the mid-nineteenth century, in what proved to be a profoundly important development, Moravian missionaries from Germany began arriving on the Mosquito Coast. Originally the Moravians, whose doctrine is close to Lutheranism, came to minister to a colony of Prussians that had been established in Bluefields, but soon they turned their attention to the Miskito Indians. In classic missionary style, they devoted themselves to "civilizing" the Indians, persuading them to abandon polygamy, wear clothing, and adopt Western-style work habits. Within half a century after their arrival, they had converted virtually the entire Miskito people, and made enormous contributions to the Miskitos' material well-being. They built schools and hospitals, introduced basic sanitation techniques, and codified the Miskito language for the first time. Many of the most capable and intelligent Indians, as well as many Creoles, became Moravian ministers or lay pastors. As the twentieth century dawned, the Moravian church was the most important institution on the Atlantic coast—in fact, the only unifying institution of any significance. By then most Moravian missionaries were from the United States, and their good works reinforced the region's already strong pro-American sentiment.

American influence was welcomed in Bluefields and everywhere else in the Mosquito Reserve, where people looked to the United States as informal successor to the departed British. Thousands of coast people either worked for Americans or made their living indirectly from the American presence. American products filled the grocery shelves, and American money circulated freely.

As the Nicaraguan nation consolidated itself, its leaders inevitably confronted the reality that nearly half the national territory was not under their control. Under terms of the 1860 treaty with Britain, the "Mosquito Reserve" enjoyed considerable autonomy. Nicaraguan authorities could not collect taxes on goods exported from the Caribbean shore, and had no power to grant logging, mining, or farming rights there. When the nation-builder José Santos Zelaya took Nicaragua's presidency in 1893, he resolved to end Miskito autonomy and definitively incorporate the vast Indian homeland as part of Nicaragua.

Early in 1894, President Zelaya ordered Nicaraguan troops to occupy Bluefields. Soldiers commanded by one of his most trusted officers, General Rigoberto Cabezas, swept up from the banks of the Escondido River late on the night of February 11–12. They pulled down the Miskito flag and replaced it with Nicaragua's blue-and-white banner, declared martial law, and stripped indigenous authorities of all their legal power.

It was a great triumph for the new Liberal government. Nicaragua had lost entire provinces in past wars, but was now showing itself as an assertive power, determined to rule every inch of its territory. There were festive celebrations in Managua, though in Bluefields most people were alarmed and outraged.

"The Nicaraguans have no sympathy for the inhabitants of the Mosquito Reserve," one resident wrote to the American consul. "They are jealous of the prosperity of the reserve. We do not speak the same language, we do not profess the same religion, and our institutions and laws and manners and customs are not agreeable to them, and their manner of life and mode of government are obnoxious to us; and both Indians and foreigners within the Mosquito Reservation are unwilling that these men shall have the rule over us."

Faced with this emergency, Miskito leaders drew up a petition asking Britain to resume its role as their "protector power." There was no reply from London, and finally residents of Bluefields took matters into their own hands. They overran the small military garrison, declared their independence from Nicaragua, and appealed to Britain and the United States for support.

Several weeks later, a company of United States Marines debarked at Bluefields. Residents at first greeted them as saviors, and were crushed to learn that they had come on behalf of the Managua government. President Zelaya, then still in Washington's good graces, had requested American help to suppress the Miskito rebellion, and the response was quick and decisive.

Once American troops were ashore, further resistance was futile. A group of about one hundred fifty rebels, unwilling to accept the new order, asked for and were granted asylum in Jamaica. They departed aboard a British vessel, and as it disappeared over the eastern horizon it carried away the last remnants of the old Miskito kingdom.

When General Cabezas returned to Bluefields, he convened a meeting of Miskito leaders and cajoled them into signing a document accepting Nicaraguan sovereignty. The final article in the Bluefields agreement was symbolic but still important: "As a show of gratitude to the great President of the Republic, General don J. Santos Zelaya, to whose efforts we owe our enjoyment of freedom, what was heretofore known as the "Mosquito Reserve" shall from this day forth be known as the DEPARTMENT OF ZELAYA."

Zelaya's government was less than scrupulous in keeping its promises to Miskito Indians. Export duties collected along the Atlantic coast were not applied to local development projects, as the government had promised. Indians around the booming town of Puerto Cabezas found their land rights threatened when the Bragman's Bluff Lumber Company, a subsidiary of Standard Fruit, was awarded a 50,000-acre concession that extended deep into their traditional homeland. Even the government's pledge to respect local traditions was broken when authorities banned the use of English in Moravian schools. Rather than comply, the Moravians temporarily shut their schools, leaving most children in the region without access to formal education.

By the 1930s most of the Atlantic coast region had entered into a long period of decline. The worldwide depression forced many businesses to close, and freighters from New Orleans and other foreign ports began arriving less frequently. Soil exhaustion and plant diseases took a heavy toll on the banana plantations, and mines became depleted. In March 1931, guerrillas loyal to Augusto César Sandino attacked the Bragman's Bluff plantation, looting, burning, and spreading panic among foreigners. Bluefields, whose local authorities had become lax and corrupt, degenerated into a den of pestilence and crime. The once-booming town of San Juan del Norte was virtually abandoned after the United States decided to build its canal across Panama instead of Nicaragua, and its harbor slowly filled with silt and debris. Indians and other coast people fell back into their traditional patterns of village life, entirely isolated from the rest of the country. It was in this state that the victorious Sandinistas found them in 1979.

The Sandinista revolution was made by men and women who, like nearly all Nicaraguans, knew nothing about the Atlantic coast. It was not their ignorance, however, that produced the Miskito tragedy of the 1980s, but their messianic arrogance, their certainty that they knew the answers to all of the nation's problems. In my travels through the coast region, I often heard people compare the arrival of the Sandinistas in 1979 to the arrival of a violent motorcycle gang in a peaceful country town.

None of the passions that sparked the Sandinista revolution was particularly strong in eastern Nicaragua. There were no rich capitalists, no disinherited masses, no impoverished factory workers. National Guardsmen had been confined to a few sleepy outposts, and were rarely known to act brutally. The Somoza regime had not been especially popular, but it was not resented or hated with the passion that many Spanish-speaking Nicaraguans felt.

Coast people listen to American, Honduran, and Costa Rican radio stations, and their instinctive anti-Communism has been strengthened by years of news reports about oppression in Fidel Castro's Cuba. Nearly all are strongly pro-American, full of fond memories of the days when stores were full of American products and there was always work available at some American-owned business. They do not deny that those were days of injustice and racial prejudice, days of low wages earned in the hot sun or deep in poisonous mine shafts, but still their memories are sweet.

The national uprising against Anastasio Somoza Debayle that shook Nicaragua in 1978 and 1979 was almost a foreign news story to people in Bluefields and Puerto Cabezas. In smaller and more remote towns, many people were hardly even aware that it was underway. Coast people had been watching "the Spanish" fight among themselves for centuries, and the Sandinista-led rebellion seemed to them just another contest between competing "Spanish" power elites. History suggested that no matter who emerged victorious, the Atlantic coast would remain isolated and ignored.

The Sandinista takeover coincided with the emergence of a renewed sense of nationhood among Miskito Indians, sparked by developments in the indigenous world during the 1960s and 1970s. A new generation of educated Miskito leaders had come into contact with Indians from other countries where struggles for indigenous rights were being waged. In trying to understand their common heritage, they developed the theory that Indians constituted a "fourth world" whose problems were entirely distinct from those of capitalist, Communist, or developing nations. Capitalists and Marxists, they asserted, disagreed only on superficial issues of how to divide the spoils of a ravaged earth; indigenous peoples, in contrast, sought to live in harmony with the elements, not to dominate them. Miskito leaders closely studied the success of indigenous campaigns for autonomy in Panama, Australia, Canada, and Greenland, and when the Sandinistas came to power, they decided the time was right to launch their own campaign.

At the time of the Sandinista victory, there were perhaps one hundred thousand Miskito Indians living in Nicaragua, mostly in the northern part of Zelaya province. Several thousand were concentrated in Puerto Cabezas, but most lived in small, ancient villages on the swampy savannah, or overlooking the broad Coco River. The Coco was the center of their tribal world, not just a home but an eternal source of spiritual sustenance. Sixty of the most important Miskito villages were on its banks, and there the Miskitos had forged their identity and nourished it for centuries. Part of the essence of being a Miskito was to be near the Coco, to see it, to bathe in it, and to absorb its mystic power.

On November 11, 1979, less than four months after the Sandinistas swept to power, five hundred Indians converged on Puerto Cabezas for a convention to form a new ethnic-based political action group. Several Sandinista leaders attended, among them junta member Daniel Ortega. They urged the Indians to join Sandinista "mass organizations," but soon realized that Indians were in no mood to join groups directed from Managua. Many convention delegates spoke in sweeping terms of their right to national self-determination, their historic autonomy, and the separate path of development they envisioned for eastern Nicaragua. At one point Ortega, who had not expected the militance he encountered, sparked a heated argument by suggesting that most of the delegates were college-educated young people out of touch with Indian needs, and urging them to step aside so "true leaders" could come forward.

From the contentious Puerto Cabezas convention emerged a new, wholly indigenous organization determined to assert and defend the rights of Miskito Indians, and of the smaller Sumo and Rama tribes. The organization was called Misurasata, an acronym for Miskito words meaning "Miskito, Sumo, Rama, Sandinista, All Together." After some hesitation, the Sandinistas officially recognized Misurasata's legitimacy, awarding it a seat on the Council of State, which went to an emerging Miskito leader, Steadman Fagoth.

The arguments that broke out during the Puerto Cabezas convention were hints of trouble to come. Sandinista leaders who arrived to take political control of the Miskito region showed themselves highly insensitive to patterns of life that had been in place there for generations. They confiscated businesses and farms, expropriated foreign-owned companies, and imposed a mass of new commercial regulations. Even in small villages, where Indians had farmed together for centuries in what was essentially a form of pure communism, Sandinistas decreed the establishment of state-sponsored cooperatives. Just as in the rest of the country, they sought to dictate what crops should be grown on which farms, and to require that all produce be sold to government agencies at fixed prices. Their blundering reinforced coast people's worst stereotypes of "the Spanish."

In the southern part of Zelaya province, where black Creoles rather than Indians are the main ethnic group, resentment of the new Sandinista regime grew just as quickly. The local political organization, Southern Indigenous Creole Community, was so rabidly anti-Sandinista that the government refused to recognize or deal with it. Many Creoles, like many Indians, viewed Sandinista authorities as a hostile occupying force, and the Sandinista takeover as a nightmare come true.

By the middle of 1980, tensions along the Mosquito Coast were crackling. Organizers from Misurasata, among them several Moravian pastors, had fanned through the region and were spreading the word that an Indian revival was at hand. A group of militant Sumo Indians disrupted Sandinista efforts to establish a logging camp in their traditional homeland, and other land conflicts soon followed. In Puerto Cabezas, Indians who worked for government-run companies began to demand salary increases, and when their demands were ignored they launched a crippling labor slowdown.

As authorities were trying to decide how to deal with the Puerto Cabezas strike, violence exploded in Bluefields. Parents there had been refusing to send their children to school as a protest against the arrival of Cuban teachers, who they accused of teaching atheism and Marxism. In September 1980, groups of them took to the streets, carrying anti-Cuban signs and chanting slogans. Their protest quickly mushroomed, and large crowds assembled under a giant homemade banner reading, "The Atlantic Coast Demands Justice Without Communism."

There had been no such challenge to Sandinista rule anywhere in the country, and authorities moved quickly to suppress it. Reinforced police and army units were summoned, and they attacked the crowd with nightsticks. Many demonstrators were injured, and protest organizers were arrested. Several were forced to kneel in front of groups of Cubans and beg forgiveness.

Sandinista leaders were alarmed at the wave of defiance in the coast region. Their concern mounted when Indian leaders met in the village of Bilwaskarma and vowed to resist the establishment of lumber camps and other enterprises in their traditional homeland. Former National Guardsmen in Miami were already announcing the beginnings of their counter-revolution, and Sandinista *comandantes* were in a nervous state. Still not comprehending the nature and dimension of the Indian movement, they tried to crush it. In February 1981 they ordered the arrest of more than thirty Miskito leaders on charges that they were plotting to dismember the Nicaraguan state.

All but one of the arrested Miskito leaders were released after two weeks in jail, receiving stern warnings to refrain from further organizing. The last, Steadman Fagoth, who had quit his seat on the Council of State to protest what he said was Sandinista indifference to Indian demands, spent two months in Sandinista custody. He was finally released after promising to leave Nicaragua and accept a scholarship to study in the Soviet Union. Soon after his release, however, he reneged on his promise and announced that he was joining the incipient contra movement.

A wave of Indian protests followed the arrests of Fagoth and other Misurasata leaders. The Sandinistas responded with a new crackdown, arresting village elders and others they believed were collaborating with a supposed plot to declare eastern Nicaragua autonomous or independent. In the town of Prinzapolka, four Indians and four Sandinistas were killed when police tried to arrest a suspected separatist. Rumor inflated the Prinzapolka killings, along with other incidents, into a systematic terror campaign directed by Cubans, and Indian fear of the Sandinista began turning to hatred.

Sandinista *comandantes* held a stormy meeting with Misurasata leaders in August 1981, and after it dissolved in acrimony, they announced that they no longer recognized the organization's existence. The angry encounter was significant not only because it led to the banning of Misurasata, but also because it marked the emergence of a new Miskito leader, Brooklyn Rivera. Young and charismatic, devoted to the developing ideology of Indian revival, Rivera soon became the most widely respected spokesman for his threatened people.

The break between Sandinista and Indian leaders drove many Miskitos to panic, and large numbers of them began fleeing across the Coco River. They had always considered the river the heart of their ancient homeland, but since 1960, as a result of a World Court decision, it had formed the official boundary between Nicaragua and Honduras. Thus to escape the Sandinistas, Indian villagers needed only to float themselves and their belongings across to Honduran territory. During the early 1980s, several entire villages picked up and moved, often in the face of Sandinista efforts to prevent them from doing so. In some places, armed Indians formed raiding parties on the Honduran side, and then crossed back into Nicaragua to attack Sandinista garrisons, whooping for "Indianekarnika"—Indian power. Authorities blamed villagers for aiding the guerrillas, and launched yet another wave of arrests. As a result, many more Miskitos fled across the Coco and turned definitively anti-Sandinista.

THE Indian attacks that began in November 1981 became known as the "Red Christmas" campaign. Sandinista leaders took the campaign very seriously, believing that it was the beginning of a coordinated, CIA-directed effort to establish a breakaway state in the Miskito region. Several dozen Sandinista soldiers were killed in the attacks, and *comandantes* in Managua were pushed beyond the limits of their tolerance. They realized that Indian villagers along the Coco River would always be disposed to help Indian fighters, no matter what efforts the regime made to win them over. Convinced that they needed to act decisively to avoid losing control over the northeast part of their country, they embarked on a cruel campaign of forced relocation that became the greatest collective trauma in Miskito history.

Beginning in the first days of 1982, battalions of heavily armed Sandinista troops swept along the high Coco River bank, herding residents into trucks and driving them away from their homeland. To assure that guerrillas would not be able to use the evacuated villages as base camps, soldiers burned them to the ground. They also destroyed large amounts of stored grain and other foods, machine-gunned hundreds of farm animals, and reduced innumerable orchards to ashes. Distraught villagers looked on in horror, hugging each other and singing Christian hymns through their tears.

As word of the evacuation campaign flashed along the river bank, more than half the Indians who lived there, a total of about ten thousand, chose to flee across the river into Honduras. The rest, about 8,500 of them, were brought to a large jungle clearing fifty miles from the river, given food rations and rudimentary building supplies, and told to make new homes for themselves.

The forced removal of the Miskitos from their ancient homeland marked a military success for the Sandinistas. By depopulating the river bank, they deprived Indian rebels of a vital base of support. In the process, they also created a vast free-fire zone that could be bombed and strafed without danger to civilians. But in every sense other than military, the removal was catastrophic. It embittered an entire generation of Indians, and even outraged many Spanish-speaking Nicaraguans. Roman Catholic bishops issued a strongly worded pastoral letter declaring that the Indians' inalienable rights had been unjustly violated. Many foreign governments joined in what became a worldwide chorus of protest and condemnation.

The Reagan administration, watching from Washington, saw political opportunity in the tragedy, and moved quickly to exploit it. In the early months of 1982, CIA agents circulated among Miskito refugees in Honduras, trying to recruit them into the contra movement. Their efforts sparked a split between two of the most prominent Indian leaders. Steadman Fagoth eagerly accepted CIA overtures, agreeing to fight under the guidance of the Nicaraguan Democratic Force, the principal contra army. Fagoth's onetime ally Brooklyn Rivera, however, struck out on a different path. Rivera claimed he had seen Fagoth become "psychopathic" in Miskito refugee camps, brutally mistreating young Indians and becoming "totally blinded and sick with power and personal ambition." He refused to submerge his cause to that of the contras, whose leaders he scorned as brutes. To Rivera, as to many Miskitos, the contra war was just another case of "Spaniards" fighting among themselves for power. Indians had little in common with the Sandinistas, he argued, and it was foolish to believe they would have more in common with the CIA or the contras.

Because Fagoth was allied with the CIA, he never lacked for money or supplies. Rivera, however, had no such patron. In search of allies, he turned to another anti-Sandinista leader who had refused to take CIA orders, the flamboyant Edén Pastora. After some resistance, Pastora and his civilian partner, former junta member Alfonso Robelo, agreed to support the concept of Indian autonomy, and a deal was struck. Their alliance seemed promising; Pastora was an authentic hero, Robelo a shrewd political operator, and Rivera a charismatic Indian. All three were revolutionaries at heart, and together they represented an attractive alternative for Nicaragua. For a time their Democratic Revolutionary Alliance received a modest CIA stipend, but it was cut off when they refused to make common cause with the contras.

Through most of the mid-1980s, while Indian refugees remained huddled in refugee camps, war ravaged the Mosquito Coast. There was never any question of the outcome, since the total number of insurgents fighting there, counting Indians, Creoles, and Spanish-speaking fighters loyal to Edén Pastora, never exceeded a few thousand. Behind the curtain of an enforced news blackout and tight travel restrictions, Sandinista soldiers militarized most villages and used mortar fire and aerial bombarment to punish those they believed were harboring guerrillas. Scores of Indians suspected of being guerrillas, including more than a dozen Moravian pastors, were arrested and jailed, along with hundreds of civilians charged as collaborators. Occasionally there were reports of Indian victories over Sandinista troops, but they were rare. More symbolic of the course of the war were accounts of Indians armed with only bows and arrows, trying to overrun heavily defended government garrisons.

Nicaragua has more than four hundred miles of Atlantic coast, and none of it was spared the cost of war. The conflict there never became as relentlessly cruel as the contra war being fought in Spanish-speaking Nicaragua, but both sides were nonetheless guilty of brutal abuses. Each tried to deprive the other of its popular base, with abduction, torture, and murder among the acceptable tactics. Sandinistas fighting along the Atlantic coast held an overwhelming advantage in manpower and weaponry, but no matter how successful they were on the battlefield, they could never feel secure, living as they did among people who detested them so completely.

Sandinista authorities required anyone visiting the Atlantic coast to carry an official permit, and permits were difficult to obtain. As part of the loosening of political restrictions that preceded the 1984 election, however, the coast region became more accessible, and in September of that year, several journalists were notified that our longstanding applications to visit Bluefields had been approved. There was no road to Bluefields, and scheduled air service was highly unreliable. Virtually the only way for outsiders to visit the coast was by charter plane, and I hired one to fly me over the jungle.

From Managua to Bluefields is only 150 miles by air, but in an aging Piper the trip took nearly two hours. I was the only passenger, and sat next to the pilot. The last half of the flight was over dense rain forest. When finally Bluefields appeared below, it seemed an entirely foreign place.

About 25,000 people lived in and around Bluefields in the 1980s, most of them black Creoles but also some Indians and even some Spanish-speaking Nicara-guans who had emigrated from Managua or other parts of the Pacific plain. The town is classically Caribbean, dominated by wood frame houses set above a shallow harbor. A single main street runs parallel to the waterfront, and beyond it are decaying wharves, the harbor, and the open sea. Rain falls almost every day, and people ducking under cover to wait out the downpours turn quickly to uninhibited conversation. On the streets, women wear striking jewelry made from black coral, and men greet each other by pointing and saying, "Right here, man!" Latin America seems very far away.

Sandinista soldiers were very much in evidence around Bluefields, and there was no mistaking the hostility with which many residents regarded them. In other parts of Nicaragua, even in areas where Sandinista policies were especially unpopular, soldiers mixed fairly well with local people; most were young draftees, and could have been any Nicaraguan's sons. Along the Atlantic coast, however, soldiers were perceived as an occupying army, foreign in race, language, religion, and culture. It was rare to see them in conversation with anyone besides other soldiers. More than once, I saw people stand up and leave cafés as soon as someone in a Sandinista uniform came through the door.

Everyone in Bluefields, it seemed, had something bad to say about the regime. Many had lost their jobs at the local seafood processing plant, which the Sandinistas had expropriated from its American owners soon after taking power. Others blamed the Sandinistas for scaring away not only foreign companies, but also the tramp steamers that for years had been reliable sources of food and consumer goods. Hunters and fishermen were angry because Sandinista travel restrictions had sharply reduced their freedom of movement. Clergymen warned that the Sandinistas were Communist, and as such inherently untrustworthy.

My first morning in Bluefields was sunny, and I spent several hours around the docks. From there, the town's shabbiness was unmistakable. Piers were crumbling, and hulks of abandoned vessels lay scattered along the shoreline. Houses along the water were in dire need of repair and repainting. With the exception of the regal Moravian school, whose white clapboard bell tower dominated the modest skyline, every building in town seemed to be falling down.

A shirtless laborer, dark-skinned and about thirty-five years old, was unloading plantains from a canoe. After watching him for a minute or two, I approached and struck up a conversation. He had not a single good word for the Sandinistas. When I asked him what he resented most about their rule, he shook his head and replied, "Everything."

"Give me one example," I pressed. He looked at me for a moment, and then leaned forward as if taking me into his confidence. His first complaint was about food rationing.

"Used to be you could get two, three, five, ten, twenty bag of rice, man," he said with a scowl. "Know what they give you now? One *pound,* man. *One fucking pound!*"

On a good day in Bluefields, a load of giant sea turtles would arrive at the dock. One morning while I was there, the *Elena J.,* a thirty-foot trapper whose paint was peeling and whose timbers were beginning to rot, eased toward one of the central piers carrying more than forty of the creatures, each of them weighing fifty pounds or more. Customers looking forward to steaks, soup, and stew crowded around. As a crew member deftly cut the turtles apart with a long knife, women carrying shopping bags shouted "Three pounds!" or "Five pounds!" The flippers, said to contain the tastiest meat, were most sought after. Meat of any kind was hard to find in Bluefields, and the arrival of the *Elena J.* was considered a felicitous event, so I tried to forget that giant sea turtles were on their way to extinction, just as I did when I saw their eggs for sale at markets in Bluefields and other Atlantic coast towns.

When the turtles had been finally dispatched, a crew member invited me aboard the *Elena J.* He and his mates were full of stories about the good old days. Several had been dock workers at a time when freighters from New Orleans arrived in Bluefields every week, and they spoke of the United States as if they were discussing an old and dear friend. All were anti-Sandinista, but they recognized that they were going to have to live under Sandinista rule for some time to come. Creoles like these were not moved by the millenarian fervor that lent fire to the Indian rebellion, and many were slowly forcing themselves to adapt to the new order.

"The way I see it," one of the crewmen told me, "if a man come with a gun and tell you to come, you go with him. Then the other guy with a gun come, and you go with him, too. Don't say no to nobody, man."

Not everyone in Bluefields accepted the Sandinistas so philosophically. A few days before I arrived, townspeople told me, several hundred students had marched on the local Sandinista headquarters to protest the military draft. Pro-government demonstrators were summoned to confront them, fights broke out, and a rock-throwing melee ensued. One evening during my stay, local Sandinista officials called a rally to denounce the anti-draft protesters. The crowd was small, but the rhetoric, all in Spanish, was hot enough to cut through the persistent drizzle.

"These streets of Bluefields belong to the revolution!" boomed one of the Sandinista speakers, a young woman in combat fatigues. "We will defend the streets! We are not willing to turn them over to the counter-revolution!"

Sandinista demonstrators did not seem very motivated that night, and most of them soon drifted toward the nightclub where Nicaragua's most popular band, *Dimensión Costeña,* played on weekends. The eight-piece band, all of whose members were black Creoles from the Bluefields area, struck up a pulsating beat, and townspeople danced to reggae, calypso, and Afro-Caribbean sounds until long after midnight. Anthony Matthews, boisterous leader of the band, put on a great show, dancing across the stage while singing original tunes like "Everything I Do, That Monkey Can Do."

Matthews was a local celebrity of the first order, and the next morning I dropped by to see him at the local radio station, where he worked as a disk jockey. He greeted me with a friendly grin and a handshake, and we talked as he spun records for the radio audience.

"If you're from Bluefields and all the band members are English-speakers," I began, "how come the band has a Spanish name?"

"We are Coastal Dimension, man!" Matthews cried. "We know where we're from, don't you worry about that—right here in Bluefields. People buying records in Managua want a Spanish name, so we give them one. We are beyond language, man. We sing in English, Spanish, even in Haitian French. True Coastal Dimension, man!"

Matthews shared the local dissatisfaction with Sandinista rule, and did not shy away from political discussion. But he and the band had been well treated by the ministry of culture, which had bought them a new set of instruments and amplifiers and sent them on several foreign tours.

"There's a bad situation out here, that's for sure," Matthews reflected after announcing a Stevie Wonder tune. "What the band can do is help people survive through it, man. We represent the happiness of the coast people. Playing takes away that bad feeling people have about the war situation. You feel so good, you want to dance!"

Dimensión Costeña had indeed lifted many spirits in Bluefields, but the reality of war was still inescapable. The same day I met Anthony Matthews, military authorities reported that a force of more than two hundred guerrillas had attacked the nearby town of La Cruz del Rio Grande, leaving fourteen dead. Two days later, the head of a farm cooperative less than ten miles from Blue-fields, who had urged his neighbors to cooperate with Sandinista authorities, was killed in an ambush. Then news was received that Ray Hooker, a prominent local figure and one of the few Creoles who sympathized with Sandinista rule, had been kidnapped by guerrillas while on an organizing trip.

Hooker was later released after an international outcry, but Indian fighters continued to target those they considered collaborators with the regime. Their victims included health workers, coordinators of Sandinista youth groups, and administrators of state-run cooperatives. Once they captured three American journalists and led them to believe they were facing death.

The journalists—veteran Juan Tamayo of the *Miami Herald,* free-lance correspondent Nancy Nusser, and Reuters photographer Lou DeMatteis—were visiting Indian villages near Puerto Cabezas in mid-1985 when suddenly a band of heavily armed guerrillas burst from the forest. They surrounded the journalists and brusquely ordered them to lie face-down on the ground. All feared the worst.

"Juan, do you think they're going to kill us?" Nancy managed to whisper.

"Nancy, I don't know if they're going to kill us," Juan whispered back.

The three were made to lie still until a guerrilla commander appeared. He let them sit up and smoke cigarettes while he examined their passports. All seemed well until the commander noticed that Juan's passport listed his birthplace in Cuba. Immediately the guerrillas became very excited, talking loudly among themselves in their native tongue. All that the reporters could make out was the word "Cuba," which the guerrillas used repeatedly while pointing their rifles at Juan. Apparently they believed he was a Cuban military advisor masquerading as a journalist. He tried to explain that he had left Cuba as a small child and grown up in Connecticut, but to no avail.

"We need to investigate you people some more," the commander finally told them. "For now, you have to come with us into the woods."

Terrified that they were being led toward execution, the journalists began pleading with their captors. They made no headway. As they were about to be marched away, however, something quite remarkable happened. A group of Miskito women from a nearby village appeared and began to reason quietly with the guerrillas. They seemed to be vouching for the journalists' integrity and urging the guerrillas to release them. Slowly and palpably, the tension began to ease. Finally the three were allowed to go free, willingly leaving behind a ransom of boots and radios.

"I'm sure those women saved our lives," Nancy reported after returning to Managua. "Until they showed up, we thought it was all over." Juan, who had been covering wars and trouble spots for years, was equally shaken. "Definitely the scariest moment of my life," he later said.

As war escalated along the Atlantic coast, Miskito Indian leaders chose different paths. Steadman Fagoth and his followers strengthened their alliance with the CIA and its Nicaraguan Democratic Force, arguing that the only hope for Indian redemption lay in destroying the Sandinista state. But Fagoth's rival for Indian leadership, Brooklyn Rivera, rejected that argument. Rivera always insisted that he was not a contra, and bitterly denounced Fagoth for having sold out to the CIA and "the dirtiest, most assassinating right-wing elements of the Honduran army." Though he hated the Sandinistas for what they had done to his people, he still considered himself very much a revolutionary.

"Of course the revolution made this whole movement possible," Rivera once acknowledged. "The fervor of the revolutionary triumph injected into the soul, heart, and atmosphere that everybody could express themselves and participate. Before, there was no incentive . . . We were just asleep."

Rivera was an instantly appealing figure, introverted by nature but highly intelligent, able to move in both the native and non-native worlds. He had been born and raised in the placid coastal village of Sandy Bay, ancient seat of Miskito kings. Child of a Miskito woman and a Spanish-speaking Nicaraguan, he studied in Puerto Cabezas and Bluefields, and then traveled to Managua to enroll at the National University, from which he graduated with a degree in mathematics.

In the months that followed the 1979 Sandinista victory, Rivera, like other Miskito leaders, ingenuously believed that the new regime would accept Indian demands for sweeping autonomy and "self-determination." He was one of the leaders arrested in February 1981 on charges of plotting separatism, and after his release, he had made his way to Honduras and begun to build a following among Miskito refugees there. But his refusal to ally himself with CIA-sponsored contras soon led Honduran authorities to expel him, and for most of the 1980s he was based in Costa Rica, along with his ally Edén Pastora.

Pastora's struggling guerrilla campaign came to an abrupt halt after he was nearly killed in the May 1984 bombing at La Penca. During the months that followed, Rivera made several private overtures to the Sandinista government. Moravian pastors, who served as intermediaries, urged both sides to work for a compromise, and in December the Sandinistas made an astonishing and unprecedented announcement: they would open peace talks with Rivera and Misurasata. Never before had they recognized the legitimacy of a guerrilla group, or acknowledged that any anti-Sandinista insurgents might have legitimate grievances. Now they were sending *Comandante* Luis Carrión to Bogotá, Colombia, to sit across a table from leaders of the four-year-old Miskito rebellion.

There were three stormy rounds of talks in Colombia, and another in Mexico City. Rivera demanded that the Sandinistas withdraw their troops from Indian villages, and Luis Carrión refused even to entertain the idea.

"The proposal is completely beyond any political or military reality," Carrión said upon returning to Managua after the talks collapsed in May. "Besides being politically unacceptable because it would limit government authority over national territory, militarily it would give every advantage to the groups fighting there. What they are seeking is almost a state within a state."

Rivera was equally gloomy. "The government delegation completely refused to discuss fundamental issues such as land rights, cultural identity, natural resources, and the political organization of indigenous people," he told reporters. "They continually deny our aboriginal rights."

The poverty in which Rivera and his supporters were forced to live was evident not only in their chronic lack of military supplies, but also in their personal circumstances. Whenever I called Rivera in Costa Rica to arrange an interview, he suggested that we meet for the lunch buffet at my hotel. He would arrive with two diminutive Indian bodyguards, and at the buffet table, the three of them would heap enormous piles of food onto their plates. They ate slowly and methodically, never leaving a single scrap, and then consumed several desserts apiece. I often had the feeling I was feeding them for the week.

In 1985 Sandinista *comandantes* made a decision that was to have profound effect on the Atlantic coast for years to come. Henceforth, they decreed, all policy toward Indians, and all policy toward the coast region, would be handled personally by Interior Minister Tomás Borge. From that moment, Borge became the effective governor of Zelaya province, the ultimate authority in matters great and small. No one had held such sweeping power over the coast region since the era of General Rigoberto Cabezas, ninety years before.

Like General Cabezas, the Sandinistas at first believed they could crush resistance in the coast region through the sustained application of brute force. But like Cabezas, they finally came to realize that force alone could not resolve an ethnic or racial conflict, and they resolved to try a different approach. For the daunting, long-term assignment of winning back the confidence of coast people, Tomás Borge, the self-proclaimed champion of seduction, was an ideal choice. Borge had lost out to Daniel Ortega in the struggle for leadership of the Sandinista Front, and would never be president of Nicaragua. But now he had his own kingdom to rule, sparsely populated to be sure, but vast in size and very much at the center of world attention.

The policy that Borge designed for the coast region was a masterful blend of resolve and compromise. Rather than continue negotiating only with politicized Misurasata leaders like Brooklyn Rivera, who dreamed of turning the region into an autonomous, self-governing Indian reserve, he set out to seduce individual villages, and even individual Indians, hoping to woo them away from their leaders by resolving their particular problems. He and his agents traveled through the region assessing local needs, and soon many long-postponed projects began to materialize. In one village, a decaying pier was repaired; in another, a schoolteacher arrived; in a third, new outboard motors were distributed. Coast people were also offered special incentives to join government security forces, and soon some of the police patrolling Bluefields and Puerto Cabezas were English-speaking local residents. Borge encouraged the emergence of new Indian and Creole leaders who acknowledged the reality of Sandinista rule, and gave them the resources they needed to build their credibility. More important, he listened to their advice.

At the same time he was working to win the hearts and minds of villagers, Borge made direct appeals to Indian fighters. The Miskito army had never been conventionally structured, and obeyed no central command. Its leaders were tribal warlords, each of whom commanded a few score or a few hundred men. Many professed solidarity with Brooklyn Rivera, and others considered themselves followers of Steadman Fagoth, but most took orders only when they chose to. Borge began sending them messages offering to talk peace, and several accepted. He made them a startling offer, one that would have been unthinkable anywhere else in Nicaragua. Any Miskito combat commander who agreed to stop fighting, he said, would be allowed to return, with all his fighters and all his weaponry, to his native village. There he would be placed in charge of local security, and all Sandinista authorities, including police and soldiers, would be withdrawn.

No anti-Sandinista guerrillas had ever been offered such a deal. Borge was making an enormous concession, implicitly recognizing a form of Indian sovereignty and acknowledging that Sandinista troops were outsiders in Miskito territory. But he was also achieving a key Sandinista goal, which was to end the Indian war without giving in to Brooklyn Rivera's demands for land rights and quasi-independence. Several important Indian commanders accepted his offer.

There had never been such a thing as a rebel-controlled village in Sandinista Nicaragua, and in mid-1985 I decided to travel to the Atlantic coast to see one. Because Borge had eased travel restrictions, I was able to obtain a permit to fly to Puerto Cabezas by plane. Accomodations there were poor, limited to a few dank, rundown guest houses. There was running water for only a few hours each week, and after a while visitors, like residents, had to adapt themselves to living under layers of sweat and dirt. As elsewhere along the Mosquito Coast, insect life was luxuriant and endlessly varied, and I always returned from my trips covered with bites and painful swellings.

After some inquiring around Puerto Cabezas, I found a young man with a pickup truck who was willing to drive me out through the tropical savannah. Our route took us first to the Wawa River, where a pulley-operated barge ferried us across, and then through a stretch of palm forest. After about half an hour, we emerged onto the damp, swampy lowland. Standing in the back of the truck with the humid wind at my face, I could see the Miskito homeland stretching for miles in every direction.

Our destination was the village of Yulu, the largest of about a dozen villages that had been turned over to Indian rebels. At mid-morning Yulu finally appeared on the horizon, looking not a bit like any village where Spanish-speaking Nicaraguans lived. Houses were spaced far apart, and set above the ground on posts or stilts. There were no streets, no sidewalks, and, of course, no motor vehicles. Children played in the shade of regal palm trees, and everything in sight was verdant green. Most remarkable of all, there were armed men in charge, and they were not Sandinistas.

Children crowded around and adults looked up from their labors as we slowed to a stop beside Yulu's modest Moravian church. Indian fighters dressed in green fatigues, assault rifles slung casually over their shoulders, eyed us uncertainly. We asked for their commander, and after a few minutes we were greeted by a slight young man, in uniform but unarmed, with a thick mane of jet-black hair, who told us his name was Rubio.

Rubio, whose real name was Uriel Vanegas, was just twenty-one years old, but he had been at war for four years. He told us he commanded three hundred men, and from the respectful attitudes of those in Yulu, we could tell he had authority. Many gathered to listen as he sat on a wooden step and answered our questions.

Since abandoning his studies to take up arms, Rubio said, he had been in many battles and killed his share of Sandinista soldiers. He acknowledged Brooklyn Rivera as his leader, but said Rivera had not been able to keep him and his men supplied with food or medicine. When the Sandinistas offered him a safe-conduct pass to Puerto Cabezas, he accepted, and there he negotiated his deal. Sandinista troops pulled out of Yulu, and Rubio's men replaced them. For the time being, at least, his war was over.

"We're in a temporary cease-fire," Rubio told us. "The idea is that our political leaders will negotiate some permanent agreement, if they can. Otherwise we're ready to start fighting again."

Rubio's men murmured approval as he made his threat. But without a reliable source of provisions and war supplies, he and his fellow Miskito commanders had little hope of launching a serious offensive. He seemed to understand that, and as we were parting, he told me he had thought of going to college someday.

"What would you like to study?" I asked.

"Literature," he replied immediately.

Tomás Borge's new approach to the Atlantic coast was beginning to work. He won over, or at least neutralized, a number of Creoles and Indians, both civilians and guerrilla fighters. And in 1985, in a brilliant maneuver, he suddenly announced a dramatic turnaround in the government's attitude toward autonomy. With typical audacity, he declared that he was not only going to stop arresting people for supporting autonomy, but that he himself now supported it.

"We are going to have the best and the strongest autonomy law in the world!" he promised.

Borge realized that there would be no peace in eastern Nicaragua as long as thousands of Indians from the Coco River remained penned in refugee camps. Originally the Sandinistas had intended to keep the Coco River bank permanently uninhabited, and to resettle Indians elsewhere. But Borge had come to recognize the mystic importance of the river in Miskito culture, and ordered that policy reversed.

In June 1985, authorities at the sprawling complex of Indian refugee camps began summoning refugees to give them news that some had despaired of ever hearing: the government was allowing them to return home. Many were at first incredulous and afraid. All understood that there was no longer any kind of food or shelter available along the river, and that they would have to reclaim their villages from the voracious jungle. But some were so desperate that they responded immediately, clamoring to leave the camps as soon as possible. The first of them were brought to Puerto Cabezas in mid-July, and when I arrived there on July 23 I found the streets crowded with Indian families, most of them sitting alongside bags that contained all their worldly possessions, waiting to be taken back to their sacred river. The first truckload of settlers, I was told, had left that day for the site of Waspam, once the main town along the Coco.

Early the next morning, I set out by jeep toward the river, a young Creole at the wheel. The road north had been widened and graded to accommodate army trucks, and we made good time. As we approached the river, the foliage became thicker. We passed a settlement that had once been an American-owned logging camp, now abandoned except for a few Sandinista soldiers, and soon found ourselves driving through a fragrant pine forest. The last few miles of the drive were rugged, as the road tapered almost to nothing, but finally we saw signs of life ahead. We had arrived where Waspam once stood.

For many decades, Waspam had been the center of life along the Coco River. It stood on a bluff overlooking the broad, majestic waterway, facing the forests of Honduras on the other side. Once it had been a busy commercial center, where Indians from up and down the river converged to sell and trade. Seven thousand people had been living in Waspam when the Sandinistas launched their forced evacuation plan three and a half years earlier.

We parked our jeep under a grove of palm trees, and I began walking toward the river bank. I could make out where a main street had once run, and see paving blocks beneath the thick brush. A few shells of cement buildings, and the remains of a Texaco station, proved that human beings had once lived here, but the rest of Waspam had been devoured. As I walked, I felt as if I were an archeologist from the future, stumbling on remains of twentieth-century life.

The first person I saw was an elderly Indian standing on the bluff, gazing out at the river. I kept my distance, not wanting to disturb his solitude. After a few moments, he turned and looked at me, and slowly began to smile.

"Wangki," he sang, using the Miskito name for the Coco River. And then again, crossing his wrists over his heart, "Wangki."

About fifty Indians had made their way back to Waspam by then. I saw men clearing land with machetes, and digging post holes for houses. They told me that they were not only determined to rebuild a community here, but that each of them was planning to build his new house on the precise spot where his old house had stood.

"Churches, theaters, stores, markets, horses to ride, an airstrip, schools, clinics—we had everything in those days," a middle-aged Indian named Diego Lucas remembered. "Now it's all gone and burned. If it can ever come back, I don't know."

From behind a crumbling concrete wall, I heard the sound of laughter. A young Indian woman was operating a kind of day care center for children whose fathers were clearing brush while their mothers foraged for food in the jungle. She told me she was Silvia Miguel, twenty-four years old, and that she had come home to Waspam to be a schoolteacher. The fact that there was no school seemed not to daunt her at all.

"When our ancestors first came here, they had to build Waspam from nothing," she reminded me. "We have to do the same thing. It's going to be a hard life for a few years, but at least we're back at home. You should have seen the joy when we first got here. On the first day, people were running into the river with their clothes on, singing and crying. We've been waiting for so long, and so many died before they could see the river again. Any kind of problem, we can handle it if we are here with Wangki. We could never be happy outside this place."

Miskito Indians were not given to public displays of emotion, at least not in the presence of outsiders, but I could sense a strong spirit at work among them that day in Waspam. After finishing my interviews, I put away my notebook, walked to the edge of the bluff, and looked down at the wide river. Indians had told me tales about its power, and that day it looked powerful indeed. I was seized by an impulse to sample its richness.

Back in the jeep, I dug out a pair of bathing trunks and pulled them on. With some difficulty, I managed to climb down the bluff to the river's edge, and dove in. My idea had been to swim to the other side and back, thereby making a technically illegal trip into Honduran territory. But the current was too strong, and I settled for a short dip near the shore. It turned out not to be true that, as I had been told, anyone who swims in the Coco emerges with the ability to speak Miskito. Nonetheless, I felt I had been initiated a bit more fully into the Indian world.

Several weeks later, when I had all but forgotten the incident, I was in Costa Rica, and arranged to interview Brooklyn Rivera. As usual, he joined me at my hotel for the buffet lunch. He had been under renewed pressure from the CIA, and I had much to ask him. But before I could begin, he spoke.

"I heard you took a swim in the Wangki," he said.

I was puzzled at first, and then astonished. We were sitting in a fancy hotel in Costa Rica. The river was five hundred miles away, and only a few dozen miserable refugees were living there. I stared at Rivera for a minute.

"As a matter of fact, I did swim in the Wangki," I said finally. "How did you know?"

Rivera grinned and shook his head.

"We don't get many people other than Indians swimming in our river," he told me cryptically. "Whenever one does, Indians talk about it. I heard that a newspaperman showed up in a jeep asking a lot of questions, and then went swimming. I figured it was probably you."

PEOPLE had been telling me for years what a close family the Miskitos were, and I was beginning to understand. Their resilience was almost unbelievable, as I saw at Waspam and again when I visited the refugee complex where thousands of them had been living since 1982. Sandinista authorities had given the complex a Miskito name, Tasba Pri, which means "free land," but for the nearly ten thousand Indians who spent the early 1980s there, there was little free about it.

Tasba Pri was deep in the bush, a hard ride from Puerto Cabezas. The day I arrived there in mid-1985, my first sight was a group of about six Indian families sitting along a muddy dirt road. They were surrounded not only by bags of possessions, but also by corrugated zinc roofing panels, which they were hoping to take home with them.

"Where are you from?" I asked a man named Rodolfo Herman.

"Downriver," he replied. Indians traditionally divided the Coco River villages between those that were east or "downriver" from Waspam, and those that were west or "upriver."

"What village, exactly?"

"Saklin," he said. "It's between Klark and Tuskro Tara. Or at least, it used to be."

"When are you supposed to be going back?"

"Four days ago, sir."

"Four days *ago?*"

"Yes, sir."

"What happened?"

"We don't know. They said that people from Saklin who wanted to go home should be here Monday morning. We arrived before dawn, and we've been sitting here since then."

Rodolfo Herman and his neighbors were a pitiful sight. After nearly four years at Tasba Pri, they were aching to see their river again. Their last few days must have been especially trying, since they had taken their homes apart and thus had no shelter from the elements. Herman decided he should try to make his way to Puerto Cabezas to see what had gone wrong, and I agreed to drive him.

Before heading back, I took a walk around one of the nearby settlements. Sandinista authorities had given the Indians wood and zinc to build homes, as well as seeds and fertilizer so they could grow some of their own food. They had also made efforts to establish schools and health centers in the camps. Indians had not been actual prisoners, though travel outside the camp usually required a permit, and camp administrators were generally sympathetic. Some were Miskitos themselves, like Riley Sanders, twenty-eight years old, who was busy at his tiny office when I walked in. He told me he was urging people not to try traveling back to the Coco just yet.

"There are no conditions for an immediate movement of these people," Sanders said. "It's not just that we don't have trucks to bring them to Waspam, or boats to carry them upriver or downriver. It's that there's nothing up there, nothing at all—no food, no houses, nothing! And besides, the whole river bank is full of land mines; we've already had people killed by mines up there. I keep explaining all this, and the people hear what I'm saying. They believe me. They know how bad the situation is up there. But a lot of them just want to go back anyway."

Sanders's expression softened as he looked out at Indians dismantling their shacks and packing their meager belongings.

"You can't blame them, I guess," he sighed. "The whole thing has just been so sad. *Trabil nani.*"

"Trabil nani" had been one of the first Miskito expressions I learned. Indians often used it when I asked them how they were doing. It means "lots of trouble."

Naturally there was a Moravian pastor at the refugee settlement I visited. I tracked him down at his wood shack, where he was sitting with a group of neighbors. Like most Indians I met, these men and women were filled with hope that they might now be allowed to resume their shattered lives. The worst thing about Tasba Pri, they repeated over and over, was the close confinement and lack of privacy. They had been brought up in open spaces, with plenty of room all around, and were suffocated by having to live the way "Spaniards" lived.

"Everyone is waiting to leave, and happy to get out of this place," the pastor told me. "But we know there are so many problems. Just getting back to the river again is next to impossible, and then we'll have to start building a town all over again, just like we did when we came here. One thing will be different, though. We'll be by the river."

Most of the Indians I met during those weeks had very bad memories of the forced evacuation in 1982. Many told of being made to walk long distances, sometimes under harsh conditions that led to exhaustion, injuries, and deaths. At least some believed the Miskitos' final judgment had arrived, and that they were being marched to mass slaughter. It had been a merciless trek, harsh beyond all necessity, as the Sandinistas themselves came to admit. Daniel Ortega told me in an interview years later that more than twenty Sandinista soldiers had been given prison terms for abuses committed during the evacuation, and that at least five had been executed. Without any public announcement, the government also began making cash payments in 1985 to the families of more that one hundred Indians who, it acknowledged, had been killed by Sandinista soldiers or police during the evacuation of the Coco River or other Sandinista operations.

I wanted to keep up with the Indians' progress as they emptied the camps at Tasba Pri and returned to their native land along the river bank, but that proved difficult. Tomás Borge's office quietly stopped issuing travel permits to journalists seeking to visit the river; apparently Borge hoped to avoid a new round of stories that would remind the world of past Sandinista abuses. I knew conditions must be difficult for the returning Indians—they could not possibly be otherwise—and I was anxious to visit them again. There was only the problem of the travel ban.

Borge was still allowing journalists to fly to Puerto Cabezas, so one option would be to make that trip and then try somehow to proceed northward to the river. Experience told me that option was unpromising. Even if I could find a vehicle, a driver, and gasoline in Puerto Cabezas, there was only one road out of town, and soldiers had erected a barrier across it, allowing no one to pass without a permit.

It didn't take long for me to realize that this was my chance to take a trip I had been imagining since first arriving in Nicaragua, overland from coast to coast. Maps showed a dirt road running from Matagalpa eastward through mining country and on to Puerto Cabezas, though few people I knew had ever traveled it. Often I had passed a kilometer marker in Puerto Cabezas that carried the number 565, signifying that it was 565 kilometers to Managua, and wondered what kind of trip that must be. Now was my chance to find out. My plan was to drive halfway across the country in one day, stay overnight in one of the old mining towns, and from there continue straight to the Coco, without entering Puerto Cabezas.

I broached the idea to my companion Guillermo, and he was immediately enthusiastic. He warned me, however, that since we had no permit we were likely to be stopped and turned back at any point. We needed to invent a cover story credible enough to get us through military roadblocks. Guillermo had often bluffed his way through checkpoints by yelling briskly that he was "with the project" or "from the ministry," but for this trip, something more inventive was required.

Borge had been publicly appealing to foreign governments and relief agencies to aid the resettlement of Indians along the Coco. Here was a perfect opportunity to combine my reporting responsibilities with humanitarian concern for the needy. When Guillermo and I finally departed on our long trip, we were carrying not only food, drink, extra diesel fuel, and other necessities, but also four fifty-pound bags of rice. The rice was stacked prominently on top of our other cargo, and we hoped it would be our ticket to the river.

Guillermo backed the trusty Land Cruiser out of its parking spot before dawn on the appointed morning, and we set off. Before two hours had passed, we were in Matagalpa, where a faded wooden sign at one intersection pointed the way eastward, as if daring drivers to attempt the trip. A few miles further on, the road turned to gravel and then to dirt. All day we pressed ahead, passing across the clandestine corridors that contras used to enter and leave Nicaragua. Militarized farm cooperatives lined the road, some showing signs of recent combat.

Slowly the land grew more barren. We were entering into the Sumo Indian homeland, and approaching the gold mines where Sumos had for years done the dirtiest and most dangerous work. Finally we approached the town of Siuna, once a busy mining center but now in decline. This was as far as outsiders were allowed to travel.

As we expected, soldiers had built a barrier across the road in Siuna. Luckily, the barrier was manned that day by only a single soldier. When he asked us for our travel permit, Guillermo smiled broadly.

"Don't worry about it," he told the soldier. "We're going to the Coco to bring supplies to those poor Indians—responding to *Comandante* Borge's appeal, you know."

"Sorry," came the reply. "I can't let anyone through without a permit."

Guillermo and I had spent much of the day rehearsing for this moment, and now was show time. I remained mute and smiled dumbly as Guillermo went into his act.

"We're from Rice for Peace, brother," he told the soldier reassuringly. "This guy here is a big shot. Rice for Peace, you know? Peace!"

We had invented this name, Rice for Peace, because in Nicaragua the word "peace" had become a Sandinista code word, just as "reconciliation" had become a contra word. Any public figure who called for peace was signalling his pro-Sandinista sentiments, and any organization with the word "peace" in its name was presumed to be pro-Sandinista. The soldier manning our roadblock understood this, and I could sense his resolve weakening.

"Rice for Peace?" he asked tentatively. "What's that?"

"What's that?" Guillermo laughed. "Didn't you see the *Comandante* on television last night?"

Television reception was very poor in Siuna, and in any case Sandinista infantrymen, we knew, did not spend much time watching. The soldier weakened further.

"You're supposed to have a permit," was all he could say.

"Hey, *compañero*, you don't want to stop this guy, believe me," Guillermo told him reassuringly. "This guy is Rice for Peace—you understand what I'm telling you? It's for peace! The Indians are starving to death up there. We don't want the imperialists to say we're blockading their food!"

The soldier looked carefully in the back of the jeep, and seemed suitably impressed by our bright white sacks of rice. He had no two-way radio, and no one nearby to consult.

"Rice for Peace, you say?" he asked, one last time.

"For peace, *compañero*, that's right. Rice for Peace."

The soldier smiled uncertainly, and then slowly raised the heavy barrier that blocked our road. As we drove through, Guillermo waved his fist through his open window and gave a Sandinista cheer.

"*Patria Libre!*" he shouted.

"*O Morir!*" the soldier shouted back, raising his own fist.

Guillermo and I didn't want to spend the night in Siuna for fear of being discovered by State Security agents, so we pressed on to the next town, Rosita, another once-bustling mining center. It was dark when we arrived there, and we were exhausted. We collapsed onto bunks at the town's only rooming house, and slept until roosters awoke us at dawn.

There was no breakfast available, so I walked to the jeep to dig out a piece of fruit. A man was sitting on the running board, and when I approached, he asked, "Is this your jeep?"

"Yes, it's mine."

"Where you headed?"

"Out for a ride," I said tentatively. "You live here?"

"Not exactly."

"So who are you?"

"*Hombre,* I'm from State Security. We'd like you to stop by our office for a chat before you leave town."

I agreed, trying to act casually, and after a few minutes I slipped back inside to consult with Guillermo about how to deal with this unexpected intrusion. We agreed to visit the State Security agents together, and when we arrived at their shack, Guillermo motioned for me to stay outside. He closed the door behind him, and I could hear only snatches of his argument. The agents kept asking for our travel permit, and Guillermo kept talking about peace. I heard him mention suffering Indians, rice, *Comandante* Borge, and the need for Nicaragua to "unmask imperialist lies." After about twenty minutes, he emerged with one of the agents beside him. They shook hands warmly, and Guillermo walked toward the jeep.

"*Vámonos!*" he called to me. We climbed aboard, waved goodbye to our State Security friends, and headed back to the main road, another obstacle behind us.

We met no more Sandinista agents, but when we reached the Wawa River, about fifty miles south of the Coco, we found another surprise: the ferry was out of service. This was a serious problem, because the river was far too wide and deep for us to attempt driving across. On the opposite bank, we could see the immobilized ferry, as well as the ferryman, who was asleep in the high grass.

Guillermo and I considered our options for a minute or two. First we needed a full understanding of the problem, so I stripped off my outer clothing, dove into the river, and swam across to consult with the ferryman. He told me that the ferry's motor had died, and that until it was started again, there could be no service.

I swam back and explained the situation to Guillermo, who came up with a brilliant solution. He opened the hood of our jeep, disconnected the battery, and removed it. As he worked, I found a local Indian with a canoe who agreed to row Guillermo and the battery across to the other side. There Guillermo connected the battery to the ferry motor, and as the amazed ferryman watched, started it purring. He then rode the ferry back across, the lone passenger, grinning broadly and waving his clasped hands above his head as if he had just won a prizefight. Once back on my side of the river, he replaced the battery, started the jeep, and drove it onto the ferry. We crossed the Wawa, and were on our way again.

As we pressed northward toward Waspam, the last leg of our long trip, Guillermo told me he was becoming worried about our fuel supply. We had filled the jeep before leaving Managua, but we had come a long way, and still had to think about our return trip. There was no hope of finding a service station, so we had to improvise. It didn't take long before Guillermo had his chance.

Because of Borge's travel ban, the road to the Coco was all but abandoned. The only vehicle we encountered along the way was a Sandinista army truck parked beside the road. We pulled to a stop behind it. Two young recruits were sitting in the shade, and as I watched, Guillermo approached them and began talking. At first I couldn't guess his plan, but after a minute or two, he came back to the jeep and explained it.

"We've got a deal," he told me. "Six Marlboros for all their diesel."

As I watched, Guillermo dug six packs of cigarettes from our supply chest and presented them to the grateful soldiers. Then, using a section of garden hose that we always carried for such emergencies, he siphoned twenty gallons of fuel from their truck into spare containers we were carrying.

"These soldiers fill up the truck every time they go back to their base," Guillermo told me as we sped away. "Nobody ever checks how much they use. They were happy to help Rice for Peace."

Soon we were on our way northward through the pine forest again, and before long we reached Waspam. I could see immediately that Indians had made great progress in their first few months back from Tasba Pri. There were hundreds of people around, some planning to stay in Waspam and others waiting for a chance to return to their native villages upriver or downriver. Many families had built temporary shelters, and some were living in concrete foundations where homes had once stood. People told me that some relief aid had been reaching them, but that food was still their greatest need. Then I remembered I had two hundred pounds of rice in the back of my jeep.

I had bought the rice as a gimmick, but now that I was in Waspam where people were actually going hungry, it was a life-giving cargo. At the local Moravian church, I found volunteers sorting through a pile of second-hand clothes, and I told the pastor I had some rice to donate. At first he didn't quite understand or believe me, but when he saw the bulging sacks, his eyes lit up.

"What group did you say you were with?" he asked as we carried the sacks inside. I almost told him Rice for Peace.

"No group," I said. "Actually, it's the *New York Times*."

"*New York Times*," the pastor repeated, as if making a mental note. "Well, good for them."

After a couple of hours in Waspam, Guillermo and I packed ourselves back into the jeep and headed south toward Puerto Cabezas, where we hoped to spend the night. We made good time, but as we drove we discussed the prospect of more trouble ahead. As a foreigner on the streets of Puerto Cabezas, I would probably be quickly stopped by State Security agents, and if they found out what I had been up to, they might well hold me in town for days.

Sure enough, even before we had reached the center of Puerto Cabezas, our jeep was stopped by suspicious agents. We promised to proceed to State Security headquarters for questioning as soon as we had registered at our rooming house.

"This isn't good," Guillermo told me. "I'm Nicaraguan, so they don't care about me. But you're a gringo. They aren't going to let you out of here until they get a direct approval from Borge, and he could be in Cuba or anyplace!"

We fell silent. A few minutes passed, and then, ever so faintly at first, I began to hear the sound of an approaching airplane. Soon I could make out a silhouette in the sky, looming larger as it approached the airstrip outside of town. It dawned on me that the plane might be my ticket out of trouble, and Guillermo and I jumped into our jeep. We were at the airstrip in time to see a small passenger plane from the national airline, Aeronica, touch down and pull to a stop on the tarmac. This was a stroke of great good fortune, because Aeronica planes arrived in Puerto Cabezas only two or three times a week, at highly irregular intervals.

A clerk inside the small terminal building told me the plane would be discharging cargo and passengers and then heading straight back to Managua. If I could pay in dollars, she said, she would happily sell me a ticket. Guillermo and I rummaged through the jeep and came up with forty-five dollars, which was accepted. Half an hour later I was airborne.

I told Guillermo to take his time coming home with the jeep. Three days later he walked into the bureau in Managua, gleeful at our triumph.

"State Security stopped me right after your plane took off," he reported. "When they asked where you were, I just pointed up at the plane. They tried to call it back, but they couldn't make radio contact. I told them where we'd been, and they kept asking how we got through Siuna, where we found fuel for the jeep, all that stuff. They were angry, but I kept smiling and saying we were from the *New York Times*. After a few hours, they gave up and let me go."

Guillermo paused for a moment, and then spoke again more seriously, summing up what the episode had taught him.

"*El New York Times es un árbol que da mucha sombra,*" he said. The *New York Times* is a tree that gives much shade.

By allowing the Miskitos to return to their homeland and by responding to some of their material needs, Borge hoped to split them away from their political leaders, especially Brooklyn Rivera. He refused to allow Rivera to enter Nicaragua, hoping that Indians would forget him. For a time the strategy seemed to be working, and the frustrated Rivera occupied himself by shuttling among foreign capitals begging support for his cause. By the end of 1985 he could bear his exile no longer, and in January 1986 he crossed clandestinely into Nicaragua. For two weeks he traveled secretly through the Miskito homeland, accompanied by several foreign-born Indians, including Russell Means of the American Indian Movement, who had led the Indian siege at Wounded Knee, South Dakota, in 1973.

Tomás Borge never appreciated being taunted, and now he believed Rivera was taunting him. He ordered State Security agents to track the furtive Indian party, and discovered that the Indians were encamped with a band of guerrillas near the aboriginal village of Layasiksa, twenty miles southwest of Puerto Cabezas. Without hesitating, Borge ordered the campsite bombarded. Helicopters and small planes dove out of the sky over Layasiksa, carpeting the lush countryside with 250- and 500-pound bombs. Terrified villagers raced into the bush, where many of them hid for days. Several were killed, but Rivera and his party escaped, making their way to the coast and then sailing to the Colombian island of Providencia. Borge had narrowly missed them, but his message was clear. He was in charge of the coast region, and would not have his authority defied.

The sad story of Miskito travails was repeated, on a smaller scale but with no less tragedy, in the Sumo and Rama tribes. The Sumos numbered less than ten thousand when the Sandinistas took power, most of them living in about thirty communities in north-central Nicaragua. They were not only marginalized as Indians in a non-Indian country, but also suffered discrimination at the hands of Miskitos, who were their ancient rivals.

While the Miskitos' abuse at the hands of Sandinistas and contras received world attention, the Sumos suffered anonymously. Their principal town, Musawas, was invaded in mid-1982 by several hundred rampaging Sandinistas searching for military recruits. One of their first acts was to capture a twenty-five-year-old Indian suspected of collaborating with the contras, and torture him to death over a period of hours, while anguished townspeople listened to his screams of pain. After a violent three-day occupation, the Sandinistas carried thirty-two youths away in a helicopter. Remaining residents fled at the first opportunity, most making their way to the Coco River, thirty miles north, and crossing into Honduras. News of the assault spread quickly, and soon the refugees from Musawas were followed by virtually the entire Sumo tribe.

Contras were not much kinder to the Sumo Indians than Sandinistas had been. Once in Honduras, many Sumo men were pressured to join Steadman Fagoth's contra units, under threat of harm to themselves or their families. In some cases, the threats were carried out. The Sumos were caught between warring armies, afraid to stay in Honduras but also afraid to return to Nicaragua.

Some ethnologists who worked with Nicaraguan Indians in the 1980s believed the Sumos might be able to withstand the traumas inflicted on them, and survive as a people. Few were so sanguine about the prospects facing the country's smallest tribe, the Ramas. Less than one thousand of them remained in 1984 when I traveled to their lush island home, Rama Cay. It was in ruins and all but deserted, a ghost town in paradise.

The Ramas' tribal origin is shrouded in mystery, but Rama Cay has been their home for centuries. Just twelve miles off the coast of Bluefields, the island was an idyllic world. General Rigoberto Cabezas visited there in 1894, soon after his bold "reincorporation" of the Mosquito Coast, and was amazed by what he found. "All the Indians know how to read and write," he reported. "The church is handsome, and the island as amiable and picturesque as can be imagined."

Sandinista authorities barely knew Rama Cay existed, and for a few years Rama Indians managed to keep themselves apart from the upheaval afflicting the rest of Nicaragua. Inevitably, however, their island became a strategic prize for armies more interested in victory than in preserving ancient ways of life. Its peace was finally shattered, and with it the Ramas' fragile world.

In July 1984, Indian guerrillas landed on Rama Cay aboard small launches, and began to build fortified defenses along the shore. A few were Ramas themselves and natives of the island, the rest Miskitos. Their presence, they knew, would soon attract a Sandinista assault, and they advised residents to leave in order to avoid being caught in crossfire. No persuasion was necessary, and in a small-scale but poignant exodus, the several hundred islanders packed what they could aboard canoes and motorboats, and departed for Bluefields.

Sandinista troops soon launched their expected assault on Rama Cay. For two days, they were unable to land because of hostile fire. On the third day, they ordered the island bombed from the air, not knowing that the Indian guerrillas had slipped away the night before. Bombs thus devastated an island on which there was not a single soul.

I traveled to Bluefields two months later, and there I found families of Rama Indians, once the freest of Nicaraguans, encamped in mud-soaked tents behind the Moravian church. They had been reduced to living on donated food and wandering around Bluefields in search of odd jobs. All were afraid to go back to Rama Cay while Sandinista troops were stationed there, and the troops weren't leaving.

"I want to die rather than take this charity," one of the Rama refugees told me. "But I try to stay alive so I can see the day when we all go home."

The Rama chief, Rufino Omier Daniel, was among the refugees. Middle-aged and taciturn, he had become deeply heartsick, and seemed unable to deal with the tragedy unfolding around him. A younger Indian, Cleveland MacCray, had become the tribe's spokesman, but MacCray, also depressed and unwell, had refused to assume the title of chief. Neither had been back to the island since fleeing in July, and they agreed to accompany me on a visit.

I found a boatman willing to take us to Rama Cay, and we set out on on a cloudy morning. The trip took an hour, and when we arrived, a contingent of Sandinista soldiers greeted us. They saw that we meant no harm, and allowed us to stroll about.

Immediately I could see why the Ramas had chosen this place. Mango trees soared above wildflower groves, herons gambled along the sandy shore, and a sea breeze softened the tropical heat. Footpaths were paved with oyster shells. Oranges, limes, pears, breadfruit, and coconuts abounded.

Bombardment and looting had laid most of Rama Cay to waste. I followed MacCray to his home, and watched as he pulled a hymnal out from under some trash in what had once been his bedroom.

"I don't really blame the government," he told me softly. "Some of the people they sent to occupy our island are so young. They don't have the right experience to be soldiers. They do things they shouldn't do."

Chief Rufino was disconsolate as he poked through the remains of the home where he and his children were born.

"It's very hard for us," he finally said. "Once this Rama Cay was named happy home, but now it's not happy any more."

Back in Bluefields, I called on Bishop John Wilson, the senior Moravian clergyman in Nicaragua. Rama Indians considered him their protector, their link with the outside world, the savior who would ultimately find a way to end their sad exile. He told me, though, that he harbored little hope for their future. Even before their flight from Rama Cay, only about twenty of them still spoke the tribal language, and their prospects as a people were not bright.

"I am doing whatever I can, and I try my very best to avoid confrontations," the Bishop said, shaking his head in frustration. "You have to have the patience of Job."

NOT every trip I took from Bluefields was as sad as the one to Rama Cay. Sometimes I was able to persuade local officials to issue me a permit to travel to romantic-sounding villages like Monkey Point, Set Net Bay, and Pearl Lagoon, and those were adventures in Eden. I would rent a skiff, usually with an Indian boatman, and navigate the winding streams and bayous. All life there centered on the water, and almost every town faced either a river or the open sea. Supplies moved only by water, and anyone who wanted to travel needed a vessel of some sort.

As I made my way northward toward the centuries-old village of Pearl Lagoon one day, I saw Indians and Creoles paddling small canoes along the shore, some laden with bananas or other produce. Occasionally we passed motorized launches carrying people or goods from one village to another. Children dove from the hulks of derelicts swamped along the banks.

War intruded even here, however. Sandinista soldiers were quartered in most towns, and guerrillas lurked in the weeds and marshes. As we turned a bend in the Kukra River, we suddenly saw one of Nicaragua's few Navy patrol boats speeding toward us, soldiers deployed across the bow, scanning the shoreline with rifles in hand. They waved as they passed us, shouting greetings in Spanish.

I never found a prettier town in Nicaragua than Pearl Lagoon. It was lush and tranquil, and its three thousand residents, most of them Creoles, seemed untouched by modern life. Every one I met invited me for fruit drinks or conversation.

"We hustle our own food, fishing in the river, growing rice, picking all the oysters you want, just an hour's paddle from here," Ainsworth Fox told me. "We live a better life here than plenty of people, daddy."

There was something endearing about being called "daddy" by a seventy-seven-year-old man. Ainsworth Fox was a wonderful character, born in Pearl Lagoon to parents who had also been born there. He told me that his son Erskine, then forty-two, had never been to school, but nonetheless made boats, fashioned his own tools and fishing equipment, and had built a large home for his family.

Sandinista soldiers were posted at a newly built garrison near Pearl Lagoon, and they wandered freely around town. Ainsworth Fox seemed to have adjusted to their presence.

"In any Army there are some bad boys, but we do need protection," he said. "We Creoles are a cowardly people. We're not fighters like the Indians or the Spanish. We live in harmony in this place, and we'd like to keep it that way, daddy."

Ainsworth Fox was not the oldest resident of Pearl Lagoon, not nearly. After a few inquiries, I learned that there was in that town a man born before the Atlantic coast was incorporated into Nicaragua in 1894. I found him reclining on a sofa inside his home. His name was Robert Temple, and he told me that he had been one year old when General Rigoberto Cabezas seized control of the coast region in Nicaragua's name.

White-haired and frail, Robert Temple lived by himself but kept his door open all day so he could watch what was happening outside. Other villagers treated him as a revered elder. He was still quite sharp, and had become sort of a free-lance counsellor, advising his neighbors on matters from farming and fishing to romance. Children brought him food and water and did his other chores.

"It's been such a very long time," Temple remembered softly. "Sometimes I look out at the cannon and think about it."

Later that afternoon, as I was preparing to leave Pearl Lagoon, I asked a local boy if there was a cannon anywhere around. He took me to the edge of the bluff that overlooked the peaceful lagoon, and there sat an iron cannon. Embossed on its black barrel was the seal of the lion and unicorn, symbol of British imperial rule.

The warm sunshine and rich greenery around us on the ride back to Bluefields was exhilarating, and I asked the boatman if he would slow down so I could jump overboard for a swim. He pointed to a spot ahead where the water was deep, and when we arrived there, he cut the engine. I stood up and began stripping off my clothes, but just as I was about to dive in, a burst of automatic rifle fire erupted from an unseen place along the bank. Evidently someone did not want us stopping there.

"Let's try swimming a little further downstream," the boatman suggested, and we did.

SUCH unexpected encounters were common under the tropical sky of eastern Nicaragua. In Bluefields, when *Dimensión Costeña* was not in town, I sometimes spent my evenings at a restaurant called Chez Michel, the only place in town that offered a taste of what the old days might have been like. Waiters wore black bow ties, and though the ice often looked highly suspicious, there was usually Johnny Walker scotch to pour over it. Few Bluefields residents could afford to eat at Chez Michel, but its savory seafood attracted foreigners unerringly. It was there, late in 1986, that I met Zahari Zahariev and the other Bulgarians.

Bulgarian surveyors had come to Bluefields three years before, charged with helping to fulfill Nicaragua's age-old dream of building a deep-water port on the Atlantic. Soon they were joined by teams of engineers and other specialists. Elaborate plans were drawn up and large labor crews hired. Sandinista leaders depicted the massive project, which was fully financed by the Soviet bloc, as strictly civilian in nature. Pentagon planners feared otherwise, fretfully envisioning hostile submarines and arms-laden Soviet freighters someday calling at Bluefields.

The Bulgarians were happy to see a fresh face at Chez Michel, and welcomed my idea of traveling across the harbor to see their project. One morning I found a seat in an open skiff headed toward El Bluff, the peninsula which protects Bluefields harbor, and in fifteen minutes I was there. El Bluff had once been an unofficial American reservation, and I found remnants of the formerly American-owned seafood packing plant still in use. Giant fuel storage tanks bearing the Texaco logo dominated the landscape.

Zahariev showed me drawings of what this muddy sandbar would look like after it was made into an international seaport. As we spoke, workmen were blasting through a basalt deposit nearby to make boulders for a long breakwater. Others were at work dredging a mile-long channel across the peninsula, deep and wide enough to accommodate 20,000-ton freighters.

The Sandinistas, visionaries that they were, loved giant projects like this one.

I could not help wondering if it would ever come to fruition, and Zahariev had been in Nicaragua long enough to feel the same skepticism. When I asked him if he actually expected the project ever to be completed, he laughed, and answered obliquely.

"There are, uh, what should I say, a lot of, let's say, *differences* between this and what I'm used to," Zahariev said. "There are no machine shops here. Some people don't work too hard, and—what else could I say?—it rains at least ten times more than it does in Bulgaria."

It was raining at that moment, and had not let up by the time I boarded the skiff back to Bluefields. On board I struck up a conversation with a young customs inspector. Like most people in Bluefields, he had no use for the Sandinistas. As we were approaching dry land, he invited me to come visit him that night, in the section of Bluefields called Old Bank. I eagerly accepted, because I had heard stories about Old Bank. Supposedly it was the most anti-Sandinista neighborhood in all of Nicaragua, a place where Sandinista police entered, if at all, only in groups.

That evening, I met my friend under a streetlight. We walked along the waterfront, away from the center of town, and after a few minutes we turned off the paved street onto a muddy alleyway. Old Bank was a jumble of unsteady shacks set on the side of a gently sloping hill, and at my friend's place, several people had already gathered. When we arrived, they were sipping beer and listening to reggae music on a battered cassette player.

"No poli-tricks here, man," said one of them, a resplendently dreadlocked Rastafarian. "Just the music and sweet feelings, right?"

Never did I find it harder to believe I was in Nicaragua than that evening. For several hours, my friend and I wandered through Old Bank, stopping at various houses and at a couple of unmarked bars where juke boxes played loudly. I never heard a word of Spanish spoken, and never saw a sign of Sandinista authority. It had been nearly a century since Nicaragua took control of the Mosquito Coast, but the news apparently never reached this enclave.

ON one of Bluefields' main streets, there was a barber shop that offered the finest shave I ever had in Nicaragua. Under the barber's hot lather and skillful hand, a man could briefly forget he was in a shabby, out-of-the-way town where life was hard and even finding a bar of soap was a challenge. On one wall of the barber shop hung a life-sized portrait of Lenin, but all the other pictures were of American sports heroes.

In Nicaragua as everywhere else, barber shops are great places to talk and listen. The Sandinistas had for years prohibited the gathering of news along the Atlantic coast, and I found the Bluefields barber shop a good place to catch up on events. It was there that I first learned what had happened in May 1985, after guerrillas unsuccessfully attacked the local army base.

"The next day, everyone was told to go to the park and see what happens to enemies of the people," the barber told me. "When we got there, they drove up a truck with thirty or thirty-five bodies, and they threw the bodies onto the ground as if they were animals. When the mothers asked for the bodies, they said dogs did not deserve to be buried in the cemetery. They loaded them up and dumped them in a pit outside town."

The incident, I later determined, had indeed taken place. Immediately afterward, Tomás Borge had flown to Bluefields, convened a public assembly, and apologized for the behavior of his troops, swearing that they had acted far beyond their orders. But in such cases, as Borge must have understood, no apology could undo the damage.

As the Atlantic coast settled into a sort of peace during the late 1980s, Borge could claim that his policies had been at least partially successful. By persuading many Indian fighters to abandon their rebellion, he had calmed a confrontation that was costing the Sandinistas enormous amounts of good will around the world. He never claimed to have won the affection of coast people, but through a combination of carrot and stick he had at least quieted them.

Left behind by Borge's success were Brooklyn Rivera and the group of Miskito leaders gathered around him. Rivera still had broad support, both within Nicaragua and among Indian rights advocates around the world, but as years passed, his demands that the coast region be given genuine self-rule seemed less and less plausible. He was seeking to convert the region into "a self-governing autonomous territory" where the authority of the central government would be strictly limited, and where Indians would control "the use, occupation, development and possession of the land, subsoil, rivers, lagoons, cays, islands, adjacent seas, seabed, fish, wildlife and natural resources."

In the modern world, demands of indigenous peoples for rights over their ancestral homelands are considered anachronistic, incompatible with the needs of the nation-state. Rivera himself acknowledged that acceptance of his proposal would constitute "the most far-reaching manifestation of Indian self-determination in this hemisphere." The very purity of his cause was what made it so appealing and, at the same time, so unpromising. He and Indian leaders like him were trying to call the world back to a different time, but the world was not listening.

IT was raining in Bluefields one afternoon as I sat in a corner café, reflecting on the chasm of understanding that separated coast people from other Nicaraguans. A young Creole walked by, saw me, and came inside. He asked if he could join me, and I slid aside to make room. We chatted for a few minutes, and then he offered a proposition.

"You want to buy an old coin, man?" he asked.

"A coin? What kind?"

"If you're interested, I'll go and get it for you, man."

"Sure," I told him. "I'm interested."

He disappeared, and ten minutes later was back at my side. From his pocket he withdrew a folded white paper, and handed it to me. Inside I found an American silver dollar. It was in excellent condition, with the date 1891 clearly legible. The mint mark signified that it had been struck in New Orleans.

Turning the coin over in my hand, I began to imagine its history. Probably it had been brought to Bluefields soon after being minted, aboard one of the steamships that then plied the New Orleans-to-Bluefields route. Perhaps it was used to pay for a meal at some luxurious restaurant, or given as pay to a local workman. Quite possibly, this silver dollar had been in Bluefields in the momentous year of 1894, when General Rigoberto Cabezas definitively incorporated the Mosquito Coast into Nicaragua. It must have been kept in a jewelry box, or at the back of a drawer, for many decades, half-forgotten like the coast region itself.

Any silver dollar of that period is handsome-looking, but this particular one transfixed me. I stared at the date for a long time, and then spoke.

"How much do you want for it?"

"You got dollars?" he asked.

"Yes, I do."

"Then give me fifteen dollars, man."

Fifteen dollars it was, and I came home from that trip with a keepsake I treasured forever.

The century since that coin was minted had not been kind to coast people, who were still defending themselves against "the Spanish," still grasping for a way to preserve their heritage in a hostile world. They suffered greatly during the 1980s, but emerged from their ordeal with a renewed sense of pride, determined to preserve their old ways of life. Painfully and at enormous cost, they had taught the Sandinista Front and the world a great political and moral lesson.

17

BLOODSTAINS

VIOLENCE OVERWHELMED Nicaragua as the contra war dragged on. Guerrilla raiders swept through the countryside blowing up bridges, ambushing military patrols, attacking farm cooperatives, and capturing and killing Sandinista officials. Burned-out hulks of military trucks littered many country roadsides. Soldiers were everywhere, and hospitals were full to overflowing. By the middle of 1985, the war had taken twelve thousand Nicaraguan lives, and no one could escape its awful shadow.

In many parts of the country, funerals became part of everyday life. I attended more than a hundred. Some were military funerals, at which angry speakers denounced the United States, and caskets were draped in red-and-black Sandinista flags. Others were for the civilian dead, luckless victims of ambush or crossfire. Most victims were young people, many of them teenagers. Always there were sobbing relatives, soothing words from a clergyman, and then a sad walk to the cemetery.

The war's devastation was no longer felt only by poor peasants. In Managua and other cities, many living rooms were dominated by enlarged photographs of lost sons or daughters. So many died that cemeteries began running out of burial plots. On the streets, the sight of young men in wheelchairs, or blinded, or missing a limb, became pathetically common.

One day in early 1985, I received a terse Sandinista communiqué reporting that contras had ambushed a bus near the Honduran border, killing two young women. The victims were schoolteachers who had volunteered for assignment to war zones and had been working in the remote town of El Cuá. They were returning from a Christmas holiday in Managua, carrying rifles and riding in a van marked as property of the agrarian reform ministry, when they were ambushed. Both returned enemy fire before being killed by grenades. They were buried in separate funerals. A few days afterward, I sought out their mothers.

Alba María Siezar was a fruit vendor in Managua, and I found her sitting in a nylon hammock behind a stack of pineapples. She kept her hands crossed over her heart as she talked quietly about her daughter Sandra, who had been nineteen years old.

"With my daughter dead, my spirit is also dead," she said, trying to maintain her composure.

Sitting with Mrs. Siezar was one of her surviving daughters. She told me the family had pleaded with Sandra not to return to her teaching job in El Cuá.

"Mom did everything but get down on her knees and beg Sandra not to go," she said. "We told her she was only one step away from death up there."

I asked who the family held responsible for Sandra's death. Mrs. Siezar blamed both contras and Sandinistas.

"The people who kill with Reagan's support are beasts," she spat. "But these people are also animals. They are sending innocent lambs off to die. Here in Nicaragua, we have never had a government worth defending."

In another poor neighborhood on the opposite side of Managua, I found Zoila Rosa Dominguez, mother of the other victim. Beside her modest pedicure salon was a weathered plaque commemorating the heroic death of a Sandinista martyr, *Comandante* Johnny. Neighbors had told me that Johnny was Mrs. Dominguez's only son, born in 1960 and killed in combat during the 1979 insurrection. Her only daughter had been Estrella Dolores Dominguez, now dead at the age of twenty-two.

"My daughter gave her life fighting for freedom, like my son did in the insurrection," Mrs. Dominguez told me through an iron grate, crying freely. "Losing a child is like losing your life."

She stopped for a moment to wipe her cheeks, and then looked up again. "My children were my whole life," she said. "My daughter never hurt anyone. All she was doing was teaching poor children in the mountains how to read."

"Who do you consider responsible for Estrella's death?" I asked.

"The blame is with imperialism," she replied immediately. "It was the work of the jackal who governs the United States."

WHAT made the Nicaraguan war especially cruel was that its purpose was so vague and undefined. The contras, hopelessly outmanned and outgunned, never had the slightest chance of military victory. Yet American policymakers believed the war was worth fighting because of what it symbolized. By supporting the contras, they argued, the United States was sending the world a powerful message of resolve and determination.

Of all the contras' supporters, none was more vocal than President Reagan himself. His speeches were full of inspirational tributes to contra bravery, usually coupled with frightening warnings about the Sandinista threat. One day he called contras "the moral equivalent of our founding fathers and the brave men and women of the French resistance." Asked if he did not consider them to be counter-revolutionary, he replied, "I guess they are counter-revolutionary, and God bless them for being that way. And I guess that makes them contras, and so it makes me a contra, too."

With these rhetorical flourishes and others like them, President Reagan made his sympathies unmistakably clear. Yet the closest he came to enunciating a goal for the contras was to suggest once that they might be able to make the Sandinista government "say uncle." Officially the president favored a diplomatic settlement, and claimed Nicaragua had rejected "meaningful negotiations." But in fact, the Sandinistas had repeatedly asked for talks with Washington, and offered to enter into them without pre-conditions, only to be rebuffed time and again.

After a time it became clear that there was no strategy for winning the contra war, and hence no real objective to it other than simply to bleed Nicaragua. The war was an exorcism of demons that had plagued some American politicians since the Vietnam debacle. It was being fought not for victory, but simply to make a point.

Early in 1985 President Reagan asked Congress to vote new aid for the contras. In a series of public statements, he wove a vivid picture of the Sandinista threat. On February 15, he told a national radio audience that the Sandinistas had imposed a "brutal dictatorship" in Nicaragua and had "moved quickly to suppress internal dissent, clamp down on a free press, persecute the church and labor unions, and betray their pledge to hold free elections." A few weeks later he asserted in a Washington speech that the Sandinistas planned "to turn Central America into a beachhead of Soviet aggression that could spread terror and instability north and south, disrupt our vital sea lanes, cripple our ability to carry out our commitments to our European allies, and send tens of millions of refugees streaming in a human tidal wave across the border."

Despite the president's colorful rhetoric, many members of Congress remained unconvinced. Some were against supporting foreign insurgencies of any kind, and others were troubled by reports of contra atrocities and human rights abuses. More than a few were outraged at the revelation that the CIA had prepared training manuals for the contras that not only explained the rudiments of small-scale sabotage, but also advised guerrillas to "neutralize carefully selected and planned targets, such as court judges, magistrates, police and state security officials, etc."

When the $14 million contra aid proposal was first brought to a vote on April 23, the Senate favored it but the House of Representatives turned it down by a wide 248–180 margin. President Reagan was stung by the rebuff. To signify his determination to press ahead with his anti-Sandinista crusade, he issued an executive order banning all trade with Nicaragua. He justified the embargo on the grounds that the Sandinistas posed "an unusual and extraordinary threat to the national security and foreign policy of the United States."

A few days later, President Daniel Ortega left Managua for a twenty-five-day tour of Eastern and Western Europe, including what was to be a fateful stop in Moscow. He had been there several times before, and had never hidden his identification with the Soviet bloc, but this time his trip provoked howls of protest from Washington. Influential members of Congress believed that because they had recently rejected contra aid, Ortega was now obligated to make a reciprocal gesture of friendship. When he flew off to the Kremlin instead, they took it as an insult and a gesture of defiance. Sensing a change in mood, President Reagan renewed his campaign for aid to the contras.

Some members of Congress now found themselves in a familiar trap, reluctant to support the contras but afraid of being labeled unpatriotic, weak-willed, or soft on Communism. Two years earlier, they had resolved their doubts by creating a fiction, approving money for the contra war with the ingenuous stipulation that the money be used only to interdict Sandinista arms shipments to El Salvador. Now they sought a similar subterfuge, and President Reagan happily cooperated. In a letter to Representative David McCurdy, Reagan swore that the contras were not trying to overthrow the Nicaraguan government.

"My administration is determined to pursue political, not military, solutions in Central America," he wrote. "We do not seek the military overthrow of the Sandinista government, or to put in its place a government based on supporters of the old Somoza regime."

Debate in the House of Representatives on June 12 was heated. "To fail to recognize the threat the Sandinista government poses to Central America and the United States is to bury our heads in the sand," warned Representative Bill Chapell. "If we allow the Soviets and Cubans to develop this powerful beachhead in Central America, and that ferment spreads, our nation will know a security threat that we cannot abide."

Opponents of the aid package countered by decrying the carnage the war was causing. "[T]he pressure is not on the government," Representative George Miller reminded his colleagues. "It is not on the Sandinistas. The pressure is on the peasants and the plain people of Nicaragua . . . Those are the people who are dying at the hands of the contras who are supported by this government."

When debate finally ended, the House of Representatives approved a compromise aid package. By a margin of 248–184, it voted to send the contras $27 million worth of "humanitarian aid"—mostly food, clothing, and medicine. The aid was to be disbursed by a new State Department agency called the Nicaraguan Humanitarian Assistance Office.

The vote was a victory for the contras because it meant they would soon begin receving badly needed supplies. In addition, the new law contained a little-noticed but immensely valuable provision allowing the CIA to share intelligence data with contra commanders. But Congress had given the contras a decidedly halfhearted endorsement, agreeing to send them food and uniforms but refusing them the weaponry they needed in order to have a chance at victory. Colonel Enrique Bermúdez, the contra commander, was understandably frustrated.

"How can we win a war with humanitarian aid?" Bermúdez fumed in Miami after the vote. "You think we are going to win with enough medicine for the wounded?"

During the June congressional debate, many legislators condemned Ortega for his trip to the Soviet Union. From the Sandinista perspective, however, the trip was vital. Nicaragua was running out of oil, and could no longer afford to pay even concessionary rates offered by Venezuela and Mexico. The Sandinistas had no choice but to appeal for Soviet help.

"Our country is a sovereign country," Ortega had said at an airport press conference. "We are not a satellite of the United States. We are not obliged to ask permission of the American president or the American Congress—I don't know what the American laws are in this respect—to go to Moscow, Montevideo, Brasilia, Paris, or Rome."

Sandinista leaders, by insisting on upholding their "sovereign" rights, once again showed their determination not to adjust their policies to suit the political climate in Washington. They also gave Congress an excuse to vote for new contra aid. By doing so, they passed up a chance to cripple the contras.

WHILE politicians debated in Washington, war raged through the Nicaraguan countryside. Much of the fighting was in the north, where contras could operate close to their Honduran sanctuaries. But by 1985 a contra unit called the Jorge Salazar Task Force had established itself deep inside Nicaragua, in the ranching provinces of Boaco and Chontales. People who lived in those provinces considered themselves frontier people, cowboys and hillbillies who loved open spaces and bridled at government regulation. Many sympathized with the contras, which meant that contra units operating there had sources of food and shelter that they did not have in other areas.

In August 1985, Guillermo and I spent several days driving the back roads of Chontales. We found the region torn by violence. Sandinista troops, determined to eliminate the contras' support base, had forcibly evicted thousands of peasants from their homes and moved them into wretched settlements clustered near military garrisons. In the depopulated countryside, Sandinista mortar shells and helicopter-launched rockets rained down on lush hillsides where contras were believed to be hiding. Yet the contras not only survived, but were able to build at least one semi-permanent camp in the region. Several ranchers I met were willing to admit, on condition of anonymity, that they sometimes offered food and other help to passing contras.

One of the Chontales towns I wanted to visit was La Libertad, where both Daniel Ortega and Cardinal Obando were born. The ride was rough, and we saw only military trucks along the way. La Libertad turned out to be just as miserable an outpost as one would to expect to find in the hills of central Nicaragua. I had read that it was once a prosperous gold-mining center, but its glory days were long past.

There was a drab café off the main street, and the elderly proprietor said he had beds upstairs. His wife made us a dinner of rice, beans, and tortillas, and as we ate, he told us what life was like in La Libertad.

"We're in the middle of the war," he lamented. "Every day the helicopters fly out of here, and then we hear bombing. Sometimes we feel the ground shake. We're terrified. The roads are too dangerous to use, so people don't leave town. Nobody knows where the contras are, but . . ."

"But what?" I asked.

"But I think we're surrounded."

In was nighttime in a war zone, and that always made Guillermo uneasy. He would drive anywhere during daylight hours, but at night he sensed more danger. When I rose to go to bed, he shook his head.

"I'm going to sleep in the jeep," he said. "I don't want anything to happen to it."

The night was peaceful, but I slept only lightly. At dawn we rose and took our leave. After a few hours of driving we arrived at Cuapa, where the Virgin Mary had appeared in a series of apparitions several years before. Contras had recently attacked there, and had managed to capture the town and hold it for several hours. Their first act had been to summon all residents to the town square. They had captured the Sandinista mayor, Hollman Martínez, and asked townspeople what should be done with him.

Martínez was a Cuapa native. Residents pleaded for his life, and he was spared. But other Sandinista activists, all of whom had been sent from Managua or other areas, were given no reprieve. Twelve were marched out of town and executed.

Upon learning that Cuapa was under attack, Sandinista commanders in Juigalpa, the provincial capital, had immediately dispatched a truckload of reinforcements. Contras ambushed the truck and killed nearly all of the forty soldiers aboard. By the time a second wave of reinforcements was able to reach Cuapa, the contras were gone.

IT was standard contra practice to attack lightly defended targets and then withdraw before government troops arrived. Militarily they were underdogs, and they knew it. The Sandinistas, with generous help from the Soviet bloc, had built a potent war machine, by far the strongest ever seen in Central America. They had trucks, tanks, armored personnel carriers, helicopters, and heavy artillery pieces. Their supplies of machine guns, grenade launchers, and automatic rifles were unlimited, and their soldiers never ran short of ammunition. Many of their operations were planned by a group of senior Cuban officers headed by General Arnaldo Ochoa, who had formerly commanded all Cuban forces in Angola.

Besides counting on an enormous advantage in mobility and firepower, the Sandinista army was always several times larger than the contra force, numbering at least sixty thousand fighting men and women on active duty. At its core were fifteen to twenty "irregular fighting battalions," each about 750 strong and composed mainly of draftees. These were the units that journalists often encountered deep in the bush, either fresh from action or in search of it. Most had no fixed base, and commonly operated for months without seeing a paved road or tasting hot food. These units took most of the Sandinista casualties, and were justly praised in the official press for their ability to operate in punishing conditions.

What Sandinista newspapers did not report, however, was that while the irregular battalions were slogging through the mud and facing mortal danger every day, most of the army was being held in reserve, assigned to defend Managua and other cities in case of an American invasion. The *comandantes* were never able to shake their fear that contra guerrillas were really only an advance guard for United States troops, intended to serve as bait to lure the Sandinista army away from its urban defenses. So for the entire duration of the war, many crack Sandinista units remained quartered in or near urban centers, while semi-trained draftees bore the brunt of combat.

Throughout the war, Sandinista leaders waged a campaign to portray contra fighters as "beasts," bloodthirsty mercenaries interested only in turning back the clock to the days of dictatorship. At the beginning, when most contras were ex-Guardsmen, that portrayal was largely accurate. But as years passed, the nature of the contra force changed. Most of its members were young Nicaraguan peasants and workers, driven by Sandinista policies to the point of rebellion.

I met many contra fighters during the course of the war, and was always struck by how much they resembled Sandinista fighters. Both armies were made up of young boys, almost exclusively from the poorest social classes. Each side had its slogans, and few fighters ever questioned them.

When I asked young contras why they had abandoned their homes to fight, they told me they had found life under Sandinista rule intolerable. Most said they had enlisted because Sandinistas had seized their family's land, or tried to force them to join farm cooperatives, or otherwise interfered with their traditional rural lives. Others told me they considered the Sandinistas to be anti-Christian. And there were those who would have preferred not to fight at all, but who joined the contras to avoid conscription. Nearly all were too young to have belonged to the National Guard, or even to remember the Somoza years.

As the contra army broadened its base, however, its leadership remained stagnant. Several times, moderate civilians tried and failed to wrest control of the movement away from ex-Guardsmen. As a result of their failure, the contras remained under the control of soldiers who had served the Somoza dictatorship. Many were not motivated by commitments to justice or freedom, but rather by thirst for revenge, and for a return to the days of property and privilege. They were a fearsome group, not the sort of people Nicaraguans wanted to entrust with the government of their country.

Although Sandinista leaders were confident of their military advantage, they were less certain of their hold on public opinion. Their government lost popularity during the mid-1980s, though not nearly as precipitously as some in Washington liked to imagine. Determined to avoid the fate of Salvador Allende, whose Chilean government was overthrown in 1973 after a CIA-directed "destabilization" campaign, they announced a new crackdown.

On the morning of October 16, 1985, the official newspaper *Barricada* carried a banner headline: "Enough Impunity! We Cannot Permit Agents of Imperialism to Continue Sabotaging National Defense." The accompanying article reported that the government had decided to impose sweeping new restrictions on civil liberties. The rights to assembly and free speech, the right to strike, the right to travel freely, and a series of other guarantees were suspended. President Ortega was quoted as saying that the restrictions were necessary to prevent the contras from forming an "internal front" and provoking "discontent and confusion among the masses."

The curbs sounded onerous, but they altered the terms of political debate only slightly. The Sandinistas had decreed a "state of economic and social emergency" in September 1981, and a more comprehensive military emergency in March 1982. Under those decrees authorities already had the right to ban political activity that displeased them, and they often exercised it.

Some Sandinistas told me the new decree was valuable because it gave police the legal right to open mail and tap telephones. But Sandinista police needed no such authorization. They had long been monitoring my calls, as I learned one night while trying to telephone my New York office.

That night, I dialed the international operator's number, 116, about thirty times. It was busy each time, but I kept trying. Finally I was lucky enough to hear a ring at the other end.

There was usually a long wait for the operator to reply, so I occupied myself with some work at my desk, cradling the phone on my shoulder. The phone rang steadily for fifteen minutes, and then another fifteen minutes. Suddenly, for a few seconds, all static and noise disappeared from my line. This happened several times, and I perked up. Finally I heard a revealing conversation.

"Who's he talking to now?" I heard one man ask in Spanish.

"He's not talking to anyone," another man replied. "He's still waiting for an international operator. I don't know what takes those operators so long!"

THE new curbs were most seriously felt at the opposition newspaper *La Prensa*. Even before they were imposed, President Ortega had warned that "restricted freedom of the press" was all Nicaragua could afford during wartime. Already about one-third of the articles *La Prensa* sought to print were being banned by censors, and now the proportion rose to two-thirds. Photocopies of banned articles circulated among journalists and foreign diplomats, and their headlines reflected the tensions afflicting Nicaraguan society: "Sandinista and Independent Student Groups Clash"; "Human Rights Commission Reports Increase In Complaints"; "Security Police Interrogate Church, Business, Labor Leaders."

In January 1986 the chief Sandinista censor, Captain Nelba Blandón, gave an interview to Eloy Aguilar of the Associated Press in which she eloquently defended her role.

"Censorship is an instrument to defend our revolution," Blandón said. "We understand the international political cost of these measures. Censorship is uncomfortable, difficult to understand in other countries where situations are normal . . . But we can't permit the press to become a destabilizing force in our society simply out of fear of the reaction from abroad."

When *La Prensa* received the Associated Press story over its wire, editors decided to print it. To their surprise, Blandón refused permission. I had never heard of a censor banning his or her own words, and the next time I saw Blandón, I asked her about it.

"What I said was intended for audiences outside Nicaragua," she told me. "Inside the country, we don't talk about censorship."

A few months later, the editor of *La Prensa,* Jaime Chamorro, brother of the slain Pedro Joaquín, received a startling overture from the Sandinistas. It came in the form of an offer by his surviving brother Xavier, editor of the pro-Sandinista newspaper *Nuevo Diario.* The two brothers had for several years headed opposing factions in the Chamorro family. Now Xavier wanted to buy *La Prensa* for "a very good price," in the millions of dollars.

Since Xavier Chamorro had no access to such funds, it seemed clear that he was making his offer on behalf of the government. Had the gambit succeeded, it would have eliminated one of the most potent anti-Sandinista institutions in Nicaragua, and fundamentally shifted the political balance. But editors of *La Prensa* refused to sell.

"The implication of my brother's offer was very clear," Jaime Chamorro told me a few days later. "He was saying that the paper probably won't last very long in any case, and that I ought to make some money out of it while there's still time. The strategy didn't work, but the fact that it was attempted makes me fear that they're looking for a way to close *La Prensa.*"

The Sandinistas were not irritated at *La Prensa* for publishing objectionable material, because it did not—censors saw to that. They did not even really care that *La Prensa* was receiving aid from the National Endowment for Democracy, a quasi-independent foundation funded by the United States Congress. The paper's true sin was its refusal to condemn the contras.

In the first months of 1986, as President Reagan launched a campaign to win approval of $100 million in new contra aid, Sandinista leaders demanded that all patriotic Nicaraguans join in condemning the aid proposal. Not only did *La Prensa* refuse, but Jaime Chamorro went so far as to write an article for the *Washington Post* that seemed to justify the aid request. The Sandinistas, he wrote, were "taking a nationalist movement and turning it into a beachhead for Communist expansion."

EDITORS of *La Prensa* were not the only Nicaraguans who refused to join the anti-contra campaign. Roman Catholic bishops were energized when Pope John Paul II elevated Archbishop Miguel Obando y Bravo to the rank of Cardinal in June 1985, and their clash with the Sandinistas slowly escalated to a new crescendo. On the last day of 1985, the Roman Catholic radio station in Managua failed to join a mandatory national radio hookup transmitting President Ortega's year-end speech. As punishment, authorities ordered the station shut indefinitely on the grounds that it was "threatening public order."

Soon the most prominent Sandinista priest, Foreign Minister Miguel D'Escoto, began denouncing Cardinal Obando in increasingly vivid terms. The Cardinal, like the editors of *La Prensa,* had refused to urge Congress to reject contra aid, and for that Sandinista leaders reviled him. In February D'Escoto announced that he would take a leave of absence from his job as foreign minister to begin a "march for peace and life" through northern Nicaragua. At villages along the way, he stopped to deliver speeches condemning the United States, Roman Catholic bishops, and especially Cardinal Obando. In one tirade broadcast on Sandinista television, he damned Obando as an "accomplice to murder," and asked, "Could there ever be a more abominable sin in the history of humanity?"

D'Escoto's televised messages to Cardinal Obando were not the only way the

Sandinistas conveyed their disgust for him. The official press maintained a steady drumbeat of criticism, calling him "the Cardinal of intervention" and "the CIA Cardinal." When President Reagan, during a radio address in mid-March, singled him out as a brave critic of Sandinista oppression, the official newspaper *Barricada* carried the headline, "Obando's Lies Support Reagan's Hatred."

Both Cardinal Obando and Bishop Pablo Antonio Vega of Chontales visited Washington in early 1986, while the debate over renewed contra aid was underway. They not only refused to denounce the aid proposal, but in some of their comments appeared to support it. *Barricada* asserted that they had "openly and dangerously placed the Nicaraguan [Catholic] hierarchy alongside the traitors who are selling themselves to Yankee power for $100 million."

With the vote in Washington only weeks away, Sandinista anger at the bishops, and especially at Cardinal Obando, grew still more intense. In an interview on Sandinista television, Foreign Minister D'Escoto pointed out, probably correctly, that if the Cardinal were to raise his voice against contra aid, the aid would be rejected. His failure to do so, D'Escoto said, placed him in "a situation of sin" and made him "the principal accomplice of aggression against our people.

"The people of Nicaragua have refused to burn incense before the idol, and for that, the empire is attacking us," D'Escoto told the television audience. "The only ones willing to burn incense at the feet of the empire are our bishops."

By the stridency of their attacks, the Sandinistas were forcing Nicaraguans to choose between following their bishops or following the government. As was eminently predictable, many chose to side with the bishops. Church attendance rose steadily, and when Cardinal Obando appeared in public, crowds were bigger and more enthusiastic than ever.

One evening I watched the Cardinal celebrate Mass in the gymnasium of a Catholic high school in Managua. I arrived an hour early, but the gym was already packed to overflowing, with at least five thousand people inside and more arriving. When the Cardinal finally appeared, the applause was deafening. It lasted for several minutes, punctuated by chants of "O-ban-do, O-ban-do."

In his homily, the Cardinal insisted that it was Christian to care for contras, as well as for Sandinistas. He did not mention D'Escoto by name, but warned, "The devil can come in the form of people who want to divide the church. The devil can walk among us in disguise, like a lion hunting for meat. The devil comes with lies or half-truths.

"They said we went to ask for the $100 million, they said we have blood on our hands, and that is slander!" the Cardinal boomed, his voice amplified by powerful loudspeakers. "They attack us, they slander us, they say our hands are drenched in blood! But fortunately, our people are intelligent and mature, and know how to interpret this."

* * *

As tension increased within Nicaragua during early 1986, Congress pressed ahead with its consideration of President Reagan's request for new contra aid. The House of Representatives turned down the request in a preliminary vote March 20, setting off alarm bells at the White House. Officials knew that once again, they needed a gimmick to win the votes of undecided legislators.

Late in March, several hundred Sandinista troops crossed into Honduras to raid contra camps. There had been several such incursions before, but it was in the interest of all parties to pretend they had not happened. The Sandinistas could not admit that their troops had crossed a border, because that is a violation of international law. Contra commanders could hardly complain that they were being attacked in Honduras, since they were maintaining the fiction that all their bases were inside Nicaragua. And for the Honduran government, any protest would be an admission that it had lost control over part of its territory.

The March 1986 incursion might have gone unreported if President Reagan and his aides had not been anxious at that moment to stir passions in Congress. Affecting great alarm, they declared that Nicaragua had launched an invasion of Honduras. Once again, they charged, the Sandinistas were threatening their pro-American neighbors.

Reporters in Managua barraged the government press office for comment, but no one in authority would speak to us. Pressure from Washington intensified, and finally President Ortega called a news conference. As journalists waited for him to appear, we wondered whether he would try to deny the obvious. He did not.

"Our forces are only defending themselves in the border area," Ortega said, choosing his words carefully. "Honduras has lost sovereignty over part of its territory as counter-revolutionaries have taken it over. It has been transformed into a war zone . . . What Nicaragua has done is to defend itself against attacks by the counter-revolution, which is based in Honduras. This is a legitimate right which Nicaragua will continue to exercise."

The Reagan administration wanted to respond to the Sandinista incursion with a show of American force in Honduras. Honduran President José Azcona, however, showed no interest in soliciting such a display, and urged that the episode be forgotten. Honduran military commanders did not even want to call an alert. But Assistant Secretary of State Elliott Abrams, who was emerging as one of the leading anti-Sandinista ideologues in the Reagan administration, was adamant. He ordered the new American ambassador in Honduras, John Ferch, to insist.

"You have got to tell them to declare there was an incursion!" Abrams demanded.

It was Holy Week, the week before Easter, and like most people in Central

America, President Azcona was looking forward to a few days of rest. Ambassador Ferch visited him at his home early on Tuesday morning, March 25, and explained what Abrams wanted.

"You don't have a choice on this one," Ferch told Azcona sympathetically. "You've got to get a letter up there right now. They're going bonkers up there. This is absurd, but you've got to do it."

Azcona grasped the situation, and knew he had to play his part in the charade.

"I formally and urgently request military assistance from the United States of America to repel Sandinista forces and to prevent these attacks from occurring in the future," he wrote to President Reagan that day. Then, acting not much like a head of state whose country was being invaded, he left to spend the rest of Holy Week at the beach.

The moment Azcona's letter was received in Washington, sabers began to rattle. On March 26, 1986, the Pentagon ostentatiously sent six hundred troops to Honduras. The next day the Senate voted 53–47 in favor of President Reagan's contra aid proposal.

The theatrical dispatch of troops to Honduras had impressed some legislators, but the Reagan administration was still a few votes shy of victory in the House. Many members were still uncomfortable with the contras, and particularly with their leaders. Arturo Cruz, who had joined the contra directorate in June 1985, astonishing those who had heard him swear he would never do such a thing, had been frustrated by his inability to "reform" the contras and was preparing to resign. Since Cruz was the only contra leader with broad credibility in Washington, his departure at that moment would have been a serious blow. To keep him from quitting while the congressional debate was underway, the CIA arranged a round of talks in Miami aimed at "reforming" the contra leadership.

No reforms ever materialized, and Cruz, who like other senior contras was receiving a handsome CIA retainer, finally decided to quit the contra movement. But the bogus "contra reform talks" served their purpose, persuading a few credulous legislators to change their votes. Several others were brought aboard by the administration's decision to combine the contra aid request with a request for $300 million in economic aid to Guatemala, El Salvador, Honduras, and Costa Rica.

On June 25 the House finally succumbed, voting 221–209 to appropriate $100 million for the contras. Seventy million dollars was earmarked for the purchase of military supplies, making this the first time Congress had voted to buy guns and bullets for the contras. The vote marked a great political victory for President Reagan. Congress had explicitly endorsed the contra cause, and thereby assumed part of the responsibility for the carnage to come.

"I fear there may be blood on the hands of this body," Representative Gerry Studds lamented afterward.

In Managua, reporters understood that we were now going to be seeing more suffering, more blood, and more dead bodies. Covering this conflict had already become emotionally draining because of the horrors we so often had to witness in the countryside, and now it was sure to become worse. I dreaded the prospect.

After the House vote, Elliott Abrams moved immediately to fire Ambassador Ferch, in whom he detected insufficient enthusiasm for the contra cause. It was an extraordinary act of political reprisal against a career diplomat, and surprised even President Azcona.

"I thought this happened only in Honduras," Azcona remarked when he learned of it.

In Managua, President Ortega said he was not surprised by the vote. It was, he told reporters who located him that night, "nothing more than the ratification of the United States' criminal policy of war against Nicaragua." He warned that he would not allow contra sympathizers to maintain an anti-Sandinista "internal front."

"The people will know how to deal with these accomplices," Ortega told us.

We inferred that some new blow was about to be struck, and we were right. The next afternoon, I was sitting in my office when a news bulletin came over the radio. In one of its most dramatic acts, the Sandinista government had decided to shut *La Prensa*. Notice came in a two-sentence letter from press censor Nelba Blandón.

"Acting on superior orders, I notify you that as of this date, the newspaper *La Prensa* is indefinitely closed," she wrote. "With nothing else to add, I take advantage of the occasion to reiterate my considerations."

At *La Prensa*'s ugly warehouse complex along the airport road, the Nicaraguan flag was lowered to half-staff. When I arrived, walls were decorated with signs reading "Down With the Totalitarian Regime!" and "Only Unpopular Regimes Impose Their Will By Force." I found Violeta Chamorro, former junta member now turned anti-Sandinista publisher, sitting alone in the office where I had interviewed her martyred husband ten years before.

"My husband gave his life so Nicaragua could be free," she reflected. "This is not the kind of government he dreamed of."

La Prensa had already been emasculated by heavy censorship, and its closure was above all symbolic, a message to the world that the Sandinistas were prepared for battle and willing to take whatever steps they believed were necessary to assure victory. A week later, the Sandinistas delivered the same message again, with equal force. This time the victims were the popular Father Bismarck Carballo, spokesman for Cardinal Obando, who was prevented from re-entering Nicaragua after a trip abroad, and Bishop Pablo Antonio Vega, who was brusquely arrested and deported on July 4.

While the war raged, no suggestion was more abominable to the Sandinistas than that they negotiate with contra leaders. Bishop Vega had repeatedly violated that taboo. In Managua and in Washington, he publicly asserted that the Soviet Union was as guilty as the United States for turning Nicaragua into a battleground; that the Sandinistas were repressive rulers who abused prisoners and persecuted religion; and that the contra war was not the product of foreign intervention, but rather a logical response to oppression.

At such a tense moment, Sandinista leaders considered these statements too provocative to ignore. Still, expelling a Roman Catholic bishop was a drastic step. The Sandinistas justified it on the grounds that Bishop Vega's "unpatriotic and criminal attitude" had made clear that he "does not deserve to be Nicaraguan."

Both the Contadora Group and the Organization of American States offered new peace initiatives in 1986, but the Reagan administration rejected them. When the International Court of Justice, an arm of the United Nations, ruled in June that the United States was breaking international law "by training, arming, equipping, financing, and supplying the contra forces," administration officials paid no heed. They likewise turned aside appeals from allies in Europe and elsewhere. President Reagan and members of his inner circle considered the Sandinistas irretrievably evil, and were determined to overthrow them or, failing that, to inflict pain on their country.

The pain was felt not only by the wounded and maimed, but by those whose bodies survived intact while their spirits were broken. As I walked through the streets of ruined Managua and traveled to country villages, I often tried to imagine the trauma and heartbreak that had been visited on the people I met. Many had been forced from their homes and lost everything that defined their lives. Many more were mourning for loved ones. Most had more bad times ahead.

Political conflict split many families, among them many of Nicaragua's most prominent. The four children of the late Pedro Joaquín Chamorro and his wife Violeta were equally divided, two holding important Sandinista posts and two others strongly anti-Sandinista. Contra spokeswoman Marta Sacasa was the sister of Captain Rosa Pasos, spokeswoman for the Sandinista army. And Luis Carrión, a member of the Sandinista National Directorate, was a nephew of Arturo Cruz, the anti-Sandinista presidential candidate who became a contra leader.

"I don't consider Arturo a relative any more," *Comandante* Carrión told me once. "What he is doing is bringing war, death, and destruction to this country."

"Luis is brilliant and very sincere," Cruz retorted when I told him of his nephew's comment. "But because of his attitude toward me, saying I am an imperialist agent or a CIA mercenary, I don't consider him a relative. He may be my sister's son, but he's no relative to me."

Among the casualties of war were many of the social programs of which the Sandinistas had once been so proud. The health care system, which had wiped out polio by 1983 and cut the infant mortality rate almost in half, began to fall apart. Schoolchildren had no books or pencils, and many were being taught by inexperienced teachers barely older than themselves. Food was in shorter supply than ever, even after the Sandinistas abandoned features of their land reform program that many peasants found objectionable, and inflation was raging at the rate of one thousand percent annually.

By shutting *La Prensa* and expelling Bishop Vega, and by continuing to rule by fiat, the Sandinistas earned worldwide condemnation. Even many of their harshest critics, however, acknowledged reality as it appeared from Managua. The Sandinista government faced a large-scale insurgency sponsored by a foreign power, and its survival was at stake. At moments of comparable crisis, many nations, not excluding the United States, had taken drastic measures against real or imagined enemies.

No lover of freedom could endorse the closure of newspapers, nor could any advocate of reconciliation cheer when religious leaders were forced into exile. Yet even at their most repressive, the Sandinistas never ruled with anything near the level of savagery that was accepted as routine in other parts of Central America. Many political leaders in Washington, including President Reagan, chose to ignore this reality. They praised regimes in Guatemala and El Salvador, where military-backed death squads roamed with impunity, while condemning the Sandinistas for leading Nicaragua toward, as Secretary of State Shultz once put it, "the endless darkness of Communist tyranny."

BY imposing economic policies that had already failed in every country on earth where they had been tried, the Sandinistas wreaked enormous damage on Nicaragua. They might well have driven the country to bankruptcy even if there had been no contra war. But the United States pushed them beyond mere bankruptcy to the point of complete economic collapse.

The trade embargo which President Reagan imposed in May 1985 was his most publicized act of economic war against Nicaragua. The embargo banned all commercial contact between the United States and Nicaragua, and although the Sandinistas were able to circumvent it by buying many American-made goods through Panama or other friendly countries, it contributed to Nicaragua's economic decline. But the embargo was hardly the only form of economic pressure applied from Washington.

In capitals throughout Europe and Latin America, United States diplomats encouraged friendly governments not to send aid to Nicaragua. Banking officials in the United States advised private lenders that while Guatemala, El Salvador, and Honduras were good credit risks, Nicaragua was not. And at multilateral lending agencies, the Reagan administration succeeded in killing several loan packages for Nicaragua, ignoring long-established rules designed to insulate loan decisions from political pressure.

Largely as a result of American pressure, the World Bank ceased granting credits to Nicaragua in November 1982, despite an internal report concluding that World Bank programs there had been "extraordinarily successful." At the Inter-American Development Bank, the United States vetoed a proposed $500,000 loan to buy tractors and livestock for farm cooperatives, and another one for $2.2 million to build a road between the remote villages of Abisinia and El Cuá. Secretary of State Shultz personally intervened in January 1985 to prevent approval of a $59.8 million loan which was to support a large-scale agricultural project. Economists for the bank had judged the project "viable technically, institutionally, financially, economically, and legally." In order to block it, Shultz had to write an unusually frank letter to bank president Antonio Ortiz Mena.

"We are all too well aware of the increasing difficulties involved in gaining congressional appropriations for the international financial institutions, such as the Inter-American Development Bank," Shultz wrote. "[O]ur joint long-term goal of strengthening the Inter-American Development Bank and expanding its resource base would be undercut by Board approval of this proposed loan."

The threat was clear enough. Final consideration of the proposed loan was indefinitely postponed. Several member nations complained, but to no avail.

WHILE Secretary Shultz worked to isolate the Sandinistas politically and economically, the Pentagon sought to intimidate them by launching a series of large-scale military maneuvers in Honduras. The maneuvers, many of them staged near the Nicaraguan border, were intended as warnings to the Sandinistas, and the warnings were clearly received. But like the contra war itself, they had no real strategic point. They were not part of a grand strategy designed to achieve a particular result in Nicaragua, for the White House had no such strategy. War games in Honduras were simply another way for the Reagan administration to threaten Managua.

The maneuvers began soon after President Reagan's inauguration, and steadily escalated in scale through the mid-1980s. Tens of thousands of American troops rotated through Honduras, learning the terrain and practicing bomber raids, sea landings, infantry tactics, and commando operations. After each maneuver, they left airstrips, warehouses, and other facilities that were useful not just to the Honduran army, but also to the contras.

Within Nicaragua, the CIA and other intelligence agencies were busily going about their clandestine work. No one could know precisely what they were doing, but we never doubted their presence. When two important Sandinista installations in Managua were destroyed in conflagrations, reporters immediately wondered whether an unseen hand was at work.

Before dawn on October 12, 1985, a spectacular fire swept through a warehouse where the agrarian reform ministry stored vital supplies of seeds, fertilizers, and insecticides. Six hundred firefighters battled the blaze for twelve hours, and thick, putrid smoke covered nearby neighborhoods. Several senior Sandinistas appeared at the scene. One of them, Minister of Agrarian Reform Jaime Wheelock, struggled to hold back tears. Losses totaled seven million dollars. Investigators said an electrical malfunction was to blame, and no evidence to the contrary ever emerged.

Five months later, on March 6, 1986, a tremendous explosion destroyed an arms depot adjacent to the military hospital and El Chipote prison. Debris was blown onto surrounding streets. Windows were blown out of many homes, including mine, which was a block and a half away. There was a great commotion inside, but reporters were kept away. The government announced the next day that the explosion had been set off by a short circuit. Years later it was revealed in Washington that a CIA-hired commando team had actually been responsible.

The CIA station in Managua was active, but from what outsiders could glean, it was never very successful. Several times the government charged American diplomats with espionage and expelled them. In at least some cases, the charges were undoubtedly accurate.

Nicaraguan citizens found guilty of spying, of course, faced punishments far harsher than expulsion. In what may have been the only successful operation of its kind, the CIA once managed to recruit two interior ministry officers as spies. Agents provided them with a set of code books, a tiny camera concealed in a cigarette lighter, and dissolving pills that made invisible messages appear on specially treated paper. Both were arrested in March 1986. One of them, Reynaldo Aguado, was brought before news correspondents to confess his crimes, and was later tried and sentenced to thirty years in jail. The other, José Eduardo Trejos, who apparently refused to confess, died soon afterward in his jail cell at El Chipote, a reported suicide.

In 1986 the CIA began equipping contra units with land mines, and soon the mines began exploding under trucks and buses in northern Nicaragua. Sandinista patrols equipped with metal detectors were sent out early each morning to sweep the roads, and they disarmed many mines. Every few weeks, though, there was another explosion. Some were highly publicized, like one on May 24 in which a Spanish medical worker and seven Nicaraguans were killed near San José de Bocay, and one on July 2 that killed thirty-four people outside El Cuá. Others, particularly those in which Sandinista soldiers died, were kept quiet. The dirt roads of the north became highly dangerous, and the only people who traveled them were those whose business required it.

One of the many victims of mine explosions I met in northern Nicaragua was a sixty-year-old grandmother named Francisca Sobalbarro. I found her sitting in a wheelchair outside her home near the village of Pantasma, both her legs amputated at the thigh. Neighbors still called her "the seamstress" because she was renowned for her ability at the sewing machine. But her machine was powered by pedals, and because there was no electric power in Pantasma for sewing machines or anything else, she could no longer work. She was composed and highly dignified as we spoke and sat tall in her wheelchair.

"Planting that mine was a crime against people who were innocent and not involved in anything," Mrs. Sobalbarro told me. "If this war continues, we are all going to die."

Meeting and talking with disfigured war victims like Mrs. Sobalbarro was the most wrenching aspect of my job. In Managua, I lived near a rehabilitation center for crippled veterans, and my conversations with them always filled me with sadness. The carnage was even more pathetic in war zones, because so many of the victims were civilians whose only crime was to have boarded the wrong bus.

Soon after the contras began receiving land mines, the CIA started sending them Stinger anti-aircraft missiles. The Stingers were portable, weighed less than thirty-five pounds when loaded, and could be fired from the shoulder. They proved extremely effective against Sandinista helicopters. The number of copters reported to have crashed due to "bad weather" or "mechanical imperfections" increased dramatically, and we knew that at least some of them had actually been hit by Stinger missiles.

News of these crashes was especially disturbing to journalists, because we ourselves often flew aboard Sandinista helicopters. After the Stingers appeared in Nicaragua, those flights became very scary. Every time I looked down, I wondered if someone below was preparing to fire a missile at me.

My moments of greatest tension in Nicaragua were during those helicopter flights, and during jeep rides over mined roads. These were moments even more terrifying than being under fire. Noncombatants can survive firefights by running, hiding, or lying close to the ground. But when a Stinger missile hit a helicopter, or when a mine exploded beneath a jeep, there was no escape.

When Guillermo and I traveled on mined roads we accepted no passengers. Once, however, we were persuaded to make an exception to our rule. The woman who traveled with us that week was an American human rights worker based in El Cuá, in the heart of a war zone. She fully understood the perils of the trip.

As we drove, her forehead probably began to throb as mine did, and perhaps she was shivering despite the heat, like me, but she never said a word. When finally the village of Abisinia appeared below us, meaning that we were emerging from the mined zone, her emotions broke loose.

"Oh, Guillermo, you got us through!" she shouted suddenly, flinging her arms around him from the back seat. "Oh, that's so great! We made it! Wow! Guillermo, you're so great! We got through!"

At Abisinia, we paused to catch our breath and wipe the sweat from our bodies. We found a small stream, knelt to splash water on our faces, and then sat silently for a few minutes. I thought of how horrific it was to be surrounded by such random violence, and how fortunate I was to be able to escape it simply by driving away. Many poor peasants had no such escape, and lived each day knowing that it might be their last. It was with their blood that Nicaragua was paying the price of war.

18

PLANE CRASH

USUALLY THE skies over Nicaragua's vast jungles and forests are heavy with clouds, but once I flew home from Puerto Cabezas on a completely clear day. Only one other passenger was aboard the cramped four-seat Cessna. Our route took us over regions where contras were fighting, and as I gazed down I imagined them trudging through the mud and plotting their next attacks. It was August 1985, Congress had not sent the contras any military aid for nearly two years and President Reagan's request for $100 million in new aid was still pending. Yet strangely, their war was as intense as ever.

The pilot interrupted my musing with a nudge. "Look down there," he pointed.

I looked, but could see only treetops. After a few moments my fellow passenger, a Nicaraguan schoolteacher, let out a gasp. I could still see nothing.

"Look right where I'm pointing," the pilot urged. "Just above the trees." Finally I was able to make out the silhouettes of two small airplanes flying zigzag patterns several thousand feet below us.

"Who are they?" I asked.

"Contra supply planes looking for their drop zone," the pilot replied with the aplomb of a jaded tour guide. "We see them all the time."

Cut off from United States military aid and facing an increasingly powerful

Sandinista army, the contras might logically have been expected to collapse during 1985. But they did not. They made no measurable progress in the field, but still managed to remain quite active and destructive. Not only did they wage steady campaigns along both borders, but in the Chontales area deep inside the country, the Jorge Salazar Task Force rampaged relentlessly, hitting government cooperatives, supply depots, and other lightly guarded targets. Obviously the contras were receiving fresh supplies from somewhere.

During 1985 and 1986, common sense led journalists and diplomats in Central America to certain logical conclusions about how the contras were managing to survive. What we could see around us suggested that something large and probably illegal was underway. At military bases in countries near Nicaragua, the United States was making improvements that were clearly intended to transform the bases into part of a contra supply network. The two bases most clearly involved were Aguacate, a once-sleepy Honduran airstrip that the Americans had turned into a modern facility beyond any conceivable use to Honduras, and Ilopango, formerly El Salvador's international airport, now under military control. So many sightings of unidentified aircraft over Nicaragua, so much unexplained night traffic out of Aguacate and Ilopango, and such resilience on the part of the contras, we reasoned, could not be unrelated.

Some American officials seemed at times to tease news correspondents for our inability to prove that a clandestine supply operation was underway. They revelled in their open secret. Clues were all around us, as I recognized one day in 1986 when I stepped off a Taca Airlines flight in El Salvador. Just ahead of me, dressed in a dark business suit, I noticed the contra commander, Colonel Enrique Bermúdez. Out of curiosity I followed him. Before reaching passport control, he was met by a man in civilian clothes who escorted him through without any of the normal formalities. As they waited for Bermúdez's luggage downstairs, I edged over to see who the man was, and was not surprised to recognize a senior United States military advisor. His official job was to help Salvadoran officers suppress a domestic insurgency, but evidently he had business with Bermúdez.

Shortly after noon on October 5, 1986, in the jungle of southern Nicaragua, a fantastic train of events began unfolding. At that hour, a ragged nineteen-year-old draftee, José Fernando Canales, raised a Soviet anti-aircraft weapon to his shoulder and fired it at an unmarked plane that was descending out of the clouds. Until he squeezed the trigger, most of what was known about the contra supply operation was in the realm of supposition, perhaps solidly based but not quite fit to print. All of that changed in the wake of Canales's shot.

Testifying in court later, Canales said that on the fateful day, he and the other members of his anti-aircraft patrol "were resting as usual, some guys cooking bananas and animals from the forest," when their squad leaders heard something and jumped.

"They heard a noise, the noise of an airplane," he testified. "They immediately pulled out binoculars to find the plane and see what kind it was. When they saw it wasn't one of ours, they ordered me to fire . . . After I shot, we saw the rocket hit the plane's right wing. The plane started to maneuver . . . We saw it explode in the air, and we saw it go down covered with flames."

Pictures of Canales and the other members of his squad were splashed on the front pages of Sandinista newspapers for days. All received medals from President Ortega, and Canales was invited to throw out the first ball for the 1986–87 baseball season. Reporters at the game asked him how he felt as he watched the plane explode.

"I couldn't believe it," he told us. "The plane just kept falling. I thought I was dreaming."

Canales's sure shot was no dream. It set off a chain of events that not only confirmed much of what had been suspected about the contra supply operation, but also revealed the existence of secrets no one could have imagined.

Two Americans and a Nicaraguan died as the lumbering C-123 cargo plane crashed near the village of El Tule, twenty miles from the border town of San Carlos. The fourth crew member, Eugene Hasenfus, managed to parachute to safety. Disoriented and alone, he made no effort to flee toward Costa Rica, nor did he make his way back to the wreckage to destroy compromising documents. Instead he waited to be found, and when soldiers captured him the day after the crash, he was lying in a hammock peeling a tropical fruit. His captor was Raúl Acevedo, the fifth of eight children from a poor family in the coastal province of Carazo, a draftee nearing the end of his two-year service. Acevedo was of dark complexion and unmistakable Indian features, his hair uncut and a large wooden cross hanging from his neck. A photo of him leading Hasenfus through the jungle to captivity was published around the world.

Until Hasenfus was shot down, the contra supply operation had gone remarkably smoothly, and had in fact been one of the few success stories of the war. As many as five hundred shipments of supplies had been secretly dropped into Nicaragua, and nearly all reached their intended recipients. The ill-fated Hasenfus flight was to have been one of the last. Only weeks before, Congress had voted to send the contras $100 million of new aid. The aid bill included language allowing the CIA to supervise supply flights, taking the operation out of the hands of amateurs like Hasenfus.

Perhaps knowing that their operation was coming to an end, planners of the clandestine flights became careless. They sent the Hasenfus plane to fly in broad daylight over territory that was constantly patrolled by anti-aircraft squads. Sandinista anti-aircraft missiles were heat-seeking, and C-123s like the one Hasenfus was flying were known for emitting unusually hot exhaust, making them magnets for such missiles. Navigation was by landmarks like trees and wrecked boats rather than by maps and radio coordination, so the plane was flying much lower than it should have. It was an embarrassingly unprofessional operation.

The capture and trial of Eugene Hasenfus marked a turning point in Sandinista history. To the great discomfort of many in Washington, Hasenfus spoke freely to his captors and to the press, and much of what he said was reinforced by the trove of revealing documents found in the wreckage of his plane. In the weeks following his capture, he provided a vivid picture of a secret supply operation that had kept the contra army alive when it might otherwise have expired. His trial, besides laying the groundwork for what were to be even more spectacular revelations in Washington, was an entirely original piece of political theater.

Four days after Hasenfus's cargo plane was shot out of the sky, correspondents were summoned to the government press center in Managua to hear his story. In appearance, the prisoner lived up to his gleeful billing on Radio Sandino: "tall, blond, and strong, just as we always imagined a pure gringo would be." He took a seat and spoke in a flat monotone, a translator at his side for the benefit of local reporters.

"My name is Eugene Hasenfus," he began. "I am a native of Marinette, Wisconsin. I have a wife named Sally, and three children, Sarah, Eugene and Adam. After I graduated from high school, I immediately enlisted in the United States Marine Corps. I was in for five years. I was Airborne, the air delivery section. This was from 1960 to '65. After my discharge from the Marine Corps, I took employment with a company called Air America. This company worked in Southeast Asia, where I was working as an air freight specialist."

Air America was owned by the CIA, so already the plot was thickening. Hasenfus said he had left Asia in 1973, returned to the United States, and married. He worked as a construction laborer and metal finisher, but by the mid-1980s found himself only intermittently employed. In June 1986 one of his buddies from Air America, a pilot named Bill Cooper, telephoned him "and asked if I would be interested in flying in Central America."

Hasenfus, then forty-five years old, jumped at the chance. On Cooper's instructions, he flew to Miami, telling his wife he had found temporary work with a furniture company there. From Miami he traveled on to El Salvador, where he learned details of his mission.

"I was told we were working out of the Salvadoran air force base at Ilopango," he said. "We would be flying into Honduras to an air base named Aguacate, and there we would load up small arms and ammunition, and fly into Nicaragua. There it would be dropped to the contra."

The supply operation, Hasenfus continued, was run under arrangement with two CIA-connected companies, Southern Air Transport and Corporate Air Service, which led him to assume that it had official sanction. His pay was not great, but attractive enough for an unemployed and perhaps restless middle-aged veteran: three thousand dollars per month, plus a $750 bonus for every mission into Nicaragua.

During his days in jail, Hasenfus had been interrogated by a team of Nicaraguan and Cuban intelligence agents. The Cubans, who had apparently penetrated the supply operation at Ilopango, showed him a series of surveillance photos, and from the photos he identified two Cuban exiles who were directing the operation. One of the exiles, who called himself Max Gomez but was christened Felix Rodriguez, was a lifelong anti-Communist fighter who had been part of the ill-fated Bay of Pigs invasion force in 1961. He was one of about two hundred Bay of Pigs officers given commissions in the United States Army, and in the late 1960s he turned up as a counter-insurgency advisor in Bolivia, apparently working for the CIA. There he helped capture and interrogate the legendary guerrilla Che Guevara, whose wristwatch he wore as a souvenir.

In El Salvador, Felix Rodriguez had helped the air force commander, General Juan Rafael Bustillo, design helicopter tactics for use against Marxist insurgents. Later he joined the contra supply effort, in which General Bustillo played a discreet but vital role. His partner, also a Cuban exile, was known to Hasenfus as Ramon Medina.

From photographs supplied by the Cuban intelligence service, Hasenfus had been able to identify "Medina" as the fugitive terrorist Luis Posada Carriles. A chill ran down my spine when I heard that name. Luis Posada Carriles had once almost succeeded in killing me.

Ten years had passed since my near-fatal brush with Posada in October 1976, hardly enough time for me to have forgotten it. I was on a free-lance reporting trip through the Caribbean and had bought a ticket for a Cubana Airlines flight to Havana, which was to be my final stop. My trip had gone well and I was running ahead of schedule, so I decided to exchange my ticket and fly to Cuba on an earlier flight. Two days after arriving there, I was chatting with the poolside bartender at the Havana Riviera hotel when another reporter arrived with stunning news. The Cubana flight on which I was originally booked had exploded in midair and crashed into the sea off Barbados, killing all seventy-three people aboard.

This savage crime was the work of anti-Castro terrorists who believed that it would somehow hasten the end of Communist rule in Cuba. Four were arrested in Venezuela, where the bomb had been placed in the airliner's rest room. Among them was Luis Posada Carriles.

Posada had participated in the Bay of Pigs invasion, and was among those captured and jailed when the invasion failed. After his release from Cuban custody, he enlisted in the CIA's secret anti-Castro army, then based in the Florida Keys. Later he moved to Venezuela, where, without cutting his ties to the CIA, he became a senior officer in the security police. After the Cubana bombing he was tried, found guilty, sentenced, and imprisoned in Venezuela.

He spent several years in a comfortable jail cell, and then one day in August 1985 he disappeared.

After his mysterious escape, it was later determined, Posada left Venezuela on a false Salvadoran passport, changed his name and reportedly altered his appearance through plastic surgery. He told a journalist who found him in El Salvador that he was engaged in "a fight against international Communism, against Castro in all parts of the world." Apparently the CIA had welcomed him back to the ranks. Some of his old comrades may even have considered him something of a hero. He was an apt symbol of the moral level on which the contra war was being waged.

Eugene Hasenfus, it turned out, knew little of how the supply operation was run at the top. But after he finished his first statement to the press, reporters were shown the remarkable collection of documents found in the wreckage of his C-123. Most were dog-eared cards found stuffed in wallets, many bearing scrawled telephone numbers and cryptic notes. Some, like Hasenfus's Wisconsin fishing license and his Sears credit card, were innocent enough. But others were more tantalizing, such as business cards bearing the name of Robert W. Owen, an associate of Lieutenant Colonel Oliver North of the National Security Council staff, and P. J. Buechler, an employee of the State Department's Nicaragua Humanitarian Affairs Office. There were also logbooks carrying detailed descriptions of previous supply flights from airports in El Salvador and Honduras, naming more than thirty crew members and listing the type and quantity of weapons dropped during each flight.

As reporters pressed close to examine the evidence, Major Ricardo Wheelock, chief of Sandinista military intelligence, read out a telephone number. He said it was a number in El Salvador that Hasenfus had been told to call in case of trouble. Reporters who called that day found no one home.

Sandinista leaders recognized that Hasenfus's revelations were of enormous propaganda value, and wanted the whole world to hear what he had to say. In the days following his capture, they made him available for private interviews with selected news correspondents. Public relations consultants based in New York advised the Sandinistas to give Mike Wallace of CBS television the first crack, and they did. Wallace flew to Managua for the occasion.

As uniformed Sandinista guards stood by, the insistent Wallace prodded Hasenfus to confess that he was a CIA agent. He was triumphant when Hasenfus admitted he had worked for Air America in Southeast Asia with Bill Cooper, who had died in the C-123 crash.

"He was CIA, you were CIA!" Wallace cried.

The soft-spoken prisoner demurred. All he would admit was that he suspected the supply operation was "tied in with the Company." He said he felt guilty about making a "selfish mistake" that would hurt his family.

"I am down here as a job," Hasenfus said. "I am not down here as a soldier, so this is not my war. I don't believe it's an American war."

The few American officials who knew that Hasenfus had been working for a government-backed operation were angry at him for cooperating so fully with his captors. Secretary of State George Shultz, one of those who did not know, at first swore that Hasenfus had been "hired by private people" and had "no connection with the U.S. government at all." Hasenfus was quite right when he told one interviewer that some people in Washington probably wished he had been killed in the crash. As he put it, "Dead men don't tell tales."

Soon after Hasenfus was captured, Sandinista authorities announced that he would not be tried in a civilian court, but before the People's Anti-Somozist Tribunal, which had been established in 1983 to judge those suspected of aiding the contras. The People's Tribunal was just the kind of court one would expect to find in a besieged third world country. Some defendants were captured contra footsoldiers, but most were impoverished peasants from remote areas. They were charged with giving information about Sandinista troop movements to passing contras, or supplying contras with food, or hiding their weapons, or carrying their messages.

Many of those brought before the People's Tribunal had been arrested on the basis of secret accusations, and were never given the chance to confront their accusers. It was a system made for abuse. Security agents did not hesitate to use it to punish political activists and others who, in their judgment, were transgressing the acceptable limits of dissent. Informants used it as a form of revenge against people they disliked. Defendants had few rights, and conviction was virtually guaranteed.

The People's Tribunal, of course, did not punish only innocent peasants and honest dissidents. In all the years of contra war, no urban sabotage campaign was ever successful, no important Sandinista events were ever disrupted, and there were no attempts against the lives of government leaders. That remarkable record was largely a result of Sandinista vigilance. Police and security forces, using the People's Tribunal to legalize their actions, arrested and imprisoned everyone they suspected of ties to the contras. By doing so, they disrupted every contra effort to bring the war into Managua and other cities. Human rights advocates were entirely justified in complaining that the People's Tribunal routinely sent defendants to jail on the basis of flimsy evidence or hearsay. At least some of those convicted, however, really were contra collaborators, and the Sandinistas were quite prepared to imprison innocent Nicaraguans if that was the price of apprehending the guilty.

For the Hasenfus trial, the People's Tribunal dusted off its rule book and abided by regulations which it normally honored only in the breach. Most startling was its announcement that this trial would be conducted within strict time limits. Under official rules, prosecutors were required to present charges within eight days of an arrest, and defendants then had two days to answer. After that, a judge could take no more than eleven days to reach a verdict. Lawyers had never known these regulations to be observed before. Detainees were normally held for weeks or months before being brought before a magistrate, and sentencing sometimes took a year or longer. The decision to treat the Hasenfus case so differently underscored its extraordinary importance to the Sandinistas.

In theory, proceedings of the People's Tribunal were open to the public, but because no docket was ever published it was practically impossible to find out what cases were pending, or when they would be heard. For that reason, and because most of the defendants were poor unknowns, few journalists ever followed cases there. But suddenly, with the appearance of an American defendant apprehended under such spectacular circumstances, the People's Tribunal became a focus of world attention. Journalists were not only invited to cover the trial, but permitted to use cameras and tape recorders, normally forbidden in Sandinista courts.

Each morning while the trial was underway, I was one of scores of reporters who assembled in the dusty, unadorned courtroom. Windows were left open in a vain effort to ease the oppressive heat, and testimony was often drowned out by the roar of passing trucks and other street noises. Hasenfus arrived at every session in an armored wagon. As he emerged, he would instantly be surrounded by news photographers and correspondents yelling silly questions like, "Think you can beat the rap, Gene?"

Hasenfus's wife and brother flew to Managua for the trial. They appeared in court every day, looking increasingly haggard as time passed. The defendant himself was soft-spoken and compliant. He never became angry, never complained about the unfairness of the proceedings, never lamented the injustice of his fate. At one point, in fact, one of his lawyers suggested that a bit of emotion might make him seem more human.

Choosing lawyers to defend Hasenfus was a tricky business. His relatives, acting on suggestions from Washington, decided to seek out a prominent American political figure, preferably one with liberal credentials. They first approached former Senator Walter Mondale, but he declined, correctly surmising that what he had learned in law school would be of little use before the People's Tribunal. Finally they settled on Griffin Bell, a former federal judge from Atlanta who had been attorney general in the Carter administration.

Bell arrived to head a defense team whose most prominent local member was Enrique Sotelo Borgen, a volatile anti-Sandinista politician. The two made an odd pair. Neither spoke the other's language. Bell, courtly and correct, drew on a lifetime of experience in the law, but seemed uncomfortable in Managua. He dressed always in a suit and tie even though no one in Nicaragua ever dressed that way. Sotelo, in contrast, was prickly, argumentative, and excitable. As a member of the National Assembly from the Conservative party, he was one of the small band of legislators who rose predictably to oppose every Sandinista initiative.

Several times Sotelo's dissidence had provoked the ire of Interior Minister Tomás Borge, and once Borge had ordered him arrested and brought to El Chipote prison. After some hours in a cell, he was brought to an office where Borge himself was waiting. Borge always had a deal to offer, and he had one for Sotelo. If Sotelo would become a Sandinista agent inside the Conservative party, fomenting division and keeping police informed of internal party developments, Borge said, he would be rewarded with a new car and a regular cash retainer. He refused. Borge then warned him that his name was on a secret list of enemies of the regime, all of whom would be sought out and executed in the event of an American invasion. Sotelo was not intimidated, however, and in fact became more outrageous than ever. To him, the Hasenfus trial was an opportunity to ridicule and condemn the Sandinista judicial system and, by extension, Sandinista rule itself.

Sotelo's first step in the Hasenfus defense was to challenge the legality of the People's Tribunal. The trial had been underway for only a few minutes when he stood to face the three magistrates and boomed, "Your appointments are illegal and absolutely null!" He was quickly ruled out of order.

Given the political climate in Nicaragua, not to mention the weight of evidence, it was perfectly obvious from the beginning that Hasenfus was going to be declared guilty and sentenced to the maximum prison term of thirty years. The main charge against him, the one that carried the thirty-year jail term, was that he had violated the same "public security" law used to convict most defendants before the People's Tribunal. This peculiar statute did not ban any specific act; instead it outlawed "actions aimed at subjecting the nation totally or partially to foreign domination, or infringing on its independence or integrity." The prosecutor, Rodrigo Reyes, who was also Minister of Justice, asserted in his opening statement that Hasenfus was foreign intervention incarnate.

After opening statements were completed, Sotelo leaned over to whisper something to Hasenfus. The magistrate immediately banged his gavel, and sternly warned Sotelo that he was forbidden to speak to his client in court. Furthermore, he ruled, no lawyers would be allowed to question witnesses directly. All questions would instead be directed to the magistrate himself, and if the magistrate considered them appropriate, he would repeat them to the witness.

On the witness stand, Hasenfus played his role well, confessing and apologizing for his acts. He repeated his earlier explanations of how the cache of automatic rifles, bullets, boots, and other military supplies came to be found in the wreckage of his plane, and admitted to having made four successful supply runs before being shot down. But although he talked freely, he insisted that he was only a low-ranking employee of the supply operation. He admitted knowing full well that his plane was carrying lethal cargo for the contras, but insisted that his work was "only that of a loadmaster."

The defense lawyer, Sotelo, had to address his client through the magistrate. His first questions were designed to show how insignificant a role Hasenfus had played in the supply operation.

"Did you plan the route of flight?" he asked Hasenfus.

"The prisoner will say whether he planned the route of flight," the magistrate repeated.

"No, I did not," Hasenfus replied.

"Did you choose the cargo?" Sotelo continued.

"The prisoner will say whether he chose the cargo."

"No, I did not."

So it went, with Sotelo establishing that his client had been hired only to load planes and then to work as a "kicker," the person who pushes supplies out the cargo hatch. Sotelo also noted that Hasenfus had been unarmed, did not resist arrest, and had cooperated fully with interrogators. He drew from Hasenfus a flat denial that he was a CIA agent, and the prosecutor, Rodrigo Reyes, accepted the denial.

"Whether he has or does not have anything to do with the CIA is irrelevant to my case," Reyes told reporters during a break.

The Hasenfus testimony, which took only half a day, was the high point of the trial. During one of the other sessions, José Fernando Canales and other members of the crew that had shot down the C-123 gave their accounts. On another day, crates full of arms and other supplies taken from the wreckage were brought to court for the benefit of photographers.

Although the shooting down of Hasenfus's cargo plane had been big news around the world, the trial turned out to be quite dull, which made the stifling heat in the courtroom even more oppressive. Since a guilty verdict was certain, the proceedings took on a stylized, unreal quality. Even Griffin Bell sometimes seemed distracted, his attention wandering around the room.

Bell came up with several unorthodox plans that he hoped would speed Hasenfus's release after the expected conviction. One of his oddest ideas was to inquire if Nicaraguan officials would be interested in a prisoner exchange involving some of the fifteen or twenty Nicaraguan citizens jailed in federal penitentiaries in the United States. When that idea failed to spark a response, Bell enlisted the help of his fellow Atlantan Joseph Lowery, a clergyman and civil rights leader who had once sponsored a reception for Daniel Ortega in Atlanta. Reverend Lowery met with all parties in the case, and while he did not explicitly urge a pardon, he suggested that justice be tempered with mercy.

"I want to use this tragedy to say to the American people that our policy toward Central America is disastrous," he told me over breakfast at the Intercontinental one morning.

Outside the courtroom, Griffin Bell was free with his opinions. He held periodic news conferences, during which he perspired heavily and paused every minute or two to wipe his brow. Not surprisingly, he was especially piqued at CBS interviewer Mike Wallace, who, he said, had asked "leading questions trying to connect the defendant to the CIA," thereby aiding the prosecution.

"It's a disgrace for American journalists to be in with the police," Bell fumed at one point.

Bell was serious and intelligent, albeit somewhat out of his element. Yet like many Americans without first-hand experience in Nicaragua, he had never been forced to come to grips with the realities of the contra war. At his news conferences, he faced journalists who were witnessing the brutality of the war every day, and some lost patience with his lawyerly manner. Once someone asked him how he could insist that Hasenfus was not a terrorist, since the weapons he had helped transport were so often used in attacks on civilian targets.

"I thought the contras were a revolutionary movement trying to overthrow the government here in Nicaragua," he replied with a touch of irritation. "I did not know they were terrorists."

After testimony was completed, and after Griffin Bell, Joseph Lowery, and other American visitors had returned to their homes, the penultimate acts in the Hasenfus drama, the conviction and sentencing, were played out. It was a Saturday morning, November 15, when reporters were convened at the tribunal to record the preordained result. A throng turned out, and no seats were available for latecomers like me. The verdict took more than an hour to read in Spanish, and was then read in English for the defendant's benefit. He sat motionless, dressed in blue jeans, sneakers, and an embroidered white shirt, as he heard himself found guilty and sentenced to thirty years in jail.

After we heard the verdict in both languages, the magistrate asked Hasenfus if he wished to file an appeal to a higher People's Tribunal.

"May I consult my lawyer?" he asked.

"No, you may not," the magistrate replied.

Sotelo jumped from his seat indignantly. "I want to speak to the prisoner!" he called out, as the magistrate banged his gavel. "I want to speak to my client!"

Sotelo was ordered silent, and finally took his seat. Hasenfus, after a moment's thought, decided he wanted to appeal. The magistrate took due note, and then declared the proceedings closed. The prisoner was led through a crowd of unruly journalists, locked into a paddy wagon, and driven away.

"Verdict Is Condemnation of United States" was the banner headline in the Sunday edition of *Barricada*. Minister of Defense Humberto Ortega lauded the People's Tribunal for condemning "the unjust and irrational policy of the

Reagan administration." And the victorious prosecutor, Rodrigo Reyes, urged that the verdict be read as a warning to those who might be tempted to join the contras.

"We are not fooling around here," Reyes said sternly. "This is not a game."

Despite the heavy coverage the case received in the official press, however, few ordinary Nicaraguans considered Hasenfus himself a bad fellow. Even the top Sandinista leader, President Daniel Ortega, had good words for him.

"Hasenfus is a victim of American policy, just as those who were sent to Vietnam were victims," Ortega told an assembly of workers one evening at the Coca-Cola bottling plant formerly managed by Adolfo Calero. "If the government of the United States had been able to guarantee a job and a salary to a man who has three children and a wife, then this man would not be engaged in mercenary activity."

Not every Nicaraguan was so understanding. A vocal group of militant Sandinistas, including combat veterans and relatives of war victims, began insisting that Hasenfus be forced to serve his full jail term. Many were appalled at Daniel Ortega's comments, which they took as a hint that a pardon was in the works.

An inquiring reporter from *Nuevo Diario* found several Nicaraguans with ideas for Hasenfus. "I would torture him," one young woman told the reporter. "I wouldn't give him any food so he would die of hunger, and feel in his own body what thousands of Nicaraguans felt as they were killed by his people."

The prosecutor, Rodrigo Reyes, never advocated such extreme measures, but he too wanted to see Hasenfus punished. "I don't see any possibility of a pardon," Reyes told *Nuevo Diario*. "If there was a pardon, the people would reject it, and the political authorities would have to explain themselves very well."

A few days after the trial, I attended an outdoor meeting at which Daniel Ortega and other senior Sandinistas fielded questions from a public audience. One of the first to rise was a woman who said she was the mother of a soldier on active duty, and was speaking on behalf of local Sandinista Defense Committees.

"We have felt the pain of losing our children," she said in a strong voice. "They shed their blood to defend this little piece of land that is Nicaragua. In no way should Hasenfus be pardoned. He brought weapons here to kill our people."

There was loud applause, during which Ortega remained impassive. When it subsided, he said he understood the woman's point of view, but expected that loyal Sandinistas would accept "with great maturity" whatever decision the National Directorate made regarding a pardon. We understood then that Hasenfus would soon be freed.

As the Hasenfus trial was ending, another even more bizarre political scandal began to capture the world's attention. At the beginning of November, the Lebanese magazine *Al-Shiraa* published an outlandish story asserting that the Reagan administration had been secretly selling sophisticated weapons to Ayatollah Khomeini's radical Islamic regime in Iran. Furthermore, the magazine reported, President Reagan's national security advisor, Robert MacFarlane, had travelled to Teheran bearing gifts for Iranian leaders, including a Bible inscribed by President Reagan.

The story was incredible but true. In the hope of winning freedom for American hostages held by pro-Iranian terrorists in Lebanon, the Reagan administration was selling modern missile systems to the relentlessly anti-Western Ayatollah. President Reagan had allowed the scheme to go forward over the objections of Secretary of State Shultz and Secretary of Defense Caspar Weinberger. On his copy of the memo proposing the idea, Weinberger had written, "This is almost too absurd to comment on."

The Iran scandal was of only passing interest to people in Central America until November 25, 1986. On that date, about fifty mid-ranking contras were meeting at the Cariari Hotel in San José, Costa Rica. I happened to be in San José, and dropped by to see what was happening.

When I arrived at mid-morning, about half the group was inside, listening to meaningless proposals for yet another reorganization of the contra leadership. Others were chatting in small groups beside the pool, or sipping drinks at the bar. A television was on, and when normal programming was interrupted for a news bulletin, conversation stopped. The news was amazing. Attorney General Edwin Meese had just announced in Washington that a portion of profits from the sale of arms to Iran had been used to finance the contras.

The assembly in Costa Rica was stunned by the news. People gaped at each other in disbelief. No one knew what to make of what they had heard. Most raced toward their offices, or toward hotel telephones. Their meeting dissolved in pandemonium without anyone bothering to adjourn it.

Revelations that followed taxed the credulity of even many Reagan supporters. A congressional investigating committee found that senior American officials had secretly solicited private funds to carry on the contra war during 1985 and 1986. The funds came from wealthy American citizens; from foreign nations, principally Saudi Arabia and Taiwan; and from money the Ayatollah Khomeni paid for the American missiles he was secretly buying. That was the money that paid Eugene Hasenfus and the men with whom he worked, and bought the weapons they dropped to contra task forces.

Robert MacFarlane, who left his post as national security advisor in December 1985, confessed to the investigating committee that President Reagan's decision to launch the contra war had been made "in a policy vacuum."

"There is something wrong about the way this country makes foreign policy," MacFarlane told the committee. "Policymakers who create conditions like this must bear some of the moral responsibilities for the failures that follow."

The capture of Eugene Hasenfus and subsequent revelations about arms sales to Iran were not the only blows to President Reagan's Nicaragua policy during the final months of 1986. In mid-term elections on November 4, the Democratic party scored major victories, taking control of the Senate and strengthening its majority in the House of Representatives. Then on December 15, the man who had done more for the contra cause than any other American, CIA Director William Casey, was hospitalized with what turned out to be a fatal brain tumor.

This turn of events devastated the contras. Like so many Nicaraguan crusades, theirs had been fueled from Washington. Now that their American friends were crippled, their own future suddenly looked quite bleak.

In Managua, President Ortega was anxious to take advantage of the new political climate. Releasing Hasenfus, he concluded, would be an appropriately conciliatory sign. It would win him not only political points, but a certain amount of emotional capital as well, represented most vividly by Sally Hasenfus. After her husband's conviction, Mrs. Hasenfus had tearfully announced that she had "only love and gratitude for the people of Nicaragua."

"Gene realizes that in accepting this job, he has made a terrible mistake, a mistake for which we have all paid dearly," she said in a public appeal. "The hearts of my children, as well as my own, are locked in your prison. I pray that your government will be compassionate."

One day in mid-December, I received a telephone call from an aide to Senator Christopher Dodd, a prominent member of the Senate Foreign Relations Committee who had strenuously opposed the contras. The aide told me Dodd was in Managua as part of a Central American tour, and wanted to meet with me. Dodd had an "important dinner" the next evening, the aide said, and would see me afterward, at 10:30 at the Mirador Tiscapa restaurant.

I agreed, and arrived at the appointed hour. I had never liked the Mirador Tiscapa. It was Tomás Borge's favorite restaurant, and I had been told that the interior ministry either owned or controlled it. The outdoor terrace was designed so that diners had a view of not only the Tiscapa lagoon, but also the foreboding hill under which Borge's political prison, El Chipote, was buried. Staring at the hill and wondering which unfortunates might be confined inside, I always found it difficult to enjoy myself there.

Dodd was nowhere to be seen. I ordered a drink, and then another, sipping them slowly. Nearly two hours had passed when I finally realized that Dodd was not going to appear. As I paid my bill, I guessed that he was at that moment discussing the Hasenfus affair with President Ortega. His failure to keep our date, I presumed, meant negotiations were going well.

The next day, in a whirlwind of announcements and proclamations, Hasenfus was pardoned. He appeared at a news conference with Ortega, and the two shook hands.

"We want to turn citizen Hasenfus over to the American people, and we are doing so through the person of Senator Dodd," Ortega announced.

Hasenfus himself, brought from jail only moments before, was beaming. Tomás Borge had sent him the key to his cell as a souvenir, and now Ortega was wishing him well.

"Today has been a great day, a day I'll remember in my heart forever," he said with a broad smile.

Police quickly whisked Hasenfus to the airport, and he was back in Wisconsin in time to take his children shopping for a Christmas tree. After his first reunion with family and friends, a reporter asked him what he was thinking.

"It's great to be standing here drinking my third beer," he replied.

Some Sandinistas were angered by the pardon. The official newspaper, *Barricada,* acknowledged that critics had a point. It quoted some people asking, "Why fight in the mountains if the prisoners are going to be freed later on?"

The Sandinistas handled Hasenfus's trial and subsequent release with considerable good sense. Although they had caught him red-handed, they saw no point in holding him after he had told his tale in court. As the Iran-contra scandal mushroomed, Hasenfus was becoming irrelevant. When he was shot down, neither he nor anyone else could have imagined that his trial would lead to such astonishing revelations. The scandal it sparked not only debilitated President Reagan for the remainder of his term, but sounded the contras' death knell.

19

AN AMERICAN MARTYR

IN THE Nicaraguan north, where some of the country's poorest people live, mist hovers over the coffee fields and mules are still the only reliable way to travel most places. Many peasants live in isolated shacks miles from any settlement, cut off from contact with the outside world, toiling like beasts as if the twentieth century had never dawned. Rates of illiteracy and disease are among the highest in the Western hemisphere, and life can be as short as it is sad. Any Nicaraguan government dedicated to the public welfare, regardless of ideology, would try to concentrate its resources in the north.

The Sandinistas had grand plans for transforming life in the northern provinces of Estelí, Madriz, Nueva Segovia, Matagalpa, and Jinotega, but war and economic crisis crippled them. In the village of El Cuá, for example, set in the hills of Jinotega far from the nearest paved road, where things had hardly changed in the lifetimes of the oldest residents, the Sandinistas in 1980 began work on a small hydroelectric project. It was scheduled to open in July 1981, but on that date it was less than half finished and all but abandoned.

With a population of about three thousand souls, half of them recent arrivals from nearby war zones, El Cuá qualified as one of northern Jinotega's principal settlements. "Going to El Cuá is a lot like going to a small town in the western United States in 1830," Benjamin Linder wrote home while he was living there

324

in 1986. "The main street is dusty, two bars, one hotel, a military command post that looks like it came right out of a western."

Ben Linder was to become the most famous person ever to pass through El Cuá. His efforts there, aimed at helping to pull the region out of poverty, cost him his life. As the only American to be killed in Nicaragua by contra gunfire, he instantly became the stuff of legend. He was an extraordinary figure whose life spoke reassuringly to Americans about the better side of their character. In death, he became a symbol of the kind of war that was being waged in Nicaragua.

Linder was born in 1959, meaning that by strict definition he was too young to have been part of the generation whose protests shook the United States during the 1960s. But he grew up in a household where liberal activism was a tradition, and participated in several demonstrations. In 1977 he was arrested at a sit-in outside the Trojan nuclear power station near his home town of Portland, Oregon. Later, while an engineering student at the University of Washington in Seattle, he helped organize a committee of activists opposed to United States policy toward El Salvador. In the classroom, he studied the theory and practice of rudimentary, small-scale development, not a field with great earnings potential. He had already decided that he was going to devote himself to working on behalf of poor people far from his home.

Ben Linder was one of more than one hundred thousand Americans who traveled to Nicaragua during the decade of Sandinista rule. The visitors fell into various categories. Many were café radicals who traipsed to Sandinista rallies, spent an hour protesting in front of the American embassy, perhaps hit a beach or two, and then returned home to preach about the glories of life in the revolutionary state. Others came as part of organized groups, sponsored by churches or relief agencies. A large portion were blindly pro-Sandinista, so outraged by what the Reagan administration was doing in Nicaragua that they came to believe the *comandantes* could do no wrong. Most were motivated by altruism and compassion, but many Nicaraguans came to resent them as ignorant meddlers.

Besides these political tourists, there was a smaller but infinitely more productive group of Americans who made tangible contributions to Nicaragua's development. I often ran into them during trips through the countryside or found evidence of their good works, like the clinic in Niquinohomo built by volunteers from Rhode Island, or the playground in Puerto Cabezas paid for by donations from Burlington, Vermont. Yet even the Americans who supported those efforts were making only a temporary commitment to Nicaragua. Ben Linder was resolved to do more. By coming to Nicaragua, he hoped not only to put his knowledge to work, but also to make a political statement against his government's foreign policy.

Linder arrived in Nicaragua soon after receiving his mechanical engineering degree in 1983. His introduction to Sandinista bureaucracy was classic; he had to wait three months for the government to process his application for residency and give him permission to donate his skills. Temporarily unable to begin his engineering work, he occupied himself by practicing his hobby, circus performing. He appeared as a juggler and clown with a local circus company, and spent some of his weekend afternoons pedaling through the Riguero section of Managua on a unicycle, dressed in his clown suit, delighting children along the way.

When Linder's papers were finally ready in November 1983, he began work at the Nicaraguan Energy Institute, the state-owned electric company. His job was helping to plan rural electrification projects, but after two years he came to recognize that in countries like Nicaragua, where both materials and expertise are scarce, planners are only effective if they are also doers. He asked the energy institute to transfer him out of the central office in Managua, and send him to northern Jinotega to design and direct what he called an "integral development program" for the region. Impressed with his seriousness and ability, his superiors agreed to send him to El Cuá to complete the stalled hydroelectric project there. I met him while passing through El Cuá once, and found him quiet, hardworking and much appreciated.

The 100-kilowatt power plant was finally completed in mid-1986, and it was inaugurated amid great celebration. Linder viewed completion of the plant as just the beginning of his work. He was bubbling over with plans. Soon, he wrote in one letter home, El Cuá might have a sawmill, a metal shop, and a factory for building bricks and roof tiles.

Before turning fully to those projects, Linder wanted to build a second small hydroelectric plant, similar to the one in El Cuá, outside the area's other important town, San José de Bocay. The plants, serving the two population centers in rugged northern Jinotega, would provide the base for what Linder conceived as a grass-roots development campaign. But while he was sitting in his tiny office in the wood shanty that served as Sandinista headquarters in El Cuá, or traveling in the countryside, other people with other interests were also casting their eyes on Jinotega. In December 1986 contra footsoldiers began moving back into Nicaragua from the Honduran bases where they had been languishing. They were well-armed thanks to new American aid, and led by field commanders fresh from training in the United States. By early 1987, several thousand contras had re-established themselves in many parts of Nicaragua, including Jinotega.

The towns of El Cuá and San José de Bocay were normally full of Sandinista soldiers, which made them unlikely targets for attack. But the contras' infiltration corridors were not far away. Peasants would often report seeing many contras, as well as Sandinista troops tracking them, moving through the hills. Often the sound of Sandinista artillery echoed nearby. Military casualties were heavy on both sides, and for civilians, danger lurked everywhere.

It was against this background that Ben Linder set out from San José de Bocay early on the morning of April 28, 1987. With him were six men detailed from a local farm cooperative. Their plan that day was to set a weir in a stream south of town, to measure the flow of water and see if the stream was strong enough to power an electric generator. Of the seven men in the group, five were carrying automatic rifles, including Linder.

The men arrived at the stream around seven o'clock, and set to work. They had been there less than an hour when contras burst from the bush, firing rifles and grenades.

"Linder died immediately when a grenade exploded near his head," one of the wounded survivors later recalled. "When the shooting and the explosions began, we all ran. We never had a chance to pick up our guns and fire back, and everyone left their weapons behind."

The ambush was like many other contra attacks, and would probably not have attracted much notice if the two Nicaraguans who died, Pablo Rosales and Sergio Hernández, had been the only casualties. But because Linder was also killed, it sparked a passionate debate.

In the hours that followed the ambush, conflicting reports flashed through Managua. Foreign Minister Miguel D'Escoto fired off a letter to Secretary of State George Shultz asserting mistakenly that "a group of counter-revolutionaries under contract to your government kidnapped and later murdered an American citizen from Washington State." The truth was sad enough. Linder lived in an area of constant fighting, and ventured regularly into areas where contras prowled. He had probably been more exposed to danger than any other American citizen in Nicaragua at that time. Ironically, the Sandinistas had recently ordered the withdrawal of foreign volunteers from such war zones, but Linder was not affected because he was working directly for the government.

On several occasions, Linder had spoken to friends about the dangers he faced, and had told them that if the worst happened, he wanted to be buried in Nicaragua. No one was surprised to learn that he had considered the prospect of sudden death.

"It's something that everyone in the area knows and accepts, and then decides whether to keep working or not," he wrote. "Many Nicaraguan engineers don't want to go out in the field."

In Honduras, the Nicaraguan Democratic Force issued a statement acknowledging responsibility for the ambush in which Linder was killed. It falsely described the ambush as "a firefight between one of our patrols and a group of militia of the Sandinista army," and charged that the Sandinistas had exposed Linder to death "by allowing him to enter an area of civil war in our country." The statement also advised all foreigners to leave Nicaragua for their own protection.

For those opposed to the contras, Linder's death crystallized the nature of the Nicaraguan war. They saw an idealistic young American, together with two Nicaraguan co-workers, cut down by bullets bought with American tax dollars. But there was more to his sacrifice than that.

Linder had made a profound ideological leap by agreeing to carry a rifle and wear olive green fatigues in a country at war. It had not been an easy decision, friends said later, because he knew it made him into a kind of soldier. He had decided that Sandinista rule was best for Nicaragua, and he must have known that not everyone accepted his right, as a foreigner, to make that decision.

The day after Linder's death, a group of Americans held an angry protest rally in front of the American embassy in Managua. Friends sobbed and embraced each other. One woman held a poster depicting a happy clown, and carrying the legend, "Ben Linder, Engineer, Juggler, Martyr."

In the crowd, I noticed Howard Hiner, a middle-aged American activist who had known Linder well.

"Last time I talked to him," Hiner said softly, "he was talking about starting a forestry project, and wanted me to come up and work with him. He was always coming up with something."

Ben Linder's parents, looking every bit as devastated as one would expect, arrived in Nicaragua soon after his death, accompanied by his brother and sister. The mother, a refugee who had fled Nazi repression in Czechoslovakia, and the father, a tall, distinguished-looking physician, did not hesitate to fix blame for their son's death. Immediately after they arrived at the Managua airport, Dr. David Linder was asked who he thought had killed his son. His voice breaking, he replied, "Someone who paid someone who paid someone who paid someone, and so on down the line to the president of the United States."

Later Linder's family appeared at a large May Day rally in Managua. Thousands of Sandinista workers warmly applauded them. "This war must end, and it must end now!" Miriam Linder told the crowd. She said her brother had lived "a full and meaningful life," and urged her listeners, "Keep your vision clear, and continue your good work."

The main speaker at the rally was *Comandante* Victor Tirado, a member of the Sandinista National Directorate. He compared Ben Linder to John Reed, another Portland native who traveled abroad to support revolutionary regimes.

"Linder represents the democratic, internationalist spirit of the American people," Tirado said. "Linder symbolizes the future of relations between Nicaragua and the United States, which will be based on friendship, cooperation, and mutual respect."

After the rally, government radio stations announced that Ben Linder had been posthumously awarded the country's highest civilian medal for heroism. Later, his brother John read a statement to reporters.

"In this case, the true criminal is the government of the United States," he asserted. "The contras who killed Ben were hired guns. The real killers are in

Washington, enjoying a pleasant lunch or perhaps a game of golf, while my brother lies dead at the age of twenty-seven . . . The Reagan administration had Oliver North sneaking around in the White House basement because it was afraid to tell the truth to the American people about their illegal and immoral war against Nicaragua. Everything they have told us about Nicaragua is a lie."

Linder was buried in Matagalpa, the principal city in the region where he died. The funeral cortege was long, and as some people wept, a couple of clowns juggled bowling pins to amuse young children. President Daniel Ortega, who was among the pallbearers, spoke over the open grave, his voice filled with emotion. He eulogized Linder as "an American citizen who, full of love and joy, gave his life for the poor people of Nicaragua."

A few days after the funeral, with Guillermo at the wheel, I set out toward El Cuá to see what mark Ben Linder had left there. It was a Sunday, and when we arrived at the Matagalpa cemetery, visitors were placing flowers and reciting prayers at the graves of loved ones. Several stopped to pay respects at Linder's fresh gravesite. As I stood there, I heard a woman ask her companion, "What reason did he have to come and live here with us, when he was so comfortable in his own country?"

As we left Matagalpa, two ferocious-looking Sandinista helicopters, their rocket pods fully loaded, appeared overhead, circled lazily for a few minutes, and then flew on. We could sense the war close at hand, and when we reached the town of Abisinia, we learned just how close it was. Abisinia had once been a fairly prosperous farm outpost, but most of its residents had fled the war, and only a few hundred unhappy peasants remained. On the morning we arrived in our bright white jeep, half a dozen battered trucks were pulled to the side of the road, waiting for permission to proceed. A young soldier told us contras had been spotted nearby, and that traffic was halted until further notice. It was time for Guillermo, who knew all the right code words, to go into his act.

"We're on an international mission," he told the soldier, gesturing plaintively. "This is a very important foreigner. He has to get through. It's for peace, compañero. For peace."

The soldier looked pained, apologized, and told us that only the lieutenant in charge could grant an exception. Guillermo glanced quickly at me, scooped two packs of American cigarettes into his pockets, and headed toward the command post. He emerged about ten minutes later, climbed back aboard, and started the ignition. At a signal from the lieutenant, the roadblock was pushed aside, and we drove through. As soon as we were out of earshot, we congratulated ourselves loudly.

"Marlboro es la clave," Guillermo confided. Marlboro is the key.

We made our way north along one of the twisting roads where dozens of Nicaraguans had been killed by land mine explosions during the past months.

There was no other traffic, but a few miles past Abisinia we encountered a patrol of Sandinista soldiers on full combat alert, crouching, listening, their fingers taut on the triggers of their rifles. All were teenagers, and all were sweating profusely. They told us contras had been spotted on the road just ahead.

None of the soldiers tried to stop us, or even expressed the slightest interest in whether we pulled over or proceeded. We drove slowly ahead, holding our breath at each bend in the road. Around one turn, we found the road littered with mimeographed leaflets. "Troops of the Dictatorship, Surrender, Your Life Will Be Respected," they said. "There Is Still Time."

Contras had obviously passed this way, but they seemed to have faded into the bush. After a few minutes, the Sandinista soldiers we had passed appeared from behind us. They seemed relieved as they collected the leaflets, but kept peering over their shoulders into the dense forest. There could be no doubt that the war was nearby.

As we pressed on toward El Cuá, peasants swinging machetes and children carrying loads of wood stopped to stare at our white jeep. Few passenger vehicles passed this way any more, and those that did were objects of great curiosity. People waved at us, often shouting, *"Vaya con Dios!"* After several hours, we reached our destination, the wretched settlement where Ben Linder had come from Oregon to live.

El Cuá was far from such luxuries as paved streets, telephones, and running water. It was a backward, dirty, unhealthy place where children ran naked through the mud and refuse was dumped into the same river from which people drank. Nonetheless, it qualified as one of the principal towns in northern Jinotega. The first shack we encountered had been painted in the Sandinista colors, red and black, as an obvious message of defiance to the contras. It was the home of Cosme Castro, at that time seventy-one years old. He had fought occupying United States Marines as a member of Sandino's rebel army more than half a century before.

The day we arrived, Cosme Castro was wearing fatigues and sporting a pin recognizing him as a "historic collaborator" with the Sandinista Front. He had painted his house red and black after a contra attack "to show the bastards where to shoot," one of his friends told me. When Linder needed a place to stay in El Cuá, Don Cosme, as he was locally known, offered him a room.

At Don Cosme's place, one of Linder's friends, Dr. Tim Takaro, a young American physician who worked as a medical volunteer in Jinotega, was packing Linder's belongings to be sent back to Oregon. A cot was the only piece of furniture in the small room. Linder had owned a single-burner gas stove, and on a crossbeam there were plastic vials containing oregano, sage, paprika, cayenne pepper, and other spices. Paperback books, ranging from Che Guevara's guerrilla diary to novels by popular American writers like William Styron and James Michener, were stacked in one corner. Most of what Linder had brought to El Cuá fit into his single red plastic suitcase, which Dr. Takaro was filling bit by bit.

I walked down the road to Uriarte's diner, which also served as a general store and social hangout. It was a dark, dingy, fly-infested place, and I rarely saw anyone eat there. Still, it was across from the town's only bus stop, and so people congregated out front.

Everyone at Uriarte's remembered Linder. There had never been a clown in El Cuá, much less one who was red-headed, bearded, American, and able to charm children into the clinic on vaccination day by picking them up at their homes on his unicycle. Most people I talked to knew that Linder had been involved in the hydroelectric project, but had no idea he was an engineer.

Peasants who lived in El Cuá were in many ways intensely conservative, not the raw material for revolution. The local Sandinista political officer, Captain Miguel Angel Castro, was under no illusions about local sentiment.

"A lot of people are confused," Captain Castro told me, using the code word for those who opposed Sandinista rule. "Some sympathize with the contras because they have relatives out there. Many people in this area haven't understood our message."

Near a rustic bar absurdly named Café Central, I found a young woman sitting with her husband outside a rickety shack. She told me her brother was a contra, and that she hoped the contras would win their war. I asked why.

"The Sandinistas wouldn't let us have our own farm, or grow what we wanted, or sell to who we wanted," she replied. "They repressed us."

Even this woman, though, remembered Ben Linder fondly, mostly because he was able to make children laugh. "They used to beg him to put on his clown suit," she remembered.

Walking along El Cuá's dusty main street, I saw one of Linder's American co-workers, Mira Brown, who had delivered a speech at the protest rally in Managua several days earlier. "The project goes ahead," she assured me resolutely. "We're going to finish what Ben started."

A while later, I noticed Brown with an AK-47 rifle slung over her shoulder. It was the first time I had seen an American civilian carrying a weapon of war in a foreign country. Linder had also carried an AK-47, and contras later said that by doing so, he had given up all pretense of neutrality and made himself a fair target.

The handful of people in El Cuá who knew just how much Linder had hoped to contribute to the region's development plans were the most somber of those I met. To them, Linder had been a gift. A person with his skills and commitment might not come to northern Jinotega again for many years.

"Everyone in this town has lost a loved one, or loved ones, during this war, but this was an especially hard blow, because there just aren't people with that kind of training who will come to places like this," said Beatriz Granada, the town treasurer. "Besides, no one here had ever seen a unicycle before Benjamin came."

Later, on my way out of town, I stopped one more time at the red-and-black shanty that had been Ben Linder's last home. Dr. Takaro was still sorting through folders, deciding what to pack and what to throw away.

"Ben stayed with us for a week because his leg was infected," he told me without looking up. "We had him on i.v. all week, and we were so close to sending him home. In fact, the day he went out toward Bocay was the first time he had put on his boots since the swelling went down."

As the doctor spoke, a printed leaflet from one of Linder's folders fluttered to the floor. It carried the heading, "Visit Nicaragua and Learn About Central America First-Hand."

20

OLIVER NORTH IN NICARAGUA

THE SUMMER of 1987 was the moment of Lieutenant Colonel Oliver North, the earnest and eager Marine officer whose go-get-'em forthrightness briefly charmed the American public during the televised Iran-contra hearings. North was a quintessentially American character, combining naive missionary zeal with indignant frustration at bureaucratic rules and the petty functionaries who enforce them. Politically, he was a faithful and perhaps even inevitable reflection of the Reagan administration's approach to the developing world.

Though he knew nothing of Latin American history, culture, or traditions, North became one of those officials in Washington absolutely convinced that Sandinista Nicaragua was nothing more or less than a Soviet neo-colony whose very existence posed a mortal threat to the United States. His world view was appealing for its insistent simplicity. He believed that superpowers were determining the future of the world in a series of duels over countries like Nicaragua, and that to view the Nicaraguan conflict in any other light was ingenuous to the point of treason.

The Sandinistas, North told Congress and a national television audience, had built "a Soviet client state on the mainland of this hemisphere" whose survival "will be disastrous for our foreign policy." If the Sandinistas were not soon overthrown, he predicted, "you will see democracy perish in the rest of Central

America, a flood of refugees crossing the American borders, and potentially the construction of a Berlin-type wall across the Río Grande to keep people out . . . You're talking about something in the nature of ten million refugees, the potential for drawing down on NATO support in order to defend our own southern border, and ultimately, with the consolidation of Communism in Central America, the commitment of American troops, the very thing we sought to prevent."

If North's view of the Sandinista threat was frighteningly apocalyptic, his perception of the contras and their cause was so idealized that it must have stimulated at least some viewers to want to enlist. To him, the contras were a brotherhood of dispossessed peasants secretly beloved by a terrorized population awaiting liberation, authentic heroes engaged in "a desperate struggle for liberty" despite Washington's callous indifference. They were a "democratic resistance" movement challenging a despotic regime that forced workers to join "a state-controlled, state-operated, state-managed, state-directed union."

Toward the end of his Congressional testimony, North described a slide show he had produced as part of his campaign to raise private funds for the contras:

> There are two photographs showing the arms captured after the M-19 assault on the Supreme Court, in which the entire Supreme Court of Colombia was murdered. . . . All of the weapons in those photographs originated in Nicaragua. Then a photograph that starts a series on what has happened to the people of Nicaragua. . . . A photograph of one of the victims, with his face terribly burned from having been trussed, bound, thrown into his Pentecostal church, and set afire while he was alive . . . A photograph . . . showing an entire town which fled in their Sunday best across the border, simply to go to church on Sunday, wearing everything they had because they could never go home. A series of photographs showing the dislocation of the Miskito Indians, 25,000 to 30,000 of which have been driven from tribal homelands across the border into Costa Rica and Honduras, bringing with them their entire culture, left alone for hundreds of years. These people can no longer go home.
>
> Then some photographs of the Nicaraguan resistance. It shows the young men and women who have taken up arms because they've been denied any other recourse in their own country. It shows the 57-year-old coffee farmer who I described earlier, who came home and found his entire family murdered by the Sandinistas because they had given water to a passing contra patrol . . . And then finally a photograph showing the grave of a resistance fighter. And the conclusion of the briefing is, gentlemen, we've got to offer them something more than the chance to die for their own country and the freedoms that we believe in.

It was an obviously heartfelt appeal, and it naturally led many Americans to wonder why their government had not rallied more vigorously around such a noble cause. North had a familiar explanation. "It is a very difficult thing to get out the straight story on the Nicaraguan resistance and the true perversion of the revolution undertaken by the Sandinistas," he told the investigating committee. "Their propaganda machine is very, very effective. And it is difficult to get the straight story out, on either the repression of the Sandinistas, the threat that they pose to their neighbors, or the realities about the Nicaraguan resistance."

In expressing frustration with press coverage of Nicaragua, North also returned to a theme he brought up several times during his testimony, his service in Vietnam. The war there had marked him deeply, and he had apparently never stopped brooding over it. In Vietnam, he said, "we won all the battles, but lost the war." Vietnam was a place where the paralyzing cowardice of small-minded politicians had denied brave men a chance at victory. Caught in the grip of the Vietnam experience, utterly innocent of the tides of Nicaraguan history, North saw Central America as another tropical outpost where the Soviet Union was testing American mettle. From his position at the National Security Council, he tried to provide Nicaragua's "freedom fighters" with the support nobody had given him and his comrades in Vietnam.

To someone living in Nicaragua, what was most striking in North's testimony was the vast difference between the real Nicaragua and the one he described. His exaggerations and misstatements, such as the suggestion that Sandinistas were involved in the massacre of Colombian judges, or the intimation that it was impossible to work in Nicaragua without joining an official union, were secondary. More depressing was the alacrity with which he constructed a good-versus-evil confrontation so simple it might have sprung from a children's fable.

Here was the living result of a foreign policy process in which factual assessments by professionals in the field had been systematically ignored, while lurid rumors were accepted as gospel. North was the ultimate example of what happens when policy planners refuse to be guided by reality, and instead sift selectively in order to find facts that fit their own views. This kind of contempt for truth tainted the Reagan administration's policies in Central America, stacking the intelligence deck in favor of pre-determined conclusions. It could not have been otherwise in an administration infused with President Reagan's view that for the United States, Nicaragua represented "one of the greatest moral challenges in post-war history."

North had enthusiastically supported the secret sale of arms to Iran, and told congressional investigators he considered it "a neat idea" to divert part of the profits for contra aid. Rivals with cooler heads managed to prevent him from carrying out some of his other bizarre schemes. On one occasion, he sought to arrange the sinking of a Nicaraguan merchant vessel on the high seas, arguing that it was a fair target since it was apparently carrying weapons for the Sandinista government. Another time, he designed an elaborate plan for contra leaders to rent a yacht called the *Sea Goddess* and hold a "constitutional convention" modelled after the one in Philadelphia in 1787. The plan called for contras to adopt a constitution modelled after that of the United States, and then to proclaim it either on the island of Grenada or in Boston or Philadelphia.

From North's narrow perspective, Nicaragua was not a nation with its own heritage, but a battleground where he could take revenge on international Communism for having defeated him and the men with whom he served in Vietnam. Yet he ignored vital lessons of the Vietnam debacle. In Nicaragua, he helped to sponsor a foreign adventure which the American people were not prepared to support. To the enormous propaganda benefit of anti-American elements throughout the hemisphere and the world, he and the Reagan administration placed the United States in the role of a cruel bully, waging a dirty war to defend security interests that even its closest allies did not believe were truly threatened.

In the world of Oliver North and Ronald Reagan, Nicaragua had joined Libya, Cuba, North Korea, and Iran as heads of a poisonous hydra that had to be subdued before it destroyed America. President Reagan once referred to the leaders of those countries as "the strangest collection of misfits, looney tunes, and squalid criminals since the advent of the Third Reich." Frustrated at their inability to strike at the more powerful "looney tunes," Reagan and his aides set their sights on Nicaragua. That was where they would live out their dream of confronting and punishing their enemies.

Despite the ignorance that underlay North's view of Nicaragua, however, the final impression he left was not one of malice or cruelty. He was a military man in his early forties who had risen to power by showing valor in combat and resolute loyalty to lofty principles. Perhaps as a result of his military training, he found it difficult to recognize that his truth was not the only truth, that different people perceive reality differently. He was never above adjusting the truth to serve what he believed to be the greater good. Over the years, he had come to believe that obedience to principle was more important than obedience to law.

That remarkable combination of qualities was very familiar to people in Nicaragua, because it was the same formula that made a successful Sandinista. If Oliver North had been born to Nicaraguan parents, and had come of age in Managua instead of on Maple Avenue in Philmont, New York, his idealism, his courage, and his hatred of tyranny might well have led him to join the Sandinista Front. Young, fearless, mystically convinced of his righteousness, ready to assume the thankless responsibility of making unpleasant decisions in secret, and certain that only knaves and traitors would stand in his way, North would have made a fine Sandinista.

North's testimony, which led to the short-lived phenomenon of "Olliemania" in some quarters, ended Tuesday, July 14, 1987. At that moment, contras inside Nicaragua were on the move. On July 16, according to their excited spokesmen in Miami, contra fighters scored a major military victory at San José de Bocay, not far from where Benjamin Linder had met his death three months earlier.

Contras claimed to have overrun the town, which was serving as a Sandinista command post, and destroyed its military installations, including an airstrip from which MI-24 helicopters often launched deadly raids.

Contra guerrillas had acquired an unsavory reputation for attacking unguarded civilian targets and abusing defenseless victims, but by the mid-1980s their apologists were insisting that such brutality was a thing of the past. They told anyone who would listen that the contras had reformed, that they now attacked military targets rather than clinics and state farms, and shot at soldiers instead of civilians. North's testimony that week had been a powerful assertion that the contras were true people's fighters. I had seen no evidence of a change in the contras' field tactics, but it was impossible to ignore their claim to have struck an important blow at San José de Bocay. As dawn broke the next morning, Guillermo and I were on our way northward.

That day was July 17, two days before the annual commemoration of the 1979 Sandinista takeover. The main celebration was to take place in the city of Matagalpa, through which I would have to pass on my way to San José de Bocay. Along the ninety-mile stretch of pockmarked road between Managua and Matagalpa, security was extraordinarily heavy. A soldier was posted every hundred yards, and we had to show our papers repeatedly.

At the entrance to Matagalpa itself, we were stopped at a barricade manned by a large military detachment. A somber-looking lieutenant was in charge. After our papers were checked, he approached, carrying something I could never remember having seen in Nicaragua: a clipboard. He told us crisply that he was recording the license plate numbers of all vehicles that passed through, and then moved to the front of our jeep.

Like many vehicles in Nicaragua, our jeep had only one license plate, mounted on the rear. On the front, I had affixed a souvenir plate with the name of my home town in Massachusetts. The lieutenant stared at it for a few moments, and then copied laboriously from what he must have assumed was a foreign plate: "Truro, Cape Cod." He took so long that Guillermo guessed he was also drawing the lighthouse that appeared on the plate. We kept straight faces, and said nothing. Finally, without ever looking at our real plate, the lieutenant briskly waved us on.

As we left Matagalpa behind and began to climb slowly through the coffee plantations, the heavy warmth that enveloped the lowlands gave way to cool mist. Dense clouds shrouded nearby mountain peaks, and hillsides were covered with verdant overgrowth. Brilliant scarlet birds flitted across the road as we passed La Fundadora, a giant coffee plantation once owned by the Somozas. At what is called the "city" of Jinotega, we talked our way past a final checkpoint, assuring our passage by judicious distribution of candy and cigarettes.

Beyond Jinotega, the road turned to dirt and rock, deteriorating as it wound north. River beds that had been dry a few months earlier were now swollen.

Several bridges had been destroyed or washed out, and we had to drive across free-flowing streams whose waters reached the jeep's hood. Women washing clothes and children diving from river banks stopped to stare as we passed.

We pressed north through intermittent rain, passing through small settlements I had visited before. I recognized several weatherbeaten peasants whose reports of military activity in the hinterlands had found their way into one or another of my dispatches. Most of them could probably not imagine Oliver North any more clearly than he had imagined them.

It was midday when we reached San José de Bocay. The sun was hidden behind heavy clouds, breaking through only for brief moments between rain squalls. Mud covered everything.

In a country of miserable villages, San José de Bocay was one of the most miserable. As the war had forced dirt-poor subsistence farmers from their plots on nearby mountainsides, they had descended to Bocay, swelling its population from five hundred in 1980 to twenty-five hundred in 1987. Many of the refugees, afraid to venture far from town and therefore unable to grow food, were plainly overwhelmed by the violence and upheaval that had engulfed them. Bocay had no electricity, no running water, no paved streets, not even any solid buildings. Arriving there was something like it must have been to arrive in Macondo, the fictional village created by Gabriel García Márquez, at the most primitive point in Macondo's history.

We pulled up to the grain depot on Bocay's only street and stepped out of our jeep, stiff from the rough ride but anxious to see what damage the contras had managed to inflict. Perhaps this place would mark some sort of turning point in the war, a crossroads at which the contras would finally have shown real military power. But at first glance, we could see no damage at all, no evidence that a battle had been fought.

Through the drizzle, I saw villagers milling quietly around the entrance to the depot. I strolled over and stepped inside. In the half-darkness I could at first make out only shadows, but soon a stark tableau came into focus. Contras had indeed passed this way.

Thirteen rough-hewn coffins were lying side by side on the dirt floor. Around them people stood in small groups, clutching each other's hands and whispering softly. Some gathered near the open door to escape the ripening smell.

I watched a man open one of the coffins, gaze at the pregnant woman inside, and then shut it, turning away with a muted sob. Then he edged toward three smaller coffins lying together, and opened one briefly. Neighbors told me his name was Domingo Martínez, and that his wife and three-year-old son had been killed in the previous day's attack. I remembered that during hearings in Washington, it was revealed that one of the pseudonyms Oliver North used in secret messages was "BG," for "blood and guts."

"I understand what war is, but it's unjust to kill civilians like this," Domingo

Martínez murmured as he gazed down at the coffins. His fingers twitched in slight spasms, but otherwise he seemed almost composed.

The spectacle was overpowering. I retreated back outside to escape it. Rain was falling again, and muddy currents were cascading toward the banks of a nearby stream. Another trip in search of the "new" contras had been in vain. Instead of the aftermath of a military raid, all that awaited in San José de Bocay were dead villagers in leaky coffins.

Shellshocked residents told me what had happened the day before. A squad of about one hundred contras had attacked just before dawn, firing mortars and automatic weapons from the surrounding hills. But despite nearly eight hours of fighting, they had not been able to enter the town, much less destroy its military installations.

When the shooting finally stopped, villagers counted their dead. They were nine militiamen, three children, and Mrs. Martínez. She was eighteen years old and in the fifth month of her third pregnancy.

In a ragged tent that was serving as a field hospital, Dr. Manuel García was treating thirty injured victims, most of them civilians. Among them was Maria Cecilia Novoa, a twelve-year-old girl with shrapnel lodged in her throat. One of her sisters was among the dead.

"A bunch of contras just shot machine guns into my house," the girls' father told me. "My little girl was hit, and died right away."

Suddenly a shout went up outside. Moments later, a new victim was carried in. He was a contra who had been badly wounded, and was found quietly bleeding to death in a clump of bushes. Sandinista officers said they had found the bodies of twenty-one contras nearby. Four of them, twisted into grotesque postures, lay beside the muddy road. I glanced at the corpses quickly, and then turned away. Guillermo stared for a few more moments.

On a bluff near the center of town, the rickety complex of wood shacks that served as Sandinista military headquarters stood undamaged. Also intact was the gravel airstrip that contras claimed to have destroyed. But more vulnerable targets had been hit. Beyond the airstrip, beyond the protection of soldiers, I found blank-faced peasants standing outside ruined hovels in what had been a government cooperative. A few of the shacks were still smoldering despite the rain, which had begun to fall in torrents.

Elvira Arauz, a mother of seven, stared blankly at the wreckage of her hut. Contras had burned it to the ground. Even worse, they had stolen her cow, meaning that she now had no source of milk for her young children.

"There isn't any army out this far, so we had no one to protect us," Mrs. Arauz said, obviously devastated but already trying to gather her wits. "We came down here from the mountains to escape the contras. We can't go back, because they'll kill us. But here we have no food, no clothes, absolutely nothing. We're wiped out."

Half a mile further out, I found a leathery grandfather named Raymundo Castillo sitting outside his ruined home, absently sharpening a machete. Several small children played in the rubble as he told me his sad tale. He said contras had made a mistake burning his house, which they believed was a state cooperative.

"They came and set fire to my place with everything inside," he sighed, seeming closer to resignation than rage. "They shouted that this was a state farm, and that they were burning everything owned by the state. I told them they were wrong, but it wasn't possible to explain."

By late afternoon, the bodies of the thirteen dead villagers had still not been moved from the grain depot. Someone said a priest was on his way to offer a funeral Mass, but someone else was saying that the bodies would have to be buried by nightfall, priest or no priest. In a sea of deep-lined faces, all bearing witness to lifetimes of toil, the saddest and most pathetic expressions were from mourners who stopped to touch the three small coffins containing the bodies of the youngest victims.

One woman, probably not past forty but already looking sick and used up, stared directly at me as she lay her hands on one of the coffins. I thought she was going to accuse me, or at least appeal for succor. Instead she managed a thin smile, and tried to reassure me.

"We will survive," she said. "We are praying to God to protect us."

In his testimony to Congress, Oliver North complained that a powerful disinformation network had prevented Americans from learning the truth of what was happening in Nicaragua. But he and the officials with whom he worked developed such an intense anti-Sandinista fervor that they never understood, or else chose to ignore, the nature of the war they were unleashing. They not only convinced themselves that the Sandinista regime was a demon sprung to life from America's worst nightmares, but apparently also concluded that inflicting pain on villages like San José de Bocay was necessary in order to extract a price for Sandinista defiance.

21

"PEACE IS A PROCESS"

THE AMBUSH in which Benjamin Linder was killed and the contra raid on San José de Bocay were just passing news events in a war that now gripped all of Nicaragua. Each day brought reports of new tragedy, and people had no choice but to adjust to life in a world of terror. Many Nicaraguans came to fear that peace might never come, that theirs had become one of those unfortunate nations condemned to an eternity of fratricidal conflict.

From a secret air base on Swan Island, off the coast of Honduras, the CIA kept contras equipped with weapons, ammunition, and other supplies. During 1987, the year following Eugene Hasenfus's crash, CIA pilots flew more than three hundred supply missions over Nicaragua without a mishap. The arms they delivered allowed contra units to intensify their war, and as I traveled through the countryside I could plainly see the results. Hospitals were full of victims, and in many parts of the country every village had been made to suffer.

Sandinista *comandantes* had made clear that as long as the war continued, they would tolerate dissent only within strict limits. A new constitution guaranteeing broad political freedom came into effect in January 1987, but President Ortega immediately suspended most of its important provisions. In February he extended the five-year-old state of emergency for another year. Among the rights that remained suspended were the right to strike, the right to hold outdoor public meetings, the right to be presumed innocent until proven guilty, and the right to publish uncensored news.

Opposition leaders became increasingly defiant, daring police to arrest them. Most of the time, police complied. When a group of them tried to leave a Catholic church in Managua for a protest rally in March, police moved in, broke up the crowd, and arrested ten organizers. A week later, a protest demonstration was violently suppressed in Boaco, and three anti-Sandinista organizers were jailed.

Nicaragua, with eager help from outside powers, was tearing itself apart. In battle zones, young men shot and killed each other every day. Normal political life was impossible, economic propects were bleak, and the emotion with which Nicaraguans had come to hate each other was more intense than ever. The decade that was to have witnessed the liberation of Nicaragua had instead seen its devastation, and all that loomed ahead was darkness.

There had been no lack of peace efforts over the years. The four-nation Contadora Group had produced a series of draft treaties. Several European leaders, notably Prime Minister Felipe González of Spain, had tried private initiatives. The secretaries-general of the Organization of American States and the United Nations had even toured the region in search of a formula for peace. All these efforts failed, principally because the thought of compromise was still anathema to the parties in conflict.

The Sandinistas repeatedly offered to enter peace talks, but there was a catch: they would talk only to the United States. They argued, as they had argued for years, that the contras were nothing more than mercenaries. To negotiate with them would be to legitimize them, to accept them as an independent force.

"We want to negotiate with the owner of the circus, not with the clowns," *Comandante* Bayardo Arce liked to say.

Washington turned a deaf ear to every Sandinista proposal for peace talks. President Reagan and the officials directing his Nicaragua policy maintained that if the Sandinistas wanted to negotiate, they should negotiate with contra leaders. Since the Sandinistas had vowed never to do that, the parties were at a deadlock. For lack of an acceptable negotiating formula, Nicaraguans continued to kill each other.

Journalists based in Nicaragua were consumed with the task of covering civil war and social upheaval, and sometimes we paid less than full attention to developments in nearby countries. Many of us had traveled to Costa Rica in 1986 to cover the presidential campaign in which Oscar Arias was elected, but we didn't expect much from Arias. We presumed he would behave like other Costa Rican presidents.

Costa Rican politics, like politics in other Central American countries, was conducted within certain unspoken rules. All Costa Rican politicians were expected to proclaim their love of peace, and both candidates in the 1986 election did so, as had the outgoing leader, Luis Alberto Monge. But Monge, while mouthing these cliches, had been quietly helping the CIA in its anti-Sandinista war for years. There was every reason to expect that Arias would do the same. Instead, he became the peacemaker for whom Nicaraguans had waited so long, the statesman who would finally show them a way out of war.

Arias was born in 1941 to a prosperous coffee-growing family. In his high school yearbook, he wrote that his goal in life was to be elected president. After graduating from the University of Costa Rica, he made a decision that profoundly shaped his life. Rather than move to the United States for a few years, as did many young Costa Ricans from wealthy families, he moved to England. During his years there, he studied at the London School of Economics and the University of Essex. More important than anything he learned there was what he did not learn. By not being educated in the United States, he did not assimilate the United States' view of Latin America, and he never came to perceive Costa Rica or Latin America as part of Washington's sphere of influence.

After returning from England, Arias became a professor of political science at the University of Costa Rica. In 1972 he was named vice president of the central bank, and from there he rose through both government ranks and the ranks of his National Liberation party. He never made any secret of his presidential ambitions, but even many of his friends considered him too stiff and intellectual to win a national election. Older party leaders tried to block his 1986 candidacy by proposing that former President José Figueres be drafted to head the ticket. Figueres, a revered figure in Costa Rica, expressed interest despite his advanced age, but Arias refused to make way for him.

Arias waged a decent campaign, but was widely considered the underdog. His opponent, Rafael Angel Calderón, was the son of a popular former president, and a rising star in his own right. Calderón staked out positions that placed him somewhat to Arias's right, but for most of the campaign, both candidates used much the same rhetoric. Both condemned the Sandinistas, but swore that they would never compromise Costa Rican neutrality by helping the contras. Their pledges had the ring of cynicism, because Costa Rica had long since abandoned its neutrality. Costa Rican leaders liked to pretend that their country was still the demilitarized paradise of years past, but secretly they worked with the CIA and permitted contras to launch a host of operations from Costa Rican soil.

By the mid-1980s this mendacity had become an accepted fact of Costa Rican political life. Oscar Arias had campaigned on familiar platitudes that journalists had heard time and time again: Costa Rica was made for peace, Costa Rica would do nothing to support war, Costa Rica must always be truly neutral. In the last weeks of his campaign, when he seemed headed for defeat, he made a special effort to portray himself as the peace candidate, pledging to keep his country out of the conflicts shaking Central America. Later he attributed his victory to that maneuver. But even at the moment of his inauguration in May 1986, there was no way of knowing that he took Costa Rica's noble principles so seriously.

Arias had not even taken office when Assistant Secretary of State Elliott Abrams flew to Costa Rica for the first of several confrontations with him. Abrams asked Arias to turn a blind eye to contra activity in Costa Rica, as President Monge had done. To his surprise, Arias firmly refused.

Soon after Arias assumed the presidency, Costa Rican police began arresting and disarming suspected contras. The health ministry shut down a clinic outside San José where wounded contras were being treated. Immigration authorities refused to allow Adolfo Calero or other senior contra leaders to enter Costa Rica. And in public statements, Arias began suggesting that United States aid to Central America would be more welcome if it supported development projects instead of guerrilla armies.

As the CIA intensified its anti-Sandinista war during the mid-1980s, Costa Rica had assumed great strategic importance. President Monge, who served from 1982 to 1986, had faced deep economic troubles, and his presidency was saved by the infusion of hundreds of millions of dollars in American aid. By 1985 more than one-third of Costa Rica's budget was being underwritten by the United States.

Monge was not ungrateful. When the CIA and the contras began building a "southern front" in Costa Rica, he raised no objection. His Minister of Public Security, Benjamin Piza, cooperated so fully with the Americans that he was rewarded with a private photo session in Washington with President Reagan.

With Monge and Piza in their pockets, CIA planners felt free to expand their activities in Costa Rica. In 1985, working through a series of dummy companies, they built a "secret" 6,520-foot dirt airstrip at a place called Santa Elena, just twelve miles from the Nicaraguan border. It was to be the base for a new anti-Sandinista campaign aimed at turning the southern part of Nicaragua into as violent a battleground as the north.

At first, the CIA's greatest problem in Costa Rica was not the government but the temperament of the flamboyant Costa Rica-based contra leader Edén Pastora, who had recovered from the wounds he suffered in the attempt on his life at La Penca and was eager to fight again. Never one to accept orders, Pastora feuded endlessly with his CIA handlers. To punish him, the CIA cut off all his subsisidies and induced six of his lieutenants to defect and join a more cooperative contra unit. Finally in March 1986, tired and frustrated, Pastora announced he was retiring from guerrilla life.

"There is no reason for one more Nicaraguan to die, because there is no possibility of military victory," he said in a farewell statement.

Pastora's retirement rid CIA strategists of one of their least favorite characters. President Arias, however, was about to present them with far more serious problems. Soon after his inauguration Arias learned about the Santa Elena airstrip, and he sent private messages to the United States embassy insisting that it be shut down. Embassy officials did not take him seriously at first. They assured him the strip would be closed, but continued to use it. When Arias discovered what was happening, he was furious. He scheduled a news conference to announce that he was dispatching Costa Rican police to shut the airstrip.

From Washington, Assistant Secretary Abrams and his military counterpart, Lieutenant Colonel Oliver North, struck back. Upon learning that Arias had called a news conference, they telephoned United States Ambassador Lewis Tambs in San José and directed him to visit Arias immediately. They told him to threaten Arias with a cutoff of all American aid if he went ahead with his plans. Tambs's notes of the conversation were later made public: "Tell Arias: Never set foot in W. H. [White House]. Never get 5 [cents] of $80M promised by [AID Director Peter] McPherson."

Arias, who had a good sense of when to press forward and when to yield, called off his news conference. But journalists soon discovered the airstrip on their own, and on September 26 Arias officially announced he was shutting it down. Reagan administration officials were livid, and CIA Director William Casey himself decided it was time for a trip to San José. When he arrived on October 6, Arias refused to receive him, sending his foreign minister instead.

Two months later, when Arias was on a visit to Washington, Casey approached him again, inviting him to a private chat at CIA headquarters. Arias declined, but offered to receive Casey at the presidential suite of the Westin Hotel, where he was staying. Casey agreed.

Upon entering the suite, Casey was surprised to find a crowd of Costa Rican diplomats and other officials. Arias was present, but made no move to invite Casey aside so they could talk in private. The spymaster fumed for half an hour before realizing that a bit of a joke had been played on him. He left in disgust.

Arias's decision to shut the CIA airstrip was dramatic news, bordering on the unthinkable. Central American presidents normally did not defy the United States so boldly. I was anxious to meet and talk with the new president, and after he was settled into office I travelled to San José for an interview.

The presidential palace in Costa Rica looks nothing like a palace. If it did not have an iron fence around the front, it might easily be taken as part of the chocolate factory across the street. A single guard was posted outside on the day I arrived, and when I told him I had come to meet the president he waved me through.

Arias could smile broadly when necessary, but his natural expression was one of gloom. When we met, he greeted me with a firm handshake, and ushered me into his office. His desk was cluttered with books and papers, held down by a heavy plaque reading, *"La Paz Construye"*—Peace Builds. With bushy eyebrows, jowly face, and drooping shoulders, he seemed more like a preoccupied university professor than a politician.

As I was sitting down, he asked in English whether I would prefer to speak English or Spanish. I told him Spanish would be fine. Without any further prompting, he began a monologue about his plans for Costa Rica.

I listened as Arias told me of Costa Rica's commitment to social justice and peace. It was a country where fifteen percent of the gross national product was spent for education and health care, and where land was more fairly distributed than anywhere else in Latin America. Thirty-eight years before, Arias reminded me, Costa Ricans had abolished their army and pledged themselves to peace.

"This tradition of peace is the greatest inheritance our forefathers left us," he said. "It is the best thing I can hope to leave to my children and grandchildren."

Arias spoke proudly about Costa Rica's heritage. When he finished, I asked him his opinion of the Sandinista regime next door.

"Costa Ricans would prefer a different government in Nicaragua," he replied. "We feel deceived by the Sandinistas, the same way the rest of the world does. What they are doing is not what people want, and not what they themselves promised . . . I would like to see them change, to evolve to the point where they would permit a more open, pluralist system, be tolerant, and keep the promises they made to the OAS in 1979. But reality tells me something else. With the passage of time, the regime has become less pluralist, less tolerant. It's all very sad."

"So you dislike the Sandinistas, but you won't help to overthrow them?"

As I held my pen poised above my notebook, Arias paused for a moment to gather his thoughts. He was always careful to avoid directly criticizing the United States, and liked to frame his views in strictly Costa Rican terms.

"Costa Rica must be truly neutral, not just neutral in rhetoric," he said. "It is the desire of Costa Ricans that their territory not be used to fight against other regimes in Central America, and I want that to be respected. I can guarantee that I will not permit any foreigners to act militarily from our territory."

"Does that mean you oppose American aid to the contras?"

"Look, the purpose of the aid was to force Ortega to negotiate, to change. What has actually happened? What's the reality? The more you give the contras, the more Ortega gets from the Soviets. What do you do if the contras can't win with $100 million? Give them $200 million, or $400 million? I'm thinking of my country, of the consequences that insurrectional violence in Nicaragua has for my people. It threatens our stability and our democracy."

"Given your attitude, do you think the United States still considers Costa Rica a friend?"

"Friendship should not mean being servile. A friend who does everything you want is not a friend, but a slave."

Despite his lack of charm, Arias had great persuasive power. In that interview and in many that followed, I found him refreshingly candid on all subjects save one. It was his firm policy, regardless of the facts, always to deny that the United States had ever threatened or pressured him in any way. Stories of his confrontations with American officials were widely reported, but in public he unfailingly embraced the United States. He indignantly dismissed suggestions that the Reagan administration might cut aid to Costa Rica as punishment for his defiance.

"The United States is a great democracy," he liked to say. "Democracies don't punish other democracies."

Perhaps only a man so sure of himself could have assumed the role into which Arias was now stepping. In the course of a few months, he had ruined the CIA's plan to open a "southern front" against the Sandinistas. With that accomplished, he set out on an even more ambitious project: designing a plan to end the Nicaraguan war.

The timing was propitious for a new initiative when Arias began his quiet peace campaign at the beginning of 1987. Contras were no closer to victory than ever, and their most important patron, William Casey, had died. President Reagan and many of his closest advisors were preoccupied with the unfolding Iran-contra scandal. Inside Nicaragua, the pace of economic decline had accelerated dramatically, and people were restive.

Arias set out to resolve Nicaragua's conflict by drafting a regional treaty that would apply to all five Central American countries. His greatest dream was to produce a plan that would lead to resolution of not only the contra war, but also guerrilla insurgencies in Guatemala and El Salvador. From the beginning, however, his Central American peace initiative was designed principally for Nicaragua.

In February 1987 Arias invited the presidents of Guatemala, Honduras, and El Salvador to San José for a summit. There the four leaders agreed in principle to a peace formula that Arias proposed. The formula seemed utopian in its simplicity. Each Central American government would negotiate a cease-fire with insurgents, declare an amnesty, and hold free elections. Outside powers, for their part, would be asked to cut off aid to all guerrillas. Similar proposals had been circulating for years, and at first this one seemed no more promising than the others.

After the San José summit, Arias set out to persuade world leaders that the moment was ripe for a serious peace effort in Central America. He toured Latin America and Europe, impressing heads of state with his intelligence and seriousness of purpose. Then he visited Washington, where he found influential Democrats especially encouraging. They were searching for a workable alternative to the failed contra policy, and Arias seemed to be offering them a way out.

Reduced to its essentials, his plan called for insurgents to stop fighting and for governments to respect democracy. Everyone could embrace that formula, and the Senate voted 97–1 for a resolution supporting it.

Among those who now began to take Arias more seriously were the Sandinista *comandantes.* They were highly suspicious of his motives at first, and their public statements were full of scorn for Costa Rica's "so-called democracy." But as they reviewed the peace plan more carefully, they saw that it might be the vehicle by which they could accomplish their transcendent goal of destroying the contras. One of the plan's major provisions was a call on outside powers to stop all arms shipments to "irregular forces." That provision would not be binding, but it would certainly carry heavy moral weight in Washington. Congress could hardly vote more aid to the contras if all five Central American presidents asked them not to.

The Central American presidents met again on May 24–25, this time with Daniel Ortega also participating. Their summit, held at Esquipulas, Guatemala, ended inconclusively. The presidents issued a statement lauding the principles of democracy and human rights, but committed themselves to nothing except another round of talks.

Arias was paying an unofficial visit to Indianapolis in June 1987 when he was summoned to the White House. He presumed that President Reagan simply wanted to greet him and be photographed with him. But when he entered the Oval Office he found himself facing not only Reagan, but also Vice President George Bush, National Security Advisor Frank Carlucci, White House chief of staff Howard Baker, Assistant Secretary of State Abrams, and other senior officials.

President Reagan and his aides told Arias that his peace initiative was undermining United States policy toward Nicaragua. For more than an hour they pressed him to alter his course. The confrontation, according to one published report, was "sharp, tense, and blunt," but Arias did not budge.

By bringing the five Central American presidents together for negotiations, Arias had accomplished something new and valuable. But the political distances among them still seemed vast, and when they arrived in Guatemala City on August 6 for the summit called Esquipulas II, expectations were low. The prospect was for another round of recriminations, perhaps another meaningless proclamation, and a return to war as usual.

On the evening of August 4, I was at the San José airport waiting for a flight back to Managua. In the terminal I ran into Alfonso Robelo, the former Sandinista junta member who was now a contra leader. We sat in the coffee shop together, and he told me he was on his way to Washington, where he and other senior contras were to meet with President Reagan. He shared the general view that the Arias initiative was about to fail, and assured me that the contras would fight on.

"We have the equipment now, and we have the men," Robelo told me. "We're going to start bringing the war down into populated areas. We've got to make ourselves felt in every part of the country."

Robelo was as surprised as everyone else when he learned the next day that President Reagan and Speaker of the House Jim Wright had issued a Central American peace proposal of their own. Their proposal was a patchwork job, containing some elements of the Arias plan and some new ones. Though it was not coherent enough to have formed the basis of a treaty, it had a sobering effect on the Central American presidents gathering for their summit in Guatemala City. They began to fear that politicians in the United States were preparing to impose a solution on them.

The Guatemala talks were held in an upstairs suite at the fashionable Camino Real hotel. Arias, a student of human nature as well as history, had arranged that the five leaders meet alone, with no aides present. He had read a biography of Franklin Roosevelt in which he learned that Roosevelt sometimes resolved conflicts among his advisors by locking them in a room together and not allowing them to emerge until they had reached an agreement. At the Camino Real he adopted that technique. After a few hours of bargaining, one of the presidents suggested a dinner break, but Arias vigorously objected. Meals were instead delivered by hotel room service, and the entire negotiation was conducted in a single marathon session.

"I didn't want them going downstairs and talking to the generals and foreign ministers down there," Arias told me later. "That would have been the end of everything."

Reporters in Guatemala awoke on the morning of August 7 to the astonishing news that a breakthrough had been reached during the night. Before anyone could quite believe what was happening, the five leaders appeared together at Guatemala's presidential palace, announced that they had decided to make peace, and affixed their signatures to an agreement. Then they walked across the plaza to the ornate Roman Catholic cathedral. Archbishop Próspero Penados del Barrio officiated at a special Mass of Thanksgiving.

In his homily, Archbishop Penados ignored the congregation and directly confronted the five presidents.

"Your own names, not just those of your governments and your epochs, are going to be remembered," he warned them. "You will either be corrupt tyrants who betrayed the people who believed in you, or heroes who brought our isthmus out of its misery and suffering, and set it on the path to true freedom and peace."

The peace accord signed in Guatemala committed each government to promote "an authentic pluralist and participatory democratic process." Specifically, the five governments pledged to permit full freedom for political parties and full press freedom, and to hold periodic elections monitored by the United

Nations and the Organization of American States. In addition, countries facing "deep social divisions" were to begin dialogue with opposition groups, offer amnesty to enemies, and enter into cease-fire negotiations.

Each country's internal dialogue was to be guided by a four-member National Reconciliation Commission, made up of a government representative, an opposition leader, a Roman Catholic bishop, and an independent figure chosen by the president. States of emergency existing in any country—Nicaragua was the only one—were to be lifted. All constitutional guarantees were to be fully respected.

By accepting these provisions, Daniel Ortega was making astonishing concessions. He was agreeing not only to ease pressure on dissidents, but to reshape the nature of Sandinista rule. The political system outlined in the Guatemala accord was not at all the one that Sandinistas had originally envisioned. It was, in fact, the "bourgeois democracy" that they had scorned for years.

Ortega's decision to sign the treaty was based in part on his recognition that the political system he had hoped to implant in Nicaragua was failing. But he would never have agreed to such sweeping commitments if the accord had not offered him a chance to reach his great goal: defeating the contras. The accord contained two provisions that would, if respected, end the contra insurgency. One required all Central American governments to forbid the use of their territory by "irregular forces or insurrectional movements." The other was an unprecedented joint plea for a cutoff of American aid to the contras.

The accord did not specifically mention the United States, but its language was clear enough: "The governments of the five Central American states will ask governments in the region, and extra-regional governments which openly or covertly provide military, logistical, financial, or propaganda aid in manpower, arms, munitions, and supplies to irregular forces or insurrectional movements, to cease such aid, as an indispensable element in the achievement of a stable and lasting peace in the region."

There was another, unwritten aspect of the peace accord which Ortega perceived as highly favorable to his government. One of its basic premises was that "irregular forces" like the contras were not legitimate, and should be disbanded. By signing, the five presidents were effectively certifying each other's legitimacy and, by logical extension, condemning all insurgents as enemies of peace.

None of the five presidents who signed the accord was taking greater risks than Ortega. Aboard the airliner that carried him back to Managua on the evening of August 7, he told reporters that the accord represented "a first great, transcendent, and historic step" toward peace. But when he landed in Managua, he found himself facing a rebellious National Directorate. Other *comandantes* were stunned at the concessions he had made. The Directorate, still the country's top decision-making body, convened an emergency meeting to hear his explanation.

Before Ortega's departure for the Guatemala talks, the National Directorate had given him a private vote of confidence. But the content of the accord he signed was as shocking to his fellow *comandantes* as to everyone else. Instead of immediately endorsing it, the Directorate maintained an ominous silence for several days. Tomás Borge later said he and other *comandantes* had subjected Ortega to "very deep and very serious questioning."

Finally, three days after the accord was signed, Ortega's aides summoned journalists to a 10 A.M. news conference. We were anxious to hear what he would say, and many of us arrived early. But ten, eleven, and twelve o'clock passed, and there was no sign of Ortega. He was still locked in argument with other *comandantes.*

After years of experience covering Sandinista Nicaragua, most reporters came to news conferences prepared for such long delays. I had brought a book, and several of my colleagues were contentedly listening to music on Walkman tape players. Waiters in white shirts circulated among us offering small cups of coffee, and then returned later with soft drinks.

At long last, an aide appeared to announce that the news conference had been postponed until 4 P.M. We returned at that hour, took our seats once again, and waited. At 5:30 there was another announcement. Ortega's news conference, we were told, was now definitively set for 6 P.M., but it would be held at Sandino Airport, eight miles away.

No one knew what to make of this development. Television crews quickly folded up their equipment and packed it into waiting vans. We raced toward the airport, and assembled there to wait. Suddenly, someone looking out the window over the tarmac noticed Daniel Ortega walking toward a small, unmarked airplane. We tried to chase him, but security agents blocked our way. Then Ortega's press secretary walked in and read a brief communqué announcing that Ortega was on his way to Cuba.

Faced with incipient rebellion from his fellow *comandantes,* Ortega had decided to appeal to Fidel Castro, the highest authority in the Latin American revolutionary firmament. Castro, like Ortega, viewed the peace accord as an instrument by which the contras could finally be destroyed. He warmly welcomed Ortega, and the two leaders posed for a photo that was flashed back to Managua and published on the front page of *Barricada.* Immediately the internal debate among Sandinistas ended. Within hours after Ortega's return from Havana the next day, the National Directorate formally endorsed the peace plan signed in Guatemala. *Barricada* reported the endorsement under the banner headline, "Sandinista Front Monolithically Supports Accords."

Oscar Arias, architect of the peace plan, was welcomed home far more fervently than Ortega. A jubilant crowd awaited him at the San José airport, church bells pealed, and Costa Rican flags flew from many homes and offices.

It was a great moment not only for Arias, but for the nation whose principles he so admirably personified.

Though the crowds that welcomed Arias home were rightfully thrilled, he himself was fully aware of the difficulties ahead.

"If today we are raising a hope, there are also a thousand obstacles before us," he warned his admirers at the airport. "Each time we think we have completed a task, the horizon recedes and we face a greater challenge."

A week after the accord was signed, I traveled to San José for an interview with Arias. He was still basking in the glow of victory. His smile was infectious, and I shook his hand warmly.

"So, Mr. President," I began, "what is responsible for this miracle?"

"My powers of persuasion," he replied, at least half seriously.

We talked at length, and I was struck by his open admission that his plan was essentially anti-Sandinista. If Daniel Ortega lived up to his new commitments and allowed full freedom to Nicaraguans, Arias kept saying, the days of Sandinista rule were numbered.

"The lesson of history is so clear," he said, spreading his palms skyward. "No Communist system can survive with freedom of the press."

Although Arias could never say so publicly, he believed he was presenting the United States with an ideal solution to its Nicaragua problem. He was certain that if the peace accord was implemented, the Sandinistas would inevitably lose their hold on power, which was the Reagan administration's main goal. Yet he was never able to win the White House to his side. President Reagan sent him a congratulatory message after the accord was signed, but the message promised only that the White House would study the accord "with great interest." Soon afterward, in a televised speech, Reagan reiterated that he was "totally committed to the democratic resistance, the freedom fighters, and their pursuit of democracy in Nicaragua."

As soon as Nicaraguan opposition leaders grasped the potential significance of the new accord, they set out to test it. On August 15, eight days after the accord was signed, several hundred protesters tried to gather for a rally in Managua. Police not only dispersed them, but did so with unusual force, resorting for the first time to the use of electric prods. Two outspoken critics of the regime, human rights activist Lino Hernández and bar association president Alberto Saborío, were arrested and jailed for three weeks. Many suspected that Tomás Borge, acting on his own, was sending a message to friends and enemies alike. Accord or no accord, he was not yet prepared to allow anti-Sandinista groups to take to the streets in protest.

Borge made several speeches during August, all suggesting dissatisfaction with the peace accord. "We are not and will not be prepared to forget our principles," he insisted during a visit to Bluefields. "We have not been defeated, and we are not going to be defeated."

For a time it seemed Borge might pose a real threat to the peace process in Nicaragua, and he fed such speculation by refusing all requests to be interviewed on the subject. But in mid-September, he traveled to Havana for meetings with Fidel Castro. Apparently Castro was persuasive, because Borge never again raised the issue.

The peace plan's most vigorous opponents turned out to be President Reagan and his advisors. On September 10, barely a month after the five Central American presidents had called on foreign powers to stop funding "irregular forces" in the region, Secretary of State Shultz announced that the Reagan administration was seeking $270 million in new aid for the contras. Central American leaders were bound by the new accord to oppose such aid, and they did.

"It would end the peace process," Salvadoran Foreign Minister Ricardo Acevedo Peralta said simply. "The Sandinistas could use the new aid package as an excuse not to comply with the accords. They could say that now that the contras are getting new U.S. aid, they are no longer bound to move toward democracy."

The peace accord required each country to take steps toward democracy within ninety days. In Managua, expectations built steadily as the November 7 deadline approached. Amid much fanfare, Ortega announced the formation of Nicaragua's National Reconciliation Commission, naming Cardinal Obando as its chairman. Then in late September came an announcement many had feared they would never hear: *La Prensa* would be permitted to reopen after sixteen months of enforced silence. Next came a decree allowing the Roman Catholic radio station to reopen, and another lifting orders of exile against Bishop Pablo Antonio Vega and Father Bismarck Carballo. The Sandinistas were now restoring rights they had suspended, something they had never done before.

"A few months ago, the future of the country was more aggression," *Comandante* Jaime Wheelock told party faithful at a rally. "Today a new possibility is being opened."

The first edition of the revived *La Prensa* was published on October 1. A front-page editorial made clear that the paper's political line had not softened.

"In the name of the people of Nicaragua," it said, "*La Prensa* today tells the Sandinista Front that Nicaraguans have never wanted and do not want a Communist-style totalitarian dictatorship."

In its first weeks back in business, *La Prensa* published relentless attacks on the government, sparking renewed Sandinista charges that its editors were cooperating with the United States to destabilize Nicaragua. Editors acknowledged that they were receiving aid from the National Endowment for Democracy, a congressionally-funded foundation that served the Reagan administration's goals abroad. The Endowment donated $98,000 to *La Prensa* for the purchase of ink and other supplies in the months after it reopened in 1987, bringing the total of its contributions to $254,000 since 1980.

Although Sandinista leaders seemed to be accepting the inevitability of political change, there remained two basic questions on which they swore they would never compromise. Vice President Sergio Ramírez summarized them succinctly in a speech in León.

"We will never talk to the armed mercenaries," Ramírez vowed. "Nor will there be amnesty for the Guardsmen who killed people."

Cardinal Obando and other Catholic bishops protested this narrow interpretation of the peace accord. In a pastoral letter, they urged the government to open talks with contra leaders, offering Obando as an intermediary. They also called for an end to military conscription and a sweeping amnesty for all anti-Sandinista prisoners.

The bishops were challenging cherished Sandinista principles, and Sandinista leaders reacted strongly. "The enemy has proposed the absolute forgetting of crimes, ignoring the rivers of blood and tears left by half a century of tyranny," the National Directorate said in a formal statement. "Such suggestions are intolerable. . . . The people of Nicaragua and the Sandinista National Liberation Front declare that never, in any way, in any place, through any intermediary, will there be direct or indirect political dialogue with the counter-revolutionary leadership."

Such rhetoric, and the inflexibility it seemed to represent, underscored the enormous obstacles that still blocked the path to peace. Harsh reality was setting in. Aides to President Arias recognized that some kind of new push was needed, something to give renewed momentum to the peace process. Very quietly, they came up with the idea of proposing Arias for the Nobel Peace Prize.

To campaign publicly for the prize would have been unseemly, but in several capitals Costa Rican diplomats broached the subject with Scandinavian counterparts. The initial response was favorable. Arias's advisors were led to believe that he was a serious contender.

Often the Nobel Prize is awarded to men and women who have devoted lifetimes to the cause of peace, recognizing not specific achievements but the accumulated work of decades. Such awards, while justly recognizing great peacemakers, do little to affect the course of immediate history. But in 1987 jurors had a chance to make a different kind of award. By recognizing Arias they would not only be rewarding a principled pacifist, but quite possibly rescuing the Central American peace process from failure.

As I reflected on this from my post in Managua, I became convinced that Arias was going to win. After several telephone calls to Norway, I learned that the prize was to be awarded on October 13. On the afternoon of the 12th I boarded a flight for San José. After arriving at my hotel there, I called Lyle Prescott, an intrepid local reporter who had helped discover the secret CIA airstrip at Santa Elena a year earlier. Lyle knew Costa Rica intimately, and during my visits there I sometimes hired her to help me research stories.

"We're going to have a busy day tomorrow," I told her. "Arias is going to win the Nobel Prize."

"What time is it being announced?" she asked.

"Four o'clock in the morning, Costa Rica time."

"No problem. I'll wake up early and turn on the radio. If he wins, I'll call you."

Dawn had not broken the next morning when I awoke to the sound of a ringing telephone. As soon as I opened my eyes and realized where I was, I knew who was calling.

"He got it," was all Lyle said.

"So what happens today?" I asked.

"I don't know. Let me check around, and I'll call you back."

Arias was on a retreat with his family at a remote beach home where there was no telephone. He learned of the prize by radio. Aides finally reached him, and a plane was dispatched to bring him back to San José.

Arias's plane was to land not at San José's international airport, but rather at a small airstrip used mainly by private pilots. Two dozen journalists, most of them Costa Rican, assembled there to wait. Finally a small plane appeared in the sky. It approached, landed, and coasted to a stop. We pressed around as the door opened, but the only passengers were Arias's mother and his two young children. There were not enough seats aboard the plane for everyone, and Arias had chosen to stay behind. The pilot told us we would have to wait at least another hour.

Some journalists conducted interviews with the Arias children, and the rest of us retreated into the shade to wait. Cabinet ministers began arriving, smiling broadly and slapping each other on the back. After a while someone heard a buzz in the air, and soon the plane we had been awaiting was on the ground. Arias, dressed in casual clothes and beaming, stepped out and waved. He embraced a few close friends, and then turned to the waiting journalists.

"The accord we signed in Guatemala was a triumph of reason over madness," he told us. "It represents the hope that war and other problems can be resolved through dialogue and negotiation. Dialogue is the way civilized people should resolve their conflicts."

Arias made his way home, and a few hours later arrived at the presidential palace for a hastily called news conference. All regular business there had been abandoned in the jubilation. Office workers swarmed around the president as soon as he appeared. Lines of schoolchildren, freed from class for the occasion, stood outside and waved Costa Rican flags.

I found myself next to a vivacious young teacher named Elizabeth Chacon, who reminded me that Costa Rica was the only country in Latin America without an army, that education had been free and compulsory since 1869, and that the death penalty had been abolished in 1882.

"Part of our basic curriculum is teaching children the importance of peace," she told me proudly. "Costa Ricans are often accused of being cowards because we are pacifists. Now, with this prize, we're going to be able to show our young people that peace has its rewards."

Arias stopped briefly to acknowledge the cheers. As he waved, someone shouted, "Costa Rica has been heard around the world!"

"This is the happiest day of my life," the president confessed.

Several hundred people were packed into the auditorium where Arias was to meet the press. Only a small number were reporters. The rest were government workers and private citizens who wanted to share the historic moment. Arias, now formally dressed, spoke seriously.

"This prize was not given to someone who arranged peace, but to someone who is struggling to arrange it," he told us. "They are giving us this prize so that we will redouble our work for peace. Peace has not yet happened. It is about to happen."

All afternoon and evening, the presidential palace was alive with euphoric celebration. At dusk cases of champagne appeared, and before long people were giddily dancing in the corridors. Arias agreed to grant private interviews to each of the major Costa Rican television stations, and he invited me to sit and listen. He said nothing new in the interviews, but after the first one was over, I saw his mask drop revealingly.

The television crew had packed and left. In the president's office, waiting for the next crew to arrive, were Arias and two of his closest friends and advisors, John Biehl and Fernando Zumbado. Perhaps for the first time that day, Arias enjoyed a moment of silence. The three men looked at each other, sharing their triumph. I could sense the intimacy among them. They had forged the strategy which propelled Arias to the presidency, and then, against all odds, produced a peace accord which held out the hope of reshaping Central American history. Now they had brought a Nobel Prize to Costa Rica.

"How do you think they took this news at the White House?" Biehl asked.

"Como un golpe en los meros huevos," Arias replied with a broad grin. Like a kick right in the balls.

For once, albeit in private, Arias had acknowledged that his peace plan was a direct challenge to President Reagan's policy in Central America. Reagan wanted to continue the anti-Sandinista war, while Arias sought to end it. But at its heart, the Arias peace plan was designed with United States security interests very much in mind. Had the Reagan administration been more open-minded, it might have embraced the Guatemala accord as a great victory. It committed the Sandinistas to adopt fundamental political reforms, precisely the goal for which contras said they were fighting. Arias repeatedly tried to make the Reagan administration understand that his plan was in essence anti-Sandinista, but he never succeeded.

The fact that Arias was now a Nobel Prize winner made no difference to Reagan aides in Washington, who were working systematically to undermine his peace plan. When they learned that the Costa Rican ambassador in Washington, Guido Fernández, was visiting members of Congress to explain the plan's merits, they forced Arias to recall him. Soon afterward, they orchestrated a pressure campaign that led to John Biehl's resignation from his position with the United Nations Development Program. They also sought to tarnish Arias's image at home by leaking information, later found to be inaccurate, that his government had misspent millions of dollars in American aid. A State Department official reported that the Reagan administration had reacted to Arias's prize with "unbridled disgust," and that administration officials had begun derisively referring to him as "the laureate."

SOME aspects of the peace plan also worried the Sandinistas. Under its provisions, they had no choice but to permit *La Prensa* and the Catholic radio station to reopen. After taking those steps, however, they resolved to go no further. They forbade the Catholic station to broadcast news, refused to authorize the reappearance of more than twenty other radio news programs shut down since 1982, and ignored appeals that they authorize a non-Sandinista television channel.

Though the Sandinistas dragged their feet, they did far more to comply with the peace accord than any other government in Central America. Guatemalan negotiators met once with guerrillas, and broke off talks when the guerrillas refused to surrender. Salvadoran leaders, in a hideous perversion of the peace accord, used its amnesty provision to justify freeing not only many guerillas, but also dozens of imprisoned death squad members. And Honduran authorities, who were committed to closing contra bases on their territory, made no effort to do so.

"Honduras has not assumed new international political obligations," Honduran Foreign Minister Carlos López Contreras piously told the press.

All involved in the regional peace process, however, recognized that its central goal was to stop the war in Nicaragua. Soon after the accord was signed, the Sandinista government unilaterally declared a cease-fire in three zones where contras were concentrated. Inside the zones, which covered about two percent of Nicaraguan territory, they hoped to persuade contra fighters to lay down their weapons and return to civilian life. As a show of good faith they withdrew their troops from the zones. Contras were free to move within them.

The idea of contras walking peacefully along roadsides without fear of attack was jarring. It was a sight I wanted to see, so one morning in early October Guillermo and I set out for the northern border, where two of the three zones had been established. At Quilalí, on the edge of one zone, I found Sandinista troops quartered as usual. Residents told us contras were nearby, and we drove slowly eastward.

At a bend in the road just three miles from the last Sandinista outpost, we ran into a band of contras commanded by an agitated young man named Norland. He was angry at us for finding him, and began shouting threats. A Red Cross worker who was accompanying us turned pale as Norland stopped directly in front of him.

"No Red Cross, no journalists!" the guerrilla commander shouted, waving his M-16 menacingly. "If I see you again, I'll burn your jeeps!"

Norland and other contras had reason to be nervous. They faced a situation unlike any they had experienced before. Sandinista radio stations were proclaiming the war over, and urging them to surrender. Yet their senior military commander, Enrique Bermúdez, was telling them to "remain firm" and not disarm.

I looked at Guillermo, who was at the wheel, and for once he looked a bit pale. Norland was a frightening character, seemingly out of control. He was threatening not only us but our jeep, and Guillermo didn't like people threatening the jeep. The situation felt volatile and dangerous. I jumped back into the jeep and told Guillermo, *"Vámonos, hombre."* He threw the jeep into reverse, and we sped away, backwards, into the relative safety of the bush.

Outside the three cease-fire zones, war raged much as before. In several parts of the country, contras took the offensive. In September they cut the country's principal east-west road for two days, and their anti-aircraft units shot down two more Sandinista helicopters, bringing their total for 1987 to at least six. On October 15 they attacked several towns in Chontales, and when I traveled there a week later, I found destroyed bridges and freshly burned military trucks. In the town of San Pedro de Lóvago, contras methodically burned the mayor's office, the telephone company office, and the military garrison, and then withdrew. The mayor, Augusto Vega, told me he had hidden in a bathroom during the attack.

"They completely took over the town," Vega said. "We see they aren't as weak as we thought they were."

In Miami, contra spokesman Bosco Matamoros declared the offensive a great success. "We showed in Chontales that we can launch coordinated attacks, and destroy strategic targets," he told reporters. "We're ready to talk to the Sandinistas without conditions, but they are not interested."

Foreign Minister Miguel D'Escoto replied on behalf of the government, again rejecting the idea of negotiating with contras.

"The one we talk to has to be the one paying the bills, the one who is making war on us," D'Escoto insisted. "That is the only one we talk to."

* * *

THE November 7 deadline for compliance with the peace accord was fast approaching. Diplomats from several Western countries urged President Ortega to show flexibility, and Cardinal Obando repeated his offer to serve as an intermediary between the warring parties. Then on October 31, Ortega unexpectedly departed for a quick trip to Moscow. Conditions had begun to change there since the ascension of Mikhail Gorbachev. The Soviets were still supplying Nicaragua with weapons, but were now also urging the Sandinistas to seek a negotiated settlement.

"We have not closed ourselves off from seeking an agreement," Ortega said cryptically before leaving Managua. "On November 5 we will be making some new announcements."

The Sandinistas called a public rally for the evening of November 5, and Ortega returned from Moscow just hours before it was to begin. Organizers hung banners all over Managua with slogans like "Total Amnesty Never, Never, Never" and "For Our Heroes and Martyrs, No Dialogue With Contra Leaders." Thousands of people gathered. As I walked through the crowd, I didn't sense much support for compromise.

Ortega began with familiar rhetoric, and after speaking for about twenty minutes finally came to the question of amnesty. To show his intent to comply with the accord, he said, he was prepared to grant amnesty to 981 prisoners, about ten percent of those believed incarcerated. The applause that followed was half-hearted at best. All were waiting to see what Ortega would say about peace talks.

"We are going to negotiate a cease-fire through an intermediary," he finally declared.

Demonstrators were thunderstruck. The thousand-times-repeated promise never to negotiate with contras was being abruptly broken. When the rally ended, people drifted away in confused silence.

The next day Ortega met for forty minutes with Cardinal Obando. When the meeting ended, he announced that the Cardinal would serve as intermediary between Sandinista and contra leaders, an assignment he described as "transcendently important for peace in our country." Obando said nothing, but in his homily the following Sunday, he warned both sides that he was not prepared for lengthy negotiations.

"If they bring irrational proposals, that means the mediation will take years, and during those years rivers of blood will flow in our country," he boomed. "We cannot play games while the blood of young Nicaraguans is flowing."

Ortega had taken a dramatic initiative, one that upset and angered many Sandinistas. The fact that he had been able to persuade the National Directorate to support him on such a major policy shift reflected his ever-growing individual power, which was essential to the success of the peace accord. As President Arias often pointed out, the accord was not a treaty among nations, since it had never been ratified by any legislative body, but rather a set of commitments accepted by five individuals. Ortega's ability to control his government encouraged Arias and other supporters of the peace process, because it reduced the possibility that the accord might be upset by more militant *comandantes.*

All the concessions that Ortega and his government made in the months following their acceptance of the peace accord were aimed at a single end: destroying the contras. Ortega had finally come to understand that he could not destroy them with guns and bombs. By accepting the Arias peace proposal, he was setting out on an uncharted new path. Sympathetic members of Congress, led by Senator Christopher Dodd and Speaker of the House Jim Wright, had told him that if he made political concessions to his opponents, Congress might vote against further aid to the contras. Now that he had taken their advice, he decided to fly to Washington to press his case.

The day before Ortega departed, one of his aides telephoned me and asked if I would like to come along on the plane. I immediately accepted. The next day, for the first and last time, I enjoyed a nonstop flight from Managua to Washington, courtesy of the Sandinista government.

Our plane was a jetliner on loan from Cubana airlines. The front section had been altered to provide a comfortable lounge where Ortega and Foreign Minister D'Escoto were seated. I shared the cavernous rear section with a handful of bodyguards and other aides, and members of an NBC television crew who were also aboard for an interview. The TV crew was invited forward soon after takeoff, and spent nearly an hour with Ortega. Soon after they emerged, I was summoned.

Journalists had been invited aboard the flight because Ortega had a point he wanted to make. The future of peace efforts in Nicaragua, he insisted, depended on the United States Congress, which at that moment was considering President Reagan's request for $270 million in new aid to the contras.

"If the $270 million is approved, all political space in Nicaragua would close immediately," Ortega warned. "The situation cannot stabilize until the war ends."

United States aviation authorities had denied Ortega's plane the right to fly over American territory, and so our route took us eastward across the Caribbean, and then north. The flight dragged on for hour after hour. I had asked Ortega all I needed to ask, but he invited me to stay and talk.

During dozens of interviews and other encounters over the years, we had exhausted most political topics. This time we talked about our backgrounds and home towns. When I mentioned that I had studied the history of the American revolution, he asked me to tell him something of how the revolution was fought and won. He listened intently to stories about the Minutemen, the Committees of Correspondence, the Boston massacre, the skirmishes at Lexington and Concord, and the hauling of cannon from Fort Ticonderoga to Dorchester Heights in 1776.

"Are any of those battlefields still preserved?" Ortega asked as we approached Washington. "Can people visit them?"

Foreign Minister D'Escoto, who had once lived in Massachusetts, was following our discussion, and he answered before I could speak.

"Definitely!" D'Escoto said. "They have parks where people can tour the battlefields. I've visited some of them myself."

"Maybe we'll have parks like that someday," Ortega reflected.

At Dulles Airport, our plane was directed to park on a distant runway. As we stepped into the raw Washington autumn, carloads of federal agents watched from a distance. Ortega sped away to begin a whirlwind round of meetings.

His most important target was House Speaker Jim Wright, who had emerged as the key congressional figure on matters relating to Nicaragua. Wright commanded the respect of many moderate Democrats in Congress, and Ortega was eager to persuade him that Nicaragua was taking genuine steps toward peace. In all of his meetings, and in appearances at the Organization of American States and the National Press Club, Ortega portrayed himself as open-minded and willing to compromise.

Although the Sandinistas had finally decided to negotiate with contra leaders, they were still avoiding the full implications of their decision. They insisted that the talks could not be held in Nicaragua, finally settling on the Dominican Republic as a neutral site. Their negotiator, deputy foreign minister Victor Hugo Tinoco, had strict instructions to discuss only matters relating to cease-fire, and not to respond to proposals for political reform in Nicaragua. And they announced that Tinoco would not sit face-to-face with contra negotiators. He would deal with them only through Cardinal Obando.

Under such conditions, progress was all but impossible. The parties arrived in the Dominican Republic as agreed. On the evening of December 3, Obando met with contra negotiators and presented a peace proposal of his own. It called for a truce during which the government would decree a general amnesty, lift remaining restrictions on press freedom, and end the state of emergency. The contras agreed in principle, and the next morning, Cardinal Obando called on Sandinista negotiators. As he had feared, they rejected his proposal out of hand. He did not hide his irritation.

"I would say we are at a dead point," he told reporters before returning to Managua. "I am going to talk directly to President Ortega to try to make him see that to accelerate these negotiations, there has to be direct dialogue between the parties in conflict."

One comment Cardinal Obando made at his news conference rang in my ears for a long time afterward. When a reporter asked him why he saw such urgency in the talks, he replied simply, "Fifty young Nicaraguans are dying every day."

By the end of 1987, I had been living in Nicaragua for four years, and had seen enough human blood to last a lifetime. Like the nation itself, I was surrounded and enveloped by tragedy. Almost everyone I met was mourning the loss of a son or brother or close friend. In much of the countryside, people lived not only in misery but in constant fear that violence would explode without warning and shatter what was left of their wretched lives. Political leaders had pushed Nicaragua to war against itself, and as they bickered over procedural details, their nation was bleeding horribly.

In January 1988 the five Central American presidents met again, this time in Costa Rica. After their summit, President Ortega announced that his government would, as required by the peace accord, lift the state of emergency that had been in effect for nearly six years. But that same day, as if to show Nicaraguans that the announcement was not to be taken too seriously, Sandinista police arrested and briefly jailed eleven opposition leaders, charging them with having been in contact with contras. Later that week, rock-throwing Sandinista demonstrators attacked an opposition meeting in Managua. I happened to be there, and had to use a folding chair as a shield against rocks that rained down around me.

On February 3, in a historic vote, the House of Representatives rejected further aid to the contras. Rather than seize on the vote as a point of departure for new concessions, Ortega reacted as if he had won a victory and was now free to crack down. His negotiators at the "national dialogue" among political parties rejected virtually every proposal for political reform. At a new round of talks with contra negotiators in Guatemala in mid-February, the Sandinistas offered nothing new. Cardinal Obando, angered by Sandinista intransigence, abruptly adjourned the Guatemala talks only hours after they began. "The one who has power feels obligated to repress others in order to conserve it," he lamented.

The National Assembly opened its 1988 session on February 21, and President Ortega used the occasion to lash out at his critics once again. Those who were demanding political concessions at such a delicate moment, he asserted, were "seeking to blackmail the government of Nicaragua."

"This is called treason," Ortega told the Assembly. "Now is not the time to be taking our country's situation lightly."

Many non-Sandinista legislators had boycotted the inaugural session to protest the Sandinistas' hard line. One of them was Mauricio Díaz, who had supported the Sandinistas during their early years in power and who had been chosen by President Ortega to sit on the National Reconciliation Commission. Díaz watched Ortega's speech on television, and when I visited him later in the day, he was in despair.

"If the government keeps acting this way," he told me, "ultimately all of us will have no alternative but to become contras."

HAVING lived among Nicaraguans during such a searing period of their history, and having seen so much tragedy and death, reporters posted in Managua could not help but be emotionally involved in the drama unfolding around them. Many of us found the first months of 1988 the worst period of our assignments there. Hopes for peace seemed to be slipping away, and the prospect ahead was for more war and more repression. In six years, more than thirty thousand Nicaraguans had died violently. Foreigners who witnessed the carnage could not help but ask ourselves how many more years of upheaval, and how many more deaths, would be necessary before Nicaraguans would come to their senses.

One day I visited the Velez Paiz Hospital in Managua, which like every health care facility in Nicaragua was filthy, woefully understaffed, and lacking even the most basic medical supplies. Awful screams echoed through the corridors, and I followed them. Soon I found myself in the ward where wounded and maimed children were attended.

Alfredo Orozco, ten years old, and his brother Bayardo, who was five, were screaming the loudest. As their father, a Sumo Indian, sat helplessly between them, the two children writhed in their cots, crying out continuously in a combination of pain and delirium. The father told me his sons had been playing near their home in a remote village when they uncovered a buried land mine. Both of their small bodies were covered with fresh scars and deep burns, and doctors said they might never see again.

In another ward I met Harold Rosales, thirteen years old, who told me he spent his days reading and rereading a comic book of Bible stories he had found. Harold had a shoulder wound that seemed to be healing, but when I inquired about it, he pulled aside his sheet to show the real damage. Most of his right thigh had been torn away, and his leg looked as though it might require amputation.

"My brother is in the military service," Harold told me. "He didn't have the safety on his rifle, and it went off in the house."

I stayed in the children's ward as long as I could bear it. Each young patient had a more heart-rending story than the one before. One of them, Casimiro Pérez, who was twelve and slept with a stuffed animal given to him by a Canadian visitor, smiled through a face disfigured by shrapnel. Another, Josefa Gutierrez, sat in a wheelchair and stared into space.

Josefa, the stump of her right leg wrapped in gauze, told me she had been walking by an electric plant near the city of Jinotega when a mine blew her leg off. As I struggled to maintain my composure, she told me she knew she would never walk again. She seemed not resigned, not enraged, but simply disoriented and overwhelmed.

A couple of days later I found myself covering the aftermath of a contra attack near Matagalpa. I arrived at the scene less than twelve hours after the shooting stopped. Bodies of six people, naked and stiff, were laid out on a grassy hillside. Four were members of a single family: mother, father, son, and daughter. Several nearby shacks lay in ruins. For years I had been seeing horrific scenes like this, and on that morning I began to think that I had seen enough.

A week after those episodes, before I had fully regained my equilibrium, I heard news that a contra land mine had exploded beneath a bus near Quilalí, twenty-five miles from the Honduran border. Guillermo and I had driven many times over the spot where the mine exploded, and might as easily have been victims as those aboard the destroyed bus. As we rode toward Quilalí I tried to put that thought out of my mind, but it was not easy.

A mass funeral was underway when we arrived in Quilalí at midday. Seventeen people had been killed in the mine explosion. The victims were ten men, two women, and five children.

"These are seventeen new victims of the criminal policy of the American administration," a local Sandinista official, Carlos Gusen, told a hushed crowd gathered in the central plaza. "Those who kill innocent people do not want peace!"

As I watched from a distance, stoic mothers approached the open coffins for final views of their sons. Men wearing cowboy hats gently led them away, toward the cemetery.

In an outlying part of town, at the end of a muddy road where pigs and children played together, I found a more private funeral underway. Aunts, uncles, and cousins were sitting around a rough-hewn table where lay the tiny corpse of a baby named Juan Carlos Peralta. He had been carried aboard the bus by his father, who died in the explosion, and his mother, who was seriously wounded. Now, at four months of age, Juan Carlos Peralta had become the youngest victim of Nicaragua's war. His body was swaddled in a white shawl. Flowers had been arranged around the corpse, and a single candle burned at his feet.

On the way home from Quilalí that evening, I decided to ask for a week of vacation. I cabled editors in New York with my request, and the next day received a negative reply. Editors did not think this was a good moment for me to be off duty.

I tried to tell myself that I could endure a bit more, but there was still a year remaining on my agreed-upon tour of duty, and I began to wonder if I would make it. It had become more and more difficult, and ultimately impossible, to shut out the horror around me. Even my sleeping hours were filled with images of dead bodies and sobbing peasants. Another year of this, I feared, might be too much.

Besides the emotional toll the war took on me and other correspondents, the physical risks began to seem greater as time passed. I had been exposed to my share of danger in Nicaragua, but I had always felt that fortune was with me. Now I began to fear otherwise. Runs of luck always end sometime, and I sensed that I had taken enough chances.

One day in February my next-door neighbor, free-lance reporter Mary Speck, returned home with a harrowing tale of how she and a photographer traveling near Quilalí had been ambushed by contras. Their jeep was raked with automatic weapons fire, and they managed to jump to safety just before it was hit by a rocket-propelled grenade. I had traveled those roads too many times, flown too often over war zones in military helicopters. To continue for much longer would be to tempt fate.

As fighting and killing continued apace during those first months of 1988, Sandinista rhetoric became angrier. President Ortega announced new wage and price controls, and warned that vendors who refused to accept them would be arrested. Police swept through marketplaces confiscating merchandise said to be overpriced, and smashed into "clandestine warehouses" used by unlicensed vendors. Nicaraguans, who never became accustomed to such controls, reacted angrily, launching a wave of wildcat strikes in Managua and other cities.

Sensing that political developments were escaping from their control, Sandinista leaders decided to take the offensive. One morning in early March, they sent a squad of thugs to break up a meeting in Managua where several hundred striking union members were discussing ways to coordinate their protests. That afternoon, truckloads of workers from state-owned factories arrived at *La Prensa,* shouting slogans and throwing rocks. A prominent Sandinista union organizer, Damaso Vargas, gave a fiery speech warning that those who joined labor protests would lose their jobs and be replaced by "others who want to work and are also ready to defend the revolution." A few days later, when friends and relatives of prisoners staged a march through Masaya, gangs of young Sandinistas attacked them and sent them running. The *comandantes* seemed to be abandoning their commitment, enshrined in the peace accord, to create "the conditions inherent in any democracy."

Cardinal Obando, still officially recognized as the mediator between Sandinistas and contras, was sorely distressed at the unravelling of peace efforts. To break the deadlock, he proposed that the government fix a date by which it would accept "unrestricted freedom of expression" and decree "total and unconditional amnesty." This suggestion was so radical that the Sandinistas not only rejected it, but announced that they would no longer accept Cardinal Obando as a mediator.

Dismissing the cardinal was a shocking move, and some feared it marked the death knell for the peace process. But as President Ortega announced it, he also made a new offer. If contras were still interested in talking, Ortega said, he was willing to do so without an intermediary. Furthermore, he said, he was now prepared to name his brother Humberto, the Minister of Defense, as chief Sandinista negotiator. He even said the talks could be held in Nicaragua, and suggested the village of Sapoá, on the Costa Rican border.

In mid-March, Sandinista troops launched a sweep through a remote section of the Nicaragua-Honduras border, north of San José de Bocay. A community of contras and their families had been living in an 85-square-mile area along the Coco River, and the Sandinistas had been sent to clear them out. It was a major operation, involving heavy bombing and large infantry forces. The United States tried to portray it as another Sandinista "invasion" of Honduras, but Honduran authorities reported that conditions on their side of the border were normal.

After much fighting, the contras were forced to retreat across the Coco River, back to their camps in Honduras. The Sandinistas were anxious to show off their victory, and invited a handful of reporters and photographers to travel to the scene aboard an army helicopter. On the morning of March 18, we gathered at dawn at the military airfield in Managua and piled aboard a Soviet-made copter.

It was a long ride to the border. The roar of the engine and the constant vibrations induced several passengers to nausea. After an hour in the air, our pilot brought the copter down to treetop level, and accelerated to top speed. This was a maneuver designed to make it harder for contras with anti-aircraft weapons to hit us, but I never found it encouraging. It meant the pilot was acknowledging danger below.

The copter landed in a clearing, and as soon as we climbed off, it sped away toward safety. Soldiers escorted us through the overgrowth to a rustic campsite. There a Sandinista officer, Lieutenant Colonel Javier Carrión, briefed us on the just-concluded operation.

"We have retaken a portion of our territory that was occupied by mercenaries," he told us.

When the briefing was over, journalists were free to wander until the copter returned. We were in one of the most remote and inaccessible parts of Central America. Impenetrable walls of green stretched for miles in every direction. Ahead of us flowed the Coco, not as wide as in other sections but still a formidable natural boundary.

In the overgrowth I found empty ration cans, spent cartridges, and other residue of war. Under one tree, I came across a heavy plastic pouch full of 7.62 millimeter bullets, the kind used in many automatic rifles. On an impulse I decided to take the pouch home as a souvenir, and dropped it into the overnight bag slung over my shoulder.

Eventually we found our way down to the sandy river shore. Television crews were filming the scene, and the rest of us talked lazily among ourselves, wondering when our copter would return. Then, very faintly, we began to hear the faraway buzz of an approaching aircraft. But it was not coming from inside Nicaragua. It was coming from Honduras.

For about thirty seconds, we scanned the sky as the drone grew louder. Finally we could make out the silhouette of a plane coming in our direction. I doubted it could be a civilian airliner, since we were far from any safe air corridor. As we watched, the plane grew larger, and seemed to dip toward us. It passed almost directly above, and we heard a loud whistle followed by a tremendous, ear-splitting explosion. Sand and rock was blasted high into the sky, and I could feel the ground shake below me.

We dashed wildly away from the river bank and dove for cover. The plane made a second pass, and I saw a bomb land on the Honduran shore of the river, less than a hundred yards from where we were cowering. Again the earth shook violently at the impact.

The planes obviously belonged to some anti-Sandinista force, and as I lay waiting for the next bombing pass, I was struck with a terrifying thought. Perhaps, I imagined, someone had decided to punish the Sandinistas for expelling contras from this area. Perhaps they were going to lay waste to it with carpet bombing. Seconds passed excruciatingly slowly, but there were no more explosions. Overhead, the plane circled a couple of times and then flew off.

A few minutes later, our helicopter appeared. As it descended, soldiers shouted for us to run from our hiding places toward the clearing. We were desperate to escape, and all ran as fast as we could. The copter hovered above the ground, and we had to fight the wind churned up by its powerful rotors. The moment the last of us was aboard, the pilot pulled up and away.

I found myself strapped in next to Maria Morrison, a photographer for *Agence France-Presse*. Maria had come on this outing even though she had a four-month-old baby in Managua, expecting only a placid stroll through the countryside. Now she was sweating and shaking.

"I can't be doing this any more," I heard her say. "I'm a mother now. I can't be doing this."

The bombs, dropped from what later turned out to be a Honduran Air Force plane, had been a warning to the Sandinistas to stay on their side of the river. Probably the pilot had no idea there were civilians below. It had been another close call, too close.

DURING the early days of March, Sandinista and contra leaders exchanged a series of messages by telefax. Soon it became clear that the Sandinista offer of direct peace talks was serious. The *comandantes* were still snarling at their critics, and their police agents were still arresting protesters. But slowly, at first in private and then increasingly in public, some of them began to acknowledge that Nicaraguans needed a more open political system.

"There is a reality in our country, and it is that certain forms of thought, even thought from the Somoza period, have not disappeared," President Ortega conceded in one speech. "There are people who defend different economic systems, different ideologies, and social policies. There is even a school of thought that favors submission to imperialism. There are those who oppose our mixed economy and favor a return to private capitalism. These schools of thought exist, whether or not they are expressed. They cannot be eliminated by decree. This is a reality."

Such statements were a far cry from the venomous discourse that had dominated Nicaraguan politics for years. They seemed designed to reassure the contras that it would be worth their while to attend talks in Sapoá. Contra leaders were at first uncertain how to respond, but one evening the voice of the best-known contra, Adolfo Calero, came crackling over the clandestine contra radio frequency. The United States Congress, he said, had dealt the contras a crippling blow, and had left them no choice but to bargain.

"We are ready to go to Sapoá for the meeting President Ortega has proposed," Calero announced. "The cutoff of aid to the Nicaraguan resistance is affecting us more each day . . . In the long run the cutoff could be fatal."

The peace talks were set to begin in Sapoá on Monday, March 21, 1988. Guillermo and I left Managua early that morning, but not early enough. Crowds of Sandinista demonstrators had been up all night, clogging the highway south to Sapoá. Ostensibly they were showing support for Humberto Ortega and the other government negotiators, but many had still not reconciled themselves to the idea of peace talks. Near Masaya, one group gathered under a banner that read, "We Demand Total Surrender of the Contras—Nothing Less!" Further along the road, others had hung a large sign warning, "Contras: Give Up or We Destroy You."

We were running late as we approached Rivas, the last big town on the road to Sapoá. Hundreds of demonstrators crowded the highway there, and I began to worry that I might miss the opening of the talks. People were in a surly mood, and wouldn't move out of our way. Finally Guillermo became exasperated.

"If this man doesn't get through, the talks can't begin!" he shouted authoritatively.

"Better that they don't begin!" shot back several demonstrators.

Sandinista leaders had so often promised never to negotiate with contras that the promise had become a central article of Sandinista faith. Tomás Borge had once sworn that the sun would rise in the west and set in the east, and that rivers would begin running upstream, before Sandinistas would talk peace with contras. The abrupt abandonment of that commitment opened new hopes for peace, and thus was welcomed by many Nicaraguans. But in Sandinista ranks it sparked confusion and bewilderment.

When we arrived at Sapoá after three hours on the road, contra negotiators were overdue. They were based at a hotel in the Costa Rican town of Liberia, about fifty miles from the border, and their bus was expected to arrive at any moment. More than two hundred journalists and photographers were waiting, flown in from all over the world. Also on hand was a delegation of American activists, among them the singer Kris Kristofferson, who had come to show support for the Sandinistas. Security agents prevented anyone else from approaching.

Journalists crowded around the contras' bus when it finally appeared. It was the first time in years that any contra leader had set foot inside Nicaragua, and we all wanted to witness the moment. One of the more emotional Sandinista reporters, Emigdio Suárez, could not contain his emotion.

"*Ustedes son Guardia!*" he began screaming at the arriving contras. You are Guardsmen!

Adolfo Calero, the chief contra negotiator, was unruffled by the disturbance. Only one contra, a small, dapper-looking older man who I did not recognize, took the bait.

"You Communists have destroyed Nicaragua!" he shouted back at Suárez.

"Murderers!" Suárez shrieked. "You take blood money from the Americans! Isn't it true that Americans were killers in Vietnam and killers in Grenada?"

"Nicaragua has gone a generation backward under the Sandinista government!" came the shouted reply.

The two antagonists were finally separated, and I asked one of my Nicaraguan colleagues who the excitable contra was. I was astonished to learn that he was Fernando Agüero, a onetime anti-Somoza leader who had betrayed his followers in 1967 by signing a political pact with the dictatorship. He still had a small coterie of followers in Miami, and with their help he had won a spot on the contra negotiating team. His voice was an echo from an almost prehistoric era of Nicaraguan politics.

There was no town at Sapoá, only a cluster of buildings used by customs and immigration authorities. Arriving contras were escorted into a low wooden building that had once been a cafeteria. There they sat cloistered with Sandinista negotiators for hour after hour, while the press corps waited in a reserved area nearby. At lunchtime that first day, a Sandinista spokesman emerged to tell us that the warring parties had agreed to observe a cease-fire during their three days of talks. That was the only news.

Sandinista and contra leaders had been bitterly denouncing each other for years in the most vitriolic terms, and the thought of them sitting around a table and talking peace was difficult to assimilate. Reporters were not allowed into the salon where talks were underway, but a handful of photographers were briefly admitted, and they told us the atmosphere seemed quite civil. When the first day of talks ended, leaders of the two delegations told us they were getting along fine.

"I did not feel any antagonism," Adolfo Calero said before heading back to his hotel in Costa Rica.

"We had no great problems facing them," agreed Humberto Ortega, who emerged a few minutes later.

The sun was setting as Guillermo and I drove off. Because there were no accomodations at Sapoá, reporters scattered at the end of the day. I had rented a room in a private home at the seaside resort of San Juan del Sur, twenty-five miles away.

I typed my story onto a laptop computer as we bounced along the road, and when we arrived at San Juan del Sur I was ready to file. Placing a call from there to New York was not easy, and involved Guillermo running over to the local telephone office and negotiating with the sole operator on duty. It was dangerously close to my deadline when I was finally connected.

After dictating my story, I gazed out my window at the beckoning Pacific. I changed into bathing trunks, jogged a mile or two down the beach, and then dove into the warm surf. Later Guillermo and I found a restaurant that served succulent red snapper.

The second day of talks, so far as reporters could tell, went much like the first. None of us dared to guess what was happening inside, but there were signs of progress. The Sandinistas, we were told, had accepted the principle that they had to make political concessions if they wanted to end the war. That was a vital step. When Calero emerged from the sesssion, he sounded optimistic.

"There are points of coincidence," he said. "I think it's been a fruitful day. Tomorrow could be even better."

For the first time it began to seem possible that a treaty might be signed. I wanted to know more about what was going on in the negotiating sessions. Humberto Ortega and other Sandinista negotiators were cloistered at a house in San Juan del Sur, discussing strategy with President Daniel Ortega and Vice President Sergio Ramírez, and I knew I would not be welcome there. So I decided to follow the contras in my jeep—Guillermo would not be allowed to cross the border—and try to interview them at their hotel in Costa Rica.

Las Espuelas, where contra leaders were staying, was a sprawling, ranch-style hotel by the side of a main highway. It was late in the evening when I arrived. From the lobby I telephoned Alfredo César, a former Sandinista official who had emerged as one of the brightest and most ambitious contra leaders. He invited me to his room, which was at the end of a long corridor where bodyguards sat silently outside most doors.

"How are the talks going?" I asked.

"They're going well," César replied. "We've narrowed the issues quite a bit. We're ready to agree to a cease-fire if the Sandinistas will give us a little democracy."

"That sounds great," I said. "Does it mean the war is over?"

"It could be," César said slowly. His wife brought him a glass of scotch, and after taking a sip he repeated softly, "It could be."

I stood silent for a moment, absorbing what César had said. The prospect that the bloodshed might soon end was jarring. Images of mothers crying over open coffins flashed through my mind. I asked Mrs. César to pour me a drink, and she did. Still not quite believing what seemed to be happening, I held my glass high and toasted peace.

"Que la paz sea en nuestra sufrida Nicaragua," I said. César smiled, lifted his glass and replied, *"La paz!"*

The final day of the talks was Wednesday, March 23. I left the hotel shortly after dawn. When I arrived at the border, immigration officers had not yet shown up for work. They appeared an hour later, at eight o'clock, and waved me across.

At Sapoá I joined the large and restless crowd of reporters. Contra negotiators arrived on schedule and then disappeared into the conference center. We settled into a third hot and boring day, reading, dozing, playing cards, and otherwise amusing ourselves as we waited. Someone produced a bottle of bourbon. Sandinista agents who maintained dossiers on journalists circulated through the crowd, watching and listening.

The talks were set to end at sundown, but they did not. My first deadline was approaching, and I filed a story saying simply that talks were continuing amid signs of progress. Darkness fell, and the stifling heat broke. There was still no clue to what was happening inside.

Shortly before ten o'clock, Sandinista spokesman Manuel Espinoza appeared. With him were a handful of workmen carrying furniture. They set up a long table and arranged three wooden chairs behind it. Then, without saying a word to us, they left.

It was a promising development, we agreed. Perhaps one chair was for Humberto Ortega, another for Adolfo Calero, and the third for Cardinal Obando, who was serving as one of two official witnesses to the talks. We gathered expectantly before the raised stage.

An hour went by without any further activity. Then Espinoza appeared again, and added two more chairs. We yelled for an explanation, but he waved us off. Five chairs instead of three—what could it mean?

It was nearly midnight when Espinoza showed up for a third time. As we watched uncomprehending, his workmen cleared all the furniture from the stage, and then brought out two small tables and two wicker-seated chairs.

Two chairs could be a good sign, presuming they were for Ortega and Calero.

But they could also be, as some pessimists suggested, seats for the two witnesses, Cardinal Obando and OAS Secretary General João Baena Soares, who might be called upon to announce the talks' failure. No one knew what to think.

Our speculation was suddenly hushed when we saw movement from inside. Television lights flashed on, and journalists scurried to our places. The entire negotiating teams from both sides were walking toward us. With them was Daniel Ortega. Immediately we guessed that there had been a breakthrough, and a surge of excitement crackled through the crowd.

At this moment, my first thought was not of history but of my newspaper deadline. It was midnight, which made it two o'clock in New York. The final deadline for the last edition of the *Times* was 2:45.

There were only eight telephones at Sapoá. As soon as I comprehended what was happening, I dashed to one of them and asked the operator to connect me to the *Times* foreign desk. It took ten minutes for her to place the call, and while I waited, I watched an unbelievable spectacle. The senior Sandinista leaders, Daniel and Humberto Ortega, accompanied by their aides, filed in and stood before us. Beside them stood Adolfo Calero, Alfredo César, and other contra leaders. All snapped to attention as the recorded strains of the national anthem boomed from a loudspeaker.

> Save you, Nicaragua! On your soil
> The sound of the cannon echoes no more;
> And the blood of brothers no longer stains
> Your glorious blue and white banner.

Jaws dropped and eyes opened wide in amazement as Sandinista and contra leaders sang the anthem together. Nicaraguan journalists seemed especially stunned. It was a sight many had never imagined.

As João Baena Soares, the OAS Secretary General, stepped to the microphone to read the text of the peace agreement, I was told that my call to New York had been connected. I grabbed the phone and breathlessly explained to a night editor what was happening. He agreed to take down a story as I dictated it.

The rest of the correspondents at Sapoá, most of whom had deadlines different from mine, were listening carefully and taking notes as Baena read the treaty. But I was on the phone, trying to hear Baena while composing and dictating a news story. After each new clause I shouted another sentence into the receiver, rushing to finish so I could hear the next clause. Somehow we finished in time, and the late edition of the *Times* carried the news at the top of the front page.

Other reporters were by now clamoring for telephones, and I surrendered mine to Tifani Roberts of NBC. Baena had finished reading the agreement, and leaders of the two sides were making statements. As Daniel Ortega stepped to the microphone, a gust of wind blew through his hair.

"Brother Nicaraguans, I speak to you as constitutional president of the nation of Sandino and Darío," he said. "We have reached an agreement based on the spirit of peace that is within all Nicaraguans, and we are determined to bury the weapons of war and raise the olive branch of peace."

Adolfo Calero, who had sung the national anthem more loudly than anyone, spoke next.

"We have reached a sincere and viable agreement," Calero began. "We cannot say that this has been a victory for either side, but we can say that it has created prospects of peace and freedom for the Nicaraguan people . . . I hope and believe that today we have taken the first real step toward ending this fratricidal war. We cannot continue killing each other, because we are children of the same nation, children of the same mother."

Representatives of the two sides then stepped forward to sign their peace agreement. It was probably too much to expect them to embrace, and not so much as a handshake was exchanged publicly. Yet none of the countless Nicaraguans who were following live television and radio broadcasts from Sapoá could fail to grasp the ceremony's transcendent importance. It was an answer to every Nicaraguan's most fervent prayer, the sudden bursting of dawn after a long black night.

I found Guillermo in the crowd, and we sped off toward Managua. He had heard the news on radio, but like the rest of us could not quite believe that the war might be ending.

"They signed," he kept repeating. "I can't believe they signed."

As we drove, we listened to radio announcers repeating and analyzing the triumphant news. Many openly expressed their astonishment.

"This story comes straight from Ripley's Believe It or Not," said one. "Leaders of the two Nicaraguan armies that have spread so much misery across Nicaragua have now signed a cease-fire agreement. So much hatred, so much death and pain, has been put aside. Finally we can hope for peace again."

I slept for a few hours, and then soon after dawn began telephoning opposition leaders to ask their reactions. All were positive. The first one I reached, Virgilio Godoy, pronounced himself "very impressed," and the next, Mauricio Díaz, praised the *comandantes* for making "concessions that most of us political leaders thought they would never make." The pro-Sandinista newspaper *Nuevo Diario* carried a banner headline asking the question on every Nicaraguan's lips: "Is Peace Breaking Out?"

Under terms of the Sapoá agreement, the Sandinista government agreed to legalize all forms of peaceful dissent and guarantee "unrestricted freedom of expression"; to invite exiles to return home without fear of persecution; and to begin freeing anti-Sandinista prisoners being held in Nicaraguan jails, including former National Guardsmen. The contras made even more astonishing concessions. They accepted a formula aimed ultimately at their own disarmament, and agreed to stop receiving military aid from the United States or anyone else.

Both sides thus abandoned fundamental principles to which they had clung blindly during six years of war. The contras accepted the fact that they had no hope of military victory, and recognized the legitimacy of President Ortega's government. Sandinista leaders gave up on their Marxist dream, and agreed to allow Nicaragua to move toward Western-style democracy.

"No victors or vanquished emerged from this encounter," *La Prensa* said in an editorial. "For Nicaragua, it means a new beginning in the way we conduct politics. It has always been normal that political struggle take place on the battlefield. What is new is that now the adversaries prefer to resolve their difference through intelligence, persuasion, and reason. This frees us from the karma of the rifle, which has been a plague on our history."

Contra leaders admitted that they had been forced to the bargaining table by the congressional vote cutting off their American aid. The Sandinistas' motives were more complex. Nicaragua's economy had collapsed. Most Western countries had cut or sharply curtailed their aid programs, and the Soviet Union was becoming less generous. As long as war continued, the Sandinistas faced only the prospect of ruling an unhappy and rebellious people.

Three days after the Sapoá accord was signed, Guillermo and I drove northward to a Sandinista army base near the Honduran border. Several hundred draftees who had completed their two-year hitches were to be mustered out of the service, and I wanted to hear their reactions to the news from Sapoá. Every one I talked to was thrilled. Some admitted to residual anger at the contras, but all believed they could overcome it.

"Hearing about the cease-fire was very emotional," an eighteen-year-old soldier named Jorge Arturo Pantos told me. "I'm sure the contras feel the same way. We've lost friends and they've lost friends. We're all Nicaraguans. We all have a right to live."

The next day, Palm Sunday, reporters were called to a prison near Managua to witness the release of the first one hundred anti-Sandinista prisoners. Tomás Borge made a brief speech describing the decision to free prisoners as "dramatic and painful," and then he pronounced the lucky one hundred free.

All of the released prisoners had been arrested for anti-Sandinista activity during the 1980s. A few were political activists like Juan de Dios Aguinaga, a member of the Independent Liberal party, who had spent forty months in jail for having urged people not to vote in the 1984 election. One was a contra pilot captured after his plane was shot down, and another was a physician who had been convicted of plotting to assassinate Sandinista leaders. The rest were peasants accused of collaborating with contras.

The sight of these prisoners walking through a wire gate to freedom and being embraced by sobbing relatives symbolized how much had suddenly changed in Nicaragua. Many details still remained to be negotiated, and no one underestimated the obstacles ahead. Yet the cycle of war and repression had been broken. I felt exhilarated, and when I visited Costa Rica a few weeks later to interview Oscar Arias, I began by congratulating him. He stared at me from behind his dark oak desk.

"Admit it," he demanded with a scowl, pointing his index finger at me. "You didn't think this would happen. You were cynical."

"I guess I was," I shrugged. "A lot of people were."

"Let me explain something to you," he said, adopting his professorial tone. "Peace is not something you reach or don't reach. Peace is a process. It's an outlook, a way to live. You can never say that peace is lost, or that hopes for peace are lost. Peace is always waiting for us. Dialogue is the only way to resolve problems. Sooner or later, even Nicaraguans recognize that."

22

ENDINGS

THE GUNS of Nicaragua finally fell silent following the agreement at Sapoá. After years of killing each other, Nicaraguans dared to hope that they could begin resolving their disputes peacefully. A nation torn by war slowly stopped bleeding.

One morning a few weeks after the agreement was signed, I traveled north to the provincial capital of Estelí. War had raged unceasingly in the surrounding hills, and funerals had been routine events there. But a few weeks of peace, I found, had completely changed people's mood.

"Things have been awful here, but it's all different now," a middle-aged woman named Maria Degama told me from behind the counter of her general store. "For the first time I see a real hope for peace. It may take a while, but it's going to happen. The war has gone on for too long."

It had been a very long time since I had heard a Nicaraguan say anything like that. As I walked through town, I met peasants from outlying villages who told me they were returning to farms they had not tilled for years. They said that bulldozers and tractors were now being used in areas where, in the past, contras had burned such equipment on sight.

The highlight of my visit to Estelí was a stop at the public hospital. Dr.

Marlon Amador told me that for the first time since he had been named director of the hospital in 1985, he was not treating a single war victim.

"The cease-fire has made all the difference in our work," Dr. Amador told me as we walked through the wards. "Right now we have no patients who have been shot, no victims of land mines, nobody with shrapnel wounds. All our beds are occupied by civilians who have normal illnesses or who have suffered trauma not related to fighting."

The war's end, however, did nothing to resolve Nicaragua's all-encompassing economic crisis. By 1988, the signs of devastation were everywhere. Massive currency devaluations, coupled with selective freeing of wages and prices, had jolted the economy and left one-third of the work force unemployed. Inflation reached the numbing rate of thirty thousand percent annually. Managua and other cities were swept by waves of violent crime, much of it perpetrated by gangs of hungry youths. At the city's fetid garbage dumps, poor people scavenged like rats for scraps of food. When the health ministry surveyed 2,829 randomly selected schoolchildren, it found seventy-five percent of them suffering from malnutrition.

One day I visited La Mascota, the main children's hospital in Managua. Several wards were full of acutely malnourished infants, many of them suffering from cases of diarrhea that would soon prove fatal. Wide-eyed and listless, with only thin layers of skin covering their tiny bones, they looked like victims of an African famine.

"They live in filth, they have no clean water, and they eat out of garbage dumps," the hospital's director, Dr. Fernando Silva, told me when I stopped by his office. "We can't even estimate how many get sick and die without coming to the hospital."

The depth to which Nicaragua had fallen was reflected pathetically when a rumor swept through the northern hills that the Canadian government was sending a passenger vessel to Corinto, and that anyone who wanted to emigrate to Canada would be welcome aboard. Whole families, in some cases even whole villages, packed their miserable belongings into burlap sacks and made their way to Corinto. There they camped for days, refusing to believe that no Canadian ship was coming. When the truth finally sunk in, they had no choice but to return, defeated once again, to the homes they had so eagerly sought to abandon.

In April 1988, soon after that sad episode, shock waves spread through political circles when the mayor of Managua, Moisés Hassan, was removed from his post after announcing that he was quitting the Sandinista Front. Hassan had been a Sandinista for most of his adult life, and was one of the five members of the first revolutionary junta. Not since the defection of Edén Pastora had such a senior figure decided to abandon the Sandinista cause.

I visited Hassan soon after learning of his startling decision. His home was full of flowering plants, and he sat beneath one as we spoke. The Sandinistas, he told me, had become ideological dogmatists and had lost touch with the Nicaraguan people.

"When you are part of the power elite, there's a great temptation to begin relating only to other members of the elite," he said. "Too many groups within the Sandinista Front have become isolated, cut off from the daily lives of normal people. You begin to believe everything is the way you would like it to be."

Sandinista leaders, however, could not help but recognize the overwhelming crisis confronting their country. As early as the mid-1980s they had begun abandoning their misguided economic policies, lifting many government controls on commerce and agriculture. But their measures were half-hearted, and opposition political parties gained strength as the economy collapsed. After the Sapoá treaty was signed, emboldened anti-Sandinista leaders convoked rallies in several provincial capitals. The turnouts were surprisingly large. For the first time, the *comandantes* faced the prospect of broad-based political opposition from people with empty stomachs.

Reflecting the growing discontent, unionized workers began walking off their jobs in the first months of 1988, among them several thousand construction workers. The construction workers' strike was laden with symbolism. Their union was one of the oldest and most combative labor organizations in Nicaragua, and was widely admired for its courageous defiance of the Somoza dictatorship.

Striking construction workers gathered each day at their union hall in Managua. During one of my visits there in April, a month after the Sapoá treaty was signed, I met a laborer who told me that the government had fixed his salary at twenty-six córdobas per day, which on the black market was then the equivalent of about forty cents. A cheap lunch cost thirty córdobas, a pack of filter cigarettes was thirty-nine, and an inexpensive pair of shoes sold for at least four hundred.

To maintain morale, union leaders gave speeches to their striking brethren several times each day. They spoke before a banner reading, "We Prefer to Die of Hunger Fighting For Dignity Than to Die Working Like Slaves." One day when I walked into the hall, a union official named Roberto Moreno was speaking.

"The Sandinistas believe that all workers should belong to a single federation and follow orders from above," he told a crowd of about two hundred strikers. "That does not fit the reality of Nicaragua. We are in a terrible political, social, and economic crisis. They should be negotiating with us, not fighting us, because without national unity Nicaragua is not going to be able to resolve this giant crisis we are facing."

Tensions rose as the strike continued, and President Ortega began denouncing strikers as "false revolutionaries" and "servile lackeys of the bourgeoisie and American imperialism." He insisted that they drop their demands for better wages, which he said would only fuel inflation. When they refused, he accused them of having "no class consciousness."

At the end of April, thirty-eight strikers began a fast inside the union hall. They were seeking to focus attention on their plight, and they succeeded. Crowds began to gather outside to show support, and police reacted harshly. They cordoned off the building, refusing to allow anyone to approach and dragging off those who ventured too close. I was among them. As I tried to peer into the union hall from across the street one day, I was grabbed by two young officers and pulled roughly away. I avoided arrest by showing my press credentials, but was warned to be more obedient in the future.

The conflict soon turned ugly. Elite police agents in black berets and riot gear, accompanied by fierce-looking attack dogs, were posted in front of the union hall day and night. They cut the strikers' telephones, then their electricity, and then their water supply.

World attention began to focus on the rundown union hall. Television crews from as far away as Italy and Japan arrived to cover the strike. Finally Sandinista leaders recognized that they were being made to look very bad, and decided to negotiate a compromise. They agreed to free the more than thirty union members who had been arrested during the strike, and to open new wage negotiations. In exchange, the union called off its hunger strike. It was the angriest labor protest the Sandinistas had faced, and it left deep scars.

As the Sandinistas were dealing with unhappy construction workers and other protesters, they were also engaged in delicate peace talks with contra leaders. Under terms of the treaty signed at Sapoá in March, leaders of the warring factions were required to negotiate a permanent cease-fire and fix a timetable for political reforms. Not surprisingly, the negotiations proved quite difficult.

Four rounds of talks were held in Managua, but when the fourth round ended on June 9, no agreement had been reached. Contra leaders refused to order their troops to disarm until they had iron-clad guarantees of sweeping political reform. The Sandinistas were not prepared to offer any such concessions before a complete contra surrender.

"They should be grateful that we are not offering them the guillotine or the firing squad, which is what they deserve," President Ortega railed in a speech while the talks were underway.

Ortega's sharp words reflected a growing realization among Sandinista leaders that they were losing control of events. Economic conditions were disastrous and social tensions were rising. Among those most frustrated was Interior Minister Tomás Borge. He decided that the Nicaraguan press was becoming too negative, and imposed new censorship rules that included a ban on the phrase "economic crisis."

The Nicaraguan economist Francisco Mayorga was closely monitoring his country's decline, and one morning in June 1988, three months after the Sapoá peace treaty was signed, he accepted an invitation to meet with foreign correspondents. Mayorga, brisk and Yale-educated, was virtually the only non-Sandinista economist still working in Nicaragua. Over breakfast that morning, he gave us statistics that confirmed the dimensions of the catastrophe. The living standard of the average Nicaraguan, he showed us with charts and graphs, had fallen to less than half of what it had been forty years earlier. Since the Sandinista takeover, peasants had lost seventy-five percent of their purchasing power. In 1979 the average daily wage in the countryside was enough to buy thirty eggs, but now it bought just two.

"This economy has become a black hole," Mayorga told us sadly.

As more and more Nicaraguans reached the point of desperation, the flow of citizens seeking to leave the country grew into a flood. At the office where visas and passports were issued, lines often began forming before dawn. Doctors, farm administrators, and white-collar workers, including many who had once worked for the Sandinista government, led the parade out. By mid-1988 there were only 250 engineers left in the country, and the situation in other professions was equally acute.

Most of the Nicaraguans abandoning their homeland, however, were poor people. Those unable to obtain proper permits trekked overland into Honduras or Costa Rica, where they filled refugee camps to overflowing. Of a population that numbered about three million, perhaps three hundred thousand fled during the 1980s. Everyone had a friend or relative who had left.

Many of Nicaragua's leading radio commentators had begun to denounce the Sandinistas relentlessly. One day Borge summoned José Castillo Osejo, the country's best-known radio news director, to his office for a reprimand. He began by angrily lecturing Castillo, telling him that his broadcasts were inciting violence and insurrection. Then he started shouting, threw an ash tray and charged at his guest, punching him several times. Castillo, a former boxer, ducked away. Borge began hurling furniture at him, and at the commotion several aides burst in. Finally Borge calmed down. Castillo was allowed to leave. His face had been cut in several places, but he was not seriously hurt.

Sandinista frustration was fed by continued violations of the cease-fire. Most contras had retreated to their bases inside Honduras, but about fifteen hundred remained in Nicaragua. Every week or so a group of them clashed with Sandinista troops. One of these skirmishes took the life of Major Xavier Hidalgo, a top Sandinista counter-insurgency officer in Chontales. Hidalgo had been on the front line for years, and was an invaluable repository of strategic knowledge and experience. He had met with groups of contras several times in the weeks following the signing at Sapoá. One of the invitations he received turned out to be a trap. Apparently one contra unit could not resist the temptation to kill someone who had been a hated adversary for so long.

Into this volatile situation stepped a new American ambassador, Richard Melton, who arrived at the end of April to take up a post that had been left vacant for nearly a year. Unlike the three other Americans who had been ambassadors to the Sandinista government, Melton arrived in Managua bent on confrontation. He began inviting groups of opposition figures to dine with him at his official residence. At the end of these meals, he would deliver a brief speech unequivocally endorsing the anti-Sandinista cause. No one who heard him could have harbored any doubt about where the embassy now stood. It was no longer functioning as a listening post, but rather as part of the anti-Sandinista political movement.

Viewing Melton's attitude against the background of economic chaos and continuing contra attacks, the *comandantes* succumbed to panic. Whether they were acting to prevent an explosion of domestic protest, or out of fear that the expiring Reagan administration might launch a last-gasp invasion, or whether they were simply swept away by an impulse to repress, would later be much debated. Whatever the reason, during a week of rapid-fire action they lashed out against their critics with a vigor and enthusiasm they had not shown for years.

ONE day in early July 1988, the telephone rang in the office of Luis Humberto Guzmán, a leader of the center-left Popular Social Christian party. The caller was *Comandante* William Ramírez, a senior Sandinista leader who had been assigned to maintain contact with the Popular Social Christians.

"Some new repression is coming," the *comandante* warned Guzmán. "We've decided to crack down. Don't send your people to Nandaime. We're going to kick ass down there."

Opposition parties had convoked a rally for Sunday, July 10, in the farm town of Nandaime, and there had been signs the Sandinistas were preparing to disrupt it. They were in a combative mood, and Nandaime seemed an opportune place to draw a line in the dirt. It was the same town where Alfonso Robelo had tried to hold a protest demonstration seven years earlier, only to be thwarted by Sandinista violence.

During the first days of July, Sandinista news commentators began hinting that the Nandaime protest would not be allowed to proceed peacefully. Pro-government television and radio stations carried interviews with "patriotic youths" pledging to disrupt it.

"Remember, there was a time when we burned down a house to prevent reactionaries from taking over the streets of Nandaime," one angry Sandinista warned on television, referring to the torching of Robelo's headquarters in 1981. "This time we're ready to burn ten houses!"

I drove to Nandaime alone on the appointed day, guessing that the Sandinistas would not be so foolish as to unleash violence against protesters. The Sapoá agreement had ushered in an era of greater political freedom, and a serious act of repression at this moment could undermine all that had been so painstakingly achieved. I did not know that William Ramírez and other senior Sandinistas had been warning friends to stay away from Nandaime.

Soon after leaving Managua I came across two trucks and a bus, all filled with would-be protesters, pulled over to the roadside. A police officer was explaining that the vehicles could not proceed. Opposition organizers produced a copy of the government permit authorizing the Nandaime march, but the officer kept repeating that he could not let them pass.

"Every vehicle needs a permit from the transport ministry," he told them.

"Anyone has the right to use the roads!" shouted one disgusted passenger.

"Only if you have permission," the officer retorted.

He was obviously under orders. The orders did not require him to stop automobiles, however, and he made no effort to detain me. Half an hour later I reached the outskirts of Nandaime. I pulled my car off the road and walked toward the gathering crowd.

It took only a moment to see that police were preparing for something extraordinary. Previous protest marches had been permitted to proceed with minimal police presence, but this time hundreds of officers lined the streets. They seemed prepared for all-out war. Each carried an AK-47 assault rifle and extra ammunition clips. Some wore gas masks and bulletproof vests, which I had never seen in Nicaragua.

Police shouted at demonstrators as they gathered, and swung their nightsticks freely. Their attitude was hostile and aggressive, a marked contrast to the studied calm they usually displayed at such events. They had come to teach the opposition a lesson, to show that henceforth protesters would have to pay not only a political price for their defiance, but a personal, physical price as well.

More than five thousand protesters assembled that morning. None seemed intimidated by the show of police force. At a signal from their leaders, they began marching through the unpaved streets. They passed the birthplace of General José Dolores Estrada, hero of the war against William Walker, and the bust of Rubén Darío that adorns the central plaza. Authorities had forbidden them to stop in the plaza, so they doubled back toward the edge of town. They taunted police with rhythmic chants.

"*Qué quiere la gente? Que se vaya el Frente!*" they cried. What do people want? To be rid of the Sandinista Front!

And then, even more loudly: "*Dónde está el terror? En el Ministerio del Interior!*" Where is the terror? In the Interior Ministry!

I stood on the back of a flatbed truck and watched the crowds of marchers file past. They seemed confident and almost festive. Among them I saw my friend Emilio Álvarez Montalván, a vigorous seventy-year-old opthalmologist who had been one of Pedro Joaquín Chamorro's closest friends.

"*Buenas días, Doctor!*" I called out.

"*Hola, Stephen,* he replied with a wave. "Take a look at this! People aren't afraid any more. It means the Sandinistas' days are numbered!"

In front of a decaying wooden stadium once used for rodeos and horse shows, the marchers began assembling to hear their leaders speak. The first to take the microphone was the diminutive but passionate Conservative leader Myriam Argüello. As she began, police were shoving marchers at the rear of the column. They apparently had orders to escalate their provocations until there was a violent response.

Finally the inevitable happened. Argüello had been speaking less than five minutes when a scuffle broke out at the back of the crowd.

"Here comes the *turba!*" she yelled.

Marchers and police momentarily drew apart from each other, and marchers began throwing rocks and sticks. The police were perfectly disciplined. They stood motionless for about fifteen seconds, and then suddenly exploded in fury. With clubs flying, they charged into the crowd. After a minute or two they began firing tear gas, something Sandinista police had never done before.

It took only a few gas grenades to disrupt the rally, and the whole episode might have ended there. But police were not satisfied with that. They fired volley after volley of the grenades, and soon all Nandaime was under a paralyzing cloud. Protesters and bystanders alike ran through the streets trying to escape, many of them covering their eyes and screaming in pain. Police chased them across yards and fields, clubbing those they could catch.

Staggered by the gas, I made my way toward the edge of town. From a low bluff, I could see Sandinista police officers kicking and beating people. Never had they broken up a protest with such sustained violence.

Suddenly one officer looked my way and, to my horror, began charging at me, his rifle at the ready.

"*Periodista! Periodista!*" I shouted, holding my hands high. I'm a journalist!

He never broke his stride, and in a flash I realized he was not interested in my professional status. I turned to run, but it was too late. With tremendous force, the officer smashed his rifle butt between my shoulder blades. I felt a shock of pain, and then my knees buckled.

For a few moments I staggered forward, tear gas burning my eyes and the mud below me fading out of focus. My attacker, apparently satisfied by what he had done, had moved on to find other transgressors. His single blow had knocked me senseless.

I never was able to figure out how much time passed before I regained consciousness. Someone was calling my name. I was being carried across a beanfield by Adolfo Pastrán, a hefty opposition journalist and organizer. We circled the town to avoid police, and Adolfo helped me onto a half-full bus whose terrified driver was weaving his way through the mayhem in the direction of Managua.

It was past midday, and I began to worry about my newspaper deadline. I took out my notebook and painfully started writing my report in longhand, barely able to hold my pen. There were twenty-one dazed protesters aboard with me. Twelve showed cuts or bruises.

After an hour-long bus ride, I was dropped off a mile from home. I staggered the rest of the way, anxious not to miss my deadline. Once at home, I was able to telephone New York and file my story before collapsing into bed.

I awoke in time to watch the Sandinista news on television. Its correspondent in Nandaime reported that protesters had wantonly assaulted police officers there. Footage of police being pelted with rocks, and interviews with bandaged officers, conveyed an impression directly contrary to the truth.

More than thirty-five protesters were arrested that day, among them Myriam Argüello and several other opposition leaders. Only one of the organizers, Roger Guevara, a European-educated lawyer, managed to escape and make his way home to Managua. Two days later, State Security agents arrived at his home and presented his wife with a summons ordering him to surrender himself at El Chipote. He did, and was placed under arrest.

The outburst of police violence at Nandaime, it turned out, was just the first of several shocks the government was planning that week. On Monday morning the interior ministry ordered the Roman Catholic radio station off the air, charging that it had covered the protest inaccurately. Hours later *La Prensa* appeared, its front page covered with graphic photos of the police assault, and authorities ordered it shut for fifteen days as punishment. Then, late Monday afternoon, reporters learned that Ambassador Melton had been summoned to the foreign ministry.

I was about to leave for the ministry when my telephone rang. Tomás Borge was calling. He had received a protest from the *Times* about my treatment in Nandaime.

"Caramba, hombre, que te pasó?" Borge asked. What happened to you?

I recounted the unpleasant sequence of events. Borge listened with interest, and even asked a couple of questions about what I had seen in Nandaime, but was careful not to apologize. Before he could hang up, I asked him what was about to happen to Melton.

"Are you expelling him?" I guessed.

"Something like that," Borge replied.

Promptly at 5 P.M., Melton and his tight-lipped press aide arrived at the foreign ministry. They were ushered directly into Foreign Minister D'Escoto's office for a session that lasted less than five minutes. D'Escoto curtly told them that Melton and seven other United States diplomats were no longer welcome in Nicaragua, and were being expelled.

On his way out, Melton brushed by a knot of about twenty journalists without comment. Soon afterwards D'Escoto appeared. He was characteristically quotable.

"Mr. Melton said this was a strong measure," D'Escoto reported. "We told him it was nothing compared to the systematic policy of murder and terror that Mr. Reagan's government has carried out against Nicaragua."

Three days later the Sandinistas struck again. This time their target was the largest and oldest private business in Nicaragua, the San Antonio sugar complex. They ordered the complex confiscated from the Pellas family, which had owned it since its foundation in 1890. Although their government was under siege, they seemed to be saying, they could still act decisively against perceived enemies.

One of my friends in the Sandinista government, Dionisio Marenco, a business school graduate who had become a close advisor to President Ortega, had once been a manager of the San Antonio complex. I arranged to interview him a few days after it was expropriated. In his office at the Department of Agitation and Propaganda, which he headed, we debated the wisdom of the Sandinista crackdown. He insisted that the regime was acting to foil a new American-sponsored destabilization plan.

"The revolution has a right to defend itself with the weapons at hand," Marenco argued. "We were being made fools of. With the economic situation bad and deteriorating, we had to do something to show our people that we were not going to sit back and be beaten."

"But what you did is a sign of weakness, not strength," I countered. "Now, for the first time, I can sense that I'm going to see the fall of the Sandinista regime."

"Que mal presagio," he replied. What a bad prediction.

Among those most upset by the crackdown in Managua was the father of the peace process, Oscar Arias. "While in Costa Rica we give our children computers, the Sandinistas give their children machine guns," he told me angrily during an interview in August. "They have taken off their mask. They were not really honest when they promised to democratize and advance toward a pluralist society."

President Reagan responded to the expulsion of Ambassador Melton by ordering Nicaraguan Ambassador Carlos Tunnerman out of the United States. Relations between Managua and Washington reached another new low. Within Nicaragua, political conflict grew steadily more intense. In a lengthy interview published by *Barricada,* Interior Minister Borge vowed that he would not permit "the suicide of the revolution."

"We can be flexible and tolerant, but not to the point of killing the revolution," Borge warned. "That would not be tolerance. It would be stupidity."

Further clouding the political picture was an outburst of conflict among contra leaders. Some wanted to sign a final armistice with the Sandinistas, but others wanted to resume fighting. One group of field commanders rebelled against the leadership of Enrique Bermúdez, while others remained loyal to him. Like the Sandinistas, they were having trouble adjusting to the exigencies of peace.

The three dozen opposition leaders jailed since the Nandaime protest in July became symbols of Nicaragua's polarization, and calls for their release grew more insistent as months passed. Finally the Sandinistas relented, freeing the last of them on December 8. Their release was timed in part to attract the attention of George Bush, newly elected president of the United States.

A few days after the Nandaime prisoners were freed, I asked for an interview with Daniel Ortega. He received me late one night, dressed in his usual working outfit of boots, blue jeans, and black T-shirt. As I expected, he had Bush on his mind. He was hoping the United States might finally be prepared to negotiate seriously with Nicaragua.

"I am Mr. Bush," Ortega mused. "I have the experience of eight years under President Reagan. I, George Bush, have watched his policy in Latin America and Central America, and I can see that it did not achieve the desired results. As president of the United States, I can't afford to make the same mistakes. I can't work from the same script the Reagan administration used. If I want to have a realistic policy, I have to take this experience into account, and work for an alternative that favors negotiation."

That interview with Ortega turned out to be my last. I had been posted in Nicaragua for five years, a long stretch by *New York Times* standards. Finally my term had expired.

I decided to throw a farewell party, and sent Guillermo around with invitations. Practically everyone I knew showed up. We spent the evening eating, drinking, and wishing each other well. The next day, *La Prensa* ran a photo of me and my designated successor, Mark Uhlig, on the front page.

By mid-January 1989, Uhlig had finished his crash Spanish course and was ready to take over the bureau. I spent one long day and night packing, slept fitfully, and awoke before dawn. Guillermo was already waiting outside. As we drove through the half-light toward the airport, I told him I'd be back for a visit before long. We embraced at the departure gate.

"I couldn't have done it without you," I told him.

"*Adiós, jefe,*" he replied.

SOON after President Bush took office, a stunning series of political events shook the world, and public attention began shifting decisively away from Central America. The collapse of Communist regimes in Europe and the radical shift in Soviet foreign policy profoundly affected Nicaragua. Daniel Ortega had met and embraced the Marxist leaders of Poland, Czechoslovakia, East Germany,

Bulgaria, Hungary, and Romania, and all of them had sent valuable aid to his regime. Suddenly, in the space of a few months, all were deposed. And in Moscow, Mikhail Gorbachev was declaring that the Soviet Union was no longer interested in promoting world revolution.

The Sandinistas now counted on only two unconditional allies, Cuba and North Korea. Ruling Communist parties in those countries had rejected Gorbachev's example and refused to accept political reforms. Sandinista leaders, however, did not have the political or economic strength to follow that course. They had to liberalize their regime or else lose all hope of aid from either East or West.

The Sandinistas faced an identity crisis during the late 1980s. For years they had considered themselves the "vanguard" of the Nicaraguan people, a new kind of political force that would hold power indefinitely in the style of Cuba's Fidel Castro. But Nicaragua had proven resistant to their ambitions, and at the same time the world situation had changed dramatically. Ortega recognized that the Sandinista Front could not fight the tide of history, and slowly he began reshaping it into something resembling a conventional political party.

When Ronald Reagan left the presidency in January 1989, Ortega and his comrades had reason to feel satisfied. They had managed to survive eight years of sustained military, economic, and political attack from Washington. Attempts to resume military aid to the contras had been defeated in Congress, and most contra footsoldiers had withdrawn to camps in Honduras, where they were living off handouts from the United States. No one could doubt that the Sandinistas had defeated them.

The cost of victory, however, was staggering. Besides causing thirty thousand deaths and incalculable human suffering, the war had left Nicaragua in more desperate economic condition than any country in Latin America. Worse, it had divided Nicaraguans deeply and bitterly. While they remained so full of anger, there could be no hope of reconciliation or eventual economic recovery. Sandinista leaders recognized this truth, and committed themselves to resolving some of the conflicts that had been tearing Nicaragua apart for years. Rather than continue the policy of confrontation symbolized by police violence against political protesters and strikers, they resolved to try a different tack.

On March 17, 1989, eight months after Nandaime, Ortega appeared at the sprawling Tipitapa prison compound to preside over a ceremony for which many Nicaraguans had long been waiting. Assembled before him were 1,894 former members of the deposed National Guard, all of whom had been serving long jail terms. Each of their names was read aloud, and then Ortega pronounced them free. In an effort to heal wounds in Nicaraguan society, he had issued an unconditional amnesty for ex-Guardsmen, excepting only thirty-nine former officers accused of odious crimes.

In the months that followed, Nicaraguans enjoyed more political freedom than they had known in a decade. The anti-Sandinista press flourished free of censorship, and political dissidents were allowed to protest without interference. Taking advantage of this new climate, critics of the regime, supported by some foreign governments, began pressing Ortega for a new concession. If he was really serious about democratizing Nicaragua, they said, he should cut short his presidential term and call an early election.

To everyone's surprise, Ortega agreed. He set the election for February 25, 1990, nine months earlier than required by law. By launching an honest campaign and winning, he believed, he could show the world that Nicaragua was a true democracy.

The election that Ortega had in mind was nothing like the charade played out against the backdrop of war in 1984. Though the Sandinistas were naturally not prepared to surrender the enormous benefits of incumbency, they vowed that this time they were going to give the opposition a fair chance to win. In a remarkable interview during the campaign, Vice President Sergio Ramírez said the Sandinista Front was in a process of "political evolution," and admitted that it was "futile" for Sandinistas to continue pretending they were Nicaragua's vanguard.

"The most important task for Nicaragua is economic reconstruction, and that requires cooperation among all factions," Ramírez said. "We need to make a very great effort to wipe away every kind of polarization, to put aside ideological questions, and find policies we can all support."

As soon as the Sandinistas announced plans to call an early election, opposition leaders began the process of selecting a presidential candidate. Fourteen anti-Sandinista parties, spanning the ideological spectrum from Conservative to Communist, banded together into a coalition called the National Opposition Union. After a period of maneuvering in which no favorite candidate emerged, party leaders convened a marathon nominating sesssion and made a remarkable choice. Their candidate against Ortega would be Violeta Chamorro, widow of the publisher martyred a decade before.

Because she was not a member of any political party, Mrs. Chamorro was able to unite disparate political parties behind her candidacy and hold her fragile coalition together during the six-month campaign. Most Nicaraguans perceived her not as a political leader or even as a potential president, but rather as a symbol. She was not only the widow of Nicaragua's most outstanding contemporary figure, but also a former official of the Sandinista government who had resigned for reasons of principle. As publisher of *La Prensa,* she had been subject to an official campaign of vilification that only enhanced her stature as an anti-Sandinista leader. No one claimed that she was especially well prepared for the task of governing, but her status as an incarnation of dissent was unique.

The day Mrs. Chamorro was nominated was Labor Day in the United States. I was in Boston, enjoying a leave of absence from the *Times* and looking forward to an afternoon Red Sox game at Fenway Park. At mid-morning my telephone rang. An editor from the *Times* foreign desk in New York was calling.

"We need your help on a story," he began. Immediately I sensed that the Red Sox were going to have to play without me that day.

It turned out that the correspondent who had replaced me in Managua, Mark Uhlig, was on vacation and unavailable. The *Times* needed a story about Mrs. Chamorro, and I had been drafted to write it.

The new candidate was at home when I telephoned later that morning. I congratulated her, and then asked her if she felt ready to rule Nicaragua.

"Of course I am," she replied, as if surprised by the question. "I have enormous faith in God. He will illuminate me and show me how to do what my conscience dictates."

"And do you think you have a real chance of defeating the Sandinistas?"

"Forget about the Sandinistas. They're obsolete."

Chastened by their experience in 1984, Sandinista *comandantes* were determined to mount an election that the world would accept as legitimate. They allowed the United Nations and the Organization of American States to send large delegations of election monitors, and although there were several outbreaks of violence during the campaign, it was conducted more freely than any election campaign in Nicaraguan history.

"We are not interested simply in winning the elections," Managua Mayor Carlos Carrión told one group of Sandinista activists. "We want to win them in such a way that they will be recognized by the great majority of countries and by large groups in the United States. That will give us a domestic and international power base much broader than the one we have now."

Mrs. Chamorro and her running mate, Virgilio Godoy, based their campaign not on a specific political program, but simply on opposition to Sandinista rule. They sought to tie their campaign to pro-democracy movements that were springing up around the world, and to paint the Sandinista regime as repressive and incompetent.

"All over the world, people like you are burying Communism and proclaiming democracy!" Mrs. Chamorro told an enthusiastic crowd in Granada. "So set your watches! Set them to the same hour as Poland, as Bulgaria, as Czechoslovakia, as Chile! Because this is the hour of democracy and freedom—this is the hour of the people!"

Rather than defend themselves against charges that they had mismanaged the country and squandered their chance to pull it out of poverty, the Sandinistas chose to look to the future. With the war finally ended, Daniel Ortega and Sergio Ramírez said in campaign speeches, Nicaragua was poised for recovery. Their slogan was, "Everything Will Be Better!"

"Everything will be better with a president who listens to the people," read one Sandinista advertisement. "A president who takes our opinions into account, so he can resolve problems and guarantee everyone's well-being. Everything will be better with a simple, human, caring president. A loyal and revolutionary president, a working man. For peace, everyone with Daniel!"

In a clumsy attempt to help Mrs. Chamorro, the United States Congress appropriated $9 million to be spent on election-related projects in Nicaragua. Much of it wound up in the coffers of the Sandinista-controlled Supreme Electoral Council, though at least $3 million found its way to the Chamorro campaign. Yet the campaign was amateurish, hardly a match for the Sandinista juggernaut.

I was anxious to see a bit of the campaign, and in January 1990, a year after leaving my post in Managua, I returned for a week-long visit. Guillermo drove me around to some of my old haunts. I found people relieved that the war had actually ended, but worn down by great economic hardship. Nearly everybody I met was planning to vote for Mrs. Chamorro. No one, however, thought she had a chance of winning. She had appeared only sporadically in public, and her campaign rallies were poorly prepared and sparsely attended.

Ortega rallies, by contrast, were choreographed as if they had been planned by Hollywood consultants. The candidate arrived surrounded by musicians, often riding on horseback. Aides with Polaroid cameras took photos of him greeting local voters, and distributed them as souvenirs. Others handed out T-shirts, caps, kerchiefs, key rings, and other paraphernalia bearing the bold slogan, "Everything Will Be Better!" Spectators were encouraged to press around the mobile stage from which Ortega spoke, and often he would lean down to clasp people's outstretched hands. On good days, the effect was electric.

Sandinista campaigners had free access to as many trucks and buses as they needed, and thus their rallies were always larger than opposition rallies. They were also able to use the powers of office to resolve local problems on the spot. With seemingly unlimited funds—they officially put the cost of their campaign at $6.4 million dollars, most of it provided by unidentified foreign donors—the Sandinistas lacked for nothing. They mobilized more than sixty thousand full-time volunteers, established headquarters in every city and town, and designed an advertising campaign more sophisticated than any in Nicaraguan history.

A huge crowd, estimated at more than half a million, jammed the *Plaza de la Revolución* in Managua for Ortega's final campaign speech on February 21. Many of those present were government employees given the day off in order to attend, and many others were peasants trucked in from state-owned cooperatives. They waved banners, chanted slogans, cheered, and applauded. To many who watched, and probably to Ortega himself, the rally was proof that despite everything that had gone wrong, Nicaraguans still wanted to be ruled by the Sandinista Front.

A few, however, could not help but remember May Day 1979, when an equally tumultuous crowd filled that same plaza to cheer President Anastasio Somoza Debayle. On that day, Somoza seemed overwhelmingly popular, and the deafening chant was, *"No te vas, te quedás!"*—You're not going, you're staying! Less than three months later, Somoza was defeated and in exile.

Mrs. Chamorro seemed to gain support in the closing days of the campaign. Cardinal Obando obliquely endorsed her during one of his Sunday homilies, telling voters that they should vote the way Jesus Christ would have voted. Yet polls showed her running far behind, and even many of her supporters privately doubted that she could win. Most Nicaraguans and most foreign observers believed her defeat was inevitable. No one believed it more completely than Daniel Ortega and his fellow Sandinistas.

It was past midnight when the first election results were announced. Soon a stunning and all but unbelievable pattern began to emerge. The opposition ticket was winning in every part of the country.

Not only were Ortega and the Sandinistas defeated, but they were defeated overwhelmingly. Final tabulations showed that fifty-five percent of the electorate had voted for Mrs. Chamorro, with just forty-two percent casting ballots for the Sandinistas. Some of the most shocking results came from polling places adjacent to military bases, where soldiers who had been expected to vote almost unanimously for the regime instead cast thousands of votes for the opposition.

Shortly after three o'clock in the morning, Mrs. Chamorro arrived at her campaign headquarters, where an ecstatic crowd was waiting. Her face radiated jubilation as she claimed victory.

"We have given the world an example of civic duty, showing that we Nicaraguans want to live in democracy, want to live in peace, and above all, that we want to live in freedom!" she told her supporters, many of whom could still not believe what had happened. "I knew that in a free election, like the one we have had, the people of Nicaragua would vote to create the democratic republic that my husband, Pedro Joaquín Chamorro, always dreamed of . . . This is an election that will not produce exiles or political prisoners or confiscations, because here there are no victors or vanquished. Today we all deserve to congratulate ourselves with a fraternal embrace, because Nicaragua will be a Republic again!"

Across town, at the convention center where stunned Sandinistas were watching the results, tears flowed freely. Emotions ran beyond astonishment and disappointment, because the defeat was more than simply the defeat of a candidate. It was a repudiation of ten years of revolutionary rule, a resounding vote of no confidence in a regime that had convinced itself it represented Nicaragua's deepest aspirations. Sandinistas had never doubted that they would not only win the election, but would rule their country for the rest of the century and beyond. None had conceived of the possibility of defeat, least of all Daniel Ortega.

Three hours after Mrs. Chamorro's victory speech, the defeated president appeared before his supporters to concede that he had lost. Stunned aides and comrades stood nearby, many of them pale with shock. Some seemed lost in their nightmare, barely able to hear their leader's concession.

"The president of Nicaragua and the government of Nicaragua are going to respect and obey the popular mandate of these elections," Ortega began, struggling to maintain his composure. "We leave victorious. Because we Sandinistas have sacrificed, have spilled blood and sweat, not to cling to government posts but to bring Nicaragua something it has been denied since independence in 1821. . . . We feel proud, in this unjust world divided between weak and strong, to be giving Nicaragua and Latin America a little bit of dignity, a little bit of democracy, a little bit of social justice."

For years the Sandinistas had been living in an unreal cocoon of their own making, a Nicaragua far different from the one other people saw. They were living in a country of militants, a country where people waved their fists and shouted slogans, where people were ready to sacrifice whatever necessary to support the cause of revolution. The real Nicaragua, however, was a nation exhausted by years of war and deprivation.

The most obvious reason voters threw the Sandinistas out of power was the poverty into which they had plunged Nicaragua. People who could not afford to feed and clothe themselves, and who had to hear their children crying for food day after day, could not have been expected to support the regime. Even many Nicaraguans who considered themselves revolutionaries had come to believe that their country was condemned to eternal deprivation as long as the Sandinistas were in power, and they voted accordingly.

Besides the collapse of the national economy, Nicaraguans had another reason to vote against the Sandinista government. All of the Sandinista *comandantes* were soldiers, and all were militarists at heart. In public they liked to carry firearms and wear the olive green uniforms which, to many Nicaraguans, symbolized only suffering and death. Under their rule the size of the combined military services and reserves had grown to three hundred thousand, more than ten percent of the population. That made Nicaragua one of the most militarized countries on earth, a distinction many of its citizens found repugnant.

After more than a decade of virtually uninterrupted war, Nicaraguans could not bear the prospect of continuing to send their sons and brothers off to military service. The peace and prosperity that neighboring Costa Rica had enjoyed after abolishing its army symbolized one of their most profound hopes. When Violeta Chamorro promised during her campaign that she would end conscription and steadily reduce the army's size and influence, she was promising to reverse the tide of Nicaraguan history. It was a pledge that won her the votes of not only many mothers and fathers, but also many young people desperate for the chance to live normal, peaceful lives.

When Nicaraguans were finally given the chance to choose what kind of a regime they wanted to live under, they overwhelmingly chose one that promised to rebuild the economy and dismantle the huge military machine. Just as important, they voted for a candidate who offered them what the Sandinistas had originally offered: liberty. Like the peoples of a dozen other nations who rebelled against unpopular regimes in 1989 and 1990, Nicaraguans wanted leaders who would allow them to live their lives as they saw fit. They voted for an end to suffocating social and political controls, an end to authoriarianism and polarizing rhetoric.

The great myth that drove the Sandinista regime, the same one proclaimed by a host of other self-described revolutionaries, was that governments could create a "new man" to serve their will. This "new man" would submit happily to authority, forsake individualism and personal ambition, and accept the right of government to dictate the direction of his life. But the great lesson of the political cataclysms that shook Nicaragua and the world in 1989 and 1990 was that the human spirit resists and will always resist such assaults. The nobility of the human spirit is precisely the impulse to choose, to rebel, to say no. By trying to repress that impulse, the Sandinistas lost the confidence of the people they so desperately wanted to help.

The Sandinistas' great failures had been evident for years before their fall from power. Their domestic policies were based on three colossal misjudgments. First and most important, they believed they could build Nicaragua into a prosperous country without deferring to the principles of free enterprise. Second, they grossly underestimated the moral influence of Catholic bishops and, in particular, the esteem in which Nicaraguans held their spiritual leader, Cardinal Obando. Third, they abused Miskito Indians and other ethnic minorities who had lived peaceably for centuries along the Atlantic coast, provoking a rebellion that attracted widespread sympathy both within Nicaragua and around the world.

The premises on which Sandinista foreign policy was based were also disastrously misconceived. The *comandantes* rode to power on a wave of enthusiasm for the idea of guerrilla war. They shared Fidel Castro's outlandish dream that Marxist insurgents could topple the regime in El Salvador and then proceed to win victories in the rest of Latin America. Their anti-Yankee convictions led them to sympathize with oppressive regimes in the Soviet Union and other Communist countries. The political model they sought to follow became obsolete, and when regimes in Eastern Europe collapsed at the end of the 1980s they suddenly found themselves almost alone.

Alongside these failures, however, the Sandinistas could claim epochal successes. The most profound was their destruction of the Somoza regime and the political/economic structure that sustained it. Only by comparing the history of Nicaragua in the 1980s to that of nearby countries was it possible to appreciate the scope of that success.

Nicaragua shook off its dictatorship at about the same time that military rulers in Guatemala, Honduras, and El Salvador were replaced by civilians. In those countries, the transition was peaceful, and the old elite was able to retain all of its privileges. Armies which had brutalized their populations and kept them in misery for generations remained intact, and political fanatics who directed death squads and other forms of violent repression continued to act with impunity. By no honest standard could those countries be considered democracies, nor was there any real prospect that they could evolve toward democracy. Their civilian presidents were no more than figureheads, forced to rule within limits fixed by reactionary oligarchs and military officers.

By many standards the Sandinista regime was undemocratic, though it never resorted to the kind of savagery common in nearby countries. But by destroying the repressive apparatus of the Somoza family, the Sandinistas at least provided a basis on which a genuine democracy could be built. They made it possible for Nicaraguans to go peacefully to the polls and choose the kind of government they wanted, something that was unthinkable in Guatemala, El Salvador, or Honduras. Had they done nothing more than that, they would deserve a place of historic honor.

Sandinista leaders could claim other successes as well. They encouraged Nicaraguans to take pride in their nationality and their heritage. They destroyed the rigid class structure that had confined Nicaraguans since time immemorial. And their policies, however misguided, were based on the premise that government's greatest responsibility was to the poor and dispossessed. No Nicaraguan regime to come, even the most avowedly anti-Sandinista, would be able to ignore those advances.

Because their long struggle against the Somoza dictatorship ended with such a spectacular victory, Sandinista *comandantes* came to believe that they had special powers of insight beyond those of other Nicaraguans. Their self-assurance, their certainty that they knew what was best for their country, fed an arrogance that ultimately led to their downfall. Like many revolutions, theirs succeeded in destroying an old and unjust order, but remained stalled in that infantile stage and was never able to proceed to the next one. Their errors were enormous, and cost Nicaragua incalculable amounts of treasure and blood. Yet their government was moved always by patriotism, never by lust for money or power. Any remaining doubt of that was erased by their willingness to hold the freest election in Nicaraguan history and to abide by its shocking result. Ultimately they showed themselves worthy of the legacy of Nicaragua's heroes, among them the visionary poet Rubén Darío, who wrote: *A través de las páginas fatales de la historia,/Nuestra tierra está hecha de vigor y de gloria,/Nuestra tierra está hecha para la humanidad.* Through the fatal pages of history, our land is made of vigor and glory, our land is made for humanity.

NOTES

Many of the events described in this book were covered extensively by Nicaraguan newspapers, but in these notes there are references only to a few articles from the Nicaraguan press, those which provide specific details not elsewhere reported. When Kinzer articles provide more detail, they are noted. Author's interviews were conducted in 1989 unless otherwise noted.

Chapter One—Arrival

Christmas party assault: Pataky, László, *Llegaron los que No Estaban Invitados: La Sombra de Sandino* (Managua: Editorial Pereira, 1975); also, García Márquez, Gabriel, *El Asalto: El Operativo con que el FSLN se Lanzó al Mundo* (Managua: Editorial Nueva Nicaragua, 1983); also, García Márquez, *Crónica del Asalto a la "Casa de los Chanchos"* in García Márquez, et. al., *Los Sandinistas* (Bogota: La Oveja Negra, 1979); also, Diederich, Bernard, *Somoza and the Legacy of U. S. Involvement in Central America,* (New York: Dutton, 1981), pp. 106–114; also, *New York Times,* December 29–31, 1974; January 3, 5, and 13, 1975; and January 7, 1985.

Pedro Joaquín Chamorro background and imprisonment: Chamorro, *Estirpe Sangriente: Los Somoza* (Managua: Artes Gráficas, 1978); also, Chamorro, *La Patria de Pedro* (Managua: La Prensa, 1981); also, Edmisten, Patricia Taylor, *Nicaragua Divided: La Prensa and the Chamorro Legacy* (Pensacola: University of West Florida, 1990); also, Diederich, op. cit., 153–175.

Fernando Cardenal on his clandestine activities: Belli, Humberto, *Breaking Faith: The Sandinista Revolution and Its Impact on Freedom and Christian Faith in Nicaragua* (Westchester, Ill.: Crossways, 1985), p. 23.

Chapter Two—"Gun the Bandits Down"

Exploits of William Walker: Bolaños Geyer, Alejandro, *William Walker: The Grey-Eyed Man of Destiny,* five volumes (Lake St. Louis, Mo.: Privately printed, 1989–90); also, Bolaños Geyer, *James C. Jamison: Con Walker en Nicaragua* (Managua: Editorial San José, 1977); also, Bolaños Geyer, *El Filibustero Clinton Rollins* (Managua: Editorial San José, 1976); also, Rosengarten Frederic, Jr., *Freebooters Must Die!* (Wayne, Pa.: Haverford House, 1976); also, Allen, Merritt Parmelee, *William Walker, Filibustero* (New York: Harper & Bros., 1932); also, Carr, Albert Z., *The World and William Walker* (New York: Harper & Row, 1963); also, Doubleday, C. W., *Reminiscences of the "Filibuster" War in Nicaragua* (New York: Putnam, 1886); also, Gerson, Noel, *Sad Swashbuckler* (Nashville: Thomas Nelson, 1976); also, Scroggs, William O., *Filibusters and Financiers: The Story of William Walker and his Associates* (New York: Macmillan, 1916); also, Houston, Robert, *The Nation Thief* (New York: Pantheon, 1984). Quotes from Walker are from his memoirs, *The War in Nicaragua* (Tucson: University of Arizona, 1985).

For contemporary views of Sandino by Undersecretary of State Robert Olds and U.S. envoy to Nicaragua Henry L. Stimson, see Leiken, Robert S. and Barry Rubin, *Central America Crisis Reader* (New York: Summit, 1987); pp. 83–85.

Nicaragua in the second half of the nineteenth century: Perhaps the best book to be published about Nicaragua in this period was an account by a mining engineer and amateur naturalist, Thomas Belt, which was praised by no less an authority than Charles Darwin as "the best of all natural history journals which have ever been published." Belt spent four years in Chontales running a gold mine. Like Squier before him, he found Nicaragua endlessly fascinating. Some of his observations are as valid in the late twentieth century as they were in the late nineteenth:

"Of patriotism I never saw any symptom in Central America, nothing but selfish partisanship, willing at any moment to set the country in a state of war if there was only a prospect of a little spoil," Belt wrote. "The states of Central America are republics in name only; in reality, they are tyrannical oligarchies. They have excellent constitutions and laws on paper, but both their statesmen and their judges are corrupt, with some honorable exceptions, I must admit, but not enough to stem the current of abuse. Of real liberty there is none. The party in power is able to control the elections, and to put their partisans into all the municipal and other offices. Some of the presidents have not hesitated to throw their political opponents into jail at the time of an election . . . A change of rulers can only be effected by a so-called revolution; with all the machinery of a republic, the will of the people can only be known by the issue of a civil war." (Belt, Thomas, *The Naturalist in Nicaragua* [Chicago: University of Chicago, 1985], p. 343.)

Nicaragua Canal: "The place most nineteenth-century North Americans expected the canal to be built, including the President, was Nicaragua . . . The earliest authoritative study of the problem, or rather the first to be taken as authoritative, appeared in 1811 and designated Nicaragua as the route possessing the fewest difficulties . . . Here was an enchanting land of blue lakes and trade winds, towering volcanic mountains, rolling green savannahs and grazing cattle . . . The United States and Great Britain had come close to war over Nicaragua, in fact, so great was Nicaragua's importance as the canal site regarded on both sides of the Atlantic." (McCullough, David, *Path Between The Seas: The Construction of the Panama Canal 1870–1914* [New York: Touchstone, 1978]).

Also, Simmons, William E., *Uncle Sam's New Waterway* (New York: F. T. Neely, 1899); also, Walker, J. W. G., *Ocean to Ocean: An Account Personal and Historical of Nicaragua and Its People;* also, Miner, Dwight Carroll, *The Fight for the Panama Route: The Story of the Spooner Act & the Hay-Heran Treaty* (New York: Columbia University, 1940).

Presidency of José Santos Zelaya: An American military engineer who spent two years in Nicaragua studying possible canal routes, Admiral John Walker, came to know Zelaya well. He made his observations in 1898, but they could have been made at virtually any time during the nineteenth or twentieth century:

"Nicaragua is a military despotism masquerading as a republic. The President, though nominally elected, is almost invariably a successful military man who forces himself into office and maintains his supremacy with a strong hand . . . The present incumbent, General Zelaya, is an able, broad-minded man whose strong personality and indomitable energy have enabled him to administer a restless and unappreciative country for eight troubled years. He represents the Liberal party, and, since one of its most notable achievements has been the curbing of the power of the clergy in temporal affairs, it is needless to say that the sympathies of the priesthood are in general with his Conservative opponents, the chief of whom live in exile, whence they direct abortive insurrections against the existing government . . . The government is despotic, but perhaps none other would be less so." (Walker, J. W. G., *Ocean to Ocean: An Account Personal and Historical of Nicaragua and its People* (Chicago: A. C. McClurg, 1902).

See also Aquino, Enrique, *La Personalidad Política del General José Santos Zelaya* (Managua: Talleres Gráficos Pérez, 1944); also, Zelaya, José Santos, *La Revolución de Nicaragua y los Estados Unidos* (Madrid: Imprenta B. Rodriguez, 1910).

American authorities were startled in November 1913 when Zelaya turned up in New York City. Reporters, politicians and Latin American exiles clamored to meet him. A large portrait of him dominated the cover of the *New York Times Magazine* on Sunday, November 23, 1913. "Zelaya Blames Dollar Diplomacy for his Troubles," read the banner headline. "Exiled President of Nicaragua, Now Here, Says American 'Big Business' Is Really Forcing an Unacceptable Government on His Country." The reporter who interviewed him, George MacAdam, found that he still radiated the qualities that had first propelled him onto the world stage. "It takes no second glance, no scrutiny, to see that this is a man of courage, a man of action, a man who has been commissioned by Nature, a leader of men. Eyes, chin and mouth, the set of head and shoulders, but particularly his eyes, all fit into one's preconceived mental picture of a dictator. He looks as though he would be equally at home in a presidential chair or cavalry saddle, as though he could sign a death warrant between dinner courses without any interference with his digestion. And yet there is no suggestion in his personality of brutality."

Zelaya's charges that he had been unjustly ousted by American power struck a chord in the United States, and authorities sought an excuse to deport him. They arranged for criminal charges to be brought against him in Nicaragua, and a few days after the *New York Times* story about him appeared, he was arrested at an apartment on the corner of West End Avenue and 92nd Street. He spent a week at the Tombs prison, and was finally freed on condition that he leave the United States. He sailed for Le Havre and obscurity on December 23.

Several years later, claiming he had business deals to attend to in the United States, Zelaya made his way back to New York. Depressed, sick, and all but broke, he settled into an apartment at 3000 Broadway, where he died in May 1919.

Benjamin Zeledón uprising and letters: Ministerio de Educación, *Doctor y General Benjamin F. Zeledón* (Managua: Editorial Union, 1980). Among the Marine officers who pursued Zeledón was outspoken Smedley Butler. His accounts are cited extensively in Schmidt, Hans, *Maverick Marine: General Smedley Butler and the Contradictions of American Military History* (Lexington, Ky.: University of Kentucky, 1987).

Guerrilla war led by Augusto César Sandino: Sandino's writings are collected in Ramírez, Sergio, *Augusto César Sandino, El Pensamiento Vivo,* two volumes (Managua: Editorial Nueva Nicaragua, 1982). See also Ramírez, *Sandino es Indohispano y No Tiene Fronteras en America Latina* (Managua: IES, 1984); Ramírez, *Sandino Siempre* (León: UNAN, 1980); Ramírez, *El Muchacho de Niquinohomo* (Managua: Editorial Vanguardia, 1988).

Also, Alemán Bolaños, Gustavo, *Sandino el Libertador: Biografía del Héroe Americano* (San José: IMCUSA, 1980); Arellano, Jorge Eduardo, *Lecciones de Sandino* (Managua: Distribuidora Cultural, 1983); Campos Ponce, Xavier, *Sandino: Biografía de un Héroe* (Mexico: EDAMEX, 1979); De la Selva, Salomón, *La Guerra de Sandino, o Pueblo Desnudo* (Managua: Editorial Nueva Nicaragua, 1985); Fabela, Isidro, *El Rebelde de America* (Managua: Editorial Nueva Nicaragua, 1979); Galeano, Eduardo, *Ventana Sobre Sandino* (Managua: Ediciones Raití, 1985); Kaman, William, *Search for Stability: United States Diplomacy Toward Nicaragua 1925–1933* (Notre Dame, Ind.: University of Notre Dame, 1968); López, Santos, *Memorias del Coronel Santos López* (Managua: Secretaria Nacional de Propaganda y Educación Política, FSLN, 1981?); Macauley, Neil, *The Sandino Affair* (Chicago: Quadrangle, 1967); Román, José, *Maldito Pais* (Managua: Pez y Serpiente, 1983); Selser, Gregorio, *El Pequeño Ejército Loco: Sandino y la Operación Mexico-Nicaragua* (Managua: Editorial Nueva Nicaragua, 1986); Selser, *Sandino* (New York: Monthly Review, 1981); Wheeler, Senator Burton K., *Dollar Diplomacy at Work in Mexico and Nicaragua* (Washington: Government Printing Office, 1927); also, Belausteguigoitia, Ramon de, *Con Sandino en Nicaragua* (Managua: Editorial Nueva Nicaragua, 1985).

Ocotal battle: Four days before the battle, the Marine commander in Ocotal, Captain G. D. Hatfield, sent Sandino a letter offering him "one more opportunity to surrender with honor." Sandino replied with one of his most famous short texts. "I received your communication of yesterday and fully understand it," he wrote. "I will not surrender, and await you here. I want a free country or death. I am not afraid of you; I rely on the patriotic ardor of those who accompany me." (Selser, op. cit., pp. 78–80.)

An official Marine report of the battle included this account: "Ocotal detachment was attacked by an overwhelming force of about 400 men under Sandino . . . A five-plane formation from Managua, under command of Major Rowell, flew to Ocotal and attacked Sandino's force with bombs and machine-gun fire, completely routing the bandits. . . . Bandit loss undetermined." (*Use of the United States Navy in Nicaragua,* Hearings before Senate Foreign Relations Committee, February 11 and 18, 1928. Washington: Government Printing Office, 1928).

Account of Sandino's murder: Pérez-Valle, Edmundo, *La Muerte de Sandino: El Martirio del Héroe* (Managua: ENIEC, 1984).

Somoza family regime: Millett, Richard, *Guardians of the Dynasty: A History of the US-Created Guardia Nacional de Nicaragua and the Somoza Family;* also, Tierney, John J., *Somoza and the Sandinistas: The United States and Nicaragua in the Twentieth Century* (Washington: Council on Inter-American Security, 1982); also, Somoza Debayle, Anastasio (as told to Jack Cox), *Nicaragua Betrayed* (Boston: Western Islands, 1980).

Somozas' wealth: Laino, Domingo, *Somoza: El General Comerciante* (Asunción: Editorial Intercontinental, 1989). At the time of his overthrow in 1979, Anastasio Somoza Debayle was worth an estimated $900 million *(New York Times,* July 22, 1979).

Somoza as a drug dealer: In a 1984 book, a Mexican-American drug dealer named Andrew Starhill Vallejo told of his dealings with the regime. "Somoza was a dictator's dictator," he recalled. "Everything of value in his country was owned by some other member of his family . . . [Once] I met with Anastasio in the privacy of his office. I gave him $250,000 in cash—all in one-hundred-dollar bills—and he agreed to allow my clients unencumbered use of three Nicaraguan airports as well as several Pacific ports . . . Later, when he grew a moustache, he would reach up and curl the edges when he spoke of his love of the United States and capitalism, and his eyes would shine brightly. He would say, 'I know my friends in your country will take care of me and my country, if we ever need them badly.' . . . My own dealings with the Somoza government amounted to giving them a total of more than $13.5 million over a period of about ten years. All was paid in cash to Anastasio or Luis, or other family members." (Greenshaw, Wayne, *Flying High: Inside Big-Time Drug Smuggling* [New York: Dodd, Mead & Co.,1984]).

Chapter Three—A Nation Rebels

President Somoza on Pedro Joaquín Chamorro: Somoza Debayle, Anastasio (as told to Jack Cox), *Nicaragua Betrayed* (Boston: Western Islands, 1980), p. 27.

Elie Abel on Chamorro: Diederich, Bernard, *Somoza and the Legacy of U.S. Involvement in Central America* (New York: Dutton, 1981), p. 154.

Chamorro assassination: Vélez Barcenas, Jacinto, *Dr. Pedro Joaquín Chamorro C. Asesinado* (Managua: Trejos Hermanos, 1979).

Monimbó uprising: Briones Torres, Ignacio, *Monimbó Rebelde,* essay appearing in Márquez, Gabriel García, et. al., *Los Sandinistas* (Bogota: La Oveja Negra), pp. 49–59.

Nora Astorga episode: Interview with Astorga in Randall, Margaret, *Sandino's Daughters: Testimonies of Nicaraguan Women in Struggle* (Vancouver: New Star, 1981), pp. 116–128; also, *Los Sandinistas,* op. cit., pp. 101–102. Various parties have told the story of General Pérez Vega's murder differently. Sandinista leaders say their plan was only to kidnap the general in hopes of exchanging him for imprisoned comrades, but that when he resisted violently, commandos were forced to kill him. Friends and relatives of the victim, however, allege that he was tortured to death, and his body mutilated.

Nora Astorga died of cancer ten years after the killing, in February 1988, at the age of thirty-nine. She was then serving as Nicaragua's ambassador to the United Nations.

Somoza as "devilish man": Diederich, Bernard, op. cit., p. 162.

Disagreements between Jimmy Carter and Carlos Andrés Pérez, and Carter letter to Somoza: Pastor, Robert, *Condemned to Repetition* (Princeton: Princeton University Press, 1987), pp. 64–70; also, Christian, Shirley, *Nicaragua: Revolution in the Family* (New York: Random House, 1985), pp. 57–58; also, Somoza Debayle, op. cit., pp. 143–145.

Carter wrote his unfortunate letter to Somoza after Somoza announced on June 19 that he would allow the dissident Group of Twelve to return to Nicaragua, permit human rights investigators from the OAS to visit the country, and consider decreeing some form of amnesty. At that moment, unequivocal United States pressure could probably have forced Somoza from power. By encouraging him, by dealing with him as a legitimate leader with a long-term political future, the United States stiffened his resolve and thereby assured that the struggle to depose him would be longer and bloodier. This was what Carter wrote:

"I read your statements to the press on June 19 with great interest and appreciation. The steps toward respecting human rights that you are considering are important and heartening signs; and, as they are translated into actions, will mark a major advance for your nation in answering some of the criticisms recently aimed at the Nicaraguan government . . .

"You have spoken about a possible amnesty for Nicaraguans being held in jail for political reasons. I urge you to take the promising steps you have suggested; they would serve to improve the image abroad of the human rights situation in Nicaragua.

"I was also encouraged to hear your suggestion for a reform of the electoral system in order to ensure fair and free elections in which all political parties could compete fairly. This step is essential to the functioning of a democracy . . .

"I look forward to hearing of the implementation of your decisions and appreciate very much your announcements of these constructive actions. I hope that you will continue to communicate fully with my ambassador, Mauricio Solaun, who enjoys my complete confidence."

Palace Assault: García Márquez, Gabriel, et. al., op. cit., pp. 29–48; also, Somoza Debayle, Anastasio, op. cit., pp. 150–168; also, *Barricada,* Aug. 21–22, 1988.

September 1978 insurrection: García Márquez, Gabriel, op. cit., pp. 61–98; also, Somoza Debayle, Anastasio, op. cit., pp. 181–195; also, Universidad Nacional de Nicaragua, Departamento de Ciencias Sociales, *Apuntes de Historia de Nicaragua,* Vol. II, pp. 302–316; also interview with Humberto Ortega, *Barricada,* Sept. 9, 1988.

Chapter Four—Triumph

Carter administration debate over Nicaragua: Pastor, Robert, *Condemned to Repetition* (Princeton: Princeton University, 1987); also, Lake, Anthony, *Somoza Falling* (Boston: Houghton Mifflin, 1989).

Carlos Andrés Pérez warning to Carter: Pastor, op. cit., pp. 86–87.

Omar Torrijos warning to Carter: Pastor, op. cit., pp. 89–90.

Sandinista call to rebellion: Núñez Téllez, Carlos, *Un Pueblo en Armas* (Managua: Editorial Vanguardia, 1986), pp. 43–45.

Bill Stewart murder: Mendieta Alfaro, Roger, *El Último Marine, La Caída de Somoza* (Managua: Editorial Union, 1980), pp. 171–178; also, Diederich, Bernard, *Somoza and the Legacy of U.S. Involvement in Central America* (New York: Dutton, 1981), pp. 269–280.

Vance speech to OAS: *New York Times,* June 22, 1979. A week later, Sandinista leaders pledged to the OAS that once in power, they would adhere to OAS and UN human rights resolutions, recognize the separation of legislative, judicial, and executive power, pursue a non-aligned foreign policy, and guarantee freedom of speech, religion, and assembly (*New York Times,* June 28, 1979).

Masaya uprising: Kinzer story in *Boston Globe,* June 26, 1979; account of Macho Negro execution from Núñez Téllez, op. cit., pp. 182–185.

Retreat from Managua to Masaya: Núñez Téllez, op. cit., pp. 95–118; also, Mendieta Alfaro, op. cit., pp. 211–262; also, Morales, Arqueles, *Con el Corazón en el Disparador* (Managua: Editorial Vanguardia, 1986), pp. 93–120.

Managua following Sandinista withdrawal: Kinzer story in *Washington Post,* June 30, 1979.

Meeting between Somoza and Pezzullo: Somoza Debayle, Anastasio (as told to Jack Cox), *Nicaragua Betrayed* (Boston: Western Islands, 1980), pp. 333–349. Somoza secretly taped his meetings with Pezzullo, and published the transcripts as an appendix to his memoirs.

Chapter Five—Sandinista Dreams

Early Sandinista history: Nolan, David, *FSLN: The Ideology of the Sandinistas and the Nicaraguan Revolution* (Miami: University of Miami, 1984), pp. 13–43; also, Leiken, Robert S. and Barry Rubin, *Central America Crisis Reader* (New York: Summit, 1987), pp. 139–145; also, Guadamúz, Carlos José, *Y Las Casas se Quedaron Llenas de Humo* (Managua: Editorial Nueva Nicaragua, 1986); also, Hernández, Plutarco, *El FSLN Por Dentro: Relatos de un Combatiente* (San José: Privately printed, 1982).

Carlos Fonseca background and views: Instituto de Estudios del Sandinismo, *Carlos, El Eslabón Vital: Cronología Básica de Carlos Fonseca, Jefe de la Revolución 1936–1976* (Managua: Editorial Nueva Nicaragua, 1985); also, Borge, Tomás, *Carlos, El Amanecer*

Ya No Es Una Tentación (Havana: Casa de las Americas, 1980); also, Rius (Eduardo del Rio), *Carlos Para Todos* (Managua: Editorial Vanguardia, 1987); also, Fonseca's works published by the Sandinista DEPEP in Managua, 1984.

Tomás Borge on Castro victory: Borge, op. cit., p. 27.

Raití and other early Sandinista military campaigns: Lozano, Lucrecia, *De Sandino al Triunfo de la Revolución* (Mexico: Siglo XXI, 1979), pp. 51–56; also, Ortega, Humberto, *50 Años de Lucha Sandinista* (Managua: Ciencias Sociales, 1980), pp. 147–148; also, *Barricada,* October 27, 1988.

Killing of Gonzalo Lacayo: Author's interviews with Daniel Ortega and Oscar René Vargas.

Vargas brothers in Europe: Author's interview with Oscar René Vargas.

Sandinista activities in the Mideast: Author's interviews with Oscar René Vargas, Leticia Herrera (1984), and Moisés Hassan; also, U.S. Department of State, *The Sandinistas and Middle East Radicals* (Washington: Department of State, 1985); also, Payne, Douglas W., *The "Mantos" of Sandinista Deception,* published in *Strategic Review,* Spring 1985.

Omar Cabezas on joining the Sandinista Front: Cabezas, Omar, *Fire From the Mountain: The Making of a Sandinista,* translated by Kathleen Weaver (New York: Crown, 1985).

Somoza García arms deal with Israel: Urcuyo Maliaños, Francisco, *Solos: Los Últimos 43 Horas en el Bunker de Somoza* (Guatemala: Edita, 1979), pp. 83–85.

Herty Lewites gunrunning operation: Author's interview with Lewites.

Dora María Téllez background and statements: Author's interview with Téllez (1984); also, Randall, Margaret, *Sandino's Daughters: Testimonies of Nicaraguan Women in Struggle* (Vancouver: New Star, 1981), pp. 40–54.

Sandinista oath: Nolan, op. cit., p. 35.

Luis Carrión background and statements: Author's interviews with Carrión (1986) and his father, Luis Carrión Montoya (1986).

Factional disputes among Sandinista leaders: Nolan, David, op. cit., pp. 56–58; also, author's interviews with Moisés Hassan and Ignacio Briones Torres; also, Leiken and Rubin, op. cit., pp. 158–164; also, Belli, Humberto, *Breaking Faith: The Sandinista Revolution and Its Impact on Freedom and Christian Faith in Nicaragua* (Westchester, Ill.: Crossway, 1985), pp. 26–40.

Carlos Fonseca's return to Nicaragua: Hernández, op. cit., pp. 81–83; also, Ramírez, Sergio, *La Marca del Zorro: Hazañas del Comandante Francisco Rivera Quintero* (Managua: Editorial Nueva Nicaragua, 1989), pp. 109–123.

"Political-military platform" circulated by Ortega faction: Nolan, op. cit., pp. 78–79.

Fernando Cardenal on the Group of Twelve: Black, George, *Triumph of the People: The Sandinista Revolution in Nicaragua* (London: Zed, 1981), p. 104.

Kidnapping of journalists for Sandinista news conference: Author's interview with Fila-delfo Martínez (1990); also, Núñez Téllez, Carlos, *Un Pueblo en Armas* (Managua: Editorial Vanguardia, 1986), pp. 21–23.

Chapter Six—Guerrillas in Power

Events of July 1979: Christian, Shirley, *Nicaragua: Revolution in the Family* (New York: Random House, 1985), pp. 108–118; also, Urcuyo Maliaños, Francisco, *Solos: Los Últimos 43 Horas en el Bunker de Somoza* (Guatemala: Edita, 1979), pp. 90–144; also, Diederich, Bernard, *Somoza and the Legacy of U. S. Involvement in Nicaragua* (New York: Dutton, 1981), pp. 310–328; also, Pastor, Robert, *Condemned to Repetition* (Princeton: Princeton University, 1987), pp. 128–137.

Somoza comment in Florida: *New York Times,* July 18, 1979.

Warren Christopher call to Somoza: Urcuyo Maliaños, op. cit., pp. 132–133; also, Pastor, op. cit., p. 186.

Somoza call to Urcuyo: Urcuyo Maliaños, op. cit., p. 117.

Conversation between Urcuyo and Lawrence Pezzullo, and circumstances of Urcuyo's departure: Urcuyo Maliaños, ibid., pp. 137–144.

Quotes from Oscar René Vargas and Jaime Wheelock: Author's interview with Vargas, who was present at the National Palace meeting on July 19.

Living conditions in Nicaragua: Articles by Thomas John Bossert (p. 347) and Deborah Barndt (p. 317) in Walker, Thomas W. (ed.), *Nicaragua: The First Five Years* (Boulder: Westview, 1986).

Literacy campaign: Black, George, *Triumph of the People: The Sandinista Revolution in Nicaragua* (London: Zed, 1981), pp. 311–316; also, Belli, Humberto, *Breaking Faith: The Sandinista Revolution and Its Impact on Freedom and Christian Faith in Nicaragua* (Westchester, Ill.: Crossway, 1985), pp. 102–105; also, Pastor, op. cit., p. 215; also, the newsletter of the campaign, *La Cruzada en Marcha,* Numbers 1–16; also, the teaching text, *Manual del Brigadista: Ejército Popular de Alfabetizadores* (Managua: Ministerio de Educación, 1980).

Jaime Wheelock on agrarian reform: Collins, Joseph, et. al., *Nicaragua: What Difference Could a Revolution Make? Food and Farming in the New Nicaragua* (San Francisco: Institute for Food and Development Policy, 1985), p. 80.

Sergio Ramírez at ceremonies nationalizing the mining industry: Ramírez, Sergio, *Estás en Nicaragua* (Barcelona: Muchnik, 1985), pp. 104–109.

Early Sandinista plans: Beginning on September 21, 1979, a group of about one hundred senior Sandinistas, the men and women who had directed the insurrection, did something they had never before been able to do: they met together. For three days they gathered behind closed doors, listening as the nine-man National Directorate outlined its plans for building a revolutionary state. Several months later, copies of the document that emerged from that meeting fell into the hands of outsiders. Sandinista leaders had not intended it to become public, but they did not disavow it. The 72-Hour Document, as it came to be known, provided early insights into the Sandinista mind.

In many passages, the 72-Hour Document speaks frankly of the shock with which the Sandinistas greeted their complete victory. They attributed it to "a spectacular diplomatic struggle" that isolated Somoza and prevented the emergence of non-Sandinista alternatives to his tyranny:

"The National Guard was not even dissolved by decree, as some expected," they wrote. "After suffering a series of humiliating defeats, the National Guard collapsed like a house of cards, its tyrants, chieftains and pseudo-heroes fleeing in a shameful stampede. Few victories in the annals of revolution have been as complete as the Sandinista victory. Every phenomenon that defines defeat befell the Guard: military rout on the battlefield, loss of urban centers, the defeat of senior officers, the flight of commanders, the massive capture of war prisoners, the general disarmament and then the final dissolution. Nothing remained of this army but shame, smoke and ashes. It was completely wiped out."

Because of the "absolute Sandinista victory," Sandinista leaders proclaimed that they were entitled to "an extraordinary quota of power." They saw no force able to stand in their way. They unequivocally singled out the United States as "the true enemy," but in a grave misjudgment, concluded that the Americans were powerless to act against them.

"Imperialism has lost its armed instrument in Nicaragua, and for the moment has no way to pursue a reactionary project," they told their followers. "The kind of military victory achieved against the dictatorship makes an aggression by the defeated National Guard practically impossible for now . . . Imperialism is destroyed in Nicaragua. An interventionist aggression is not imminent."

Moisés Hassan on Sandinista intentions: Author's interview with Hassan.

Debate over Alfonso Robelo and his Nicaraguan Democratic Movement: Kinzer stories in *Boston Globe*, March 28 and May 4, 1980; also, Christian, op. cit., pp. 147–154.

Political clashes at *La Prensa*: Chamorro, Jaime, *Frente a Dos Dictaduras: La Lucha por la Libertad de Expresión* (San José: Libre Libre, 1987); also, Kinzer story in *Boston Globe*, May 4, 1980; also, Christian, op. cit., pp. 150–154.

White House meeting between Jimmy Carter and Daniel Ortega: Pastor, op. cit., pp. 206–7.

First anniversary celebration in Managua: Kinzer story in *Boston Globe*, July 20, 1980; also, Christian, op. cit., pp. 161–169.

Humberto Ortega speech August 23, 1980: Christian, ibid., pp. 170–171.

Somoza assassination: Diederich, op. cit., pp. 329–334. Diederich reports that at 10:05 A.M., a team of four to six commandos opened fire on Somoza's limousine as it passed along Avenida España near the center of Asunción. "The top of the Mercedes was ripped apart. The decapitated, armless torso of driver Gallardo was ejected twenty yards into the street by the force of the explosion. Somoza, seated on the rear right side of the car, had eighteen bullets in his body. By the time the rocket hit the car he was dead . . . The hit team had carried out their work well. They had carried out the attack with meticulous precision and speed, making good their escape . . . Somoza's burial in Miami's Woodlawn Cemetery turned into a political rally for Republican presidential candidate Ronald Reagan, with Nicaraguan and Cuban exiles shouting, 'Down with Carter,' whom they accused of 'betraying Nicaragua.' All their 'vivas' were for Reagan, upon whom they had placed their hopes for a better future."

Tomás Borge warning to Robelo: Christian, op. cit., p. 179.

Killing of Jorge Salazar: A detailed United States intelligence report on the case was inserted into the Congressional Record five years later. Nicaraguans close to the case confirmed its principal points:

"In the fall of 1980, the National Directorate of the Sandinista National Liberation Front (FSLN) made a political decision to assassinate private sector leader Jorge Salazar," the report began. "Salazar had become an outspoken critic of the FSLN within the private sector, and had been attending meetings with other anti-Sandinista businessmen. These meetings took place in the home of Dora María Lau, former consul of Nicaragua in Japan under the government of Anastasio Somoza . . . Lau attempted to recruit her nephew, Nestor Moncada Lau, for the private sector cause, not knowing that he was an assistant to Lenin Cerna, chief of the General Directorate of State Security . . . She told him about the meetings and asked him to seek out members of the EPS [Sandinista army] who were opposed to the Sandinista regime and would work with business leaders. Moncada reported the information to Cerna, who in turn reported it to the FSLN National Directorate. The Directorate decided to send two agents posing as disaffected EPS members to the meetings with Salazar and the business leaders . . . The DGSE agents told Salazar and the businessmen that a plan was being prepared within the EPS to overthrow the Sandinista government. The DGSE then drew up the purported plan for the agents to present to the businessmen, who offered to financially back the plot.

"On 17 November 1980, after the DGSE had accumulated information on the anti-Sandinista activities of Salazar and the businessmen, a high-level meeting was held among FSLN National Directorate members and DGSE leaders. Those present at the meeting included Minister of Interior Tomás Borge; Vice Minister of Interior Luis Carrión; chief of the DGSE Cerna; deputy chief of the DGSE Juan José Ubeda; Minister of Defense Humberto Ortega; chief of [DGSE] operations Raul Cordón; DGSE deputy chief of security Roger Mayorga; chief of the Cuban intelligence mission Carlos Lingote; and other National Directorate members . . . During the meeting, Ortega stated that a political decision had been made by the Directorate to assassinate Salazar as an example to other private sector leaders . . . After Ortega's statement, Lingote told the Sandinista leadership that he viewed their decision as a mistake. He said that it would be a grave error that would have political repercussions. Ortega declined to accept the Cuban's advice, saying that the decision had been made. Lingote then left the meeting to consult with his superiors in Cuba. When he returned, he again tried unsuccessfully to dissuade the Sandinista leadership from enacting their plan to kill Salazar, saying the Cuban government did not approve of the plan.

"At the 17 November meeting, Ubeda was put in charge of the operation to assassinate Salazar. He initially gave Cordón the mission of eliminating the businessman, but Cordón protested, saying that he could not do it because he was a friend of Salazar's. Because of Cordón's reaction, Ubeda decided to take responsibility for the assassination himself. On 18 November 1980, Moncada called Salazar, saying that he had important information and needed to talk to Salazar privately as soon as possible. Ubeda accompanied Moncada to the meeting site at El Crucero, on the outskirts of Managua, where the former hid himself. Moncada took a duffle bag of M-16 automatic rifles, which he was to plant in Salazar's car to make the latter appear guilty of possession of arms for use in a coup attempt. When Salazar arrived at the meeting site, Moncada placed the weapons in his car, and Salazar began to protest, saying that he could not carry such items in his possession. Moncada then drew his weapon and fired shots in the air to give the impression to any witnesses within earshot of the incident that a firefight had taken place between the DGSE and Salazar. Ubeda came forward from his hiding place and shot Salazar. Moncada suffered a nervous breakdown as a result of this operation, and has had psychological problems ever since." (*Congressional Record,* April 23, 1985, p. H2365.)

Also, see Christian, op. cit., pp. 175–184.

El Papalonál as transshipment point: Author's interview with Daniel Ortega (1986); also, Pastor, op. cit., pp. 226–228.

In November 1989, two planes laden with arms crashed in El Salvador. Journalists found that the planes had taken off from a Sandinista airstrip at Montelimar, on the Pacific coast. (*Washington Post,* December 4, 1989.)

Foreign Minister Miguel D'Escoto admitted in an interview after the 1990 Sandinista defeat that the Sandinistas had given Salvadoran guerrillas "a direct level of support in regard to weapons." (*National Catholic Reporter,* September 14, 1990.)

Chapter Seven—Me and E. G. Squier

Shaping of Republican platform: Gutman, Roy, *Banana Diplomacy: The Making of American Policy in Nicaragua 1981–1987* (New York: Touchstone, 1988), pp. 19–21. Gutman reports that the plank on Nicaragua was produced by Senator Jesse Helms.

E. G. Squier background: Squier was born in Bethlehem, New York, son of a Methodist minister. "He had little opportunity for formal schooling beyond the grades, but through study by himself he became a scholar of distinction. As a child he worked on a farm, and in his early youth taught school and studied civil engineering; but the panic of 1836–1837 made engineering unprofitable, and he soon turned to journalism and literature . . . In 1847 and 1848 he was clerk of the Ohio House of Representatives."

Squier was named to his diplomatic post in Central America in 1849, and remained there for a year and a half. Later he was United States Commissioner to Peru, and after his return he served as general consul of Honduras in New York City.

"He was honored at home and abroad as one of the most distinguished Americanists of the nineteenth century, and is perhaps the best single authority on the Central America of this period. He was handsome and distinguished in appearance, with waving hair, full beard, and fine features. He was sociable, somewhat fond of gayety, slightly vain, but had a saving sense of humor and a strong altruistic bent, and in the performance of duty was conscientious as well as energetic." (Malone, Dumas [ed.], *Dictionary of American Biography* [New York: Charles Scribner's Sons, 1935], vol. IX, p. 489.)

Chapter Eight—Looking for Contras

Thomas Enders's visit to Managua: Christian, Shirley, *Nicaragua: Revolution in the Family* (New York: Random House, 1985), pp. 198–199.

"The gist of Enders' message at that time was this," Foreign Minister Miguel D'Escoto later recalled. " 'The United States respects the self-determination of countries. We don't care what you do in your country. But you've been accused of exporting revolution, and we want to tell you that we will not stand for such a policy, exporting revolution.' " (*National Catholic Reporter,* September 14, 1990.)

Raids of March 15, 1982: Christian, op. cit., p. 201; also, Gutman, Roy, *Banana Diplomacy: The Making of American Policy in Nicaragua 1981–1987* (New York: Touchstone, 1988), p. 104.

William Casey appearance before congressional committees, and subsequent passage of Boland Amendment: Gutman, ibid., pp. 114—117.

Daniel Ortega on Reagan visit: Kinzer story in *Boston Globe,* December 5, 1982.

Discovery of contra camp: Kinzer story in *New York Times,* March 28, 1983.

Alan Romberg comment: *New York Times,* March 29, 1983.

Security Council debate: Verbatim transcripts, March 28–29, 1983.

Chapter Nine—Bureau Chief

Comments by Congressman Toricelli and Bedell: Kinzer story in *New York Times,* April 12, 1983.

President Reagan news conference: *New York Times,* April 15, 1983.

Conditions in San José de Bocay: Kinzer story in *New York Times,* April 17, 1983.

Plot against Miguel D'Escoto: Kinzer story in *New York Times,* June 7, 1983.

Chapter Ten—CIA and Friends

Killing of *Comandante Bravo:* Dickey, Christopher, *With the Contras: A Reporter in the Wilds of Nicaragua* (New York: Simon and Schuster, 1985), pp. 65–67; also, Cruz, Arturo, Jr., *Memoirs of a Counterrevolutionary: Life With the Contras, the Sandinistas and the CIA* (New York: Doubleday, 1989), pp. 122–123.

Enrique Bermúdez meetings with Luis Pallais Debayle: Christian, Shirley, *Nicaragua: Revolution in the Family* (New York: Random House, 1985), p. 176.

Somoza promises $1 million to contras: Gutman, Roy, *Banana Diplomacy: The Making of American Policy in Nicaragua 1981–1987* (New York: Touchstone, 1988), p. 41.

Pallais meeting with Alfredo Stroessner: Gutman, ibid., p. 41.

Quote from Jorge Rafael Videla, and account of Argentina under his rule: Kinzer article in *The New Republic,* December 23, 1978.

Gustavo Álvarez trip to Washington: Gutman, op. cit., pp. 46–49.

Bermúdez trip to Buenos Aires: Gutman, ibid., pp. 52–53.

United States payment to Argentina: *New York Times,* May 3, 1987.

Duane Clarridge activities and background: Gutman, op. cit., pp. 55–58, 154–157, 203–206; also, author's interview with Edgar Chamorro; also, Cruz, op. cit., p. 132.

Meeting to formalize *la tripartita:* Gutman, op. cit., p. 57; also, Cruz, op. cit., p. 130.

Nicaraguans sent to Argentina for training: Affadavit of Edgar Chamorro before the World Court, published in Vandermeer, John and Peter Rosset (eds.), *Nicaragua: Unfinished Revolution—The New Nicaragua Reader* (New York: Grove, 1986), p. 235.

Reagan's "finding:" Gutman, op. cit., p. 85; also, *New York Times,* May 3, 1987.

Álvarez terror campaign: Years afterward, the Inter-American Court of Human Rights, an arm of the Organization of American States, conducted an extraordinary investigation into the kidnap/murder apparatus that General Álvarez devised and administered. The court was investigating a complaint filed on behalf of a single disappeared Honduran, but its decision included an exhaustive account of how Álvarez's repressive system worked. The court estimated the number of victims at between one hundred and one hundred fifty, and said they had been captured and killed in a strikingly similar manner. All were abducted by men in civilian clothes, blindfolded, and brought to clandestine jails. One witness, an ex-prisoner who had escaped, testified that while in detention, "she was tied up and beaten, she was naked most of the time, she was not given food for many days, she suffered electric shocks, chokings, intents to strangle, threats with firearms, threats that her eyes would be burned, burns on her legs, skin perforations with needles, administration of drugs and sexual abuse." Kinzer story in *New York Times,* July 30, 1988.

After his overthrow, Álvarez became a consultant to the United States Department of Defense, which paid him more than $50,000 during the mid-1980s. Claiming to have become a born-again Christian, he began traveling regularly back to Honduras, stirring fears that he was seeking a return to power. In January 1989 he was assassinated by unknown gunmen on the streets of Tegucigalpa.

CIA involvement in bridge bombings: Dickey, op. cit., p. 131; also, Gutman, op. cit., p. 104.

William Casey pronunciation: Gutman, ibid., p. 115.

Formation of FDN leadership and Edgar Chamorro: Chamorro affidavit in Rosset and Vandermeer, op. cit., pp. 235–237.

Krill and Barreda case: Dickey, op. cit., pp. 166–171.

For lengthy newspaper accounts of the contras' development: *New York Times,* November 27, 1986 and May 3, 1987; also, *Miami Herald,* March 2 and July 12, 1987; also, *Washington Post,* July 23, 1987.

Chapter Eleven—Life During Wartime

Plastic bags: Kinzer story in *New York Times,* August 27, 1986.

Raquel Fernández article: *Nuevo Diario,* December 4, 1988.

Rainstorms: Kinzer story in *New York Times,* May 8, 1987; also, Pallais, Azarias, *Los Caminos Después de las Lluvias,* in Arellano, Jorge Eduardo (ed.), *Antología General de la Poesía Nicaragüense* (Managua: Distribuidora Cultural, 1984), p. 182.

Chapter Twelve—*Comandantes*

Edén Pastora quits Sandinista Front: Christian, Shirley, *Nicaragua: Revolution in the Family* (New York: Random House, 1985), pp. 268–277.

Tomás Borge on Karl May: *Playboy,* September 1983.

State Security apparatus and El Chipote prison: Kinzer story in *New York Times,* August 24, 1986.

Interrogation of Sofonías Cisneros: Victim's statement published by Permanent Commission on Human Rights, Managua, 1985. After the Sandinistas were voted out of power in 1990, Sofonías Cisneros was named Minister of Education.

Borge on women: Interview with Borge broadcast on Sandinista television, December 27, 1989.

Daniel Ortega on Americans, and on experiences as prisoner in Guatemala: *Playboy,* November 1987.

Chapter Thirteen—The Faithful

Jailing of business leaders: In October 1981, Defense Minister Humberto Ortega made a speech asserting that anti-Sandinista entepreneurs were collaborating with "imperialism" and, in the event of an American invasion, would be "the first to be hanged by the people along the roads and highways." The business coalition COSEP responded with an indignant letter to Daniel Ortega:

"The national economy is collapsing," they warned. "As we observe the government's domestic and foreign policies, we see an unmistakable Marxist-Leninist ideological line, which is confirmed in speeches by members of the National Directorate . . . Nicaragua's destruction is at hand. We are reaching a point of no return from which the government will have great difficulty reclaiming its legitimacy. The nationalism of an entire people is being threatened by a radical and fanatic minority."

Sandinista response to the letter was swift. Authorities ordered all six business leaders who signed it arrested and jailed. One sought asylum in the Venezuelan embassy, and two others had left the country after signing the letter, but the remaining three were arrested and held for several weeks without charge.

Murder of Bishop Valdivieso: Quintana, Ofsman, *Apuntes de Historia de Nicaragua* (Managua: Fanatex, 1977), p. 57. For early history of Nicaraguan Catholicism, see Zúñiga, Edgar, *Historia Eclesiástica de Nicaragua* (Managua: Editorial Unión, 1982).

Archbishop Obando: Kinzer story in the *New York Times Magazine,* November 18, 1984; also, Obando y Bravo, Miguel Cardinal, *Agonía en el Bunker* (Managua: Coprosa, 1990); also, Obando, *Libres Como Rios: Homilias de Monseñor Miguel Obando y Bravo* (Managua: Coprosa, 1984).

Bishops' statement following 1979 Sandinista takeover (excerpts from text): "We are asked what we think of socialism . . . If it means, as it should, that the interests of the majority of Nicaraguans are paramount, and if its economic system is planned with national interests in mind, if it encourages people's participation . . . we deem it just. . . . If socialism implies that power is used on behalf of the great majority, and that it is increasingly shared with the people . . . again it will find . . . only our encouragement and support.

"[But if] socialism becomes adulterated, robbing . . . the people of their right to shape their own history; if it attempts to force people blindly to submit to the manipulation and dictates of those who would arbitrarily exercise power, such false socialism we could not accept . . .

"We also have confidence that the revolutionary process will be something original, creative, entirely our own, and that it will be in no way imitative. Because what we seek, together with most Nicaraguans, is a process that will result in a society completely and truly Nicaraguan, one that is neither capitalist, nor dependent, nor totalitarian . . .

"If through fear and mistrust, through the insecurity of some in the face of radical social change, or through the desire to defend personal interests, we neglect this crucial opportunity to commit ourselves to the poor . . . we would be in serious violation of the Gospel's teaching."

Ernesto Cardenal baptism: Belli, Humberto, *Breaking Faith: The Sandinista Revolution and Its Impact on Freedom and Christian Faith in Nicaragua* (Westchester, Ill.: Crossway, 1985), p. 160.

Reynaldo Tefel criticizes bishops: Tefel, Reynaldo Antonio, *Cristianismo y Revolución* (Managua: Centro Ecuménico Antonio Valdivieso, 1985?). Excerpts:
"For 2,000 years, Christianity has been developing along two paths, one progressive and revolutionary and the other conservative and reactionary. The first, the revolutionary, begins with the Sermon on the Mount, a true manifestation of Christian humanism, and with Christ's dramatic action lashing and expelling merchants from the temple. . . . The second path is by nature counter-revolutionary, conservative and devoid of conscience. It begins with Judas's betrayal, the selling of Christ to imperialist political and economic power, a sale that has been repeated many times in these 2,000 years of Christian history . . .

"The revolutionary road was embodied by Bishop Valdivieso and Friar Bartolomé de las Casas, who defended the Indians against the ravages and cruelties of the conquerors.

. . . The other way is represented by the perpetrators, Pedrarias and the Contreras brothers, who enslaved the Indians in God's name, just as today the counter-revolution kills our brothers in the name of that same God . . .

"Once again we see two paths: one interpreting the liberating values of the Gospel, and the other manipulating the Gospel to condemn Latin American revolutionary movements and serve the Empire."

Other Sandinista warnings to bishops: In 1983, Interior Minister Tomás Borge insisted that the Catholic hierarchy could not remain neutral in the escalating war. "The options are clear," he said. "You either defend the oppressive giant, or you side with the small but worthy country that is under attack. You are either with David, or you take aim alongside Goliath. There is no other alternative, none at all." (Borge, et. al., *El Axioma de la Esperanza* [Bilbao: Editorial Desclée de Brouwer, 1984], p. 114.)

Army Chief of Staff Joaquín Cuadra Lacayo raised the possibility that Nicaraguan bishops might one day be expelled from the country, and that the regime would name pro-Sandinista clerics to replace them. "It would be counter-productive," Cuadra said in an interview, "to promote a confrontation now which would end up . . . in the church splitting, perhaps into two churches, thus forcing the Nicaraguan government to say, well, this one is the church that we recognize, the others must go . . . But historically it seems to me that this has to happen someday." (Belli, op. cit., p. 236.)

Papal visit to Managua: Belli, Humberto, op. cit., pp. 211–221; also, Christian, Shirley, *Nicaragua: Revolution in the Family* (New York: Random House, 1985), pp. 230–231.

Shortly before the Pope's visit, the Sandinistas convened an "act of the masses" in Managua to commemorate the victims of a recent contra attack in San Francisco del Norte. The principal speaker was a militantly pro-Sandinista cleric, José Arias Caldera. Standing above a row of flag-draped coffins and facing several thousand sympathetic mourners, Father Arias ridiculed the bishops' insistence that Sandinistas, not contras, posed the real threat to Nicaragua:

"Is it the Nicaraguan people, the militias or the people's Sandinista army that is cutting the hearts out of peaceful and simple peasants living along the border? Is it people like you who profane God's name? Is it you who uses God's name to proclaim 'Death to Communism'? Is Communism a real person, something concrete? What about the deaths of these fourteen or fifteen peasants massacred in San Francisco del Norte? . . .

"When the bishops pray with their hands outstretched, I avert my eyes so as not to see them. Their prayers multiply, but I do not hear them, because there is blood on their hands. Cleanse yourselves! Purify yourselves!" (Pochet, Rosa María, and Martínez, Abelino, *Nicaragua: Iglesia: ¿ Manipulación o Profecía?* [San Jose: DEI, 1987], p. 61.)

Ernesto Cardenal on Papal visit: Episcopal Secretariat of Central America, *Juan Pablo II en America Central* (San José: Sedac, 1984), p. 144.

Bishops' opposition to military conscription: The anti-draft letter was issued August 29, 1983. Defense Minister Humberto Ortega said it showed that Archbishop Obando was being "used by American imperialism." Reynaldo Tefel wrote a pamphlet denouncing it.

"This document contains nothing of theology, and even less of Christianity," Tefel wrote. "It will be remembered as one of the blackest pages in church history, like those that tell the stories of the Inquisition and the condemnation of Galileo, because it seeks to leave an entire people defenseless in the face of United States invasion."

Edward Kennedy quote: Belli, op. cit., p. 224.

Chapter Fourteen—Baseball and Other Passions

History of Nicaraguan baseball: Federación Nicaragüense de Beisbol Amateur, *Historia del Beisbol Nicaragüense: Antiguo, Moderno y Contemporaneo* (Managua: Artes Gráficas, 1976); also, Tijerino, Edgard, *El Mundial Nica* (Managua: Copiaco, 1973); also, Tijerino, Edgard, *Doble Play* (Managua: Editorial Vanguardia, 1989). Kinzer articles in *New York Times,* September 3, 1983, August 8, 1987, and April 15, 1988.

Ballpark as Sunday meeting place: Black, George, *The Good Neighbor: How the United States wrote the History of Central America and the Caribbean* (New York: Pantheon, 1989), p. 150.

Nicaraguan victory over Cuba: Tijerino, *El Mundial Nica,* op. cit., pp. 114–117.

Spanish explorers' reaction to Masaya volcano: Squier, E. G., *Nicaragua: Its People, Scenery, Monuments, Resources, Conditions, and the Proposed Canal* (New York: Harper & Bros., 1860), p. 197.

John Lloyd Stephens on Masaya volcano: Cited in Black, op. cit., p. 15.

Squier on ancient monuments: Squier, op. cit., pp. 446–490. Kinzer article on monuments, *New York Times,* January 20, 1987.

Kinzer article on trip to Chontales, with photo of wounded child in La Embajada: *New York Times,* September 13, 1987.

Rafaela Herrera and conflicts between Spain and Britain in Central America: Floyd, Troy S., *The Anglo-Spanish Struggle for the Mosquitia* (Albuquerque: University of New Mexico, 1967); also, Dozier, Craig L., *Nicaragua's Mosquito Shore: The Years of British and American Presence* (University, Alabama: University of Alabama, 1985), pp. 6–29; also, Quintana, Ofsman, *Apuntes de Historia de Nicaragua* (Managua: Fanatex, 1977), p. 72 & pp. 86–87.

"Never was there so complete a ruin," wrote the British commander, Lt. Col. Stephen Kemble, in his account of the failed campaign to seize Central America from Spain. His reports are collected as *The Kemble Papers, 1773–1789* (New York: N. Y. Historical Society, 1885).

History text on Rafaela Herrera: Quintana, op. cit., p. 87.

Kinzer article on El Castillo: *New York Times,* May 23, 1988; on Solentiname painters: May 18, 1988.

Mark Twain on the San Juan River: Twain sailed from San Francisco to New York along the so-called "Nicaragua route" during the winter of 1866–67, and wrote an account of his trip that was later included in a collection called "Travels with Mr. Brown." The ride down the San Juan set Twain to rhapsody:

"[W]e started down the broad and beautiful river in the grey dawn of the balmy summer morning. In a little while all parties were absorbed in noting the scenery on shore—trees like cypress; other trees with large red blossoms; great feathery tree ferns and giant cactuses; clumps of tall bamboo; all manner of trees and bushes, in fact, webbed together with vines; occasionally a vista that opened, stretched its carpet of fresh grass far within the jungle, then slowly closed again . . . All gazed in rapt and silent admiration for a long time as the exquisite panorama unfolded itself . . . Now and then a rollicking monkey scampered into view, or a bird of splendid plumage floated through the sultry air, or the music of some invisible songster welled up out of the forest depths. The changing vistas of the river ever renewed the intoxicating picture. . . . all manner of quaint and beautiful figures!"

Rubén Darío: Torres, Edelberto, *La Dramática Vida de Rubén Darío* (Managua: Editorial Nueva Nicaragua, 1983); also, Oliver, Antonio, *Este Otro Rubén Darío* (Barcelona: Editorial Aedos, 1960). Kinzer articles on Darío in the *New York Times,* May 14, 1985 and January 18, 1987.

In the Oliver book, I found this excerpt from one of Darío's letters, written in 1915 after a visit to the United States: "Unfortunately, those who believe that the Yankees are not serious thinkers are mistaken. They know about everything. They amass millions of dollars, write books, build railroads, produce poems, and launch new scientific doctrines which the world respects and accepts."

Chapter Fifteen—Action Democracy

Arturo Cruz background: Author's interviews with Cruz, Reynaldo Tefel, and Emilio Álvarez Montalván; also, Cruz, Arturo, Jr., *Memoirs of a Counterrevolutionary: Life With the Contras, the Sandinistas, and the CIA* (New York: Doubleday, 1988) pp. 31–43.

Mining of Corinto: Kinzer story in *New York Times,* March 16, 1984; also, Gutman, Roy, *Banana Diplomacy: The Making of American Policy in Nicaragua 1981–1987* (New York: Touchstone, 1988), pp. 197–199. Gutman reports: "The mines selected for the job were 'bottom sitters' containing about 300 pounds of explosives . . . [T]he CIA had them assembled to its own design specifications at a workshop in Honduras." Also, Cruz, Arturo, Jr., op. cit., pp. 164–165.

Barry Goldwater letter: Gutman, op. cit., pp. 199–200.

Edén Pastora on the CIA: *Washington Post,* July 5, 1987.

Bomb attack on Pastora: Avirgan, Tony, and Martha Honey (eds.), *La Penca: On Trial in Costa Rica;* also, Kinzer stories in *New York Times,* June 1 and June 2, 1984. "For several months, the CIA has been preparing the ground, mounting a campaign against me, saying I am the only obstacle to unity with the Nicaraguan Democratic Force," Pastora said the day after the bombing. "This attack is punishment for not yielding."

Six years after the bombing, the Costa Rican Judicial Police issued a report that led to murder charges being filed against John Hull, an American linked to the CIA who had once owned a farm in northern Costa Rica, and Felipe Vidal, an anti-Castro Cuban. Hull and Vidal were charged with planning the La Penca attack together with contras and CIA collaborators. For accounts of Hull's activities, see the *Wall Street Journal,* May 21, 1987, and the *Miami Herald,* July 11, 1987.

George Shultz meeting with Daniel Ortega: Kinzer story in *New York Times,* June 3, 1984; also, Gutman, op. cit., p. 211.

Selection of presidential candidate: Gutman, op. cit., p. 238.

Tomás Borge on democracy: Borge, et. al., *El Axioma de la Esperanza* (Bilbao: Editorial Desclée de Brouwer, 1984), p. 89.

Cruz campaign: Kinzer stories in *New York Times,* July 23, 26, 29, August 15, 22, 26, September 21, 24, October 7, 22, 23, 30, 31, November 3, 4, 5, 7 and 11, 1984; also, Cruz, Arturo, *Nicaragua's Continuing Struggle* (New York: Freedom House, 1988).
  I interviewed Cruz in 1988 at his Miami home, and he said he regretted quitting the 1984 presidential campaign. "That was a fundamental error," he said. "We should have stayed in the race no matter what happened . . . That would have been constructive for Nicaragua." (*New York Times,* January 8, 1988.)

Sandinista view of presidential campaign: As the campaign was beginning, the Sandinista campaign manager, *Comandante* Bayardo Arce, visited the headquarters of the Socialist party to deliver a supposedly secret speech outlining "the focus that we Communists should give to the electoral process":
  "We think the electoral process, which we announced and committed ourselves to as part of our revolutionary program, was and is a valuable tool in our offensive against United States policy . . . From our perspective, the elections are a nuisance, just as a number of things that make up our revolution are a nuisance. But from a realistic standpoint, being in a war with the United States, these things become weapons of the revolution . . .
  "Imperialism asks three things of us: to abandon interventionism, to abandon our strategic ties with the Soviet Union and the socialist community, and to be democratic. We cannot stop being internationalists without ceasing to be revolutionaries; nor can we cut off strategic relationships without ceasing to be revolutionaries. It is impossible even to consider this. But the other matter, democracy as they call it, has an element which we can manage, and that can even help the construction of socialism in Nicaragua. . . . We are using an instrument claimed by the bourgeoisie, which disarms the international bourgeoisie, in order to move ahead on matters that are strategic to us . . . We see the election as one more weapon of the revolution to bring its historical objectives gradually into reality." *(Comandante Bayardo Arce's Secret Speech before the Nicaraguan Socialist Party* [Washington: Department of State, 1986]).

Rio de Janeiro summit: Gutman, op. cit., pp. 247–253. Also, Cruz Jr., op. cit., pp. 186–187.

Virgilio Godoy meeting with Harry Bergold: Author's interviews with Godoy and Bergold (1984).

Interior Ministry guidelines to *La Prensa* (full text):
  "1. Absolute prohibition to refer to the November 4 elections in terms that directly

or indirectly express or suggest citizens' abstentions, fraud, manipulation of figures, or lack of confidence in electoral authorities. Anything referring to the elections must meet the Media Office's criteria.

"2. Absolute prohibition of all news and comment on all military matters, other than that released by the Defense Ministry, Interior Ministry or government junta.

"3. Absolute prohibition of all news from abroad that contains attacks or unfavorable comments tending to weaken the Nicaraguan government, the Sandinista party, or the people's Sandinista revolution, whether from individuals, prominent persons, or foreign governments or organizations, above all the United States.

"4. Absolute prohibition of news headlines that do not exactly coincide with the body of the article.

"5. Absolute prohibition of all items on labor problems or strikes.

"6. Obligation to publish the dispatches of the Defense and Interior Ministries and the government junta."

Alleged shipment of Soviet jets: Kinzer stories in *New York Times,* September 8–9, 1984.

Bergold visit to foreign ministry: Gutman, op. cit., p. 255.

Chapter Sixteen—*Trabil Nani:* The Miskito War

Early history of Mosquito Coast: Dozier, Craig, *Nicaragua's Mosquito Shore: The Years of British and American Presence* (University, Alabama: University of Alabama, 1985); also, Floyd, Troy S., *The Anglo-Spanish Struggle for the Mosquitia* (Albuquerque: University of New Mexico, 1967); also, Smutko, Gregorio, *La Mosquitia: Historia y Cultura de la Costa Atlántica* (Managua: Editorial La Ocarina, 1985); also, Montenegro, Sofia, *Memorias del Atlántico* (Managua: Editorial Nuevo Amanecer, 1986).

Advertisement in *Bluefields Messenger:* Dozier, op. cit., p. 146.

Early conflicts between coast people and Sandinistas: One of the first Sandinista organizers sent to the coast region, Jorge Jenkins, later sought to explain government policies during the early 1980s.

"At the beginning, many Misurasata leaders undoubtedly acted in good faith," he wrote. "But they lacked the political vision necessary to see that they were being manipulated to take confrontational attitudes toward the government and the Sandinista Front. Many naively sought to apply in Nicaragua arguments that they had picked up at international conferences . . .

"The Indian leaders became ethnicists . . . Their separatist work made great progress, manipulating ethno-populist sentiments with slogans like, "Only the Indian Will Save the Indian" and "Atlantic Coast for the Coast People." Government delegates were made to look ridiculous when they attended Miskito meetings, where Indian leaders, speaking in their own language, hurled accusations at the government and even at the delegates themselves. By doing this, Misurasata leaders were showing the Indians that they were the 'true' defenders against the intrusions of 'Spaniards' from the Pacific coast. . . .

"Misurasata led its supporters to believe that the government was reaping enormous profits along the Atlantic, sending all of it to the Pacific side and leaving nothing for the local population. The truth was exactly contrary . . . The cost of developing an enormous region that represents forty percent of the national territory, and only ten percent of its people, has been nothing short of colossal . . .

"[Misurasata leaders] completely forgot that their demands had to be conciliated with the many problems facing the rest of the population, which was desperately trying to recover from Somoza's tyranny, and from the destruction left after the national liberation war. Misurasata did not care about the national situation. They wanted their demands met immediately because they were in a special category as Indians. Because they were Indians, they felt they deserved the most extraordinary and undivided attention . . .

"In all of these events leading up to the critical situation of February 1981, mention must be made of the errors the government and Sandinista Front committed, all of which were used by Misurasata leaders to foment animosity against the revolution. In the first place, it must be said that from the beginning, the people sent by the government to take charge of the Atlantic region were totally ignorant of the socio-economic reality there. This ignorance was even more glaring when it came to indigenous groups, about whom almost nothing was known . . . There was not even a realization that it was important to understand the Miskito . . .

"By the beginning of 1981, Misurasata had managed to consolidate a basic conspiratorial structure, even copying some of the Sandinista Front's own techniques. It had great popular support, and with the help of many Moravian pastors, it had created an anti-government and anti-Sandinista attitude among the indigenous population, with which it alone could communicate . . . Misurasata's leaders were no longer interested in dialogue or in reaching any understanding. They wanted confrontation." (Jenkins Molieri, Jorge, *El Desafío Indígena en Nicaragua: El Caso de los Miskitos* [Managua: Editorial Vanguardia, 1986], pp. 275–331.)

One of the few Miskito physicians, Dr. Kenneth Serapio, was in his native village of Raití, on the bank of the Coco River, during much of this period. In an interview several years later, he reflected on how the Sandinistas lost their moral authority over Nicaragua's Indians:

"They underappreciated my people's identity, my people's history, well, our whole culture. The less they knew about our village, the more they pretended to know. And every time they made a mistake, every time our people responded to their ideas with suspicion or reluctance, they became more hostile, and blamed us for their failure to convince us. They were so worried about control, and so in a hurry, they didn't do anything but make us mad. Our most sacred concerns, about food subsistence and our land base, they trampled on. It was inevitable that my people would become hostile. . . .

"I remember a small incident, while in Raití, after one of the first attacks on the garrison. Afterward, the army gathered the whole village. The Sandinista official spoke harshly to everyone. He accused the village of backing the combatants, and then of supporting American imperialism, and [said] Yankee imperialism must be erased from the face of the earth. Annihilate first the supporters and later the roots, he said. They got the whole community together to tell them this. In a harsh voice, not the sweet voice of before. A military threat, and a true one, because the cannons of the garrison were now pointed in the direction of the village. It is true. I was the translator. The military had the whole village surrounded." [Akwesasne Notes, vol. 17, #3 and 4, Summer 1985 and Late Summer 1985.)

Evacuation of Miskitos and their conditions during the early 1980s: Americas Watch, *The Miskitos in Nicaragua, 1981–1984* (New York: Americas Watch, 1984); also, Nietschman, Bernard, *The Unknown War: The Miskito Nation, Nicaragua and the United States* (New York: Freedom House, 1989).

Brooklyn Rivera comments on Steadman Fagoth and Sandinistas: Philippe Bourgeois article in Vandermeer, John and Peter Rosset (eds.), *Nicaragua, Unfinished Revolution: The New Nicaragua Reader* (New York: Grove, 1986), p. 463.

Rivera and Luis Carrión after peace talks: Kinzer story in *New York Times,* May 30, 1985.

Visit to Yulu: Kinzer story in *New York Times,* July 29, 1985. Further information on Rubio: Kinzer stories in *New York Times,* October 6 and 8, 1987.

Sandinistas support autonomy: Kinzer stories in *New York Times,* June 26 and August 30, 1985.

Indians' return to Coco River: Kinzer stories in *New York Times,* June 25, July 24 and 27, and August 22, 1985.

Rivera's clandestine trip into Nicaragua: At a news conference in Costa Rica, Russell Means and other Indian activists from the United States declared their support for the Miskito rebellion. They accused the Sandinista regime of subjecting Nicaragua to an "unconscionably racist, soulless Marxist experiment," and said the regime was "fast forfeiting the claim of any right or say in the future of the Atlantic coast's indigenous people and territories." Kinzer story in *New York Times,* November 11, 1985. Also, Kinzer story from Layasiksa in *New York Times,* February 8, 1986.

Sumo Indians: Americas Watch, *The Sumos in Nicaragua: An Endangered People* (New York: Americas Watch, 1987).

Travels from Bluefields: Kinzer stories in the *New York Times,* September 13, 1984 (Rama Cay) and October 29, 1986 (Pearl Lagoon).

Bulgarians in Bluefields: Kinzer story in *New York Times,* December 12, 1986. The deep-water port project was virtually destroyed by the force of Hurricane Joan, which devastated the Atlantic coast region in October 1988.

Chapter Seventeen—Bloodstains

Mothers' grief: Kinzer story in *New York Times,* January 15, 1985.

Reagan quotes: Sklar, Holly, *Washington's War on Nicaragua* (Boston: South End, 1988), pp. 217, 261, 308.

Reagan radio broadcast and Washington speech: *New York Times,* February 16 and March 25, 1985.

CIA training manual: Kornbluh, Peter, *Nicaragua, The Price of Intervention: Reagan's War Against the Sandinistas* (Washington: Institute for Policy Studies, 1987), p. 45.

Congressional votes on contra aid: Gutman, Roy, *Banana Diplomacy: The Making of American Policy in Nicaragua 1981–1987* (New York: Touchstone, 1988), p. 284.

Bill Chapell and George Miller quotes: *Congressional Record,* June 12, 1985, pp. H4166, H4128.

Enrique Bermúdez on humanitarian aid: Gutman, op. cit., p. 291.

Daniel Ortega returns from Moscow: Kinzer story in *New York Times,* May 21, 1985.

General Ochoa: Throughout the Contra war, Ochoa was the Sandinistas' key military strategist. After the war ended, he returned to Cuba where he had won wide popularity. President Fidel Castro apparently considered him a threat. In 1989 Ochoa was arrested and charged with corruption and treason. After a military trial, he was sentenced to death and executed.

Offer to buy *La Prensa:* Kinzer story in *New York Times,* April 18, 1986.

Jaime Chamorro article (excerpts): "[T]he Sandinistas are transforming the Nicaraguan revolution, fought for by all Nicaraguans, into a revolution that serves the purpose of Marxism-Leninism. That is to say, they are taking a nationalist movement and turning it into a beachhead for communist expansion . . .

"Before the Sandinistas can reach this goal, those Nicaraguans who are fighting for democracy have a right to ask for help from wherever they can get it . . . The future of the freedom of generations of Nicaraguans hangs in the balance.

"Those who would argue that to give aid to the Nicaraguan rebels would be a violation of the 'principle of a people's right to self-determination' are mistaken. These people seem to ignore or perhaps forget deliberately that self-determination applies to peoples, not oppressive governments that do not legitimately represent the will of the people." (*Washington Post,* May 3, 1986.)

Miguel D'Escoto attacks on Cardinal Obando: Several of D'Escoto's speeches were broadcast on Sandinista television. One included these comments:

"That poor human being born in Nicaragua and ordained to the priesthood, Miguel Obando, tells the legislators, 'Don't worry, because I, I am Cardinal, and I cannot condemn aggression!' Could there ever be a more abominable sin in the history of humanity? I believe, dear brethren, that there is no word uttered by human mouth, no adjective that could truly describe the horror, the disgust produced by this brother of ours . . .

"If you are at your television or radio, don't turn it off! Don't turn it off, Miguel Obando! The Lord, through his humble people—the peasants who suffer the aggression of which you have been the principal accomplice—that God, the God of life, the God of love, of justice but also of mercy, has had mercy on you, Miguel Obando . . . The Lord, therefore, is giving you an opportunity. Meanwhile, listen carefully: In the name of God and with the authority that comes from God, we tell you that you must immediately abstain from again celebrating the Holy Sacrifice of the Mass. Because it is sacrilegious for an accomplice to murder to celebrate the Sacrifice, and it deeply offends the faith of our people."

March 1986 incursion: Gutman, op. cit., pp. 324–325; also, *Miami Herald,* January 8, 1987.

Arturo Cruz quits contra leadership: Sklar, op. cit., p. 219. Later Cruz came to regret having accepted a retainer from the CIA. "Everyone was getting it," he said. "It was a tremendous mistake." (Kinzer story in *New York Times,* January 8, 1988.)

Gerry Studds comment: Sklar, op. cit., p. 131.

President Azcona responds to firing of Ambassador Ferch: Gutman, op. cit., p. 335.

Closure of *La Prensa:* Soon after announcing the closure, the Sandinistas issued an official communiqué.

"The Press Directorate of the Interior Ministry informs the Nicaraguan people:

"(1) That the American administration's immoral approval of the $110 million [sic] for counter-revolutionary forces means continuation of the war of aggression, which within our own country has been encouraged and defended by some unpatriotic groups.

"(2) That as our people prepare to confront and defeat imperialist aggression, which has brought death and destruction to Nicaragua, the newspaper *La Prensa,* acting as spokesman for the interests of the aggressive power, has been escalating the level of its provocation and disinformation, seeking thereby to justify United States aggression, denying the validity of the Contadora Group as the only possible solution for peace in Central America.

"(3) That the newspaper *La Prensa* has never lived up to its social, ethical or professional responsibility, and has not reflected the common goals of Nicaraguan society, which is the obligation of the press to its people.

"(4) That it has repeatedly violated orders of this Directorate by publishing expressly prohibited material.

"(5) That despite preventive warnings, editors of *La Prensa* continue to behave defiantly, and to disturb order and public safety.

"(6) That on the basis of the foregoing, based on Decree 130 of October 31, 1985, and Articles 1, 2 and 3 of the provisional press law, and articles 42, 43 and 46 of rules under said law, the Directorate has resolved to suspend the publication of *La Prensa* indefinitely."

Expulsion of Bishop Vega: In Vega's last public statement in Managua before his expulsion, he told journalists that under some circumstances there existed a "right to insurrection." He said there were "totalitarian regimes" that were even more oppressive than traditional dictatorships.

"In some dictatorships, man can defend himself and say what he feels," Vega said. "In contrast, under the totalitarian ideology man has no voice, no form of personal expression. He is reduced to a simple instrument of work without any rights of his own." (Kinzer stories in *New York Times,* July 7 and 17, 1986.)

Family divisions: Kinzer stories in the *New York Times,* May 22, 1986 (Cruz/Carrión family), September 22, 1986 (Chamorro family).

George Shultz on the Sandinistas: Sklar, op. cit., p. 261.

American opposition to Nicaraguan loans: Kornbluh, op. cit., pp. 93–121.

Military maneuvers in Honduras: During the first maneuvers, held in October 1981 and July 1982, American and Honduran troops practiced amphibious and air-mobile operations in areas twenty-five miles from the Nicaraguan border. The maneuvers steadily escalated in scale. In February 1983 a force of 1,600 American troops, accompanied by more than forty aircraft, joined four thousand Honduran soldiers in fending off a staged invasion by the nation of "Corinto."

That exercise lasted six days. The next one lasted six months, longer than any military maneuver in American history. Five thousand American troops and six thousand Hondurans spent from August 1983 to March 1984 practicing bomber raids, sea landings, infantry tactics, and commando operations. The cost was officially reported at $76.9 million.

Maneuvers aimed at intimidating the Sandinistas were held not only on Honduran soil, but also at sea. During 1983 and 1984, small armadas of American warships appeared off both Nicaraguan coasts. Among them were not simply frigates and destroyers, but also giant aircraft carriers that dispatched F-14 fighter jets up and down the coastlines. (Kornbluh, op. cit., pp. 140–142.) For full list of maneuvers through 1986, see Lowenthal, Abraham F. (ed.), *Latin America and Caribbean Record,* vol. 5, 1985–86 (New York: Holmes & Meier, 1988) p. B378.

March 1986 explosion: Gutman, op. cit., p. 306.

Francisca Sobalbarro: Kinzer story in *New York Times,* August 16, 1987.

Chapter Eighteen—Plane Crash

Kinzer stories on Hasenfus case in *New York Times:* November 2, 3, 6, 14, 16, 23, and December 20, 1986.

Luis Posada Carriles: *The Nation,* November 15, 1986; also, *Los Angeles Times,* January 9, 1989.

Caspar Weinberger on proposed arms deal: Burns, Bradford E., *At War in Nicaragua: The Reagan Administration and the Politics of Nostalgia* (New York: Harper & Row, 1987), p. 309.

Robert MacFarlane on US foreign policy: Gutman, Roy, *Banana Diplomacy: The Making of American Policy in Nicaragua 1981–1987* (New York: Touchstone, 1988), p. 341.

Daniel Ortega statement on pardoning Hasenfus: *Barricada,* December 18, 1986.

Chapter Nineteen—An American Martyr

Ben Linder background and letters home: Mimeographed memorial leaflets passed out in Managua following his death. After completing the electric plant in El Cuá, Linder wrote this in a letter:

"The idea is not just to put electricity into a town; that's easy and can happen anywhere. The important thing is also to deal with the social-technical problems that go with it . . .

"It's amazing to us, being from the States, the lack of basic experience these people have. While most men in the US, and now more women, have used a wrench, most people in El Cuá have never seen one . . . The people who gained experience with tools on the job will serve as mechanics not only for the plant, but for the surrounding area as a whole. We'll take some of the people from this project and put them with new workers so we don't lose the experience, and they keep getting better training. After another generation, in 20 years, there should be a marked increase in the technical ability in this area.

"The new plant will make a variety of development projects possible. Right now, wood is cut in the hills around El Cuá, taken to Jinotega [city] and cut into boards, and then brought back. By then the price is too high for any of the local construction needs. So we're putting in a sawmill. To take care of the coffee harvest equipment and the sawmill, we're putting in a complete metal shop, and a carpentry shop; also facilities for making cement blocks, bricks and roof tiles . . . There are also plans to put in several fish ponds as part of [the government's] local fish breeding project, which would be good because there's a definite protein shortage in the area . . . The traditional stream for washing clothes is always short of water during the dry season, so we're going to put in a good washing area, with actual washboards and sinks . . .

"Another part of the plan is to conduct an energy conservation program when we hook up the houses. Most people in the town have never had electricity in their house, so we have the opportunity of promoting energy consciousness from day one. The idea is to use the project to promote a whole series of small solutions that come with good planning. And we'll find our mistakes, and on the next plant we'll avoid them."

Survivor's account of raid: *Dallas Morning News,* April 30, 1987. There were conflicting accounts of how Linder died. His father charged at a news conference that contra raiders had only wounded him at first, and then "blew his brains out at gunpoint, there as he lay wounded at the site."

Also, Kinzer stories in *New York Times,* April 30 and May 6, 1987.

Chapter Twenty—Oliver North in Nicaragua

Oliver North testimony: *Taking the Stand: The Testimony of Oliver North* (New York: Pocket Books, 1987); for background on North, see Bradlee, Ben, Jr., *Guts and Glory: The Oliver North Story* (New York: D. I. Fine, 1988).

Reagan on Sandinistas as "moral challenge": Gutman, Roy, *Banana Diplomacy: The Making of American Policy in Nicaragua 1981–1987* (New York: Touchstone, 1988), p. 284.

North calls diversion a "neat idea:" Burns, Bradford E., *At War in Nicaragua: The Reagan Administration and the Politics of Nostalgia* (New York: Harper & Row, 1987), p. 320.

Plans for constitutional convention, and other North projects: *Los Angeles Times,* March 21, 1987; also, *Washington Post,* May 4, 1987. At North's 1989 trial, the government released previously classified information about the contra project and North's role in it. See *New York Times,* April 7, 1989. For a detailed account of the trial, see *The New Yorker,* October 16, 1989.

Raid on San José de Bocay: Kinzer story in *New York Times,* July 19, 1987.

Chapter Twenty-one—"Peace Is a Process"

CIA airdrops to Contras: *New York Times,* January 27, 1988.

Spain offers peace plan: Kinzer story in the *New York Times,* December 25, 1985.

Edén Pastora retires: Sklar, Holly, *Washington's War on Nicaragua* (Boston: South End, 1988), p. 279.

Oscar Arias presidential campaign: Fernández, Guido, *El Primer Domingo en Febrero* (San José: Editorial Costa Rica, 1986).

Efforts of William Casey to meet Arias: Fernández, Guido, *El Desafío de la Paz en Centroamerica* (San Jose: Editorial Costa Rica, 1989), pp. 50–53.

Santa Elena airstrip: Fernández, ibid., pp. 62–63; also, *New York Times,* May 3, 1987.

Interview with Arias: Kinzer story in *New York Times,* September 10, 1986.

Early Arias efforts to forge peace plan: Kinzer stories in *New York Times,* February 22 and April 26, 1987.

Signing of peace plan and immediate effects: Kinzer stories in *New York Times,* August 9, 14, 23, 24, 26, 30, September 3, 5, 9, 10, 12, 15, 16, 19, 23, 25, 29, 30, October 3, 17, 20, 22, 25–31, November 4, 1987. Arias comments after signing: Kinzer story in *New York Times,* August 12, 1987.

President Reagan seeks new aid for the contras after Central American presidents sign peace accord: Two months after the Guatemala accord was signed, Reagan spoke to the Organization of American States in Washington. "Today, we are called upon to face one of the most serious challenges that has ever confronted our hemisphere," he said. "I am talking about the efforts of the democratic nations of Central, South and North America to bring Nicaragua into the embrace of freedom . . . Nicaraguans have known only tyranny. They have seen one dictator fall, only to be replaced by nine *comandantes* who are far worse . . . And I make a solemn vow—as long as there is breath in this body, I will speak and work, strive and struggle, for the cause of the Nicaraguan freedom fighters . . . I will request and fight for a $270 million package of renewed military and humanitarian assistance for the freedom fighters." (*New York Times,* October 8, 1987.)

Arias wins Nobel Prize: Kinzer stories in *New York Times,* October 14 and 15, 1987.

Reagan administration's attitude toward Arias: Kinzer and Robert Pear story in *New York Times,* August 7, 1988. "Publicly, the Reagan administration refers to Arias in a cordial, friendly fashion," acknowledged Jose Sorzano of the National Security Council staff. "But actually, privately, they have a low opinion of him that borders on despising him."

Carlos López Contreras on Honduran obligations: *Miami Herald,* August 22, 1987.

Encounter with Norland: Kinzer story, with photo, in *New York Times,* October 11, 1987.

Ortega agrees to meet contras, then flies to Washington: Kinzer stories in *New York Times,* November 6, 7, & 11, 1987.

Negotiations in the Dominican Republic: Kinzer stories in *New York Times,* December 4–5, 1987.

Wounded children: Kinzer story in *New York Times,* January 28, 1988.

Attack on Mary Speck: *Baltimore Sun,* February 21, 1988.

Bombing at Coco River: Kinzer story in *New York Times,* March 18, 1988.

Sapoá talks and aftermath: Kinzer stories in *New York Times,* March 21–31, 1988.

Release of prisoners: Kinzer stories in *New York Times,* March 28 and April 3, 1988.

Chapter Twenty-two—Endings

Estelí at peace: Kinzer story in *New York Times,* June 6, 1988.

Moisés Hassan quits Sandinista Front: Kinzer story in *New York Times,* May 8, 1988. "Among Sandinistas, you become somewhat undesirable when you disagree with certain policies and actions," Hassan said. "I'm not a fanatic. I can't be locked into a box."

Labor protests: Kinzer stories in *New York Times,* April 16, 29, May 3, 5, 7, 1988.

Daniel Ortega on contras: Kinzer story in *New York Times,* May 2, 1988.

Nandaime protest: Kinzer stories in *New York Times,* June 9, 11, 1988.

Expulsion of Ambassador Melton and Sandinista crackdown: Kinzer stories in *New York Times,* July 14, 15, 17, 18, 1988.

Tomás Borge on flexibility: Kinzer story in *New York Times,* July 18, 1988.

Interview with Sergio Ramírez: *Crónica,* January 3–10, 1988.

Violeta Chamorro in Granada: *New York Times Magazine,* February 11, 1988.

Carlos Carrión on elections, and Sandinista electoral strategy: Carrión, *Plan de Campaña del FSLN—Region 3* (mimeo, August 9, 1989); also, Arce, Bayardo, *La Coyuntura Actual y el Proceso Electoral* (mimeo, August 26, 1989).

BIBLIOGRAPHY

Acuña Escobar, Francisco. *Biografía del General Rigoberto Cabezas.* Masaya: El Espectador, 1940.

Alaniz Pinell, Jorge. *Nicaragua, Una Revolución Reaccionaria.* Panama: Kosmos, 1985.

Alegría, Claribel, and D. J. Plakoll. *Nicaragua: La Revolución Sandinista, Una Cronología Política 1855–1979.* Mexico: ERA, 1982.

Alemán Bolaños, Gustavo. *El Pueblo de Nicaragua y los Estados Unidos.* Managua: Heurberger, 1923.

———. *Sandino el Libertador: Biografía del Héroe Americano.* San José: IMCUSA, 1980.

Alfaro, Olmedo. *El Filibustero Walker en Nicaragua.* Panama: Editorial La Moderna, 1932.

Alfaro Alvarado, Mario. *Agonía en Rojo y Negro: Los Derechos Humanos en Nicaragua.* San José: Trejos Hermanos, 1986.

Allen, Merritt Parmelee, *William Walker, Filibustero.* New York: Harper & Bros, 1932.

Álvarez, Miguel Ángel. *De Cómo Perdimos las Provincias de Nicoya y Guanacaste.* Granada: Tipografía Salesiana, 1942.

Álvarez Lejarza, Emilio. *Las Constituciones de Nicaragua.* Madrid: Ediciones Cultura Hispánica, 1958.

Amador, Armando. *El Exilio y Las Banderas de Nicaragua.* Mexico: Federación Editorial Mexicana, 1987.

425

──── . *Sandino y la Derrota Militar de los Estados Unidos en Nicaragua.* Mexico: Federación Editorial Mexicana, 1987.

Americas Watch. *Freedom of Expression in Nicaragua During the Election Period 1984.* New York: Americas Watch, 1984.

──── . *Human Rights in Nicaragua.* New York: Americas Watch, 1984.

──── . *Human Rights in Nicaragua 1985–1986.* New York: Americas Watch, 1986.

──── . *Human Rights in Nicaragua 1986.* New York: Americas Watch, 1987.

──── . *Human Rights in Nicaragua: Reagan, Rhetoric and Reality.* New York: Americas Watch, 1985.

──── . *Land Mines in Nicaragua and El Salvador.* New York: Americas Watch, 1986.

──── . *May 1987 Supplement to the Report on Violations of the Rules of War by Both Sides in Nicaragua.* New York: Americas Watch, 1987.

──── . *The Miskitos in Nicaragua 1981–1984.* New York: Americas Watch, 1984.

──── . *Nicaragua: A Human Rights Chronology July 1979–July 1989.* New York: Americas Watch, 1989.

──── . *The Sumos in Nicaragua: An Endangered People.* New York: Americas Watch, 1987.

──── . *Violations of the Rules of War by Both Sides in Nicaragua 1981–1985.* New York: Americas Watch, 1985.

Aquino, Enrique. *La Personalidad Política del General José Santos Zelaya.* Managua: Talleres Gráficos Pérez, 1944.

Arce, Bayardo. *Política de la Revolución Sandinista: Una Respuesta Ante la Política Agresiva de la Administración Reagan.* Managua: Centro de Comunicación Internacional, 1985.

──── . *Sandinismo y Política Imperialista.* Managua: Editorial Nueva Nicaragua, 1985.

Arellano, Jorge Eduardo, ed. *Antología General de la Poesía Nicaragüense.* Managua: Distribuidora Cultural, 1984.

──── . *Lecciones de Sandino.* Managua: Distribuidora Cultural, 1983.

──── . *Panorama de la Literatura Nicaragüense.* Managua: Editorial Nueva Nicaragua, 1982.

Argüello, Álvaro, ed. *Fe Cristiana y Revolución Sandinista en Nicaragua.* San José: Artes Gráficas, 1980.

Argüello, Rosendo. *Doy Testimonio: Conspiraciones y Traiciones en el Caribe.* Managua: CIRA, 1982.

──── . *El Filibusterismo Diplomático Ante la Conciencia Política.* San José: CIRA, 1982.

Arias, Pilar. *Nicaragua en Revolución: Relatos de Combatientes del Frente Sandinista.* Mexico: Siglo XXI, 1980.

Avirgan, Tony, and Honey, Martha, eds. *La Penca: On Trial in Costa Rica.* San José: Editorial Porvenir, 1987.

Ayon, Tomás. *Historia de Nicaragua Desde los Tiempos Más Remotos Hasta el Año de 1852.* Granada: El Centroamericano, 1889.

Barahona, Amaru. *Estudio Sobre la Historia de Nicaragua del Auge Cafetalero al Triunfo de la Revolución.* Managua: INIES, 1989.

Barreto, Pablo Emilio. *44 Años de Dictadura Somocista.* Managua: La Prensa, 1980.

Barry, Tom, and Deb Preusch, eds. *The Central America Fact Book.* New York: Grove, 1986.

Beals, Carleton. *Con Sandino en Nicaragua.* León: Editorial Universitaria, 1980.

———. *Banana Gold. American Imperialism: Viewpoints of United States Foreign Policy 1898–1941* Salem, N.H.: Ayer, 1970.

Belausteguigoitia, Ramon de. *Con Sandino en Nicaragua.* Managua: Editorial Nueva Nicaragua, 1985.

Bell, Belden, ed. *Nicaragua, An Ally Under Siege.* Washington: Council on American Affairs, 1978.

Belli, Gioconda. *Amor Insurrecto.* Managua: Editorial Nueva Nicaragua, 1984.

———. *De la Costilla de Eva.* Managua: Editorial Nueva Nicaragua, 1986.

———. *La Mujer Habitada.* Managua: Editorial Vanguardia, 1988.

Belli, Humberto. *Breaking Faith: The Sandinista Revolution and Its Impact on Freedom and Christian Faith in Nicaragua.* Westchester, Ill.: Crossway, 1985.

Belt, Thomas. *The Naturalist in Nicaragua.* Chicago: University of Chicago, 1985.

Bemis, Samuel Flagg. *The Latin American Policy of the United States: An Historical Interpretation.* New York: Harcourt, Brace, 1943.

Berman, Karl. *Under the Big Stick: Nicaragua and the United States Since 1848.* Boston: South End, 1986.

Blachman, Morris J, et. al., eds. *Confronting Revolution Through Security and Diplomacy in Central America.* New York: Pantheon, 1986.

Black, George. *The Good Neighbor: How the United States Wrote the History of Central America and the Caribbean.* New York: Pantheon, 1989.

———. *Triumph of the People: The Sandinista Revolution in Nicaragua.* London: Zed, 1981.

Blandón, Jesús M. *Entre Sandino y Fonseca.* Managua: Departamento de Agitación y Propaganda, FSLN, 1981.

Bolaños, Pio. *La Situación Económica de Nicaragua: La Intervención Norteamericana y sus Consequencias.* San José: Lehman, 1915.

Bolaños Geyer, Alejandro. *El Filibustero Clinton Rollins.* Managua: Editorial San José, 1976.

———. *James C. Jamison: Con Walker en Nicaragua.* Managua: Editorial San José, 1977.

———. *1984 en Nicaragua: Las Elecciones Sandinistas.* St. Charles, Mo.: Privately printed, 1988.

———. *William Walker: The Grey-Eyed Man of Destiny.* Five volumes. Lake St. Louis, Mo.: Privately printed, 1989–1990.

Booth, John A. *The End and the Beginning: The Nicaraguan Revolution.* Boulder: Westview, 1982.

Borge, Tomás, et. al. *El Axioma de la Esperanza.* Bilbao: Editorial Desclée de Brouwer, 1984.

———, et. al. *Sandinistas Speak: Speeches, Writings and Interviews With the Leaders of Nicaragua's Revolution.* New York: Pathfinder, 1982.

———. *Carlos, El Amanecer Ya No Es una Tentación.* Managua: Editorial Nueva Nicaragua, 1982.

————. *Carlos, Te Seguimos Viendo.* Managua: Ministerio del Interior, 1984.

————. *La Mujer y la Revolución Nicaragüense.* New York: Pathfinder, 1984?

————. *No Pedimos Que Elogien la Revolución, Sino que Digan y Divulguen la Verdad.* Managua: DEPEP, 1981.

————. *Ocho Tesis Equivocadas: Principales Tesis del Imperialismo Sobre Nicaragua.* Managua: Ministerio del Interior, 1985.

————. *La Revolución Combate la Teología de la Muerte: Discursos Cristianos de un Comandante Sandinista.* Managua: Ministerio del Interior, 1986?

————. *Tasba Pri: A Seis Meses de Trabajo.* Managua: INNICA, 1982.

Bourgeois, Phillipe, and Jorge Grunberg. *La Mosquitia y la Revolución: Informe de una Investigación Rural en la Costa Atlántica Norte.* Managua: INRA, 1980.

Bovallius, Carl. *Nicaraguan Antiquities.* Managua: Editorial San José, 1970.

Boyle, Frederick. *A Ride Across the Continent: A Personal Narrative of Wanderings Through Costa Rica and Nicaragua.* London: R. Bentley, 1868.

Bradlee, Ben, Jr. *Guts and Glory: The Oliver North Story.* New York: D. I. Fine, 1988.

Bradstock, Andrew. *Saints and Sandinistas: The Catholic Church in Nicaragua and Its Response to Revolution.* London: Epworth, 1987.

Brody, Reed. *Contra Terror in Nicaragua: Report of a Fact-Finding Mission September 1984–January 1985.* Boston: South End, 1985.

Burns, Bradford E. *At War in Nicaragua: The Reagan Administration and the Politics of Nostalgia.* New York: Harper & Row, 1987.

Butterworth, Hezikiah. *Lost in Nicaragua, or Among Coffee Farms and Banana Lands.* Boston: W. A. Wilde, 1898.

Cabestrero, Teofilo. *Ministros de Dios, Ministros del Pueblo: Testimonio de Tres Sacerdotes en el Gobierno Revolucionario de Nicaragua.* Barcelona: Desclée de Brouwer, 1983.

Cabezas, Omar. *Canción de Amor Para los Hombres.* Managua: Editorial Nueva Nicaragua, 1988.

————. *La Montaña es Algo Más que un Enorme Estepa Verde.* Managua: Editorial Nueva Nicaragua, 1982. Published in the United States as *Fire From the Mountain: The Making of a Sandinista* (translated by Kathleen Weaver). New York: Crown, 1985.

Campos Ponce, Xavier. *Sandino: Biografía de un Héroe.* Mexico: EDAMEX, 1979.

Cardenal, Ernesto. *Antología.* Managua: Editorial Nueva Nicaragua, 1983.

————, et. al. *La Batalla de Nicaragua.* México: Bruguera, 1980?

————. *La Democratización de la Cultura.* Managua: Ministerio de Cultura, 1982.

————. *El Estrecho Dudoso.* Managua: Editorial Nueva Nicaragua, 1985.

————, (editor). *Poesía Nicaragüense.* Managua: Editorial Nueva Nicaragua, 1981.

Carr, Albert Z. *The World and William Walker.* New York: Harper & Row, 1963.

Carrión, Luis. *Austeridad: Principio y Norma de Nuestro Pueblo.* Managua: DEPEP, 1981.

————. *Realizar los Sueños del General Sandino.* Managua: Ministerio del Interior, 1984.

Castañeda, Jorge. *Nicaragua: Contradicciónes en la Revolución.* Mexico: Tiempo Extra, 1981.

Castrillo Gamez, Manuel. *Estudios Históricos de Nicaragua.* Managua: Editorial Asel, 1947.

Castro, J. A. *Las Milicias en Acción: El Pueblo y su Defensa.* Matagalpa: Junta de Reconstrucción de Matagalpa, 1982.

Chamorro, Edgar. *Packaging the Contras: A Case of CIA Disinformation.* New York: Institute for Media Analysis, 1987.

Chamorro, Emiliano, *El Último Caudillo.* Managua: Editorial Unión, 1983.

Chamorro, Jaime. *Frente a Dos Dictaduras: La Lucha por la Libertad de Expresión.* San José: Libro Libre, 1987.

Chamorro, Pedro Joaquín. *Diario de un Preso.* Managua: Nuevos Horizontes, 1963.

———. *Estirpe Sangriente: Los Somoza.* Managua: Artes Gráficas, 1978.

———. *La Patria de Pedro.* Managua: La Prensa, 1981.

———. *Los Pies Descalzos de Nicaragua.* Managua: La Prensa, 1975?

———. *Nuestra Frontera Recortada.* Managua: La Prensa, 1976?

———. *Relatos Completos.* Managua: Pez y Serpiente, 1985.

———. *Richter 7.* Managua: Pez y Serpiente, 1981.

Christian, Shirley, *Nicaragua: Revolution in the Family.* New York: Random House, 1985.

Close, David H. *Nicaragua: Politics, Economics, and Society.* London: Pinter, 1988.

Cockburn, Leslie. *Out of Control.* New York: Atlantic Monthly, 1987.

Cohn, Betsy, et. al. *US-Nicaraguan Relations: Chronology of Policy and Impact.* Washington: Central American Cultural Institute, Georgetown University, 1984?

Congress, Rick. *The Afro-Nicaraguans: The Revolution and Autonomy.* Atlanta: Atlanta Committee on Latin America, 1987?

Colburn, Forest D. *Post-Revolutionary Nicaragua: State, Class and the Dilemmas of Agrarian Policy.* Berkeley: University of California Press, 1986.

Collins, Joseph, et. al. *Nicaragua: What Difference Could a Revolution Make? Food and Farming in the New Nicaragua.* San Francisco: Institute for Food and Development Policy, 1985.

Conzemius, Eduardo. *Miskitos y Sumos de Honduras y Nicaragua.* San José: Libro Libre, 1984.

Córdova Rivas, Rafael. *Contribución a la Revolución.* Managua: CPASA, 1983.

Coronel Urtecho, José. *Conversaciones con Carlos.* Managua: Editorial Vanguardia, 1986.

———. *Reflexiones Sobre la Historia de Nicaragua de Gainza a Somoza.* 2 vols. León: Instituto Histórico Centroamericano, 1942.

Corragio, José Luis. *Nicaragua: Revolution and Democracy.* Boston: Allen & Unwin, 1986.

Cortázar, Julio. *Nicaragua, Tan Violentamente Dulce.* Managua: Editorial Nueva Nicaragua, 1983.

Cox, Isaac J. *Nicaragua and the United States.* New York: Gordon Prange, 1976.

Cramer, Floyd. *Our Neighbor Nicaragua.* New York: Frederick A. Stokes, 1929.

Crawley, Eduardo. *Dictators Never Die: Nicaragua and the Somoza Dynasty.* New York: St. Martin's, 1979.

Cruz, Arturo. *Nicaragua's Continuing Struggle.* New York: Freedom House, 1988.

Cruz, Arturo, Jr. *Memoirs of a Counterrevolutionary: Life With the Contras, the Sandinistas and the CIA.* New York: Doubleday, 1989.

Cuadra, Abelardo. *Hombre del Caribe.* San José: Educa, 1981.

Cuadra, Pablo Antonio. *El Nicaragüense.* Managua: Pez y Serpiente, 1981.

Darío, Rubén. *Al Libertador Bolivar: Oda.* Managua: Ministerio de Educación, 1983.

———. *Autobiografía.* Managua: Distribuidora Cultural, 1983.

———. *Azul.* Managua: Editorial Nueva Nicaragua, 1988.

———. *Cuentos.* San José: Libro Libre, 1986.

———. *Historia de Mis Libros.* Managua: Editorial Nueva Nicaragua, 1988.

———. *Nuestro Rubén Darío.* Managua: Ministerio de Cultura, 1982.

———. *Obras Completas.* Madrid: Afrodisio Aguado, 1953.

———. *Prosas Profanas.* Managua: Distribuidora Cultural, 1984.

———. *Tantos Vigores Dispersos.* Managua: Centro de Publicaciones de Avanzada, 1983.

———. *Unión Centroamericana.* Managua: Ediciones Arellano/Jiron, 1983.

———. *El Viaje a Nicaragua, e Intermezzo Tropical.* Managua: Ministerio de Cultura, 1983?

Davila Bolaños, Alejandro. *El Interrogatorio.* Masaya: Librería Loaisiga, 1979.

Davis, Peter. *Where is Nicaragua?* New York: Simon & Schuster, 1987.

Davis, Richard Harding. *Three Gringos in Venezuela and Central America.* New York: Harper & Brown, 1903.

De la Selva, Salomón. *La Guerra de Sandino, o Pueblo Desnudo.* Managua: Editorial Nueva Nicaragua, 1985.

Denny, Harold Norman. *Dollars for Bullets: The Story of American Rule in Nicaragua.* New York: Dial, 1929.

Departamento de Propaganda y Educación Política [Departamento de Agitación y Propaganda] del FSLN. *Carlos Fonseca Siempre.* Managua: DEPEP, 1982.

———. *Datos Básicos Sobre Nicaragua.* Managua: DEPEP, 1981.

———. *Francisco Meza Rojas: Datos Biográficos.* Managua: DEPEP, 1980.

———. *Introducción al Pensamiento Sandinista.* Managua: DEPEP, 1981.

———. *Juan de Dios Muñoz: Datos Biográficos.* Managua: DEPEP, 1980.

———. *Nelson Suárez: Datos Biográficos.* Managua: DEPEP, 1980.

———. *Ricardo Morales Aviles: Datos Biográficos.* Managua: DEPEP, 1980.

Dickey, Christopher. *With the Contras: A Reporter in the Wilds of Nicaragua.* New York: Simon & Schuster, 1985.

Diederich, Bernard. *Somoza and the Legacy of U. S. Involvement in Central America.* New York: Dutton, 1981.

Dirección de Planificación Nacional. *La Costa Atlántica, Geografía Física y Política, Situación Económica y Social.* Managua: Dirección de Planificación Nacional, 1976.

Diskin, Martin, et. al. *Peace and Autonomy on the Atlantic Coast of Nicaragua.* Pittsburgh: Latin American Studies Association, 1986.

Donaldson, Lois. *Nicaragua in Story and Pictures.* Chicago: A. Whitman, 1943.

Doubleday, C. W. *Reminiscences of the "Filibuster" War in Nicaragua.* New York: Putnam, 1886.

Dozier, Craig L. *Nicaragua's Mosquito Shore: The Years of British and American Presence.* University, Alabama: University of Alabama Press, 1985.

Dunkerly, James. *Power in the Isthmus.* London: Verso, 1988.

Edmisten, Patricia Taylor. *Nicaragua Divided: La Prensa and the Chamorro Legacy.* Pensacola: University of West Florida, 1990.

Escobar, José Benito. *Ideario Sandinista.* Managua: DEPEP, 1984.

Eich, Dieter, and Rincón, Carlos, eds. *The Contras: Interviews With Anti-Sandinistas.* South Hadley, Ma.: Bergon & Garvey, 1986.

Ejército Popular Sandinista. *Preparación Política.* Managua: Seccion de Formación Política y Cultural del EPS, 1981?

———. *Preparacion Política de Clases y Soldados.* Managua: Dirección Política del EPS, 1986.

Everett, Melissa. *Bearing Witness, Building Bridges: Interviews With North Americans Living and Working in Nicaragua.* Philadelphia: New Society, 1986.

Fabela, Isidro. *El Rebelde de América.* Managua: Editorial Nueva Nicaragua, 1979.

Federacion Nicaragüense de Beisbol Amateur. *Historia del Beisbol Nicaragüense: Antiguo, Moderno y Contemporáneo.* Managua: Artes Gráficas, 1976.

Ferlinghetti, Lawrence. *Seven Days in Nicaragua Libre.* San Francisco: City Lights, 1984.

Fernández, Francisco de Asís, ed. *Poesía Política de Nicaragua.* Managua: Ministerio de Cultura, 1986.

Fernández, Guido. *El Primer Domingo en Febrero.* San José: Editorial Costa Rica, 1986.

———. *El Desafío de la Paz en Centroamérica.* San José: Editorial Costa Rica, 1989.

Floyd, Troy S. *The Anglo-Spanish Struggle for the Mosquitia.* Albequerque: University of New Mexico Press, 1967.

Fonseca, Carlos. *Escritos.* Managua: EPS, 1979.

———. *Ideología Política de Augusto César Sandino.* Managua: DEPEP, 1984.

———. *Programa Histórico del FSLN.* Managua: DEPEP, 1984.

———. *Sandino: Guerrilla Proletaria.* Managua: DEPEP, 1984.

———. *Viva Sandino.* Managua: DEPEP, 1984.

Gadea Mantilla, Fabio. *Editoriales de Ayer y Hoy.* San José: 10 En Punto, 1985.

Galeano, Eduardo. *Ventana Sobre Sandino.* Managua: Ediciones Raití, 1985.

Gámez, José Dolores. *Historia de Nicaragua Desde los Tiempos Prehistóricos Hasta el Año 1860.* Managua: Banco de America, 1975.

Gámez, Mario. *Compendio de Historia de Nicaragua.* Managua: Tipografía Perez, 1936.

García Márquez, Gabriel. *El Asalto: El Operativo con que el FSLN se Lanzó al Mundo.* Managua: Editorial Nueva Nicaragua, 1983.

———, et. al. *Los Sandinistas.* Bogota: La Oveja Negra, 1980?

Garinzzo, Alicia. *El Café en Nicaragua: Los Pequeños Productores de Matagalpa y Carazo.* Managua: INIES, 1984.

Gerson, Noel B. *Sad Swashbuckler.* Nashville: Thomas Nelson, 1976.

Gilbert, Dennis. *Sandinistas: The Party and the Revolution.* New York: Blackwell, 1988.

Gispert-Sauch, Ana, ed. *Nicaragua a Un año de la Victoria: Documentos, Testimonios, Reflecciones.* Lima: Centro de Estudios y Publicaciones, 1980.

Gómez Espinosa, Margarita. *Así es Nicaragua.* Madrid: Paraninfo, 1973.

González Bermejo, Ernesto. *Vengo de Nicaragua.* Montevideo: Librosur, 1986?

González R., José Esteban. *Nicaragua: Una Revolución Amenazada.* Tegucigalpa: Editorial Unión, 1982.

Grande Preza, José Luis. *Nicaragua: Seis Años Después.* San Salvador: Editorial Época, 1987.

Greene, Laurence. *The Filibuster.* New York: Bobbs-Merrill, 1937.

Greenshaw, Wayne. *Flying High: Inside Big-Time Drug Smuggling.* New York: Dodd, Mead & Co., 1984.

Grossman, Guido. *La Costa Atlántica de Nicaragua.* Managua: Editorial La Ocarina, 1988.

Grossman, Karl. *Nicaragua: America's New Vietnam.* Sag Harbor, N.Y.: Permanent, 1985.

Guadamúz, Carlos José. *Y Las Casas se Quedaron Llenas de Humo.* Managua: Editorial Nueva Nicaragua, 1986.

Guerrero, Julián N. *Geografía y Historia de Nicaragua.* Managua: Librería Cultural, 1963.

Guerrero, Julián N., and Lola Soriano de Guerrero. *100 Biografías Centroamericanas.* Managua: Artes Gráficas, 1971.

———. *Diccionario Nicaragüense: Geografía y Historia.* Managua: Editorial Somarriba, 1985.

———, (editors). *Tres Naturalistas en Nicaragua: Oviedo y Valdez, Thomas Belt, y Rubén Darío.* Managua: Editorial Somarriba, 1983.

Guido, Clemente. *El Chipote.* Managua: Editorial Unión, 1982.

———. *Conservatismo en Nicaragua.* Managua: Editorial Unión, 1982.

Gullette, David, ed. *Nicaraguan Peasant Poetry from Solentiname.* Albequerque: West End, 1988.

Gunther, John. *Inside Latin America.* New York: Harper & Bros., 1940.

Gutiérrez, Pedro Rafael. *Calero, El Contra.* San José: Ediciones Lena, 1987.

Gutman, Roy. *Banana Diplomacy: The Making of American Policy in Nicaragua 1981–1987.* New York: Touchstone, 1988.

Harnecker, Marta. *Pueblos en Armas.* Managua: Editorial Nueva Nicaragua, 1985.

Haslam, David. *Faith in Struggle: The Protestant Churches in Nicaragua and Their Response to the Revolution.* London: Epworth, 1987.

Hernández, Plutarco. *El FSLN Por Dentro: Relatos de un Combatiente.* San José: Privately printed, 1982.

Hodges, Donald C. *Intellectual Foundations of the Nicaraguan Revolution.* Austin: University of Texas Press, 1986.

Houston, Robert. *The Nation Thief.* New York: Pantheon, 1984.

Hurtado González, Armando. *Sandino Desconocido.* San José: Ediciones Populares Nicaragüenses, 1984?

Instituto de Estudios del Sandinismo. *Ahora Sé que Sandino Manda.* Managua: Editorial Nueva Nicaragua, 1986.

———. *Carlos, El Eslabón Vital: Cronología Básica de Carlos Fonseca, Jefe de la Revolución 1936–1976.* Managua: Editorial Nueva Nicaragua, 1985.

————. *General Augusto César Sandino, Padre de la Revolución Popular Anti-Imperialista, 1895–1934.* Managua: Editorial Nueva Nicaragua, 1986.

————. *El Sandinismo: Documentos Básicos.* Managua: Editorial Nueva Nicaragua, 1985.

International Bank for Reconstruction and Development. *The Economic Development of Nicaragua.* Baltimore: Johns Hopkins University Press, 1953.

Invernizzi, Gabriele, et. al., eds. *Sandinistas: Entrevistas con Humberto Ortega Saavedra, Jaime Wheelock Román y Bayardo Arce Castaño.* Managua: Editorial Vanguardia, 1986.

Jenkins Molieri, Jorge. *El Desafío Indígena en Nicaragua: El Caso de los Miskitos.* Managua: Editorial Vanguardia, 1986.

Jirón, Manuel. *Contra Dos Dictaduras.* San José: Ediciones Radio Amor, 1982.

————. *Exilio, S. A.: Vivencias de un Nicaragüense en el Exilio.* San José: Ediciones Radio Amor, 1983.

————. *Pasado, Presente y Futuro de la Libertad de Expresión en Nicaragua.* San José: Ediciones Radio Amor, 1983.

————. *Quién es Quién en Nicaragua.* San José: Ediciones Radio Amor, 1986.

Jirón Terán, José, and Jorge Eduardo Arellano. *Rubén Darío Primogenio.* Managua: Ediciones Convivio, 1984.

Jones, William Carey. *Documentos Diplomáticos de William Carey Jones, Enviado Especial de los Estados Unidos Ante Nicaragua y Costa Rica 1857–1858.* Managua: Banco de América, 1974.

Junta de Gobierno de Reconstrucción Nacional. *Un Año Después: Entrevistas con la JGRN.* Managua: JGRN, 1980.

Kaman, William. *Search for Stability: United States Diplomacy Toward Nicaragua 1925–1933.* Notre Dame, In.: University of Notre Dame, 1968.

Karnes, Thomas L. *The Failure of Union: Central America 1824–1975.* Chapel Hill: University of North Carolina Press, 1961.

Kemble, Lt. Col. Stephen. *The Kemble Papers, 1773–1789.* New York: N. Y. Historical Society, 1885.

Kornbluh, Peter. *Nicaragua, The Price of Intervention: Reagan's War Against the Sandinistas.* Washington: Institute for Policy Studies, 1987.

Lacayo Nuñez, Donald. *Profile of a Democrat.* Miami: Nicaraguan Democratic Force, 1986?

LaFeber, Walter. *Inevitable Revolutions: The United States in Central America.* New York: W. W. Norton, 1983.

Lainez, Francisco. *Nicaragua: Colonialismo Español, Yanki y Ruso.* Guatemala: Serviprensa, 1987.

————. *Terremoto 1972: Elites y Pueblo.* Managua: Editorial Unión, 1977.

Laino, Domingo. *Somoza: El General Comerciante.* Asunción: Editorial Intercontinental, 1989.

Lake, Anthony. *Somoza Falling.* New York: Houghton Mifflin, 1989.

Lancaster, Roger N. *Thanks to God and the Revolution: Popular Religion and Class Consciousness in the New Nicaragua.* New York: Columbia University, 1988.

Leiken, Robert S., ed. *Central America: Anatomy of Conflict.* New York: Pergamon, 1984.

———, and Barry Rubin, eds. *The Central America Crisis Reader.* New York: Summit, 1987.

López, Santos. *Memorias del Coronel Santos López.* Managua: Secretaría Nacional de Propaganda y Educación Política, FSLN, 1981?

Lozano, Lucrecia. *De Sandino al Triunfo de la Revolución.* Mexico: Siglo XXI, 1979.

Macaulay, Neil. *The Sandino Affair.* Chicago: Quadrangle, 1967.

Maier, Elizabeth. *Los Sandinistas.* México: Cultura Popular, 1985.

Maraboto, Emigdio E. *Sandino Ante el Coloso.* Managua: Ediciones Patria y Libertad, 1980.

Marcoleta, José de. *Documentos Diplomáticos de José de Marcoleta, Ministro de Nicaragua en los Estados Unidos 1854.* Managua: Banco de América, 1974.

Marcus, Bruce, ed. *Nicaragua: The Sandinista People's Revolution.* New York: Pathfinder, 1985.

Matagalpa, Juan. *Sandino, Somoza, y los Nueve Comandantes Sandinistas.* Tegucigalpa: Editorial Industrial, 1984.

Mayorga, Francisco. *The Economic Trajectory of Nicaragua 1980–1984: An Overview.* Miami: Florida International University, 1985.

McCullough, David. *Path Between the Seas: The Construction of the Panama Canal 1870–1914.* New York: Touchstone, 1978.

McIntyre, Alexander H. *Political and Electoral Confrontation in Revolutionary Nicaragua.* Miami: University of Miami, 1985.

McNeil, Frank. *War and Peace in Central America.* New York: Scribner's, 1988.

Medina, Alberto. *Efemérides Nicaragüenses 1509–1941.* Managua: Editorial Nueva Prensa, 1945.

Meléndez, Carlos. *Hernández de Córdoba, Capitán de Conquista en Nicaragua.* Managua: Talleres San José, 1976.

Melrose, Dianna. *Nicaragua: The Threat of a Good Example?* Oxford, U. K.: Oxfam, 1985.

Mendieta Alfaro, Roger. *El Último Marine, La Caída de Somoza.* Managua: Editorial Unión, 1980.

Meyer, Harvey K. *Historical Dictionary of Nicaragua.* Metuchen, N. J.: Scarecrow, 1972.

Millett, Richard. *Guardians of the Dynasty: A History of the US-Created Guardia Nacional de Nicaragua and the Somoza Family.* Maryknoll, N. Y.: Orbis, 1977.

Miner, Dwight Carroll. *The Fight for the Panama Route: The Story of the Spooner Act and the Hay-Herán Treaty.* New York: Columbia University, 1940.

Ministerio de Educación. *El Amanecer de un Pueblo: Cuaderno de Educación Popular Básica.* Managua: MED, 1981?

———. *Doctor y General Benjamin F. Zeledón.* Managua: Editorial Unión, 1980.

———. *Manual del Brigadista: Ejército Popular de Alfabetizadores.* Managua: MED, 1980.

Ministerio del Interior. *El FSLN: Vanguardia de la Revolución Popular Sandinista.* Managua: MINT, 1980?

Ministerio de Relaciones Exteriores. *Nicaragua Denuncia Agresiones que Sufre Desde el Territorio de Honduras, 1980–1982.* Managua: MINEX, 1982.

Mondragón, Rafael, and Carlos Decker Molina. *Participación Popular en Nicaragua.* México: Claves Latinoamericanos, 1986.

Montenegro, Sofía. *Memorias del Atlántico.* Managua: Editorial Nuevo Amanecer, 1986.

Morales, Arqueles. *Con el Corazón en el Disparador.* Managua: Editorial Vanguardia, 1986.

Morales Aviles, Ricardo. *La Dominación Imperialista en Nicaragua.* Managua: Secretaria Nacional de Propaganda y Educación Política del FSLN, 1980.

———. *No Pararemos de Andar Jamás.* Managua: Editorial Nueva Nicaragua, 1983.

Morley, Morris, and James Petras. *The Reagan Administration and Nicaragua: How the United States Constructs its Case for Counterrevolution in Central America.* New York: Institute for Media Analysis, 1987.

Muravchik, Joshua. *News Coverage of the Sandinista Revolution.* Washington: American Enterprise Institute, 1988.

Murillo, Rosario. *Amar es Combatir.* Managua: Editorial Nueva Nicaragua, 1982.

———. *Un Deber de Cantar.* Managua: Ministerio de Cultura, 1981.

Muro Rodríguez, Mirtha, et. al. *Nicaragua y la Revolución Sandinista.* Havana: Ciencias Sociales, 1984.

Najlis, Michelle. *El Viento Armado.* Managua: Editorial Nueva Nicaragua, 1982.

Navas Zepeda, Máximo. *Los Cancilleres de Nicaragua 1838–1936: Influencias y Reminiscencias.* Managua: Pinsa, 1976.

Nietschman, Bernard. *The Unknown War: The Miskito Nation, Nicaragua and the United States.* New York: Freedom House, 1989.

Nogales, Rafael de. *The Looting of Nicaragua.* New York: Robert McBride & Co., 1928.

Nolan, David. *FSLN: The Ideology of the Sandinistas and the Nicaraguan Revolution.* Miami: University of Miami, 1984.

North, Oliver. *Taking the Stand: The Testimony of Oliver North.* New York: Pocket Books, 1987.

Núñez Tellez, Carlos, et. al. *Día de la Dignidad Nacional: Instalación del Consejo de Estado.* Managua: Consejo del Estado, 1980.

———. *Un Pueblo en Armas.* Managua: Editorial Vanguardia, 1986.

Obando y Bravo, Miguel. *Agonía en el Bunker.* Managua: COPROSA, 1990.

———. *Libres Como Ríos: Homilias de Monseñor Miguel Obando y Bravo.* Managua: COPROSA, 1984.

Oliver, Antonio. *Este Otro Rubén Darío.* Barcelona: Editorial Aedos, 1960.

Ortega Saavedra, Daniel. *Las Armas: Instrumentos de Paz en las Manos del Pueblo.* Managua: Presidencia de la República, 1986.

———. *Con Jóvenes Latinoamericanos y del Caribe.* Managua: Presidencia de la República, 1986.

———. *Discursos Pronunciados en las Naciones Unidas.* Managua: Ministerio del Exterior, 1983.

———. *El Sandinismo: El Más Alto Grado de Organización del Pueblo.* Managua: Editorial Nueva Nicaragua, 1987.

————. *Las Reglas del Juego las Dicta el Pueblo.* Managua: DEPEP, 1981.

————. *Proclama de la Dirección Nacional del FSLN.* Managua: Editorial Vanguardia, 1986.

————. *Seguiremos Defendiendo Esta Democracia.* Managua: Presidencia de la República, 1986.

Ortega Saavedra, Humberto. *50 Años de Lucha Sandinista.* Managua, Ciencias Sociales, 1980.

Oviedo, Jose Miguel. *Musas en Guerra: Poesía, Arte y Cultura en la Nueva Nicaragua (1974–1986).* México: Joaquín Moritz, 1987.

Paiz Castillo, Ricardo. *Breve Historia del Partido Conservador de Nicaragua.* Managua: Editorial Unión, 1984.

Palmer, Frederick. *Central America and Its Problems: An Account of a Journey from the Rio Grande to Panama.* New York: Moffat, Yard & Co., 1913.

Palmer, Mervyn. *Through Unknown Nicaragua: The Adventures of a Naturalist on a Wild-Goose Chase.* London: Jarrolds, 1945.

Pashke, Barbara, and David Volpendesta, eds. *Clamor of Innocence: Stories from Central America.* San Francisco: City Lights, 1988.

Pastor, Robert. *Condemned to Repetition.* Princeton: Princeton University, 1987.

Pataky, László. *Llegaron los que No Estaban Invitados: La Sombra de Sandino.* Managua: Editorial Pereira, 1975.

————. *Nicaragua Desconocida.* Managua: Editorial Universal, 1956.

Pérez, Paola. *Diez Años de Investigaciones Sobre la Mujer en Nicaragua, 1976–1986.* Managua: Ministerio de la Presidencia, 1986.

Pérez-Valle, Edmundo. *El Asesinato de Sandino: Documentos Testimoniales.* Managua: Ministerio de Cultura, 1986.

————. *La Muerte de Sandino: El Martirio del Héroe.* Managua: ENIEC, 1984.

Pochet, Rosa María, and Martínez, Abelino. *Nicaragua: Iglesia: ¿Manipulación o Profecía? San José: DEI, 1987.*

Puebla Institute. *Nicaragua, Civil Liberties, and the Central American Peace Plan.* Washington: Puebla Institute, 1988.

Quintana, Ofsman. *Apuntes de Historia de Nicaragua.* Managua: Fanatex, 1977.

Rabe, Stephen G. *Eisenhower and Latin America: The Foreign Policy of Anti-Communism.* Chapel Hill: University of North Carolina Press, 1988.

Ramírez, José M. *José de Marcoleta, Padre de la Diplomacia Nicaragüenese.* Managua: Imprenta Nacional, 1975.

Ramírez, Sergio. *El Alba de Oro: La Historia Viva de Nicaragua.* Mexico: Siglo XXI, 1983.

———— (editor). *Augusto César Sandino, El Pensamiento Vivo.* Two volumes. Managua: Editorial Nueva Nicaragua, 1984.

———— (editor). *Cuentos Nicaragüenses.* Buenos Aires: Editorial Nueva America, 1985.

————. *Castigo Divino.* Managua: Editorial Nueva Nicaragua, 1988.

————. *Charles Atlas También Muere.* Managua: Editorial Nueva Nicaragua, 1982.

————. *Estás en Nicaragua.* Barcelona: Muchnik, 1985.

————. *Las Armas del Futuro.* Managua, Editorial Nueva Nicaragua, 1987.

————. *Mensaje de la Junta de Gobierno de Reconstrucción Nacional al Pueblo Nicaragüense.* Managua, DEPEP, 1980.

———— (editor). *Queremos Tanto a Julio: 20 Autores Para Cortázar.* Managua: Editorial Nueva Nicaragua, 1984.

————. *Sandino es Indohispano y No Tiene Fronteras en America Latina.* Managua: IES, 1984.

————. *Sandino Siempre.* León: UNAN, 1980.

————. *Sandino y los Partidos Políticos.* Managua: UNAN, 1984.

Randall, Margaret. *Cristianos en la Revolución.* Managua: Editorial Nueva Nicaragua, 1983.

————. *Risking a Somersault in the Air: Conversations With Nicaraguan Writers.* San Francisco: Solidarity, 1984.

————. *Sandino's Daughters: Testimonies of Nicaraguan Women in Struggle.* Vancouver: New Star, 1981.

Rius (Eduardo del Rio). *Carlos Para Todos.* Managua: Editorial Vanguardia, 1987.

————. *Nicaragua for Beginners.* New York: Writers and Readers, 1984.

Robinson, William, and Kent Norsworthy. *David and Goliath: The U. S. War Against Nicaragua.* New York: Monthly Review, 1987.

Rodríguez, Ileana. *Primer Inventario del Invasor.* Managua: Editorial Nueva Nicaragua, 1984.

Rodríguez, René M., and Espinosa, Antonio Acevedo, eds. *La Insurrección en Nicaragua 1978–79: La Lucha Armada del FSLN y el Pueblo Contra la Dictadura Somocista, En la Prensa Nacional y Extranjera.* Managua: Banco Central, 1979.

Rodríguez Porras, Armando. *Juan Rafael Mora Porras y la Guerra Contra los Filibusteros.* Alajuela, Costa Rica: Museo Cultural Juan Santamaría, 1986.

Rodríguez R., Magdalena de. *Estelí 79.* Managua: Editorial Alemana, 1979.

Román, José. *Maldito País.* Managua: Pez y Serpiente, 1983.

Rosengarten, Frederic, Jr. *Freebooters Must Die!* Wayne, Pa.: Haverford House, 1976.

Rothschuh Tablada, Guillermo. *El Retorno del Cisne: Ensayos.* Managua: Distribuidora Cultural, 1983.

Ruchwarger, Gary. *People in Power: Forging a Grassroots Democracy in Nicaragua.* South Hadley, Ma.: Bergin & Garvey, 1987.

Rugama, Leonel. *La Tierra es un Satélite de la Luna.* Managua: Editorial Nueva Nicaragua, 1983.

Ruhl, Arthur J. *The Central Americans: Adventures and Impressions Between Mexico and Panama.* New York: Charles Scribner's Sons, 1928.

Rushdie, Salman. *The Jaguar Smile: A Nicaraguan Journey.* New York: Viking, 1987.

Sacasa, Juan Bautista. *Cómo y Por Qué Caí del Poder.* León: Eco Nacional, 1946.

Salinas, Pedro. *La Poesía de Rubén Darío.* Barcelona: Seix Barral, 1975.

Salvatierra, Sofonías. *Sandino: La Tragedia de un Pueblo.* Madrid: Europa, 1934.

Sanabria, Octavio and Elvira. *Nicaragua: Diagnóstico de Una Traición: El FSLN en el Poder.* Barcelona: Plaza & Janes, 1986.

Sánchez, Rodrigo. *Panorama Político de Nicaragua.* Managua: Talleres Gráficos Pérez, 1940.

Sanchez Arguello, Hector. *Perfil de Nicaragua.* San José: Multiprint, 1988.

Sánchez Fuentes, Julio César. *Documentos de Apoyo para el Area de Sociales.* San José: Editorial Unión, 1986.

Santos, Rosario, ed. *And We Sold the Rain: Contemporary Fiction from Central America.* New York: Four Walls Eight Windows, 1988.

Santos Rivera, Jose, ed. *Retratos de Sandino.* Managua: Ministerio de Educación, 1984.

Sapio, Raúl, ed. *Nicaragua's Guide for Tourists, Businessmen, and Travellers.* New York: River Plate, 1940.

Schmidt, Hans. *Maverick Marine: General Smedley D. Butler and the Contradictions of American Military History.* Lexington, Ky.: University of Kentucky, 1987.

Schneider, Robin. *Nicaragua's Atlantic Coast.* Berlin: Berlin Institute for Comparative Social Research, 1989.

Schonherr, Dietmar. *Nicaragua Mi Amor: Diario de un Viaje.* Managua: Ministerio de Cultura, 1986.

Schulz, Hermann. *Una Tierra de Pólvora y Miel.* Managua: Ministerio de Cultura, 1983.

Scroggs, William O. *Filibusters and Financiers: The Story of William Walker and his Associates.* New York: MacMillan, 1916.

Selser, Gregorio. *Apuntes Sobre Nicaragua.* Mexico: Nueva Imagen, 1981.

————. *El Pequeño Ejército Loco: Sandino y la Operación Mexico-Nicaragua.* Managua: Editorial Nueva Nicaragua, 1986.

————. *Sandino.* New York: Monthly Review, 1981.

Sheehan, Edward R. F. *Agony in the Garden: A Stranger in Central America.* Boston: Houghton Mifflin, 1989.

Simmons, William E. *Uncle Sam's New Waterway.* New York: F. T. Neely, 1899.

Sklar, Holly. *Washington's War on Nicaragua.* Boston: South End, 1988.

Smutko, Gregorio. *La Mosquitia: Historia y Cultura de la Costa Atlántica.* Managua: Editorial La Ocarina, 1985.

Somoza Debayle, Anastasio (as told to Jack Cox). *Nicaragua Betrayed.* Boston: Western Islands, 1980.

Somoza García, Anastasio. *El Verdadero Sandino, o El Calvario de las Segovias.* Managua: Tipografía Robelo, 1936.

Soto Hall, Máximo. *Nicaragua y el Imperialismo Norteamericano.* Buenos Aires: Artes y Letras, 1928.

Spadafora, Hugo. *Las Derrotas Somocista y Comunista en Nicaragua.* San José: Privately printed, 1985?

Squier, E. G. *Nicaragua: Its People, Scenery, Monuments, Resources, Conditions, and the Proposed Canal.* New York: Harper & Bros., 1860.

Stephens, John Lloyd. *Incidents of Travel in Central America, Chiapas and Yucatan.* New Brunswick, N.J.: Rutgers University, 1949.

Stimson, Henry L. *American Policy in Nicaragua.* Salem, N.H.: Ayer, 1970.

Tapia Barquero, Humberto. *Nicaragua: Maíz y Folklore.* Managua: Papelería Industrial, 1981.

Tefel, Reynaldo Antonio. *Cristianismo y Revolución.* Managua: Centro Ecuménico Antonio Valdivieso, 1985?

———. *El Infierno de los Pobres: Diagnóstico Social de los Barrios Marginales de Managua*. Managua: Pez y Serpiente, 1978.

———. *Nicaragua: Las Condiciones Estaban Dadas y Sonó el Detonante*. Managua: CINASE, 1979.

Tierney, John J. *Somoza and Sandinistas: The United States and Nicaragua in the Twentieth Century*. Washington: Council on Inter-American Security, 1982.

Tijerino, Doris (as told to Margaret Randall). *Inside the Nicaraguan Revolution*. Vancouver: New Star, 1978.

Tijerino, Edgard. *El Mundial Nica*. Managua: Copiaco, 1973.

———. *Doble Play*. Managua: Editorial Vanguardia, 1989.

Tijerino, Toribio. *El Tratado Chamorro-Bryan y sus Proyecciones en la América Central*. Managua: La Prensa, 1935.

Tirado, Victor. *La Primera Gran Conquista: La Toma del Poder Político*. Managua: Central de Trabajadores Sandinistas, 1985.

Toledo Ortiz, Alberto. *Grandes Reportajes Históricos de Nicaragua: Lo Que Ocurrió Hace 40, 30, 20, 10 y 5 Años*. Managua: Editorial Alemana, 1972.

Torres, Edelberto. *La Dramática Vida de Rubén Darío*. Managua: Editorial Nueva Nicaragua, 1982.

———. *Sandino y sus Pares*. Managua: Editorial Nueva Nicaragua, 1983.

Torres, Rosa María. *Nicaragua: Revolución Popular, Educación Popular*. Managua: INIES, 1985.

Torres Bodet, Jaime, ed. *Antología de Rubén Darío*. México: Fondo de Cultura Económica, 1966.

Tower, John, et. al. *The Tower Commission Report: The Full Text of the President's Special Review Board*. New York: Times Books, 1987.

Tullberg, Steven. *Report on the Nicaraguan Indian Peace Initiative: A Search for Indian Rights Within the Arias Peace Plan*. Washington: Indian Law Resource Center, 1988.

United States Department of State. *A Brief History of the Relations Between the United States and Nicaragua, 1909–1928*. Washington: Government Printing Office, 1928.

———. *Comandante Bayardo Arce's Secret Speech Before the Nicaraguan Socialist Party*. Washington: Department of State, 1986.

———. *Inside the Sandinista Regime: A Special Investigator's Perspective*. Washington: Department of State, 1986.

———. *Nicaraguan Biographies: A Resource Book*. Washington: Department of State, 1988.

———. *The Sandinista Constitution*. Washington: Department of State, 1987.

———. *The Sandinistas and Middle East Radicals*. Washington: Department of State, 1985.

———. *The Soviet-Cuban Connection in Central America and the Caribbean*. Washington: Department of State, 1985.

———. *The United States and Nicaragua: A Survey of Relations from 1909 to 1932*. Washington: Government Printing Office, 1932.

Universidad Nacional de Nicaragua, Departamento de Ciencias Sociales. *Apuntes de Historia de Nicaragua.* Two volumes. Managua: UNAN, 1980?

———. *Curso Sobre la Problemática Actual.* Managua: UNAN, 1981?

Urcuyo Maliaños, Francisco. *Solos: Los Últimos 43 Horas en el Bunker de Somoza.* Guatemala: Edita, 1979.

Valle, Marco Antonio: *La Dictadura Somocista.* Managua: UNAN, 1980.

Vandermeer, John, and Peter Rosset, eds. *Nicaragua, Unfinished Revolution: The New Nicaragua Reader.* New York: Grove, 1986.

Vargas, Oscar René. *Elecciones Presidenciales en Nicaragua 1912–1932: Análisis Socio-Político.* Managua: Editorial Manolo Morales, 1990.

———. *La Intervención Norteamericana y Sus Consequencias, Nicaragua 1910–1925.* Managua: DILESA, 1989.

———. *Partidos Políticos y la Búsqueda de un Nuevo Modelo Político.* Managua: CONSA, 1990.

Velásquez, José Luis. *Nicaragua: Sociedad Civil y Dictadura.* San José: Libro Libre, 1986.

Vélez Bárcenas, Jacinto. *Dr. Pedro Joaquín Chamorro C.: Asesinado.* Managua: Trejos Hermanos, 1979.

Vilas, Carlos María. *The Sandinista Revolution: National Liberation and Social Transformation in Nicaragua.* New York: Monthly Review, 1986.

Vogl Baldizón, Alberto. *Nicaragua con Amor y Humor.* Managua: COMPANIC, 1985.

Volpini, Federico. *Desde Managua.* Barcelona: Plaza & James, 1987.

Walker, J. W. G. *Ocean to Ocean: An Account Personal and Historical of Nicaragua and Its People.* Chicago: A. C. McClurg, 1902.

Walker, Thomas A. *Nicaragua, Land of Sandino.* Boulder: Westview, 1981.

Walker, Thomas W. *Reagan versus the Sandinistas.* New York: Praeger, 1985.

——— (editor). *Nicaragua: The First Five Years.* Boulder: Westview, 1986.

Walker, William. *The War in Nicaragua.* Tucson: University of Arizona, 1985.

Weber, Henri. *Nicaragua: The Sandinista Revolution.* London: Verso, 1981.

Wheeler, Senator Burton K. *Dollar Diplomacy at Work in Mexico and Nicaragua.* Washington: Government Printing Office, 1927.

Wheeler, John Hill. *Diario de John Hill Wheeler, Ministro de los Estados Unidos en Nicaragua 1854–1857.* Managua: Banco de América, 1974.

Wheelock Román, Jaime. *Con Trabajadores Agrícolas.* Managua: Presidencia de la República, 1986.

———. *El Gran Desafío.* Managua: Editorial Nueva Nicaragua, 1983.

———. *Frente Sandinista: Hacia la Ofensiva Final.* Havana: Ciencias Sociales, 1980. Also published as *Diciembre Victorioso.* Managua: Editorial Nueva Nicaragua, 1982.

———. *Imperialismo y Dictadura.* Mexico: Siglo XXI, 1979.

———. *Jaime Wheelock Román on the Nicaraguan Revolution.* San Francisco: Institute for the Study of Militarism and Economic Crisis, 1985.

———. *Raíces Indígenas de la Lucha Anti-Colonialista en Nicaragua.* Mexico: Siglo XXI, 1974.

White, Steven F. ed. *Poets of Nicaragua: A Bilingual Anthology.* Greensboro: Unicorn, 1982.

Witness for Peace. *Bitter Witness: Nicaraguans and the 'Covert War.'* Santa Cruz, Ca.: Witness for Peace Documentation Project, 1984.

Yatama. *Proposal for a Treaty of Peace Between the Republic of Nicaragua and the Indian Nations of Yapti Tasba.* San José?: Privately printed, 1988.

Zamora, Daisy. *La Violenta Espuma.* Managua: Ministerio de Cultura, 1981.

Zavala, Xavier, et. al. *1984 Nicaragua.* San José: Libro Libre, 1985.

Zelaya, José M. *El Estado Sandinista.* Managua: Editorial Unión, 1985.

Zelaya, José Santos. *La Revolución de Nicaragua y los Estados Unidos.* Madrid: Imprenta B. Rodriguez, 1910.

Zepeda-Henríquez, Eduardo. *Mitología Nicaragüense.* Managua: Editorial Manolo Morales, 1987.

Zimmerman, Marc, ed. *Nicaragua in Reconstruction and War: The People Speak.* Minneapolis: MEP Publications, 1985.

Zúñiga, Edgar. *Historia Eclesiástica de Nicaragua.* Managua: Editorial Unión, 1982.

INDEX

ABC, 47
Abel, Elie, 36–37
Abisinia, 305, 307–08, 329–30
Abrams, Elliott, 300–302, 344, 345, 348
Acan-Efe, 67
Acevedo, Raúl, 311
Acevedo Peralta, Ricardo, 353
Achuapa, 120, 122–23
Agence France-Presse, 367
Agency for International Development, 198, 345
Aguado, Reynaldo, 306
Agüero, Fernando, 369
Aguilar, Eloy, 297
Aguinaga, Juan de Dios, 374
Aid Committee for Nicaraguan Refugees, 137
Air America, 312–14
Alfonsín, Raúl, 128, 148
Algeria, 174, 177
Allende, Hortensia, 81
Allende, Salvador, 296
Al-Shiraa, 321
Altamirano, José, 181
Álvarez, Gustavo, 138–40, 142–44, 146, 148, 231, 408
Álvarez Montalván, Emilio, 382–83
Alyea, Brant, 212
Amador, Samuel, 120
American Indian Movement, 281
Andrés Pérez, Carlos, 40, 44, 67, 81, 243
Anduray Palma, Plutarco, 181
Angola, 295
Arafat, Yasir, 81
Arana, Frank, 231
Arce, Bayardo, 68, 79, 96, 176, 249, 342
    1984 election, 243, 244, 414
Argentina, 59, 83, 128, 138, 144, 165
    contras and, 139–43, 147, 148
    Falklands war, 86, 91, 92, 147–48
    U.S. and, 140–43, 147–48
Argüello, Leonardo, 31–32, 126, 223
Argüello, Myriam, 118, 383, 384
Argüello, Patricio, 60
Arias, Oscar, 342–44
    interviews with, 345–47, 352, 375, 385
    Nobel Peace Prize for, 354–57
    peace plan of, 343, 346–57, 359–60, 362
Associated Press (AP), 109, 110, 233, 297
Astorga, Nora, 38–39, 78
Australia, 258
Avance, 247
Azcona, José, 300–302

Baena Soares, João, 372
Baker, Howard, 348
Baltodano, Alvaro, 118
Bárcenas, Martin, 45, 50–51
Barreda, Felipe, and Mary (Maria), 146–147
Barreto, Martin, 126–28
Barricada, 77, 207, 296, 299, 319, 323, 351, 385
BBC, 45
Beals, Carleton, 30
Bedell, Berkley, 117
Bell, Griffin, 316–19
Bergold, Harry, 245, 250
Bermúdez, Enrique, 138, 141, 145, 146, 230, 234–35, 293, 310, 358, 386
    interview with, 231–32
Betancur, Belisario, 243
Biehl, John, 356, 357
Bishop, Maurice, 81
Blandón, Nelba, 297, 302
Bluefields, 255–258, 260, 263, 267, 269, 282, 283, 285–288, 352
    baseball in, 210
    mining of harbor, 229
Boaco, 293, 342
Boccanera, Silio, 45
Boland, Edward, 117
Boland Amendment, 97–98, 117
Bolaños, Enrique, 238, 240
Borge, Tomás, 17, 42, 57, 58, 73–74, 83, 84, 132, 137–38, 208, 236–39, 247, 317, 322, 323, 368–69, 351–53, 374, 379, 380, 384, 385
    background and character of, 177–85, 188–89
    Catholic Church and, 198, 199, 207
    interviews with, 179–80, 182
    Miskito Indians and, 269–71, 275–81, 287
    Sandinista split and, 65, 66, 68
Boston Globe, 38, 45, 46, 81, 89, 98, 128, 227
    decision to leave, 91–93, 113
Bowdler, William, 43–44
Brandt, Willy, 244
Brattle Book Shop, 89
Brazil, 128, 165, 196
Brezhnev, Leonid, 48
Britain, 26, 148, 215–16, 254–56, 285, 343
    Falklands war, 86, 91, 92, 147–48
Brown, Mira, 331
Buechler, P. J., 314
Bulgaria, 152, 153, 389
    Sandinistas and, 177, 185, 249, 285–86, 387
Bush, George, 348, 386
Bustillo, Juan Rafael, 313

Cabezas, Omar, 63–64, 157
Cabezas, Rigoberto, 256, 257, 269, 282, 284, 288
Cajina, Francisco, 228–29
Calderón, Rafael Angel, 343
Calero, Adolfo, 44, 145, 238, 320, 344, 368–73
Callejas, Alfonso, 145
Canales, José Fernando, 310–11, 318
Carazo (Province), 311
Carazo, Rodrigo, 67
Carballo, Bismarck, 199, 200, 203–4, 302, 353
Cardenal, Ernesto, 197, 201, 202, 217
Cardenal, Fernando, 21–22, 63, 67, 75, 197
Cárdenas, Adán, 210
Carlucci, Frank, 348
Carrión, Carlos, 389
Carrión, Javier, 246, 366
Carrión, Luis, 64–65, 68, 79, 176, 268, 303
Carter, Jimmy, 40, 43, 44, 48, 71, 140, 316
    Sandinistas and, 80–81, 84–85, 87
Casas, Bartolomé de las, 193
Casey, William, 97, 140, 142–44, 229, 248, 345
    death of, 347
    hospitalization of, 322
Castillo, José María, 17
Castillo Osejo, José, 380
Castro, Fidel, 44, 56–58, 75, 177, 258, 387
    Sandinistas and, 60, 67, 77, 82, 173, 188, 351, 353, 393
    U.S. and, 82, 89, 313, 314
Castro, Miguel Angel, 331
Catholic Church
    contras and, 199–202, 206–7
    Sandinistas and, 115–16, 192–204, 206–8, 217, 226, 237, 262, 298–99, 302–4, 353, 354, 357, 384, 393
    Somoza and, 33, 41, 115, 194–96, 207, 217
CBS, 240, 314–15, 319
Central American University (UCA), 194
Central Bank, Nicaraguan, 224, 225
Cerna, Lenin, 124–25, 179, 181–82, 188
César, Alfredo, 370–72
Chacón, Juan, 81
Chamorro, Edgar, 88, 145–46, 231
Chamorro, Jaime, 297–98
Chamorro, Pedro Joaquín, 32, 44, 88, 180, 222, 224, 297, 302, 303, 382, 388, 391
    accomplishments of, 18–19, 36–37
    assassination of, 37–40, 48, 87, 200
    interview with, 19–20
Chamorro, Violeta, 19, 37, 303
    interviews with, 302, 389
    as junta member, 48, 73, 79, 172, 198, 225
    La Prensa and, 80, 302, 388
    1990 election, 388–92
Chamorro, Xavier, 297–98
Chapell, Bill, 292
Chile, 64, 128, 131, 296, 389
Chinandega, 42, 43
Chontales (Province), 204, 214, 293, 294, 299, 310, 358, 380
Christian Revolutionary Movement, 63
Christopher, Warren, 71, 80

CIA (Central Intelligence Agency), 296
    Castro and, 89, 313, 314
    contras and, 87–89, 97–99, 102, 105, 140, 142–46, 148, 179, 228–30, 232, 234–35, 248, 253, 262, 267, 268, 291–93, 301, 306–7, 311–23, 341, 343–45, 347
    Costa Rica and, 343–45, 347, 354–55
    El Salvador and, 312–14
    Hasenfus affair, 311–23, 341
    Honduras and, 314, 341
    Miskito Indians and, 253, 261, 262, 267, 273
    Nicaragua and, 52, 87–89, 97–99, 102, 124–25, 139, 140, 142–46, 148, 155, 179, 180, 202, 224–25, 228–30, 232, 234–35, 237, 239, 240, 248, 249, 253, 261, 262, 267, 268, 273, 291–93, 299, 301, 303, 305–7, 311–23, 341, 343–45, 347, 354–55
Cisneros, Omar, 213
Cisneros, Sofonias, 181–82
Clarridge, Duane, 142, 143
Clemente, Roberto, 15
Coca-Cola, 44, 186, 320
Coco River, 28, 58, 258–259, 261, 271–279, 281, 366
Colombia, 179, 196, 211, 268
    M-19 in, 334
    Sandinistas and, 208, 243, 334, 335
Columbus, Christopher, 254
Communist party, 247, 388
Congress, 26, 40–41, 52, 55, 70, 138
Conservative party, 24, 25, 118, 210, 224, 225, 245, 317, 383, 388
Contadora Group, 208, 239, 303, 342
Contras, 96
    Argentina and, 139–43, 147, 148
    beginnings of, 87–89, 137–48
    brutality of, 146–47, 199–200, 204–6, 230, 291–92, 294, 295, 306–7, 337–40, 364, 365
    Catholic Church and, 199–202, 206–7
    cease-fire, 357–58, 361, 369, 371, 373, 374, 377, 379, 380
    Costa Rica and, 230–32, 321, 343–47, 369–71
    El Salvador and, 310, 312, 314
    Guatemala and, 87, 141–42
    Honduras and, 88, 97–113, 117, 118, 120, 122, 140–44, 146–48, 204, 229–31, 262, 267, 268, 281, 290, 293, 300–301, 305, 310, 312, 314, 326, 341, 357, 366, 380, 387
    Iran-contra affair, 321–23, 333–38, 340, 347
    La Penca bombing, 233–34, 237, 268, 344
    peace talks and, 358, 359, 361, 362, 365–75
    postwar period, 377, 379, 380, 386
    Sandinista war, 97–171, 179, 199–208, 210, 213–15, 222–50, 253, 262, 263, 267, 268, 277, 281, 289–375
    Saudi Arabia and, 321
    split in ranks of, 230–33, 386
    U.S. and, 87–89, 97–102, 105, 108–14, 117, 140–48, 228–32, 234–35, 248, 250, 253, 262, 267, 268, 290–93, 295, 298–303,

305–7, 309–38, 340–48, 350, 352, 353, 356, 360, 362, 368, 369, 374, 387
visit to a secret contra base, 102–11
Contreras, Rodrigo de, 193
Coolidge, Calvin, 30
Cooper, Bill, 312, 314
Córdova Rivas, Rafael, 225, 245
Corinto, 164, 211, 249, 377
mining of harbor, 228–229
Corporate Air Service, 312–13
Cortázar, Julio, 76
COSEP, 83, 238
Costa Rica, 19, 23, 25, 33, 45, 66, 67, 72, 75, 157, 158, 162, 175, 179, 203, 236, 258, 311, 334, 375, 380, 392
Arias peace plan, 343, 346–57, 359–60, 362
contras and, 230–32, 321, 343–47, 369–71
National Liberation party, 343
1986 Costa Rican election, 342–44
Sandinistas and, 67, 81, 343, 346–52, 356–57, 385
U.S. and, 301, 343–48, 352, 354–57
Council of State, 79, 203, 259, 260
Cruz, Arturo, 73, 222–24, 301, 303
interviews with, 224–27
1984 election, 227, 238, 240–45, 247
Cuapa, 226, 294–95
Virgin appears at, 190–93
Cuba, 56, 57, 84, 91, 159, 163, 179, 211, 227, 248, 258, 260, 267, 280
Bay of Pigs, 142, 313
Sandinistas and, 17, 44, 59, 60, 65, 67, 75, 77–78, 82, 96, 173, 174, 185, 188, 237, 239, 292, 295, 313, 351, 353, 360, 387, 393
U.S. and, 71, 82, 89, 142, 313, 314, 336
Cuevas, Freddy, 110
Czechoslovakia, 77, 386–87, 389

Daniel, Rufino Omier, 282, 283
Danlí, 102, 103, 106, 108
Darío, 219–221
Darío, Rubén, 218–21, 373, 382, 394
Davico, Mario, 142
Day, Dorothy, 200
DeMatteis, Lou, 266–67
Democratic Coordinator, 241, 242
Democratic Revolutionary Alliance, 262
D'Escoto, Miguel, 123–25, 197, 249, 298–99, 327, 358, 360, 361, 384–85
DeYoung, Karen, 45
Díaz, Mauricio, 362–63, 373
Diederich, Bernard, 39, 45, 46
Diriamba, 49, 153
Diriangén, 23, 213
Dodd, Christopher, 322–23, 360
Domínguez, Estrella Dolores, 290
Domínguez, Zoila Rosa, 290
Dominican Republic, 45, 75, 138, 246, 361
Dulles, John Foster, 32
Dunne, Edward, 29
Duvalier, François ("Papa Doc"), 45

East Germany, 78, 185, 386–87
Echaverry, Emilio, 138
Eisenhower, Dwight D., 223
El Castillo, 215–217
El Chipote prison, 180–82, 225, 317, 322, 384
El Crucero, 83
El Cuá, 290, 305–307
Ben Linder at, 324–326, 330, 331
El Papalonal, 84
El Salvador, 23, 25, 59, 86, 91, 92, 100, 101, 113, 128, 156–57, 167–68, 196, 236, 394
Arias peace plan, 347–50, 353, 357, 362
contras and, 310, 312, 314
Sandinistas and, 80–82, 84–85, 97, 117, 292, 393
U.S. and, 84–85, 97, 117, 143, 301, 304, 310, 312–14, 325
El Tule, 311
Emory Company, G. D., 26
Enders, Thomas, 96–98
Escondido River, 256
Espinoza, Manuel, 371
Estelí, 42, 43, 55, 60–61, 376–77
Estelí (Province), 324
Barredas captured in, 147
Estrada, José Dolores, 382
Eugarrios, Manuel, 41

Fagoth, Steadman, 259, 260, 262, 267, 269, 281
Feland, Logan, 28
Ferch, John, 300–302
Fernández, Guido, 357
Fernández, Raquel, 167
Ferrey, Azucena, 238
Figueres, José, 81, 343
Fonseca, Carlos, 22, 57–61, 177, 182, 213
death of, 65–67, 173
Frazier, Linda, 233
Frederick, George Augustus, 254–55

García, Dr. Manuel, 339
García, Romeo Lucas, 72
García Lorca, Federico, 180, 221
García Márquez, Gabriel, 81, 221, 338
Godoy, Virgilio, 244–45, 373, 389
Goldwater, Barry, 229
Gomez, Max (Felix Rodriguez), 313
Gómez, Roberto, 153
González, Felipe, 342
González y Robleto, Vicente, 196
Gorbachev, Mikhail, 359, 387
Granada (city of), 37, 88, 90, 186, 196, 212, 214, 247
Granma, 77
Greenway, David, 91
Grenada, 81, 131, 133, 186, 369
Group of Twelve, 66–67, 73, 224
Guadamúz, Carlos, 187
Guadamúz Pineda, Eylin, 218
Guatemala, 23, 25, 33, 72, 158, 174, 187, 236, 301, 304, 394
Arias peace plan, 347–51, 353, 355–57, 362
contras and, 87, 141–42
ORPA, 174

Guevara, Ernesto ("Che"), 62, 313, 330
Guevara, Roger, 384
Guido, Clemente, 245
Gusen, Carlos, 364
Guthrie, Alvin, 241
Guzmán, Luis Humberto, 381

Hasenfus, Eugene, 311–23, 341
Hasenfus, Sally, 312, 316, 322
Hassan, Moisés, 48, 73, 78, 377–78
Hernández, Lino, 352
Hernández, Sergio, 327
Herrera, Julio César ("Krill"), 139, 146, 147
Herrera, Leticia, 132
Herrera, Rafaela, 215–16
Hidalgo, Xavier, 380
Hiner, Howard, 328
Hoge, Warren, 128–29
Honduras, 23, 25, 28, 33, 58, 61, 62, 65, 72,
    124, 130, 137–38, 157, 158, 179, 203,
    206, 236, 258, 261, 334, 364, 367, 374,
    394
  Arias peace plan, 347–50, 353, 357, 362
  Association for Honduran Progress, 148
  contras and, 88, 97–113, 117, 118, 120, 122,
    140–44, 146–48, 204, 229–31, 262, 267,
    268, 281, 290, 293, 300–301, 305, 310,
    312, 314, 326, 341, 357, 366, 380, 387
  FUSEP, 138
  U.S. and, 98, 100–102, 108–13, 127, 140,
    143–44, 147, 300–302, 304, 305, 310,
    312, 314, 341, 366
Hood, Cookie, 240
Hooker, Ray, 266
Hoover, Herbert, 30
Hughes, Howard, 32–33

Independent Liberal party, 245, 374
Inter-American Development Bank, 73, 224,
    227, 305
International Court of Justice, 229, 261, 303
Iran-contra affair, 321–23, 333–38, 340, 347

Jagger, Bianca, 246–47
Jalapa, 99, 102, 122
Jamaica, 253, 254, 257
Jarquín, Edmundo, 46
Jinotega, 55, 204, 337
  conditions in 1983, 120–22
Jinotega (Province), 214, 246, 324, 326, 330,
    331, 363
Jinotepe, 223
Jirón Terán, José, 221
John Paul II, Pope, 95–96, 99, 198, 298
  Nicaragua visit, 201–3, 207, 411
Johnstone, L. Craig, 238–39
Jordan, 60

Kennedy, Edward, 207
Khadaffy, Muammar, 165, 174
Khomeini, Ayatollah Ruhollah, 321
Kim Il Sung, 60
Kirkpatrick, Jeane, 148, 239
Kissinger, Henry, 151

Knox, Philander, 26
Kristofferson, Kris, 369

Lacayo, Gonzalo, 59, 187–88
La Embajada, 214
La Libertad, 186, 195, 294
Lantigua, John, 251–52
La Penca, 233, 244, 344
La Prensa, 44, 218, 353–54, 374, 386
  Sandinistas and, 79–80, 192, 212, 236–38,
    248, 297–98, 302, 304, 353, 357, 365,
    384, 388, 414–15, 419
  Somoza and, 18–20, 36, 41, 54–55
Largaespada, Fulgencio, 72
Larios, Barnardino, 73
Layasiksa, 281
Lebanon, 60, 321
Lebrón, Lolita, 81
Léon, 90, 193, 201, 219, 221, 354
  anti-Somoza activities in, 42, 43, 49, 55, 61–3,
    65
Léon (Province), 84
Lewites, Herty, 61, 159–63
Liberal party, 24–27, 32, 145, 210, 223, 256
Liberia, 370
Libya, 165, 174, 177, 249, 336
Linder, Benjamin, 324–32, 336, 341, 420–21
López, Ernesto, 209
López, Luis, 156
López Contreras, Carlos, 357
López Pérez, Rigoberto, 32
Lowery, Joseph, 318–19
Lowman, Shepard, 110

MacCray, Cleveland, 282–83
McCurdy, David, 292
MacFarlane, Robert, 321–22
McPherson, Peter, 345
Madriz (Province), 324
Managua, 13–18, 20, 22, 26, 30, 32, 34, 35, 37,
    39–40, 44, 81, 84, 85, 88, 98, 99, 110,
    114, 115–18, 120, 123, 124, 126,
    129–136, 140, 142, 174, 175, 180, 183,
    186–88, 192, 194, 199, 204, 208, 215–17,
    219, 233, 225–28, 230, 233, 237, 238,
    240, 241, 243, 244, 246, 248–50, 289,
    292, 294, 295, 298–307, 312, 314–16,
    322, 326–28, 331, 336, 337, 342, 348,
    350–54, 359–363, 365, 368, 374, 377–79,
    381–85, 389, 390
  anti-Somoza activity in, 42, 58, 61, 63, 65
  conditions during 1980s, 150–56, 158–171,
    209–10
  conditions during 1979, 45–47, 49–50, 52,
    54–55, 67–69, 71, 72, 74, 77, 78
  Enders's visit to, 96
  Hasenfus in, 312, 314–16, 322
  Papal visit to, 201–3, 207–13
  relationships with Atlantic Coast, 251, 256,
    259, 261, 263, 266–68, 276, 279, 280
Mangione, Chuck, 127
Marcia, Guillermo, 162, 164, 165, 214–16, 245,
    247, 276–80, 293–94, 307–8, 329–30,

337–39, 357–58, 364, 368, 370, 373, 374, 386, 390
first proves self as driver, 156–58
Marenco, Dionisio, 133, 236, 385
Martínez, Bernardo, 190–92
Martínez, Denis, 212–13
Martínez, Domingo, 338–39
Martínez, Filadelfo, 67–68
Martínez, Hollman, 294
Martínez Rivas, Carlos, 220
Masatepe, 60, 184
Masaya, 27, 368
  anti-Sandinista activity in, 199, 203, 365
  anti-Somoza activity in, 42, 43, 52–55
Masaya volcano, 13–14, 90, 213–14
Matagalpa, 121, 178, 194, 196, 246, 276, 329, 337, 364
  anti-Somoza activity in, 43, 55, 57, 60–61, 65
Matagalpa (Province), 83, 127, 324
Matamoros, Bosco, 358
Matasano, 104–09
Matthews, Anthony, 265–66
May, Karl, 178
Mayorga, Francisco, 379–80
Mayorga, Silvio, 57, 58
Means, Russell, 281
Medina, Ramon (Luis Posada Carriles), 313–14
Meese, Edwin, 321
Melton, Richard, 381, 384–85
Mena, José, 131
Mercedes-Benz, 69, 82, 166
Mexico, 24, 28, 46, 163, 179, 196, 239, 268
  Sandinistas and, 208, 293
Miami, 70, 138, 141, 159, 293
Miller, George, 292
Miskito Indians, 251–59
  CIA and, 253, 261, 262, 267, 273
  Sandinista war, 253, 257–88, 334, 394
Misurasata, 259–61, 268, 269
Moncada, Marlena, 124–25
Moncada, Nestor, 83–84
Mondale, Walter, 248, 316
Monge, Luis Alberto, 343, 344
Monimbo, 38
Moon, Sun Myung, 148
Moreno, Roberto, 378
Morgan, Susan, 233–34
Morrison, Maria, 367
Moynihan, Daniel Patrick, 229

Najlis, Michelle, 218
Nation, The, 30
National Assembly, 227, 244, 317, 362
National Emergency Committee, 33, 194
National Endowment for Democracy, 298, 353–54
National Guard, 20, 33, 37–39, 58, 60, 65–66, 72–73, 112, 137, 138, 140, 141, 145, 186, 187, 217, 230, 232, 235, 258, 260, 295, 296, 354, 369, 374, 387
  brutality of, 21, 42–49, 51–55, 59, 78, 87, 146, 147, 187–88, 195

Sandinista insurrection (1978–79) and, 42–56, 68, 70, 72–73, 87, 195
Sandinista National Palace raid and, 41, 175
Sandinista trials of Guardsmen, 78–79
Sandino assassination and, 30–31
National Opposition Union, 388
National Reconciliation Commission, 353, 362
National Theater, 163
National University, 267
NATO (North Atlantic Treaty Organization), 334
Natorf, Wlodzimierz, 112
NBC, 156, 360, 372
Negroponte, John, 100, 108, 110, 143, 148
Neruda, Pablo, 221
Netherlands, 208, 228, 229
Neutrality Act (U.S.), 145
Newsweek, 98, 234
New York Times, 39, 45, 46, 94–96, 109–14, 128, 134, 135, 149–52, 156, 164, 210, 279, 280, 372, 384, 386, 388–89
  decision to join, 91–93
  named bureau chief for, 128–29
Nicaraguan Democratic Force (FDN), 141–42, 327
  CIA and, 87, 88, 145, 230, 262, 267
  split in ranks of, 230–32
Nicaraguan Democratic Movement (MDN), 79, 83
Nicaraguan Energy Institute, 326
Nicaraguan Humanitarian Assistance Office, 293
Niquinohomo, 115, 123
Nixon, Richard, 32–33, 100, 128
Nordland, Rod, 233–34
Norland, 358
North, Oliver, 314, 329, 333–38, 340, 345
North Korea, 179, 336
  Sandinistas and, 60, 65, 77, 81, 249, 387
Novedades, 22, 52
Nueva Segovia, 324
Nuevo Diario, 80, 132, 133, 167, 192, 249, 320, 373
Núñez, Carlos, 68, 79, 176, 249
Núñez, Daniel, 130
Nusser, Nancy, 266–67

Obando y Bravo, Miguel, 114–15, 117, 123, 192, 226, 294
  contras and, 199–200, 299, 361
  elevated to rank of cardinal, 298
  interviews with, 116, 197–98
  1984 election, 242
  1990 election, 391
  peace efforts, 353, 354, 359, 361–62, 365–66, 372
  Sandinistas and, 115–16, 126, 193, 195–204, 206–7, 242, 298–99, 302, 353, 354, 361, 362, 365–66, 393
  Somoza and, 33, 41, 115, 194–95, 207
Ochoa, Arnaldo, 295
Ocotal, 28, 29, 204–05, 206, 235

Organization of American States (OAS), 44, 48–49, 197, 303, 346
  1990 Nicaraguan election, 389
  peace efforts, 342, 350, 361, 372
Ortega, Daniel, 80, 98, 171, 176, 195, 223, 235, 239, 244, 249, 269, 294, 297, 318
  Arias peace plan, 348, 350–53, 359–60, 362
  background and character of, 177–78, 185–89
  early Sandinista years, 17, 59, 66, 159, 187–88
  economy/agriculture and, 132, 378–79
  European trip (1985), 292, 293
  Hasenfus affair and, 320, 322–23
  interviews with, 275, 360–61, 386
  as junta member, 48, 73, 74, 76, 82, 84, 178, 188, 259
  Latin American trip (1983), 208
  Miskito Indians and, 259, 275
  1984 election, 238, 242, 244, 246, 247, 250
  1990 election, 388–92
  peace talks and, 359, 361, 366, 368, 370–73
  postwar period, 378–79, 386–92
  as president, 219, 292, 293, 296, 298, 300, 302, 311, 320, 322–23, 329, 341–43, 346, 348, 350–53, 359–62, 365, 366, 368, 370–74, 378–79, 385–92
  rise to power, 185, 188–89
  Sandinista split and, 66, 68
Ortega, Humberto, 66, 68, 79, 82, 83, 133, 176, 185, 212, 319–20
  peace talks and, 366, 368, 370–72
Ortez Colindres, Enrique, 112, 113
Ortiz Mena, Antonio, 305
Owen, Robert W., 314

Pacific News Service, 22, 35
Pak, Bo Hi, 148
Palestine Liberation Organization (PLO), 60, 81
Pallais, Azarias, 171
Pallais, Leon, 194
Pallais Debayle, Luis, 41, 138–39
Panama, 99, 159, 161, 173–74, 216
  Sandinistas and, 67, 74, 208, 304
  U.S. and, 25, 44, 257
Pantasma, 306
Pantos, Jorge Arturo, 374
Paraguay, 59, 82, 138–39
Parrales, Edgard, 197
Pasos, Rosa, 303
Pastora, Edén, 46, 178
  as anti-Sandinista leader, 173–77, 230–34, 237, 238, 262, 263, 268, 344, 377
  as anti-Somoza leader, 41, 42, 45, 49, 67
  bomb attack on, 233–34, 237, 268, 344
  interview with, 175
  retirement from guerrilla life, 344–45
Pastrán, Adolfo, 383
Pataky, László, 16–18, 36
Peace Corps, 75
Pearl Lagoon, 283–84
Pedrarias, 23, 193
Pellas family, 385
Penados del Barrio, Próspero, 349

Peña Gómez, José Francisco, 246–47
People's Anti-Somozist Tribunal, 315–20
Peralta, Juan Carlos, 364
Pérez, Casimiro, 363
Pérez Vega, Reynaldo, 38–40, 78
Pezzullo, Lawrence, 55, 70, 84
Pinochet, Augusto, 128
Piza, Benjamin, 344
Plasmaferesis, 36, 37
Poland, 112, 202, 386–87, 389
Ponce, José Ignacio, 29
Popular Social Christian party, 381
Posada Carriles, Luis (Ramon Medina), 313–14
Prescott, Lyle, 354–55
Prinzapolka, 260
Puerto Sandino, 228, 229

Quezada, Juan José, 63–64
Quilalí, 358, 364, 365

Radio Havana, 45
Radio Liberación, 85
Radio Sandino, 42, 45, 312
Raití, 58, 416–17
Rama Cay, 282, 283
Rama Indians, 281–83
Ramírez, Sergio, 45, 48, 66–67, 354, 370
  as junta member, 73, 74, 76–77, 207
  1990 election, 388, 389
Ramírez, William, 381, 382
Ramos, Pedro, 37
Reagan, Ronald, 84, 85, 148, 225, 325, 348, 349
  contras and, 97–98, 100–102, 117, 142–44, 229–30, 290–92, 298, 300–301, 303, 309, 321–23, 329, 333–37, 344, 345, 352, 353, 356, 360, 387
  Grenada invasion and, 133
  Iran-contra affair, 321–23, 333–38, 340, 347
  Miskito Indians and, 253, 262
  1984 Nicaraguan election, 238–39
  1984 U.S. election, 248
  Sandinistas and, 87, 89, 91, 93, 96, 97, 137, 202–3, 208, 235, 239, 246, 248–50, 291, 292, 299, 303–5, 320–23, 333–37, 352, 356–57, 381, 385–87
Red Cross, 78, 134, 215, 238, 358
Reuters, 266
Reyes, Ismael, 238
Reyes, Rodrigo, 317, 318, 320
Ribeiro, Osvaldo, 141
Riding, Alan, 39, 45, 135
Righetti, Dave, 127–28
Riguero, 47
Rio de Janeiro, 243
Rio San Juan,
Rivas, 37, 49, 55, 243, 268
Rivas Gasteazoro, Eduardo, 238
Rivera, Brooklyn, 261, 262, 267–71, 280–81, 287
  interviews with, 268, 273
Robelo, Alfonso, 83, 88, 262, 238, 348–49, 381
  as junta member, 48, 73, 79, 172, 198, 225
Roberts, Tifani, 372

Robleto, Octavio, 171
Rodriguez, Felix (Max Gomez), 313
Rodriguez, Indalecio, 145
Romberg, Alan, 111–12
Roosevelt, Franklin D., 31, 349
Rosales, Pablo, 327
Rosenthal, A. M., 92
Rousseau, Henri, 217
Ruiz, Henry ("Modesto"), 68, 79, 176–77, 249

Saavedra, Lidia, 186, 188
Saborío, Alberto, 352
Sacasa, Juan Bautista, 30, 31
Salazar, Jorge, 83–84, 145
Salazar, Lucia, 145
Salazar, Pablo Emilio, 137–38
Salgado, Jose, 205
Sampson, Dinorah, 82, 83
San Albino, 28
San Carlos, 216, 217, 311
Sánchez, Humberto, 71
Sanchez, Nestor, 98
Sanders, Riley, 274–75
Sandinista National Liberation Front (FSLN),
    36, 115, 170–71, 219
  achievements and failures summarized, 393–94
  Arias peace plan, 343, 346–57, 359–60, 362
  background and organization of, 56–68
  Bulgaria and, 177, 185, 249, 285–86, 387
  Catholic Church and, 115–16, 192–204,
    206–8, 217, 226, 237, 262, 298–99,
    302–4, 353, 357, 384, 393
  cease-fire, 357–59, 361, 369, 371, 373, 374,
    377, 379, 380
  Chamorro's death, aftermath of, 37–39
  Christmas party raid, 16–17, 22, 61, 64, 66
  Colombia and, 208, 243, 334, 335
  contra war, 97–171, 179, 199–208, 210,
    213–15, 222–50, 253, 262, 263, 267, 268,
    277, 281, 289–375
  Costa Rica and, 67, 81, 343, 346–52, 356–57,
    385
  Cuba and, 17, 44, 59, 60, 65, 67, 75, 77–78,
    82, 96, 173, 174, 185, 188, 237, 239, 292,
    295, 313, 351, 353, 360, 387, 393
  Defense Committees, 77, 132, 320
  economy/agriculture and, 76, 120–23,
    129–33, 150, 152–55, 157–67, 176, 177,
    224, 228, 235–36, 246, 259, 264–65, 296,
    304–5, 324, 326, 374, 377–81, 385,
    387–90, 392, 393
  El Salvador and, 80–82, 84–85, 97, 117, 292,
    393
  Hasenfus affair, 311–23, 341
  insurrection (1978–79), 42–57, 67–73, 87, 88,
    118, 131, 135, 138, 154, 161, 172, 173,
    195, 224, 231, 243, 258, 290
  Iran-contra affair, 321–23, 333–38, 340, 347
  junta and, 48–49, 73–79, 172, 178, 188, 198,
    207, 225, 259
  La Prensa and, 79–80, 192, 212, 236–38, 248,
    297, 302, 304, 353, 357, 365, 384, 388
  Libya and, 165, 177, 249
  military draft and, 133, 203, 296, 354
  Miskito Indian war, 253, 257–88, 334, 394
  National Directorate, 78, 79, 84, 145, 172–89,
    201, 303, 320, 328, 350–51, 354, 359
  National Palace raid, 40–42, 55, 67, 82, 175
  newly in control of Nicaragua, 73–88,
    172–73, 185, 188, 212, 224, 231, 239,
    253, 268, 393
  news conferences, 81–82, 123–24, 351
  1984 Nicaraguan election, 208, 222–23, 227,
    230, 235–50, 389
  1990 Nicaraguan election, 388–93
  North Korea and, 60, 65, 77, 81, 249, 387
  Panama and, 67, 174, 208, 304
  peace talks and, 358, 359, 361, 362, 365–75
  postwar period, 376–94
  secrecy and, 20–22, 62–63, 79, 159–60
  Soviet Union and, 77, 81, 96, 98, 117, 174,
    176, 177, 206, 228, 237, 239, 248–49,
    285, 292, 293, 295, 303, 310, 335, 346,
    359, 366, 393
  split in ranks of, 65, 66, 68, 173, 198
  State Security police, 124, 147, 179–82, 204,
    277, 278, 280, 281, 384
  U.S. and, 28–30, 48–49, 78, 80–82, 84–85,
    87–89, 91, 93, 96, 97, 112, 116, 117, 119,
    120, 122, 124–25, 127, 130–31, 133, 137,
    152, 161, 176, 177, 179, 202–3, 207, 208,
    212, 220, 225–27, 235, 238–39, 246–50,
    291–93, 295, 296, 299, 303–6, 311–23,
    325, 326, 333–38, 340–42, 352, 356–57,
    364, 366, 378, 381, 384–87, 389, 390
  Venezuela and, 67, 81, 208, 243, 293
Sandino, Augusto César, 57, 58, 62, 96, 98, 115,
    163, 200, 205, 213, 226, 246, 373
  assassination of, 30–31, 80, 186
  as rebel, 27–31, 123, 185, 186, 257, 330
San José de Bocay, 117, 306, 326–27, 336–41,
    366
San Juan del Norte, 25, 257
San Juan del Sur, 370
San Juan River, 216, 232, 233
San Judas, 116
San Rafael del Norte, 28
Santa Elena, 344–45, 354
Sapoá, 366, 368–74, 376, 378–81
Saupuka, 251–52
Schoures, Larry, 180
Sébaco, 120
September 15 Legion, 87, 138
Shelton, Turner, 33
Shultz, George, 304, 305, 315, 327, 353
  Iran-contra affair and, 321
  1984 Nicaraguan election, 238–39
  Ortega meeting with, 235, 239
Silva, Dr. Fernando, 377
Silva, Maria, 217
Silverman, Ken, 102–11
Siuna, 76–77, 276–77
Sobalbarro, Francisca, 306–7
Social Christian party, 158, 238
Solaún, Mauricio, 44
Solentiname Archipelago, 217–18

Somoza, Bernabé, 90–91
Somoza, Hope, 163
Somoza Abrego, José, 41
Somoza Debayle, Anastasio, 20, 46, 61, 64, 66,
    73, 77, 80, 86, 87, 91, 96, 99, 112, 116,
    147, 149, 177, 179, 183, 187, 211–12,
    219, 222, 223, 226, 236, 296, 368, 369,
    378, 391
  assassination of, 82–83, 138, 182
  brutality of, 13, 19, 21, 22, 32, 42–49, 51–56,
    59, 74, 75, 88, 115, 146, 178, 180, 394
  Catholic Church and, 33, 41, 115, 194–96,
    207, 217
  Chamorro's death, aftermath of, 37–40
  fall of, 55–57, 69–70, 72, 114, 115, 137, 172,
    224, 253, 393
  foreign journalists and, 35–36, 39–40, 47–48
  heart attack suffered by, 34
  La Prensa and, 18–20, 36, 41, 54–55
  martial law imposed by, 17
  news conferences, 35–36, 40, 47–48
  rise to power, 32
  Sandinista insurrection (1978–79) and, 42–57,
    67–70, 118, 131, 173, 195, 224, 231,
    258
  Sandinista National Palace raid and, 41–42,
    55, 82, 175
  U.S. and, 19–20, 22, 32–33, 40, 43–44, 55,
    58, 65, 70–71, 119, 178, 186, 223
  wealth of, 33–34, 71, 76, 123, 130, 166, 167
Somoza Debayle, Luis, 32, 68
Somoza García, Anastasio, 60, 185–86, 224
  Argüello overthrown by, 31–32, 126
  assassination of, 19, 32, 57, 179
  rise to power, 30–31
  Sandino assassination ordered by, 30
  U.S. support for, 31, 32
Somoza Portocarrero, Anastasio, 37
Sotelo Borgen, Enrique, 316–18
Southern Air Transport, 312–13
Soviet Union, 57, 163–64, 260, 387
  Cuba and, 248
  Sandinistas and, 77, 96, 98, 117, 174, 176,
    177, 206, 228, 237, 239, 248–49, 285,
    292, 293, 295, 303, 310, 335, 346, 359,
    366
  U.S. and, 48, 291, 335
Spain, 46, 75
  colonialism, 23, 193, 213, 214, 254
  peace efforts, 342
  Sandinistas and, 207, 208, 342
Speck, Mary, 365
Squier, E. G., 89–91, 93, 214, 216, 406–07
State Security Police, 124, 147, 179–82, 204,
    277, 278, 280, 281, 384
Stephens, John Lloyd, 213–14
Stewart, Bill, 47–48, 51
Stoltenberg, Thorwald, 243, 244
Stroessner, Alfredo, 82, 139
Studds, Gerry, 301
Student Revolutionary Front (FER), 63
Suárez, Emigdio, 369
Suazo Córdova, Roberto, 143–44

Sumo Indians, 260, 281–82
Supreme Electoral Council, 242, 390
Swan Island, 341

Taft, William Howard, 26
Takaro, Tim, 330–32
Tamayo, Juan, 266–67
Tambs, Lewis, 345
Tasba Pri, 273–74
Tefel, Reynaldo, 200–201, 224
Tegucigalpa, 88, 98–101, 107–12, 137, 138, 143,
    148, 158, 230–31
Téllez, Dora María, 61–62
Teotecacinte, 99, 122
Tico Times, 233
Tiffer, Pablo, 47
Tijerino, Edgard, 211
Time, 39, 45, 46, 149
Tinoco, Victor Hugo, 112, 361
Tirado, Victor, 68, 176, 328
Torres-Arias, Rafael, 142
Torricelli, Robert, 117
Torrijos, Omar, 44, 67, 174, 175
Trejos, José Eduardo, 306
Trujillo, Rafael, 45
Tunnerman, Carlos, 73, 385
Twain, Mark, 216, 412

Uhlig, Mark, 385, 389
United Fruit, 28
United Nations, 60, 112, 229, 244, 303, 389
  Development Program, 357
  peace efforts, 342, 349–50
United Provinces of Central America, 23
United States, 158–60, 162
  Argentina and, 140–43, 147–48
  Bolivia and, 313
  Britain and, 148
  Costa Rica and, 301, 343–48, 352, 354–57
  Cuba and, 71, 82, 89, 142, 313, 314, 336
  Dominican Republic and, 138
  El Salvador and, 84–85, 97, 117, 143, 301,
    304, 310, 312–14, 325
  Grenada, invasion of, 131, 133, 369
  Guatemala and, 301, 304
  Honduras and, 98, 100–102, 108–13, 127,
    140, 143–44, 147, 262, 300–302, 304,
    305, 310, 312, 314, 341, 366
  Lebanon and, 321
  Libya and, 336
  Namibia and, 40
  North Korea and, 336
  Panama and, 25, 44, 257
  Philippines and, 40
  Saudi Arabia and, 321
  Soviet Union and, 48, 291, 335
  Taiwan and, 321
  Vietnam War and, 291, 335, 336, 369
United States, Nicaraguan relations with, 138,
    149, 153, 185–86, 222–24, 289, 353
  Agency for International Development, 198,
    345
  Arias peace plan, 343, 346–57, 359–60, 362

Boland Amendment, 97–98, 117
CIA, 52, 87–89, 97–99, 102, 105, 124–25,
    139, 140, 142–46, 148, 155, 179, 180,
    202, 228–30, 232, 234–35, 237, 239, 240,
    248, 249, 253, 261, 262, 267, 268, 273,
    291–92, 299, 301, 303, 305–7, 311–23,
    341, 343–45, 347, 354–55
Congress, 21, 80–81, 97–98, 112, 113, 117,
    143, 228–30, 291–93, 298–302, 309, 311,
    321, 322, 333–38, 340, 348, 357, 360–62,
    368, 374, 387
contras and, 87–89, 97–102, 105, 108–14,
    117, 140–48, 228–32, 234–35, 248, 250,
    253, 262, 267, 268, 290–93, 295,
    298–303, 305–7, 309–38, 340–48, 350,
    352, 353, 356, 360, 362, 366, 368, 369,
    374, 387
Defense Department, 97–98, 285, 301, 305
Hasenfus affair, 311–23, 341
Iran-contra affair, 321–23, 333–38, 340, 347
Knox Note, 26, 98
Marines, 13, 26–30, 122, 186, 210, 256–57, 330
Mosquito Coast and, 253, 255–58, 261, 262,
    264, 265, 267, 272, 273, 285, 286, 288
National Security Council, 98, 314, 335
Neutrality Act, 145
1984 Nicaraguan election, 238–40, 242,
    245–50
1990 Nicaraguan election, 389
Peace Corps, 75
Sandinistas and, 48–49, 78, 80–81, 84–85,
    87–89, 91, 93, 96, 97, 112, 116, 117, 119,
    120, 124–25, 127, 130–31, 133, 137, 152,
    161, 176, 177, 179, 202–3, 207, 208, 212,
    220, 225–27, 235, 238–39, 246–50,
    291–93, 295, 296, 299, 303–6, 311–23,
    325, 326, 333–38, 340–42, 347, 352,
    356–57, 364, 366, 378, 381, 384–87, 389,
    390
Somoza and, 19–20, 22, 31–33, 40, 43–44, 55,
    58, 65, 70–71, 96, 119, 178, 186, 223
State Department, 71, 80, 96, 111–12, 235,
    238–39, 293, 300, 304, 305, 314, 315,
    327, 344, 345, 348, 353, 357
Walker's adventures, 13, 23–25, 96, 217, 382
Zelaya government forced from power, 26,
    220
Urcuyo, Francisco, 55, 70–72

Valdivieso, Antonio de, 193
Valin, Alberto, 141

Vallecillo, Juan Manuel ("Jaguita"), 211
Vance, Cyrus, 48–49
Vanegas, Uriel ("Rubio"), 270–71
Vargas, Damaso, 365
Vargas, Gustavo Adolfo, 59–60
Vargas, Oscar René, 59–60, 73
Vargas Llosa, Mario, 151
Vega, Augusto, 358
Vega, Pablo Antonio, 204, 299, 302–4,
    353
Velasquez, Luis Alfonso, 182
Venezuela, 40, 44, 163, 313–14
    Sandinistas and, 67, 81, 208, 243, 293
Videla, Jorge Rafael, 139
Vietnam, 81, 82, 291, 335, 336, 369
Vilchez, Pedro, 204
Villarreina, José, 77
Vivas, Bosco, 192
Voice of America, 45
Voz de Nicaragua, 186–87

Walker, William, 13, 23–25, 96, 217, 382
Wallace, Mike, 314–15, 319
Washington Post, 45, 46, 252, 298
Waspam, 271, 272–73, 274, 279
Weinberger, Caspar, 321
West Germany, 238, 243, 244
Wheelock, Jaime, 64, 65, 68, 73, 76, 79, 306,
    353
    economy/agriculture and, 122–23, 129, 176,
        177
    interviews with, 119–20, 202
Wheelock, Ricardo, 314
Whelan, Thomas, 32
Whitney, Craig, 91–93, 95–96, 128
Wilson, Bishop John, 283
Wischnewski, Hans-Jurgen, 243
World Bank, 305
World Inter-Parliamentary Union, 170
Wright, Jim, 349, 360, 361
Wuanbuco, 146

Yulu, 270

Zelaya, José Santos, 25–27, 96, 210, 220,
    256
Zelaya (Province), 65, 257, 258, 259, 269
Zeledón, Benjamin, 27, 96, 98, 213
Zeledón, Marco, 145
Zinica, 66
Zumbado, Fernando, 356